102 057 964 1

OXFORD MONOGRAPHS IN
INTERNATIONAL LAW

General Editor: Professor Vaughan Lowe
*Chichele Professor of Public International Law in
the University of Oxford and Fellow of All Souls College, Oxford*

DEFINING TERRORISM IN INTERNATIONAL LAW

D1612463

OXFORD MONOGRAPHS IN INTERNATIONAL LAW

The aim of this series is to publish important and original pieces
of research on all aspects of international law. Topics that are
given particular prominence are those which, while of interest to
the academic lawyer, also have important bearing on issues
which touch upon the actual conduct of international relations.
Nonetheless, the series is wide in scope and includes monographs on the history and philosophical foundations of international law.

RECENT TITLES IN THE SERIES

Jurisdiction in International Law
Cedric Ryngaert

The Fair and Equitable Treatment Standard in International Foreign Investment Law
Ioana Tudor

**The Immunity of States and Their Officials in International Criminal Law
and International Human Rights Law**
Rosanne Van Alebeek

Targeted Killing in International Law
Nils Melzer

Diplomatic Protection
Chittharanjan F. Amerasinghe

Human Rights and Non-Discrimination in the 'War on Terror'
Daniel Moeckli

The Decolonization of International Law
Matthew Craven

Investment Treaty Arbitration and Public Law
Gus van Harten

International Organizations and their Exercise of Sovereign Powers
Dan Sarooshi

Peremptory Norms in International Law
Alexander Orakhelashvili

DEFINING TERRORISM IN INTERNATIONAL LAW

BEN SAUL

OXFORD
UNIVERSITY PRESS

This book has been printed digitally and produced in a standard specification in order to ensure its continuing availability

OXFORD
UNIVERSITY PRESS

Great Clarendon Street, Oxford OX2 6DP

Oxford University Press is a department of the University of Oxford.
It furthers the University's objective of excellence in research, scholarship,
and education by publishing worldwide in

Oxford New York

Auckland Cape Town Dar es Salaam Hong Kong Karachi
Kuala Lumpur Madrid Melbourne Mexico City Nairobi
New Delhi Shanghai Taipei Toronto
With offices in
Argentina Austria Brazil Chile Czech Republic France Greece
Guatemala Hungary Italy Japan South Korea Poland Portugal
Singapore Switzerland Thailand Turkey Ukraine Vietnam

Oxford is a registered trade mark of Oxford University Press
in the UK and in certain other countries

Published in the United States
by Oxford University Press Inc., New York

ISBN 978-0-19-953547-7

General Editor's Preface

Naming and defining are acts of almost totemic significance to lawyers. Whether, as is widely thought, they are essential preconditions to the exercise of control of the phenomenon to which they relate or temporary substitutes for it, there can be no doubting their importance. In 2005 the UN High Level Panel on Threats, Challenges and Change reported that the absence of a definition of 'terrorism' undermined the normative and moral stance against terrorism and called the adoption of such a definition a 'political imperative'. Dr Saul's study analyses the practice of the international community in labelling actions as 'terrorist' and considers the implications of, and alternatives to, that labelling. It is an important and timely contribution to the debate on what has become a central issue of contemporary political life.

AVL
Oxford
March 2006

Acknowledgements

For assistance and encouragement of various kinds in Oxford, I thank my Doctor of Philosophy supervisor at All Souls College, Dr Guy Goodwin-Gill; my DPhil examiners, Professor Vaughan Lowe (Oxford) and Professor Conor Gearty (LSE); my supervisors at Magdalen College, Professor Colin Tapper and Dr Katharine Grevling; the President of Magdalen, Mr Anthony Smith; and Sir Frank Berman, Professor Adam Roberts, Dr Dan Sarooshi, Dr Stefan Talmon, Professor Stephen Castles, Mr Kaveh Moussavi, and the Oxford Public Interest Lawyers; the Bodleian Law Library and Official Papers; Amir Fuchs; Gyorgy Lissauer; Michael Sanderson; and the postgraduate community at Magdalen. In Geneva, I thank Emanuela Gillard and Jean-Marie Henckaerts at the ICRC; Professor Ivan Shearer of the UN Human Rights Committee (and the University of Sydney); Markus Schmidt at the Office of the UN High Commissioner for Human Rights; John Pace; Chris Sidoti at the International Federation of Human Rights; Dr Daniel Warner at the Graduate Institute for International Studies, and Mme Pejovic at the League of Nations Archives, Palais des Nations. In Australia, I thank the Faculty of Law at the University of New South Wales (especially Professor David Dixon); the Gilbert + Tobin Centre for Public Law at UNSW (particularly Professor George Williams, Dr Andrew Lynch, Tessa Meyrick, and Belinda McDonald); Dr Mary Crock at the Faculty of Law, University of Sydney; the University of Sydney Law Library; Justice John Dowd of the International Commission of Jurists; Jessica Wyndham; and my family at Meadow Flat. Elsewhere I thank Professor Surya Subedi (Middlesex), Dr Rosemary Byrne (Dublin); Professor Robert McCorquodale (Nottingham); Professor Manuel Becerra (Mexico City), Professor Antonio Cassese (Florence), Professor Iain Scobbie (London), Ms Elizabeth Wilmshurst (RIIA), Mr Anthony Aust (London), Professor John Dugard (Leiden), Mr Vaclav Mikulka at the UN Office of Legal Affairs (New York), Ms Jarna Petman (Helsinki), Jelena Pejic (ICRC), and Marina Anderson (New Zealand High Commission in Canberra). I also thank my publishers John Louth, Gwen Booth, and Darcy Ahl. Most of all I thank my partner, Jane McAdam, for all her support. For financial assistance, I thank the Commonwealth Scholarship Commission (2001–04); the Foundation for Young Australians; Europaeum; the Refugee Studies Centre Oxford; Oxford Law Faculty; the European Society of International Law; and the Czech Helsinki Committee. I also benefited from attending the All Souls–Freshfields conference on terrorism (Oxford, 2004), the Oxford Public Interest Lawyers terrorism conference (2004), the UN Committee on the Inalienable Rights of the Palestinian People International Meeting on the Israel Wall (2004), the ASIL

Annual Meeting (Washington, DC, 2004), the ESIL inaugural conference (Florence, 2004), the Sussex University conference on terrorism (2003), the New School conference on terrorism (New York, 2002), and a Club of 3 conference (London, 2002).

                                                                    BS

In Memoriam
In memory of my school mate, Charles Van Renen, 26, killed in the Bali bombing on 12 October 2002.

Note on Previous Publication and Presentation

Some of this research has been published in earlier forms: 'International Terrorism as a European Crime: The Policy Rationale for Criminalization' (2003) 11 *European Journal of Crime, Criminal Law and Criminal Justice* 323; 'Attempts to Define "Terrorism" in International Law' (2005) 52 Netherlands ILR 57; 'Definition of "Terrorism" in the UN Security Council: 1985–2004' (2005) 4 Chinese JIL 141; 'Crimes and Prohibitions of "Terror" and "Terrorism" in Armed Conflict: 1919–2005' (2005) 4 *Journal of the International Law of Peace and Armed Conflict* 264; 'The Legal Response of the League of Nations to Terrorism' (2006) 4 JICJ 78; 'Reasons for Defining and Criminalizing Terrorism in International Law' (2006) 6 *Mexican Yearbook of International Law* 419; 'Speaking of Terror: Criminalizing Incitement to Violence' (2005) 28 *University of New South Wales Law Journal* 868; 'Two Justifications for Terrorism: A Moral Legal Response' (2005) 30 *Alternative Law Journal* 219; 'Defining Terrorism to Protect Human Rights' (2005) 14(2) *Human Rights Defender* 2; 'Defending "Terrorism": Justifications and Excuses for Terrorism in International Criminal Law' (forthcoming 2006) 25 *Australian Year Book of International Law*; 'Defining Terrorism to Protect Human Rights', FRIDE Working Paper (Spanish Foundation for International Relations and Foreign Dialogue), February 2006.

Some of this research has been previously presented at the European Society of International Law Inaugural Conference (Florence, 2004); the Czech Helsinki Committee EU Accession Conference on Asylum (Prague, 2004); the International Congress on Law and Mental Health (Sydney, 2003 and Paris, 2005); the Australian New Zealand Society of International Law Annual Conference (Canberra, 2005 and Wellington, 2006); the Department of International Law and International Relations at the University of Vienna (2005); the Human Rights Initiative of the Central European University (Budapest, 2005); the Gilbert + Tobin Centre for Public Law Terrorism Workshop (Sydney, 2005); the Department of Critical and Cultural Studies at Macquarie University (Sydney, 2005); the Department of Government and International Relations at the University of Sydney (2005); the Centre for Peace and Conflict Studies at the University of Sydney (2006); the Gilbert + Tobin Centre/University College London Terrorism Conference (London, 2005); the Australian National University Terrorism Workshop (Canberra, 2006); and the Asian Law Institute Annual Conferences (Bangkok, 2005 and Shanghai, 2006).

Contents—Summary

Contents—Outline

Table of Cases

US DECISIONS

OTHER NATIONAL DECISIONS

Table of Treaties and Other Instruments

TREATIES

OTHER INSTRUMENTS

List of Abbreviations

General	
AAP	Australian Associated Press
AFP	*Agence France Presse*
AP	Associated Press
ASEAN	Association of South East Asian Nations
ASIL	American Society of International Law
AU	African Union (formerly Organization of African Unity)
BIICL	British Institute of International and Comparative Law
CIRT	Committee for the International Repression of Terrorism (League of Nations)
CIS	Commonwealth of Independent States
CTC	Counter-Terrorism Committee
DPP	Director of Public Prosecutions
ECHR	European Convention on Human Rights
EcoSoc	Economic and Social Council
ESIL	European Society of International Law
IACHR	Inter-American Court of Human Rights
IAEA	International Atomic Energy Agency
ICAO	International Civil Aviation Organization
ICC	International Criminal Court
ICCPR	International Covenant on Civil and Political Rights 1966
ICESCR	International Covenant on Economic, Social and Cultural Rights 1966
ICJ	International Court of Justice
ICRC	International Committee of the Red Cross
ICTR	International Criminal Tribunal for Rwanda
ICTY	International Criminal Tribunal for the former Yugoslavia
IHL	international humanitarian law
IIHL	International Institute of Humanitarian Law
ILC	International Law Commission
IMO	International Maritime Organization
IMT	International Military Tribunal at Nuremberg
IPA	International Peace Academy
KLA	Kosovo Liberation Army
LoN	League of Nations
LTTE	Liberation Tigers of Tamil Eelam (Tamil Tigers)
NAM	Non-Aligned Movement
NATO	North Atlantic Treaty Organization
NGO	non-governmental organization
OAS	Organization of American States

OAU	Organization of African Unity (see AU above)
OIC	Organization of the Islamic Conference
OSCE	Organization for Security and Cooperation in Europe
Pres Stat	Presidential Statement
RICO	Racketeer Influences and Corrupt Organizations
SAARC	South Asian Association for Regional Cooperation
SCO	Shanghai Cooperation Organization
UDHR	Universal Declaration of Human Rights
UNCLOS	United Nations Convention on the Law of the Sea
UNComHR	United Nations Commission on Human Rights
UNDP	United Nations Development Programme
UNGA	United Nations General Assembly
UNHCR	United Nations High Commissioner for Refugees
UNHRC	United Nations Human Rights Committee
UNODC	United Nations Office on Drugs and Crime
UNSC	United Nations Security Council
UNSubComHR	United Nations Sub-Commission on the Promotion and Protection of Human Rights
UNWCC	United Nations War Crimes Commission
UPU	Universal Postal Union

Publications

AJIAD	*African Journal of International Affairs and Development*
AJIL	*American Journal of International Law*
Ariz JICL	*Arizona Journal of International and Comparative Law*
AUILR	*American University International Law Review*
AULR	*American University Law Review*
AUJILP	*American University Journal of International Law and Policy*
Austrian RIEL	*Austrian Review of International and European Law*
BC EALR	*Boston College Environmental Affairs Law Review*
BC ICLR	*Boston College International and Comparative Law Review*
BUILJ	*Boston University International Law Journal*
BYBIL	*British Yearbook of International Law*
Can JLJ	*Canadian Journal of Law and Jurisprudence*
Can YBIL	*Canadian Yearbook of International Law*
Col HRLR	*Columbia Human Rights Law Review*
Col JTL	*Columbia Journal of Transnational Law*
Den JILP	*Denver Journal of International Law and Policy*
Duke JCIL	*Duke Journal of International and Comparative Law*
EHLR	*European Human Rights Law Review*
EJIL	*European Journal of International Law*
ELR	*European Law Review*
FMR	*Forced Migration Review*
Geo JICL	*Georgia Journal of International and Comparative Law*

HRLJ	*Human Rights Law Journal*
ICLQ	*International and Comparative Law Quarterly*
IJRL	*International Journal of Refugee Law*
ILF	*International Law Forum*
ILJ	International Law Journal (as part of journal title)
ILR	International Law Review (as part of journal title)
ILSA JICL	*ILSA Journal of International and Comparative Law*
IRRC	*International Review of the Red Cross*
IYBHR	*Israel Yearbook on Human Rights*
JACL	*Journal of Armed Conflict Law*
JCLC	*Journal of Criminal Law and Criminology*
JCSL	*Journal of Conflict and Security Law*
JICJ	*Journal of International Criminal Justice*
JIL	Journal of International Law (as part of journal title)
JTLP	*Journal of Transnational Law and Policy*
KCLJ	*King's College Law Journal*
Mich YBLIS	*Michigan Yearbook of International Legal Studies*
MLR	*Modern Law Review*
Neth YBIL	*Netherlands Yearbook of International Law*
NLJ	*New Law Journal*
NYU JILP	*New York University Journal of International Law and Politics*
NYU LR	*New York University Law Review*
Ohio NULR	*Ohio Northern University Law Review*
Ohio SLJ	*Ohio State Law Journal*
OJ	Official Journal
OJLS	*Oxford Journal of Legal Studies*
OR	Official Records
PL	*Public Law*
Pol YBIL	*Polish Yearbook of International Law*
Stan JIL	*Stanford Journal of International Law*
Stan JIS	*Stanford Journal of International Studies*
Syra JILC	*Syracuse Journal of International Law and Commerce*
TWC	*Trials of War Criminals before the Nuremberg Military Tribunals under Control Council Law No 10* (US Government Printing Office, Washington, DC, 1950)
UNYB	*United Nations Yearbook*
Van JIL	*Vanderbilt Journal of International Law*
Van JTL	*Vanderbilt Journal of Transnational Law*
Yale HRDLJ	*Yale Human Rights and Development Law Journal*

INTRODUCTION
Concepts of Terrorism

Semantic instability, irreducible trouble spots on the borders between concepts, indecision in the very concept of the border: all this must not only be analysed as a speculative disorder, a conceptual chaos or zone of passing turbulence in public or political language. We must also recognize here strategies and relations of force. The dominant power is the one that manages to impose and, thus, to legitimate, indeed to legalize (for it is always a question of law) on a national or world stage, the terminology and thus the interpretation that best suits it in a given situation.*

Few words are plagued by so much indeterminacy, subjectivity, and political disagreement as 'terror', 'terrorize', 'terrorism', and 'terrorist'. The ordinary linguistic meanings of these variant terms are instantly evocative and highly emotive,[1] referring at a literal level to intense fear, fright, or dread.[2] By itself, a literal meaning is not particularly instructive in distilling a legal concept of terrorism, since 'every form of violence is potentially terror-inspiring to its victim',[3] from mugging to warfare.

This deceptively simple, literal meaning is overlaid with centuries of political connotations in specific historical circumstances. While the word 'terror' stems from Latin, entering French and English in the fourteenth century, the notions of 'terrorism' and 'terrorist' entered political discourse in the late eighteenth century, referring to the system of intimidation and repression implemented by the Jacobins (the 'Red Terror' or 'Reign of Terror') in the French Revolution.[4] The idea of terrorism as an instrument of State control persisted until the end of the Second World War. Bismarck

---

* J Derrida, quoted in G Borradori, *Philosophy in a Time of Terror: Dialogues with Jürgen Habermas and Jacques Derrida* (University of Chicago Press, Chicago, 2003) 105.

[1] P Wilkinson, *Terrorism and the Liberal State* (Macmillan, London, 1977) 48; J Lambert, *Terrorism and Hostages in International Law* (Grotius, Cambridge, 1990) 13; P Van Krieken (ed), *Terrorism and the International Legal Order* (Asser Press, The Hague, 2002) 14.

[2] Oxford English Dictionary Online: definition of 'terror'; see also G Guillaume, 'Terrorism and International Law', Grotius Lecture, BIICL, London, 13 Nov 2003, 2; J-M Sorel, 'Some Questions About the Definition of Terrorism and the Fight against its Financing' (2003) 14 AJIL 365, 371.

[3] MC Bassiouni, 'A Policy-Oriented Inquiry into the Different Forms and Manifestations of "International Terrorism"' in MC Bassiouni (ed), *Legal Responses to International Terrorism* (Martinus Nijhoff, Dordrecht, 1988) xv, xv; also C Gearty, *The Future of Terrorism* (Phoenix, London, 1997) 16.

[4] V Johnson, 'The Declaration of the Rights of Man and of Citizens of 1789, the Reign of Terror, and the Revolutionary Tribunal of Paris' (1990) 13 BC ICLR 1, 19–22.

'terrorized' Prussia by using the army as a means of social control;[5] Nazi Germany imposed a reign of terror across Europe;[6] German and Allied air forces resorted to 'terror bombing' in the Second World War;[7] and Stalin ruled Russia by terror.[8]

Gradually terrorism also came to refer to non-State practices. In the late nineteenth century, revolutionaries and anarchists in tsarist Russia were commonly known as terrorists.[9] The Bolshevik seizure of power is often described as revolutionary terror, and communists embraced terrorism as a means of class struggle.[10] In the Balkans, ethnic separatists assassinated Archduke Franz Ferdinand in 1914, precipitating the First World War, and King Alexander of Yugoslavia in 1934, leading to a diplomatic crisis in the League of Nations. In the 1940s, Jewish extremists hastened Israeli independence by assassinating Lord Moyne in Cairo,[11] and the UN mediator, Count Bernadotte,[12] and by acts such as bombing Jerusalem's King David Hotel.

After the Second World War, 'terrorism' became mired in the ideological cleavages and proxy violence of the Cold War. Whereas developed States focused on non-State terrorism, developing and socialist States emphasized 'State terrorism' by imperial powers, and regarded anti-colonial violence either as an exception to terrorism, or as justified by colonialism. Much post-war 'terrorism' was linked to specific situations of decolonization, and dissipated on independence, as in Algeria, although Palestinian self-determination remains a stumbling block. Allegations of terrorism were also used as a pretext for intervention; the Soviet Union was 'invited' into Afghanistan to suppress Afghan and mujahadeen 'terrorists'. The magnitude, internationalization, and indiscrimination of modern terrorism set it apart from the targeted assassinations of the nineteenth century.

By the late twentieth century, new forms of fundamentalist religious terrorism emerged (such as Al-Qaeda), decoupled from particular territorial claims, specific demands like the release of prisoners, or restraint in tactics.[13]

---

[5] OED, n 2.   [6] See Ch 5 below.

[7] M Walzer, *Just and Unjust Wars* (3rd edn, Basic Books, NY, 2000) 198.

[8] R Conquest, *The Great Terror* (Pelican, Middlesex, 1971).

[9] UNComHR (53rd Sess), Terrorism and Human Rights: Progress Report by Special Rapporteur K Koufa, 27 June 2001, UN Doc E/CN.4/Sub.2/2001/31, 8, 11.

[10] L Trotsky, *Terrorism and Communism: A Reply to Karl Kautsky* (New Park, London, 1975) 75–79, 84; K Marx and F Engels, *Collected Works: vol 8* (Progress, Moscow, 1977) 161; I Blish-chenko and N Zhdanov, *Terrorism and International Law* (Progress, Moscow, 1984) 22–23, 40, 49, 53, 64–75.

[11] I Abu-Lughod, 'Unconventional Violence and International Politics' (1973) 67 ASIL Proceedings 100, 101.

[12] *Reparation for Injuries* case (1949) ICJ Reports 174.

[13] F Mégret, 'Justice in Times of Violence' (2003) 14 EJIL 327, 329–330; R Falk, *The Great Terror War* (Arris, Gloucestershire, 2003) 45; S Simon and D Benjamin, 'The Terror' (2002) 43 *Survival* 5, 6; J Stevenson, 'Pragmatic Counter-terrorism' (2002) 43 *Survival* 35.

At the same time, 'traditional' assassinations continued to be used with devastating effect: the shooting down of an aircraft carrying Rwandan and Burundian leaders in 1994 was a flashpoint for the Rwandan genocide; the assassination of Laurent Kabila helped to bring peace to Congo.[14] After 11 September 2001, there was a remarkable tendency to conflate disparate terrorist threats into an homogenous global pandemic,[15] erasing the specificity of the concrete conditions giving rise to different situations of violence.

Despite the shifting and contested meanings of 'terrorism' over time, the peculiar semantic power of the term, beyond its literal signification, is its capacity to stigmatize, delegitimize,[16] denigrate, and dehumanize those at whom it is directed, including legitimate political opponents. The term is ideologically and politically loaded;[17] pejorative;[18] implies moral, social, and value judgment;[19] and is 'slippery and much-abused'.[20] In the absence of a definition of terrorism, the struggle over the representation of a violent act is a struggle over its legitimacy.[21] The more confused a concept, the more it lends itself to opportunistic appropriation.[22]

The term 'terrorism' has been erratically deployed to describe all manner of evils, such as the nuclear 'balance of terror';[23] rape by 'sex terrorists';[24] and the Spanish inquisition.[25] It has also been used to describe things that are not evils at all: refugees in Sabra and Shatilla;[26] loggers who caused flooding in Sumatra;[27] and even parliamentary colleagues who sought to release asylum

---

[14] cf T Lumumba-Kasongo, 'Laurent-Desire Kabila's Assassination: An Attempt to End Three Decades of a Nationalist's Political Struggle' (2001) 6 AJIAD 19.

[15] J Record, 'Threat Confusion and its Penalties' (2004) 46 *Survival* 51, 53–54.

[16] Sorel, n 2, 366.

[17] Lambert, n 1, 13; T Franck and B Lockwood, 'Preliminary Thoughts Towards an International Convention on Terrorism' (1974) 68 AJIL 69, 89.

[18] Sorel, n 2, 366; Wilkinson, n 1, 51; T Kapitan, 'The Terrorism of "Terrorism" ' in J Sterba (ed), *Terrorism and International Justice* (OUP, Oxford, 2003) 47, 49.

[19] Koufa, n 9, 8.

[20] Wilkinson, n 1, 47.

[21] M Bhatia, 'Fighting Words: Naming Terrorists, Bandits, Rebels and Other Violent Actors' (2005) 26 *Third World Quarterly* 5, 13.

[22] J Derrida, 'Autoimmunity: Real and Symbolic Suicides', in G Borradori (ed), *Philosophy in a Time of Terror: Dialogues with Jürgen Habermas and Jacques Derrida* (University of Chicago Press, Chicago, 2003), 86, 104.

[23] M Koskenniemi, 'The Police in the Temple: Order, Justice and the UN: A Dialectical View' (1995) 6 EJIL 325, 339; A Carty, 'The Terrors of Freedom: The Sovereignty of States and the Freedom to Fear' in J Strawson (ed), *Law after Ground Zero* (GlassHouse, London, 2002) 44, 55.

[24] 'Gang rape case inflames anti-American passions', *Sydney Morning Herald*, 9 Nov 2005; see also C Card, 'Rape as a Terrorist Institution' in R Frey and C Morris (eds), *Violence, Terrorism, and Justice* (CUP, Cambridge, 1991) 296; A Ray, 'The Shame of It: Gender-Based Terrorism in the Former Yugoslavia' (1997) 46 AULR 793.

[25] G Bouthoul, 'Definitions of Terrorism' in D Carlton and C Schaerf (eds), *International Terrorism and World Security* (Croom Helm, London, 1975) 50, 54.

[26] Kapitan, n 18, 58 (referring to Israeli statements).

[27] AAP, 'Indonesia reels after flood disaster', *Sydney Morning Herald*, 7 Nov 2003.

seekers from detention.[28] What is not called terrorism is equally instructive;
UK Prime Minister Thatcher was reluctant to label as terrorism the bombing
in New Zealand of the Greenpeace ship, *Rainbow Warrior*, for fear of alienat-
ing France, despite her Transport Secretary calling it 'an outrageous act of
terrorism'.[29] It is clear that public or official attitudes 'can change radically
toward certain political crimes when their immorality and harmful quality
become dubious or ambiguous'.[30]

In the light of the kaleidoscopic uses of the term, it is fallacious to assert
pragmatically that terrorism is recognizable without difficulty,[31] or to claim
intuitively that 'what looks, smells and kills like terrorism is terrorism'.[32]
Disagreement about terrorism runs much deeper than technical disputes
about drafting; it reflects doctrinal, ideological, and jurisprudential arguments about who is entitled to exercise violence, against whom, and for what
purposes.

The resilience of the term terrorism testifies not only to its political utility,
but also to its popular symbolic resonance. The term is seductive because it
seems to encapsulate a phenomenon of political violence widely condemned
in many societies as anti-social, amoral, inhumane, and deviant. If criminal
law is designed to protect social values, express popular repugnance at
unjustifiable violence, and stigmatize immorality, the idea of terrorism serves
as a symbolic draw-card embodying many such judgments. The prosecution
of an individual for 'terrorism', *as such* (rather than for common crimes like
murder), might go some way towards satisfying public indignation at terrorist
acts, and placating popular demands for justice. Dismissing 'terrorism' as
inherently legally useless is unproductive, since the term serves popular
expressive functions in the national and international communities.

On the other hand, terrorism currently lacks the precision, objectivity, and
certainty demanded by legal discourse. Criminal law strives to avoid emotive
terms to prevent prejudice to an accused, and shuns ambiguous or subjective
terms as incompatible with principles of non-retroactivity and specificity
in criminal law. If the law is to admit such concepts, advance definition is
essential on grounds of fairness. Legal definition could plausibly retrieve
terrorism from the ideological quagmire, by severing an agreed legal meaning
from the remainder of the elastic, political concept.

---

[28] 'Rebel MPs behaving like "political terrorists" ', *Sydney Morning Herald*, 15 June 2005.
[29] H Muir and M Milner, 'Ministers seek to broker BA strike deal', *Guardian Weekly*, 26 Aug–
1 Sept 2005, 10.
[30] B Ingraham, *Political Crime in Europe* (University of California Press, Berkeley,
1979) 36.
[31] D Freestone, 'Legal Responses to Terrorism: Towards European Cooperation?' in J Lodge
(ed), *Terrorism: A Challenge to the State* (Martin Robertson, Oxford, 1981) 195, 195.
[32] UNGAOR (56th Sess), 12th plenary mtg record, 1 Oct 2001, UN Doc A/56/PV.12,
18 (UK).

This is no easy task. In the past, international attempts to define terrorism in legal terms have been exceedingly difficult, for ideological and political reasons, but also because of the 'prodigious' technical difficulties of definition.[33] There are no clean lines between terrorism and other forms of political violence,[34] and the debate about defining terrorism is also a debate about the classification of political violence in all its myriad forms: riot, revolt, rebellion, war, conflict, uprising, revolution, subversion, intervention, guerilla warfare, and so on. Analysis is clouded by the absence of international agreement on 'the circumstances in which it is legitimate to use violence for political ends',[35] typified by the great variation in national interpretations of the political offence exception to extradition.

Even so, there is new urgency to the quest for definition. Previously, the lack of definition was legally inconsequential—no international rights or duties hinged on the term 'terrorism'. Since 11 September 2001, that has changed. The Security Council has *required* States to implement measures against *terrorist acts* and *terrorists*, according those terms operative legal significance without defining them.

Whether one is sceptical of definitions,[36] or regrets that the term was 'ever inflicted upon us',[37] is irrelevant; the term now has legal consequences and cannot be ignored, as merely of academic interest, or wished away. Defining terrorism would help to confine the term and prevent its abuse. The absence of definition enables States to unilaterally and subjectively determine what constitutes terrorist activity, and to take advantage of the public panic and anxiety engendered by the designation of conduct as terroristic to pursue arbitrary and excessive counter-terrorism responses.

Plainly, the problem of terrorism touches on a great many areas of international law, and the focus of this book is on defining terrorism in international criminal law, drawing on other branches of international law where relevant, and mindful that criminal law is only one facet of the overall response to terrorism. There is a vast and often repetitive legal literature on terrorism, much of it focusing on national extradition law, the use of force, domestic legal measures (including civil remedies), and national human rights and civil liberties concerns. US and Israeli practice naturally dominates, given those States' frequent targeting by terrorists. While the practice of such specially affected States requires particular attention in

---

[33] R Higgins, 'The General International Law of Terrorism' in R Higgins and M Flory (eds), *Terrorism and International Law* (Routledge, London, 1997) 13, 14.

[34] Wilkinson, n 1, 32–33, 56–57; Y Alexander, 'Democracy and Terrorism: Threats and Responses' (1996) 26 IYBHR 253, 253.

[35] Freestone, n 31.

[36] A Roberts, 'Can We Define Terrorism?' (2002) 14 *Oxford Today* 18.

[37] R Baxter, 'A Skeptical Look at the Concept of Terrorism' (1974) 7 *Akron Law Review* 380.

the assessment of customary norms on terrorism,[38] caution is warranted since the legal literature may be distorted by the preponderance of US writers and interests.

There is often a lack of clarity in discussion of terrorism,[39] not to mention an over-emphasis on spectacular events and the manufacturing of a pervasive atmosphere of crisis.[40] In particular, the rapidly expanding literature exudes an infatuation with the novelty of terrorist weapons or methods, especially 'weapons of mass destruction', and everything from 'cyberterrorism' and 'eco-terrorism'[41] to 'narco-terrorism' and 'agro-terrorism'.[42] It is also marked by intemperate and hyperbolic language, exemplified by terms such as 'hyperterrorism'[43] and 'megaterrorism';[44] an ahistorical emphasis on the 'radical newness of the problem';[45] and the labelling of terrorists as 'apocalyptic', 'eschatological', and 'nihilists'.[46]

The literature is also (unavoidably) reactive to specific incidents. At this distance, whether the attacks of 11 September 2001 are a seismic normative shift or an aberration remains to be seen. Certainly a previously intermittent problem has moved to the centre of international relations, and there has been a 'staggering acceleration' in measures against terrorism,[47] and particularly a blurring or hybridization of, or vacillation between, traditional criminal justice and war paradigms.[48]

---

[38] *North Sea Continental Shelf* cases (1969) ICJ Reports 3, 43, para 74.

[39] V Lowe, 'The Iraq Crisis: What Now?' (2003) 52 ICLQ 859, 860. Interdisciplinary academic interest in terrorism expanded rapidly after 11 September 2001: see A Gordon, 'Terrorism as an Academic Subject after 9/11' (2005) 28 *Studies in Conflict and Terrorism* 45.

[40] See generally H Charlesworth, 'International Law: A Discipline of Crisis' (2002) 65 MLR 377.

[41] eg D Denning, 'Cyberwarriors: Activists and Terrorists Turn to Cyberspace' (2001) 23 Harvard ILR 70; T Schofield, 'The Environment as an Ideological Weapon: A Proposal to Criminalize Environmental Terrorism' (1999) 26 BC EALR 619.

[42] D Marshall, 'Narco-Terrorism: The New Discovery of an Old Connection' (2002) 35 Cornell ILJ 599; US Dept Justice (FBI), *Terrorism in the US 1999* (DOJ, Washington, DC, 2000) 38.

[43] Mégret, n 13, 329.

[44] Falk, n 13, 7–12, 38–60; G Gutierrez, 'The Ambiguity of "Megaterrorism" ' (2003) Cornell ILJ 367.

[45] S Holmes, 'Why International Justice Limps' (2002) 69 *Social Research* 1055, 1055; cf I Duyvesteyn, 'How New is the New Terrorism?' (2004) 27 *Studies in Conflict and Terrorism* 439 (exploring the historical continuities between contemporary and earlier terrorism).

[46] Mégret, n 13, 329–330; M Ignatieff, 'Human Rights, the Laws of War, and Terrorism' (2002) 69 *Social Research* 1137, 1147.

[47] Koufa, n 9, 7.

[48] G Abi-Saab, 'The Proper Role of International Law in Combating Terrorism' (2002) 1 Chinese JIL 305, 307; R Dworkin, 'Terror and the Attack on Civil Liberties', *NY Rev Books*, 6 Nov 2003; W Lietzau, 'Combating Terrorism: Law Enforcement or War?' in M Schmitt and G Beruto (eds), *Terrorism and International Law* (IIHL and George C Marshall European Center for Security Studies, San Remo, 2003) 75; K Hayward and W Morrison, 'Locating "Ground Zero": Caught between the Narratives of Crime and War' in Strawson (ed), n 23, 139; T Ansah, 'War: Rhetoric and Norm-Creation in Response to Terror (2003) 43 Virginia JIL 797; F Mégret, ' "War"? Legal Semantics and the Move to Violence' (2002) 13 EJIL 361, 386.

Yet crises are often bad paradigms,[49] and there is danger in being mesmerized by the scale, symbolism, and emotional resonance of those attacks, and thereby acceding to unnecessary or imprudent modifications of international law. Many claims about the legal novelty of those events misstate the scope of, or underestimate the durability and flexibility of, the existing law, and it is important not to overstate the normative effects of those events.

DEFINING TERRORISM IN INTERNATIONAL LAW

In the absence of a specific international crime of terrorism, Chapter 1 explains the policy rationale for defining and criminalizing terrorism—*why*, rather than *how*, to define it. Much of the international disagreement about defining terrorism stems from a more fundamental confusion about the underlying reasons for definition. By identifying precisely what is so objectionable about terrorism, it then becomes easier to define it technically to encapsulate those policy judgments. Since many of the physical acts comprising terrorist conduct are already domestic crimes or sectoral treaty offences, or fall within existing international crimes, it is vital to articulate why terrorism *per se* deserves special treatment.

The core rationale for definition and criminalization is that terrorism seriously undermines fundamental human rights, jeopardizes the State and peaceful politics, and threatens international peace and security. Defining terrorism as a discrete crime normatively recognizes and protects vital international community values and interests, symbolically expresses community condemnation, and stigmatizes offenders. The overreach inherent in sectoral treaties would be clarified by a more calibrated response which differentiates political from private violence. Arguments for criminalization are grounded in an examination of the basic characteristics of international crimes, the purposes of criminological policy, and the need to prevent the proliferation of unnecessary offences. The case for internationally criminalizing both domestic and international terrorism is also made, before a basic definition of terrorism is deduced from the policy reasons underlying its definition.

While the international community has repeatedly condemned terrorism as criminal and unjustifiable, that does not preclude the existence of exceptions to terrorism, or the idea that some terrorism may be *excusable*, and there is little evidence of absolute liability for it. Accordingly, Chapter 2 examines the range of justifications, excuses, and defences available to answer a terrorist charge, as well as purported exceptions (such as self-determination struggles). The first part outlines debates about the relevance of the causes of terrorism in evaluating responsibility for it. It then distinguishes permissible

---

[49] M Nussbaum, 'Compassion and Terror' in Sterba (ed), n 18, 229, 248.

self-determination violence from terrorism, and argues for the extension of international humanitarian law (IHL) as an appropriate normative framework for all self-determination struggles, as well as for certain internal rebellions.

The second part examines how the individual criminal defences of self-defence and duress/necessity may excuse some terrorist acts, and argues further that non-State group actors should be entitled to plead circumstances precluding wrongfulness, drawn analogously from the law of State responsibility, in defence of terrorism. While a narrow class of terrorist acts may be excused by individual or group defences, some acts considered justifiable may still fall outside the scope of defences. To maintain the law's legitimacy, the final part argues that limited acts of 'terrorism', in collective defence of human rights, could be regarded as 'illegal but justifiable'. In addition, political amnesties or pardons may be necessary in carefully limited circumstances in order to secure higher values of peace or national reconciliation.

In the absence of an accepted international definition of terrorism, Chapter 3 examines the international community's response to terrorism in treaty law. Since the 1960s, numerous anti-terrorism (or sectoral) treaties have objectively regulated specific activities often described politically as terroristic, without creating a distinct generic crime of terrorism, or differentiating political from private violence. Regional treaty law followed a similar pattern until recently, when a number of treaties established wide generic terrorist offences, some indistinguishable from other forms of political violence. The second part of this chapter sketches numerous unsuccessful efforts since the 1920s to generically define and criminalize terrorism in treaty form. The many attempts at definition suggest that the international community has repeatedly attached importance to it, and illustrate the basic elements on which the definition debate has focused, including in the debate since 2000 about a UN Draft Comprehensive Convention.

Close analysis of customary international law in Chapter 4 confirms that there is no generic international crime, or distinct legal concept, of terrorism. Early attempts in the General Assembly to define terrorism were unsuccessful and a much-reiterated working definition of 1994 signals nascent political consensus, rather than firm legal agreement. There also remains disagreement over proposals for a national liberation exception to any legal prohibition of terrorism, although the adoption of the 1977 Geneva Protocols and the end of the Cold War dissipated some of the more paralysing and ideological features of the debate about the liberation exception.

In the Security Council, 'terrorism' was not mentioned in resolutions until 1985, after which time the Council increasingly designated a range of particular acts and incidents as 'terrorist', and condemned them as threats to international peace and security. After 11 September 2001, more generalized references to terrorism in Council resolutions have triggered serious legal consequences, without any definition of terrorism in Council practice. A working definition of terrorism in a resolution of late 2004[50] does not cure this deficiency, given its non-binding status, and the latitude accorded to States in implementing resolutions.

Most international judicial decisions dealing with terrorist subject matter are silent on its legal status and instead treat the issue by recourse to existing legal norms. A number of national decisions concur, although some decisions have accepted international definitions for limited, non-criminal purposes. While some national laws define terrorism, most definitions serve administrative rather than criminal law purposes, and those containing generic terrorism offences are too diverse to support a customary international definition.

Finally, Chapter 5 explores the long history of attempts in IHL to regulate terrorism in armed conflict, especially in the context of air warfare, from the end of the First World War, through the inter-war period and the Second World War. A number of little-known prohibitions on terrorism, acts spreading terror, and acts of terrorism, are found in the 1949 Geneva Conventions and 1977 Protocols, and aim to enhance the protection of non-combatants in armed conflict. While those treaties do not define terrorism, its meaning in the different provisions can be derived from the drafting history, ordinary principles of textual interpretation, and a small number of judicial decisions. The meaning of terrorism in IHL is distinct from its meaning outside armed conflict, and embodies an interpretation of terrorism at its most literal—instilling extreme fear (in protected persons). There is, however, no wider concept of terrorism as politically motivated violence designed to coerce or intimidate governments or international organizations, despite attempts by the US to conflate peace-time definitions of terrorism with IHL. This chapter also examines justifications for these discrete prohibitions on terrorism, and special evidentiary difficulties arising from them.

---

[50] UNSC Resolution 1566 (2004) para 3.

1

Reasons for Defining and Criminalizing Terrorism

... the reduction of fear is precious—in itself and in the productive possibilities it allows. For fear is not only frightening; it is typically also degrading, humiliating and paralysing. There is nothing to be said for it. Fear degrades those who suffer it, and equally those who inflict it.*

A. INTRODUCTION

Much of the international legal debate on terrorism has focused on ideological disputes, or technical mechanics, of definition, rather than on the underlying policy question of why—or whether—terrorism should be internationally criminalized. Since most terrorist acts are already punishable as ordinary criminal offences in national legal systems,[1] it is vital to explore whether—and articulate why—certain acts should be treated or classified as terrorist offences rather than as ordinary national crimes such as murder, assault, or arson. Equally, it is important to explain why terrorist acts should be treated separately from existing *international* crimes in cases where conduct overlaps different categories (particularly crimes against humanity, war crimes, and the existing sectoral anti-terrorism treaty offences).

In State practice, viewed through the lenses of UN organs and regional organizations, the bases of criminalization are that terrorism severely undermines: (1) basic human rights; (2) the State and the political process (but not exclusively democracy); and (3) international peace and security. Definition would also help to distinguish political from private violence, eliminating the overreach of the many 'sectoral' anti-terrorism treaties and ensuring a more calibrated international response to different types of violence. A definition could also help to confine the scope of Security Council Resolutions since 11 September 2001, which have encouraged States to pursue unilateral, excessive, and unpredictable counter-terrorism measures. Treating terrorism

---

* M Krygier, *Civil Passions: Selected Writings* (Black Inc, Melbourne, 2005) 149.
[1] J Murphy, 'Defining International Terrorism: A Way Out of the Quagmire' (1989) 19 IYBHR 13, 23–25; J Murphy, 'United States Proposals on the Control and Repression of Terrorism' in MC Bassiouni (ed), *International Terrorism and Political Crimes* (Charles C Thomas, Illinois, 1975) 493, 503; MC Bassiouni, 'Methodological Options for International Legal Control of Terrorism', in Bassiouni (ed), above, 485, 487.

as a distinct category of criminal harm symbolically expresses the international community's desire to condemn and stigmatize 'terrorism', as such, beyond its ordinary criminal characteristics. Doing so normatively recognizes and protects vital international community values and interests. Once consensus is reached on what is considered wrongful about terrorism, it is then easier to progress (in the last part of this chapter) to define the elements of terrorist offences with sufficient legal precision.

The rationale for criminalization is anchored in an examination of the common features of international crimes and the objectives of international criminological policy. This chapter is mindful of avoiding the proliferation of international offences and addresses problems of multiple charges and convictions. The rationale for definition depends on the purpose of definition, and the emphasis here is on definition in international criminal law, rather than in other branches of law (such as international humanitarian law (IHL), human rights, the use of force, refugee law, or extradition law). Ultimately, a coherent legal definition of terrorism might help to confine the unilateral misuse of the term by national governments against their political opponents and in ways which seriously undermine basic human rights.

B. NATURE OF INTERNATIONAL CRIMES

An international crime is conduct prohibited by the international community as criminal. This bland positivist account merely identifies a crime by its source (State consent in a treaty, or through custom formation), but does not explain *why* the international community chooses to stigmatize conduct as deserving of international (or transnational)[2] criminal prohibition and punishment. The policy rationale for criminalization is often obscure, and the 'rapid expansion' of the criminal law's 'material scope has not been complemented (or complicated) by general discussion of coherent principles justifying or constraining criminalization, like individual autonomy, welfare, harm and minimalism'.[3]

1. Grave conduct of international concern

One general explanation for criminalization was suggested in the *Hostages* case, in which the US Military Tribunal at Nuremberg stated that: 'An inter-

---

[2] A distinction can be drawn between international (customary) crimes of universal jurisdiction and more limited transnational (treaty) crimes (or 'crimes of international concern'): G Goodwin-Gill, 'Crime in International Law' in G Goodwin-Gill and S Talmon (eds), *The Reality of International Law* (Clarendon, Oxford, 1999) 199, 205–208; see also N Boister, 'Transnational Criminal Law?' (2003) 14 EJIL 953; T Meron, 'Is International Law Moving Towards Criminalization?' (1998) 9 EJIL 18.

[3] Boister, n 2, 957.

national crime is such act universally recognized as criminal, which is considered a grave matter of international concern and for some valid reason
cannot be left within the exclusive jurisdiction of the State that would have
control over it under ordinary circumstances.'[4] The prohibition of conduct
as criminal is ordinarily a matter falling within the reserved domain of
domestic jurisdiction, and there is value in preventing the proliferation
of superfluous or duplicate international offences—and unnecessary liabilities on individuals—to ensure the systemic integrity and coherence of international criminal law.

However, as the Tribunal noted, conduct is internationally criminalized
where it is of such gravity that it attracts international concern. Conduct may
be of international concern because it has transboundary effects or threatens
'the peace, security and well-being of the world';[5] causes or threatens public
harm of great magnitude;[6] or violates natural or moral law and 'shocks the
conscience' of humanity.[7] International criminal law thus seeks to protect the
shared values considered important by the international community,[8] rather
than comprising socially expedient or technical rules.[9] As a result, 'a greater
degree of moral turpitude attaches' to an international crime,[10] which is not
merely the product of social prejudice, indignation, distaste, or disgust.[11]

There is inevitable subjectivity in identifying universal values, or in
appealing to natural law as the basis of criminalization,[12] and 'make-believe
universalism' undermines the law's authority.[13] Despite cultural differences
between States and their communities, over time consensus has emerged on

[4] *Hostages* case (1953) 15 Ann Dig 632, 636.
[5] 1998 Rome Statute, preamble; MC Bassiouni, *Crimes Against Humanity* (Martinus Nijhoff, Dordrecht, 1992) 46–47. Criminalization of piracy is warranted since it occurs beyond territorial jurisdiction, on the high seas.
[6] A Cassese, *International Criminal Law* (OUP, Oxford, 2003) 22.
[7] ibid; *Eichmann* (1961) 36 ILR 5 (Dist Ct Jerus), para 12; *R v Finta* [1994] 1 SCR 701, 812; H Lauterpacht (ed), *Oppenheim's International Law: vol I Peace* (8th edn, Longmans, Green and Co, London, 1955) 753.
[8] MC Bassiouni, 'A Policy-Oriented Inquiry into the Different Forms and Manifestations of "International Terrorism" ' in MC Bassiouni (ed), *Legal Responses to International Terrorism* (Martinus Nijhoff, Dordrecht, 1988) xv, xl; Cassese, n 6, 22–23; Bassiouni, n 5, 46; MC Bassiouni, *International Criminal Law* (Sijthoff and Noordhoff, Groningen, 1980) 1, 13, 17, 19; MC Bassiouni, 'Criminological Policy' in A Evans and J Murphy (eds), *Legal Aspects of International Terrorism* (ASIL, Washington, DC, 1979) 523; C Jones, *Global Justice* (OUP, Oxford, 2001) 176–179.
[9] J Smith, *Smith and Hogan: Criminal Law* (10th edn, Butterworths, London, 2002) 17; H Hart, *The Concept of Law* (2nd edn, OUP, Oxford, 1997) 229–230.
[10] *Tadic (Appeal)*, ICTY–94–1 (15 July 1999) 271.
[11] A Ashworth, *Principles of Criminal Law* (3rd edn, OUP, Oxford, 1999) 43; H Hart, 'Immorality and Treason' in R Dworkin (ed), *The Philosophy of Law* (OUP, Oxford, 1986) 83, 85.
[12] I Tallgren, 'The Sense and Sensibility of International Criminal Law' (2002) 13 EJIL 561, 564; Boister, n 2, 969–970.
[13] M McDougal and H Lasswell, 'The Identification and Appraisal of Diverse Systems of Public Order' (1959) 53 AJIL 1.

core international crimes, evolving in an ad hoc and piecemeal fashion rather than by a systematic policy of criminalization.[14] International moral agreement is not innate, but varies over time,[15] shaped by community concerns about public safety and social order. As with other crimes, there is nothing *intrinsically* criminal about terrorism (as opposed to the physical criminal acts that it often comprises), which is situated in its own historical and political context.

2. *International element*

In the *Hostages* case, the US Military Tribunal laid down the criterion that conduct must be of such a nature that its suppression in domestic law alone would not be sufficient. Sectoral anti-terrorism treaties typically apply only where there is an international element to conduct. For example, the 1997 Terrorist Bombings Convention and the 1999 Terrorist Financing Convention do not apply where an offence is committed in a single State, the alleged offender is in the territory of that State, and no other State has a Convention basis to exercise jurisdiction.[16] There is a similar provision in the Draft Comprehensive Convention, which also stipulates that the victims must not be nationals of the State where the offence is committed.[17]

Although international crimes require an international element,[18] this does not mean that prohibited conduct must always physically or materially transcend national boundaries, although domestic terrorism may threaten regional peace and security 'owing to spill-over effects' such as cross-border violence and refugee outflows.[19] Genocide, war crimes and crimes against humanity may be wholly committed in a single jurisdiction. While these crimes often involve State action because of their scale or gravity, such involvement is not essential. Further, conduct need not threaten peace and security to constitute an international crime, where such conduct infringes international values.[20]

---

[14] Bassiouni, n 5, 45; see also MC Bassiouni, 'The Penal Characteristics of Conventional International Criminal Law' (1983) 15 Case Western Reserve JIL 27, 32; E Greppi, 'The Evolution of Individual Criminal Responsibility under International Law' (1999) 81 IRRC 531. Although the ILC attempted to codify and progressively develop international crimes in its 1954 and 1996 Draft Codes of Offences against the Peace and Security of Mankind: ILC Reports (1954) UN Doc A/2693 and (1996) UN Doc A/51/10.
[15] K Kittichaisaree, *International Criminal Law* (OUP, Oxford, 2001) 3.
[16] 1997 Terrorist Bombings Convention, Art 3; 1999 Terrorist Financing Convention, Art 3.
[17] Draft Comprehensive Convention, Art 3.
[18] Bassiouni, n 5, 46–47; Bassiouni, 'A Policy-Oriented Inquiry', n 8, xxiv.
[19] Report of the Policy Working Group on the UN and Terrorism, UN Doc A/57/273, S/2002/875, para 12.
[20] P Macklem, 'Canada's Obligations at International Criminal Law' in R Daniels, P Macklem, and K Roach (eds), *The Security of Freedom* (University of Toronto Press, Toronto, 2001) 353, 355.

Thus if terrorism injures values or interests deserving international protection—such as certain human rights[21]—then domestic and international varieties should be equally criminalized. This is the approach followed regionally in the EU Framework Decision, which does not differentiate between the criminalization of domestic or international terrorism, as long as motive elements of altering or destroying a State, or intimidating a people, are satisfied. It is not the existence of a *physical* international element which attracts international jurisdiction; but the egregious nature of the interests affected. On the other hand, the international consensus favours only defining and criminalizing *international* terrorism, leaving crimes of domestic terrorism to the discretion of States. The construction of an international element to terrorist offences is considered at the end of this chapter.

3. The 'international community'

In national legal systems, the criminal law underpins, serves, and protects the values and interests of the national community.[22] While domestic analogies should be cautiously drawn, international criminal law similarly presupposes an international community,[23] as constructed by its members,[24] and even though it may lack clarity.[25] Those who doubt the coherence of the international community, and thus decry the weakness of international criminal justice,[26] overstate those problems. First, many modern, pluralist national communities also lack coherence, since power, authority, identity, and values are contested by diverse sub-national groups.

Second, individuals in national communities can still appreciate and adhere to international values, since national citizenship is not an exclusive marker of personal identity or allegiance.[27] It is possible to assert the primacy of national law while concurrently realizing the value of the Nuremberg principles; indeed, the Rome Statute of the International Criminal Court (ICC)

---

[21] UNSubComHR (53rd Sess), Terrorism and Human Rights: Progress Report by Special Rapporteur K Koufa, 27 June 2001, UN Doc E/CN.4/Sub.2/2001/31, 13; D Partan, 'Terrorism: An International Law Offence' (1987) 19 *Connecticut Law Review* 751, 763; cf M Flory, 'International Law: An Instrument to Combat Terrorism' in R Higgins and M Flory (eds), *Terrorism and International Law* (Routledge, London, 1997) 30 (international law is only concerned with cross-border terrorism).

[22] R Muellerson, *Ordering Anarchy* (Martinus Nijhoff, The Hague, 2000) 88.

[23] P Allott, 'The Concept of International Law' (1999) 10 EJIL 31, 50.

[24] B Anderson, *Imagined Communities* (Verso, London, 1983) 15; H Seton-Watson, *Nations and States* (Westview Press, Colorado, 1977) 5.

[25] A Paulus, 'The Influence of the United States on the Concept of the "International Community"' in M Byers and G Nolte (eds), *United States Hegemony* (CUP, Cambridge, 2003) 57, 58, 60.

[26] S Holmes, 'Why International Justice Limps' (2002) 69 *Social Research* 1055, 1066.

[27] C Schmitt, quoted in J Habermas, *The Inclusion of the Other* (Polity, Cambridge, 2002) 181; see also J Finnis, 'Natural Law: The Classical Theory' in J Coleman and S Shapiro (eds), *Oxford Handbook of Jurisprudence and Legal Philosophy* (OUP, Oxford, 2002) 1.

accords such primacy to national courts. Third, when national communities uniformly demand vengeance, international trials may become most important to ensure fair prosecutions[28]—particularly against 'terrorists'.[29]

A more difficult problem lies in identifying the 'international community' which designs, and is served by, international criminal law. Kennedy claims the 'international community' is a 'fantasy' of objective agreement, when it is really the product of a small bureaucratic technical class.[30] Clearly, a positivist account is insufficient—if States 'make' international law and comprise its community, it is unsurprising that States will seek to outlaw anti-State violence (including terrorism). There is a danger that the morality or national interests of dominant States may be disguised as a shared international morality of common interests;[31] a hegemonic State may 'arrogate to itself the exclusive power to lay down the definitive interpretation of the universal'.[32] As Habermas warns: 'the universalistic discourses of law and morality can be abused as a particularly insidious form of legitimation since particular interests can hide behind the glimmering façade of reasonable universality'.[33]

In considering whether (and how) to criminalize terrorism, the views and interests of a wider range of participants in the international system must be taken into account, so that regulation of terrorism does not descend into a Statist technique of illiberal control. As Lauterpacht writes, 'if there is law to be found in every community, law . . . must not be wholly identified with the law of States'.[34] The international community comprises a 'whole array of other actors whose actions influence the development of international legal rules'.[35] For Habermas, while 'there is not yet a global public sphere', there are now 'actors who confront states from within the network of an international civil society'.[36]

Diversity in a decentralized community does not preclude the existence of the community; international criminal law does not presuppose a monolithic community, just as national law does not depend on a homogenous society. As Abi-Saab writes: 'Rather than referring to a group as a community in general, it is better, for the sake of precision, to speak of the degree

---

[28] G Robertson, 'Lynch mob justice or a proper trial', *The Guardian*, 5 Oct 2001.

[29] J Paust, 'Antiterrorism Military Commissions: Courting Illegality' (2001) 23 Michigan JIL 1.

[30] D Kennedy, 'The Disciplines of International Law and Policy' (2000) 12 Leiden JIL 9, 83–84.

[31] N Krisch, 'Hegemony and the Law on the Use of Force', Paper at ESIL Conference, Florence, 13–15 May 2004, 5; Boister, n 2, 973.

[32] C Douzinas, 'Postmodern Just Wars' in Strawson J (ed), *Law after Ground Zero* (Glass-House Press, London, 2002) 29.

[33] J Habermas, 'Fundamentalism and Terror: A Dialogue with Jürgen Habermas' in G Borradori, *Philosophy in a Time of Terror: Dialogues with Jürgen Habermas and Jacques Derrida* (University of Chicago Press, Chicago, 2003) 25, 42.

[34] Lauterpacht, n 7, 10; see also Allott, n 23, 50.

[35] E Kwakwa, 'The International Community, International Law, and the United States' in Byers and Nolte (eds), n 25, 25, 27.

[36] Habermas, n 27, 177.

of community existing within the group in relation to a given subject, at a given moment.'[37] Terrorism, for instance, is a global danger that has 'united the world into an involuntary community of shared risks'.[38]

4. Legal politics and political laws

A question remains as to whether terrorism is too 'political' for agreement to be reached on definition. It would be a mistake for any law against terrorism to attempt to 'remain neutral in respect to competing values, and claims', as Bassiouni suggests.[39] International criminal justice is not a 'technical-instrumental-oriented enterprise', but is densely implicated in international politics.[40] Just as other international crimes partly rest on an 'intuitive-moralistic' foundation,[41] so too can it not be expected that terrorism is capable of definition by objective calculation or rational deduction.

The absence of any immutable content of 'terrorism' is no reason to refrain from forging a political consensus on definition; less still is it a basis for believing that terrorism is *inherently* indefinable.[42] In the past, liberal and illiberal States have supported the criminalization of other conduct,[43] demonstrating that consensus is possible even where it interferes in sovereign criminal jurisdiction. Further, that terrorism was historically directed against few States, such as the US, the UK, France, and Israel, is not fatal to the broader appeal of a prohibition. Indeed, 'a system of thought may be true, and hence non-relativistic, even though it has developed within a tradition that is historically and culturally specific'.[44] Certain values may be 'universalizable', if not yet universal.[45]

There must, however, be an awareness that criminalizing politics (or judicializing the public sphere by punishing political enemies)[46] 'strengthens the hand of those who are in a position to determine what acts count as

---

[37] G Abi-Saab, 'Whither the International Community' (1998) 9 EJIL 248, 249; Boister, n 2, 972.
[38] Habermas, n 27, 186.
[39] Bassiouni, 'Methodological Options', n 1, 485.
[40] F Mégret, 'The Politics of International Criminal Justice' (2002) 13 EJIL 1261, 1280.
[41] Tallgren, n 12, 564.
[42] cf G Sliwowski, 'Legal Aspects of Terrorism' in D Carlton and C Schaerf (eds), *International Terrorism and World Security* (Croom Helm, London, 1975) 69, 76.
[43] Mégret, n 40, 1268.
[44] D Rodin, *War and Self-Defense* (Clarendon, Oxford, 2002) 8.
[45] M Reisman, 'Aftershocks: Reflections on the Implications of September 11' (2003) 6 Yale HRDLJ 81. Or as Koskenniemi puts it: 'From the fact that law has no shape of its own, but always comes to us in the shape of particular traditions or preferences, it does not follow that we cannot choose between better or worse preferences, traditions we have more or less reason to hope to generalise': M Koskenniemi, 'International Law in Europe: Between Tradition and Renewal' (2005) 16 EJIL 113, 119.
[46] T Todorov, 'The Limitations of Justice' (2004) 2 JICJ 711, 714.

"crimes" and who are able to send in the police'.[47] What is then important are principles of transparency and broad participation in the politics of law-making, to determine 'the common interest of society'[48] and to avoid a 'democratic deficit' in law-making.[49] Only through an inclusive process is definition of terrorism likely to be widely regarded as legitimate, and not 'wielded to fit the interest or the whim of any one member of the community'.[50]

C. INTERNATIONAL CRIMINOLOGICAL POLICY

1. Criminological purposes of criminalization

In domestic criminal law, criminalization is often said to advance certain criminological or policy purposes: punishment or retribution; incapacitation; rehabilitation; and general and specific deterrence.[51] Ashworth identifies the three main purposes of criminal law as declaratory, preventive, and censuring.[52] International criminal law seeks to secure similar objectives, although its criminology is underdeveloped,[53] and its sentencing policy confused.[54] In *Simic (Sentencing)*, the 'main general sentencing factors' in the jurisprudence of the International Criminal Tribunal for the former Yugoslavia (ICTY) were found to be 'deterrence and retribution',[55] and the Rome Statute's preamble affirms that punishment and prevention of crimes are key purposes of the International Criminal Court.

While imprisonment promotes punishment and deterrence, criminalization also furthers these goals by expressing community repugnance at conduct and invoking 'social censure and shame'.[56] The purposes served by

[47] M Koskenniemi, 'Hersch Lauterpacht and the Development of International Criminal Law' (2004) 2 JICJ 810, 825.

[48] Allott, n 23, 32.

[49] Boister, n 2, 957–958.

[50] P Jessup, 'Diversity and Uniformity in the Law of Nations' (1964) 58 AJIL 341, 352.

[51] See generally T Honderich, *Punishment: The Supposed Justifications* (Polity, Cambridge, 1989).

[52] Ashworth, n 11, 36.

[53] P Roberts and N McMillan, 'For Criminology in International Criminal Justice' (2003) 1 JICJ 315, 318; Tallgren, n 12, 564; D Zolo, 'Peace through Criminal Law?' (2004) 2 JICJ 727, 728.

[54] R Henham, 'The Philosophical Foundations of International Sentencing' (2003) 1 JICJ 64, 65; A Carcano, 'Sentencing and the Gravity of the Offence in International Criminal Law' (2002) 51 ICLQ 583.

[55] *Simic (Sentencing)* ICTY–95–9/2 (17 Oct 2002) paras 32–33; see also *Todorovic (Sentencing)* ICTY–95–9/1 (31 July 2001) paras 28–29; *Krnojelac* ICTY–97–25–T (12 Mar 2002) para 508; *Kunarac* ICTY–96–23 and ICTY–96–23/1–T (22 Feb 2001) para 838; *Kunarac* ICTY–96–23 and ICTY–96–23/1–A (12 June 2002) para 142; *Celebici (Appeal)* ICTY–96–21–A (20 Feb 2001) para 806; *Furundzija* ICTY–95–17/1–T (10 Dec 1998) para 288; *Tadic (Sentencing)* IT–94–1–Tbis–R117 (11 Nov 1999) para 9.

[56] Australian Law Reform Commission, *Principled Regulation* (Report 95, Sydney, 2002) 65.

criminalization may, however, vary in different contexts, and pluralistic ideas of justice should not be sacrificed to 'western ethical aggression'.[57] For example, prosecutions in post-conflict societies may contribute to national reconciliation and rehabilitation, while in other contexts restorative or alternative models of justice may be more appropriate.[58]

Unlike in domestic law, international criminal law has no unified or systematic law enforcement and judicial machinery. Even the establishment of the ICC does not entirely remedy this deficiency, since its criminal jurisdiction is established by treaty, not universal customary law, and is limited to enforcement among State Parties (excepting Security Council referrals). Thus national courts necessarily play a leading role in enforcing international criminal law, facilitated by judicial cooperation and assistance.

Proscription may still be effective despite the absence of a universal enforcement system. While international criminal law primarily has a repressive function,[59] its normative role should not be understated.[60] The mere existence of a criminal prohibition has normative value—signifying condemnation and stigmatization of conduct—irrespective of prosecutions.[61] The identification of a crime, multilateral support for it, and its dissemination are non-prosecutorial modes of giving weight to a prohibition, producing 'general pressure' to conform.[62] As Lemkin wrote of genocide, 'if the law was in place it would have an effect—sooner or later'.[63] Inevitably, ineffective enforcement undermines the normative weight and deterrent value of a prohibition.[64] Yet even scarce prosecutions may support a prohibition, if they are appropriately targeted and publicized, and conducted by the principled exercise of prosecutorial discretion.

Criminalizing terrorism has a number of criminological implications. Bassiouni argues that incapacitation, through imprisonment, is one of the most credible theories of punishment for terrorists, since it neutralizes the threat of reoffending.[65] Yet incapacitation is already served by prosecuting terrorism as ordinary crime, so this rationale does not specifically justify criminalizing terrorism, unless terrorist offences trigger enhanced penalties and thus prolong incapacitation. International criminal law historically prohibited conduct without agreeing on penalties, 'due to widely differing

---

[57] A Garapon, 'Three Challenges for International Criminal Justice' (2004) 2 JICJ 716, 720.

[58] See, eg, S Chesterman, 'No Justice Without Peace? International Criminal Law and the Decision to Prosecute' in S Chesterman (ed), *Civilians in War* (Lynne Rienner, Colorado, 2001) 145.

[59] Cassese, n 6, 20.   [60] ibid.   [61] Ashworth, n 11, 36.   [62] Hart, n 9, 220.

[63] Rosenthal, quoted in S Power, *A Problem from Hell* (Flamingo, London, 2003) 55.

[64] G Blewitt, 'The Necessity for Enforcement of International Humanitarian Law' (1995) 89 ASIL Proceedings 298; R Goldstone, 'International Law and Justice and America's War on Terrorism' (2002) 69 *Social Research* 1045, 1046.

[65] Bassiouni, 'Criminological Policy', n 8, 527–528.

views' on the gravity of crimes and the harshness of punishment.[66] Yet as Ashworth writes, 'one of the main functions of criminal law is to express the *degree* of wrongdoing, not simply the fact of wrongdoing'.[67] An international treaty could, however, specify special penalties for terrorism, as in the 2002 EU Framework Decision.[68]

Retribution or punishment is the most significant factor supporting the distinct criminalization of terrorism, since conviction socially stigmatizes and condemns the offender and provides some sense of justice for victims.[69] In contrast, it is doubtful whether some terrorists are likely to be deterred by either imprisonment or condemnation by legal systems whose legitimacy they reject.[70] The publicity gained by detention may even be beneficial to an ideologically-motivated offender's cause, or have a martyr effect.[71] Suicide bombers are particularly unlikely to be concerned about apprehension and prosecution. It is also for these reasons that rehabilitation is often inapplicable to an offender 'opposed . . . to the social system into which he is to be resocialized'.[72]

Nevertheless, criminalization is a useful symbolic mechanism for condemning and stigmatizing unacceptable behaviour.[73] It may be too much to expect that the criminal law alone will effectively suppress terrorism, and such expectation may be an exercise in deception, irrationality, or quasi-religious hope.[74] Criminalization is only one small part of the overall international response to terrorism.[75] Further, Baudrillard fittingly warns that 'though we can range a great machinery of repression and deterrence against physical insecurity and terrorism, nothing will protect us from this mental insecurity'.[76]

---

[66] Cassese, n 6, 157.   [67] Ashworth, n 11, 37.

[68] 2002 EU Framework Decision, Art 5.

[69] Bassiouni, 'A Policy-Oriented Inquiry', n 8, xlii; Bassiouni, 'Criminological Policy', n 8, 527–528.

[70] A Rubin, 'Terrorism, "Grave Breaches" and the 1977 Geneva Protocols' (1980) 74 ASIL Proceedings 192, 193; Bassiouni, 'Criminological Policy', n 8, 525–527; see also A Dershowitz, *Why Terrorism Works: Understanding the Threat, Responding to the Challenge* (Yale University Press, New Haven, 2002) 15–33; P Wilkinson, *Terrorism and the Liberal State* (Macmillan, London, 1977) 66, 180.

[71] Bassiouni, 'A Policy-Oriented Inquiry', n 8, xlii, xxxiii; see also Rubin, ibid, 193.

[72] Bassiouni, ibid, xli–xlii; see also Rubin, ibid, 193.

[73] C Walter, 'Defining Terrorism in National and International Law' in C Walter et al (eds), *Terrorism as a Challenge for National and International Law* (Springer, Heidelberg, 2004) 23, 45.

[74] Tallgren, n 12.

[75] D Freestone, 'Legal Responses to Terrorism: Towards European Cooperation?' in J Lodge (ed), *Terrorism: A Challenge to the State* (Martin Robertson, Oxford, 1981) 195, 200; see UNODC, 'Classification of Counter-Terrorism Measures' (2002), classifying responses in these categories: I. Politics and Governance; II. Economic and Social; III. Psychological-communication-educational; IV. Military; V. Judicial and Legal; VI. Police and Prison System; VII. Intelligence and Secret Service; VIII. Other.

[76] J Baudrillard, 'Hypotheses on Terrorism' in J Baudrillard, *The Spirit of Terrorism and Other Essays* (trans C Turner, Verson, London, 2003) 49, 81.

Yet turning even an irrational hope against terrorism is not mere impotence: 'norm setting eventually changes reality, however arduous the process'.[77] Criminalization is valuable if it helps the international community to recognize and condemn violence for what it is—even if it is known that such violence is likely to continue. While punishment of terrorists may not meet 'basic requirements of deterrence, retribution, incapacitation and resocialization', 'no alternative solutions . . . have yet been found'[78]—other than defensive, pre-emptive, or centrifugal wars. When asked if a piece of paper would stop Hitler or Stalin, Lemkin exclaimed: 'Only man has law . . . You must build the law!'[79]

2. *Vengeance and the problem of evil*

Criminalization should not, however, serve as an instrument of populist vengeance. The exemplary function of international criminal justice risks degrading or victimizing an accused on the altar of popular values, while the law's retributive function may primitively inflict suffering without any broader correctional purpose.[80] Invidious moralization tends to accompany reference to terrorism, casting it as a titanic, Manichean, existential struggle of polarities: humanity and inhumanity; civilization and barbarism; freedom and fear; modernity and pre-modernity; liberal democracy and apocalyptic, eschatological, phantasmagorical nihilism; the rational and the pathological; law and outlaw; friend and enemy; the West and Others; Christianity and Islam; light and dark; good and evil.[81]

Clearly, the term terrorism is imbricated in a dense ideological discourse.[82] Habermas warns that 'moralization brands opponents as enemies, and the resulting criminalization . . . gives inhumanity a completely free hand'.[83] A State will often seek 'to usurp a universal concept in its struggle against its enemy, in the same way that one can misuse peace, justice, progress, and

---

[77] D Rieff, 'Fables of Redemption in an Age of Barbarism' (2002) 69 *Social Research* 1159, 1168.
[78] C Van den Wijngaert, *The Political Offence Exception to Extradition* (Kluwer, Boston, 1980) 220.
[79] Quoted in Power, n 63, 55.
[80] Zolo, n 53, 731–733.
[81] See, eg, US President Bush, Address to UNGA, New York, 23 Sept 2003; Spanish PM Aznar (CTC Chair), quoted in 'Defeating Terror Requires Dedication by All, Spanish Leader Tells Security Council', UN News Service, New York, 6 May 2003; R Holbrooke, 'Just and Unjust Wars: A Diplomat's Perspective' (2002) 69 *Social Research* 915, 917. For criticism of this discourse, see J Petman, 'The Problem of Evil in International Law' in J Petman and J Klabbers (eds), *Nordic Cosmopolitanism* (Martinus Nijhoff, Leiden, 2003) 111; S Chan, *Out of Evil: International Politics and the New Doctrine of War* (IB Tauris, London, 2004); Krisch, n 31, 23–24; P Berman, *Terror and Liberalism* (Norton, London, 2003) 182–183.
[82] J Mertus, ' "Terrorism" as Ideology: Implications for Intervention' (1999) 93 ASIL *Proceedings* 78.
[83] Habermas, n 27, 189.

civilization'.[84] Regarding terrorism as a human rights violation encourages just wars against terrorism 'in the name of a globalised humanity',[85] and fosters the instrumentalization of human rights.[86] For Schmitt, subsuming political relations within moral categories of good and evil turns the enemy into 'an inhuman monster that must not only be repulsed but must be totally annihilated'[87]—positing terrorism as a new enemy of humanity (*hostis humani generis*).[88] In the words of the UN legal counsel, terrorism 'threatens all States, every society and each individual'.[89]

Thus in 1986, it was possible for Friedlander hysterically to urge Old Testament justice upon terrorists—public execution to humiliate and degrade them—to 'Treat them as the monsters that they really are'; to 'metaphorically spit in their bestial faces'; and to 'terrorize the terrorist barbarians'.[90] Others have called for the abandonment of reactive criminal law responses in favour of offensive military action,[91] or for terrorists to be treated as pirates or 'outlaws'.[92] In the UK, the Archbishop of Canterbury cited Jesus in calling for terrorists who harm children to have millstones placed around their necks and be cast into the sea.[93] If terrorism is presented as an absolute threat, then counter-terrorism measures must also be unlimited.[94] Labelling opponents as terrorists de-legitimizes, discredits, dehumanizes, and demonizes them,[95] casting them as fanatics who cannot be reasoned with.[96]

Yet it is precisely because terrorism remains undefined that it lends itself to abuse in the service of unbounded moral abstraction, ideological causes, and imperial projects. The moralizing attaching to terrorism is not, however, a reason to avoid the term, so much as a reason to define it. While the term

[84] C Schmitt, *The Concept of the Political* (trans G Schwab, University of Chicago Press, Chicago, 1996) 54; see also D Fidler, 'The Return of the Standard of Civilisation' (2001) 2 Chinese JIL 137; R Coupland, 'Humanity: What Is It and How Does It Influence International Law?' (2001) 83 IRRC 969.

[85] P Fitzpatrick, 'Enduring Right' in Strawson (ed), n 32, 37, 41; see also Douzinas, n 32, 25.

[86] C Chinkin, 'Terrorism and Human Rights', Paper at ESIL Conference, Florence, 13–15 May 2004.

[87] Schmitt, n 84, 36.

[88] Krisch, n 31, 23–24; N Schrijver, 'Responding to International Terrorism: Moving the Frontiers of International Law for "Enduring Freedom"?' (2001) 48 Netherlands ILR 271, 290.

[89] H Corell, 'The International Instruments against Terrorism', Paper at Symposium on Combating International Terrorism: The Contribution of the UN, Vienna, 3–4 Jun 2002, 2.

[90] R Friedlander, 'Punishing Terrorists' (1986) 13 *Ohio Northern University Law Review* 149, 150, 155.

[91] C Carr, *The Lessons of Terror* (Little, Brown, London, 2002) 8–9.

[92] M Forster, 'Exclusionism and Terror: May Terrorists Be Excluded from the Protection of the Human Rights Treaties?', Paper at All Souls–Freshfields Seminar, University of Oxford, 25 Mar 2004; Y Dinstein, 'Terrorism as an International Crime' (1989) 19 IYBHR 55, 56.

[93] N Paton Walsh et al, 'Putin's warning as terror deaths top 360', *Observer*, 5 Sept 2004.

[94] Krisch, n 31, 24.

[95] UN Policy Working Group, n 19, para 14.

[96] T Kapitan, 'The Terrorism of "Terrorism" ' in J Sterba (ed), *Terrorism and International Justice* (OUP, Oxford, 2003) 47, 52; R Overy, 'Like the Wehrmacht, we've descended into barbarity', *The Guardian*, 10 May 2004.

implies judgment and condemnation,[97] by defining terrorism it is possible to finally appreciate precisely what is being judged and condemned. Definition fixes a legal standard against which to test and constrain political claims that opponents are terrorists, limiting ideological and political abuse of the term. Definition can harness and tame a term that has powerful symbolic resonance for, and embodies vital social judgments by, the international community of States and peoples.

It is not sufficient simply to object that the term is too potent to ever be legally deployed, since it will continue to be aggressively used in the political and public spheres as long as it remains undefined. As such, definition may help to limit the worst excesses. Definition could provide a constructive interpretation which satisfactorily expresses the community's emotional and normative attachment to the term, but simultaneously protects those accused of terrorism from being reviled as unlimited 'personifications of evil'.[98] By sketching the contours of terrorism as an international public wrong, definition could help to foil punitive and absolutist demands that terrorists, as evil people, must surrender their human dignity.

Clearly, a legal definition cannot possibly control all uses or misuses of the term terrorism, or seek to exercise a monopoly on the meaning of public language. The term 'genocide' was invented by a lawyer for the purposes of constructing the 1948 Genocide Convention, but that term is now both abused and under-used at variance with its legal meaning.[99] In part, that is because 'genocide' was defined too narrowly (due to drafting compromises) and thus excludes some vulnerable groups from protection.[100] The term does not, therefore, accord with popular understandings of the concept as group-based extermination, regardless of the group's identity.

At the same time, misapplying the term genocide to situations where genocidal intent is lacking erodes its descriptive utility and symbolic resonance, and its moral power to stigmatize offenders, and devalues the experience of victims of genuine genocides.[101] While defining terrorism is equally unlikely to restrain all misuses of the term, definition nonetheless provides strategic leverage and critical focus in public debates about whether particular acts qualify as terrorism. It may thus help to blunt some of the more excessive misuses of the term. As the genocide example suggests, to do this most effectively is it important that a definition should correlate as far as possible with public expectations about, and understandings of, the term.

---

[97] C Gearty, *The Future of Terrorism* (Phoenix, London, 1997) 11, 31–44.
[98] Douzinas, n 32, 27.
[99] See B Saul, 'Was the Conflict in East Timor "genocide" and Why Does It Matter?' (2001) 2 Melbourne JIL 477.
[100] ibid, 503–508, 516–519; B Saul, 'The International Crime of Genocide in Australian Law' (2000) 22 *Sydney Law Review* 527, 548–552.
[101] Saul (2001), ibid, 482–483.

3. Trivialization and misuse of terrorism offences

Criminalization of terrorism should also not punish trivial infringements. Recent prosecutions and convictions for international terrorism offences illustrate this problem. In the US, investigative referrals for these offences increased five-fold from 142 persons in the two years before 11 September 2001, to 748 persons in the two years from 11 September 2001 to 30 September 2003.[102] Convictions increased seven-fold in the same period, from 24 to 184. Yet of the 184 persons convicted, 171 received minor sentences (80 received no prison sentence, and 91 less than one year in prison). Despite the large increase in convictions, fewer persons received prison sentences of five or more years (three people in 2001–03, versus six in 1999–2001).[103] These sentencing trends suggest that international terrorism offences are capturing minor conduct, even though such offences should address the most serious conduct, attracting the highest penalties.[104]

The exercise of discretion by US federal prosecutors is also revealing. Sixty per cent of (domestic and international) terrorism referrals were declined by prosecutors (1,048 cases), while 30 per cent of additional 'anti-terrorism' referrals were declined (506 cases).[105] Of all referrals declined, nearly 35 per cent were declined for lack of evidence of criminal intent or the existence of an offence, or lack of federal interest. A further 15 per cent were declined for 'weak or insufficient admissible evidence'. While the statistics reflect the difficulties of gathering evidence against terrorism, they also suggest over-zealous law enforcement, based on flimsy evidence, unverified suspicion, and racial profiling. Excessive enforcement is a response to political and public demands for action against terrorists, by-passing evidentiary controls and investigative protocols. Increased enforcement does not necessarily correlate with any increase in terrorist activity.[106]

In the UK, in the four years from 11 September 2001 to 30 September 2005, 895 were arrested under the Terrorism Act 2000 (UK) but only 26 per cent of these were charged with an offence under any UK legislation.[107]

---

[102] Transactional Records Access Clearinghouse (TRAC), 'Criminal Terrorism Enforcement since the 9/11/01 Attacks', Special Report, 8 Dec 2003.

[103] However, the majority of cases referred were still pending after 30 Sept 2003 and more complex criminal matters, potentially leading to higher sentences, take longer to prosecute.

[104] Similar patterns were recorded for domestic terrorism offences. As Ashworth, n 11, 17, writes: 'criminal law, being society's strongest form of official censure and punishment, should be concerned only with the central values and significant harms'.

[105] TRAC, n 102.   [106] ibid.

[107] UK Home Office, 'Arrests and charges made under the Terrorism Act 2000', www.homeoffice.gov.uk/security/terrorism-and-the-law/terrorism-act/ (20 Dec 2005). Of the 138 charged under the Act, 62 were also charged with offences under other legislation; 156 of the 895 were charged under other legislation (including serious ordinary offences such as murder, grievous bodily harm and the use of firearms or explosives). See also C Dyer, 'Terror cases "too complex", says DPP', *The Guardian*, 20 May 2004; D McGoldrick, *From '9–11' to the Iraq War 2003* (Hart, Oxford, 2004) 38.

Around 55 per cent of those arrested (496 people) were released without charge, while 7 per cent were referred to immigration authorities (63 people). Only 15 per cent of those arrested were charged under the Terrorism Act 2000 itself (138 people), with only twenty-three people convicted (a conviction rate of 17 per cent). These twenty-three convictions represent only 3 per cent of all people arrested under the Act. Under the earlier Prevention of Terrorism Act (UK), 97 per cent of those arrested between 1974 and 1988 were released without charge and only 1 per cent were convicted.[108] As the in US, immigration proceedings are a common way of dealing with people detained under terrorism laws, but against whom there is insufficient evidence to prosecute.[109] These trends illustrate the well-known problem of emergency powers being used to capture ordinary crimes,[110] contaminating the legal system.[111]

4. Avoiding duplication of coverage by existing laws

A potent pragmatic objection to criminalizing certain conduct as terrorism is the view that domestic laws—and international criminal law—already prohibit the same conduct, albeit under different nomenclature, and that the emphasis should be placed on enforcing the existing law rather than developing new norms.[112] Proponents of criminalizing genocide in the 1940s were faced with the same objection: Australia argued that domestic crimes like murder already adequately punished the physical elements of genocidal conduct.[113] Critics also argued that human rights law—particularly the right to life and freedom from torture—would achieve the same result of preventing genocide.[114]

There is plainly value in preventing the unnecessary proliferation of offences which duplicate existing prohibitions.[115] Individuals must be able to know prospectively, with a modicum of certainty, the scope of their legal obligations, particularly their criminal liabilities. Already, international criminal law imposes a complex array of liabilities, with the deceptively simple categories of war crimes and crimes against humanity comprising numerous

---

[108] G Younge, 'No tails or tridents', *Guardian Weekly*, 29 July–4 Aug 2005, 13.

[109] S Murphy, 'International Law, the United States, and the Non-military "War" against Terrorism' (2003) 14 AJIL 347, 357.

[110] R Dworkin, 'Terror and the Attack on Civil Liberties', *NY Rev Books*, 6 Nov 2003; C Warbrick, 'The Principles of the European Convention on Human Rights and the Response of States to Terrorism', Study for the Council of Europe, Jan 2002, 5; D Eggen, 'Scoundrels take refuge in Patriot Act', *Sydney Morning Herald*, 22 May 2003; Press Association, 'Judge's doubts on prosecution', *The Guardian*, 24 Mar 2004; E Allison, 'Police killer battles to win parole', *The Guardian*, 29 July 2004.

[111] C Gearty and J Kimbell, *Terrorism and the Rule of Law* (KCL CLRU, London, 1995) 66–67.

[112] Bassiouni, n 8, xviii.   [113] See Saul (2000), n 100.   [114] Power, n 63, 75.

[115] Bassiouni, 'A Policy-Oriented Inquiry', n 8, xxvii.

distinct (and sometimes overlapping) offences.[116] While no criminal code can be static in the face of changing circumstances, international criminal law embodies only the most serious crimes, which should not vary too greatly over time.

While the law must keep pace with public expectations and social change, gratifying public passion or vengeance is not a good reason for criminalization. As in domestic law: 'Creating a new criminal offence may often be regarded as an instantly satisfying political response to public worries about a form of conduct that has been given publicity by the newspapers and television.'[117] This critique is pertinent to terrorism, which inflames public sentiment like few other issues. For example, anti-terrorism law in Northern Ireland in the early 1990s was arguably exploited for symbolic significance to placate the electorate,[118] rather than being adopted to meet legitimate law enforcement needs.

While most physical manifestations of terrorism are covered by existing domestic and international crimes—particularly crimes against humanity[119]—there is still a persuasive case for internationally criminalizing terrorism. Beyond the physical violence of terrorism lie its unique and distinguishing characteristics—such as the specific intent to terrorize, intimidate, or coerce; and the existence of a political motive. These elements, which are additional to the physical violence of terrorism, are not adequately reflected in existing criminal prohibitions—just as the genocidal destruction of a group is not adequately embodied in crimes such as murder or even extermination.

An intermediate mode of criminalization is to categorize terrorism as a crime against humanity, as proposed at the 1998 Rome Conference, and by Russia in 2001.[120] This would avoid creating an entirely new category of international crime and integrate terrorism into the existing hierarchy (and jurisprudence) of crimes, rather than setting it apart as a crime *sui generis*. It

---

[116] The 1998 Rome Statute lists 34 separate war crimes in international armed conflict and 16 in non-international armed conflict (Art 8(2)); and 11 crimes against humanity (Art 7).

[117] Ashworth, n 11, 24.

[118] B Dickson, 'Northern Ireland's Emergency Legislation' [1992] PL 592, 597.

[119] Certain terrorist acts may qualify as crimes against humanity: J Fry, 'Terrorism as a Crime against Humanity and Genocide: The Backdoor to Universal Jurisdiction' (2003) 7 *UCLA Journal of International and Foreign Affairs* 169; A Cassese, 'Terrorism is Also Disrupting Some Crucial Legal Categories of International Law' (2001) 12 EJIL 993, 994–995; Schrijver, n 88, 287–289; H Duffy, 'Responding to September 11: The Framework of International Law', *Interrights*, Oct 2001, part IV; M Byers, 'Terrorism, the Use of Force and International Law after September 11' (2002) 51 ICLQ 401, 413; Corell, n 89, 17; D Brown, 'Holding Armed Rebel Groups and Terrorist Organisations Accountable', Åbo Akademi Institute for Human Rights, 2002, 40–42. In *Menten* (1981) ILR 75, 331, 362–363, the Netherlands Supreme Court held that crimes against humanity require conduct to form part of a system of terror, or of a policy consciously pursued against a group.

[120] 'Russia proposes that terrorism be classified as crime against humanity', Pravda, 6 Nov 2001; cf P Van Krieken (ed), *Terrorism and the International Legal Order* (Asser Press, The Hague, 2002) 107.

would also set up the crime against humanity of terrorism as a peace-time counterpart to the war crime of terrorism in armed conflict.[121] One drawback is that crimes against humanity only encompass widespread or systematic attacks on a civilian population. Although this ensures that only very serious conduct is internationally criminalized, it would drastically reduce the scope of terrorism by excluding conduct below that threshold. Another disadvantage is identified by Mégret, who argues that, 'no two equally meaningful qualifications can ever be given to the same act so that, confronted with a choice, one should always opt for the most specific description available, in accordance with the principles of sound conceptual economy'.[122] In contrast, subsuming the narrower category of terrorism under the overall label of crimes against humanity risks diluting the *lex specialis* into the *lex generalis*.[123] In this light, it is preferable to establish terrorism as a separate category of international (or transnational) crime, not coupled to the restrictive conditions of war crimes (requiring an armed conflict) or crimes against humanity (requiring widespread or systematic acts). Discrete categorization would also preserve the distinct moral condemnation attached to terrorism by the international community.

5. *Multiplicity of charges and convictions*

A further concern about the proliferation of offences is the problem of prosecuting and convicting individuals for multiple overlapping offences, based on the same conduct.[124] This problem is not unique to terrorism and international tribunals have developed recent jurisprudence on the issue.[125] The ICTY found that cumulative convictions for different offences may punish the same criminal conduct where 'each statutory provision involved has a materially distinct element not contained in the other'.[126] If each offence does not require 'proof of a fact not contained in the other', then 'a conviction should be entered only under the more specific provision . . . with the additional element'.[127]

Thus in the *Galic* case, the ICTY refused to permit convictions for the

---

[121] Some argue that terrorism should be criminalized as a peace-time equivalent of a war crime: ILA Report (60th Conf), Committee on International Terrorism: 4th Interim Report (1982), 349–356; cf Scharf M, 'Defining Terrorism as the Peace Time Equivalent of War Crimes: A Case of Too Much Convergence between International Humanitarian Law and International Criminal Law?' (2001) 7 ILSA JICL 391.

[122] F Mégret, 'Justice in Times of Violence' (2003) 14 EJIL 327, 345.   [123] ibid.

[124] Cassese, n 6, 212–218.

[125] See generally A Bogdan, 'Cumulative Charges, Convictions and Sentencing in the Ad Hoc International Tribunals for the Former Yugoslavia and Rwanda' (2002) Melbourne JIL 1.

[126] *Celebici (Appeal)* ICTY–96–21–A (20 Feb 2001) para 412; *Galic* ICTY–98–29–T (5 Dec 2003) para 158.

[127] *Celibici (Appeal)* ibid, paras 412–413; *Kupreškić* ICTY–95–16 (14 Jan 2000) paras 683–684; *Galic* ibid, para 158.

crimes of terror and attack on civilians based on the same conduct, and instead entered a conviction only for the more specific crime of terror (with the additional element of the 'primary purpose of spreading terror').[128] In contrast, cumulative convictions for the crimes of terror and murder and inhumane acts were permitted, since they were not based on the same acts.[129] Pre-trial, the ICTY allows cumulative or alternative charges to be filed for the same conduct, since before the evidence is presented at trial, it may be difficult for prosecutors to know precisely which offences will be supported by the evidence.[130]

D. TERRORISM AS A DISCRETE INTERNATIONAL CRIME

Since the early 1960s, much of the physical conduct comprising terrorist acts has been criminalized in international treaties,[131] and some terrorist acts may also qualify as other international crimes (such as war crimes, crimes against humanity, genocide, or torture) if the elements of those crimes are present. Despite the adoption of the sectoral treaties, the term 'terrorism' continues to exhibit descriptive and analytical force in international legal discussion, suggesting that, for the international community, it captures a concept beyond the mere physical, sectoral acts comprising terrorism. That term signals not merely a descriptive need of the international community, but also encapsulates a normative demand. This is so despite the vagueness and ambiguity for which the term 'terrorism' is often derided.[132]

In the first place, the international community has expressed its disapproval of 'terrorism', *as such*, on a number of grounds since the 1970s, including that terrorism: is a serious human rights violation; undermines the State and peaceful political processes; and threatens international peace and security. In particular, there is a lingering sense in international political discourse that the offences in sectoral treaties fail specifically to recognize and condemn the *political* motivations underlying the physical violence of terrorism. The nature of the Security Council's enforcement measures since September 2001 have further made the search for a common definition pragmatically urgent. Each of these grounds is considered as a basis for supporting the international criminalization of terrorism. Definition of

---

[128] *Galic* ibid, para 162.

[129] ibid, paras 163–164. The ICTY has also found that genocide does not subsume persecution and extermination, and permitted cumulative convictions: see *Krstic (Appeal)* ICTY–98–33–T (19 Apr 2004).

[130] *Delalic (Appeal)* ICTY–96–21–A (20 Feb 2001) para 400 (cumulative charging); *Kupreškić* n 127, para 727 (alternative charging).

[131] See Ch 3.

[132] See, eg, R Baxter, 'A Skeptical Look at the Concept of Terrorism' (1974) 7 *Akron Law Review* 380.

terrorism could remedy persistent concerns about its vagueness, while pre-serving the symbolic force attached to the term by the international community.

1. Terrorism as a serious human rights violation

International criminal law often prohibits conduct which infringes values protected by human rights law, without proclaiming those values directly.[133] Numerous resolutions of the UN General Assembly since the 1970s,[134] and of the Commission on Human Rights since the 1990s,[135] assert that terrorism threatens or destroys basic human rights and freedoms, particularly life, liberty, and security, but also civil and political, and economic, social, and cultural rights. Regional anti-terrorism instruments,[136] and the preamble to the Draft Comprehensive Convention,[137] support the idea that terrorism gravely violates human rights. A UN Special Rapporteur observes that 'there is probably not a single human right exempt from the impact of terrorism'.[138]

The notion of terrorism as a particularly serious human rights violation does not, by itself, constitute a compelling reason for criminalizing terrorism. Many serious domestic crimes equally endanger life and undermine human rights, so this justification does not immediately present a persuasive, exceptional reason for treating terrorist activity differently. While some terrorist acts may be particularly serious human rights violations because of their scale or effects, not all terrorist acts are of such intensity.

---

[133] Cassese, n 6, 23.

[134] UNGA Resolutions 3034 (XXVII) (1972) para 1; 32/147 (1977) para 1; 34/145 (1979) para 3; 38/130 (1983) para 1; 40/61 (1985) preamble, paras 2–3; 42/159 (1987) preamble, paras 2–3; 44/29 (1989) preamble, para 2; 46/51 (1991) preamble, para 2; 48/122 (1993) preamble, para 1; 49/60 (1994) preamble; 49/185 (1994) preamble, para 1; 50/186 (1995) preamble, para 2; 1996 Declaration, preamble; 52/133 (1997) preamble, paras 2–3; 54/164 (2000) preamble, paras 2–3; 56/160 (2002) paras 2–3; 57/219 (2003) preamble; 58/174 (2004) para 1; 58/187 (2004) preamble; 59/191 (2005) preamble; 59/195 (2005) para 1; see also 1993 Vienna Declaration and Programme of Action, UN Doc A/CONF.157/24 (Part I) ch III, s I, para 17.

[135] UNComHR Resolutions 1995/43; 1996/47; 1997/42; 1998/47; 1999/27; 1999/30; 2000/30; 2001/37; 2002/35; 2003/37; UNSubComHR Resolutions 1994/18; 1996/20; 1997/39; 1998/29; 1999/26; 2001/18; 2002/24; UN Com Status of Women Resolution 36/7 (1992) para 2.

[136] 2002 EU Framework Decision, preamble (1)–(2); 1998 Arab Convention, preamble; 1999 OIC Convention, preamble; 1971 OAS Convention, preamble; 1999 OAU Convention, pre-amble; see also OAS General Assembly, AG/RES 1840 (XXXII-O/02) preamble; OAS Declar-ation of Lima to Prevent, Combat, and Eliminate Terrorism, 26 Apr 1996, preamble and para 1; Declaration of Quito, IX Meeting of the Rio Group, Sept 1995; OAU Ministerial Communiqué on Terrorism, 11 Nov 2001, Central Organ/MEC/MIN/Ex–Ord (V) Com, para 3; Council of Europe (Committee of Ministers), Guidelines on Human Rights and the Fight against Terrorism, 11 July 2002, preamble [a]; European Parliament Resolution A5–0050/2000, 16 Mar 2000, paras 41–42; OIC (Foreign Ministers), Declaration on International Terrorism, Kuala Lumpur, 1–3 Apr 2002, para 7; NAM, XIV Ministerial Conference, Final Doc, Durban, 17–19 Aug 2004, para 100; NAM, XIII Conference of Heads of State or Government, Final Doc, Kuala Lumpur, 25 Feb 2003, para 107.

[137] UNGAOR (57th Sess), Ad Hoc Committee Report (2002), Supp 37 (A/57/37), Annex I: bureau paper.

[138] Koufa (2001), n 21, 28.

Although some resolutions have condemned terrorism for violating the right to live free from fear,[139] there is no explicit human right to freedom from fear, which a crime of terror might seek to protect. Such protection may, however, be implied from other provisions. First, the Universal Declaration of Human Rights (UDHR) preamble states that 'freedom from fear' is part of 'the highest aspiration of the common people', while the International Covenant on Civil and Political Rights (ICCPR) and the International Covenant on Economic, Social and Political Rights (ICESCR) preambles refer to 'the ideal of free human beings enjoying freedom from fear'. The idea that freedom from fear is an international value deserving of protection has also been advanced by the United Nations Development Programme (UNDP) as an aspect of human development,[140] and the new African Court on Human and People's Rights 'will address the need to build a just, united and peaceful Continent free from fear, want and ignorance'.[141]

The political ideal of 'freedom from fear' was first articulated as one of four freedoms in a speech by US President Franklin D Roosevelt in 1941, and referred to the need to reduce global armaments to eliminate aggression.[142] In 1944, the British jurist Brierly also spoke of the prospects for 'freedom from fear' in a reasonably secure international order.[143] Its inclusion in the UDHR reflects an internationalization of American aspirations, partly at the urging of Eleanor Roosevelt. These treaty provisions support the criminalization of serious violations of the nascent right to live free from fear, which is protected fairly precisely by prohibiting terrorism (as extreme fear).

Second, safeguarding the right to liberty and security of person (ICCPR, Article 9(1) and UDHR, Article 3) may support the criminalization of terrorism. Most of the jurisprudence interpreting and applying that right has focused almost exclusively on the deprivation of liberty, without elucidating any independent meaning of the right to 'security'. The text of the relevant provisions elaborates only on the content of liberty. Both the UN Human Rights Committee's General Comment explaining Article 9, and European jurisprudence interpreting the equivalent right in Article 5 of the European

---

[139] UNGA Resolutions 50/186 (1995) preamble; 52/133 (1997) preamble, para 2; 54/164 (2000) para 2; 56/160 (2002) preamble; 58/174 (2004) preamble; 59/195 (2005) preamble; UNComHR Resolutions 1996/47, preamble; 1997/42, preamble; 1998/37, preamble, para 2; 1999/27, preamble, para 2; 2000/30, preamble, para 2; 2001/37, preamble, para 2; 2002/35, preamble, paras 1–2; 2003/37, preamble, para 2; UNSubComHR Resolutions 1996/26, preamble; 2001/18, preamble; 2002/24, preamble.

[140] UNDP, *Human Development Report 1994* (OUP, New York, 1994) 23.

[141] 2003 Protocol to the African Charter on Human and Peoples' Rights on the Establishment of an African Court on Human and Peoples' Rights.

[142] US President F Roosevelt, State of the Union Address, 77th US Congress, 6 Jan 1941, (1941) 87 Congressional Record, Part I. The 'four essential human freedoms' were freedom of speech, freedom of worship, freedom from want, and freedom from fear. The ideal was also popularized in a wartime painting by Norman Rockwell, *Freedom from Fear* (1943).

[143] J Brierly, *The Outlook for International Law* (Clarendon, Oxford, 1944) 75.

Convention on Human Rights (ECHR), deal almost entirely with aspects of the deprivation of liberty.[144]

Yet an ordinary textual interpretation would give the term 'security' a meaning distinct from 'liberty'.[145] The UDHR drafting records are instructive. Some States were concerned about the vagueness and lack of definition of the right to 'security' of person in Article 3.[146] While a request for a definitive interpretation of 'security' was rejected,[147] the US explained that 'security' was chosen as the most comprehensive and concise term to express 'physical integrity',[148] and that was the prevailing interpretation.[149] Some States added, without opposition, that security also referred to 'moral integrity'.[150]

Other States objected that 'security' did not fully encompass the idea of physical integrity,[151] preferring a reference to 'integrity' instead of security,[152] but a proposal to insert 'physical integrity' into the draft provision was narrowly rejected.[153] Ultimately, the reference to liberty and security in Article 3 was adopted by 47 votes to 0, with 4 abstentions.[154] Some States voted for Article 3 on the express understanding that 'security' referred to physical integrity,[155] or physical, moral, and legal integrity.[156] Costa Rica had earlier argued that 'security' implied a conferring of legal status on US President Roosevelt's ideal of 'freedom from fear', and Haiti abstained from voting because its suggestion for an express reference to 'freedom from fear' was rejected.[157]

If the right to security means a right to physical, and possibly moral, integrity, it is arguable that terrorism attacks the right to security of person in both its physical and psychological dimensions. So much is recognized by the Organization of the Islamic Conference (OIC) Convention, which states that terrorism is a 'gross violation of human rights, in particular the right

[144] UNHRC (16th Sess), General Comment No 8: ICCPR, Art 9, 30 June 1982; *Bonzano v France*, 18 Dec 1986, Series A, (1987) 9 EHRR 297. In Europe, security has been referred to in disappearance of prisoner cases such as *Timurtas v Turkey* (App 23531/94), 13 June 2000, (2001) 33 EHRR 121.
[145] C Ovey and R White, *European Convention on Human Rights* (3rd edn, OUP, Oxford, 2002) 103.
[146] UNGAOR (3rd Sess), 3rd Committee Summary Records of Meetings, 21 Sept–8 Dec 1948, 143 (Panama), 189 (Guatemala), 190 (Cuba, Uruguay), 192 (Cuba).
[147] ibid, 190 (Philippines).   [148] ibid, 190 (US).
[149] ibid, 190 (US, France), 157 (Netherlands), 189 (Haiti), 191 (China), 192 (Guatemala), 194 (Philippines).
[150] ibid, 189 (Haiti), 192 (Chile), 193 (Venezuela). Yugoslavia gave as an example of a violation of security of person, the lynching of black Americans in the US: n 146, 158 (Yugoslavia).
[151] ibid, 164 (Cuba), 193 (Ecuador).
[152] ibid, 145 (Cuba), 174 (Belgium).
[153] ibid, 188 (19 votes to 17, with 12 abstentions).
[154] ibid, 191. The reference to the right to life was separately adopted by 49 to 0, with 2 abstentions. Art 3 as a whole was adopted by 36 to 0, with 12 abstentions: 193.
[155] ibid, 193 (Guatemala), 194 (Philippines).
[156] ibid, 192 (Chile), 193 (Venezuela).   [157] ibid, 175 (Costa Rica), 172, 193–194 (Haiti).

to . . . security'.[158] In one writer's view, human rights discourse 'recognises the danger that subversive violence poses to liberal democratic society, but recasts this as a threat to human security rather than a menace to a particular territory or sovereign space'.[159] The right to security is, however, more limited in meaning than the expansive concept of 'human security' which gained some currency in the 1990s.[160]

Few human rights violations are characterized as international crimes, and usually the remedy for a rights violation is enforcement of the right rather than criminal punishment of the violator.[161] While human rights law and international criminal law may overlap, 'states do not yet regard many violations of international humanitarian and human rights law, including some truly cruel and heinous conduct, as criminal in nature'.[162] As the Inter-American Court of Human Rights (IACHR) found in the *Velasquez Rodriguez* case, human rights law is not punitive, but remedial.[163] Human rights treaties do not require prosecution of violators as a necessary remedy,[164] although 'the obligation to ensure rights is held to encompass such a duty, at least with respect to the most serious violations'.[165] In addition, the law of State responsibility has long demanded the apprehension, prosecution, and punishment of those who injure foreign nationals.[166]

There is no doubt that human rights are, however, 'one source of principles for criminalization',[167] since the effects of conduct on human rights are part of the assessment of the seriousness and moral wrongness of that conduct. Freedom from torture is one of the few human rights which is also internationally criminalized.[168] Yet other rights violations may be worthy of criminalization if they involve serious harm to 'physical integrity, material support and amenity, freedom from humiliation or degrading treatment, and privacy and autonomy'.[169]

Some writers have questioned whether terrorism can violate human rights as a matter of law, where terrorist acts are not attributable to a

---

[158] 1999 OIC Convention, preamble.

[159] C Gearty, 'Terrorism and Human Rights', Paper at ESIL Conference, Florence, 13–15 May 2004, 2.

[160] D Newman, 'A Human Security Council? Applying a "Human Security" Agenda to Security Council Reform' (2000) 31 *Ottawa Law Review*, 213, 222.

[161] S Ratner and J Abrams, *Accountability for Human Rights Atrocities in International Law* (2nd edn, OUP, Oxford, 2001) 13.

[162] ibid, 12–13.

[163] *Velasquez Rodriguez* case, IACHR, Series C, No 4, (1988) 9 HRLJ 212, para 134.

[164] Ratner and Abrams, n 161, 152; D Shelton, *Remedies in International Human Rights Law* (OUP, Oxford, 2000) 323.

[165] Shelton, ibid, 323.

[166] See, eg, *Janes Case (US v Mexico)* (1925) 4 RIAA 82; M Whiteman, *Damages in International Law* (USGPO, Washington, DC, 1937) 639.

[167] Ashworth, n 11, 41.   [168] 1966 ICCPR, Art 7; 1984 Torture Convention, Arts 4–5.

[169] Ashworth, n 11, 41.

State.[170] The basis of this argument is that under human rights treaties, only State Parties, rather than non-State actors or individuals,[171] legally undertake 'to respect and to ensure' human rights. This position was taken by the EU, the Nordic States, and Canada, in supporting the adoption of the 1994 Declaration on terrorism, who argued that terrorism is a crime but not a rights violation, since only acts attributable to a State can violate human rights.[172] (The EU has since reversed its position in justifying the 2002 EU Framework Decision.)

Clearly, terrorist acts that are attributable to States under the law of State responsibility may violate States' human rights obligations.[173] In contrast, private persons are not parties to human rights treaties, which do not have 'direct horizontal effects' in international law and are not a substitute for domestic criminal law.[174] Nonetheless, in implementing the duty to 'ensure' rights, States must protect individuals from private violations of rights 'in so far as they are amenable to application between private persons or entities'.[175] This may require States to take positive measures of protection (including through policy, legislation, and administrative action), or to exercise due diligence to prevent, punish, investigate, or redress the harm or interference caused by private acts.[176] These duties are related to the duty to ensure effective remedies for rights violations.[177]

---

[170] T Meron, 'When Do Acts of Terrorism Violate Human Rights?' (1989) 19 IYBHR 271, 275.

[171] H Steiner, 'International Protection of Human Rights' in M Evans (ed), *International Law* (OUP, Oxford, 2003) 757, 776; S von Schorlemer, 'Human Rights: Substantive and Institutional Implications of the War on Terror' (2003) 14 EJIL 265, 265; D Pokempner, 'Terrorism and Human Rights: The Legal Framework' in M Schmitt and G Beruto (eds), *Terrorism and International Law* (IIHL and George C Marshall European Center for Security Studies, San Remo, 2003) 19, 22–23; P Hostettler, 'Human Rights and the "War" against International Terrorism' in Schmitt and Beruto (eds), above, 30, 32.

[172] UNGAOR 49th Sess, 6th Committee Report on Measures to Eliminate International Terrorism, 9 Dec 1994, UN Doc A/49/743, 19–20 (Germany for the EU and Austria; Sweden for the Nordic States; Canada); see also Sec-Gen Report, Human Rights and Terrorism, 26 Oct 1995, UN Doc A/50/685, 5 (Sweden).

[173] Meron, n 170, 274.

[174] UNHRC, General Comment No 31: Nature of the General Legal Obligation Imposed on State Parties to the Covenant, 26 May 2004, UN Doc CCPR/C/21/Rev.1/Add.13, para 8.

[175] ibid.

[176] ibid; *Velasquez-Rodriguez*, n 163, paras 172–173; T Buergenthal, 'To Respect and to Ensure: State Obligations and Permissible Derogations' in L Henkin (ed), *The International Bill of Rights* (Columbia University Press, New York, 1981) 72, 77–78; A Clapham, *Human Rights in the Private Sphere* (Clarendon, Oxford, 1996) 105–106, 119; L Condorelli, 'The Imputability to States of Acts of International Terrorism' (1989) 19 IYBHR 233, 240–241; D Shelton, 'Private Violence, Public Wrongs, and the Responsibility of States' (1990) 13 Fordham ILJ 1; G Sperduti, 'Responsibility of States for Activities of Private Law Persons' in R Bernhardt (ed), *Encyclopedia of PIL*, Installment 10 (1987) 373, 375; Shelton, n 164, 47; J Paust, 'The Link between Human Rights and Terrorism and its Implications for the Law of State Responsibility' (1987) 11 *Hastings International and Comparative Law Review* 41; Koufa (2001), n 21, 29; Schorlemer, n 171, 270.

[177] 1966 ICCPR, Art 2(3).

Thus non-State actors, including terrorists, are indirectly regulated by human rights law, by virtue of the duties on States to 'protect' and 'ensure' rights.[178] For this reason, in relation to human rights: 'Much of the significance of the State/non-State (public-private) distinction with respect to the reach of international law . . . collapses.'[179] Even so, where a private act is not attributable to the State, the State cannot be held responsible for the act itself, but only for its own failures to exercise due diligence in preventing the resulting rights violations or responding appropriately to them.[180] In the absence of State involvement in a terrorist act, the State can only be held responsible for its own failures or omissions, not for the private terrorist act itself.

While private persons are not directly legally responsible for rights violations, neither are they left entirely unregulated. The UDHR preamble states that 'every individual . . . shall strive . . . to promote respect for these rights and freedoms . . . to secure their universal recognition and observance', and this injunction has been reiterated in UN Resolutions against terrorism.[181] Article 29(1) of the UDHR further recognizes that 'everyone has duties to the community' and the *travaux préparatoires* support the view that individuals must respect human rights.[182] Similarly, the ICCPR and ICESCR preambles state that 'the individual, having duties to other individuals and to the community to which he belongs, is under a responsibility to strive for the promotion and observance of the rights recognized' in those covenants.[183]

These preambular injunctions, UDHR provisions, and Resolutions are, however, not binding. More persuasively, common Article 5(1) of the ICCPR and ICESCR states that nothing in those treaties 'may be interpreted as implying for any State, group or person any right to engage in any activity or perform any act aimed at the destruction of any of the rights and freedoms recognized herein or at their limitation to a greater extent than is provided for'.[184]

During the adoption of the 1994 Declaration, Algeria responded to the EU and Nordic States by arguing that this provision imposes legal obligations on individuals and groups to respect human rights.[185] While the provision is not framed as a positive obligation on individuals or groups to observe human rights, by necessary implication it requires as much if individuals are to avoid destroying or unjustifiably limiting rights, as stipulated. The UN Special Rapporteur regards these provisions as forbidding the abuse of human rights

[178] Steiner, n 171, 776.   [179] ibid.
[180] *Velasquez-Rodriguez*, n 163, paras 172–173.
[181] Preambles to UNGA Resolution 48/22 (1993); UNComHR Resolutions 1995/43; 1996/47; 1997/42; 1998/47; 1999/27; 2000/30; 2001/37; UNSubComHR Resolutions 1997/39; 1998/29; 1999/26; 2001/18; 2002/24.
[182] Clapham, n 176, 97–98.
[183] 1966 ICCPR and 1966 ICESCR, preambles; see also 1948 UDHR, preamble.
[184] See also 1948 UDHR, Art 30.   [185] 6th Committee Report, n 172, 21.

by individuals or groups.[186] As Clapham observes, individuals are subject to duties in other areas of international law, including IHL and international criminal law.[187]

Nonetheless, private actors have rarely been held directly accountable in human rights law for terrorist acts where no State is involved, and non-State actors are not bound by international supervisory mechanisms.[188] Exceptionally, in Central and South America, the Inter-American Commission on Human Rights condemned 'acts of political terrorism and urban or rural guerilla terrorism', by irregular armed groups in the 1960s and 1970s, for causing 'serious violations of the rights to life, personal security and physical freedom, freedom of thought, opinion and expression, and the rights to protection'.[189]

Yet following controversy in the Organization of American States (OAS) in the 1980s on the definition of terrorism and its relationship to human rights, the Inter-American Commission retreated from its earlier position. In 1991, it emphasized that it was the function of the State to prevent and punish private violence, not the role of international rights bodies. There were concerns that directly addressing private violence would confer recognition on armed groups; deprive human rights of its specificity and nexus to international protection; stretch resources; irritate governments; put workers at risk; and relieve States of responsibility.[190] There is also the practical difficulty of non-State groups assuming obligations (to 'ensure' or 'protect' rights) that they may lack the minimum organizational capacity to fulfil.[191] Most of these criticisms relate to institutional, supervisory, and remedial questions, rather than to the principle of whether private actors do, or do not, violate rights.[192]

Nevertheless, the weight of international practice suggests that it remains difficult to *legally* characterize terrorist acts by non-State actors as violations of human rights, in situations where a State has not failed to fulfil diligently its duties of prevention and protection. In such cases, the rights of victims will only be violated in a descriptive,[193] or philosophical, sense—since rights inhere in the human person by virtue of their humanity, not by virtue of a legal text—but no rights remedy will lie against the terrorist themselves or the

---

[186] UNSubComHR, Terrorism and Human Rights: Preliminary Report by Special Rapporteur K Koufa (1999), UN Doc E/CN.4/Sub.2/1999/27, paras 22–23.
[187] Clapham, n 176, 95–96; see also B Saul, 'In the Shadow of Human Rights: Human Duties, Obligations and Responsibilities' (2001) 32 *Columbia Human Rights Law Review* 565.
[188] Schorlemer, n 171, 270.
[189] IAComHR Res of 23 Apr 1970.
[190] Clapham, n 176, 122–124; IAComHR, *Annual Report 1990–91*, 504–514.
[191] See generally L Zegveld, *The Accountability of Armed Opposition Groups* (CUP, Cambridge, 2002).
[192] cf Clapham, n 176, 93–94: 'International law recognizes that individuals or private bodies are capable of committing violations of human rights'.
[193] Steiner, n 171, 776.

relevant State. While it is 'dangerous to exclude private violators of rights from the theory and practice of human rights',[194] even descriptive violations of rights are a sufficient ground on which to criminalize terrorism by non-State actors.

2. *Terrorism as a threat to democratic governance?*

In the 1990s, the General Assembly and the UN Commission on Human Rights frequently described terrorism as aimed at the destruction of democracy,[195] or the destabilizing of 'legitimately constituted Governments' and 'pluralistic civil society'.[196] Some resolutions state that terrorism 'poses a severe challenge to democracy, civil society and the rule of law'.[197] The 2002 EU Framework Decision, the 2002 Inter-American Convention, and the Draft Comprehensive Convention are similarly based on the premise that terrorism jeopardizes democracy.[198] Most regional treaties are, however, silent on the effects of terrorism on democracy—including those of the OAU, OAS, OIC, SAARC, CIS, and Council of Europe—suggesting that they do not regard terrorism as an offence specifically against democracy.[199]

The idea of terrorism as a threat to 'democracy' or 'legitimately constituted governments' seems to set terrorist acts apart from other conduct that seriously violates human rights. One plausible basis for criminalizing terrorism is that it directly undermines democratic values and institutions, especially the human rights underlying democracy such as political participation and voting, freedom of speech, opinion, expression, and association.[200] Terrorists violate the ground rules of democracy by coercing electors and candidates; wielding disproportionate and unfair power through violence;

[194] Clapham, n 176, 124.
[195] UNGA Resolutions 48/122 (1993) para 1; 49/60 (1994) para 2; 49/185 (1994) para 1; 50/186 (1995) para 2; 52/133 (1997) para 3; 54/164 (2000) paras 2–3; UNComHR Resolutions 1995/43, para 1; 1996/47, paras 1–2; 1997/42, paras 1–2; 1998/47, para 3; 1999/27, para 1; 2000/30, para 1; 2001/37, para 1; 2002/35, para 1; 2003/37, para 1; UNSubComHR Resolutions 1994/18, para 1; 1996/20, para 1; 1997/39, para 1; 2001/18, preamble; 2002/24, preamble; 1993 Vienna Declaration and Programme of Action, UN Doc A/CONF.157/24 (Part I) ch III, s I, para 17.
[196] UNGA Resolutions 48/122 (1993) para 1; 49/185 (1994) para 1; 50/186 (1995) para 2; 52/133 (1997) para 3; 54/164 (2000) paras 2–3; UNComHR Resolutions 1995/43, para 1; 1996/47, para 2; 1997/42, para 2; 1998/47, para 2; 1999/27, para 1; 2000/30, para 1; 2001/37, para 1; 2002/35, para 1; 2003/37, para 1; UNSubComHR Resolutions 1994/18, para 1; 1996/20, para 1.
[197] Preambles to UNComHR Resolutions 1998/47; 1999/27; 2000/30; 2001/31; 2002/35; 2003/37; UNSubComHR Resolutions 1999/26; 2001/18; 2002/24.
[198] 2002 EU Framework Decision, recitals 1–2; Draft Comprehensive Convention, preamble; 2002 Inter-American Convention.
[199] Although the Council of Europe stated that terrorism 'threatens democracy': Guidelines, n 136, preamble, para a.
[200] 1948 UDHR, Art 29(2); 1966 ICESCR, Arts 4, 8(1)(a); 1966 ICCPR, Arts 14(1), 21, 22(2); see UN Com Status of Women Resolution 36/7 (1992) preamble; Koufa (1999), n 186, paras 26–31.

and subverting the rule of law.[201] Terrorist violence may also undermine legitimate authority; impose ideological and political platforms on society; impede civic participation; subvert democratic pluralism, institutions and constitutionalism; hinder democratisation; undermine development; and encourage more violence.[202]

As Arendt argues, humans are political beings endowed with speech, but 'speech is helpless when confronted with violence'.[203] For Ignatieff, terrorism 'kills politics, the one process we have devised that masters violence in the name of justice'.[204] Boutros Boutros-Ghali stated that terrorism reveals the unwillingness of terrorists 'to subject their views to the test of a fair political process'.[205] Thus terrorism replaces politics with violence, and dialogue with terror. On this view, terrorism should be specially criminalized because it strikes at the constitutional framework of deliberative public institutions which make the existence of all other human rights possible. Doing so would also concretize and protect the 'emerging right to democratic governance' which is progressively coalescing around the provisions of human rights treaties:[206] 'since 1989 the international system has begun to take the notion of democratic rights seriously'.[207]

Yet this explanation for criminalizing terrorism gives rise to immediate difficulties. First, there is no entrenched legal right of democratic governance in international law. At best, such a right is emerging or 'inchoate',[208] not to mention much denied.[209] The existing right of self-determination permits peoples to choose their form of government, but it does not specify that government must be democratic and a people is free to choose authoritarian rule. International rights of participation in public affairs and voting fall far short of establishing a right to a comprehensive democratic system, unless a particularly 'thin', procedural, or formal conception of democracy is accepted.[210] Further, the customary criteria reflected in the 1933 Montevideo

---

[201] T Honderich, *Three Essays on Political Violence* (Basil Blackwell, Oxford, 1976) 103.
[202] Koufa (1999), n 186, para 32.
[203] H Arendt, *On Revolution* (Penguin, London, 1990) 19.
[204] M Ignatieff, 'Human Rights, the Laws of War, and Terrorism' (2002) 69 *Social Research* 1137, 1157; see also M Ignatieff, *The Lesser Evil: Political Ethics in an Age of Terror* (Edinburgh University Press, Edinburgh, 2005) 110–111.
[205] Quoted in Koufa (1999), n 186, para 31.
[206] T Franck, 'The Emerging Right of Democratic Governance' (1992) 86 AJIL 46; G Fox 'The Right to Political Participation in International Law' (1992) 17 Yale JIL 539; G Fox and B Roth (eds), *Democratic Governance in International Law* (CUP, Cambridge, 2000).
[207] J Crawford, 'The Right of Self-Determination in International Law: Its Development and Future' in P Alston (ed), *Peoples' Rights* (OUP, Oxford, 2001) 7, 25.
[208] S Chesterman, *Just War or Just Peace?* (OUP, Oxford, 2002) 89.
[209] In 2003, Freedom House regarded only 88 States as democratic, 55 States as part-democratic, and 49 States as 'not free': www.freedomhouse.org.
[210] For analysis of different conceptions of democracy, see S Marks, *The Riddle of All Constitutions: International Law, Democracy, and the Critique of Ideology* (OUP, Oxford, 2000) chs 3–5.

Convention do not posit democracy as a precondition of statehood. Rather, effective territorial government of a permanent population is sufficient, and international law tolerates most varieties of governance (excepting those predicated on apartheid, genocide, or colonial occupation).

As a result, terrorism can hardly be recognized as an *international* crime against democratic values when democracy is not an accepted international legal right. In contrast, within a more homogenous regional community such as the EU, member States are freer to declare that terrorism violates established community values and, indeed, democracy has emerged as a precondition of European Community membership.[211] Even still, there is significant variation between EU member States in forms of democracy, and it is not clear what it means to speak of terrorism as a crime against 'democracy' as a uniform phenomenon. It goes without saying that conceptions of democracy are radically contested in both theory and practice.[212]

Second, if terrorism is indeed characterized as a crime against 'democracy', it begs the historically intractable question of whether terrorist acts directed to subverting non-democratic regimes, or against those which trample human rights, remain permissible. It is notable that some of the above UN resolutions refer to terrorism as 'destabilizing legitimately constituted Governments', implying that terrorism is not objectionable against *illegitimate* governments, particularly those oppressing self-determination movements. Over time, UN resolutions also asserted that 'all acts, methods and practices of terrorism in all its forms and manifestations, wherever and by whomever committed' are criminal and unjustifiable. Thus even just causes pursued against authoritarian regimes were not permitted to use terrorist means: 'terrorism . . . can never be justified as a means to promote and protect human rights'.[213] Though seeming to condemn terrorism unequivocally and against *any* State, these resolutions were still not intended to apply to self-determination movements in the views of many States which voted for them.[214]

Indeed, most regional instruments view terrorism as a crime against the State and its security and stability, sovereignty and integrity, institutions and structures, or economy and development, rather than as a specific anti-democratic crime.[215] Even in a community of democracies such as the EU, the

---

[211] EC, Guidelines on the Recognition of New States in Eastern Europe and in the Soviet Union, 16 Dec 1991, in (1991) BYBIL 559.

[212] See B Roth, 'Evaluating Democratic Progress: A Normative Theoretical Perspective' (1995) 9 *Ethics and International Affairs* 55; Marks, n 210.

[213] Preambles to UNComHR Resolutions 1996/47; 1997/42; 1998/47; 1999/27; 2000/30; 2001/31; 2002/35.

[214] See Ch 4 below.

[215] 1999 OAU Convention, preamble; 1998 Arab Convention, preamble; 1999 OIC Convention, preamble; 1987 SAARC Convention, preamble; OIC Resolutions 6/31–LEG (2004) preamble; 6/10-LEG(IS) (2003) preamble; OAS General Assembly, AG/RES 1840 (XXXII–O/02) preamble; NAM Final Doc (2004), n 136, para 100; NAM Final Doc (2003), n 136, paras 107–109; NAM, XIII Ministerial Conf, Final Doc, Cartagena, 8–9 Apr 2000, paras 88–89.

distinguishing feature of terrorist offences is the underlying motive to seriously alter or destroy the political, economic, or social structures of a State, including its fundamental principles and pillars.[216]

Consequently, the balance of international opinion makes it difficult to argue that terrorism should be criminalized as an offence against democratic politics, since it must also be regarded as criminal and unjustifiable against tyrannical regimes. The minimum shared international conception of terrorism encompasses violence against politics and the State (including its security and institutions), but regardless of its democratic character. There is far less support for the narrower idea of terrorism as a threat to democracy, reflecting the international diversity of political systems.

3. *Differentiating public from private violence*

While terrorism is not universally regarded as a crime limited to attacks on democracies, there is considerable support for the view that terrorism is *political* violence. In its influential 1994 Declaration on Measures to Eliminate International Terrorism, the General Assembly distinguished terrorism from other violence because of its motivation 'for political purposes'.[217] In contrast, since the early 1960s, the numerous 'sectoral' anti-terrorism treaties have avoided any general definition of terrorism.[218] Instead, most of the treaties require States to prohibit and punish in domestic law certain physical or objective acts—such as hijacking, hostage-taking, misuse of nuclear material, or bombings—regardless of whether such acts are motivated by private or political ends. Proof of the motive(s) behind the act (as distinct from the *intention* to commit the act) is thus not required as an element of the offences.

Dealing with terrorist acts by resort to sectoral treaties or ordinary criminal offences arguably lacks 'specific focus on terrorism *per se*', since it fails to differentiate between privately motivated violence and violence committed for political reasons: 'Not all hijackings, sabotages, attacks on diplomats, or even hostage-takings are "terrorist"; such acts may be done for personal or pecuniary reasons or simply out of insanity. The international instruments that address these acts are thus "overbroad".'[219] Overreach undermines 'the moral and political force of these instruments as a

---

[216] EU Com, Proposal for a Council Framework Decision on Combating Terrorism, Brussels, 19 Sept 2001, COM(2001) 521 Final, 2001/0217 (CNS), Explanatory Memorandum, 6–7.

[217] UNGA Resolution 49/60 (1994), annexed Declaration, para 3.

[218] See Ch 3 below.

[219] G Levitt, 'Is "Terrorism" Worth Defining?' (1986) 13 Ohio NULR 97, 115. Attention-seeking is also a private motive, as was argued by one suspect, Hussein Osman, in relation to the failed London bombings of 21 July 2005: 'Entire alleged bomb ring held', *Guardian Weekly*, 5–11 Aug 2005, 8.

counter-terrorism measure'[220] and dilutes the special character of terrorism as a crime against non-violent politics. As Habermas says, terrorism 'differs from a private incident in that it deserves public interest and requires a different kind of analysis than murder out of jealousy'.[221] Prosecuting an individual for politically motivated 'terrorism', rather than for common crimes like murder or sectoral offences like hijacking, may help to satisfy public indignation at terrorist acts, better express community condemnation, and placate popular demands for justice.

Is there a moral difference between political and private violence, or between a conviction for 'terrorism' rather than murder or hijacking? Historically, many States sought to downplay and deny any such distinction, fearing that formally marking out offenders as 'political' would legitimize them or transform them into *causes célèbres*, lightning rods for dissent, or martyrs for a cause. Requiring proof of a political motive would expose fringe political claims to the judicial process, inevitably requiring the law to take serious notice of them and bringing them greater public attention. It was thought preferable to focus on the physical harm resulting from terrorist acts and, accordingly, to treat offenders as ordinary criminals.

The strength of these objections is doubtful. The political demands of terrorists will usually become prominent regardless of their ventilation in a courtroom, whether through the media or, since the mid-1990s, over the internet. While the elucidation of political motives in court may amplify them, it equally allows erroneous, misconceived, or poisonous ideas to be confronted and dissipated. The expressive function of the criminal law cannot be overstated; a conviction for *political* violence sends a symbolic message that certain kinds of violence, *as such*, cannot be tolerated, and reinforces the ethical values of the political community. For these reasons, it is important to ensure that a definition of terrorism is not overbroad and is flexible enough to exclude violent resistance that has legitimate public policy justifications.[222]

Those objections are also prudential rather than theoretical ones. Whether it is wise to differentiate political offenders in the legal system is a separate question to whether such offenders *are* morally distinguishable. In recent years, the international community has shown itself increasingly willing to differentiate different kinds of violence according to their motivation. The very idea of just war theory (surviving in the law of self-defence, and resurfacing in debates about humanitarian intervention) privileges certain kinds of violence based on motivation. More pointedly, the 2000 UN Convention against Transnational Organized Crime defines transnational organized crime as serious crime that is motivated by 'financial or other

---

[220] Levitt, ibid.   [221] Habermas, n 33, 34.   [222] See Ch 2 below.

material benefit'.[223] During its drafting, a number of States argued that the definition should not cover terrorist organizations, although other States hoped that it could be used against terrorist groups when they act for profit.[224] The resolution adopting the Convention urged the drafters of the UN Comprehensive Terrorism Convention to take the Convention into account when framing its provisions.[225] Defining terrorism by reference to its underlying political motives would help to distinguish terrorism conceptually from profit-oriented transnational organized crime.

This distinction does not necessarily imply that terrorism is morally *worse* than organized crime (a mafia hit may cause as much fear as a terrorist act), but it does suggest that it is morally *different*.[226] Such a distinction was drawn in the EU's 2002 Framework Decision on Combating Terrorism.[227] According to its drafters, because terrorism aims to intimidate countries, their institutions, or people and to seriously alter or destroy their political, economic, or social structures, 'the motivation of the offender is different . . . and, consequently, other legal rights are also affected'.[228] Terrorist acts are 'ordinary offences which become terrorist because of the motivations of the offender'.[229] A motive element distinguishes terrorism from ordinary crime which terrifies (such as armed robbery, serial rape, or mass murder).

A traditional difficulty is that in most domestic legal systems (and in international criminal law), motive is normally irrelevant to criminal

---

[223] 2000 UN Convention against Transnational Organized Crime (adopted by UNGA Resolution 55/25 (2000) on 15 Nov 2000, entered into force 29 Sept 2003; 114 parties and 147 signatories by Nov 2005), Arts 2 and 5. UNGA has often expressed concern at links between terrorist groups and violent organized crime: preambles to UNGA Resolutions 44/29 (1989); 46/51 (1991); 48/122 (1993); 49/60 (1994); 49/185 (1994); 50/186 (1995); 54/164 (2000); 58/136. Since the 1980s the categories have increasingly converged: W Laqueur, *The New Terrorism* (Phoenix Press, London, 2001) 210–225.

[224] See J Moore, ' "Umbrellas" or "Building Blocks"? Defining International Terrorism and Transnational Organised Crime in International Law' (2005) 27 Houston JIL 267.

[225] UNGA Res 55/25 (2000) para 7.

[226] cf Moore, n 224, who suggests that organized crime is a 'distinct' but also a 'lesser' crime than terrorism and thus should be kept separate.

[227] See Ch 3 below. The EU also distinguishes organized crime for profit: see EU Council, Joint Action 98/733/JHA of 21 Dec 1998 on making it a criminal offence to participate in a criminal organisation in the Member States of the EU [1998] OJ L351/1 ('whether such offences are an end in themselves or a means of obtaining material benefits and, where appropriate, of improperly influencing the operation of public authorities'); see also 1995 Europol Convention, Art 2; EU Council Decision 2002/187/JHA of 28 Feb 2002 setting up Eurojust with a view to reinforcing the fight against serious crime [2002] OJ L063/1. The proceeds of crime and terrorist financing are regulated jointly in the 2005 Council of Europe Convention on Laundering, Search, Seizure and Confiscation of the Proceeds from Crime and on the Financing of Terrorism (adopted at Warsaw, 24 June 2005). See also M Valsamis, 'Defining Organised Crime in the European Union: The Limits of European Law in an Area of "Freedom, Security and Justice" ' (2001) 26 ELR 565; S Fijnaut and L Paoli (eds), *Organised Crime in Europe* (Springer, Berlin, 2004).

[228] European Commission, Proposal for a Council Framework Decision on Combating Terrorism, 19 Sept 2001, COM(2001) 521 Final, 2001/0217 (CNS), 7.

[229] ibid, 6.

responsibility.[230] Proof of motive is not typically required as an element of an offence, although it may be relevant in other ways (such as in evidence of fact, or in the exercise of judicial discretion in sentencing, especially in mitigation or aggravation).[231] It is normally an offender's intention to commit a prohibited act that is essential to criminal responsibility,[232] rather than motives such as greed, jealousy, hatred, or revenge.

Even so, in a sophisticated criminal justice system an element of motive can promote a more finely calibrated legal response to specific types of socially unacceptable behaviour. Where society decides that certain social, ethical, or political values are worth protecting, the requirement of a motive element can more accurately target reprehensible infringements of those values.[233] There may be a powerful symbolic or moral value in condemning the motivation behind an act, quite separately from condemning the intentional physical act itself.

The key practical disadvantage of requiring motive as a mental element of a criminal offence is that it may be difficult to prove and 'creates an additional obstacle to effective prosecution'.[234] Yet, the ICTY has found that intent too 'is a mental factor which is difficult, even impossible, to determine' and consequently 'intent can be inferred from a certain number of presumptions of fact'.[235] Motive too might be inferred by reference to the context and circumstances.

Where motives are mixed (as in a hybrid criminal/terrorist organization),[236] it is arguably sufficient that the political motive constitute a *substantial* motive (rather than the sole or dominant one). The real difficulties arise where motives are undeclared, or where declared motives do not accord with actual motives. An example of the first category is when two speedboats attacked

---

[230] K Kittichaisaree, n 15, 92; J Smith, *Smith & Hogan: Criminal Law* (10th edn, Butterworths, London, 2002) 96; W Schabas, *Genocide in International Law* (CUP, Cambridge, 2002) 245.

[231] Kittichaisaree, ibid, 92.

[232] W Schabas, *An Introduction to the International Criminal Court* (CUP, Cambridge, 2001) 33; Cassese, n 6, 161–163.

[233] See A Candeub, 'Motive Crimes and Other Minds' (1994) 142 *University of Pennsylvania Law Review* 2071, 2113.

[234] ibid, 2075–2076, 2077, 2114–2115; Levitt, n 219, 112; Murphy (1989), n 1, 28; T Franck and B Lockwood, 'Preliminary Thoughts towards an International Convention on Terrorism' (1974) 68 AJIL 69, 78–79; Bassiouni, 'A Policy-Oriented Inquiry', n 8, xxix. Political motives may also be difficult to distinguish from criminal or even pathological ones: Ignatieff (2002), n 204, 1146; see also J Burke, 'What exactly does al-Qaeda want?', *Observer*, 21 Mar 2004; J Morsch, 'The Problem of Motive in Hate Crimes: The Arguments Against Presumptions of Racial Motivation' (1992) 82 JCLC 659, 661, 664–672.

[235] *Akayesu (Judgment)* ICTR–96–4–T (2 Sept 1998) para 523: including 'the general context of the perpetration of other culpable acts systematically directed against that same group . . . the scale of atrocities committed, their general nature, in a region or a country, or furthermore, the fact of deliberately and systematically targeting victims on account of their membership of a particular group, while excluding the members of other groups'.

[236] C Dishman, 'The Leaderless Nexus: When Crime and Terror Converge' (2005) 28 *Studies in Conflict and Terrorism* 237, 247–248.

the Bahamas-registered cruise ship, *Seabourn Spirit*, off the Somalian coast in late 2005, where the motives were unclear and authorities were unable to determine if the attack constituted piracy (for profit) or terrorism (for political reasons).[237] In the absence of proof of political motives, such acts could, by default, be prosecuted as maritime offences under sectoral treaties. In such cases, nothing is lost by requiring a political motive to establish terrorism, since the community has not been harmed by the element of *political* coercion that justifies distinguishing terrorism from other violence.

An example of the second category is where a criminal group feigns political motives to mask private ones (such as the pursuit of illegal profit), in the hope of legitimizing their operations or lending them respectability.[238] A related situation is where a terrorist group transforms over time into a profit-driven group.[239] This problem is foremost an evidentiary one which requires investigators to distinguish genuine motives from disingenuous ones. Yet, it also raises a conceptual problem. If a group publicly justifies its violence in political terms, then the community will inevitably perceive and experience such violence as political, not private (at least until the real motives are revealed). In such cases, it may be justifiable to prosecute such violence as terrorism, on the basis that a purported or publicly manifested political motive may still constitute a substantial one; the genuineness or objectivity of the motive need not be decisive.

Pragmatically, a definition which does not require a political motive avoids the difficulty of interpreting the term 'political'. In national extradition law, there are wide divergences in the meaning of 'political' offences,[240] and such jurisprudence may influence the interpretation of 'political' motives in terrorist offences. While no exhaustive definition of 'political' offences may be possible,[241] extradition law often excludes violence from the 'political' offence except where it is indiscriminate or atrocious,[242] or where it is too

---

[237] P Goodenough, 'Attack on Cruise Liner: Piracy or Terror?', CBS News, 7 Nov 2005.

[238] On the relationships between terrorism and organized crime, see Dishman, n 236; Moore, n 224; C Dishman, 'Terrorism, Crime, and Transformation' (2001) 24 *Studies in Conflict and Terrorism* 24; MC Bassiouni, 'Effective National and International Action against Organized Crime and Terrorist Criminal Activities' (1990) 4 Emory ILR 9.

[239] Or as Ignatieff says: 'What happens when political violence ceases to be motivated by political ideals and comes to be motivated by the emotional forces . . . [such as] *ressentiment* and envy, greed and blood lust, violence for its own sake?': Ignatieff (2005), n 204, 114.

[240] Van den Wijngaert, n 78, 191; C Van den Wyngaert, 'The Political Offence Exception to Extradition: How to Plug the Terrorist's Loophole' (1989) IYBHR 297, 301; I Stanbrook and C Stanbrook, *Extradition Law and Practice* (2nd edn, OUP, Oxford, 2000) 68; I Shearer, *Starke's International Law* (11th edn, Butterworths, London, 1994) 320.

[241] *Schtraks v Israel* [1964] AC 556, 589 (Lord Radcliffe); *R v Secretary of State for the Home Department, ex p Finivest Spa* [1997] 1 WLR 743, 760 (Simon Brown LJ).

[242] *Ellis v O'Dea* Record No 441 SS/1990 (30 July 1990), transcript, 36; *Della Savia* Swiss Federal Tribunal (26 Nov 1969) 95 ATF I, 469; *Morlacci* Swiss Federal Tribunal (12 Dec 1975), 101 ATF Ia, 605; *Re Atta (Mahmoud Abed)* (1989) 706 F Supp 1032, approved (1990) 910 F 2d 1063.

remote from, or disproportionate to, a political end.[243] (Courts have applied similar factors in interpreting the meaning of serious non-political crimes in international refugee law.)[244] Historically, acts not directed to the overthrow of a government,[245] or not committed in the course of a political disturbance,[246] were also found to be non-political, even where they had political aims in a broader policy sense. While this position has since been liberalized in some jurisdictions,[247] some States now regard acts as non-political where they attack democratic regimes.[248] In addition, terrorist acts in peacetime which would violate IHL in armed conflict have been considered non-political by some courts.[249]

These cases illustrate that the existence of a political *motive* does not decisively determine the political character of an act for extradition purposes.[250] If conduct is not 'political' in these circumstances, it might be difficult to secure a conviction for terrorist offences, since the use of indiscriminate violence deprives the conduct of its political character. Thus in *McGlinchey v Wren*, terrorist violence was considered 'the antithesis' of the political.[251] In a different context, the US Supreme Court found that cross burning by the Ku Klux Klan aims to instil fear, not to express political views,[252] even though fear was instilled for a political (racist) purpose.

The meaning of 'political' in extradition law is, however, by no means decisive of its meaning in the distinct context of criminal prosecutions. If a political motive comprises an element of an international terrorism offence, courts could carefully distinguish the meaning of 'political offences' in *national extradition law* from political motives or purposes in *international*

---

[243] *McGlinchey v Wren* [1983] Irish L Rep Monthly 169; *Shannon v Fanning* [1984] IR 548; *Folkerts v Public Prosecutor* (1978) 74 ILR 498; *Kavic, Bjelanovic and Arsenijevic* 78 ATF, I, 39 (30 Apr 1952) (Switzerland); *Eain v Wilkes* (1981) 641 F 2d 504, cert den (1981) 454 US 894; *Artukovic v Rison* (1986) 628 F Supp 1370; 784 F 2d 1354 (1986); *Re Nappi* (1952) 19 ILR 375; *Ktir v Ministère Public Fédéral* (1961) 34 ILR 123; *Re Kelly and MacFarlane* [1987] Nederlanse Jurisprudentie 931; *Gil v Canada* [1995] 1 FC 508.
[244] *T v Home Secretary* [1996] 2 All ER 865; *McMullen v INS* (1986) 788 F 2d 591; *Minister for Immigration v Singh* [2002] HCA 7; *Re Gil and Minister of Employment and Immigration* (1994) 119 DLR (4th) 497; *Zrig v Canada (Minister of Citizenship and Immigration)* (CA) [2003] 3 FC 761.
[245] *Re Castioni* (1891) 1 QB 149; *Re Meunier* (1864) 2 QB 415; *Re Ezeta* 62 F 972, 978 (ND Cal 1894).
[246] *Re Ezeta* 62 F 972 (1894) ND Cal; *Artukovic* (1956) 140 F Supp 245, (1957) 247 F 2d 198, (1958) 355 US 393, (1959) 170 F Supp 383; *Jimenez v Aristeguieta* (1962) 311 F 2d 547, cert den (1963) 375 US 48; *Re Doherty* (1984) 599 F Supp 270; *Quinn v Robinson* (1986) 783 F 2d 776.
[247] *R v Governor of Brixton Prison, ex p Kolczynski* [1955] 1 QB 540; *Schtraks*, n 241; *Re Kavic* 19 ILR 371 (Swiss Federal Tribunal, 1952); *Cheng v Governor of Pentonville Prison* [1973] AC 93; *Singh*, n 244, para 45 (Gaudron J).
[248] *Quinn v Wren* [1985] ILRM 410; *Russell v Fanning* [1988] ILRM 333.
[249] *Ahmed v Wigen* (1989) 726 F Supp 389, affirmed (1990) 910 F 2d 1063.
[250] *McMullen* n 244, 597; *Ktir* n 243, 144; *Giovanni Gatti* (1947) Ann Dig 145, 145–146.
[251] *McGlinchey* n 243, 171–172.
[252] 'Cross Burning an Issue of Hate, Not Free Speech', *Sydney Morning Herald*, 9 Apr 2003 (the Court upheld a 1952 Virginian law banning cross burning in order to intimidate).

criminal law, just as the term 'political' has distinctive meanings in the law on refugees, non-discrimination, and crimes of persecution.[253] Thus an act of terrorism may be an extraditable *non-political* offence in extradition law, because it is indiscriminate or disproportionate, but still comprise the crime of terrorism because of its *political* motivation.

Anarchic or nihilist violence, which lacks political aims and seeks only to destroy life or property, poses a special problem for any motive-based definition of terrorism. In extradition cases, courts have commonly held that anarchic violence is not 'political',[254] since politics is considered to be the process of governing rather than the destruction of government itself. Similarly, if nihilism is a belief in nothing, it follows that a nihilist motive cannot be a political one. Such analysis is arguably unsound, since it hinges on a narrow conception of politics as merely the business of governing. In a modern sense, the 'political' does not only refer to the formal institutions and processes of government, but to any movements or causes which seek to influence the public or political sphere. As the House of Lords said in the *Schtraks* case: 'The use of force, or it may be other means . . . to compel a government to change its policy may be just as political in character as the use of force to achieve a revolution.'[255] The term 'political' could, for example, cover violence by anti-abortion activists, 'eco-terrorists', animal liberationists, or between ethnic groups—even if the victims are non-State targets. It is important to protect private persons perceived to be acting politically (and targeted as such), even though they are outside government.

Ignatieff claims that Al-Qaeda are eschatological and 'apocalyptic nihilists' who provide no justifications for their actions and thus lack any demands which can be politically accommodated.[256] That crude assertion is at odds with the clear claims made by Osama bin Laden in his 'Letter to America' of 2002.[257] Some of his complaints are unremarkable and shared by liberals or conservatives in the west.[258] His demands are very specific: remove

---

[253] 1951 Refugee Convention, Art 1A(2); ICCPR and ICESCR, common Art 2(1); 1998 Rome Statute, Art 7(1)(h) (crime against humanity of persecution).

[254] *Re Meunier* (1894) 2 QB 415 (since it is not directed against a particular government); see also *Prevato v Governor Metropolitan Remand Centre* (1986) 64 ALR 37.

[255] *Schtraks*, n 241, 583.

[256] Ignatieff (2005), n 204, 99, see also 112–144.

[257] Osama bin Laden, 'Letter to America', *Observer*, 24 Nov 2002; see also the interview with Bin Laden in R Fisk, *The Great War for Civilization: The Conquest of the Middle East* (Fourth Estate, London, 2005) 22–27; G O'Boyle, 'Theories of Justification and Political Violence: Examples from Four Groups' (2002) 14 *Terrorism and Political Violence* 23, 37–41.

[258] Liberals share Bin Laden's concerns that America: refuses to sign the Kyoto Protocol; dropped an atomic bomb on Japan; exploits women; maintains weapons of mass destruction; interferes in foreign governments; disrespects international law; seeks war crimes immunity for US soldiers; supported sanctions in Iraq which killed many children; and pursues an unjust oil policy. Conservatives share Bin Laden's concerns about gambling, drugs, sexual immorality, homosexuality, and Clinton's 'immoral acts' in the Oval Office.

foreign military bases; stop supporting Israel and corrupt Muslim leaders; forbid usury; permit *shariah* law, and convert to Islam. Some of these claims may be unreasonable or excessive, but they are still *political* claims.

An alternative approach is to define terrorism not only by its political motivation, but more explicitly by a range of additional *public-oriented* motives. This is the approach to definition in UK, Canadian, Australian, and New Zealand law, which require an intention to advance a *political, religious* or *ideological* cause, while this is supplemented by 'philosophical' motives in a draft South African law.[259] In many cases, it is likely that religious or ideological motives would already be covered by giving a broad meaning to 'political',[260] but the more comprehensive approach has the dual advantages of relative prospective certainty and of capturing violence which cannot be characterized as 'political'. It also neatly covers anarchic and nihilistic violence (as ideological), or eschatological or millenarian violence (as religious). Consider, for instance, the beheadings of three Christian girls on their way to school in Sulawesi, Indonesia, in 2005, designed to strike fear into that religious community.[261]

Given the breadth of the term 'political' and of these additional categories of motive, it is arguably unnecessary to prohibit separately violence motivated by a more ambiguous category of 'social' objectives (as in the US FBI's definition).[262] On the other hand, while much ethnic violence will also have a political, religious, or ideological aspect, this is not always the case. For example, spontaneous racial or communal violence may be triggered by private disputes, historical enmities, or retribution, rather than because of political disputes (about the distribution of power, land or resources, or discrimination), ideological causes (such as eugenics or organized ethnic chauvinism or supremacy), or religious differences. It is preferable to add 'ethnic' motives as an element defining violence which precipitates terror.

4. *Terrorism as a threat to international peace and security*

A further compelling rationale for criminalizing terrorism is the threat it may present to international peace and security. Resolutions of the General

---

[259] Terrorism Act 2000 (UK), s 1(1)(c); Criminal Code 1985 (Canada), s 83.1(1); Criminal Code Act 1995 (Australia), s 100.1(1); Terrorism Suppression Act 2002 (NZ), s 5; South African Protection of Constitutional Democracy against Terrorism and Related Activities Bill 2003, cl 1(1)(xxiv)(c); see also C Walker, *Blackstone's Guide to the Anti-Terrorism Legislation* (OUP, Oxford, 2002) 20–30.

[260] Walker, ibid, 26.

[261] A Rina and T Soetjipto, 'Teenagers beheaded on the way to school', *Sydney Morning Herald*, 31 Oct 2005.

[262] Walker, n 259, 21–22 (UK law-makers thought that this expression was too broad and might cover mere blackmail or extortion).

Assembly since the 1970s,[263] and of the Commission on Human Rights since the 1990s,[264] have stated that international terrorism may threaten international peace and security, friendly relations among States, international cooperation, State security, or UN principles and purposes. The preambles to the 1999 Terrorist Financing Convention and the Draft Comprehensive Convention take a similar position, while numerous regional instruments also highlight the threat to peace and security presented by terrorism,[265] particularly given access to modern technology, weapons, transport, communications, and links to organized crime.[266]

The General Assembly has also recalled 'the role of the Security Council in combating international terrorism whenever it poses a threat to international peace and security'.[267] From the early 1990s, the Security Council increasingly acknowledged in general or specific terms that acts of international terrorism may, or do, constitute threats to international peace and security.[268] After the terrorist attacks of 11 September 2001, the Council's language shifted to regarding 'any' or 'all' acts of terrorism as a threat to peace and security[269]— regardless of their severity or international effects.

At first glance it seems obvious that, by definition, 'international' terrorism must have some negative impact on international relations. To some extent, the 11 September events attacked the 'structures and values of a system of world public order, along with the international law that sustains it'.[270] Yet such consequences cannot be assumed for all terrorist acts. Before

---

[263] UNGA Resolutions 38/130 (1983) para 1; 40/61 (1985) preamble, paras 2–3; UNGA Res 42/22 (1987) annexed Declaration on the Enhancement of the Effectiveness of the Principle of Refraining from the Threat or Use of Force in International Relations, preamble; 42/159 (1987) preamble, paras 2–3; 44/29 (1989) preamble, paras 1–2; 46/51 (1991) preamble, paras 1–2; 48/122 (1993) para 1; 49/60 (1994) preamble, paras 1–3; 49/185 (1994) para 1; 50/53 (1995) para 7; 50/186 (1995) para 2; 1996 Declaration, preamble, paras 1–2; 52/133 (1997) para 3; 54/164 (2000) paras 2–3; 56/160 (2002) para 1; 58/174 (2004) para 1; 59/195 (2005) para 1; UNGA (60th Sess), 2005 World Summit Outcome, UN Doc A/60/L.1 (20 Sept 2005) para 81.

[264] UNComHR Resolutions 1995/43, para 1; 1996/47, para 2; 1997/42, para 2; 1998/47, para 3; 1999/27, para 1; 2000/30, para 1; 2001/37, para 1; 2002/35, para 1; 2003/37, para 1; UNSubComHR Resolutions 1994/18, para 1; 1996/20, para 2; 1997/39, para 1; see also 1993 Vienna Declaration and Programme of Action, UN Doc A/CONF.157/24 (Part I), ch III, s I, para 17.

[265] 2002 Inter-American Convention, preamble; 1971 OAS Convention, preamble; 1987 SAARC Convention, preamble; Special Summit of the Americas, Declaration of Nuevo León, Mexico, 13 Jan 2004; NAM Final Doc (2004), n 136, para 100; NAM Final Doc (2003), n 136, paras 107, 110; ASEAN, Declaration on Joint Action to Counter Terrorism, Brunei Darussalam, 5 Nov 2001, preamble; OSCE, Bucharest Plan of Action for Combating Terrorism, 4 Dec 2001, MC(9).DEC/1, Annex, para 1; Decision on Combating Terrorism (MC(9).DEC/1).

[266] EU Com Proposal, n 216, 3, 8.

[267] UNGA Resolution 50/53 (1995), para 7.

[268] Preambles to UNSC Resolutions 731 (1992); 748 (1992); 1044 (1996); 1189 (1998); 1267 (1999); 1333 (1999); 1363 (2001); 1390 (2002); 1455 (2003); 1526 (2004), 1535 (2004); see also 1269 (1999) para 1.

[269] UNSC Resolutions 1368 (2001) para 1; 1611 (2005) para 1; 1617 (2005) preamble; 1618 (2005) para 1; 1624 (2005) preamble; 1636 (2005) preamble.

[270] M Reisman, 'In Defense of World Public Order' (2001) 95 AJIL 833.

11 September, the Council reserved the right to assess whether particular acts of international terrorism, in the circumstances, were serious enough to threaten peace and security. That measured and calibrated approach has been abandoned in the Council's rush to condemn any act, irrespective of its gravity, as a threat.[271]

For example, a low level international terrorist incident—such as the attempted assassination of a public official by a foreign perpetrator, without the complicity of a foreign State—may not appreciably threaten peace or security, remaining localized or contained. In the absence of advance definition of terrorism before late 2004, the Council's expansive approach condemned acts of prospectively unknown—and unknowable—scope. Even with definition in 2004, it is not clear that sectoral offences committed to provoke terror, intimidate a population, or compel a government or organization, will always be sufficiently grave to affect international peace or security.

Whereas previously the Council only referred to acts of *international* terrorism as threats to peace and security, since 2003 the Council has condemned 'any act', 'all acts', and 'all forms' of terrorism,[272] without qualifying such acts as *international*. The Council has involved itself in domestic terrorism, such as the Madrid bombing (wrongly attributed to ETA), and Chechen terrorism in Russia.[273] By expanding its sphere of concern to domestic as well as international terrorism, the Council has further pursued the liberal reading of its mandate developed in the 1990s.[274]

Yet such an interpretation is unduly elastic. While domestic terrorism *may* threaten peace and security, it claims too much to assert that *any* act of domestic terrorism does so, just as not all *international* terrorism threatens peace or security. Although all terrorism (domestic or international) is of international *concern*—if it is universally accepted that it is morally repugnant—that is not equivalent to regarding all terrorism as a threat to *peace and security* under the Charter.

To the extent that terrorist acts do threaten peace and security, criminalization is one appropriate means of suppressing it, supplementing the range of other measures available to States and the Security Council. Even where terrorism is directed against an authoritarian State, criminalization may be

---

[271] See Ch 4 below.

[272] Respectively: UNSC Resolutions 1516 (2003) para 1; 1530 (2004) para 1; 1515 (2003), preamble; and 1516 (2003) para 4; 1526 (2004), preamble; and 1530 (2004) para 4.

[273] Respectively: UNSC Resolutions 1530 (2004) para 1 (though ETA has transboundary links), 1440 (2002) para 1.

[274] See, eg, Chesterman, n 208, 121–162, examining Security Council practice in relation to internal conflicts, humanitarian crises, and disruptions of democracy; R Gordon, 'United Nations Intervention in Internal Conflicts: Iraq, Somalia and Beyond' (1994) 15 Michigan JIL 519; M Berdal, 'The Security Council, Peacekeeping and Internal Conflict after the Cold War' (1997) 7 Duke JCIL 71.

justified if it helps to avert more serious harm to international peace or security, such as the escalation of regional violence.

5. *Controlling Security Council measures*

(a) Lack of definition of terrorism in Council practice

A related argument for definition and criminalization is the pragmatic need for legal controls on political discretions in efforts against terrorism. Soon after the terrorist attacks of 11 September 2001, the Security Council exercised its enforcement powers under Chapter VII of the UN Charter to compel all States to adopt wide-ranging counter-terrorism measures.[275] Yet, terrorism was not defined in resolutions after 11 September,[276] nor were lists of terrorists established.[277] The lack of definition was deliberate, since consensus on key Resolution 1373 depended on avoiding definition.[278]

Prior to these resolutions, the lack of a definition was legally inconsequential, since no international rights or duties hinged on the term 'terrorism'. Since 11 September 2001, that has changed. The absence of a definition is not merely of theoretical interest, because the terms 'terrorism' and 'terrorist' have operative legal significance in Resolution 1373, triggering obligations to criminalize financing of *terrorism*; suppress *terrorist* groups; deny refugee status to *terrorists*; prevent the movement of *terrorists*; bring *terrorists* to justice; and, vitally, establish *terrorist acts* as serious domestic crimes. Resolutions have also implicitly referred to self-defence against terrorism, so the lack of definition may allow States to unilaterally target 'terrorists' in military operations.[279]

In supervizing implementation of Council measures, the UN Counter-Terrorism Committee (CTC) also decided not to define terrorism, 'although its members had a fair idea of what was blatant terrorism'.[280] The CTC did

---

[275] See Ch 4 below.

[276] E Rosand, 'Security Council Resolution 1373, the Counter-Terrorism Committee, and the Fight Against Terrorism' (2003) 97 AJIL 333, 339–340; J Stromseth, 'The Security Council's Counter-Terrorism Role: Continuity and Innovation' (2003) 97 ASIL Proceedings 41, 44; N Rostow, 'Before and After: The Changed UN Response to Terrorism since September 11' (2002) 35 Cornell ILJ 475, 484; S Talmon, 'The Security Council as World Legislature' (2005) 99 AJIL 35, 49.

[277] Although the CTC blithely urged States to use lists to 'eliminate the need for proof of actual involvement' in terrorism: J Wainwright, CTC Expert Opinion, 24 Nov 2002, para 8.

[278] L Bondi, 'Legitimacy and Legality: Key Issues in the Fight against Terrorism', Fund for Peace, Washington, DC, 11 Sept 2002, 25.

[279] US Congress, Authorization for Use of Military Force, Pub L 107–40, 115 Stat 224 (18 Sept 2001).

[280] CTC Chair (Ambassador Greenstock), Presentation to Symposium: 'Combating International Terrorism: The Contribution of the United Nations', Vienna, 3–4 June 2002; see also W Lacquer, 'We Can't Define "Terrorism" but We Can Fight It', *Wall Street Journal*, 12 July 2002, A12.

not want to interfere in the competence of other UN bodies by defining it, or by adjudicating on specific acts.[281] Instead, the CTC took an ad hoc approach, deciding whether an act is terrorism 'where necessary' and referring controversies to the Council or other bodies.[282] It pragmatically asserted that terrorism can be combated without agreement on its criminality in all situations.[283] While Resolution 1373 was drafted partly on the basis that sectoral treaties provided a framework definition,[284] the CTC openly allowed States to define terrorism unilaterally.[285] Commonwealth model laws to implement Resolution 1373 have defined terrorism by reference to sectoral offences but also generically.[286]

While flexibility in implementation is warranted due to variations in domestic legal systems, this effectively means that each State unilaterally defines terrorism,[287] without any outer legal boundaries set by the international community. Far from urging States to confine overly-broad legislation, the CTC has advocated that *domestic* terrorism laws be jurisdictionally widened to cover *international* terrorism,[288] even though some domestic crimes more closely resemble broad national security or public order offences. The absence of a definition also makes it difficult to resolve disputes about whether particular persons or groups qualify as terrorist.[289]

The failure to define terrorism provoked mixed reactions from Council members. Colombia believed definition was unnecessary, since terrorism was defined in Assembly Resolution 49/60.[290] Whereas Mauritius did not want to 'quibble' about definition,[291] other States have placed more value on it.[292] Syria stated that non-definition encouraged violations of human rights and IHL, and 'selective accusations of terrorism'.[293] Arab and Islamic States insist

[281] Greenstock, ibid.   [282] ibid.   [283] Rostow, n 276, 487.   [284] ibid.
[285] UNHR Committee, PR HR/CT/630, 27 Mar 2003 (CTC Expert, C Ward); C Ward, 'Building Capacity to Combat International Terrorism: The Role of the United Nations Security Council' (2003) 8 JCSL 289, 294–295.
[286] Commonwealth Secretariat, Model Legislative Provisions on Measures to Combat Terrorism, Part I.
[287] Rosand, n 276, 339–340; Stromseth, n 276, 44.
[288] Greenstock, n 280; W Gehr, 'Recurrent Issues: CTC Briefing for Member States', 4 Apr 2002.
[289] Rosand, n 276, 340.
[290] UNSC, 4845th mtg, PR SC/7900, 16 Oct 2003.
[291] UNSC, 4413th mtg, PR SC/7207, 12 Nov 2001.
[292] UNSC, 4453rd mtg, PR SC/7276, 18 Jan 2002 (including Syria; Costa Rica for the Rio Group; Morocco for the Arab Group; Qatar for the OIC; Pakistan; Israel); 4512th and 4513th mtgs, PR SC/7361, 15 Apr 2002 (Syria; Malaysia); 4792nd mtg, PR SC/7823, 23 July 2003 (Pakistan); 4845th mtg, PR SC/7900, 16 Oct 2003 (Pakistan; Libya; Yemen; Armenia).
[293] UNSC, 4512th and 4513th mtgs, PR SC/7361, 15 Apr 2002.

that terrorism be distinguished from self-determination struggles; that 'State terrorism' be covered; and that root causes be addressed.[294]

As Amnesty notes, 'the terms "terrorists" and "terrorist acts" in resolution 1373 are open to widely differing interpretations' and may facilitate rights violations.[295] National anti-terrorism laws are widely divergent, with some very broad or vague definitions in play.[296] Some States have deployed the international legitimacy conferred by Council authorization to define terrorism to repress or de-legitimize political opponents, and to conflate them with Al-Qaeda.

Thus China bluntly characterizes Uighur separatists in Xinjiang as terrorists; Russia asserts that Chechen rebels are terrorists, even though many are fighting in an internal conflict; and India seldom distinguishes militants from terrorists in Kashmir.[297] In Indonesia, insurgencies in Aceh and West Papua have been described and combated as terrorism, as have a Maoist insurgency in Nepal and an Islamist movement in Morocco.[298] Israel has identified Palestinians with Al-Qaeda, with Ariel Sharon calling Arafat 'our Bin Laden'.[299] In the Maldives, an opposition politician was convicted of terrorism offences and sentenced to ten years' imprisonment for peacefully protesting against rights violations by the government.[300] Similarly, in Uzbekistan fifteen men were convicted of vague terrorism offences for

[294] UNSC, 4453rd mtg, PR SC/7276, 18 Jan 2002 (including Syria; Qatar for the OIC; cf Israel); 4734th mtg, PR SC/7718, 4 Apr 2003 (Pakistan); Syria; 4512th and 4513th mtgs, PR SC/ 7361, 15 Apr 2002 (Malaysia); 4792nd mtg, PR SC/7823, 23 July 2003 (Pakistan); 4845th mtg, PR SC/7900, 16 Oct 2003 (Pakistan; Libya; Yemen).

[295] Amnesty International, Statement on the Implementation of UNSC Res 1373, 1 Oct 2001.

[296] See Ch 4 below.

[297] Concerning China: UNSC, 4688th mtg, PR SC/7638, 20 Jan 2003 (China); Chinese Information Office of State Council, ' "East Turkistan" Terrorist Forces Cannot Get Away with Impunity,' 21 Jan 2001; J Yardley, 'China puts minorities on terrorist watch list', *Sydney Morning Herald*, 17 Dec 2003; Amnesty International, 'Rights at Risk: Concerns Regarding Security Legislation and Law Enforcement Measures', 18 Jan 2002, AI Index ACT 30/002/2002, 5; C-P Chung, 'China's "War on Terror": September 11 and Uighur Separatism' (Aug 2002) *Foreign Affairs* 8; R Menon, 'The New Great Game in Central Asia' (2003) 45 *Survival* 187, 192, 198–199; J Watts, 'China turns war on terror to its strategic advantage', *Guardian Weekly*, 16–22 Sep 2005. Concerning Russia: UNSC, 4688th mtg, PR SC/7638, 20 Jan 2003 (Russia); 'Ivanov denies war in Chechnya, calls it fighting with terrorism', Itar-Tass, 4 Mar 2004; 'Struggle in Chechnya—struggle against international terrorism', Itar-Tass, 12 Nov 2002. In 1995 the Russian Constitutional Court declared that Chechnya was an internal armed conflict governed by Protocol II: in (1996) 17 *Human Rights Journal* 133; P Gaeta, 'The Armed Conflict in Chechnya before the Russian Constitutional Court' (1996) 7 EJIL 563. Concerning India: UNSC, 4618th mtg, PR SC/7522, 4 Oct 2002 (India).

[298] J Aglionby, 'Jakarta orders attack on Aceh', *The Guardian*, 19 May 2003; ABC TV (Australia), Foreign Correspondent, 'West Papua: Ambushed', 3 Aug 2004; R Ramesh, 'Maoists tighten grip on Kathmandu', *The Guardian*, 21 Aug 2004; Reuters, 'One thousand prisoners released for each tiny finger', *Sydney Morning Herald*, 10 May 2003.

[299] ABC News, 'Arafat accuses bin Laden of exploiting Palestinians', 15 Dec 2002; Pokempner, n 171, 23.

[300] ICJ, 'Maldives: Human rights defender Jennifer Latheef should be released immediately and unconditionally', Press Release, Geneva, 18 Oct 2005.

organizing public demonstrations, at which the government indiscriminately fired upon the crowd.[301]

The Council has initiated a fight not against terrorism, but 'different terrorisms'.[302] This devolution of discretionary power is unprincipled and dangerous. Combating terrorism 'without defining it remained possible for as long as the word itself was not uttered'.[303] In contrast, operatively deploying the term without defining it creates uncertainty and allows States to make 'unilateral determinations geared towards their own interests'.[304] Few States have objected to Council measures because they largely align (rather than interfere) with their sovereign interests.[305]

(b) Scope of Council authority to respond to 'terrorism'

The absence of a definition also raises difficult questions about the scope of the Council's authority under Article 39 of the Charter to designate a generalized, indeterminate phenomenon (rather than a specific act or incident, as in past practice)[306] as a threat to security.[307] The Resolution addresses terrorism generally, unconnected to 11 September 2001 or Al-Qaeda, and the response is not bound by temporal or geographical limits.[308] The justification for addressing terrorism generally is based on assumptions about the harmfulness of transnational terrorism.[309] As Singapore stated, 'the 11 September events had brought new responsibilities to the Council's work. Traditional definitions of threats to international peace and security no longer held'.[310]

On one hand, what constitutes a 'threat to the peace' is a continuously evolving and largely political question.[311] When Article 39 of the Charter was drafted at San Francisco in 1945, threats to the peace, or breaches of the peace, were primarily understood as referring to the use of organized military

---

[301] 'Uzbekistan: UN rights experts concerned about rights of defendants', UN News Centre, 26 Oct 2005.

[302] Laqueur, n 223, 79.

[303] G Guillaume, 'Terrorism and International Law', Grotius Lecture, British Institute of International and Comparative Law, London, 13 Nov 2003, 4–5.

[304] ibid; see also J-M Sorel, 'Some Questions about the Definition of Terrorism and the Fight against its Financing' (2003) 14 AJIL 365, 370.

[305] Krisch, n 31, 15.

[306] P Szasz, 'The Security Council Starts Legislating' (2002) 96 AJIL 901, 901–902; Stromseth, n 276, 41; M de Brichambaut, 'The Role of the United Nations Security Council in the International Legal System' in M Byers (ed), *The Role of International Law in International Politics* (OUP, Oxford, 2001) 268, 271, 275; G Abi-Saab, 'The Proper Role of International Law in Combating Terrorism' (2002) 1 Chinese JIL 305, 310; G Nolte, 'The Limits of the Security Council's Powers and its Functions in the International Legal System: Some Reflections' in Byers (ed), above, 315, 321–324; D Bowett, 'The Impact of Security Council Decisions on Dispute Settlement Procedures' (1994) 5 EJIL 89, 92.

[307] Krisch, n 31.

[308] ibid, 6; Szasz, n 306, 901; Stromseth, n 276, 43.   [309] Abi-Saab, n 306, 310.

[310] UNSC (4453rd mtg), Press Release SC/7276, 18 Jan 2002.

[311] Talmon, n 276, 40–43.

force between States (or de facto States, as in the Korean war). This meant that enforcement action under Article 41 or 42 could only be triggered by inter-State military conflict, and lesser disputes were left to be dealt with by other UN organs.[312] Article 39 was not intended to cover violence by private armed groups; internal violence and civil wars (which fell within the scope of domestic jurisdiction under Article 2(7) of the Charter); or even illegal foreign occupation of territory.[313] The concept of aggression in Article 39 was purposely left undefined so as not to restrict the Council's discretion.[314] However, it too referred to the direct or indirect application of armed force (including sending armed groups) by one State against another,[315] and thus largely overlapped with the concept of a breach of the peace.[316] Early Council practice accepted this narrow view of Article 39. In considering the problem of Franco's Spain, the Council rejected a Polish argument that 'imminent' dangers, such as domestic fascism, constituted a threat to the peace, and insisted that only 'existing' threats were within its mandate.[317]

During the Cold War, the Council seldom took enforcement action in response to threats to peace and security, not for lack of threats, but because it was frequently deadlocked or paralysed by the geopolitical rivalry of the superpowers. Throughout this period, threats to peace and security were interpreted by the international community as principally referring to inter-State conflicts. While the Council criticized apartheid in South Africa—an internal affair—for disturbing peace and security (UNSC Resolution 311 (1972)), the Resolution must be interpreted in the broader context of South Africa's military incursions into neighbouring countries.

Despite its original meaning, Article 39 of the Charter confers a wide,[318] broad,[319] elastic,[320] or even 'complete'[321] or 'full'[322] discretion on the Council to determine the existence of a threat to peace or security. The 'open-textured' terms of Article 39 were left deliberately undefined[323]—including

---

[312] B Simma (ed), *The Charter of the United Nations: A Commentary* (OUP, New York, 2002) 608.

[313] ibid, 609.

[314] ibid, 608. Aggression was defined in a non-binding resolution of the UN General Assembly in its 1974 Definition of Aggression. The Rome Statute of the ICC provides for future jurisdiction over the crime of aggression once it is defined at a future review conference.

[315] According to the law of State responsibility.

[316] Simma, n 312, 610.

[317] H Kelsen, *The Law of the United Nations* (Praeger, New York, 1950) 727–728.

[318] V Gowlland-Debbas, 'The Functions of the United Nations Security Council in the International Legal System' in Byers (ed), n 306, 277, 287; Nolte, n 306, 316.

[319] D Akande, 'The International Court of Justice and the Security Council: Is There Room for Judicial Control of Decisions of the Political Organs of the United Nations?' (1997) 46 ICLQ 309, 314.

[320] M Reisman, 'The Constitutional Crisis in the United Nations' (1993) 87 AJIL 83, 93.

[321] Kelsen, n 317, 727.

[322] *Lockerbie* (1992) ICJ Reports 3, 66 and 176 (Dissenting Opinion of Judge Weeramantry).

[323] Stromseth, n 276, 42.

'aggression'[324]—and were intended to be subjectively determined by the Council.[325] Political and factual judgments are inherent in determinations,[326] though political matters are not necessarily non-legal.[327] Political reality is the foremost constraint on Council action.[328]

Few believe that the Charter should be interpreted in a static, doctrinaire, or formalistic way, mummifying original meanings from 1945. The Charter should be interpreted flexibly, as a living instrument, to promote the values of the international community, rather than in a strict constructionist or conservative textual manner.[329] The scope of Article 39 necessarily changes according to prevailing political conditions. The 1969 Vienna Convention on the Law of Treaties accepts that the subsequent practice or agreement of parties to a treaty may establish an agreed interpretation, even if it is at variance with its original meaning.[330]

In this regard, the practice of the Security Council since the 1990s, and the acquiescence of States to its measures, supports an expanded interpretation of Article 39, and a reciprocal narrowing of the reserved domain of domestic jurisdiction under Article 2(7) of the Charter. The end of the Cold War encouraged a loosening of traditional views on the meaning of peace and security under the UN Charter, including in the practice of regional institutions.[331] As early as 1992, the Security Council acknowledged that threats to peace and security may spring from 'sources of instability in the economic, social, humanitarian and ecological field'.[332] In a range of situations in the 1990s, the Council responded actively to wider threats, beyond inter-State conflict, such as violent internal armed conflicts, humanitarian crises, disruption of democracy, mass internal displacements of people, refugee outflows,

---

[324] Akande, n 319, 339.

[325] Reisman, n 320, 93.

[326] V Gowlland-Debbas, 'Security Council Enforcement Action and Issues of State Responsibility' (1994) 43 ICLQ 55, 61.

[327] R Higgins, 'The Place of International Law in the Settlement of Disputes by the Security Council' (1970) 64 AJIL 1, 15–16.

[328] Szasz, n 306, 905; E Miller, 'The Use of Targeted Sanctions in the Fight against International Terrorism: What about Human Rights?' (2003) 97 ASIL Proceedings 46, 47.

[329] R Higgins, *Problems and Process: International Law and How We Use It* (Clarendon, Oxford, 1994) 252; see also R Wedgwood, 'Unilateral Action in the UN System' (2000) 11 EJIL 349, 352.

[330] 1969 Vienna Convention on the Law of Treaties (adopted 23 May 1969, entered into force 27 Jan 1980, 1155 UNTS 331), Art 31(3).

[331] OSCE, Helsinki Final Act 1975; J Solana, *A Secure Europe in a Better World: European Security Strategy* (European Union Institute for Security Studies, Paris, 2003); NATO, London Declaration, 6 July 1990; NATO, Rome Declaration, 8 Nov 1991; NATO, Madrid Declaration, 8 July 1997; NATO, 'The Alliance's Strategic Concept', 24 Apr 1999; NATO, 'Prague Summit Declaration', 21–22 Nov 2002; L Ponsard, 'The Dawning of a New Security Era?', *NATO Review*, Autumn 2004; Lord Robertson, 'Change and Continuity', *NATO Review*, Winter 2003; OAS, *Declaration on Security in the Americas*, OAS Doc OEA/Ser.K/XXXVIII, CES/DEC. 1/03 rev.1 (28 Oct 2003).

[332] UN Doc S/24111 (1992).

and serious violations of international criminal law.[333] Many of these cases were controversial,[334] and 'there is an obvious element of artificiality and discomfort' in characterizing internal situations as threats to international peace and security.[335]

In addition, a number of non-binding, standard-setting, or thematic Council resolutions in the 1990s addressed generalized threats to security, on matters such as the protection of civilians and children in armed conflict; women and security; HIV/AIDS and peacekeeping; the protection of UN and humanitarian workers; proliferation of small arms and mercenaries in Africa; and weapons of mass destruction (WMDs).[336] In addition to the main counter-terrorism resolutions since 2001, resolutions have also addressed the impact on children of links between conflict and terrorism and between terrorism, non-State actors and WMDs.[337] The Council has been increasingly influenced by a 'human security' agenda, reflected in proposals for UN reform,[338] despite doubts about whether such issues genuinely involve security questions.[339]

On the other hand, action against an abstract and non-specific phenomenon,[340] or against distant, speculative, or potential threats,[341] may be of questionable validity—quite apart from the distinct question whether a judicial body is competent to review Council action.[342] Despite the discretionary breadth of Article 39, interpretative flexibility, and subsequent

---

[333] eg the Balkans: UNSC Res 713 (1991), 724 (1991); Somalia: Resolution 733 (1992); Liberia: Resolution 788 (1992); Lockerbie: Resolution 748 (1992); racist Rhodesia: Resolution 217 (1965), 221 (1966); Haiti: Resolution 841 and 875 (1993); Kurds: Resolution 688 (1991); see also M Odello, 'Commentary on the United Nations High-Level Panel on Threats, Challenges and Change' (2005) 10 JCSL 231, 232–237.

[334] C Glaser, 'Future Security Arrangements for Europe: Why NATO is Still Best' in G Downs (ed), *Collective Security beyond the Cold War* (University of Michigan Press, Ann Arbor, 1994) 235.

[335] G Evans, 'The Responsibility to Protect: Evolution and Implementation', Keynote Address to the London School of Economics/King's College London Conference on Ethical Dimensions of European Foreign Policy, London, 1 July 2005.

[336] UNSC Resolutions 1265 (1999) and 1296 (2000) (civilians); 1261 (1999), 1314 (2000), 1379 (2001), 1460 (2003) and 1539 (2004) (children); 1325 (2000) (women); 1308 (2000), preamble (HIV/AIDS); 1502 (2003) (humanitarian workers); 1467 (2003) (arms and mercenaries); 255 (1968) and 984 (1995) (nuclear weapons); and 1540 (2004) (WMDs). See also D Lenefsky, 'The United Nations Security Council Resolution on Security Assurances for Non-Nuclear Weapon States' (1970) 3 NYU JIL 56.

[337] UNSC Resolutions 1379 (2001) para 6 and 1540 (2004) preamble respectively.

[338] UN High-Level Panel on Threats, Challenges and Change, *A More Secure World: Our Shared Responsibility* (2004) 2, 21–30, 52–54 (recognizing that economic and social threats (including poverty, infectious disease and environmental degradation), terrorism, and transnational organized crime threaten security).

[339] See B Saul, 'The Dangers of the United Nations' "New Security Agenda" ' (2006) 1 *Asian Journal of Comparative Law* 147.

[340] Abi-Saab, n 306, 310; de Brichambaut, n 306, 275; Nolte, n 306, 321–324; Bowett, n 306, 92.

[341] *Namibia Advisory Opinion* (1971) ICJ Reports 6, 340, para 34 (Gros J); Kelsen, n 317, 727–728.

[342] Akande, n 319, 325.

agreements among parties, the meaning of Article 39 is not legally unlimited. The legal rights and duties of individuals and States hinge on the meaning given to particular words under Chapter VII, and the legal consequence of interpretation may be a decision to authorize military violence or impose sanctions. For this reason, some degree of predictability in interpretation is essential on grounds of fairness, so that participants in the international system are not confronted by rapid changes in the rules at the behest of the fifteen members of the Council. The language of Article 39 and precision in its interpretation are vital means of ensuring predictability.

Language implies constraint and inherent or ultimate limits: 'Words are supposed to carry meanings.'[343] The 1969 Vienna Convention requires that a treaty be interpreted in good faith, according to the *ordinary meaning of its terms in context* and in the light of its object and purpose.[344] While the Charter should be viewed 'not as a static formula, but as a constitutive instrument capable of organic growth',[345] it cannot be interpreted beyond its own textual limits. That can only be achieved by amending the Charter in accordance with Articles 108 and 109. There is a danger in interpreting texts too strictly or dogmatically, but the greater danger lies in straining a text beyond the outermost limits of its natural elasticity, since then the international rule of law dissipates into nothingness. As Lowe writes: 'If one can no longer read texts . . . and take them at their face value on the basis of their ordinary meaning, diplomacy and the Rule of Law become quite literally impossible.'[346]

The language of Article 39 may be indeterminate, but it is not infinite. The Council can only possess a discretion within the textual bounds of the authority conferred on it. While it may not be possible to define prospectively all conduct threatening security—abstract lists should be viewed with suspicion[347]—it may be possible to identify what is *not* a threat within the ordinary, contextual, purposive meaning of Article 39. In the *Namibia Advisory Opinion* (1971), Judge Fitzmaurice warned of the 'all too great ease with which any acutely controversial international situation can be represented as involving a latent threat to peace and security, even where it is really too remote to genuinely constitute one'.[348] Judge Gros similarly stated that a

---

[343] Nolte, n 306, 317.

[344] 1969 Vienna Convention on the Law of Treaties, Art 31(1); see also I Brownlie, *Principles of Public International Law* (5th edn, Clarendon, Oxford, 1998) 631–638.

[345] T Franck, *Recourse to Force: State Action Against Threats and Armed Attacks* (CUP, Cambridge, 2002) 6, 177.

[346] V Lowe, 'Judgment in the Iraq Hearing: Would War be Legal?', BBC Radio 4, 19 Dec 2002: <www.bbc.co.uk/radio4/today/reports/international/iraq_judgement.shtml> (15 April 2003) para 103.

[347] Nolte, n 306, 320–321.

[348] *Namibia Advisory Opinion* (1971) ICJ Reports 6 (Dissenting Opinion of Judge Fitzmaurice) para 116.

matter that 'may have a distant repercussion on the maintenance of peace is not enough to turn the Security Council into a world government'.[349] Judge Fitzmaurice agreed that a threat must be more than 'a mere figment or pretext' and must not be 'artificially created as a pretext for the realization of ulterior purposes'.[350]

Other jurists also recognize these legal limits. Abi-Saab argues that the Council 'cannot act under Chapter VII in the abstract . . . measures have thus always to be pegged to a particular crisis or situation'.[351] The Council may not interpret the Charter 'in an abstract or context-neutral way'[352] and its action must remain 'situation specific'.[353] Moreover, Bowett argues that:

> The Council decisions are binding only in so far as they are in accordance with the Charter. They may spell out, or particularize, the obligations of members that arise from the Charter. But they may not create totally new obligations that have no basis in the Charter, for the Council is an executive organ, not a legislature. In short, the Council does not have a blank cheque.[354]

There must be some outer limit on even the most flexible and dynamic interpretation of Charter provisions conferring power on the Security Council. Otherwise, the boundaries of legal authority dissolve, undermining not only the certainty of legal relations but ultimately the legitimacy of Council authority itself. If the Council is not seen to be acting within the law, then the UN system retains little moral or legal authority to impel others to remain within the law.

Clearly, while terrorism *may* threaten peace and security, in the absence of a definition limited to grave violent acts, it is hard to accept that every terrorist act constitutes a threat. It is one thing for the Council to identify particular incidents as terrorist—as with aggression[355]—but quite another matter for it to allow States to arbitrarily do so, in the absence of any 'criteria of reference'.[356] Prudentially, the Council already suffers from legitimacy problems because of its politicized selectivity in addressing some traditional violent conflicts but not others,[357] with action distorted by the veto power of the permanent five. The Council is already overburdened with confronting

---

[349] ibid, 340, para 34 (Judge Gros).
[350] ibid, 293, para 112; 294, para 116 (Judge Fitzmaurice).
[351] Abi-Saab, n 306, 310; see also Nolte, n 306, 324: 'Security Council action is linked, by definition, to concrete circumstances and the presumption is that it does not purport to influence the existing law beyond the scope of these circumstances.'
[352] Brichambaut, n 306, 275.
[353] Nolte, n 306, 321–322.   [354] Bowett, n 306, 92.
[355] G Fitzmaurice, 'The Definition of Aggression' (1952) 1 ICLQ 137, 143–144.
[356] I Brownlie, *International Law and the Use of Force by States* (Clarendon, Oxford, 1963) 356.
[357] D Caron, 'The Legitimacy of the Collective Authority of the Security Council' (1993) 87 AJIL 552, 560.

traditional threats to security and risks being swamped by wider security threats such as terrorism, diluting its already limited capacity to prevent conflict and further eroding its legitimacy.

E. ELEMENTS OF A DEFINITION OF TERRORISM

1. Approaches to a definition of terrorism

As early as 1983, 109 different official and academic definitions of terrorism were identified in one much cited study.[358] Despite the divergence of opinion, there is no technical impossibility in defining terrorism;[359] disagreement is fundamentally political. Often, definitions differ mainly in emphasis or semantics—such as by greater or lesser specification of violent means or protected targets—than in substance. Moreover, as the authors of that pioneering 1983 study concede: 'Many definitions are enumerations of elements without clear indications which element(s) must be present for a phenomenon to be qualified as terrorism and which elements are merely regularly accompanying features of the phenomenon.'[360] For example, whether terrorism is 'random' or 'indiscriminate' (as suggested by numerous General Assembly resolutions) rather than targeted may be useful in describing and differentiating different kinds of terrorist acts, but need not be decisive in the legal definition of the act. Similarly, whether terrorism relies on mass media publicity or clandestine methods may be operationally helpful in combating terrorism, but need not define its core legal elements. Indeed, many of the definitions in that study were intended for descriptive political or academic purposes and not for the narrower international legal purpose of criminalization.

Once it is understood what is objectionable about terrorism, the technical elements of a legal definition can be extrapolated from these policy foundations. Before considering each element in turn, it must be noted that precision in definition is necessary if terrorist offences are not to infringe on freedom from retroactive criminal punishment.[361] As the European Court of Human Rights stated in *Kokkinakis v Greece*:

---

[358] A Schmid and A Jongman, *Political Terrorism* (North Holland Publishing Co, Amsterdam, 1983) 119–152.

[359] Abi-Saab, n 306, 311; Flory, n 21, 33; see generally R Mushkat, ' "Technical" Impediments on the Way to a Universal Definition of International Terrorism' (1980) 20 Indian JIL 448.

[360] Schmid and Jongman, n 358, 75; see also the 73 academic definitions identified in L Weinberg, A Pedahzur, and S Hirsch-Hoefler, 'The Challenges of Conceptualizing Terrorism' (2004) 16 *Terrorism and Political Violence* 777.

[361] ICCPR, Art 15(1): 'No one shall be held guilty of any criminal offence on account of any act or omission which did not constitute a criminal offence, under national or international law, at the time when it was committed.'

... the principle that only the law can define a crime and prescribe a penalty (*nullum crimen, nulla poena sine lege*) and the principle that the criminal law must not be extensively construed to an accused's detriment ... [requires that] an offence must be clearly defined in law. This condition is satisfied where the individual can know from the wording of the relevant provision and, if need be, from the courts' interpretation of it, what acts and omissions will make him liable.[362]

The UN Human Rights Committee found, for example, that in Belgium's 2003 definition of terrorism, references to the degree of severity of offences and the perpetrator's intended purpose do 'not entirely satisfy the principle of offences and penalties being established in law'.[363] In 2005, the Committee was also concerned about the wide definition of terrorism in Canadian law and recommended that Canada 'adopt a more precise definition of terrorist offences, so as to ensure that individuals will not be targeted on political, religious or ideological grounds'.[364]

Moreover, in 2003, the Peruvian Constitutional Court declared too broad a definition of terrorism which referred to spreading anxiety, alarm or fear in the population to change the power structure (by installing a totalitarian government).[365] This followed an earlier finding by the Inter-American Court of Human Rights that Peru's terrorism offences were too vague and violated the principle of *nullum crimen nulla poena sine lege praevia* in Article 9 of the American Convention:

... crimes must be classified and described in precise and unambiguous language that narrowly defines the punishable offense, thus giving full meaning to the principle of *nullum crimen nulla poena sine lege praevia* in criminal law. This means a clear definition of the criminalized conduct, establishing its elements and the factors that distinguish it from behaviors that are either not punishable offences or are punishable but not with imprisonment. Ambiguity in describing crimes creates doubts and the opportunity for abuse of power, particularly when it comes to ascertaining the criminal responsibility of individuals and punishing their criminal behavior with penalties that exact their toll on the things that are most precious, such as life and liberty.[366]

In contrast to the objective enumeration of offences in sectoral anti-terrorism treaties, a generic definition can capture and condemn the motive elements

---

[362] *Kokkinakis v Greece* ECHR Series A No 260–A (25 May 1993) para 52 (concerning non-retroactivity in Art 7 of the European Convention on Human Rights).

[363] Under Art 15 of the ICCPR: UN HR Committee, Concluding Observations: Belgium, 12 Aug 2004, UN Doc CCPR/CO/81/BEL, para 24.

[364] UN HR Committee, Concluding Observations: Canada, 2 Nov 2005, UN Doc CCPR/C/CAN/CO/5, para 24. Morocco's broad definition of terrorist acts as any 'grave assault by means of violence' has also been criticized: UN HR Committee, Concluding Observations: Morocco, 5 Nov 2004, UN Doc CCPR/CO/82/MAR/Rev.1, para 20.

[365] Decision of 3 Jan 2003, in UN SC CTC Report: Peru, UN Doc S/2003/896 (17 Sep 2003) 2.

[366] In *Castillo Petruzzi et al v Peru* [1999] IACHR 6 (30 May 1999) para 121.

which distinguish terrorism from ordinary crime. Generic definition avoids the rigidity of enumerative definitions,[367] which may not cover changing terrorist methods. Generic definitions are, however, wider and more ambiguous than enumerative ones,[368] although all definitions generalize[369] and the problem can be lessened by combining generic and enumerative features in a single definition. Combined definitions are narrower than enumerative ones, since listed offences only amount to terrorism if they satisfy a motive element.

2. *Elements of a definition*

It is possible to sketch the contours of a definition of terrorism based on the policy reasons for definition and criminalization discussed in this chapter. Technical concerns about particular elements of definition are discussed in Chapters 3 to 5, which examine the range of definitions in criminal law treaties, State practice, and humanitarian law. The purpose of this section is to chart the boundaries of a definition which reflects existing agreement on the wrongfulness of terrorism. To reflect fully the consensus on what is wrong with terrorism, each of the elements outlined below is necessarily conjunctive, thus increasing the specificity of terrorist offences.

(a) Prohibited means and methods: serious violence

If terrorism is thought to seriously violate human rights, a definition must contain elements reflecting this judgment. In particular, if terrorism infringes the right to life and security of person, a definition should prohibit serious violence intended to cause death or serious bodily injury to a person. The prohibition should also extend to attacks on public or private property where intended or likely to endanger people physically, including acts against essential utilities and public infrastructure. Threats to commit such acts could constitute an ancillary offence with lesser penalties, rather than being regarded as terrorist acts in themselves.[370]

To increase certainty, the element of 'serious violence' could be qualified by enumerating prohibited violent acts, such as by listing the offences in existing sectoral terrorism treaties, and specifying additional acts not covered by

---

[367] Fitzmaurice, n 355, 143–144; Brownlie, n 356, 355.

[368] ibid; A Schmid, 'Terrorism: The Definitional Problem' (2004) 36 Case Western Reserve JIL 375, 400: 'The higher the level of abstraction, the less specific the properties and attributes a definition contains'.

[369] Brownlie, n 356, 356; see also Schmid, n 368, 400: 'abstraction always involves a process of reduction'; C Coady, 'Defining Terrorism' in I Primoratz (ed), *Terrorism: The Philosophical Issues* (Palgrave Macmillan, Hampshire, 2004) 3 ('mathematical exactitude' cannot be expected and there will always be 'fuzzy edges' and 'contentious interpretations').

[370] cf the Australian Criminal Code Act 1995 (Cth), s 100.1, which defines a threat to commit a terrorist act as a terrorist act in itself, thus blurring essentially different gradations of criminal harm.

those treaties (such as murder or physical assault by any means and in any context). At the same time, the element of 'serious violence' could remain as an open-ended 'catch-all' category to ensure that offenders do not evade liability by perpetrating violence by new or unanticipated methods.

Certainty could also be increased by qualifying 'serious violence' as that which is already 'criminal' under international or national law, thus excluding violence which is lawfully justified or excused by legal defences. The seriousness of criminal violence could remain a matter of appreciation in individual cases, just as 'serious non-political crime' in exclusion cases under international refugee law is interpreted by reference to comparative national law. This approach may, however, be challengeable for lack of specificity under human rights law and a definition will be more predictable if it attempts to particularize all prohibited physical acts.

(b) Prohibited purposes or aims: motives and objectives

There are a number of possibilities for framing a definitional element to reflect the normative consensus that terrorism undermines the State and the political process. A narrow approach would be to criminalize only violence directed at State officials, institutions, or interests. This approach would fail to cover acts directed at individuals, groups, or populations unconnected to State interests and would thus omit to address a significant proportion of acts commonly understood as terrorism.

To meet this problem, a number of recent international definitions of terrorism have supported protecting both the State and the broader population, by requiring that the *purpose* of an act, 'by its nature or context', must be 'to intimidate a population, or to compel a government or an international organization to do or to abstain from doing any act'.[371] One difficulty is that mere *intimidation* of a population, or *compulsion* of a government, seems to fall short of the severe impact implied by the term 'terrorism'.[372] It may be questioned why such conduct is not described more precisely as crimes of 'intimidation' (as in some national laws)[373] or 'compulsion'. This problem is arguably cured by the EU's solution of requiring an aim to *seriously* intimidate a population or *unduly* compel a government or international

---

[371] 1999 Terrorist Financing Convention, Art 2(1)(b); see also UNSC Resolution 1566 (2004); UN High-Level Panel, n 338; UN Secretary-General's Report, *In larger freedom: towards development, security and human rights for all*, UNGA (59th Sess), 21 Mar 2005, UN Doc A/59/2005; UN Draft Comprehensive Convention, Art 2(1) (see Ch 3 below).

[372] In the UK, it is enough merely to 'influence' a government: Terrorism Act 2000 (UK), s 1(b).

[373] eg in Australia, under the Crimes Act 1900 (NSW), s 545B, the crime of 'intimidation by violence' is committed where a person uses violence or intimidation against another person to compel the person to do or abstain from doing any lawful act, carrying a penalty of two years' imprisonment.

organization.[374] Alternatively, New Zealand modifies this approach by replacing the 'intimidation' of a population with a graver intention 'to induce terror in a civilian population', while also including the EU's element of undue compulsion.[375]

Even so, it remains the case that intimidation of a population or compulsion of a government may be motivated by private concerns such as blackmail, extortion, criminal profit, or even personal disputes. Consequently, if a definition of terrorism is to reflect the real nature of the harm that terrorism inflicts on the political process, it must differentiate publicly-oriented violence from private violence. As discussed earlier, a terrorist act is committed not only where it has a political purpose,[376] but wherever there is a public motive, aim, objective, or purpose broadly defined: political, ideological, religious, ethnic, or philosophical.[377] The presence of a public motive distinguishes terrorism from private violence which also intimidates a population or compels governments.

(c) The threat to international security: an international element

If terrorism is thought to threaten international peace or security, an international definition must be limited to acts capable of that result—for instance, because of its cross-border or multinational preparation or effects, the involvement of State authorities, or injury to other vital international community values or interests. As discussed earlier, this need not preclude a definition from covering domestic terrorism, where such conduct is thought to injure international values. As discussed in Chapter 4, domestic terrorism is increasingly attracting international concern.

On the other hand, historically the weight of international opinion has only supported the definition and criminalization of *international* terrorism. The offences in the sectoral anti-terrorism treaties adopted since 1963 typically do not apply to purely domestic terrorism, although the international element required is formulated in various ways.[378] The most recent

---

[374] 2002 EU Framework Decision, Art 1(1).

[375] Terrorism Suppression Act 2002 (NZ), s 5(2)(a)–(b).

[376] UNGA Resolutions 49/60 (1994), annexed Declaration on Measures to Eliminate International Terrorism.

[377] See n 259.

[378] In relation to transport, the 1963 Tokyo Convention applies only while an aircraft is in flight or on the surface of the high seas or any other area outside the territory of any State: Art 1(3). The 1970 Hague Convention only applies if the place of take-off or actual landing is situated outside the territory of the State of registration of the aircraft, and it does not apply to offences committed on board an aircraft where the places of take-off or landing are entirely within one State (unless the offender is in another State): Art 3(4)–(5). The 1971 Montreal Convention applies in similar circumstances, but also where the offence is committed in the territory of a State other than the aircraft's State of registration (unless the offender is in another State): Art 4(2)–(4). The Rome Convention 1988 only applies to ships navigating or scheduled to navigate into, through, or from waters beyond the outer limit of the territorial sea of a State, or

sectoral treaties have followed a common formula, building on that found in the 1979 Hostages Convention. The 1997 Terrorist Bombings Convention, the 1999 Terrorist Financing Convention, and the 2005 Nuclear Terrorism Convention all do not apply where an offence is committed in a single State, the offender and victims are nationals of that State, the offender is found in the State's territory, and no other State has jurisdiction under those treaties.[379] Article 3 of the UN Draft Comprehensive Convention follows the same formula.[380]

It is clear that a relatively liberal approach has been taken to construing the international element of offences, with only purely domestic terrorism being excluded. If international regulation of terrorism is limited to international terrorist acts, then the international element of offences should encompass the diverse ways in which terrorism may affect international interests. This may include instances where an act takes place in more than one State, or outside the jurisdiction of any State, or has effects in other States; where an act affects nationals of more than one State or internationally protected persons; or where the perpetrator is a foreign national.

(d) Plain textual meaning: creating terror or extreme fear

Finally, as a matter of language, it is inherent in the term 'terrorism' that any definition must reflect that some person, or group of people, felt *terror* or were intended to feel *terror*. Otherwise, the term becomes disassociated from its linguistic origin and its ordinary or plain textual meaning. A crime of terrorism that lacks an element of terror would be better described by more accurate terminology. As mentioned earlier, proposals to define terrorism as mere 'intimidation' or 'coercion' imply much weaker conduct than 'terrorism', and might be more constructively described precisely as crimes of 'intimidation' or 'coercion'. While words do not possess fixed meanings, and are necessarily socially constructed, terrorism cannot be defined so elastically as to depart altogether from its ordinary textual foundation.

---

the lateral limits of its territorial sea with adjacent States (or when the alleged offender is within the territory of a State): Art 4(1)–(2). In other treaties, the 1973 Protected Persons Convention only covers offences against protected persons located in foreign States or in other places of protection under international law: Art 1(a)–(b). The 1979 Hostages Convention does not apply where an offence is committed within a single State, the hostage and the alleged offender are nationals of that State and the alleged offender is found in the territory of that State: Art 13. The Vienna Convention 1980 applies primarily to nuclear material in 'international nuclear transport', although much of the Convention also applies to domestic uses, storage, and transport of such material: Art 2(1)–(2). The Montreal Convention 1991 regulates many purely internal uses of unmarked plastic explosives, although it also applies to the international movement 'into or out of its territory' of explosives: Arts II and III.

[379] Common Art 3.
[380] See Ch 3 below.

There has been considerable support for including such an element in an international definition of terrorism, commonly formulated in official proposals as either an intention 'to create a state of terror',[381] or 'to provoke a state of terror',[382] in particular persons, groups of persons, or the general public. Despite the circularity in defining 'terrorism' as involving a 'state of terror', an international tribunal has recently interpreted terror as meaning 'extreme fear' and has been assisted by expert psychiatric evidence in determining the causes and symptoms of extreme fear.[383] The serious social stigma which attaches to labelling an offender a 'terrorist' should be reserved for those people who cause the grave psychological harm and distress which is signified by the term terrorism. That label should not be deployed too easily to describe violent offenders who generate lesser forms of social harm.

(e) Exceptions to a definition of terrorism

Agreement on exceptions to any definition of terrorism has proved more difficult than agreement on the definition itself. The next chapter closely examines the two key controversies which have plagued debate about definition: first, whether national liberation or self-determination movements should be excluded from liability for terrorism, and second, whether State violence causing terror should be covered.

In short, Chapter 2 argues that IHL is the appropriate legal framework for dealing with all self-determination conflicts, and for internal rebellions rising to the level of an armed conflict. Given the specialized prohibitions on terrorism in armed conflict under IHL (discussed in Chapter 5), it is therefore appropriate to exclude acts committed in connection with an international or internal armed conflict, whether by State or non-State forces. Excluding conduct in armed conflicts has the added advantage of removing the moral criterion of 'innocence' from definitions of terrorism, depoliticizing it by applying the framework of combatants and non-combatants under IHL. The language of various exclusionary provisions is considered both in the next chapter and in Chapter 3 on treaty law.

Where terrorism is committed in peacetime (or in situations not covered by IHL), in order to maintain moral symmetry[384] and broaden its legitimacy, a definition should cover acts of both State officials and non-State actors.

---

[381] 1937 League of Nations Convention, Art 1(2); 1991 ILC Draft Code, Art 24; 1998 Draft Rome Statute, Art 5.

[382] UNSC Resolution 1566 (2004); 1994 UNGA Declaration on Measures to Eliminate International Terrorism.

[383] See Ch 5 below for a discussion of the *Galic* case (2003) at the ICTY.

[384] Bassiouni, 'A Policy-Oriented Inquiry', n 8, xxxix.

Thus extrajudicial assassinations of political opponents by State officials,[385] or collusion in such killings,[386] might gainfully be qualified as terrorism, as might suicide bombings by non-State actors outside armed conflict. As Primoratz argues, acts which exhibit the 'the same morally relevant traits' should be morally understood in a similar way.[387]

Any international crime of terrorism must also accommodate reasonable justifications, excuses, and defences for a limited range of violent conduct. Individual defences in international criminal law, and group circumstances precluding responsibility, drawn by analogy from the law of State responsibility, may excuse a very limited range of terrorist-type acts. In other cases not covered by any of the forgoing exceptions—such as in internal rebellions beneath an armed conflict—the international community may still regard some terrorist-type violence as 'illegal but justifiable'. In such cases, consideration might be given to excusing such conduct, and mitigating penalties for it, where it was committed in the collective defence of human rights. Concrete examples might include the assassination of a military dictator, or politicians who forcibly refuse to cede power following defeat in a democratic election. Political amnesties and pardons may also play a role in responding to terrorism where higher public goods such as peace or reconciliation are at stake.

What can rarely, if ever, be justified, however, is the instrumental killing of non-harmful civilians, including killing to indulge religious passions. International law is a secular and pluralist normative system—which partly derives its universality from its secularity—and cannot admit monotheistic claims to violence without unravelling its own coherence. While religious doctrines find a place in some national legal systems (consider sharia

---

[385] See, eg, S Jeffery, 'Abbas accuses Israel of "terrorist" attack', *The Guardian*, 10 Jun 2003; AFP, 'Mossad switches from analysis to action', *Sydney Morning Herald*, 4 Apr 2003; W Pincus, 'Yemen aided CIA strike on 6 Al-Qaeda suspects', *International Herald Tribune*, 7 Nov 2002; J Risen and D Johnston, 'Bush has widened authority of CIA to Kill Terrorists', *New York Times*, 15 Dec 2002; D Priest, 'Drone missile kills al-Qaeda suspect', *Sydney Morning Herald*, 16 May 2005 (possibly in Pakistan and outside the conflict in Afghanistan); M Khan and C Gall, 'US strikes desert village to wipe out bin Laden deputy', *Sun-Herald* (Sydney), 15 Jan 2006, 4 (killing Al-Zawahiri in Pakistan). Where committed in armed conflict, the targeting of civilians not taking an active part in hostilities (or after they have taken part) would amount to a war crime: A Cassese, Expert Opinion on Whether Israel's Targeted Killings of Palestinian Terrorists is Consonant with International Humanitarian Law, prepared for the petitioners in the *Public Committee against Torture et al v Israel et al*, available at <www.stoptorture.org.il> (21 Dec 2005); but see D Kretzmer, 'Targeted Killing of Suspected Terrorists: Extra-Judicial Executions or Legitimate Means of Defence?' (2005) 16 EJIL 171.
[386] N Hopkins and R Cowan, 'Scandal of Ulster's secret war', *The Guardian*, 17 Apr 2003.
[387] I Primoratz, 'State Terrorism and Counter-terrorism' in I Primoratz (ed), *Terrorism: The Philosophical Issues* (Palgrave Macmillan, Hampshire, 2004) 113, 114.

punishments),[388] even religious States explicitly reject religious justifications for terrorist violence,[389] including in criminal cases.[390]

In addition to the range of exceptions and defences considered in the next chapter, some recent national definitions of terrorism create an exception for acts of advocacy, protest, dissent, or industrial action which are not intended to cause death, serious bodily harm, or serious risk to public health or safety.[391] Such exclusions are useful devices to prevent criminalizing as 'terrorism' comparatively minor harm (limited to property damage), such as when protestors at a union demonstration smashed the foyer of the Australian Parliament House in 1996; when anti-Iraq war protesters painted 'No War' on the shell of the Sydney Opera House in 2003 (requiring expensive repairs);[392] or when urban rioters cause extensive property damage, as at G8 anti-globalization protests, or in the Paris suburbs in late 2005. While such acts of destruction to property may exceed the limits of freedom of expression and amount to public order offences, they should fall short of being labelled as terrorism. This is particularly important in the construction of an international crime of terrorism, since States that are not democratic or generally rights-respecting are far less likely to exercise prosecutorial restraint in selecting appropriate criminal charges.

(f) Summary of definition

Based on the international community's identification of the underlying wrongfulness of international terrorism, terrorism can be deductively defined as follows:

(1) Any serious, violent, criminal act intended to cause death or serious bodily injury, or to endanger life, including by acts against property;

(2) where committed outside an armed conflict;

---

[388] cf *Adelaide Company of Jehovah's Witnesses Inc v Australia* (1943) 67 CLR 116 (religion is not a justification for criminal violence).

[389] 1999 OIC Convention, preamble; 1998 Arab Convention, preamble; General Pervez Musharraf, Address to the Nation (Pakistan), 12 Jan 2002: <www.pak.gov.pk/public/President_address.htm>.

[390] 'Religion doesn't justify violence: judges', *Sydney Morning Herald*, 6 Aug 2003; A Spillius, 'Bali bomber greets death sentence with thumbs-up', *Daily Telegraph*, 8 Aug 2003 (an Indonesian court found that the killing of 202 people in the Bali bombing, by Amrozi bin Nurhasyim, a member of Jemaah Islamiah, betrayed Islam).

[391] In Canada, acts against property or essential services are not regarded as terrorism where they are 'a result of advocacy, protest, dissent or stoppage of work' and they are not intended to result in death, serious bodily harm, or serious risk to the health or safety of the public: Canadian Criminal Code, s 83.01(1)(E). In Australia, an act of 'advocacy, protest, dissent or industrial action' does not constitute terrorism where it is not intended to cause death, serious physical harm to a person, or serious risk to public health or safety, or to endanger life: Australian Criminal Code, s 100.1(3). In New Zealand, engaging in 'protest, advocacy, or dissent . . . strike, lockout, or other industrial action, is not, by itself, a sufficient basis' for establishing a terrorist offence: Terrorism Suppression Act 2002 (NZ), s 5(5).

[392] M Brown, ' "No war" sail painters sent for trial', *Sydney Morning Herald*, 16 Jul 2003.

(3)   for a political, ideological, religious, or ethnic purpose; and
(4)   where intended to create extreme fear in a person, group, or the general public, and:
   (a)   seriously intimidate a population or part of a population, or
   (b)   unduly compel a government or an international organization to do or to abstain from doing any act.
(5)   Advocacy, protest, dissent or industrial action which is not intended to cause death, serious bodily harm, or serious risk to public health or safety does not constitute a terrorist act.

Such a definition embodies the international community's core normative judgments about the wrongfulness of terrorism, while minimizing interference in the existing law governing violence in armed conflicts. It also neatly correlates with some of the most common characteristics found in the 1983 study of 109 definitions of terrorism.[393] The cumulative elements of this proposed definition ensure that the stigma of the terrorist label is reserved for only the most serious kinds of unjustifiable political violence. Its limited application also prevents the symbolic power of the term from being diluted or eroded. The next chapter turns to the complex problem of the circumstances in which political violence may be justified or excused in a diverse international community. If international law is to avoid criminalizing legitimate violent resistance to political oppression, agreement on the lawful boundaries of political violence is an essential first step before agreement on definition can be properly reached. The variety of possible exceptions and defences to, and justifications and excuses for, terrorism is considered both in light of the definition outlined in this chapter, and also in relation to a range of other possible definitions of terrorism. The wider the definition of terrorism, the more likely a broader range of exceptions or defences should be available.

F. CONCLUSION

Historically, technical disputes about the intricacies of drafting an acceptable definition of terrorism have obscured more fundamental questions about the

---

[393] Of those definitions, 84% referred to violence or force; 65% to a political dimension; and 51% to fear or terror: Schmid, n 358, 76–77. On the other hand, only 6% of those definitions referred to the 'criminal' features of terrorism, and merely 17% to any element of 'intimidation'. Similarly, of 73 academic definitions surveyed in 2002, 71% referred to violence or force; 60% to a political dimension; and 22% to fear or terror: Weinberg et al, n 360, 781. In a later study by Schmid of definitions in 75 States and 13 international organizations, 85% of definitions referred to the illegal or criminal nature of the conduct; 78% to fear or terror; 53% to coercion; and 25% to a political dimension: Schmid, n 368, 405. In a study of 165 academic and non-governmental definitions, Schmid found that 68% of definitions referred to a political dimension; 59% to terror; and 38% to coercion: Schmid, n 368, 407. See also G Wardlaw, *Political Terrorism: Theory, Tactics and Counter-Measures* (CUP, Cambridge, 1982) 16.

policy rationale for defining and criminalizing it in the first place. Instead of focusing on competing definitions, by stepping back to examine *what is so bad about terrorism*, it is possible to gain a clearer picture of the kinds of conduct the international community objects to. In recent years, the EU and UN organs have fashioned common justifications for prohibiting and criminalizing terrorism, regarding it as a special crime against human rights, the State and peaceful politics, and international peace and security. Consensus on what is wrongful about terrorism allows progress to be made on legal definition, and clears the way for consideration, in the next chapter, of any justifications and excuses for terrorism.

There are also incidental benefits which flow from criminalizing terrorism, which provide subsidiary justifications for its definition. Definition encourages harmonization of national criminal laws, reducing 'differences in legal treatment' between States.[394] Definition would assist in satisfying the double criminality rule in extradition requests, and in establishing and fulfilling a 'prosecute or extradite' regime for terrorist crimes.[395] Definition might also help to confine the political offence exception to extradition for terrorist offences, should that be considered desirable by the international community.[396] Definition would further assist in excluding 'terrorists' from refugee status, if terrorism qualifies either as serious non-political crime, or is contrary to UN purposes and principles.[397] To the extent that sectoral offences are enumerated within a generic definition, definition would widen the substantive implementation of sectoral treaties.[398]

Although these rationales for criminalization are not independently persuasive, taken in conjunction they establish a principled basis on which to define and criminalize the terrorist threat. Criminalization is a powerful

---

[394] EU Com, n 216, 3. Whether harmonization is desirable as an end in itself is beyond this discussion.

[395] Murphy, 'Defining International Terrorism', n 1, 35.

[396] See generally G Gilbert, *Transnational Fugitive Offenders in International Law* (Martinus Nijhoff, Dordrecht, 1998); Van den Wyngaert (1989), n 240; Van den Wijngaert, n 78; M Bassiouni and E Wise, *Aut Dedere Aut Judicare* (Martinus Nijhoff, Dordrecht, 1995); A Sofaer, 'The Political Offence Exception and Terrorism' (1986) 15 Denver JIL 125; M Shapiro, 'Extradition in the Era of Terrorism: The Need to Abolish the Political Offence Exception' (1986) 61 NYU LR 654.

[397] 1951 Refugee Convention, Arts 1(F)(b)–(c); see also 2002 Inter-American Convention, Arts 12–13; EU Council, Common Position on Combating Terrorism (2001/930/CFSP) [2001] OJ L344/90, Arts 16–17; UNGA Resolution 49/60 (1994), para 5(f); 1994 Declaration, paras 3, 5(f); 1996 Declaration, para 3; UNSC Resolutions 1269 (1999) para 4; 1373 (2001) paras 3(f)–(g), 5; 1377 (2001) preamble; *Gurung v Home Secretary* [2003] Imm AR 115; *Pushpanathan v Canada* [1998] 1 SCR 982; *T v Home Secretary* [1996] AC 742; B Saul, 'Exclusion of Suspected Terrorists from Asylum', IIIS Discussion Paper 26, Dublin, July 2004; M Zard, 'Exclusion, Terrorism and the Refugee Convention' (2002) 13 *Forced Migration Review* 32; G Gilbert, 'Current Issues in the Application of the Exclusion Clauses' in E Feller et al (eds), *Refugee Protection in International Law* (CUP, Cambridge, 2003) 425; W Kälin and J Künzli, 'Article 1F(b): Freedom Fighters, Terrorists, and the Notion of Serious Non-Political Crimes' (2000) 12 IJRL (Spec Supp) 46.

[398] EU Com Proposal, n 216, 5.

symbolic mechanism for delineating internationally unacceptable behaviour, even if deterrence of ideologically motivated offenders is unlikely. Definition of terrorism could satisfy community demands that 'terrorists' be brought to justice, without surrendering justice to populist vengeance, or criminalizing trivial harms. By defining terrorism, it is possible to structure and control the use of a term which, historically, has been politically and ideologically much abused. Rather than remaining an ambiguous and manipulated synonym for 'evil'—justifying all manner of repressive responses—legal definition would help to confine the term within known limits.

2

Defending Terrorism: Justifications and Excuses for Terrorist Violence

'The evil in the tale may be understood, if not excused, by our circumstances.'*

A. INTRODUCTION

The international community has repeatedly condemned terrorism as 'criminal and unjustifiable', irrespective of 'considerations of a political, philosophical, ideological, racial, ethnic, religious or other nature that may be invoked to justify' it.[1] Yet, in condemning terrorism as unjustifiable, some States have persistently objected that violence in pursuit of just causes (such as self-determination) does not constitute terrorism; or even that a just cause justifies all means. There is thus a disagreement over the scope of exceptions to any potential definition of terrorism.[2]

Asserting that terrorism is *unjustifiable* does not preclude the idea that some acts of terrorism are at least *excusable*. The wider and more comprehensive a definition of terrorism, the more likely it is that some acts of terrorism may be justifiable or excusable. While the 'inner core' of terrorism, such as indiscriminate attacks on civilians, is very difficult to justify under any circumstances, the 'outer core' of terrorism—such as acts that would not be contrary to international humanitarian law (IHL) if committed by State forces in armed conflict[3]—is more susceptible to justification.

The highly-charged political atmosphere surrounding international discussions of terrorism has tended to entrench opposing ideological and rhetorical positions, often leading to neither side taking the arguments of the other seriously. Yet, if international law is not to become complicit in oppression by criminalizing legitimate political resistance, justifications for terrorist violence must be taken seriously by the law. Moreover, a failure to

---

* T Lawrence, *Seven Pillars of Wisdom: Complete 1922 Oxford Text* (J&N Wilson, London, 2004) 8.

[1] UNGA Resolutions 49/60 (1994), annexed Declaration on Measures to Eliminate International Terrorism, para 3; 50/53 (1995) para 2; 51/210 (1996) para 2; 52/165 (1997) para 2; 53/108 (1999) para 2; 54/110 (2000) para 2; 55/158 (2001) para 2; 56/88 (2002) para 2; 57/27 (2003) para 2; 58/81 (2004) para 2; UNSC Resolution 1566 (2004) para 3; 1997 Terrorist Bombings Convention, Art 5; 1999 Terrorist Financing Convention, Art 6.

[2] A Cassese, *International Criminal Law* (OUP, Oxford, 2003) 121.

[3] C Greenwood, 'Terrorism and Humanitarian Law: The Debate over Additional Protocol I' (1989) 19 IYBHR 187, 189.

take terrorist justifications seriously may itself be a cause of terrorist violence; as Habermas says: 'The spiral of violence begins as a spiral of distorted communication that leads through the spiral of uncontrolled reciprocal mistrust to the breakdown of communication'.[4]

This chapter, accordingly, considers the range of legal techniques available for accommodating genuine claims of justification or excuse. It also unravels some specific terrorist claims and rigorously subjects them to the scrutiny of existing international legal principles (particularly those of IHL) and the moral frameworks underlying those principles. Doing so helps in determining whether terrorist justifications are claims of substance, or merely claims that dress up unprincipled impulses to violence. Derrida marks the danger that: 'Every terrorist in the world claims to be responding in self-defense to a prior terrorism on the part of the state, one that simply went by other names and covered itself with all sorts of more or less credible justifications.'[5]

The first part of this chapter outlines the purported causes of terrorism advanced in the General Assembly, and the contrary views of States on their legal significance—particularly whether causes such as self-determination and national liberation ought to justify or excuse terrorist violence. In attempting to reconcile this fundamental disagreement between States, it then distinguishes self-determination violence permitted under IHL from terrorism, and argues for the extension of IHL as an appropriate normative framework for all self-determination struggles. The equal application of IHL to self-determination movements would help to depoliticize attempts to define international terrorism. Similarly, excluding internal rebel violence, through the application of combatant immunity, would assist in differentiating terrorist violence from more justifiable forms of political violence.

The second part examines how a limited range of justifications for any new international crime of terrorism could be accommodated by individual defences in international criminal law (including self-defence, and duress/ necessity). It then proposes that non-State group actors accused of terrorism should be entitled to plead 'circumstances precluding wrongfulness', drawn analogously from the law of State responsibility. While a narrow class of terrorist acts may be excused by individual or group defences, some acts considered justifiable may still fall outside the scope of defences. To maintain the law's legitimacy, the final part argues that some acts of terrorism could, in exceptional cases, be regarded as 'illegal but justifiable' (or at least, excusable) in stringently limited, objectively verifiable circumstances, possibly under the rubric of a 'collective defence of human rights'. This equitable mechanism

---

[4] Habermas, quoted in G Borradori, *Philosophy in a Time of Terror: Dialogues with Jürgen Habermas and Jacques Derrida* (University of Chicago Press, Chicago, 2003) 64.
[5] J Derrida, in 'Autoimmunity: Real and Symbolic Suicides', in Borradori, n 4, 86, 103.

could also be supplemented by the availability of political pardons or amnesties for less serious terrorist crimes, where this is necessary to secure overriding community interests such as a peace settlement or national reconciliation. Proper consideration of the potential exceptions to, and excuses and justifications for, terrorism is essential before agreement can be reached on defining 'terrorism' as an international crime.

B. COMMON JUSTIFICATIONS FOR TERRORISM

1. General Assembly's study of causes

The first concerted effort to address terrorism in the United Nations came in response to the killing of Israeli athletes at the Munich Olympics in September 1972, and earlier attacks at an Israeli airport and on a Soviet diplomat in New York. With the Security Council polarized by the Cold War, the General Assembly initiated a study of 'the underlying causes of those forms of terrorism and acts of violence which lie in misery, frustration, grievance and despair and which cause some people to sacrifice human lives, including their own, to effect radical changes'. The title of this agenda item does not assert that all terrorist acts are caused by such factors, but implies that those factors underlie at least some terrorist acts. Resolution 3034 (XXVII) of 1972 emphasized 'the underlying causes which give rise to' terrorist violence rather than focusing on the definition or prohibition of terrorism. It urged States to find 'just and peaceful solutions' to those causes and reaffirmed:

... the inalienable right to self-determination and independence of all peoples under colonial and racist regimes and other forms of alien domination and upholds the legitimacy of their struggle, in particular the struggle of national liberation movements in accordance with the principles and purposes of the Charter and the relevant resolutions of the organs of the United Nations . . .[6]

The resolution does not expressly provide that terrorism is justified in pursuit of national liberation or self-determination. However, by affirming the legitimacy of those struggles, it impliedly excludes such violence from being regarded as terrorism. In addition, the resolution condemned only State, rather than non-State, terrorism.[7]

---

[6] UNGA Resolutions 3034 (XXVII) (1972) para 3; 31/102 (1976) para 3; 32/147 (1977) para 3; 34/145 (1979) preamble; 36/109 (1981) preamble; 38/130 (1983) preamble; 40/61 (1985) preamble; 42/159 (1987) preamble; 44/29 (1989) preamble; 46/51 (1991) preamble.
[7] UNGA Resolutions 3034 (XXVII) (1972) para 4; 31/102 (1976) para 4; 32/147 (1977) para 4; 34/145 (1979) para 4.

(a) Identification and significance of causes

In the Ad Hoc Committee established by the resolution, most States agreed that it was important to address the causes of terrorism, but disagreed on identifying them and evaluating their significance. A broad range of causes was suggested, including: capitalism, neo-colonialism, racism, aggression, foreign occupation, injustice, inequality, subjugation, oppression, exploitation, discrimination, interference or intervention, subversion, disruption of development, and political destabilization.[8] Some believed that 'State terrorism' was the principal cause of individual terrorism, a form of 'reciprocity' by the people against oppressive politics, economic inequality, and social trouble.[9] The most detailed classification of causes was submitted by non-aligned States in 1979, which divided causes into 'political' and 'economic and social' ones.[10] Others suggested adding State connivance with fascist or Zionist groups.[11]

In contrast, other States believed the list was a partial and subjective pre-judgment of the causes, and unresponsive to the complex, dynamic links between terrorism and its causes.[12] Some maintained that the causes involved a myriad of factors outside the competence of the Ad Hoc Committee, lawyers, and diplomats, including scientific, social, economic, political, psychological, psychiatric, or genetic causes.[13] Others suggested that the causes were already being addressed by UN organs and by existing normative frameworks,[14] and argued that addressing terrorism should not depend on resolving all underlying injustices.[15]

In evaluating the significance of causes, some States asserted that those waging just or legitimate struggles were entitled to use any means, as a matter of last resort.[16] Other States opposed this permissive view, arguing that the end does not justify the means;[17] and that some acts, particularly violence

[8] UNGAOR (28th Sess), Ad Hoc Committee Report (1973), Supp 28, UN Doc A/9028, 8, para 26; UNGAOR (34th Sess), Ad Hoc Committee Report (1979), Supp 39, UN Doc A/34/39, 12, para 38; see also P Wilkinson, *Terrorism and the Liberal State* (Macmillan, London, 1977) 37–38.
[9] Ad Hoc Committee Report (1973), n 8, 15, para 49.
[10] Ad Hoc Committee Report (1979), n 8, 20–21, para 69 (Algeria, Barbados, India, Iran, Nigeria, Panama, Syria, Tunisia, Venezuela, Yugoslavia, Zaire, Zambia).
[11] ibid, 21, para 70.   [12] ibid, 21, para 71.
[13] Ad Hoc Committee Report (1973), n 8, 15, para 48; UNGAOR (32nd Sess), Ad Hoc Committee Report (1977), Supp 37, UN Doc A/32/37, 14–15, para 13 (Sweden); Ad Hoc Committee Report (1979), n 8, 11, para 36; 18, paras 63–65.
[14] Ad Hoc Committee Report (1973), n 8, 14–15, para 46; Ad Hoc Committee Report (1977), n 8, 13, para 9 (Uruguay); 24, para 23 (US); Ad Hoc Committee Report (1979), n 8, 11, para 36.
[15] Ad Hoc Committee Report (1977), n 8, 22, para 16 (Italy); 24, para 23 (US).
[16] Ad Hoc Committee Report (1973), n 8, 7, para 22; 8, para 24; 14, para 45; 15, para 49; Ad Hoc Committee Report (1977), n 8, 35, para 35 (Tanzania); Ad Hoc Committee Report (1979), n 8, 10, para 30; 25, para 87.
[17] Ad Hoc Committee Report (1979), n 8, 9, para 29; Ad Hoc Committee Report (1977), n 8, 16–17, para 3 (Austria).

against civilians, are so heinous that they are never justified.[18] Some analogously reasoned that just as IHL limits the permissible means of State violence in armed conflict, so too must individuals and liberation movements accept humanitarian constraints.[19]

The debate in the Ad Hoc Committee occurred at a transitional moment in the evolution of IHL. The adoption of the 1977 Protocols took place between the Committee's first meeting in 1973 and its last meeting in 1979. As a result, the debate shifted after the recognition and internationalization of self-determination movements in Protocol I.[20] States that accepted Protocol I regarded qualifying liberation movements as subject to the limits on permissible means and methods of warfare imposed by IHL, legally distinguishing such movements from terrorist groups,[21] and decriminalizing liberation violence in compliance with IHL.

Any terror-type activity by those movements could henceforth be treated as breaches of IHL.[22] Far from legitimizing or encouraging terrorism, this recognition imposed duties on liberation movements to observe IHL in armed conflicts. If national liberation groups could not lawfully target civilians in armed conflict, it became very difficult to see how civilians could be regarded as lawful targets in peacetime. The implications for States which did not accept Protocol I are explored further below.

(b) General Assembly's response to causes

Following the Ad Hoc Committee's final report in 1979, resolutions in the 1970s and 1980s urged States and UN organs to eliminate progressively 'the causes underlying international terrorism',[23] particularly colonialism, racism, 'mass and flagrant violations of human rights and fundamental freedoms', alien occupation or domination, and foreign occupation.[24] Some resolutions until 1991 also stated that nothing in those resolutions:

---

[18] Ad Hoc Committee Report (1973), n 8, 8, para 23; 14, para 44; Ad Hoc Committee Report (1977), n 8, 13, para 8 (Uruguay); 21, para 11 (Canada); 24, para 21 (US); 36, para 41 (UK); Ad Hoc Committee Report (1979), n 8, 8, para 24; 9, para 29; 10, para 31.

[19] Ad Hoc Committee Report (1973), n 8, 7–8, para 23; 14, para 45; Ad Hoc Committee Report (1977), n 8, 16–17, para 3 (Austria); 24, para 21 (US); 33, para 28 (UK); Ad Hoc Committee Report (1979), n 8, 7, para 24; 10, para 31; 25, para 89.

[20] Protocol I, Art 1(4) provides that international armed conflicts include: 'armed conflicts in which peoples are fighting against racist regimes in the exercise of their right of self-determination, as enshrined in the' UN Charter and the 1970 Declaration; see further 'B(3) Jus in Bello: Self-Determination Movements' below.

[21] Ad Hoc Committee Report (1979), n 8, 10, para 30.

[22] See Ch 5 below.

[23] UNGA Resolutions 34/145 (1979) para 6; 38/130 (1983) para 2; 40/61 (1985) para 9; 42/159 (1987) para 8; 44/29 (1989) para 6.

[24] UNGA Resolutions 40/61 (1985) para 9; 42/159 (1987) para 8; 44/29 (1989) para 6; 46/51 (1991) para 6.

... could in any way prejudice the right to self-determination, freedom and independence, *as derived from the Charter of the United Nations*, of peoples forcibly deprived of that right ... particularly peoples under colonial and racist regimes and foreign occupation or other forms of colonial domination, nor, *in accordance with the principles of the Charter and in conformity with the above-mentioned [1970] Declaration*, the right of these peoples to struggle *[legitimately]* to this end and to seek and receive support ...[25]

At first glance, this provision implicitly excludes acts in pursuit of 'just' causes from being regarded as terrorism, although the nature of the right to 'struggle' is ambiguous. This provision has often been interpreted as creating a national liberation exception to the international prohibition on terrorism.[26]

However, the no-prejudice clause is not devoid of limitations. The resolutions state that the 'right' to struggle for self-determination is derived from—and must be exercised in accordance with—the Charter and the 1970 Declaration.[27] Resolution 3034 (XXVII) itself provided that measures against terrorism must be 'in accordance with the principles and purposes of the Charter' and relevant UN resolutions.[28]

These limitations are significant and are often glossed over. Respect for human rights is a basic purpose, or 'paramount object',[29] of the United Nations in Article 1 of the Charter, which self-determination movements, as para-Statal entities,[30] must act 'in accordance' with. Some resolutions also require movements to struggle 'legitimately' for self-determination,[31] indicating limits on the permissible means of struggle.

In determining these limits, it is necessary to look at the right of self-determination, the law on the use of force, human rights law, and IHL. While there is a right of self-determination in the Charter, human rights treaties, and the 1970 Declaration (reflecting custom), none of those instruments explicitly specifies whether (a) force may be used to achieve self-determination, or (b) what kinds of force may be used by those fighting for it. If there is no *ad bellum* right to use force to secure self-determination, then any use of force by such movements may be criminalized as terrorism—as politically motivated violence designed to compel or intimidate—even if targets are strictly limited to military objectives.

---

[25] UNGA Resolutions 42/159 (1987) para 14; [44/29 (1989) para 17; 46/51 (1991) para 15] (emphasis added).

[26] See Ch 4 below.

[27] UNGA Resolutions 42/159 (1987) para 14; 44/29 (1989) para 17; 46/51 (1991) para 15.

[28] UNGA Resolutions 3034 (XXVII) (1972) para 3; 31/102 (1976) para 3; 32/147 (1977) para 3; 34/145 (1979) preamble; 36/109 (1981) preamble; 38/130 (1983) preamble; 40/61 (1985) preamble; 42/159 (1987) preamble; 44/29 (1989) preamble; 46/51 (1991) preamble.

[29] H Lauterpacht (ed), *Oppenheim's International Law: vol I* (8th edn, Longmans, Green and Co, London, 1955) 742.

[30] I Brownlie, *Principles of Public International Law* (5th edn, Clarendon, Oxford, 1998) 63.

[31] UNGA Resolutions 44/29 (1989) para 17; 46/51 (1991) para 15.

2. Jus ad bellum: self-determination movements

Despite the near-completion of decolonization, the issue is not obsolete,[32] given controversial denials of the right (in the narrow external sense) in Palestine, Western Sahara, and Tibet. There are also numerous claims of internal self-determination on the basis of ethnic or other group identity. During decolonization, developing and socialist States, and some writers, believed that 'peoples' were entitled to use force to achieve self-determination, whereas western States denied any right to use force.[33] The Charter does not authorize the use of force for decolonization,[34] and UN resolutions recognize the legitimacy of liberation struggles, but do not specify the permissible means of achieving liberation.

A legal compromise is reflected in the 1970 Declaration, which refers merely to the 'actions' and 'resistance' of movements against forcible denials of self-determination by States.[35] States must refrain from forcibly denying the right, and in resisting forcible denial, peoples 'are entitled to seek and to receive support' from third States, not including sending military forces.[36] Consequently, liberation movements have no legal right to use force to secure self-determination, but they do not breach international law by using force (defensively) against its forcible denial.[37] It is significant that the UN position was adopted in the context of concerns about intervention by third States in self-determination conflicts. The UN response was less concerned about settling the question of whether self-determination movements themselves enjoyed an independent right to resort to force in the first instance.

Recourse to force by self-determination movements is clearly treated differently from recourse to force in 'ordinary' civil wars, in which international law is silent on any right of rebels to use force against a government. Where recourse to force against denial of self-determination is permitted, the repressive State necessarily loses its entitlement to criminalize such uses of force.[38] Otherwise, national criminalization would frustrate the entitlements of self-determination movements under international law. An international crime of terrorism must, therefore, carefully exclude lawful uses of force.

---

[32] I Detter, *The Law of War* (2nd edn, CUP, Cambridge, 2000) 33. There are 16 remaining non-self governing territories: 'UN Decolonization Panel calls for Cooperation with Visiting Missions', UN News Service, New York, 3 June 2003.

[33] A Cassese, *Self-Determination of Peoples* (CUP, Cambridge, 1996) 151–152.

[34] J Dugard, 'Towards the Definition of International Terrorism' (1973) 67 ASIL Proceedings 94, 97.

[35] 1970 Declaration, Principle of Equal Rights and Self-Determination, para 5; Brownlie, n 30, 602; Cassese (1996), n 33, 153–154, 200; J Crawford, 'The Right of Self-Determination in International Law: Its Development and Future' in P Alston (ed), *Peoples' Rights* (OUP, Oxford, 2001) 7, 42.

[36] 1970 Declaration, n 35, para 8: 'Every State shall refrain from any action aimed at the partial or total disruption of the national unity and territorial integrity of any other State or country'; Cassese, n 35, 152, 199–200.

[37] Cassese, n 35, 151, 153, 198.   [38] See Detter, n 32, 102.

3. *Jus in bello: self-determination movements*

Regardless of whether self-determination movements are entitled to use
to force, IHL applies equally to all participants in an armed conflict on
humanitarian grounds. Parties to Protocol I recognize self-determination
struggles as international armed conflicts.[39] As such, the forces of parties to
such conflicts may qualify as combatants (under more relaxed conditions of
combatancy recognizing the needs of guerilla warfare),[40] and enjoy immunity
for lawful acts of war.[41] Combatants cannot be characterized as terrorists for
acts compliant with IHL; Protocol I thus decriminalizes conduct that could
formerly be regarded as terrorist. In such circumstances, liberation forces
must comply with the detailed provisions of IHL, including prohibitions on
terrorist-type acts against non-combatants and those out of combat, and the
restrictions on permissible means and methods of war.[42]

States not party to Protocol I may continue to treat national liberation
struggles as non-international armed conflicts.[43] Thus Israel commonly
regards the killing of its soldiers in the Palestinian Occupied Territories as
terrorism.[44] There is also a view that even State Parties to Protocol I may so
treat liberation struggles where the State does not recognize the liberation
movement, since interpretation of Article 1(4) is thought to be within the
subjective discretion of the relevant State.[45] That view is doubtful, since
Article 1(4) refers to the objective right of self-determination 'as enshrined'
in the UN Charter, which does not make recognition dependent on the subjective agreement of the affected State. Further, Article 96(3) of Protocol I
enables authorities representing peoples to lodge undertakings to apply the
Geneva Conventions and Protocol with the depository (Switzerland), which
triggers the application of the treaties.

While many of the protective provisions of Protocol I have entered
customary law, Article 1(4)—which 'internationalizes' self-determination
struggles—has not, being seldom applied in practice and possessing a largely
agitational or rhetorical value.[46] It has, however, influenced State practice,[47]

---

[39] Protocol I, Art 1(4); see Detter, n 32, 51–53.
[40] Protocol I, Art 44(3).
[41] L Green, *The Contemporary Law of Armed Conflict* (2nd edn, MUP, Manchester, 2000) 64.
[42] E Chadwick, *Self-Determination, Terrorism and the International Humanitarian Law of Armed Conflict* (Martinus Nijhoff, The Hague, 1996) 2, 6–9, 204–206.
[43] Green, n 41, 64.
[44] A Hass, 'Who in Israel knows or cares?', *Haaretz*, 18 June 2003.
[45] Green, n 41, 64. In practice, the UN has accepted the determination of the relevant regional organization.
[46] Cassese, n 33, 203–204. cf G Abi-Saab, 'Wars of National Liberation in the Geneva Conventions and Protocols' (1979–IV) 165 Recueil des Cours 353, 371–372; A Cassese, 'The Geneva Protocols of 1977 on the Humanitarian Law of Armed Conflict and Customary International Law' (1984) 3 *UCLA Pacific Basin Law Journal* 55, 68–71.
[47] C Greenwood, 'Scope of Application of Humanitarian Law' in D Fleck (ed), *The Handbook of Humanitarian Law in Armed Conflicts* (OUP, Oxford, 2004) 39, 43.

and may be emerging as custom.[48] The more relaxed conditions of combatancy in Article 44 of Protocol I were traditionally regarded as only
applying in occupied territories, or against colonial powers,[49] but recent
practice suggests an extension to secessionist movements,[50] encompassing
internal, rather than purely external, self-determination causes.

The non-applicability of Protocol I to some self-determination conflicts
has contradictory implications. On one hand, it frees liberation forces from
the detailed IHL constraints governing international conflicts, and subjects
them only to the more spartan rules of common Article 3 of the 1949 Geneva
Conventions, the customary rules of non-international armed conflict[51]
and, where applicable, Protocol II. On the other hand, it permits States to
deny combatant status to liberation forces and to treat them as criminals,[52]
including as 'terrorists'. In the absence of combatant immunity, such persons
could fall within an international crime of terrorism, defined as politically
motivated, coercive, or intimidatory violence.

The differential treatment of similarly situated liberation movements
undermines the consistency and coherence of IHL, and would frustrate the
equal application of an international terrorism offence. There is thus some
intellectual force in the claims of some States that the struggle for self-
determination must be differentiated from terrorism. Dealing with liberation
violence within the framework of IHL would assist in depoliticizing and
defining terrorism.[53] Until there is universal ratification of Protocol I, or
Article 1(4) enters into customary law, or key States such as Israel ratify it,
there is little hope of dissipating the force of those objections.

States are naturally 'reluctant to accept a form of international legislation
which might eventually undermine their own power structure'.[54] Yet denial
of combatant status to movements resisting the forcible denial of self-
determination implicates international law in oppression. The right of

---

[48] L Green, 'Terrorism and Armed Conflict: The Plea and the Verdict' (1989) 19 IYBHR 131,
136; M Scharf, 'Defining Terrorism as the Peacetime Equivalent of War Crimes: Problems and
Prospects' (2004) 36 Case Western Reserve JIL 359, 370.

[49] Green, n 41, 111; K Ipsen, 'Combatants and Non-combatants' in Fleck (ed), n 47, 65, 77.

[50] Greenwood, n 47, 42–43.

[51] See, eg, *Tadic (Interlocutory Appeal)* ICTY–94–1 (2 Oct 1995).

[52] Green, n 41, 64. Protocol I, Art 96(3) allows the representatives of a 'people' in an international armed conflict under Art 1(4) to declare adherence to, and thereby bring into force, the
1949 Geneva Conventions and 1977 Protocol. A letter of 21 June 1989 from the PLO committed
Palestine to the conventions, but Switzerland informed States on 13 September 1989 that it was
unable to decide if the letter was an instrument of accession, due to international uncertainty
about the existence of the State of Palestine. The existence of a Palestinian people is, however,
'no longer in issue': *Israel Wall Advisory Opinion*, ICJ Case 131, Judgment, 9 July 2004, para 118
(quoting an exchange of letters between PLO President Arafat and Israeli Prime Minister Rabin
of 9 Sept 1993, and the Israeli-Palestinian Interim Agreement on the West Bank and the Gaza
Strip of 28 Sept 1995, preamble and Arts III(1) and (2), XXII(2)).

[53] Chadwick, n 42, 204.

[54] A Cassese, *International Law in a Divided World* (Clarendon, Oxford, 1994) 92.

self-determination is of fundamental international concern, given its *erga omnes* character.[55] Yet under the guise of non-intervention in the affairs of States not party to Protocol I, international law protects oppressive regimes from popular destabilization, preferencing State sovereignty over more reasonable claims of popular sovereignty.

If international law takes self-determination seriously, it must impede human rights law to allow States to criminalize—as terrorists—those who forcibly resist its denial, and to deny them recognition as combatants. International agreement on defining terrorism must be conditioned on the exclusion of legitimate liberation movements from the scope of terrorism, by the universal application of Protocol I.

4. *Human rights limits on permissible means*

In armed conflict, IHL applies as *lex specialis* in determining if a violation of the right to life is arbitrary and therefore unlawful.[56] Lawful killings in IHL are not arbitrary deprivations of life, and Protocol I establishes the conditions under which national liberation violence is justified. In contrast, self-determination violence is not justified by IHL in conflicts where Protocol I does not apply (precluding combatant immunity), or where an armed conflict does not exist and IHL is inapplicable. The question now is whether liberation violence not governed Protocol I may ever be justified.

In the absence of primary rules of self-determination authorizing violence in these situations, human rights law must be examined. Paradoxically, terrorism violates human rights but human rights is a major justification for it.[57] Terrorists may assert that violence is the only means to secure self-determination and thus killings are not arbitrary, but legitimate restrictions on the right to life, designed to achieve a more valuable objective. There is thus a conflict of two norms of equal (*jus cogens*) status.

There is nothing theoretically novel about this conflict. The internal limitations of human rights law constrain the permissible means of pursuing rights-based causes. Common Article 5 of the International Covenant on

---

[55] *Israel Wall Advisory Opinion*, n 52, paras 88, 155–156; *East Timor case (Portugal v Australia)* (1995) ICJ Reports 102, para 29.

[56] *Legality of the Threat or Use of Nuclear Weapons* (1996) ICJ Reports 226, paras 24–25; *Israel Wall Advisory Opinion*, n 52, para 101; see also J-M Henckaerts and L Doswald-Beck (eds), *Customary International Humanitarian Law* (CUP, Cambridge, 2004) vol I: *Rules*, 299–305; E-C Gillard, 'The Complementary Nature of Human Rights Law, International Humanitarian Law and Refugee Law', M Schmitt and G Beruto (eds), *Terrorism and International Law* (IIHL and George C Marshall European Center for Security Studies, San Remo, 2003) 50; H-J Heintze, 'On the Relationship between Human Rights Law Protection and International Humanitarian Law' (2004) 86 IRRC 789, 796.

[57] M Ignatieff, 'Human Rights, the Laws of War, and Terrorism' (2002) 69 *Social Research* 1137, 1146.

Civil and Political Rights (ICCPR) and the International Covenant on Economic, Social and Political Rights (ICESCR) states that nothing in those treaties 'may be interpreted as implying for any State, group or person any right to engage in any activity or perform any act aimed at the destruction of any of the rights and freedoms recognized herein or at their limitation to a greater extent than is provided for [in those treaties]'.[58] Those treaties do not expressly permit liberation movements to violate human rights in a generic or specific manner to secure self-determination—even if only combatants are targeted—and in a series of resolutions, the UN Commission on Human Rights has declared that terrorism can never be justified 'as a means to promote and protect human rights'.[59] Nonetheless, where Protocol I does not apply, attacks by liberation forces which are limited to military objectives may be considered more justifiable than those that instrumentally kill civilians.

Where rights conflict, balancing the relative importance of competing rights is an essential function of human rights law. Restricting certain rights is permissible to secure other rights;[60] particular ends justify certain (but not any) means. What matters is whether the means protect a sufficiently important end to render those means proportionate.[61] As Ignatieff observes, 'human rights are not an ethic of quietism',[62] and some killing is justified: in self-defence; in combat; and for certain kinds of law enforcement.[63] In such cases, the threat posed by the person justifies their killing, but randomly targeting civilians is ruled out. Human rights law forbids using the lives of one group of people instrumentally to secure the happiness (or ideology) of another;[64] 'people should always be treated as ends in themselves and never merely as means'.[65]

On that basis, it is difficult to accept that the right of self-determination outweighs the right to life of (non-threatening) non-combatants. Nothing in human rights law suggests that all other rights may be sacrificed on the altar of self-determination. That argument would only make sense if all other rights depended on attaining self-determination, yet most rights can be enjoyed outside one's 'people'—a homogenizing concept which itself is open

---

[58] See also 1948 UDHR, Art 30.

[59] See preambles to UNComHR Resolutions 1996/47; 1997/42; 1998/47; 1999/27; 2000/30; 2001/37; 2002/35; 2003/37; and UNSubComHR Resolutions 2001/18; 2002/24.

[60] J Raz, *The Morality of Freedom* (Clarendon, Oxford, 1986) 425.

[61] D Rodin, *War and Self-Defense* (Clarendon, Oxford, 2002) 126.

[62] Ignatieff, n 57, 1151; M Ignatieff, *The Lesser Evil: Political Ethics in an Age of Terror* (Edinburgh University Press, Edinburgh, 2005) 90–92.

[63] See, eg, ECHR, Art 2(2); US Manual for Courts Martial 1951, para 197(b).

[64] R Dworkin, 'Terror and the Attack on Civil Liberties', *NY Rev Books*, 6 Nov 2003; J Fitzpatrick, 'Speaking Law to Power: The War against Terrorism and Human Rights' (2003) 14 EJIL 241, 243.

[65] J Glover, *Humanity: A Moral History of the Twentieth Century* (Jonathan Cape, London, 1999) 85.

to rights-based challenges.[66] Whereas self-determination presupposes life, life does not presuppose self-determination.

Even States may not use unlimited means in self-defence[67] and certain forms of violence are always impermissible under IHL.[68] As Judge Higgins wrote in the *Israel Wall Advisory Opinion*, the absolute nature of IHL obligations is 'the bedrock of humanitarian law, and those engaged in conflict have always known that it is the price of our hopes for the future that they must, whatever the provocation, fight "with one hand behind their back" and act in accordance with international law'.[69] If the preservation of the State is one of the highest international values, it would be curious if other causes justified more extreme measures than those permitted in defence of the State. Self-determination is designed to achieve Statehood, so it is not so exceptional that it warrants the conferral of rights superior to those of States. Given the para-Statal personality of self-determination movements, their use of force is fundamentally *defensive*, exercised against foreign domination. As a defensive right, any action taken must be both necessary and proportionate, and the deliberate killing of civilians will rarely qualify; it may also infringe the self-determination of others.[70]

Rodin takes the more radical view that the State right of self-defence (and by analogy, violent self-determination) sometimes may not even justify killing combatants. The tendency of escalation in war means that the suffering caused by recourse to defensive force often outweighs the value of the right sought.[71] Most wars are not genocidal and merely replace the political order, and 'populations can, and frequently do, survive the destruction of their state's sovereignty'.[72] Self-defence may cause more harm than accepting occupation (particularly after 'bloodless invasion').[73]

Self-defence may also be inconsistent with international peace and security—collective defence of Czechoslovakia against the 1968 Soviet invasion would have risked global nuclear catastrophe.[74] There is a danger in positing State sovereignty and self-determination as ultimate moral values in the international order. Although the common life is important, it is not a 'source of value independent of its value for individual persons'.[75] These provocative arguments are appealing, but demanding pacifism from invaded States (or suppressed 'peoples') encourages aggression, since it

---

[66] Rodin, n 61, 158–160.

[67] J Norton Moore, 'The Need for an International Convention' in MC Bassiouni (ed), *Legal Responses to International Terrorism* (Martinus Nijhoff, Dordrecht, 1988) 437, 438.

[68] J Rawls, *A Theory of Justice* (Clarendon, Oxford, 1972) 379; J Paust, 'The Human Right to Participate in Armed Revolution and Related Forms of Social Violence' (1983) 32 *Emory Law Journal* 545, 578.

[69] *Israel Wall Advisory Opinion*, n 52, para 14 (Separate Opinion of Higgins J).

[70] Ignatieff, n 57, 1149; Ad Hoc Committee Report (1977), n 13, 16, para 2 (Austria).

[71] Rodin, n 61, 10–11, 138–139.   [72] ibid, 124, 140, 147.

[73] ibid, 131–132.   [74] ibid, 117, 131.   [75] ibid, 143.

eliminates the broader deterrence of violence that ensues from the recognition and exercise of defensive rights.

Whatever the merits of those views, the use of atrocious means often subverts or destroys the good end sought.[76] Whereas Fanon and Sartre find personal liberation in liberation violence,[77] a practitioner of liberation, Nehru, wrote: 'Bad and immoral means often defeat the end in view.'[78] Even Marcuse argued that some forms of violence, including 'arbitrary violence, cruelty, and indiscriminate terror',[79] can never be justified 'because they negate the very end for which the revolution is a means'. As Berlin puts it: 'Most revolutionaries believe, covertly or overtly, that in order to create the ideal world eggs must be broken, otherwise one cannot obtain the omelette. Eggs are certainly broken—never more violently or ubiquitously than in our times—but the omelette is far to seek, it recedes into an infinite distance.'[80] Revolutionary restraint is necessary for moral self-respect.[81] Otherwise, all that is left is 'the darker and more paradoxical thought that, if one can defeat evil only by becoming evil, then it is impossible to defeat evil'.[82]

5. *Other politically just causes: Rebellion*

An early and persistent justification for terrorism is that violent resistance, rebellion, or revolution is justifiable against an unjust or oppressive regime.[83] Such acts are manifestations of internal self-determination and purport to justify violating the rights of others.[84] Theories of revolution and rebellion are ancient and varied, from Greece and Rome to natural law, the Enlightenment, liberalism, and human rights. Even deferential and hierarchical systems, such as Confucianism, feudalism, and some religions, have justified violent regime change in extreme circumstances.

Much of the vast literature on rebellion and revolution focuses on the existence of the right and the preconditions of its exercise, usually in a particular national order, political system, or philosophical tradition. Compara-

---

[76] ibid, 65–66.

[77] See F Fanon, *The Wretched of the Earth* (trans C Farrington, Grove Press, New York, 1963).

[78] J Nehru, *Jawaharlal Nehru: An Autobiography* (OUP, Oxford, 1989) 549.

[79] H Marcuse, 'Ethics and Revolution' in E Kent (ed), *Revolution and the Rule of Law* (Englewood Cliffs, NJ, 1971) 46, 53.

[80] I Berlin, *The First and the Last* (Granta, London, 1999) 57.

[81] M Walzer, *Just and Unjust Wars* (3rd edn, Basic Books, New York, 2000) 206.

[82] Rodin, n 61, 67.

[83] See, eg, G O'Boyle, 'Theories of Justification and Political Violence: Examples from Four Groups' (2002) 14 *Terrorism and Political Violence* 23; L Kutner, 'A Philosophical Perspective on Rebellion' in MC Bassiouni (ed), *International Terrorism and Political Crimes* (Charles C Thomas, Illinois, 1975) 51; N Strickler, 'Anti-History and Terrorism: A Philosophical Dimension' in Bassiouni (ed), above, 47; G Sorel, *Reflections on Violence* (trans T Hulme, Peter Smith, New York, 1941).

[84] Ignatieff, n 57, 1151.

tively less has been said about the status of the right in international law, and the permissible means of exercising it.[85] The most sweeping consequentialist claims assert that just causes justify all means. Classic revolutions, such as the French and American, often involved 'terrorist' methods.[86]

Both the *jus ad bellum* and *jus in bello* aspects are relevant to justifications for terrorism. If there is no right to rebel, then every internal use of violence against a State is unlawful and subject to national (and potentially international) criminalization as 'terrorism'—even if violence is limited to military objectives. If there is a right to rebel (legalizing certain *ad bellum* acts of internal violence), then the contours of permissible means and methods of violence (*in bello*) must be carefully drawn, so that terrorist acts are distinguished from lawful acts of belligerency.

(a) The right to rebel in international law

(i) Jus ad bellum: internal violence

The existence of an international legal right to resist, or rebel against, tyranny or oppression is doubtful. Certainly a 'right of revolution against oppressive regimes is central to the Western democratic tradition',[87] and is also common in other political systems. As Arendt notes, many modern political communities were founded on violence and thus originated in crime.[88] Yet a shared principle in some domestic orders does not imply the existence of a similar international right. There is no binding treaty right to rebel against oppressive regimes. At best there is a preambular reference in the Universal Declaration of Human Rights (UDHR), which states: 'Whereas it is essential, if man is not to be compelled to have recourse, as a last resource, to rebellion against tyranny and oppression, that human rights should be

---

[85] T Honoré, 'The Right to Rebel' (1988) 8 OJLS 34; A Khan, 'A Legal Theory of Revolutions' (1987) 5 BUILJ 1; R Schwartz, 'Chaos, Oppression, and Rebellion: The Use of Self-Help to Secure Individual Rights under International Law' (1994) 12 BUILJ 255; T Franck and N Rodley, 'Legitimacy and Legal Rights of Revolutionary Movements' (1970) 45 NYU LR 679; C King, 'Revolutionary War, Guerilla Warfare, and International Law' (1972) 4 Case Western Reserve JIL 91; B Röling, 'The Legal Status of Rebels and Rebellion' (1976) 13 *Journal of Peace Research* 149; W O'Brien, 'The Jus in Bello in Revolutionary War and Counterinsurgency' (1978) 18 Virginia JIL 193; Paust, n 68; J Paust 'Aggression against Authority: The Crime of Oppression, Politicide and Other Crimes against Human Rights' (1986) 18 Case Western Reserve JIL 283.

[86] J Tierney, 'Terror at Home: The American Revolution and Irregular Warfare' (1977) 12 Stan JIS 1; V Johnson, 'The Declaration of the Rights of Man and of Citizens of 1789, the Reign of Terror, and the Revolutionary Tribunal of Paris' (1990) 13 BC ICLR 1.

[87] G Fox and G Nolte, 'Intolerant Democracies' in G Fox and B Roth (eds), *Democratic Governance and International Law* (CUP, Cambridge, 2000) 389, 432. eg Art 20(4) of Germany's Basic Law (*Grundgesetz*) recognizes a right of resistance, as a last resort, against attempts to overturn the constitutional order.

[88] H Arendt, *On Revolution* (Penguin, London, 1990) 20.

protected by the rule of law'. A drafting proposal, endorsed by the UN Commission on Human Rights, to refer to a 'right' of resistance was not accepted: 'When a Government, group, or individual seriously or systematically tramples the fundamental human rights and freedoms, individuals and peoples have the right to resist oppression and tyranny.'[89] Nonetheless, Honoré argues that the UDHR preamble implies that subjects have political rights against their governments.[90] While it does not recognize a formal legal right to rebel, 'neither is it a purely informal right grounded in the conventional morality of the international community'.[91] Instead, it 'possesses an intermediate, semi-formal status', premised on human dignity and international political norms.[92]

The factual recognition in the UDHR preamble that rebellion may flow from oppression does not, however, imply that a *right* of rebellion exists. The exclusion of reference to a 'right' during the drafting, the lack of reference to such a right in the 1966 covenants, and the preambular status of the provision in a non-binding declaration weigh against the existence of a right. Only peaceful rights of political participation are expressly mentioned in the ICCPR.[93] While States occasionally exhort citizens of repressive States to 'rise up' against their leaders (consider US Presidential incitement of Kurds and 'Marsh Arabs' against Saddam Hussein's Iraq), such statements are typically framed as political positions, not as a legal right to rebel.

In addition, there are no correlative duties on affected States not to suppress or criminalize legitimate rebellions,[94] nor duties on third States to assist legitimate rebellions,[95] nor even to shield rebels from extradition for political crimes.[96] The duty on third States not to intervene in civil wars is not designed to recognize a right of rebellion,[97] so much as to defer to a matter within

---

[89] ECOSOCOR (6th Sess), Supp No 1, Report of the UNComHR, 17 Dec 1947, 19.

[90] Honoré, n 85, 43; Paust, n 68, 560.   [91] Honoré, n 85, 43.

[92] ibid, 43.   [93] eg ICCPR, Arts 18–19, 21–22, 25.

[94] Crawford, n 35, 48–49 (States are entitled to forcibly suppress rebellions); C Gray, *International Law and the Use of Force* (OUP, Oxford, 2000) 57 (States may request foreign assistance in suppressing rebellions); see also J Novogrod, 'Internal Strife, Self-Determination, and World Order' in Bassiouni (ed), n 83, 98, 103. Where a rebellion reaches the level of a civil war, third States may no longer assist the government: Crawford, above, 41; Gray, above, 57; W Werner, 'Self-Determination and Civil War' (2001) 6 JCSL 171, 190.

[95] *Nicaragua* (1986) ICJ Rep 14, 108–109, paras 206–209 (no right of third States to intervene in aid of the moral or political values of a rebellion); see also Protocol II, Art 3(2).

[96] The availability of the political offence exception to extradition is a question of national (and bilateral treaty) law rather than international law: I Stanbrook and C Stanbrook, *Extradition Law and Practice* (2nd edn, OUP, Oxford, 2000) 65; cf I Shearer, *Extradition in International Law* (MUP, Manchester, 1971) 22. The 1951 Refugee Convention requires only that a person not be returned to political persecution, not to prosecution. While many national courts uphold an exception for political offences, it commonly applies to any political offenders, regardless of the justifiability of their cause: see, eg, *Schtraks v Israel* [1964] AC 556, 583 (Lord Reid); *Quinn v Robinson* 783 F. 2d 776 (9th Cir, 1986). See also Ch 1 above on the political offence exception to extradition.

[97] cf Q Wright, 'Subversive Intervention' (1960) 54 AJIL 521, 529.

domestic jurisdiction:[98] the freedom of peoples to determine their own political status through internal self-determination.[99]

(ii) Jus in bello: internal violence

It is unnecessary to determine the existence of a right to rebel to discuss the limits on violence when it occurs.[100] The *jus in bello* of internal violence bears on justifications for terrorism in important ways. In non-international conflicts, the application of common Article 3 of the 1949 Geneva Conventions does not affect the legal status of parties.[101] Similarly, Protocol II does not affect 'the sovereignty of a State or the responsibility of the government, by all legitimate means, to maintain or re-establish law and order in the State or to defend the national unity and territorial integrity'.[102]

Accordingly, rebels in civil wars do not automatically enjoy international legal personality[103] or recognition as combatants, unless the State recognizes their belligerency,[104] informally applies IHL, or where, in exceptional cases, there exist agreements between non-State[105] parties in a conflict where the State has dissolved.[106] The conditions of combatancy for irregular forces in international armed conflicts[107] do not apply in non-international conflicts and there is no combatant immunity for non-State forces.[108] Protocol II

[98] G Draper, 'Wars of National Liberation and War Criminality' in M Howard (ed), *Restraints on War* (OUP, Oxford, 1979) 135, 141; Green, n 39, 317.

[99] 1966 ICCPR, Art 1(1); 1966 ICESCR, Art 1(1).

[100] Prohibitions on terrorism in non-international armed conflicts are examined in Ch 5 below.

[101] 1949 Geneva Conventions, common Art 3.

[102] Protocol II, Art 3(1); Green, n 41, 322; see generally A Cassese, 'The Status of Rebels under the 1977 Geneva Protocol on Non-International Armed Conflicts' (1981) 30 ICLQ 416.

[103] In *Prosecutor v Morris Kallon and Brima Buzzy Kamara (Jurisdiction)* (the *Lomé Amnesty* case), SCSL–2004–15–AR72(E) and SCSL–2004–16–AR72(E), Appeals Chamber, 13 Mar 2004, paras 37–48, the Special Court for Sierra Leone held that insurgents bound by IHL do not necessarily enjoy international legal personality, nor do their agreements with governments constitute binding treaties under international law; cf P Kooijmans, 'The Security Council and Non-State Entities as Parties to Conflicts' in K Wellens (ed), *International Law: Theory and Practice—Essays in Honour of Eric Suy* (Martinus Nijhoff, The Hague, 1998) 333, 338.

[104] A Cassese, *International Law* (OUP, Oxford, 2001) 343; Brownlie, n 30, 63; Green, n 41, 317–318.

[105] In *Tadic (Interlocutory)*, n 51, para 106, the ICTY noted the trend of States since the Spanish Civil War and in the Nigerian civil war 'to withhold recognition of belligerency but, at the same time, extend to the conflict the bulk of the body of legal rules concerning conflicts between States'.

[106] eg in *Galic*, the ICTY held that an agreement between the Republic of Bosnia-Herzegovina, the Serbian Democratic Party, and the Croatian Democratic Community to apply certain IHL provisions was binding as if it were an international treaty: *Galic* ICTY–98–29–T (5 Dec 2003) paras 20–25. Capacity to enter into treaty relations does not, however, necessarily imply full international legal personality.

[107] 1907 Hague Regs, Art 1; 1949 First Geneva Convention, Art 13; 1949 Second Geneva Convention, Art 13; 1949 Third Geneva Convention, Art 4; 1977 Protocol I, Arts 43(2) and 44(3).

[108] Cassese, n 104, 343.

contains no conditions of combatancy.[109] Similarly, in internal violence below an armed conflict (such as internal disturbances and tensions, riots, isolated and sporadic acts of violence, and other acts of a similar nature),[110] there is no combatant immunity. In practice, rebels may enjoy a partial immunity in relation to third States, although this is conditional since it may be withdrawn on political grounds.[111]

States may consequently treat violence by non-State forces as crimes under national law,[112] including violence directed solely and proportionately against military objectives,[113] and even if such forces carry arms openly, wear identifying symbols, and informally respect IHL. Thus Turkey does not recognize an armed conflict in Kurdistan,[114] nor has Russia recognized internal conflicts in Chechnya. The only legitimate rebellion is a successful one.[115] While the question of whether violence constitutes an internal armed conflict triggering IHL is an objective one, even where Protocol II applies it is still open to the affected State to treat rebels as criminals.

It is nonetheless noteworthy that fairly low level internal violence has been recognized by the Inter-American Commission in the *Abella* case as triggering IHL, which 'does not require the existence of large scale and generalized hostilities or a situation comparable to a civil war in which dissident armed groups exercise control over parts of national territory'.[116] In that case, the Commission applied IHL to an organized attack by 42 armed civilians on an Argentinian military installation in peacetime, against which Argentina deployed 1,500 soldiers using military tactics. Similarly, in *Yunis* (1991), a US court found that the the defence of superior orders may be open to an Amal militia member who, in 1985, hijacked an aircraft in Beirut (in peacetime), where the militia qualified as a military organization under the laws of war.[117]

One concession is that Protocol II urges authorities at the end of hostilities to 'endeavour to grant the broadest possible amnesty to persons who have participated in the armed conflict, or those deprived of their liberty for reasons related to the armed conflict'.[118] Similarly, if belligerents do not

[109] cf Detter, n 32, 146 (criteria in the 1949 Geneva Conventions or Protocol I apply by analogy).

[110] Protocol II, Art 1(2).

[111] A Dahl, 'The Legal Status of the Opposition Fighter in Internal Armed Conflict' (2004) 3–4 *Revue de Droit Militaire et Droit de la Guerre* 137.

[112] H Lauterpacht (ed), *Oppenheim's International Law: vol II* (8th edn, Longmans, Green and Co, London, 1955) 210–212; Green, n 41, 60, 318; Cassese, n 104, 343; Draper, n 98, 141.

[113] Protocol II, Art 6 does, however, establish minimum procedural guarantees in criminal cases.

[114] S Cayci, 'Countering Terrorism and International Law: The Turkish Experience' in Schmitt and Beruto (eds), n 56, 137, 141.

[115] A Orford, 'The Destiny of International Law' (2004) 17 Leiden JIL 441, 459.

[116] *Juan Carlos Abella v Argentina* Case 11.137, Report No 55/97, IACHR, OEA/Ser.L/V/II.95 Doc 7 rev at 271 (1997) para 152.

[117] *Fawaz Yunis*, 924 F. 2d at 1097.

[118] Protocol II, Art 6(5).

commit war crimes, 'it is in the spirit of the [Geneva] Convention that trials and executions for treason should be reduced to an indispensable minimum required by the necessities of the situation'.[119] Although prosecution is permitted, it is often impractical or unwise.[120] In practice, some States have conferred de facto recognition on non-State groups which generally comply with IHL, and third States commonly do not regard insurgents as criminals.[121] However, for rebels, discretionary treatment is little legal comfort.

(iii) Implications of jus ad bellum and jus in bello

The striking feature of non-international armed conflicts, and situations of lesser internal violence, is the discretion enjoyed by States to criminalize both recourse to force, and the conduct of hostilities, by non-State forces. Unless non-State armed forces in internal conflicts—including those where Protocol II does not apply[122]—are excluded from an international crime of terrorism, there is an acute danger of internationally legitimizing State repression of internal dissidence. If terrorism is politically motivated, coercive, or intimidatory violence, then those who rebel against oppressive regimes may be prosecuted as terrorists—even if they target only military objectives.

The limited regulation of non-international conflicts is based on non-intervention in domestic jurisdiction,[123] particularly where a State interest as vital as political authority is at stake. Yet human rights law interferes in the freedom of States to act arbitrarily towards those in their power, narrowing the reserved domain of domestic jurisdiction.[124] Where oppressive States seriously violate human rights, the treaty-based, 'soft' machinery of human rights protection and supervision may fail to secure basic rights. In the absence of an effective, binding enforcement system, or Security Council intervention, violent rebellion—as collective self-help—may be the only means of terminating rights abuses.

Honoré elegantly proposes a right to rebel as a secondary right arising as a remedy against large-scale and sustained violations of primary rights.[125] Rebellion is the right of oppressed or exploited individuals to use violence to

---

[119] Lauterpacht, n 112, 211; see also T Franck and B Lockwood, 'Preliminary Thoughts towards an International Convention on Terrorism' (1974) 68 AJIL 69, 88.

[120] J Brierly, *The Outlook for International Law* (Clarendon, Oxford, 1944) 52.

[121] N Ronzitti, 'The Law of the Sea and the Use of Force against Terrorist Activities' in N Ronzitti (ed), *Maritime Terrorism and International Law* (Martinus Nijhoff, Dordrecht, 1990) 1, 3.

[122] Although 'Many provisions of this Protocol can now be regarded as declaratory of existing rules or as having crystallised emerging rules of customary law or else as having been strongly instrumental in their evolution as general principles': *Tadic (Interlocutory)*, n 51, para 117.

[123] Green, n 48, 137.

[124] M Reisman, 'Sovereignty and Human Rights in Contemporary International Law' (1990) 84 AJIL 866; Brownlie, n 30, 557.

[125] Honoré, n 85, 38.

change the government, structures, or policies of society.[126] In its absence, human rights remain rhetorical or aspirational.[127] Serious and sustained State oppression dissolves the social bonds between the State and its subjects, and as a result, 'it is no longer open to the state to define the conditions in which subjects may lawfully use force'.[128] The State may be attacked as long as rebels respect 'the same restraints as they would be bound to observe if the rebellion were a war between states'.[129] This position has intuitive appeal and reflects the view of Lauterpacht, concerning the political offence exception to extradition, that the:

> ... international community was no longer a society for the mutual protection of governments. A revolution might be a crime against the established state, but it was no longer a crime against the international community. So long as international society did not effectively guarantee the rights of men against arbitrariness and oppression by governments, it could not oblige states to treat subversive activities . . . as a crime.[130]

Were a right to rebel based on human rights standards accepted, it would jeopardize the realization of human rights to allow serious State violators to criminalize the recourse to force by internal rebels. The objection that a right to rebel revives a subjective doctrine of just war is no more persuasive than directing the same objection at the right of self-defence, itself a vestige of just war. Like self-defence, a right to rebel is a fundamentally defensive right, exercisable only when legal preconditions are satisfied—instead of an armed attack, the serious and sustained violation of human rights.

The difficulty lies in determining when a rebellion is 'justifiable'. For Honoré, a State's breach of duty must be *weighty, crucial and severe*', such as 'sustained disinterest or contempt' or continued discrimination, oppression, or exploitation which renders life intolerable.[131] Since rebellion may entail widespread violence, it must only be considered in extreme circumstances, and not if other remedies are available in a reasonable period.[132] The likely consequences of action must also be weighed. Despite the legal (rights-based) standards involved, such determinations still invite subjective appreciation of when the right to rebel arises—and when it may be denied. Such determinations are generally more subjective than verifying if an armed attack has occurred.

Regardless of its justifiability, where a rebellion generates an armed conflict, it would thwart the realization of human rights to criminalize the conduct of hostilities (such as violent resistance against military or official targets, which complies with IHL), and even to forcibly repress rebellions. There is a powerful argument that rebel violence against an oppressive State, while respecting

---

[126] ibid, 36.   [127] ibid, 34, 38.   [128] ibid, 53–54.   [129] ibid, 54.
[130] (1954–I) ILCYB 141.   [131] Honoré, n 85, 48, 51.   [132] ibid, 38, 54.

IHL constraints, should be lawfully *justified* in international law—by conferring combatant immunity—rather than merely excused at the level of mitigation in sentencing.

To avoid the problem of distinguishing just from unjust causes during combat, combatant immunity could be conferred on any rebel forces—progressive or reactionary—as long as they comply with IHL and its conditions of combatancy, transplanted from Protocol I. Internal conflicts would then mirror international ones, in which, for humanitarian reasons, the lawfulness or justice of recourse to force does not affect the lawfulness of a combatant's participation in hostilities.[133]

Objections are that such an extension would legitimize violent non-State groups (including terrorists), by conferring international recognition on them,[134] and privatize war.[135] It would also interfere in domestic jurisdiction, beyond the limited interventions of common Article 3 of the 1949 Geneva Conventions and Protocol II. Some of these objections are similar to those raised against the adoption of Protocol I.[136] Recognition implies loss of control over territory and private violence, and a degree of governmental failure, and States are reluctant to relinquish their sovereign authority to identify and penalize 'terrorists'.[137]

Yet IHL is designed to serve neutral humanitarian purposes, not to confer political legitimacy or recognition on participants in conflict—just as recognizing the combatant immunity of an aggressor State's forces does not legitimize their cause. Further, recognizing that non-State actors have rights and duties under IHL does not make them full subjects of international law, or give them legal personality equivalent to States. Conferring combatant immunity simply ensures that there is greater incentive for non-State groups to admit and respect IHL's constraints on violence. This does not privatize war, but pragmatically concedes that private groups already fight wars, and will continue to do so, even if they are denied combatancy. It is better to regulate private violence internationally, to minimize harm in conflict, than to leave it to sovereign discretion.

To ensure civilian protection, rebels would have to comply with the conditions of combatancy, and would be liable for perfidy or other IHL breaches, although in practice it may be difficult to distinguish terrorist groups from

---

[133] Lauterpacht, n 112, 218.

[134] Chadwick, n 42, 8; A Clapham, *Human Rights in the Private Sphere* (Clarendon, Oxford, 1996) 112, 116; see also A Roberts, 'Counter-Terrorism, Armed Force and the Laws of War' (2002) 44 *Survival* 7.

[135] G Abi-Saab, 'The Proper Role of International Law in Combating Terrorism' (2002) 1 Chinese JIL 305, 308.

[136] See, eg, A Sofaer, 'Terrorism and the Law' (1986) *Foreign Affairs* 901, 912; T Franck and S Senecal, 'Porfiry's Proposition: Legitimacy and Terrorism' (1987) 20 Van JTL 195, 204–206; Chadwick, n 42, 207–208; Wilkinson, n 8, 234.

[137] Chadwick, n 42, 9, 11; Clapham, n 134, 113.

resistance and guerilla groups which sometimes use terrorist tactics.[138] Rebels would require a minimum degree of organization to enjoy combatant status, since 'structure is necessary for the activation and implementation of international norms'.[139] Loosening the conditions of combatancy further (such as permitting perfidy) would jeopardize civilian protection, by reducing the distinction between combatants and non-combatants.[140]

For instance, the French resistance woman in 1944 who, dressed in civilian clothes and concealing a revolver, cycled up to a German officer in a Paris street and shot him in the head,[141] necessarily renders all French civilians suspect, and invites drastic retaliation. Yet it is such 'freedom fighters' that the EU Council sought to exclude from the scope of terrorism under the 2002 EU Framework Decision, in a draft statement excluding 'the conduct of those who have acted in the interest of preserving or restoring . . . democratic values . . . as was notably the case in some Member States during the Second World War'.[142] Were this reasoning adopted in IHL, it would analogously justify the commission of war crimes in pursuit of just causes—a position rejected by the international community in armed conflicts. Many guerillas in the Second World War would not have complied with the more relaxed conditions of combatancy in Protocol I. While the EU's statement was not part of the legal text as adopted, it nonetheless signals political unease about criminalizing (as terrorism) the conduct of freedom fighters similar to those in Europe during the war. What is unclear is whether the EU believes that such conduct should not be regarded as criminal at all, in which case it would seem to lend support to a further liberalization of the relaxed conditions of combatancy in Protocol I.

Paradoxically, the EU's position is not dissimilar to the exclusion of liberation violence from the anti-terrorism treaties of the Arab League, the Organization of the Islamic Conference, and the African Union—even though such an exemption is the main sticking point between these organizations and western States in the negotiation of a comprehensive anti-terrorism treaty.[143] The EU's lack of empathy for similarly situated 'freedom fighters' resuscitates the persistent adage that 'one person's freedom fighter is another person's terrorist'.

[138] Detter, n 32, 145.

[139] Cassese, n 54, 93; see also B Larschan, 'Legal Aspects to the Control of Transnational Terrorism: An Overview' (1986) 13 Ohio NULR 117, 148; E Posner, 'Terrorism and the Laws of War' (2005) 5 Chinese JIL 423, 432–434 (applying conditions of symmetry and reciprocity to terrorist groups).   [140] Detter, n 32, 144.

[141] J Henley, 'You can't know how wonderful it was to finally battle in the daylight', *The Guardian*, 21 Aug 2004.

[142] EU Council, Outcome of Proceedings of 6 Dec 2001, Statement No 2, Council Doc 14845/1/02, 15. Such statements have not been accepted as binding interpretations of EU legislation: *Antonissen* Case C–292/89 [1991] ECR I–745; S Peers, 'EU Responses to Terrorism' (2003) 52 ICLQ 227, 236.

[143] See Ch 3 below.

(iv) 'Non-innocent' civilians

Even if IHL is fully extended to civil wars and all liberation movements, a different justification for terrorism rests on a challenge to IHL norms of distinction. On one view, some non-combatants are not 'innocent' and therefore become legitimate targets of violence:[144] not only police officers or government officials who enforce and implement the policies of an oppressive government, but Israeli settlers in the Palestinian Occupied Territories, *pied-noirs* in Algeria, or white South Africans during apartheid. These cases involve unlawful occupations or gravely unlawful acts under international law. Foreign settlers may be seen as instruments or beneficiaries of the State's unlawfulness. As Fanon writes: 'The appearance of the settler has meant . . . the death of the aboriginal society, cultural lethargy, and the petrification of individuals. For the native, life can only spring up again out of the rotting corpse of the settler.'[145] The argument for 'non-innocence' (or 'half-innocence')[146] is most persuasive for voluntary settlers with knowledge of the international unlawfulness (regardless of domestic legality). Children of settlers ought also be excluded, since they may have no choice but to follow their parents, and their minority may preclude informed choice.

On one hand, law sometimes prohibits violence but accepts it as morally excusable: 'when the victim is Hitler-like in character, we are likely to praise the assassin's work'.[147] Assassinations of oppressive politicians, which avoid innocent casualties, are distinguishable from random murders of innocents:[148] 'who would say that he commits a crime who assassinates a tyrant?'.[149] Courts have even recognized assassinations as proportionate political acts exempt from extradition.[150] While settlers are not oppressive politicians,[151] they are voluntary, knowing agents of oppression, displacing and impoverishing local populations. The protection of civilians in general does

---

[144] Ignatieff, n 57, 1147; Franck and Lockwood, n 119, 80.

[145] Fanon, n 77, 93.

[146] T Honderich, *After the Terror* (Edinburgh University Press, Edinburgh, 2003) 159.

[147] Walzer, n 81, 199; Honoré, n 85, 37; Shearer, n 96, 185; C Van den Wyngaert, 'The Political Offence Exception to Extradition: How to Plug the Terrorist's Loophole' (1989) IYBHR 297, 305; see, eg, AFP, 'Hitler's would-be assassin receives belated honours', *Sydney Morning Herald*, 16 May 2003.

[148] Walzer, ibid, 198–199.

[149] Cicero, 'No Fellowship with Tyrants' in W Laqueur (ed), *The Terrorism Reader* (Wildwood House, London, 1979) 16.

[150] See, eg, *Watin v Ministère Public Federal*, Swiss Federal Tribunal (1964), 72 ILR 614, 617: an attempt on the life of French President de Gaulle by a French national would be proportionate: 'Where the person aimed at practically embodies the political system of the State so that it might be thought that his disappearance will entail a change in that system.' In IHL, however, the assassination of an enemy head of State is forbidden, unless he or she is also the uniformed commander-in-chief: Green (2000), n 41, 145. But POW detention is permitted to recognize the danger such leaders pose to an adversary: Lauterpacht, n 112, 352.

[151] Walzer, n 81, 199.

not disappear if the targeting of such a limited class is accepted, just as the targeting of oppressive officials does not endanger ordinary citizens.[152]

Yet the argument for killing 'non-innocent' civilians is still unacceptable. The killing of combatants in armed conflict is justified because soldiers are militarily dangerous to an adversary.[153] Violence against combatants aims to disable them so they can no longer keep fighting.[154] Civilian munitions workers are lawful targets for the related reason that they are incidental casualties of lawful attacks on military targets (munitions factories).[155] In contrast, neither police officers[156] nor settlers are militarily harmful, although some may be if they engage in hostilities and hence lose their civilian immunity.[157]

The argument for targeting settlers rests on a different argument about their moral or legal culpability,[158] not their military threat.[159] But allowing settlers to be killed for moral, political, or legal wrongdoing is little more than vigilante justice. Punishment is a judicial function, requiring procedural fairness, and not easily given over to summary justice.[160] Extra-judicially evaluating immunity, or guilt, by standards of morality, or suspected illegality, renders civilian protection highly subjective.

Even in ideal cases of 'just assassination' such as that of Hitler,[161] assassins are entitled to moral respect, but can still be prosecuted. This is because combatants are objectively harmful, but 'the unjust or oppressive character of the official's activities is a matter of political judgment'.[162] IHL provides objective criteria of combatancy which identify harmful people in conflicts.

---

[152] ibid, 200.

[153] ibid, 145. Although as Rodin, n 61, 127–128, observes: 'soldiers fighting a defensive war are permitted to use violence against persons who pose no imminent threat to anyone. For instance, they may kill enemy soldiers who are marching, eating, sleeping, and so on, as well as uniformed support staff such as lorry drivers, cooks, and administrators'. One might also wonder whether, in an age of modern air warfare, a foot soldier is really a threat to a high-altitude bomber. The point is that their harmfulness as a whole must be assessed, not their threat to particular members of opposing forces.

[154] Lauterpacht, n 112, 338.

[155] See also 1923 Hague Draft Rules, Art 24(2); Walzer, n 81, 145–146.

[156] eg French gendarmes in Algeria, who were attacked by an Algerian political group, were considered 'unarmed', 'peaceful', 'civilian', and 'non-belligerent' persons: see *Zaouche Tahar, Abdi Arezkli and Ouakli Rabah* Court of Appeal of Brussels, 7 June 1960, (1960) 75 J Trib 467, affirmed by the Cour de Cassation, 22 July 1960, Pasicrisie I, 1263 and in a subsequent advisory opinion by the Court of Appeal of Brussels, 10 Nov 1960, Doss 26.463 E and 26.464 E.

[157] In practice, distinguishing civilian settlers from militarized settlers may be difficult, as in the Palestinian Occupied Territories, where settlers frequently carry military weapons for self-protection: see, eg, *Military Prosecutor v Jab'r et al* Ramallah/4041/81 (1987) 6 SJMC 259.

[158] Honderich, n 146, 159.

[159] Rodin, n 61, 84.

[160] Consider the many extrajudicial executions of suspected informers by Palestinian militants: eg S Goldenberg, ' "Collaborator" shot dead as jet strikes', *Sydney Morning Herald*, 16 July 2002.

[161] Walzer, n 81, 203; see also Franck and Senecal, n 136, 196.

[162] Walzer, n 81, 200. One might wonder, however, whether a foot soldier is objectively more threatening than, for instance, the head of Stalin's secret police.

While there are likewise human rights standards by which to measure the conduct of officials or settlers, such judgments entail a margin of appreciation far exceeding that involved in factually identifying a combatant.

Even more tenuous than the argument for killing settlers is Al-Qaeda's view that Americans, by being Americans, are responsible for the acts of the US, or for sustaining its power. As Osama Bin Laden said of attacks on US civilians:

> You may then dispute that all the above does not justify aggression against civilians, for crimes they did not commit . . . This argument contradicts your continuous repetition that America is the land of freedom . . . Therefore, the American people are the ones who choose their government by way of their own free will; a choice which stems from their agreement to its policies . . . The American people have the ability and choice to refuse the policies of their Government and even to change it if they want.[163]

Similarly, one of the organizers of the 7 July 2005 London bombings, Mohammed Sidique Khan, stated: 'This is how our ethical stances are dictated. Your democratically elected governments perpetrate atrocities against my people and your support of them makes you responsible, just as I am directly responsible for protecting and avenging my Muslim brothers and sisters.'[164] The idea of non-innocence stretches to different lengths, as one writer notes: 'what of the private citizens who carry the flag in trade, athletics or non-governmental organizational activities? Or, for that matter, what of every private citizen who, merely by not resisting, may be presumed to condone his government's acts?'.[165]

The views of Al-Qaeda reflect a crude doctrine of collective responsibility and punishment, where (democratic) State action is mechanically imputed to all of its citizens. Such a view not only disavows the autonomy of individuals, but it is also politically punitive; it threatens a whole people, regardless of the individual harmfulness of its members.[166] Likewise, the targeting of UN or humanitarian personnel, for supposed complicity in nourishing the US occupation of Iraq,[167] embodies a world-view which ultimately exposes every individual to terrorist harm—whether on account of their occupation, political beliefs, religious affiliation, nationality, or otherwise.

---

[163] Osama bin Laden, 'Letter to America', *Observer Worldwide*, 24 Nov 2002.

[164] V Dodd and R Norton-Taylor, '7/7 bomber's video blames Blair policy', *Guardian Weekly*, 8–15 Sept 2005, 8.

[165] R Mushkat, ' "Technical" Impediments on the Way to a Universal Definition of International Terrorism' (1980) 20 Indian JIL 448, 454.

[166] See Walzer, n 81, 193, 200. Others assert, with some exaggeration, that Al-Qaeda's view of Americans is even genocidal: R Falk, *The Great Terror War* (Arris Books, Gloucestershire, 2003) 43. One US lawyer, Nathan Lewin, has similarly supported collective punishment by calling for the execution of the families of suicide bombers: quoted in R Fisk, *The Great War for Civilization* (Fourth Estate, London, 2005) 603.

[167] E MacAskill, 'Aid agency quits Afghanistan over security fears', *The Guardian*, 29 July 2004; 'Iraqi militants slaughter 12 hostages', *Sydney Morning Herald*, 1 Sept 2004.

Another extreme challenge to IHL comes from those like the Palestinian Sheik Ahmed Yassin, who stated: 'The Jews attack and kill our civilians—we will kill theirs'.[168] Similar claims have been made by Chechen groups,[169] and by Al-Qaeda: 'The time has come for vengeance against the Zionist crusader government of Britain in response to the massacres Britain committed in Iraq and Afghanistan.'[170] Arguments for retributive killings draw no moral distinction between intended and unintended killings of non-combatants, and embody a simplistic rejection of the doctrine of double effect. Incidental civilian casualties from proportionate military operations are a tolerated cost of war, but deliberately killing non-combatants—even in reprisal under treaty law—is unlawful.[171]

Arguments for retributive killings are, however, nourished by the overwhelming preponderance of civilian casualties relative to military casualties in modern conflicts, including in recent conflicts in Kosovo, Afghanistan, Iraq, and Palestine.[172] High altitude air warfare minimizes military losses among the armed forces of technologically superior States, but may inflict

---

[168] P McGeough, 'Inside the mind of a suicide bomber', *Sydney Morning Herald*, 13 Apr 2002.

[169] J Steele, 'Bombers' justification: Russians are killing our children, so we are here to kill yours', *The Guardian*, 6 Sept 2004.

[170] M Tran and D Macleod, 'Al-Qaida in Europe claims responsibility for blasts', *The Guardian*, 7 July 2005.

[171] See 1949 Geneva Conventions, common Art 3 (minimum guarantees); 1949 First Geneva Convention, Art 45 (wounded and sick); 1949 Second Geneva Convention, Art 46 (wounded, sick and shipwrecked); 1949 Third Geneva Convention, Art 13 (prisoners of war); 1949 Fourth Geneva Convention, Arts 27 (humane treatment of protected persons), 33 (protected persons and private civilian property in occupied territory), 147 (grave breaches); Protocol I, Arts 20 (wounded, sick, shipwrecked, medical and religious personnel), 51(6) (civilian population), 52(1) (civilian objects), 53(c) (cultural objects and places of worship), 54(4) (objects indispensable to civilian survival), 55 (natural environment), 56(4) (works and installations containing dangerous forces), 75 (fundamental guarantees), 85 (repression of grave breaches); Protocol II, Arts 4 (fundamental guarantees), 13 (protection of civilian population); 1954 Hague Convention on the Protection of Cultural Property, Art 4(4). See text to nn 314–318 below on the customary law of reprisals.

[172] In the Iraq war from March 2003 to March 2005, non-combatant deaths are credibly estimated at 25,000, with 42,500 wounded: Iraq Body Count, *A Dossier of Civilian Casualties 2003–2005* (Oxford Research Group, Oxford, 2005): <http://reports.iraqbodycount.org/a_dossier_of_civilian_casualties_2003–2005.pdf> (about 37% of civilians were killed by US-led forces, 9% by insurgent forces, and 36% by post-invasion criminal violence). Another study found that direct or indirect Iraqi civilian deaths could be as high as 100,000: L Roberts, R Lafta, R Garfield, J Khudhairi, and G Burnham, 'Mortality before and after the 2003 invasion of Iraq: cluster sample survey' (2004) 364 (No 9448) *The Lancet* 1857. These figures compare with 2,252 US military deaths; 204 deaths of US allied forces; 300 deaths of coalition contractors; 80 dead journalists; and at least 4,000 Iraqi (coalition) police and military deaths: Iraq Coalition Casualty Count: <http://icasualties.org/oif/default.aspx> (as at 7 Feb 2006). It is also estimated that 5,000–6,000 Iraqi soldiers and insurgents were killed in 'major combat' between March 2003 and September 2004, though estimates of insurgents killed range up to 50,000: see P Bennis and E Leaver, 'The Iraq Quagmire: The Mounting Costs of War', A Study by the Institute for Policy Studies and Foreign Policy in Focus, 31 Aug 2005, 26. In the second intifadah in Palestine, from 2000 to 2002, 1,450 Palestinians were killed compared with 525 Israelis: Fisk, n 166, 556.

high incidental civilian casualties.[173] The high rate of civilian casualties may suggest that judgments about military necessity have become overly protective of military forces (which are prepared to assume too few risks) and underprotective of non-combatants (who are too readily accepted as 'collateral damage'). If this lack of proportionality is a cause of high civilian casualties, then it may encourage terrorists to claim that their targeting of civilians is not so morally different from States that kill civilians too casually.

C. CRIMINAL LAW DEFENCES TO TERRORISM

In the absence of any positive right to rebel against oppressive States, including by self-determination movements falling outside Protocol I, international criminal defences assume importance in accommodating claims of justification for terrorism. For serious crimes, a fair trial requires the availability of defences,[174] which recognize that 'the presumption of free will is displaced' in some circumstances.[175] There is little evidence in State practice that absolute or strict liability attaches to terrorism,[176] and as such, the full range of defences is available. Sectoral treaties do not abolish defences, and most domestic terrorism laws also do not exclude them.[177]

Just as defences are available to comparably grave charges such as genocide, war crimes, or crimes against humanity, so too should defences be available to terrorism. While criminalization expresses international disapproval of terrorism, defences moderate the law's harshness in morally exceptional cases, and allow a more refined and calibrated response to claims of justification.[178] Not all terrorism is the same, and it follows that the criminal law cannot treat all terrorist acts in the same way. The motive behind terrorism is relevant to evaluating criminal responsibility.[179]

The scope of defences in international criminal law was historically ill-defined.[180] Defences were not recognized in the Nuremberg Charter, although

---

[173] I Primoratz, 'State Terrorism and Counter-terrorism' in I Primoratz (ed), *Terrorism: The Philosophical Issues* (Palgrave Macmillan, Hampshire, 2004) 113, 124.

[174] G Knoops, *Defences in Contemporary International Criminal Law* (Transnational, New York, 2001) 9.

[175] A Ashworth, *Principles of Criminal Law* (3rd ed, OUP, Oxford, 1999) 27.

[176] C Van den Wyngaert, 'The Political Offence Exception to Extradition' (1989) 19 IYBHR 297, 302.

[177] ibid.   [178] Franck and Senecal, n 136, 201, 210–215.

[179] L Kutner, 'Constructive Notice: A Proposal to End International Terrorism' (1974) 19 *New York Law Forum* 325, 349.

[180] V Morris and M Scharf, *The International Criminal Tribunal for Rwanda: vol I* (Transnational, New York, 1998) 272–283; Cassese, n 2, 146; see generally P Okowa, 'Defences in the Jurisprudence of International Tribunals' in G Goodwin-Gill and S Talmon (eds), *The Reality of International Law* (Clarendon, Oxford, 1999) 389. See generally E van Sliedregt, *The Criminal Responsibility of Individuals for Violations of International Humanitarian Law* (CUP, Cambridge, 2003) Part III.

the Nuremberg Tribunal permitted superior orders in mitigation.[181] The International Criminal Tribunal for the former Yugoslavia (ICTY) and the International Criminal Tribunal for Rwanda (ICTR) Statutes do not mention defences,[182] and exclude official position as a defence or mitigating factor, but allow superior orders in mitigation.[183] The Rules of Procedure and Evidence of those tribunals, however, allow both alibi and 'any special defence' to be pleaded.[184]

The 1998 Rome Statute explicitly affirms grounds excluding criminal responsibility, including: (a) mental disease or defect; (b) intoxication; (c) self-defence; (d) duress; and (e) other grounds deriving from international law and general principles of law.[185] Official capacity is excluded as a defence or a mitigating factor.[186] Self-defence and duress/necessity are the defences most relevant to terrorist acts.

Civil law systems commonly distinguish between defences as *justifications* or *excuses*,[187] and there is revived interest in the distinction in the common law.[188] It is unclear if international law so distinguishes,[189] although in the 1998 Rome Statute, it has been suggested that the words 'a person shall not be criminally responsible' characterize defences as excuses.[190] Both justifications and excuses are rational explanations for wrongdoing,[191] and both may produce an acquittal. The difference lies in the greater moral stigma attaching to excused conduct, where wrongfulness is admitted,[192] but responsibility is wholly or partially refused.[193] In contrast, a justification is a positive liberty to perform an otherwise unlawful act;[194] responsibility is accepted but wrongfulness denied.[195]

---

[181] K Kittichaisaree, *International Criminal Law* (OUP, Oxford, 2001) 258. Alibi was also recognized as establishing innocence: Morris and Scharf, n 180, 272–283.

[182] Kittchaisaree, n 181, 258.

[183] ICTY Statute, Art 7; ICTR Statute, Art 6.

[184] ICTY and ICTR Rules of Evidence and Procedure, rule 67; see Kittchaisaree, n 181, 258.

[185] 1998 Rome Statute, Art 31.   [186] ibid, Art 27.   [187] Cassese, n 2, 219, 222.

[188] J Smith, *Smith and Hogan: Criminal Law* (10th edn, Butterworths, London, 2002) 210–211; J Gardner, 'The Gist of Excuses' (1997) 1 *Buffalo Criminal Law Journal* LJ 575; H Hart, 'Legal Responsibility and Excuses' in M Corrado (ed), *Justification and Excuse in the Criminal Law* (Garland, New York, 1994) 31; G Williams, 'The Theory of Excuses' [1982] *Criminal Law Review* LR 732.

[189] Cassese, n 2, 221.

[190] Knoops, n 174, 29–30. In practice, cases have not yet arisen where the legal consequences of the distinction are relevant: see Cassese, n 2, 220–222; Smith, n 188, 210.

[191] J Gardner, 'In Defence of Defences' in P Asp et al (eds), *Flores Juris et Legum* (Iustus Forlag, Uppsala, 2002) 13.

[192] Smith, n 188, 210.

[193] G Fletcher, *Rethinking Criminal Law* (Little, Brown, Boston, 1978) 759; Knoops, n 174, 29; Cassese, n 2, 220–222: examples of excuses include mental disease; intoxication; mistake of fact; mistake of law; duress; and physical compulsion.

[194] Rodin, n 61, 29; Cassese, n 2, 219–221: examples of justifications include the lawful punishment of enemy civilians or combatants; lawful belligerent reprisals; and self-defence.

[195] Fletcher, n 193, 759; Knoops, n 174, 29.

1. Self-defence

Is terrorism ever justified in self-defence, or defence of another? Self-defence is a general principle of criminal law.[196] The 1998 Rome Statute excludes criminal responsibility where: 'The person acts reasonably to defend himself or herself or another person . . . against an imminent and unlawful use of force in a manner proportionate to the degree of danger to the person or the other person.'[197] In the case of war crimes, a person may also act reasonably to defend property which is essential for the survival of the person or another person, or property which is essential for accomplishing a military mission.[198]

In addition to requirements of an imminent and unlawful attack, and proportionality, Cassese suggests that the law requires two further conditions: there is no other way of preventing the offence (otherwise known as a requirement of necessity,[199] and encompassing a duty to retreat or avoid conflict);[200] and the conduct of the aggressor is not caused by the person acting in self-defence.[201] The individual right of self-defence is distinct from the right of national self-defence exercised by States or State-like entities.[202] Indeed the Rome Statute stipulates that a person engaged in defensive military operations is not automatically absolved of criminal responsibility,[203] and the ICTY has found that such operations do not justify violations of IHL.[204]

Because self-defence aims to protect 'the legitimate interest a person has in their own continued survival and bodily integrity',[205] acts in self-defence are motivated by self-preservation, rather than by political aims, or premeditated coercive or intimidatory purposes. While killing an attacker may incidentally satisfy a political goal (if, for instance, the attacker is an agent of State policy), an act remains defensive as long as it is a reasonable and proportionate response to imminent, unlawful force. For this reason, attacks on innocent civilians can never be defensive, since such persons are not responsible for threatening imminent unlawful force. Less still are *indiscriminate* attacks on civilians justified by self-defence, because the lack of discrimination must fail the proportionality test.

---

[196] *Kordić and Čerkez* ICTY–95–14/2 (26 Feb 2001) para 449.

[197] The ECHR, Art 2(2)(a), recognizes the defence of any person from unlawful violence, where 'absolutely necessary', as a justification for deprivation of life.

[198] 1998 Rome Statute, Art 31(1)(c).

[199] Rodin, n 61, 40–41: indeed, the earlier requirement of imminence derives from necessity.

[200] Ashworth, n 175, 146; Rodin, n 61, 40. A duty to retreat is not well established in the case law and the requirement in the Rome Statute to act 'reasonably' does not seem to automatically require it.

[201] Cassese, n 2, 222.   [202] ibid, 223.

[203] 1998 Rome Statute, Art 31(1)(c); see also *Carl D O'Neal*, US Ct Military Apps, 18 Feb 1966, 16 USCMA 33; 36 CMR 189, 196 (self-defence is not available to a person engaging in mutual combat).

[204] *Kordić and Čerkez*, n 196, para 452.

[205] Rodin, n 61, 30.

Self-defence does not confer a licence to use violence in a strategic way in protest at a generalized policy of State oppression. Where an oppressive government threatens imminent and internationally unlawful force, affected individuals may exercise self-defence against the State agents or officials implementing the policy, such as the police, security services, or paramilitaries. Examples include self-defence by a detainee against an official threatening torture, enslavement, or prolonged unlawful detention;[206] or where a civilian threatened with rape wounds a soldier.[207]

However, it would be disproportionate to use lethal force against a person depriving another of the right to vote or freedom of expression,[208] or even to protect property.[209] In allowing defence of property essential to survival or to accomplishing a military mission, the drafters of the Rome Statute reached a 'disturbing compromise'[210] which may violate *jus cogens* and contradict IHL.[211] In practice, threats to property will seldom have imminent lethal consequences, since alternative means of survival will often be available, and thus killing to protect such property would seldom be proportionate. Exceptional cases may, however, arise, such as threats to destroy or steal food in situations of starvation or scorched earth policies. On the other hand, it is difficult to see any rational justification for classifying defence of property essential to a military mission as *self-defence*, since such conduct falls within the primary rules of IHL on the conduct of military operations and would, in appropriate cases, attract the ordinary application of combatant immunity.

The requirement of imminence also precludes self-defence against State officials who order, but who do not personally implement, oppressive policies. While such action might fall within a more general right to rebel, only an expanded (or preventive) right of self-defence would authorize violence against such persons.

May individuals act pre-emptively in self-defence? There is little international case law on the point, but some national courts permit pre-emption. In the English case of *Beckford*, it was held that 'a man about to be attacked does not have to wait for his assailant to strike the first blow or fire the first shot; circumstances may justify a pre-emptive strike'.[212] The rationale is that a person's vital interests cannot be protected if the person is required 'to wait until the first blow was struck'.[213]

---

[206] ibid, 48; see, eg, C Banham, 'Guantanamo escape may be justified: Kirby', *Sydney Morning Herald*, 13 Nov 2003.

[207] Cassese, n 2, 222–223.   [208] Rodin, n 61, 48.

[209] ibid, 44: other means of redress are available in relation to property which are not available in the case of death or serious personal injury.

[210] W Schabas, *An Introduction to the International Criminal Court* (CUP, Cambridge, 2002) 90.

[211] E David, *Principes de droit des conflits armés* (2nd edn, Bruylant, Brussels, 1999) 693.

[212] *Beckford v R* [1988] AC 130, 144; see Ashworth, n 175, 147–148.

[213] Ashworth, ibid, 148.

Yet the attack must still be imminent, not merely anticipated or predicted at some point in the future. Pre-emptive 'self-defence' against State oppression would rarely be justified, unless a potential victim knew, with reasonable certainty, the identity and intention of a potential attacker. Thus if a police officer was ordered to exterminate an ethnic group, and accepted those orders, members of the group may be justified in pre-emptively killing that police officer. The killing would thus be defensive, not terrorist, even though it has a political aspect. Other cases might include pre-emptive actions in defence of others, such as harm to public property intended to prevent one State using internationally unlawful force against another State.[214]

2. *Duress/Necessity*

In the General Assembly's Ad Hoc Committee, some States asserted that terrorism is the inevitable or logical outcome of underlying causes.[215] The implication is that it is unfair to punish desperate acts of necessity. In contrast, many States objected that terrorism is not an automatic consequence of even legitimate grievances,[216] emphasizing the choice involved in using terrorism over other means,[217] or even in the absence of oppression.[218]

There is evidently no strict criminal law causation between terrorism and injustice[219] and some empirical research even suggests that stable democracies are the most frequent victims of terrorism and that both the perpetrators and victims are from those States.[220] Many resolutions acknowledge the lack of causation by indicating merely that causes 'may' give rise to terrorism. Even non-aligned States observed that examining the causes of terrorism was 'not in any way intended to justify' it,[221] and no resolution after 1991 has asserted that the causes of terrorism justify it. The dissipation of the 'exception'[222] after the Cold War allowed the Assembly to make progress in later resolutions.

---

[214] See, eg, AAP, 'Opera House graffiti "an act of self defence" ', *Sydney Morning Herald*, 29 July 2004 (anti-Iraq war protesters painted a 'No War' slogan on the Sydney Opera House); R Norton-Taylor and S Hall, 'Lawyers do battle over war advice', *The Guardian*, 10 Mar 2004 (Greenpeace activists chained themselves to tanks at a UK military facility, to prevent the Iraq war, and were charged with aggravated trespass); but see *R v Jones* [2006] UKHL 16.

[215] Ad Hoc Committee Report (1973), n 8, 6, para 17; 13, para 42; Ad Hoc Committee Report (1977), n 13, 35, para 36 (Tanzania); Ad Hoc Committee Report (1979), n 8, 9, para 28; 11, para 35; 13, para 42; 24, paras 81, 86.

[216] Ad Hoc Committee Report (1979), n 8, 23, para 78; 22, para 75.

[217] ibid, 9, para 29; 23, para 78; 24, para 81.

[218] ibid, 22, para 75; 23, para 78.

[219] Wilkinson, n 8, 36; A Dershowitz, *Why Terrorism Works* (Yale University Press, New Haven, 2002) 25; A Cassese, *Terrorism, Politics and Law* (Polity Press, 1989) 137.

[220] W Eubank and L Weinberg, 'Terrorism and Democracy: Perpetrators and Victims' (2001) 13 *Terrorism and Political Violence* 155.

[221] Ad Hoc Committee Report (1979), n 8, 22, para 72.   [222] Cassese, n 2, 124.

International criminal law supports political contentions that terrorism will rarely be justified by necessity or duress. The defences of duress and necessity are often conflated as categories and there remains conceptual ambiguity about the distinction.[223] Generally, duress refers to compulsion by human threats, whereas necessity involves emergencies arising from natural forces or objective circumstances.[224] Necessity is broader than duress,[225] which it encompasses; an act performed under duress is performed out of necessity.

The trend in international criminal law is to combine duress and necessity as a single defence. The 1998 Rome Statute excuses responsibility where conduct:

. . . has been caused by duress resulting from a threat of imminent death or of continuing or imminent serious bodily harm against that person or another person, and the person acts necessarily and reasonably to avoid this threat, provided that the person does not intend to cause a greater harm than the one sought to be avoided. Such a threat may either be: (i) Made by other persons; or (ii) Constituted by other circumstances beyond that person's control.[226]

In addition to the requirements of an imminent serious threat and proportionality, Cassese adds that there must also be no other 'adequate means of averting such evil' (this includes a duty to retreat or to reasonably seek escape)[227] and 'the situation leading to duress or necessity must not have been voluntarily brought about by the person concerned'.[228] Threats to property are insufficient.[229]

(a) A limited defence to terrorism?

In civil law systems, duress is usually a complete defence.[230] In contrast, the defence is often not available at common law for serious crimes such as treason, murder or attempted murder, and is only relevant in mitigation.[231] In

---

[223] Ashworth, n 175, 153, 230; see W Chan and A Simester, 'Duress, Necessity: How Many Defences?' (2005) 16 KCLJ 121; J Horder, 'Self-Defence, Necessity and Duress: Understanding the Relationship' (1998) 11 Can JLJ 143; M Bayles, 'Reconceptualizing Necessity and Duress' in M Corrado (ed), *Justification and Excuse in the Criminal Law* (Garland, New York, 1994) 492; A Brudner, 'A Theory of Necessity' (1987) 7 OJLS 339.

[224] Knoops, n 174, 13; Cassese, n 2, 242; Ashworth, n 175, 227.

[225] Cassese, n 2, 243.　　　[226] 1998 Rome Statute, Art 31(1)(d).

[227] Amnesty International, 'The Quest for International Justice: Defining the Crimes and Defences for the International Criminal Court', 1 Feb 1997, AI Index: IOR 40/006/1997.

[228] Cassese, n 2, 242. The Canadian courts require that there be 'no reasonable opportunity for an alternative course of action that does not involve a breach of the law': *Perka* (1984) 13 DLR (4th) 1.

[229] Ashworth, n 175, 228; Smith, n 188, 257; *DPP v Lynch* [1975] AC 653, 687.

[230] Knoops, n 174, 13. The American Model Penal Code also proposes duress as a defence to all crimes, including homicide: MPC §2.09, Explanatory Note, 374–375.

[231] See, eg, *Howe* [1987] AC 417; *Gotts* [1992] 2 AC 412; *Abbott v R* [1977] AC 755; *Dudley v Stephens* (1884) 14 QBD 273; see also Smith, n 188, 252; A Reed, 'Duress and Provocation as Excuses to Murder: Salutary Lessons from Recent Anglo-American Jurisprudence' (1997) 6 JTLP 51.

Erdemovic (Appeal), the ICTY followed the common law approach in a narrow 3–2 decision, rejecting the defence for war crimes or crimes against humanity that involve the killing of innocents.[232] The traditional rationale is a policy interest in preventing the killing of innocents, even in extreme circumstances of survival. Killing innocents to save oneself is regarded as a greater harm than that which it avoids, and there is no 'absolute or unqualified necessity to preserve one's life'.[233] Self-sacrifice is expected of an 'ordinary man of reasonable fortitude'.[234]

While *Erdemovic (Appeal)* would exclude a plea of necessity to a terrorist killing, lesser terrorist acts might be excused. For example, English cases have found that the defence is available to persons who hijacked aircraft to escape from imminent threats of death or serious injury, by reason of persecution in Iraq or Afghanistan.[235] The United Nations High Commissioner for Refugees (UNHCR) likewise believes that defences of duress and self-defence are relevant in applying the refugee exclusion clauses to hijackers.[236] In the Iraq war, there have been a number of reports of people being coerced, beaten, drugged, or tricked by insurgents into attempting suicide bombings against US forces or the Iraqi authorities.[237]

An important limitation on duress is that the person must not intend to cause greater harm than that sought to be avoided. Thus a trivial fear of persecution will not excuse endangering aircraft, while the killing of passengers will rarely be excused. Like hijacking, hostage-taking may be a necessary and proportionate response to an imminent threat and may be excused by duress. As soon as hostages are killed, however, the act is likely to become disproportionate.

Other terrorist-type offences are less likely to support a plea of duress. Whereas hijacking furnishes control over transport, facilitating escape from imminent peril, other terrorist acts are not so calibrated. Bombing government buildings, shooting randomly into a crowd, or exploding aircraft are far

---

[232] *Erdemovic (Appeals)* IT–96–22 (7 Oct 1997) para 19; R Ehrenreich Brooks, 'Law in the Heart of Darkness: Atrocity and Duress' (2003) 43 Virginia JIL 861.

[233] *Dudley*, n 231, 287.

[234] Smith, n 188, 255; *Howe* [1987] 1 All ER 771, 779–781.

[235] Respectively: *R v Abdul-Hussein*, CA (Crim Div), 17 Dec 1998; [1999] Crim LR 570; *R v Safi* [2003] EWCA Crim 1809; *US v Tiede*, Criminal Case 78–001 (US Crt for Berlin) (1980) 19 ILM 179.

[236] UNHCR, Guidelines on International Protection: Application of the Exclusion Clauses, 4 Sept 2003, HCR/GIP/03/05, para 22; UNHCR, Handbook on Procedures and Criteria for Determining Refugee Status under the 1951 Convention (UNHRC, Geneva, 1992) paras 159–161; J Hathaway, *The Law of Refugee Status* (Butterworths, Toronto, 1991) 218, 221. See, eg, *R v Moussa Membar* Ct App (Crim Div) [1983] Crim L Rev 618 (aircraft hijackers to London from Tanzania were not returned due to fear of persecution);

[237] 'Forced to be a suicide bomber: captured man', *Sydney Morning Herald*, 19 Sept 2005. There are similar reports from the earlier conflict in Lebanon: see L Weinberg, A Pedahzur, and D Canetti-Nisim, 'The Social and Religious Characteristics of Suicide Bombers and Their Victims' (2003) 15 *Terrorism and Political Violence* 139, 140.

less likely to facilitate escape, though the possibility cannot be discounted in extreme circumstances.

While duress/necessity may be available for some sectoral crimes, its application to generic terrorism offences presents other problems. On one hand, if terrorism is defined by its intimidatory or coercive aims, irrespective of the underlying motive, then the defence would remain available, since coercing or intimidating others may supply a means of escape, or alleviate a peril. The defence would, however, be unavailable in the absence of an imminent peril, or where the coercion or intimidation aims not to alleviate peril, but to achieve some wider political, or other, objective.

On the other hand, if terrorism is defined by political motives, the preponderance of such motives will usually negate the basis of duress/necessity. In the above cases, aircraft were not hijacked for political reasons, in that the hijackers were not aiming to change government policies, or to advance a political cause. Rather, the reason for action was escape from persecution. If terrorism is defined by its political motives, the absence of a political motive deprives the act of its terrorist character.

In difficult cases, mixed motives may underlie an act—an intent to avoid imminent peril, coupled with broader political objectives. The concurrent presence of incidental political motives will not negate a genuine claim of duress, as long as the act is the only effective means of avoiding the peril. Conversely, where an act is committed predominantly for political motives, a claim of duress will be likely to fail.

(b) A complete defence to terrorism?

The 1998 Rome Statute departs from *Erdemovic (Appeal)*, since it *excuses* responsibility and is not limited to mitigation.[238] This position was criticized for undermining deterrence,[239] but it recognizes that in extreme cases, ordinary concepts of reasonableness may not apply.[240] Criminal law should not require heroism and it may not always be more harmful to kill an innocent.[241] As argued in dissent in *Erdemovic (Appeal)*, sometimes refusing to kill will save neither the innocent nor the refuser, so there is no real choice between self-preservation and self-sacrifice.[242]

A different situation is where killing one innocent will save two or more lives.[243] The problem with the 'lesser evil' is the 'danger of citizens trying to justify all manner of conduct by reference to overall good effects'.[244] Yet

---

[238] Cassese, n 2, 251.　　　[239] Amnesty, n 227, para 3.2.3.

[240] Ehrenreich Brooks, n 232, 869–873.

[241] Cassese, n 2, 247; Smith, n 188, 255–256; Ehrenreich Brooks, n 232, 880.

[242] Such cases of 'forced choice' typically involve a military instruction to shoot a civilian which, if refused, would be likely to result in the objector being shot along with the civilian.

[243] Ashworth, n 175, 153. (As where a person frozen in fear in a sinking ship blocks an escape route.)　　　[244] ibid.

in some cases 'the autonomy of everyone simply cannot be protected' and difficult choices must be made.[245] Clear cases do not require choosing one innocent victim from others;[246] in other cases, a fair procedure for choosing the victim may be the least worst alternative.

The 1998 Rome Statute does not exclude duress/necessity for even the most serious international crimes. If it is available as a complete defence,[247] it must be limited by strict conditions. Where the killing of innocents is involved, the defence must be strictly construed and difficult to prove, and relevant factors include whether the crime would be committed in any case by someone else, so that self-sacrifice is futile.[248] This realist position acknowledges that 'criminal liability and punishment are inefficacious where a person is subject to such acute threats'.[249]

If duress/necessity may excuse the most serious international crimes, then it may potentially excuse some terrorist killings. Thus, if killing a hostage is the only means of saving a significantly larger number of innocent persons, there is a case for necessity. The graver the peril, the greater the range of acts that may be proportionate, notwithstanding incidental political motives. But, as with self-defence, the indiscriminate violence often associated with terrorism will rarely, if ever, be proportionate, since such killings are unlikely to alleviate the peril. Often there will also be other means of redress available.

(c) Widening the range of threats?

Less serious or generalized threats—such as political oppression or foreign occupation—are not sufficient grounds for claiming duress/necessity for killing innocents; there is no concept of 'political necessity'.[250] The requirement of a threat of imminent death or bodily harm is restrictively interpreted as a threat of external physical violence. In IHL, a person charged with war crimes cannot plead 'personal necessity relating to his own life or comfort, such as that he deprived a protected person of food to preserve his own life', although this may be relevant in mitigation.[251] English courts have similarly held that admitting hunger or homelessness as an excuse for crime would open the door to 'all kinds of lawlessness and disorder'.[252]

The privileging of freedom from physical *violence* (not other harms)

---

[245] ibid, 154.
[246] ibid.
[247] See also *Ohlendorf and others* (*Einsatzgruppen* case) (1953) 15 Ann Dig 656 (duress was a defence to killing innocents).
[248] Cassese, n 2, 250.
[249] Ashworth, n 175, 233.
[250] D Brown, 'Holding Armed Rebel Groups and Terrorist Organizations Accountable for Crimes against Humanity and War Crimes, and for "Terrorist Offences" under International Anti-Terrorist Conventions', Abo Akademi Institute for Human Rights, 2002, 38.
[251] Green, n 41, 305.
[252] *Southwark London Borough v Williams* [1971] 2 All ER 175, 179 (Lord Denning).

reflects the dichotomy in human rights discourse between judicially protected rights (mainly civil and political rights, especially liberty and security of person), and those subject to progressive political realization (social, economic, and cultural rights, especially food and shelter). It also reflects western legal thinking about culpability, which underestimates the material and ideological handicaps which constrain the choices of the poor and powerless.[253]

Less spectacular affronts to bodily integrity—hunger, poverty, violations of economic, social, and cultural rights—are not considered worthy of protection by the defence of duress/necessity. This contrasts with situations arising outside the effective reach of a State's jurisdiction—such as starvation on the high seas—where necessity may still be available.[254] Within society, however, it is assumed that remedies for those ills lie in the realm of politics, policy choices, and welfare programmes.

Yet a minimum level of welfare cannot be assumed in less wealthy or benevolent societies, especially where a State fails to prevent hunger or homelessness, for reasons of ideology, discrimination, or incapacity. The greater the physical deprivation caused by poverty or hunger, the stronger the basis for necessity becomes. So much has been gradually recognized even in a developed State such as England:

'Probably it is now the law that if the taking or the entry was necessary to prevent death or serious injury through starvation or cold there would be a defence of duress of circumstances; but if it were merely to prevent hunger, or the discomforts of cold or homelessness, there would be no defence.'[255]

Even so, it is a conceptual leap from excusing theft or burglary due to hunger to excusing the terrorist killing of innocents; such acts would normally be disproportionate. But the possibility cannot be ruled out in societies experiencing extreme hardship. For example, persons who, during a famine, and to avoid starvation, kill the driver of a government lorry transporting food elsewhere, might plead duress/necessity. Similarly, villagers who kill a local mayor or commissar, to signal to a repressive or negligent government that food aid is urgently required, might plead the defence,[256] although its availability will depend on whether doing so can reasonably be seen as proximately capable of averting the threat of starvation.

In the first case, if terrorism is defined objectively as the killing of public officials, regardless of motive, then the defence may excuse terrorism. In the second case, if terrorism is defined subjectively as violence for coercive or

[253] B Hudson, 'Punishing the Poor' in A Duff et al (eds), *Penal Theory and Practice* (MUP, Manchester, 1994) 302.
[254] Dudley, n 231; *US v Holmes* 26 F Cas 360 (1842).
[255] Smith, n 188, 169.
[256] Consider Stalin's forced famine in Ukraine in the early 1930s, in which 5 million died: R Conquest, *The Great Terror* (Pelican, Middlesex, 1971) 45–46.

intimidatory aims, then the defence also excuses terrorism. Even if terrorism is defined as politically motivated violence, then the second example, involving a political statement about government responsibility for food distribution, might still be excusable. The second example illustrates the earlier point that terrorist acts with mixed motives (political and self-preserving) may still be excusable, depending on the balance of motives.

The important point is that emergency situations with incidental political aspects may sometimes justify killing innocents, but wider moral or political agendas cannot.[257] There is the greatest danger in arguing that the pursuit of abstract rights, not involving threats to life or limb, excuses the killing of innocents. As Berlin warns: 'To cause pain, to kill, to torture are in general rightly condemned; but if these things are done not for my personal benefit but for an ism—socialism, nationalism, fascism, communism, fanatically held religious belief, or progress, or the fulfillment of the laws of history—then they are in order.'[258]

(d) Attenuating 'imminence'?

A further question is whether the standard of 'imminent' serious threats to life or limb is satisfactory. If imminence is regarded as wider than an immediate threat, then terrorism against an oppressive State, which potentially causes future, unspecified, but not immediate harm, may be excused. In the *Einsatzgruppen* case, it was held that a peril need not be as imminent as a loaded gun pointed at a person's head for the defence to be available.[259] The threat must simply be 'imminent, real and inevitable'.[260]

What is less clear is how far beyond such a concrete threat the idea of imminence extends. In cases involving cannibalism by shipwrecked persons adrift on the high seas,[261] starvation was not as immediate a threat as a loaded gun—after all, a rescue ship might have sailed by at any moment. There is always room for doubt, so the question is one of probability. National courts have held that an imminent threat need not be immediate,[262] and may occur in the future,[263] although remote threats of future harm are insufficient. Persons under compulsion must first resort to protection of the law,[264] but this may be no comfort where the State itself is the source of the threat. As stated in *Abdul-Hussein*: 'if Anne Frank had stolen a car to escape from Amsterdam and been charged with theft, the tenets of English law would not, in our judgment, have denied her a defence of duress of circumstances, on the ground that she should have waited for the Gestapo's knock on the door'.[265]

---

[257] Horder, n 223, 156.   [258] Berlin, n 80, 57.
[259] *Einsatzgruppen* case, n 247, 480.   [260] ibid.
[261] See, eg, *Dudley*, n 231; *Holmes*, n 254.
[262] *Abdul-Hussein* [1999] Crim LR 570; cf *Hurst* [1995] 1 Cr App Rep 82, 93; see also Ashworth, n 175, 229; Smith, n 188, 259.
[263] Smith, ibid, 258.   [264] ibid.   [265] *Abdul-Hussein*, n 262, 254.

The less imminent the threat, the more an act assumes a pre-emptive character and loses its basis in necessity. At the same time, the requirement of imminence cannot be so narrowly drawn as to destine an individual to certain death. Acts of a terrorist nature committed to avoid a vaguely anticipated threat—such as that arising from hostile but generalized political statements directed against a social group, falling short of incitement to an international crime—would seldom be excused by necessity.

(e) An individual defence

A final constraint is that necessity does not excuse a person who voluntarily and knowingly joins a group that intends to violate IHL[266] or international criminal law. The person must have knowledge of the nature of the group, and an awareness of the risk of compulsion, although it is not necessary to foresee the particular crime.[267] In an English case, duress was not a defence to a robbery committed due to IRA threats because the defendant had freely and knowingly joined the IRA.[268] The law is similar on the defence of superior orders, which cannot excuse a person who 'voluntarily and consciously joined' a criminal organization like the Gestapo.[269]

Thus persons who voluntarily and knowingly join an unlawful terrorist group cannot plead necessity or superior orders, since such persons have elected to place themselves at risk of criminal compulsion. The fairness of this exclusion depends on the proper identification of groups as criminal, and accordingly, consideration of defences available to group actors is now necessary.

D. CIRCUMSTANCES PRECLUDING GROUP RESPONSIBILITY

Much modern terrorism is planned, financed, committed, or facilitated by organizations of different structures, composition, and objectives. Such organizations have increasingly become subjects of international and national legal regulation, independently of the liabilities of their individual members. Since the early 1990s, the international community, through the Security Council, has designated certain groups as terrorist, outlawing them and authorizing the freezing or confiscation of their assets. The international legal personality of these entities has been denied, since they have been regarded as objects of regulation, without any procedural entitlements.[270]

---

[266] Cassese, n 2, 245; *Einsatzgruppen*, n 247, 91; Amnesty, n 227, para 3.2.3; see also *Sharp* [1987] QB 853 (Lane LCJ); *Shepherd* (1988) 86 Cr App R 47.
[267] *Heath* [2000] Crim LR 109.
[268] *Fitzpatrick* [1977] NI 20.
[269] *Sipo-Brussels* case, Brussels Court Martial, 1519.
[270] See Ch 4 below.

The counterpart of the international criminal law of defences is consideration of the pleas available to group actors accused of terrorism. Whereas international criminal law supplies defences to individual liability for terrorism, there is a normative gap in relation to defences available to group actors. The denial of legal agency to group actors in the international legal system contrasts with the rights of States under the law of State responsibility. A State may plead *circumstances precluding the wrongfulness* of a breach of an international obligation. Yet the International Law Commission's (ILC's) Articles on State Responsibility are silent on the responsibility of non-State entities, noting merely that they are 'without prejudice' to the responsibility of international organizations (Article 57) or individuals (Article 58) under international law. The responsibility of other entities—whether corporations or non-government, charitable, or civil society organizations—is not contemplated. This is true of international law historically[271] and it is 'doubtful whether any *general* regime of responsibility has developed to cover' such groups.[272] Moreover:

The Security Council often addresses recommendations or demands to opposition, insurgent, or rebel groups—but without implying that these have separate personality in international law. Any international responsibility of members of such groups is probably limited to breaches of applicable international humanitarian law or even of national law, rather than general international law.[273]

As Higgins observes, 'individuals are extremely handicapped in international law from the procedural point of view'[274] and the fiction, under the diplomatic protection model, that an injury to a national is assimilable to an injury to their State is unrealistic for entities falsely proscribed as terrorist. Some other remedy is necessary to protect entities or individuals from arbitrary interference with their privacy, home, honour, and reputation,[275] resulting from erroneous proscription. The marginalization of UN treaty bodies in the 'war on terror'[276] makes this all the more necessary.

Proceeding by analogy, it is arguable that at least some of the circumstances precluding wrongfulness under the law of State responsibility should be available to entities proscribed as terrorist under international law. Of particular relevance are self-defence (Article 21) and necessity (Article 25). These defences might be raised where groups breach the international

---

[271] R McCorquodale, 'The Individual and the International Legal System' in M Evans (ed), *International Law* (OUP, Oxford, 2003) 299, 306.

[272] J Crawford and S Olleson, 'The Nature and Forms of International Responsibility' in Evans (ed), n 271, 445, 447.

[273] ibid.

[274] R Higgins, *Problems and Processes* (Clarendon, Oxford, 2003) 51.

[275] 1966 ICCPR, Art 17.

[276] J Fitzpatrick, 'Speaking Law to Power: The War against Terrorism and Human Rights' (2003) 14 EJIL 241, 260–263.

obligation, affirmed in the practice of the General Assembly and the Security Council, not to engage in terrorist activity.[277]

It is difficult to see why non-State actors should not be entitled to similar equitable dispensations as States in situations where they are being held responsible for international wrongs. This is not to treat non-State groups as international legal persons equivalent to States.[278] As the International Court of Justice (ICJ) stated in *Reparation for Injuries*: 'The subjects of law in any legal system are not necessarily identical in their nature or in the extent of their rights, and their nature depends on the needs of the community.'[279]

A group actor is,[280] like a State, 'capable of possessing international rights and duties' and has the 'capacity to maintain its rights by bringing international claims'.[281] The degree of participation of group actors depends 'on the particular area of the international legal system concerned and the activity and involvement of entities in that area'.[282] For entities proscribed as terrorist, the serious personal and financial consequences of proscription give rise to an expectation that those affected are entitled to a fair and transparent procedure before their vital interests are impaired.

1. Self-defence

ILC Article 21 precludes the wrongfulness of a lawful act of self-defence in conformity with the UN Charter. Self-defence does not preclude the wrongfulness of conduct contrary to IHL and non-derogable human rights provisions.[283] As stated in the *Nuclear Weapons Advisory Opinion*, customary IHL is 'intransgressible'.[284] Acts of self-defence must respect any rules of 'total restraint' applying in armed conflict, as well as satisfying customary requirements of necessity and proportionality.[285]

National self-defence has historically been thought of only as a right of States, or of para-Statal entities such as self-determination movements forcibly denied their rights, and as a Charter right it can only be claimed by States.[286] Yet on ethical grounds, Rodin questions 'why the right to use collective violence should be limited to States', and not be extended to other

---

[277] See Ch 4 below.
[278] Indeed, some modification of the concepts applicable to States may, however, be necessary in transposing circumstances precluding wrongfulness to non-State entities.
[279] *Reparation for Injuries (Advisory Opinion)* (1949) ICJ Reports 174, 178–179.
[280] McCorquodale, n 271, 302.
[281] *Reparation for Injuries*, n 279.
[282] McCorquodale, n 271, 303.
[283] *Legality of the Threat or Use of Nuclear Weapons* (1996) ICJ Reports 226, para 25.
[284] ibid, para 79.
[285] ibid, para 41; *Nicaragua*, n 95, paras 176, 194; J Gardam, 'Proportionality and Force in International Law' (1993) 87 AJIL 391.
[286] Cassese, n 33, 197.

human communities which 'do not coincide with the boundaries of States'[287] (nor even with the boundaries of self-determination units).

State practice does not necessarily furnish a principled answer, because it is in the interests of States to limit the right to use violence to themselves; this is also true of the Charter system of collective security, which is an expression of an international community constructed primarily by States and usually in their interests. The issue is important because non-State violence is often characterized as terrorist, especially where it is below an armed conflict, and even if humanitarian restraint is exercised.

Restricting the use of force to States is usually justified because the State embodies 'a genuine community capable of exercising a form of collective autonomy'.[288] But the legal fiction of a homogenous 'people' expressing self-determination is exploded by a cursory examination of the many other communities which attract an individual's allegiance—religious, ethnic, social, or political. It is 'difficult to see why such groups should be denied an analogous right to defend their integrity with force'.[289] (Consider violent State persecution of ethnic or religious groups, as in Kosovo, to which civil society groups respond in 'self-defence'.) The nation is but one expression of identity deserving protection, if necessary by force.

Further, the traditional objective criteria of Statehood—political independence, territorial control, and a permanent population[290]—are morally 'empty',[291] or embody the peculiar morality of *realpolitik*: 'The only test is internal naked power'.[292] States need not be coextensive with self-determination units, and the people's sovereignty has not yet displaced the sovereign's sovereignty.[293] As such, it is hard to appreciate the moral basis on which to privilege the use of force by States over other social units.

Limiting the right to use force to States might be defended because a State monopoly limits the spread of international violence. Certainly there is pragmatic appeal in preventing the privatization of violence, and the entrenchment of communal fragmentation or tribalism by force. The field of lawful violence is limited to less than 200 States, rather than encompassing many thousands of group actors. Too much diversity, if imposed by force, is objectionable on public order grounds.

Yet the opposite might equally be true: too little diversity, backed up by force, is also dangerous—if not more so. By concentrating the authority to use force in States, the destructive potential of violence is vastly magnified, since States often command greater resources and organizational capacities than other communities. Violence may occur less often, but it may cause greater harm. A group right of self-defence may help to deter the abuse of

---

[287] Rodin, n 61, 160, 158.   [288] ibid, 160.   [289] ibid.
[290] 1933 Montevideo Convention on Rights and Duties of States, Art 1.
[291] Rodin, n 61, 119.   [292] Reisman, n 124, 874.   [293] ibid, 869.

power by States. Groups will act defensively when attacked anyway, so it is better to decriminalize and structure their use of force.

At present, international law considers the use of force by non-State actors (outside armed conflict) largely as an internal affair, subject to basic human rights obligations. There is no right to collective 'self-defence' by sub-State communities. Yet if terrorism is internationally criminalized, international law can no longer ignore claims to self-defence by non-State groups, since group self-defence may be a vital justification for violence characterized by States as terrorist. The same is true of acts of group self-defence which occur across a frontier, below the level of an armed attack. A legal system that confers duties without rights will struggle to maintain legitimacy, particularly given the limited application of individual criminal defences.

Group self-defence is conceptually closer to individual self-defence than national self-defence, since requiring an 'armed attack' on a non-State community as a precondition of self-defence sets the threshold too high. For example, a State policy of genocide, or violent persecution, against an ethnic group may not amount to a conventional, military 'armed attack', yet it is clearly serious enough to trigger group self-defence. Whether conduct is necessary in self-defence should be based on a strict and objective assessment, leaving no room for discretion by the group itself, just as these requirements apply to State actors.[294] *Collective* group self-defence might also be admitted, where a group requests assistance from other groups (domestic or international), particularly given the failure of States to fulfil obligations to prevent genocide,[295] or to prevent mass human rights violations through the Security Council.

2. *Necessity: Knowing the law*

ILC Article 25 provides that necessity may not be invoked by a State unless it (a) 'is the only means for the State to safeguard an essential interest against a grave and imminent peril' and (b) it 'does not seriously impair an essential interest of the State or States towards which the obligation exists, or of the international community as a whole'.[296] Necessity may not be invoked if the international obligation excludes it, or the State has contributed to the situation of necessity.[297] While the 'existence and

---

[294] *Nicaragua*, n 95, para 242.

[295] 1948 Genocide Convention, Art 1; consider failures in Rwanda and Bosnia in the 1990s, and Cambodia in the late 1970s; see, eg, S Power, *A Problem from Hell: America and the Age of Genocide* (Flamingo, London, 2003); P Gourevitch, *We wish to inform you that tomorrow we will be killed with our families* (Picador, London, 1999).

[296] See also *Gabčíkovo-Nagymaros Project* (1997) ICJ Reports 7, paras 50–51 (those conditions reflect custom).

[297] 2001 ILC Articles on State Responsibility, Art 25(2)(a)–(b).

limits' of the plea have been controversial, on balance it is considered available.[298]

A claim of necessity precludes wrongfulness and is thus a justification.[299] It is subject to stringent conditions due to its exceptional nature. Whether an act is justified 'depends on all the circumstances, and cannot be prejudged'.[300] The peril must be 'objectively established and not merely apprehended as possible' or 'contingent', and it must be 'imminent in the sense of proximate'.[301] There must be no lawful means available to avert the danger, and any action taken must be strictly necessary.[302] The State's interest must objectively outweigh other competing considerations.[303]

Similar ethical considerations apply to the plea of necessity by non-State communities as apply to self-defence. It is possible to conceive of grave and imminent perils to the essential interests of other human communities,[304] particularly peril caused by States. State decision-making, about whether an act is required to safeguard an essential interest, is not necessarily more valid than corresponding decisions by groups. States do not always represent the interests of their populations, and smaller social units may be more responsive to the essential interests of their members.

On the other hand, the problems of recognition and representativeness of non-State groups are well known,[305] and caution against a simple extension of necessity to non-State groups. Less structured groups may have fewer lines of accountability and restraint in decision-making, although the same may be true of authoritarian States. Further, non-State actors may not be constrained by the tradition of Westphalian ethics[306] and strategies of containment and deterrence which shape State conduct.

If it were admitted, a group defence of necessity would seldom justify the killing of innocents to avert imminent danger. The dictum that 'necessity knows no law'[307] is not part of the modern law, which is circumscribed by strict legal conditions. In particular, a breach of a norm of *jus cogens* remains wrongful and unjustifiable.[308] As Lauterpacht notes, necessity 'has been

---

[298] J Crawford, *The International Law Commission's Articles on State Responsibility: Introduction, Texts and Commentaries* (CUP, Cambridge, 2002) 182–183; cf Brownlie, n 30, 468.

[299] cf Lauterpacht, n 29, 298 (there is no State right of self-preservation; necessity is only an excuse).

[300] Crawford, n 298, 183.

[301] ibid, 183–184. A long-term peril is imminent as soon as it is established that the realization of the peril is certain and inevitable: *Gabčíkovo-Nagymaros Project* (1997) ICJ Reports 7, 42, para 54.

[302] Crawford, n 298, 184.   [303] ibid.

[304] See, eg, C Coady, 'Terrorism, Morality and Supreme Emergency' in Primoratz (ed), n 173, 80, 88–93 (questioning Walzer's restriction of necessity to States).

[305] See 'E "Illegal but Justifiable" Terrorism' below.

[306] C Gearty, 'Terrorism and Human Rights', Paper at ESIL Conference, Florence, 13–15 May 2004.

[307] Von Bethmann-Hollweg, 4 Aug 1914, in (1916) III *Jahrbuch des Voelkerrechts* 728.

[308] 2001 ILC Articles on State Responsibility, Art 26.

invoked as justifying all the horrors of war, the sacrifice of human life, and the destruction of property and devastation of territory'.[309] The intentional targeting of civilians is very hard to justify and requires 'a substantial case that it is highly likely to prevent worse horrors',[310] and there is always a danger of 'moral monstrosities threatened by unbounded consequentialism'.[311]

Further, necessity 'is not intended to cover conduct which is in principle regulated by the primary obligations'.[312] Importantly, IHL expressly excludes reliance on military necessity,[313] including forbidding reprisals against protected persons under Protocol I,[314] which would now render area (or 'terror') bombing, as in the Second World War, unlawful.[315] However, the customary law on reprisals against civilians remains controversial.[316] While the provisions on reprisals in the 1949 Geneva Conventions arguably reflect customary law,[317] the wider prohibitions in Protocol I are less well established. Reprisals against civilians in unoccupied enemy territory are probably still permitted under customary law.[318] The 2004 International Committee of the Red Cross (ICRC) study of customary IHL does not claim the existence of any customary prohibition on such reprisals, merely stating in rule 145 that 'belligerent reprisals are subject to stringent conditions' where they are not prohibited by international law. Some major States continue to assert that a belligerent may violate IHL in proportion to an initial severe violation of IHL by another belligerent, to compel the violator to terminate the unlawful conduct. In internal conflicts, even the relevant treaty law (Protocol II) contains no

[309] Lauterpacht (*vol II*), n 112, 208–209.

[310] Glover, n 65, 85.

[311] Horder, n 223, 156; see generally J Taurek, 'Should the Numbers Count?' (1977) 6 *Philosophy and Public Affairs* 293; P Pettit, 'Consequentialism and Respect for Persons' (1989) 100 *Ethics* 116.

[312] Crawford, n 298, 185.

[313] ibid; Green, n 41, 305; Morris and Scharf, n 180, 279.

[314] Green, n 41, 352–353; *Kupreškić* ICTY–95–16 (14 Jan 2000) para 533; Cassese, n 102, 341; see also S Nahlik, 'Belligerent Reprisals as Seen in the Light of the Diplomatic Conference on Humanitarian Law, Geneva, 1974–1977' (1978) 42 *Law and Contemporary Problems* 36; M Bristol, 'The Laws of War and Belligerent Reprisals against Enemy Civilian Populations' (1979) 21 *Air Force Law Review* 397; R Bierzanek, 'Reprisals in Armed Conflicts' (1988) 14 Syracuse JIL and Com 829; S Darcy, 'The Evolution of the Law of Belligerent Reprisals' (2003) 175 *Military Law Review* 184.

[315] cf Green, n 41, 353. For ethical arguments against area bombing in the Second World War, see Walzer, n 81, 255–263.

[316] Detter, n 32, 299–303; S Oeter, 'Means and Methods of Combat' in Fleck (ed), n 47, 105, 207; E Kwakwa, 'Belligerent Reprisals in the Law of Armed Conflict' (1991) 27 Stan JIL 49, 52.

[317] ICRC Study, vol I, n 56, rules 146–147; A Mitchell, 'Does One Illegality Merit Another: The Law of Belligerent Reprisals in International Law' (2001) 170 *Military Law Review* 155, 163; Kwakwa, n 316, 56–58; F Hampson, 'Belligerent Reprisals and the 1977 Protocols to the Geneva Conventions of 1949' (1988) 37 ICLQ 818, 824.

[318] C Greenwood, 'The Twilight of the Law of Belligerent Reprisals' (1989) 20 Neth YBIL 35, 62–64; Oeter, n 316, 207; Kwakwa, n 316, 72; F Kalshoven, *Belligerent Reprisals* (Sijthoff, Leiden, 1971) 360–361 (prior to Protocol I); see also F Kalshoven, 'Belligerent Reprisals Revisited' (1990) 21 Neth YBIL 43, 79–80.

prohibitions at all on reprisals, although the ICRC study asserts in rule 148 that parties to non-international armed conflicts 'do not have the right to resort to belligerent reprisals'.

Moreover, in the *Nuclear Weapons Advisory Opinion*, the ICJ found that, under the law of self-defence, the use of nuclear weapons might not be unlawful in an extreme case where the survival of a State is at risk.[319] If the use of nuclear weapons by States is not always unlawful, then their similar use against civilians by non-State groups might analogously be justified where the group's survival is at risk. However, the ICJ did not clarify whether IHL norms, including those on reprisals and proportionality, could be breached (such as permitting the targeting of non-military objectives), or if pre-emptive nuclear strikes to ensure a State's survival are permitted.[320] The prohibition on reprisals in Protocol I is controversial in part because of its potential challenge to the legal validity of strategic nuclear deterrence by major States.[321] Reprisal is not precluded as a defence before the ICC.[322]

The ICJ further did not explain whether the 'survival' of a State referred to the physical survival of the State's inhabitants, or whether it also refers to its political survival. If 'survival' refers merely to maintaining political independence or territorial integrity, it is difficult to see how the destruction and irradiation of enemy civilians, territory and environment, and future generations, is justified simply to preserve a local government over a foreign one. Despite the importance of a State's political survival and the values it sustains,[323] the common life is not a 'source of value independent of its value for individual persons',[324] or as important as their survival.[325]

(a) Terror of necessity: suicide bombing

In conflicts beneath an armed conflict, where IHL does not apply, or it applies but liberation forces are unrecognized,[326] necessity may preclude the responsibility of non-State groups. Honderich defends Palestinian suicide bombing against Israel as a moral right—'terrorism for humanity'—as the only effective means for freeing Palestinians from Israeli domination.[327] A right of self-determination is meaningless without a remedy and terrorism is

---

[319] *Legality of the Threat or Use of Nuclear Weapons* (1996) ICJ Reports 226, paras 97–97.
[320] Cassese, n 102, 337.   [321] Oeter, n 316, 207.
[322] W Schabas, *An Introduction to the International Criminal Court* (CUP, Cambridge, 2002) 73, 88.
[323] B Williams, *Morality* (CUP, Cambridge, 1972) 36.   [324] Rodin, n 61, 143.
[325] Williams, n 323, 35; cf Walzer, n 81, 254, who believes that 'the survival and freedom of political communities . . . are the highest values of international society'.
[326] Although like the argument about 'non-innocent civilians' discussed above, the argument for suicide bombing also challenges the foundations of IHL itself.
[327] Honderich, n 146, 151, 170; see also T Honderich, 'Is There a Right to Terrorism?', Lecture at the University of Leipzig, 19 Oct 2003; see also Weinberg et al, n 237, 146 (summarizing similar arguments by Hamas and Islamic Jihad).

thought justifiable where it has a decent probability of achieving its ends at a cost that makes it worthwhile.[328] Honderich relies on analogies with the deliberate killing of innocents by western States in the naval blockade of Germany in the First World War and by terror and atomic bombing in the Second World War.[329]

While Israel is not party to Protocol I, Palestinian attacks on Israeli soldiers, which may be treated as terrorism under domestic law, are plainly of a different moral order than Palestinian attacks on Israeli non-combatants. On the other hand, the 'necessity' argument for Palestinian suicide bombing of Israeli civilians fails for at least five reasons. First, Palestinians do not face a 'grave and imminent peril' of the kind envisaged as necessity. The weight of opinion holds that Palestinians suffer from an oppressive military occupation, unlawful settlements, economic privations, and serious rights violations. A denial of self-determination is the denial of a peremptory norm. But Palestinians are not experiencing genocide, extermination, or a threat to their survival as grave as that anticipated by the law of necessity. Foreign occupation is an insufficient threat, and is, moreover, dealt with by the primary rules of IHL, although the absence of reciprocity as a constraint in situations of occupation may encourage more radical, exceptional responses to breaches of IHL by the occupier.

Second, permitting the deliberate targeting of Israeli civilians would impair a countervailing essential interest of both Israel and the international community as a whole—the right to life of innocent civilians. Deliberately killing Israelis is a means disproportionate to the peril it seeks to alleviate. Third, killing civilians may be too remote from the political end sought, since terrorist acts have steeled Israel's will and have probably increased, not reduced, Israeli domination of Palestinian lives.[330] Due to the political, security, and religious motives underpinning Israel's persistent claim to Palestine, Israel responds to terrorism with excessive and escalating violence of its own. This is a difficult question of political judgment; Israel's withdrawal from Gaza in 2005 might be seen as a tangible gain from decades of Palestinian terrorism. Contrarily, Israel's construction of a 'security' barrier in the West Bank, its continued expansion of unlawful settlements there, and its retreat from promises made in the Oslo Accords indicate that terrorism has not far advanced the Palestinian cause.

Fourth, unlike States, which monopolize national political decision-making, it is not clear that terrorists express the will of the Palestinian people.

[328] Honderich, n 146, 184–185.
[329] ibid, 162.
[330] Wilkinson, n 8, 186; Weinberg et al, n 237, 146, though noting, at 141, the strategic successes of suicide bombing by Hamas and Islamic Jihad (which has a psychological effect on Israelis and Palestinians; narrowed the ratio of Israeli-Palestinian fatalities in the conflict since 2001; and helped to disrupt peace negotiations between the rival Fatah-led Palestinian Authority and Israel, contributing to the defeat of the Peres government).

Fragmentation and factionalism make it difficult to identify clear lines of Palestinian political authority. Some terrorist attacks are launched by secret militant groups outside political or civilian control. Other attacks derive from extreme quasi-religious justifications of self-sacrifice and martyrdom, rather than from the political goal of self-determination. Finally, it is not obvious that alternatives to suicide bombing—including the faltering but not extinct peace process—have been exhausted. Suicide bombing to improve one's bargaining position may be strategic, but it is not of necessity.

Arguments for suicide bombing rely on a fundamental objection to the asymmetry of power between States and non-State actors. Terrorism is considered the only effective weapon[331] available to the weak and disempowered, who cannot hope to win by regular methods against modern, well-resourced, militarized States.[332] There is intuitive appeal to this view, which assumes that power disparity is unfair and that the law should redistribute power. There is also a policy argument that terrorism minimizes violence, where liberation forces tactically choose not to escalate a dispute into an armed conflict, and instead employ low-intensity terrorist methods, although it is rarely possible to predict the level of violence that is likely to ensue.[333]

Yet, it is difficult to see why the fact of unequal resources triggers an entitlement to use irregular methods, to even up the odds. Nothing in IHL presupposes equality of power between adversaries (as opposed to procedural 'fair play').[334] Conflict is intimately founded on achieving superiority of power, and to manipulate IHL to equalize power differences is simply unrealistic. There would no longer be any incentive for States to comply with IHL, and any exceptions accorded to liberation movements would be reciprocally resorted to by States.

Further, equalizing power might perversely prolong conflict and make it more destructive, since evenly matched forces may fight for longer. Focusing on asymmetry of power also conceals the extent to which tactics and strategy (such as lawful guerrilla warfare) can challenge superior power. The objections to targeting 'non-innocent' civilians were described earlier. Allowing new methods of violence would also widen the sphere of violence, without sufficient justification.

---

[331] Y Alexander, 'Democracy and Terrorism: Threats and Responses' (1996) 26 IYBHR 253, 257; Larschan, n 139, 121; cf Wilkinson, n 8, 50–51; J Lambert, *Terrorism and Hostages in International Law* (Grotius, Cambridge, 1990) 24.

[332] Ignatieff, n 57, 1150; T Pfanner, 'Asymmetrical Warfare from the Perspective of Humanitarian Law and Humanitarian Action' (2005) 87 IRRC 149; C Card, 'Making War on Terrorism in Response to 9/11' in J Sterba (ed), *Terrorism and International Justice* (OUP, Oxford, 2003) 171, 174; Lambert, n 331, 31; Cassese, n 219, 4; G Guillaume, 'Terrorism and International Law', Grotius Lecture, BIICL, London, 13 Nov 2003, 2; Alexander, n 331, 264; Walzer, n 81, 197.

[333] See, eg, R Young, 'Political Terrorism as a Weapon of the Politically Powerless' in Primoratz (ed), n 173, 55, 61. As Yasser Arafat said: 'Nobody knows how the mechanism of war develops': quoted in Fisk, n 166, 553.

[334] T Meron, 'The Humanization of Humanitarian Law' (2000) 94 AJIL 239, 240.

Finally, analogies with naval blockade, or terror and atomic bombing, are anachronistic. Starving an enemy population, as in the First World War, or indiscriminately area bombing or atomic bombing civilians, as in the Second World War, are no longer acceptable means of warfare. Because such means are forbidden by the primary rules of IHL, necessity is not available as a circumstance precluding the wrongfulness of such acts. Such analogies are also flawed, because at the time, terror and atomic bombing were justified more by arguments about targeting legitimate military objectives, and/or reprisals, than by arguments of necessity.

Even if necessity-based arguments for terror and atomic bombing are considered, such arguments fail. Such methods were used later in the war— after the 'supreme emergency' had passed—not to ensure Nazi or Japanese defeat, or even to prevent genocide—but merely to improve the speed and price (in Allied lives saved) of victory.[335] It is also difficult to appreciate how killing German civilians, to undermine morale, was related to the end of a Nazi defeat, since it may have contrarily steeled the German will to resist[336] (although exterminating a population inevitably defeats it).

At the same time, unless divine or natural law is accepted, an absolute prohibition on killing innocents is difficult to defend, since it embodies a poor sense of proportion if refusing to kill some innocents leads to the death of many more.[337] Despite the danger of 'moral monstrosities threatened by unbounded consequentialism',[338] it is 'paradoxical to justify fighting a bloody war by saying Hitler must be defeated, and then to accept absolute restrictions which may mean the war is followed by Hitler's victory'.[339] It is clear that States have often vacillated between the desirability of absolute moral prohibitions on certain types of violence and the necessity of exceptions, often justified by consequentialist reasoning. Yet, if terror bombing was not

---

[335] Walzer, n 81, 261, 263–268; Glover, n 65, 83, 89–112; F Taylor, *Dresden* (Bloomsbury, London, 2004) 403. Walzer distinguishes area bombing earlier in the war as justified by necessity, when it was the only offensive weapon available to Britain to avert the evil of a Nazi victory. By early 1945, Japan's economy was close to collapse and the US knew that Japan had approached Stalin to sue for peace.

[336] Glover, n 65, 75; S Garrett, 'Terror Bombing of German Cities in World War II' in Primoratz (ed), n 173, 141, 153; Further, in a secret police State, political authority does not depend so much on civilian support; Hitler fought on regardless of German morale, until the Soviets reached Berlin.

[337] Glover, n 65, 109. After 11 Sept 2001, the US President ordered hijacked aircraft to be shot down: O Burkeman, 'Panic and delay wrecked 9/11 response', *The Guardian*, 18 June 2004; but in 2006 the German Constitutional Court held that such an order would violate the right to life and human dignity: BVerFG, 1 BvR 357/05 (15 Feb 2006). Consider also the debate about torturing terrorists in the 'ticking bomb' scenario: see B Saul, 'Torturing Terrorists after September 11: Dershowitz' Torture Warrant' (2004) 27 *International Journal of Law and Psychiatry* 645; S Levinson (ed), *Torture: A Collection* (OUP, Oxford, 2004); Dershowitz, n 219, ch 3: 'Should the Ticking Bomb Terrorist Be Tortured?', 131–163.

[338] Horder, n 223, 156.

[339] Glover, n 65, 85.

justified by necessity in the extreme case of Nazi aggression, the justification for Palestinian suicide bombing is even less convincing, given the lesser seriousness of the Israeli threat.[340] Prudentially, if necessity is thought to excuse terrorism, then it might equally excuse other sorts of severe harm, such as torture or the use of chemical, biological, or nuclear weapons.

E. 'ILLEGAL BUT JUSTIFIABLE' TERRORISM

While there is broad support for the view that political violence is sometimes justified, there remains disagreement on *when* it is justified. Insisting on non-violence in the face of chronic injustices 'can be tantamount to confirmation and reinforcement of those injustices'.[341] From the foregoing analysis, individual criminal defences and group defences seldom justify or excuse terrorist acts, due to stringent requirements of imminence and proportionality. Further, there is no combatant immunity for internal rebels or unrecognized self-determination forces, nor in situations of internal dissent below an armed conflict. The question now is whether there is some other way of accommodating reasonable arguments for 'terrorist' violence.

One method is to regard terrorist acts as 'illegal but justifiable', where they are collectively committed in defence of fundamental human rights against an oppressive State. Recognizing such a plea is preferable to attenuating the strict conditions of existing defences to accommodate justifiable terrorist claims. Treating certain terrorist acts as criminal but justifiable is also less ambitious than developing a positive international right to rebel, or extending combatant immunity to rebels and unrecognized liberation forces. Regarding conduct as 'wrongful but excused' also strengthens the normative pull of international law.[342]

The NATO bombing of Kosovo has been defended as a case of humanitarian necessity, justifying a breach of the prohibition on the use of force.[343] Morality-based, equitable exceptions to legal rules, 'in unforeseeable and extraordinarily grave circumstances',[344] ensure the law's legitimacy, and hence

---

[340] Although in the past, Israeli leaders have advocated mass expulsion, or even extermination, of Palestinians: see B Saul, 'A Just Peace, Not Just Any Peace', Palestinian Initiative for the Promotion of Global Dialogue and Democracy, Ramallah, Oct 2003.

[341] M Reisman, 'Private Armies in a Global War System: Prologue to Decision' (1973) 14 Van JIL 1, 32–33; see also Ignatieff, n 57, 1149.

[342] V Lowe, 'Precluding Wrongfulness or Responsibility: A Plea for Excuses' (1999) 10 EJIL 405.

[343] Independent International Commission on Kosovo, *Kosovo Report: Conflict, International Response, Lessons Learned* (2000). Humanitarian intervention is not a plea of necessity, as circumstance precluding wrongfulness under the law of State of responsibility, but a purported exception to the primary rules on the use of force: Crawford, n 298, 185–186.

[344] T Franck, *Recourse to Force* (CUP, Cambridge, 2002) 185.

encourage compliance with it.[345] The legal effect of considering an act illegal but justifiable is mitigation of sanctions, rather than exculpation.[346] The justifiability of an act may be determined by the 'global jury' of UN organs.[347] That the doctrine is open to abuse is not fatal, just as abuse of self-defence does not render that right untenable.[348]

In General Assembly debates in the 1970s, there was some support for the view that terrorism is sometimes illegal but justifiable. Some States suggested that 'terrorism directed at democratic regimes where institutional means of redress existed' should be distinguished from 'popular upsurge against oppressive regimes'.[349] On this view, 'although terrorism was never justified, resort to violence was particularly inadmissible in democratic societies'.[350] The implication was that rebellion against oppressive regimes is less 'inadmissible' than violence against a democracy. Further, some States noted that while motive is irrelevant to the commission of a crime, it may be a mitigating factor determining punishment.[351]

The foremost difficulty in accepting the idea of 'illegal but justifiable' terrorism is ascertaining the criteria for distinguishing oppressive regimes from democratic (or rights-respecting) ones,[352] particularly given the variation in degree of both oppression and democracy, and subjective differences of perception.[353] Thus, in *Tehran Hostages*, Judge Tarazi argued in dissent that in weighing Iran's responsibility for the US embassy occupation, factors that should be taken into account included popular dissatisfaction with links between the Shah of Iran and 'the exigencies of American worldwide and Middle-East strategy', 'the context of the revolution', and its 'break with a past condemned as oppressive'.[354]

In spite of the subjectivity of 'oppression', international human rights law, coupled with the law of the Charter, supplies a minimum legal framework of evaluation for international organs, although the degree of oppression justifying resistance remains a matter of appreciation in a particular case. It is also possible to draw on debates about the right of rebellion, and humanitarian intervention,[355] which have grappled with the same basic problem of when

---

[345] ibid, 178; 175, 177, 185, 197, 190.
[346] ibid, 179.   [347] ibid, 186.   [348] ibid, 185.
[349] Ad Hoc Committee Report (1979), n 8, 23–24, para 80; 19–20, para 67.
[350] ibid, 23–24, para 80.   [351] ibid, 7–8, para 24.   [352] Honoré, n 85, 48.
[353] MC Bassiouni, 'A Policy-Oriented Inquiry into the Different Forms and Manifestations of "International Terrorism"' in MC Bassiouni (ed), *Legal Responses to International Terrorism* (Martinus Nijhoff, Dordrecht, 1988) xv, xxxii.
[354] *Tehran Hostages (Merits)* case, (1980) ICJ Reports 3, paras 62–63 (opinion of Tarazi J), although such 'links do not in any way justify the occupation'.
[355] S Chesterman, *Just War or Just Peace?* (OUP, Oxford, 2002) 229–232, distils the conditions of intervention from the literature, including: (1) severe and immediate rights abuses; (2) no realistic peaceful alternative; (3) collective action must have failed; (4) action must be limited to what is necessary to prevent further violations; and (5) the actor must be relatively disinterested, acting predominantly for humanitarian objectives.

rights abuses are serious enough to warrant action. At a minimum, serious, repeated, and sustained violations of fundamental rights are necessary,[356] even if violations are limited to 'systematic disenfranchisement of minorities'.[357] Even in democracies, the preferences of minorities may not always be sufficiently accommodated.[358]

A second criterion, advanced in the Ad Hoc Committee, is the availability of effective means of peaceful redress, which must be exhausted before terrorism is justifiable.[359] This condition minimizes non-State violence by regarding it as a remedy of last resort, consistent with the regulation of force in international law generally. Exhaustion of remedies is an established juridical standard in other branches of law, such as regional human rights systems,[360] and in diplomatic protection claims.[361]

While it is easier to determine whether *legal* mechanisms are exhausted (ie has a final decision been made? Is appeal futile? Has a judgment been enforced or obeyed?), the exhaustion of non-legal redress is more difficult to discern. For example, to resort prematurely to violence might be unjustified while a peace process is under way, but consider the sporadic Middle East peace process—at what point is it safe to judge that the process is exhausted?

This leads to a further problem in evaluating claims of justification—who genuinely represents a non-State group, entitled to make judgments about the resort to violence? With States, this is (usually) clear, since the lines of political authority are neatly drawn (excepting in civil conflicts where there are problems of recognition). For a valid claim of self-determination, there must be a body representative of the 'people',[362] a 'radically indeterminate' term[363] only partially clarified by the practice of recognition by the relevant regional organization and UN organs.[364]

Non-State groups are frequently riven with competing factions claiming to represent the group—consider fragmented loyalties among Palestinians, or competition between the ANC and Inkatha under apartheid. As Ashrawi says of suicide bombings: 'Nobody gave Hamas or Jihad the mandate to

[356] Ignatieff, n 57, 1156; B Palmer, 'Codification of Terrorism as an International Crime' in Bassiouni (ed), n 83, 507, 512–513; MC Bassiouni, 'Criminological Policy' in A Evans and J Murphy (eds), *Legal Aspects of International Terrorism* (ASIL, Washington, DC, 1979) 523, 530; Bassiouni, n 353, xlv; Franck and Lockwood, n 119, 88.
[357] Ignatieff, n 57, 1155.
[358] Eubank and Weinberg, n 220, 163.
[359] Ad Hoc Committee Report (1979), n 8, 19–20, para 67; see also Walzer, n 81, 204; Ignatieff, n 57, 1153, 1156; Bassiouni, n 353, xxxi; MC Bassiouni, 'Methodological Options for International Legal Control of Terrorism' in Bassiouni (ed), n 83, 485, 491; Palmer, n 356, 512–513.
[360] ECHR, Art 35(1); 1969 ACHR, Art 46(1)(a).
[361] *Interhandel* case (1959) ICJ Reports 6, 26–27; *Ambatielos Arbitration* (1956) 12 RIAA 83; *Finnish Ships Arbitration* (1934) 3 RIAA 1479, 1535; *Panevezys-Saldutiskis Railway* case (1939) PCIJ Series A/B, No 76; *El Oro Mining and Railway Co* case (1931) 5 RIAA 191; Brownlie, n 30, 496–506.
[362] Cassese, n 33, 146–147.   [363] Crawford, n 35, 18.   [364] Cassese, n 54, 94.

carry out these actions in the name of the Palestinians.'[365] The problem is accentuated where well-organized movements assume trappings of political authority (control of territory and a population, and structures of govern-ance), yet are not widely supported by the people they claim to represent—consider the Tamil Tigers, or the IRA.

Who speaks or acts in the name of whole groups of people is fundamental to the problem of terrorism. It is commonly small, radicalized sub-groups of larger populations experiencing oppression which resort to indiscriminate violence. Participatory decision-making is rarely—if ever—part of the pro-cess leading to terrorism, and clandestine, militarized operations are a hallmark of terrorist groups. While participatory politics may not always produce restraint, it is likely to generate more restraint on random killings than an absence of participation altogether.

It must be noted, however, that some groups regarded as terrorist by the international community have been popularly elected by their own constitu-ents. For example, in mid-2005, Hezbollah and the more moderate Amal organization won all 23 seats in southern Lebanon in the first general election after the withdrawal of Syrian forces.[366] While this may be perceived as popular endorsement of terrorism, many voters supported Hezbollah as a defensive militant group against any future Israeli incursions into Lebanon. Over time, it is possible that Hezbollah's participation in regular political processes may help to civilize its methods. Such a view underlies moves by some States to negotiate with Hamas after it won Palestinian elections in early 2006. Again, while Hamas has engaged in suicide bombing, its electoral support is probably more attributable to its humanitarian efforts and dissatis-faction with corruption and maladministration in the Fatah-dominated Palestinian Authority. Even so, terrorism may still be politically popular; an opinion poll by the British Ministry of Defence found that 65 per cent of Iraqis believed suicide attacks against British and American troops were justified.[367]

A defensible theory of justification for terrorist acts requires further condi-tions to be met. Logically, if the justification for violence is resistance to oppression, then the purpose of any terrorist acts must be to replace oppres-sion with freedom, rights violations with rights protection, and tyranny with democracy.[368] Thus an important measure of the legitimacy of terrorist vio-lence must be the lawful end to which it is directed. The defence does not justify special interest terrorism, nor terrorism which pursues objectives other than core legal values such as self-determination and human rights (thus

---

[365] H Ashrawi, Interview on ABC TV (Australia), Foreign Correspondent, 16 Sept 2003.
[366] 'Hezbollah sweeps to victory in south Lebanon', *Sydney Morning Herald*, 7 June 2005.
[367] S Shrader, 'Zarqawi's terrorism goes worldwide, says US', *Sydney Morning Herald*, 24 Oct 2005.
[368] Ignatieff, n 57, 1151.

excluding reactionary assassinations of democratic leaders or peace-makers). To the extent that violent groups make excessive or unreasonable claims, out of proportion to the cause, accommodation of such demands cannot be expected.

Cumulatively satisfying the four foregoing conditions (serious rights violations; exhaustion of alternatives; representativeness; and a rights-based end) is still not adequate to justify terrorism. Unless all means are admitted, any theory of justifiable terrorism must construct outer limits on the permissible means and targets of violence. Ignatieff argues that liberation violence, below an armed conflict, must analogously follow IHL on civilian immunity.[369] Yet the problem of non-innocent civilians was discussed earlier. In that light, Honoré argues that, while generally observing IHL, rebels may also target the State and responsible officials.[370] Indiscriminate attacks on non-governmental civilians would always be prohibited, and proportionality, as a general principle of law, must be respected.

Where violence satisfies the foregoing five conditions, it could be considered 'illegal but justifiable', perhaps under the umbrella of a 'collective defence of human rights'. The five conditions provide clear, narrow, and prospective criteria for internationally evaluating the moral or political justifiability of terrorism, even if they fall short of a formula for legality.[371] While such a defence may be open to abuse, it is less open to abuse than the alternative of legalizing violence (by establishing a positive right to rebel, or conferring combatant immunity on rebels), and no more open to abuse than existing rights such as self-defence.[372] In extreme cases of oppression, individuals are likely to resort to violence even if violence is absolutely prohibited. As such, this defence provides a fairer and more flexible mechanism for structuring the international response to reasonable claims.

F. DISCRETION AND LAW: NEVER NEGOTIATE WITH TERRORISTS?

Criminal law does not operate in a political vacuum and must clearly engage with discretionary political responses to individual criminal harms in some cases. Sometimes prosecution of terrorists may interfere with other national or international interests. Despite the maxim of some States to 'never negotiate with terrorists', *realpolitik* sometimes forces States to adopt a less stringent path. Negotiating with terrorists may be necessary to end peacefully or humanely particular terrorist incidents, or to resolve longstanding terrorist campaigns. At the former level, in the Achille Lauro hijacking in 1986, Egypt

---

[369] ibid, 1153; Honoré, n 85, 54.   [370] Honoré, ibid, 54.
[371] Chesterman, n 355, 232 (referring to the conditions of humanitarian intervention).
[372] Palmer, n 356, 512–513.

and Italy attempted to negotiate an end to the crisis (and save the lives of hostages), while the US used military force and declared itself 'completely averse to . . . any form of negotiation'.[373] Conversely, in 1986 US President Reagan secretly agreed to sell arms to Iran in return for promises to seek the release of US hostages.[374] It is a perennial humanitarian dilemma of governments whether to pay ransom to save hostages,[375] in the light of fears that negotiation may encourage others to resort to political violence to secure a seat at the bargaining table.

At the latter level, three iconic figures—Yasser Arafat (PLO), Gerry Adams (IRA), and Nelson Mandela (ANC)—were at some point arguably responsible for terrorism by their organizations. While their degree of responsibility differs (particularly in organizations with ostensibly separate political and military wings), it is startling how persons once regarded as terrorists were later embraced as legitimate representatives of political movements, entitled to a share of State power, or even to Nobel Prizes (Arafat in 1994, Mandela in 1993). All were absolved of criminal responsibility for terrorism, as a precondition of involvement in political settlements.

In Northern Ireland, under the 1998 Good Friday Agreement over 500 political prisoners were released by Britain and Ireland by July 2001,[376] while amnesties were conferred for the decommissioning of armaments. Ahead of the IRA's renunciation of armed struggle in July 2005, Britain released the convicted 'Shankill Road bomber', Sean Kelly, although the broader question of amnesties remains controversial,[377] as it does in Spain, following ETA's announcement of a ceasefire in March 2006. In contrast, the leader of

---

[373] Quoted in A Cassese, *Terrorism, Politics, and Law* (Polity, Cambridge, 1989) 127; see also G Gooding, 'Fighting Terrorism in the 1980's: The Interception of the Achille Lauro Hijackers' (1987) 12 Yale JIL 158. Paradoxically, Abu Abbas, organizer of the Achille Lauro action, was apprehended in Iraq in 2003 and died in US custody in 2004, even though the US had earlier revoked his international arrest warrant, and Israel had granted him immunity from prosecution in 1999: R Tait, 'Hijacking mastermind dies in Iraq', *The Guardian*, 10 Mar 2004; J Risen and D Johnston, ' '85 Hijacker is captured in Baghdad', *New York Times*, 16 Apr 2003.

[374] E McWhinney, *Aerial Piracy and International Terrorism* (Martinus Nijhoff, Dordrecht, 1987) 171.

[375] See G Sacerdoti, 'States' Agreements with Terrorists in Order to Save Hostages: Non-Binding, Void or Justified by Necessity?', in N Ronzitti (ed), *Maritime Terrorism and International Law* (Martinus Nijhoff, Dordrecht, 1990) 25; J Hooper, 'Italians ready to pay ransom for release of hostages held in Iraq', *The Guardian*, 21 Apr 2004; M Baker and C Banham, 'Arroyo pulls out troops to save a life', *Sydney Morning Herald*, 15 July 2004; J Miller, 'US Plans to Act More Rigorously in Hostage Cases', *New York Times*, 18 Feb 2002; J Forero, 'Colombia President Ready for Hostage Talks', *New York Times*, 15 Dec 2005.

[376] UK and Irish Governments, Good Friday (Belfast) Agreement, 10 Apr 1998, 'Prisoners': paras 1–5; UK and Irish Governments, 'Achievements in Implementation of the Good Friday Agreement', 14 July 2001.

[377] 'IRA's Shankill bomber released from prison', *Sydney Morning Herald*, 28 July 2005; J Button, 'Barricades fall as British troops pull back', *Sydney Morning Herald*, 30–31 July 2005, 13; A Chrisafis, 'After 35 years of bombs and blood the IRA ends its war', *Guardian Weekly*, 5–11 Aug 2005, 1. Amnesties were included in the 1962 Evian Agreements settling the conflict between France and Algeria.

the Tamil Tigers (LTTE), Velupillai Prabhakaran, was sentenced to 200 years in prison, *in absentia*, while simultaneously negotiating a Norwegian-brokered peace settlement with the Sri Lankan government,[378] while many foreign governments continued to treat the LTTE as a terrorist organization.

While domestic legal systems are infused with discretionary political concepts such as pardons, immunities, and amnesties, the availability of (domestic or international) amnesties for *international* crimes is an unsettled question,[379] which is not directly addressed in the 1998 Rome Statute.[380] International organizations have rejected and endorsed amnesties in different contexts, while State practice is variable.[381] There is no customary rule against amnesties[382] and international human rights law does not preclude them, as long as they do not result in impunity for serious rights violations.[383]

There may, however, be a trend in practice towards the restriction of amnesties for serious international crimes. For example, in 2005, Argentina's Supreme Court declared unconstitutional two laws of 1986–87 which effectively conferred amnesties on those responsible for violating human rights in Argentina's 'Dirty War' of 1976–83.[384] The Court reasoned that self-amnesty laws violated both international human rights law as well as the duty to prosecute serious international crimes under international law. Similarly, while the 1999 Lomé Peace Agreement in Sierra Leone conferred an

---

[378] A Waldman, 'Rebel leader sentenced to 200 years' jail as talks start', *Sydney Morning Herald*, 2 Nov 2002.

[379] See generally R Slye, 'The Legitimacy of Amnesties under International Law and General Principles of Anglo-American Law: Is a Legitimate Amnesty Possible?' (2003) 43 Van JIL 173; D Cassel, 'Lessons from the Americas: Guidelines for International Response to Amnesties for Atrocities' (1996) 59 *Law and Contemporary Problems* 197; K Henrard, 'The Viability of National Amnesties in View of the Increasing Recognition of Individual Criminal Responsibility at International Law' (1987) 8 Mich YBILS 595; Cassese, n 2, 312–316.

[380] On amnesties in the ICC, see J Gavron, 'Amnesties in the Light of Developments in International Law and the Establishment of the International Criminal Court' (2002) 51 ICLQ 91; D Majzub, 'Peace or Justice: Amnesties and the International Criminal Court' (2002) 3 Melbourne JIL 247.

[381] Cassese, *International Criminal Law*, n 2, 312–316.

[382] *Lomé Amnesty* case, n 103, para 82; Cassese, n 2, 315. Some writers suggest that there is a trend and presumption against national amnesties: Gavron, n 380, 116–117.

[383] See, eg, *Chumbipuma Aguirre et al v Peru* (*Barrios Altos* case) (2001) Series C, No 75, paras 41–44. In particular, self-amnesty laws were found to violate Arts 1(1) and 2 (general obligations to guarantee rights), 8 (right to a fair trial), and 25 (right to an effective remedy) of the Inter-American Convention on Human Rights; see also the concurring opinions of Judge Trindade, paras 10–11 and Judge García-Ramírez, paras 9–17; *Barrios Altos (Interpretation of Merits Judgment)*, IACHR (3 Sept 2001); *Castillo Páez (Reparations)* case (27 Nov 1998) Series C, No 43, paras 103–108 and concurring opinion of Judge García-Ramírez, paras 6–9; See also UNHR Committee, General Comment No 20 (1994).

[384] *Simón* case, Argentine Supreme Court, causa No 17.768 (14 June 2005) S.1767.XXXVIII. The decision upheld the findings of lower courts on this issue and confirmed that Argentina's Congress had validly annulled the amnesty laws in 2003; see C Bakker, 'A Full Stop to Amnesty in Argentina' (2005) 3 JICJ 1106.

'absolute and free pardon and reprieve to all combatants and collaborators in respect of anything done by them in pursuit of their objectives' between 1991 and 1999, the Statute of the Special Court for Sierra Leone precludes amnesties for crimes within its jurisdiction.[385] In the *Lomé Amnesty* case, the Special Court for Sierra Leone found that while the conferral of amnesties is within the sovereign discretion of States, a State cannot exercise that power to deprive other States of universal jurisdiction over international crimes.[386] In March 2006, former Liberian President Charles Taylor was detained in Sierra Leone while attempting to leave Nigeria, where he had been granted asylum in an earlier agreement to end Liberia's long civil war. While Taylor's apprehension might be seen as a welcome elimination of impunity (since he had been indicted by the Special Court), it gives rise to other difficulties. If dictators know that peace agreements which protect them from prosecution will not be honoured in the future, then there is no incentive for them to relinquish power—and every incentive to hold on to it, whatever the cost. A puritanical insistence on bringing dictators to justice may thus come at the price of many thousands of additional deaths which could have been averted if an earlier end to conflict had been secured by a peace agreement conferring—and guaranteeing—amnesties or asylum.

Policy objections to amnesties are that they conflict with obligations to prosecute international crimes; thwart victims' rights to a remedy; and undermine the rule of law.[387] In some cases, far from promoting peace or reconciliation, amnesties may counter-productively foster perceptions of injustice and accentuate grievances. Yet, amnesties are not a capitulation to power politics, but a necessary and pragmatic concession to the political realities which bound the operation of law. A number of principles are relevant in evaluating the propriety of amnesties.

First, amnesties must be necessary, as a last resort, to secure fundamental objectives such as peace, national reconciliation, or to save lives; or alternatively, allowing prosecution would pose a 'grave and imminent peril'.[388] A discretion not to prosecute (or extradite) may need to be exercised,[389] or amnesties or immunities conferred, to preserve fragile peace agreements or

---

[385] Peace Agreement between the Government of Sierra Leone and the Revolutionary United Front of Sierra Leone, 7 July 1999, Lomé, UN Doc S/1999/777, Art 9 (and a freedom from any 'official or judicial action'); Statute of the Special Court for Sierra Leone, Art 10.

[386] *Lomé Amnesty* case, n 103, paras 66–74; see also S Meisenberg, 'Legality of Amnesties in International Humanitarian Law: The Lomé Amnesty Decision of the Special Court for Sierra Leone' (2004) No 856 IRRC 837.

[387] Slye, n 379, 182–201.   [388] Majzub, n 380, 278.

[389] Historically, selectivity in international prosecutions has been based on unstated or opaque reasons, undermining perceptions of legitimacy: D Zolo, 'Peace through Criminal Law?' (2004) 2 JICJ 727, 730; A Garapon, 'Three Challenges for International Criminal Justice' (2004) 2 JICJ 716, 717.

the survival of transitional governments.[390] The cost of these approaches is that criminal justice—including punishment, retribution, deterrence, and satisfaction for victims—is rationally traded for other public goods.

Second, blanket amnesties are less acceptable than amnesties tailored to the specific circumstances of particular individuals following some kind of fair and transparent determination procedure, such as a national reconciliation process.[391] Such processes may also ensure alternative forms of accountability and redress for victims. Further, amnesties are more legitimate where they operate in conjunction with prosecutions for the most serious international crimes, whether for offenders who fail to fully disclose their crimes (as in post-apartheid South Africa) or for more serious crimes (as in independent East Timor).[392]

Third, amnesties conferred by national leaders upon themselves prior to leaving office are less likely to be objectively or rationally founded. Amnesties granted by democratic parliamentary processes, or through consultative processes which engage victims and the community, are more likely to produce more appropriate amnesties. As Judge García-Ramírez found in the Inter-American Court of Human Rights case of *Castillo Páez (Reparations)*:

... a distinction must be made between the so-called 'self-amnesty laws' promulgated by and for those in power, and amnesties that are the result of a peace process, with a democratic base and reasonable in scope, that preclude prosecution for acts or behaviors of members of rival factions but leave open the possibility of punishment for the kind of very egregious acts . . .[393]

Similarly, amnesties conferred by one group that benefited from the crimes of others should be precluded for bias as in the case of self-amnesties. For example, the Reconciliation, Tolerance and Unity Bill 2005 (Fiji) proposed amnesties for those involved in a racialized coup by indigenous Fijians against a democratic Indian-led government in 2000.[394] The Bill was spon-

---

[390] Y Naqvi, 'Amnesty for War Crimes: Defining the Limits of International Recognition' (2003) 85 IRRC 583, 624; R McCarthy, S Goldenberg, and N Watt, 'Amnesty for Iraqi insurgents', *The Guardian*, 5 July 2004; 'Putin sets Chechnya amnesty in train', *The Guardian*, 15 May 2003.   [391] Cassese, n 2, 316.

[392] R Goldstone, 'Past Human Rights Violations: Truth Commissions and Amnesties or Prosecutions' (2000) 51 *Northern Ireland Legal Quarterly* 164; see, eg, Promotion of National Unity and Reconciliation Act 1995 (South Africa), ss 3(1)(b), 4(c), and 16–22; UN Transitional Administration in East Timor, Reg 2001/10 on the Establishment of a Commission on Reception, Truth and Reconciliation in East Timor (13 July 2001); but note that the Report of the East Timorese Reception, Truth and Reconciliation Commission recommended prosecuting perpetrators of rights violations during the Indonesian occupation prior to 1999, but President Xanana Gusmao recommended suppressing it in the public interest: J Aglionby, 'Timorese truth may stay hidden', *Sydney Morning Herald*, 30 Nov 2005.

[393] *Castillo Páez (Reparations)* case (27 Nov 1998) Series C, No 43, para 7 (Concurring Opinion of Judge García-Ramírez), para 9.

[394] 'Fiji's indigenous leaders back release of coup plotters', *Sydney Morning Herald*, 30–31 July 2005, 15. The new State of Israel also gave amnesties to 'Stern Gang' members who assassinated the UN mediator in Palestine in 1948: see Ch 5, n 175 below.

sored by an indigenous-led government which came to power as a result of the coup. In Palestine, Irgun leaders such as Menachim Begin, a future Israeli Prime Minister, were never brought to justice for 'terrorist' crimes committed during the violent struggle to establish Israel.

Fourth, in some situations, since international crimes are matters of international concern, no single State should be permitted to decide unilaterally whether to confer amnesties. Although the views of the affected State should be accorded significant weight, they are not the exclusive consideration. It may not be acceptable to other States, for example, for Afghanistan's peace and reconciliation commission to offer an amnesty to insurgents fighting against the Afghan government and US forces where they extend to those suspected of serious crimes, such as Taliban leader Mullah Mohammad Omar and sectarian 'warlord' Gulbuddin Hekmatyar.[395] Likewise, Britain's willingness to negotiate secretly with Hamas and Hezbollah in 2005 was questioned by Israel and the US, although that case is more complex because of the success of those organizations in democratic elections in the West Bank, Gaza, and Lebanon in May and December of 2005 and January 2006.[396] Electing terrorism may be democratic, but democracy is constrained by rights-based limits precluding terrorism.

In the light of these general principles, it is important to note that amnesties for terrorism may raise different issues from those applying to other international crimes. For example, war crimes or crimes against humanity are typically more widespread and affect larger sections of the population than terrorism, and so amnesties for terrorism may not be justifiable as necessary to achieve national reconciliation or to restore harmony between rival ethnic or religious groups in the community. Indeed, prosecuting terrorism is often necessary precisely because terrorists attack the institutions of the State and the community which the State protects. It may be questioned, for example, where it was proper in 2005 for the King of Morocco to pardon seven Islamists convicted of involvement in the May 2003 terrorist attacks in Casablanca, which killed forty-five people.[397]

On the other hand, amnesties for terrorism may be appropriate where it is sectarian and affects significant parts of the population, or in specific cases where life is at imminent risk. In an effort to defuse a violent and widespread Islamist insurgency, in 1999 Algeria passed a Law on Civil Concord which offered immunity from prosecution for insurgents who demilitarized.

[395] C Gall, 'Amnesty may include Taliban leaders', *Sydney Morning Herald*, 11 May 2005.
[396] E MacAskill, 'UK ponders talking with Hamas and Hizbullah: Militants' gains at polls persuade Foreign Office to rethink policy', *The Guardian*, 20 May 2005; C McGreal, 'Israelis pressure Straw over UK contacts with Hamas', *The Guardian*, 8 June 2005; C McGreal, 'Hamas election victory sets new Middle East challenge', *Guardian Weekly*, 3–9 Feb 2006, 1; see International Crisis Group, 'Enter Hamas: The Challenges of Political Negotiation', Middle East Report No 49, Amman/Brussels, 18 Jan 2006.
[397] 'Morocco Islamists get royal pardon', Aljazeera.net, 20 Aug 2005.

Immunity was not available for those who participated in collective massacres, rapes, or public bombings. Claimants were assessed by a three-member panel of judges and officials, and received housing and integration assistance if successful. The law was overwhelmingly approved by 98 per cent of Algerian voters.[398] As a result, 4,500 insurgents laid down their weapons.

By 2005, Algeria estimated that around 1,000 insurgents remained and to entice them to demilitarize, the government put a Charter on Peace and National Reconciliation to referendum in September 2005, which was endorsed by 97 per cent of voters.[399] The Charter pardons those convicted or imprisoned for armed violence or support of terrorism. If also offers amnesties to those who: renounce violence and disarm; were involved in networks of support for terrorism and who declare their activities to the authorities; and those sought in Algeria or abroad who present themselves to the authorities. Pardons and amnesties are not available to those involved in collective massacres, rapes, or public bombings. While human rights organizations have been critical of the Charter,[400] the real concern is not so much its text as the apparent failure of Algeria to attempt seriously to bring to justice those suspected of committing the serious crimes exempt from pardon or amnesty.

Where terrorism affects multiple States, waiving prosecution or extradition should 'only be exercised in agreement between the nation and the States whose citizens and property are the object of the terrorists' acts'.[401] (In relation to the ICC, the prosecutor has a discretion in Article 53 not to proceed if 'an investigation would not serve the interests of justice'.) Illegitimate reasons for failing to bring terrorists to justice might include appeasement, fear of reprisals, or the protection of commercial interests.[402] The more serious the terrorist acts involved, the stronger the justification must be for waiving prosecution or extradition. Such decisions should not be taken arbitrarily or unilaterally, but based on a careful balancing of vital community interests, such as humanitarian needs, justice for victims, long-term peace, or sustainable political solutions.

Where terrorism threatens *international* peace and security, the Security Council is the natural body in which to consider claims of amnesty or

---

[398] On a voter turn-out of 85%: Algerian Embassy (Washington, DC), *Algeria Today*, 30 Sept 2005. The credibility of such a high affirmative vote is, however, open to doubt.

[399] On a voter turn-out of 80%: ibid; see Algerian Ministry of Foreign Affairs, 'Projet de charte pour la paix et la reconciliation nationale', 6 Sept 2005.

[400] ICJ, 'Algeria: Amnesty law risks legalizing impunity for crimes against humanity', Joint Press Statement, 14 Apr 2005; Amnesty International, 'Algeria: President calls for referendum to obliterate crimes of the past', Public Statement, 22 Aug 2005, AI Index: MDE 28/010/2005.

[401] T Franck and D Niedermeyer, 'Accommodating Terrorism: An Offence against the Law of Nations' (1989) 19 IYBHR 75, 128.

[402] S Rosen and R Frank, 'Measures against International Terrorism' in D Carlton and C Schaerf (eds), *International Terrorism and World Security* (Croom Helm, London, 1975) 60, 63.

immunity. Indeed the Charter posits peace and security as higher values than justice, given its fleeting references to human rights, the preservation of domestic jurisdiction and sovereignty, and the absence of provisions on humanitarian intervention. Charter obligations prevail over other treaty obligations,[403] and, as in the *Lockerbie* case, the certainty of treaty responses to terrorism may need to yield to security interests.[404] In that case, however, it is arguable that the Council's actions implicitly (and unlawfully) supported a breach of *jus cogens* by those States (the UK and the US) which had unlawfully threatened force against Libya if it did not comply with their demands.[405]

In relation to ICC prosecutions, Article 16 of the Rome Statute explicitly recognizes that the Council may postpone the investigation or prosecution of an international crime for a renewable twelve-month period.[406] The Council has relied on this provision temporarily to preclude the investigation or prosecution of ICC crimes by personnel from States not party to the Rome Statute engaged in UN operations.[407] This measure has been criticized on a number of legal grounds, including failure to first determine a threat under Article 39 of the Charter, exceeding the scope of Article 16 of the Rome Statute, violation of *jus cogens*, inconsistency with UN purposes and principles, and unlawful interference in treaty regimes.[408] At a minimum, the measure gives blanket immunity to a whole class of people, without specifically justifying the need for a postponement in the circumstances of an individual case.

Council interference with treaty frameworks is not to be lightly presumed, and the discontinuance of the *Lockerbie* case in the ICJ ensured that the availability and conditions of review of Council measures that conflict with other treaty obligations remain undecided. Like political decisions to grant pardons or amnesties generally, Council decisions of this kind are not outside the realm of law; indeed: 'A discretion can only exist within the law'.[409] If a duty to prosecute terrorism were to emerge as a norm of *jus cogens*, then the Council may be prohibited from conferring amnesties,[410] if it is accepted that

---

[403] UN Charter, Art 103.   [404] See Ch 4 below.

[405] A Orakhelashvili, 'The Impact of Peremptory Norms on the Interpretation and Application of United Nations Security Council Resolutions' (2005) 16 EJIL 59, 71.

[406] Although under Art 103 of the UN Charter, the Council may impose obligations over-riding States' commitments under any other treaty, which may trump Article 16's 12-month limitation period.

[407] UNSC Resolution 1422 (2002), para 1.

[408] See Amnesty International, 'International Criminal Court: The unlawful attempt by the Security Council to give US citizens permanent impunity from international justice', May 2003, AI Index: IOR 40/006/2003, 42–75.

[409] I Brownlie, 'The Decisions of the Political Organs of the United Nations and the Rule of Law' in R MacDonald (ed), *Essays in Honour of Wang Tieya* (Martinus Nijhoff, Dordrecht, 1993) 91, 95–96.

[410] Cassese, n 2, 316 (referring to international crimes generally).

the Council cannot lawfully override norms of *jus cogens*.[411] State participation in anti-terrorism treaties may also be less attractive if they do not offer
certainty and predictability, due to vulnerability to Council interference.
There is the further danger that powerful States may attempt to circumvent
treaty regimes by pursuing Council measures. At the same time, the Council's
broad discretion under the Charter cannot be unduly fettered in dealing with
serious terrorist threats to security, and criminal law responses may not
always be the appropriate solution.

G. CONCLUSION

Unless absolute liability is imposed for terrorism, sometimes acts commonly
regarded as terrorism may be justifiable, or at least excusable: 'in exceptional
circumstances that which is commonly held to be wrong is found on reflection
not to be wrong'.[412] Political violence is committed for a wide range of
reasons, and the law's legitimacy depends on its capacity to differentiate
between morally different reasons for action. IHL is an appropriate normative framework for dealing with self-determination claims and internal rebellions that cross the threshold of an armed conflict, effectively decriminalizing
non-State violence that otherwise complies with the laws of war.

Outside armed conflict, the law of international criminal defences
(self-defence, and duress/necessity), and the circumstances precluding the
wrongfulness of group actors (drawn analogously from the law of State
responsibility) may excuse a limited range of ostensibly 'terrorist' conduct.
However, some acts widely considered justifiable by the international community may still fall outside the scope of these defences. To maintain the
law's legitimacy and fairness, limited acts of 'terrorism', in collective defence
of human rights, could be regarded as 'illegal but justifiable'. This would
recognize that in the absence of collective international enforcement of
human rights, it may be necessary to licence remedial violence by victims
themselves.[413] Such equitable consideration could be supplemented by a
rational international policy on the conferral of pardons and amnesties for
less serious terrorist violence, to recognize the overriding political importance
in some cases of securing peace or reconciliation.

---

[411] *Bosnia* case [1993] ICJ Reports 440 (Lauterpacht J); A Reinisch, 'Developing Human
Rights and Humanitarian Law Accountability of the Security Council for the Imposition of
Economic Sanctions' (2001) 95 AJIL 858, 859; K Doehring, 'Unlawful Resolutions of the Secur-
ity Council and their Legal Consequences' (1997) 1 Max Planck *Yearbook of UN Law* 91, 99;
Orakhelashvili, n 405.

[412] Cicero, n 149, 16.

[413] T Franck, *The Power of Legitimacy Among Nations* (OUP, Oxford, 1990) 70.

3

Terrorism in International and Regional Treaty Law

A. INTRODUCTION

Historically the existence of a discrete prohibition, crime, or concept of terrorism in international law was much doubted.[1] The orthodox view was succinctly expressed by Baxter in 1974, who stated that 'We have to regret that a legal concept of "terrorism" was ever inflicted upon us. The term is imprecise; it is ambiguous; and above all, it serves no operative legal purpose.'[2] This view was shared by Higgins in 1997, who believed that terrorism 'is not a discrete topic of international law with its own substantive legal norms', but 'a pernicious contemporary phenomenon which . . . presents complicated legal problems'.[3] In her view: ' "Terrorism" is a term without legal significance. It is merely a convenient way of alluding to activities, whether of States or of individuals, widely disapproved of and in which either the methods used are unlawful, or the targets protected, or both.'[4]

In contrast, Cassese asserts that terrorism is a customary crime with distinct elements, deriving from a combination of mutually reinforcing sources: the definition in the 1999 Terrorist Financing Convention; the definition in a much-reiterated 1994 General Assembly Declaration; a 1937 League of Nations definition; numerous converging national law definitions; the

---

[1] R Baxter, 'A Skeptical Look at the Concept of Terrorism' (1974) 7 *Akron Law Review* 380; R Higgins, 'The General International Law of Terrorism' in R Higgins and M Flory (eds), *Terrorism and International Law* (Routledge, London, 1997) 13, 13–14; G Guillaume, 'Terrorism and International Law', Grotius Lecture, British Institute of International and Comparative Law, London, 13 Nov 2003, 6; MC Bassiouni, 'A Policy-Oriented Inquiry into the Different Forms and Manifestations of "International Terrorism" ' in MC Bassiouni (ed), *Legal Responses to International Terrorism* (Martinus Nijhoff, Dordrecht, 1988) xv, xvi; D Freestone, 'Legal Responses to Terrorism: Towards European Cooperation?' in J Lodge (ed), *Terrorism: A Challenge to the State* (Martin Robertson, Oxford, 1981) 195; J-M Sorel, 'Some Questions About the Definition of Terrorism and the Fight against its Financing' (2003) 14 AJIL 365, 370; C Gearty, *The Future of Terrorism* (Phoenix, London, 1997) 3; R Friedlander, 'Terrorism' in R Bernhardt (ed), *Encyclopaedia of PIL, vol 4* (North Holland, Amsterdam, 2000) 845; M-C Sornarajah, ' "Terrorism" Not Useful for Analyzing Random Violence' (1999) 93 ASIL Proceedings 79; H Gasser, 'Acts of Terror, "Terrorism" and International Humanitarian Law' (2002) 84 IRRC 547, 554; G Sliwowski, 'Legal Aspects of Terrorism' in D Carlton and C Schaerf, *International Terrorism and World Security* (Croom Helm, London, 1975) 69, 71.

[2] Baxter, n 1.

[3] Higgins, n 1.

[4] ibid, 28; see also I Brownlie, *Principles of Public International Law* (6th edn, OUP, Oxford, 2003) 713.

IHL prohibitions discussed in Chapter 1; and the statements and practice of States and international organizations since 11 September 2001.[5] In his view, the essence of terrorism is the commission of serious, politically motivated, criminal violence, aimed at spreading terror, regardless of the status of the perpetrator.[6] Such conduct must also have a nexus with armed conflict, or be of the magnitude of crimes against humanity, or involve State authorities and exhibit a transnational dimension, such as by jeopardizing the security of other States.[7]

Chapter 1 argued for the differentiation of terrorism from other kinds of illicit violence and Chapter 2 explored the range of exclusions, justifications, and defences for terrorism. In the absence of any explicit definition of terrorism in international law, the next three chapters evaluate the residual disagreement about the normative status of 'terrorism' as a distinct legal concept. As Higgins observes: 'Whether one regards terrorism . . . as new international law, or as the application of a constantly developing international law to new problems—is at heart a jurisprudential question.'[8] This jurisprudential question is considered through a classical investigation of the sources of international law, considering treaties in this chapter, customary law in Chapter 4, and the special concept of terrorism in the treaty and customary law of armed conflict in Chapter 5. In particular, this chapter examines how international and regional treaty law have responded to terrorism, and evaluates their contribution to customary law on terrorism. It also considers key attempts in treaty law to define terrorism.

B. TRANSNATIONAL CRIMINAL LAW TREATIES[9]

Twelve international treaties and five protocols were concluded between 1963 and 2005 to address specific types of violent conduct understood by many States as terrorist in nature.[10] Most of these conventions were adopted in reaction to particularly egregious terrorist incidents, beginning with violence against civil aircraft in the 1960s. For instance, a series of attacks on civil aviation in 1970–71 led to the adoption of the 1970 Hague Convention and

[5] A Cassese, *International Criminal Law* (OUP, Oxford, 2003) 120–131; A Cassese, 'Terrorism is Also Disrupting Some Crucial Legal Categories of International Law' (2001) 12 EJIL 993, 994.
[6] Cassese (2003), ibid, 129.
[7] ibid, 125–126, 129.
[8] Higgins, n 1, 13.
[9] The term 'transnational' treaties is explained in Ch 1, n 2 above.
[10] 1963 Tokyo Convention; 1970 Hague Convention; 1971 Montreal Convention; 1973 Protected Persons Convention; 1979 Hostages Convention; 1980 Vienna Convention; 1988 Montreal Protocol; 1988 Rome Convention; 1988 Rome Protocol; 1991 Plastic Explosives Convention; 1994 UN Personnel Convention; 1997 Terrorist Bombings Convention; 1999 Terrorist Financing Convention; 2005 Nuclear Terrorism Convention.

the 1971 Montreal Convention;[11] the 1988 Montreal Protocol was a response to terrorist attacks on international airports in Rome and Vienna in 1985; and the 1988 Rome Convention was a response to the terrorist seizure of the Italian cruise ship, *Achille Lauro*, in 1985.[12] The 1997 Terrorist Bombings Convention was initiated by the US in response to bombings against US interests in Saudi Arabia in 1996, gas attacks in Tokyo, and bombings in Sri Lanka, Israel, and Manchester in the UK.[13]

Many of these treaties were adopted to fill normative gaps in the regulation of certain activities, such as air and maritime transport, which were spread across multiple jurisdictions and in relation to which the ordinary principle of territorial jurisdiction was insufficient. Some treaties were necessary because norms regulating the subject matter were considered inadequate. Thus, the 1988 Rome Convention was necessary because the crime of piracy was inapplicable to situations like the Achille Lauro incident, where the elements of piracy—the two-ship rule and a private motive[14]— were not present.

Few of the so-called anti-terrorism treaties designate prohibited conduct as specifically 'terrorist' offences.[15] Instead, most treaties require States to prohibit and punish in domestic law certain physical acts—such as hostage-taking or hijacking—without requiring, as an element of the offence, proof of a political motive or cause behind the act,[16] or an intention to coerce, intimidate, or terrorize certain targets. The substantive provisions of these treaties never refer to the terms terrorism or terrorist.[17]

A few treaties refer to these terms in their titles or preambles. The 1979 Hostages Convention describes 'all acts of taking of hostages as manifestations of international terrorism'. The 1988 Rome Convention refers to terrorism five times in its preamble. The 1991 Plastic Explosives Convention mentions terrorism three times, signalling concerns about the terrorist use of unmarked explosives. The preambles of the 1997 Terrorist Bombing Convention, the 1999 Terrorist Financing Convention, and the 2005 Nuclear

---

[11] G Levitt, 'Collective Sanctions and Unilateral Action' in Y Alexander and E Sochor (eds), *Aerial Piracy and Aviation Security* (Martinus Nijhoff, Dordrecht, 1990) 95, 96, 100.

[12] C Joyner, 'Suppression of Terrorism on the High Seas: The 1988 IMO Convention on the Safety of Maritime Navigation' (1989) 19 IYBHR 343; M Halberstam, 'Terrorist Acts against and on Board Ships' (1989) 19 IYBHR 331, 333; see also A Cassese, *Terrorism, Politics and Law: The Achille Lauro Affair* (Polity, London, 1989).

[13] S Witten, 'The International Convention for the Suppression of Terrorist Bombings' (1998) 92 AJIL 774.

[14] 1958 Geneva Convention on the High Seas, Art 15 (reflecting custom, despite earlier controversy on its elements): I Brownlie, *Principles of Public International Law* (5th edn, Clarendon, Oxford, 1998) 236; 1982 UNCLOS, Art 101; see Halberstam, n 12, 341, 350–352. Private ends refer not only to a profit motive, but also to 'feelings of hatred or revenge': (1956–II) ILCYB 282.

[15] Witten, n 13, 775.

[16] J Lambert, *Terrorism and Hostages in International Law: A Commentary on the Hostages Convention 1979* (Grotius, Cambridge, 1990) 49.

[17] ibid.

Terrorism Convention recall General Assembly Resolution 49/60,[18] which condemned 'all acts, methods and practices of terrorism as criminal and unjustifiable, wherever and by whomever committed'. The 1999 Terrorist Financing Convention further notes that 'the number and seriousness of acts of international terrorism' depend on their financing, while the preamble to the 2005 Nuclear Terrorism Convention warns that 'acts of nuclear terrorism may result in the gravest consequences and may pose a threat to international peace and security'.

There is an abundant literature on these treaties and it is not necessary to retrace those debates here.[19] In brief, some treaties prohibit specified, violent criminal acts against especially vulnerable or politically or economically significant targets (such as international aircraft, airports, ships, fixed platforms, and internationally protected persons).[20] Sometimes this approach is coupled with prohibitions on loathsome methods or means (such as hijacking and hostage-taking).[21] A further approach is the prohibition of the use of particular weapons (such as plastic explosives, nuclear material, and bombs).[22] A recent convention also prohibits the financing of terrorist activities.[23] Most of the treaties also contain a number of ancillary offences additional to the principal crimes.[24] Other instruments are also relevant to combating the physical acts comprising terrorism,[25] which may additionally qualify as other

---

[18] UNGA Resolution 49/60 (1994) and annexed Declaration on Measures to Eliminate International Terrorism.

[19] See E McWhinney, *Aerial Piracy and International Terrorism* (Martinus Nijhoff, Dordrecht, 1987); Y Alexander and E Sochor (eds), n 11; N Ronzitti (ed), *Maritime Terrorism and International Law* (Martinus Nijhoff, Dordrecht, 1990); Joyner, n 12; Halberstam, n 12; Lambert, n 16; Higgins, n 1; G Plant, 'The Convention for the Suppression of Unlawful Acts against the Safety of Maritime Navigation' (1990) 39 ICLQ 27; A Falvey, 'Legislative Responses to International Terrorism: International and National Efforts to Deter and Punish Terrorists' (1986) 9 BC ICLR 323, 326–343; J Murphy, 'The Future of Multilateralism and Efforts to Combat International Terrorism' (1987) 25 Col JTL 35, 41–49; A Cassese, 'The International Community's "Legal" Response to Terrorism' (1989) 38 ICLQ 589, 591–596.

[20] See, eg, 1970 Hague Convention; 1971 Montreal Convention and 1988 Montreal Protocol; 1973 Protected Persons Convention; 1994 UN Personnel Convention; 1988 Rome Convention; 1988 Rome Protocol.

[21] See, eg, 1970 Hague Convention; 1971 Montreal Convention; 1979 Hostages Convention.

[22] See, eg, 1980 Vienna Convention; 1991 Montreal Convention; 1997 Terrorist Bombings Convention; 2005 Nuclear Terrorism Convention.

[23] 1999 Terrorist Financing Convention; A Aust, 'Counter-terrorism: A New Approach—The International Convention for the Suppression of the Financing of Terrorism' (2001) Max Planck *Yearbook of UN Law* 287; R Lavalle, 'The International Convention for the Suppression of the Financing of Terrorism' (2000) 60 *Zeitschrift fur auslandisches offentliches Recht and Volkerrecht* 491.

[24] Such as attempt, threats, complicity, abetting, organizing or directing, or intentionally contributing to the commission of an offence by a group of persons acting with a common purpose: see, eg, 1970 Hague Convention, Art 1; 1971 Montreal Convention, Art 1.

[25] 1972 Biological Weapons Convention; 1982 UNCLOS, Arts 100–107 (piracy, including aircraft); 1944 Chicago Convention, Art 4; 1993 Chemical Weapons Convention; 1992 Biological Weapons Convention; UPU Resolution CA 1/2001 on Combating Terrorism; ICAO Resolutions A17–1 to A17–24 (1970); ICAO (Council) Resolution (1970), ICAO Doc 8923–C/998; Joint

international crimes.[26] Two of the conventions are primarily regulatory and do not establish criminal offences.[27]

These approaches have been variously classified as object-oriented or segmented, sectoral or enumerative, functional or inductive, and incremental or piecemeal.[28] They reflect a 'pragmatic, empirical, problem-oriented, step-by-step', or ad hoc and 'roundabout' response to terrorist-type activities.[29] The international community has approached terrorism in this way precisely to avoid confronting the contentious question of a general definition.[30] This helps to explain the broad multilateral support for many of the treaties, since it evades the political and 'prodigious' technical difficulties[31] of a generic, analytic, deductive, or comprehensive definition.[32]

As terrorist violence spread from attacks mainly on western States to attacks on Arab, Communist, and Non-Aligned States,[33] broad multilateral support emerged for many of the sectoral treaties. Table 3.1 below shows the level of State participation in each of the major anti-terrorism treaties (out of 192 UN member States). After 11 September 2001, Security Council resolutions urging States to ratify the anti-terrorism treaties[34] produced a marked

Statement of Heads of State and Government on International Terrorism, Bonn Summit Meeting, 17 July 1978, (1978) 78 State Department Bulletin No 2018, 5 ('Bonn Decl'); Guidelines for the Application of the Bonn Declaration, London, 9 May 1979; NAM, XIII Conference of Heads of State or Government, Final Document, Kuala Lumpur, 25 Feb 2003.

[26] Particularly war crimes, crimes against humanity, genocide, or torture.

[27] 1963 Tokyo Convention; 1991 Plastic Explosives Convention.

[28] See, eg, N Gal-Or, *International Cooperation to Suppress Terrorism* (St Martin's Press, New York, 1985) 87; Lambert, n 16, 47–57; K Skubiszewski, 'Definition of Terrorism' (1989) 19 IYBHR 39, 40; G Levitt, 'Is "Terrorism" Worth Defining?' (1986) 13 Ohio NULR 97, 108–112, 115; McWhinney, n 19, 167; Murphy, n 19, 44, UNComHR (53rd Sess), Terrorism and Human Rights: Progress Report by Special Rapporteur K Koufa, 27 June 2001, UN Doc E/CN.4/Sub.2/2001/31, para 24.

[29] McWhinney, n 19, 107, 149 and Cassese (2003), n 5, 123, respectively.

[30] Cassese, ibid, 123; Levitt, n 28, 115; Lambert, n 16, 50; Higgins, n 1, 14. Writers have generally preferred this approach: see, eg, Bassiouni, n 1, xxii, xxx; A Rubin, 'International Terrorism and International Law' in Y Alexander and S Finger (eds), *Terrorism: Interdisciplinary Perspectives* (John Jay Press, New York, 1977) 121, 123; D Partan, 'Terrorism: An International Law Offence' (1987) 19 *Connecticut Law Review* 751, 754.

[31] Higgins, n 1, 14; also Lambert, n 16, 51; A Rubin, 'Current Legal Approaches to International Terrorism' (1985) 7 *Terrorism* 147, 158; R Mushkat, ' "Technical" Impediments on the Way to a Universal Definition of International Terrorism' (1980) 20 Indian JIL 448.

[32] J Murphy, 'Defining International Terrorism: A Way Out of the Quagmire' (1989) 19 IYBHR 13, 35; MC Bassiouni, 'Methodological Options for International Legal Control of Terrorism' in MC Bassiouni (ed), *International Terrorism and Political Crimes* (Charles C Thomas, Illinois, 1975) 486; Levitt, n 28, 108–112, 115; Falvey, n 19, 337.

[33] J Murphy, 'United Nations Proposals on the Control and Repression of Terrorism' in Bassiouni (ed), ibid, 493, 504; Higgins, n 1, 18.

[34] UNSC Resolution 1373 (2001); 1535 (2004) preamble; see also UNODC, Legislative Guide to the Universal Anti-Terrorism Conventions and Protocols (UN, New York, 2003); A Aust, Implementation Kits for the International Counter-Terrorism Conventions (Commonwealth Secretariat, London, 2002); H Corell, 'The International Instruments against Terrorism', Paper at Symposium on Combating International Terrorism: The Contribution of the UN, Vienna, 3–4 June 2002.

increase in multilateral participation in many treaties. Whereas only two States had ratified all twelve sectoral treaties before 11 September 2001, over 40 States had done so by December 2003.[35]

Table 3.1. Status of International Sectoral Treaties[36]

Convention	States Party	% of all States
1963 Tokyo Convention	180	94
1970 Hague Convention	181	94
1971 Montreal Convention	183	95
1973 Protected Persons Convention	159	83
1979 Hostages Convention	153	80
1980 Vienna Convention	116	60
2005 Amendment	2 ratifications (at 9 Jan 2006)	
1988 Montreal Protocol	155	81
1988 Rome Convention	126	65 (representing 82% of world merchant shipping tonnage)
2005 Protocol to 1988 Convention	Open for signature 14 Oct 2005	
1988 Rome Protocol	115	60 (representing 77% of world merchant shipping tonnage)
2005 Protocol to 1988 Protocol	Open for signature 14 Oct 2005	
1991 Montreal Convention	123	64
1994 UN Personnel Convention	79	41
2005 Protocol to 1994 Convention	4 signatories	
1997 Terrorist Bombings Convention	145	76
1999 Terrorist Financing Convention	150	78
2005 Nuclear Terrorism Convention (open for signature 14 Sep 2005– 31 Dec 2006)	0 (97 signatories by Nov 2005)	

With the adoption of the 1997 Terrorist Bombings Convention[37] and the 2005 Nuclear Terrorism Convention (after almost eight years of negotiation),[38] most of the physical conduct widely considered as terrorist in nature

---

[35] D McGoldrick, *From '9–11' to the Iraq War 2003* (Hart, Oxford, 2004) 26–27.

[36] Status of treaties recorded by the relevant depositories (UN, ICAO, IAEA, and IMO) at 8 Feb 2006.

[37] Witten, n 13. The vast majority of terrorist acts in the US from 1980 to 1999 were bombings: US Dept Justice (FBI), *Terrorism in the US 1999* (Counterterrorism Division, Washington, DC, 2000), 41.

[38] The 2005 Nuclear Terrorism Convention (adopted by UNGA Resolution 59/290 of 15 Apr 2005) fills lacunae left by 1980 Vienna Convention, by covering a wider range of 'targets, forms and acts of nuclear terrorism': Corell, n 34, 12. The 1980 Convention is limited to offences

is now prohibited. The result is the de facto criminalization of most acts commonly regarded as terrorism, although it is significant that only about one-quarter of States have ratified *all* sectoral treaties[39] and there consequently remain *jurisdictional* gaps in the coverage of the existing treaties.

One of the few remaining *normative* gaps in the network of treaties is the failure to criminalize internationally the terrorist killings of civilians by any method. Presently, the treaties only criminalize violence by terrorists in specific contexts or by particular methods: at airports or on board aircraft (but only where it is likely to endanger air safety); against protected persons (but only when in foreign States);[40] by nuclear material; on board ships or fixed platforms; or by explosives or other lethal devices.[41] While the 1988 Rome Convention criminalizes murder on board ships, the Hague, Montreal, and Hostages Conventions do not criminalize killings at all.[42]

Thus violence against civilians outside aerial or maritime contexts, who are not protected persons (or who are protected persons but present in their own States), and not victims of bombings or nuclear acts, is not criminalized as terrorism. Examples include the terrorist killing or assassination of civilians (such as business people, engineers, journalists, doctors, or teachers)[43] by guns or knives, including killing hostages not on board aircraft or ships. Although the 1999 Terrorist Financing Convention refers to death or serious bodily injury by terrorist acts, it does so only for the purpose of criminalizing terrorist financing rather than terrorist offences *per se*. Similarly, the 1997 Terrorist Bombings Convention covers only death or serious injury caused by bombings, not other terrorist means such as sabotage of public transport or public utilities such as water or electricity

---

relating to nuclear material while in international transport or in domestic use, storage and transport: Art 7. The 2005 Convention was drafted by the Ad Hoc Committee at the request of the General Assembly, based on a Russian draft of 1997: see UNGAOR (53rd–59th Sess), Ad Hoc Committee Reports (1997–2004), Supps 37 (A/53/37–A/59/37); UNGA (53rd Sess) (6th Committee), Measures to Eliminate International Terrorism: Working Group Report, 22 Oct 1998, UN Doc A/C.6/53/L.4. A 2005 Amendment to the 1980 Vienna Convention required State Parties to protect nuclear facilities and material in peaceful domestic use, storage, and transport, and to cooperate on prevention and enforcement: IAEA Board of Governors: General Conference, Final Act of Amendment Conference of 4–8 July 2005, 6 Sept 2005, IAEA Doc GOV/INF/2005/10-GC(49)/INF/6.

[39] M Scharf, 'Defining Terrorism as the Peacetime Equivalent of War Crimes: Problems and Prospects' (2004) 36 Case Western Reserve JIL 359, 365.

[40] 1973 Protected Persons Convention, Art 1.

[41] Respectively: 1971 Montreal Convention, Art 1 and 1988 Montreal Protocol, Art 1; 1973 Protected Persons Convention, Art 2; 1980 Vienna Convention, Art 7; 1988 Rome Convention, Art 3 and 1988 Rome Protocol, Art 2; 1997 Terrorist Bombings Convention, Art 2 (the definition of 'explosive or other lethal device' in Art 1(3) does not extend to guns or knives and similar hand weapons).

[42] Halberstam, n 12, 332 (Art 1 of the 1979 Hostages Convention prohibits only threats to kill hostages).

[43] Scharf, n 39.

supplies.[44] Further, mailing anthrax (or other biological agents) to government employees is not presently prohibited, nor are attacks on electronic systems ('cyberterrorism').[45]

Many of the existing treaties reach considerably beyond common conceptions of terrorism, since they prohibit certain acts without reference to their political motives or objectives. Thus criminal acts perpetrated for nonterrorist purposes, motives, aims, or objectives are also criminalized. For example, hostage-taking or hijacking for personal or private reasons (such as financial greed or child abduction to obtain custody) is also criminalized.[46] This inherent overreach dilutes the special nature of terrorism, which is not inherent in a physical act of violence itself.[47] The depoliticization of offences was deliberate, to minimize the availability of the political offence exception to extradition.[48]

At the same time, a few of these treaties do reflect a more comprehensive or generic approach to the definition of terrorist acts. As early as 1972, the US proposed in the United Nations a treaty to criminalize unlawful killing, causing serious bodily harm, or kidnapping where 'intended to damage the interests of or obtain a concession from a State or an international organization'.[49] That initiative did not gain much support at the time,[50] but its emphasis on the coercive aims behind violent acts is reflected in some subsequent treaties. For example, the 1979 Hostages Convention prohibits hostage-taking to compel a third party 'to do or abstain from doing any act as an explicit or implicit condition for the release of the hostage'.[51] Similarly, the 1994 UN Personnel Convention requires States to criminalize intentional threats to commit violent attacks on UN and associated personnel and their property 'with the objective of compelling a physical or juridical person to do or to refrain from doing any act'.[52]

In relation to maritime offences, the 1988 Rome Convention and 1988 Rome Protocol prohibit threats against the safety of ships or maritime installations 'aimed at compelling a physical or juridical person to do or refrain from doing any act'.[53] The Convention and Protocol are supplemented by two

---

[44] The Convention prohibits the use of an 'explosive or other lethal device', defined to include chemical and biological agents or toxins (Art 1(3)), while radioactive material is separately prohibited (Art 2); Witten, n 13, 776–777; Scharf, n 39; see also B Broomhall, 'State Actors in an International Definition of Terrorism from a Human Rights Perspective' (2004) 36 Case Western Reserve JIL 421, 426.

[45] Scharf, n 39.

[46] W Mallison and S Mallison, 'The Concept of Public Purpose Terror in International Law' in Bassiouni (ed), n 32, 67, 70.

[47] Lambert, n 16, 50.   [48] Joyner, n 12, 347.

[49] Draft Convention for the Prevention and Punishment of Certain Acts of International Terrorism to the General Assembly, UN Doc A/C.6/L.850 (1972), Art 1(d).

[50] See Ch 4 below.   [51] 1979 Hostages Convention, Art 1(1).

[52] 1994 UN Personnel Convention, Art 9(1)(c).

[53] 1988 Rome Convention, Art 3(1)(b), (c), and (e); 1988 Rome Protocol, Art 2(2)(c).

Protocols of 2005, which add new offences involving the use of biological, chemical, or nuclear weapons against ships or maritime platforms for the purposes of intimidating a population or compelling a government or international organization to do or refrain from doing any act.[54]

Further in relation to weapons of mass destruction (WMDs), the 1980 Vienna Convention (as amended in 2005) prohibits threats to steal nuclear material, or interfere with a nuclear facility, to compel a natural or legal person, international organization, or State to do or refrain from doing any act.[55] The 2005 Nuclear Terrorism Convention creates objective offences for possessing or using radioactive material or devices in certain circumstances,[56] but also establishes the offence of using such material or devices[57] with the intent to compel a natural or legal person, an international organization or a State to do or refrain from doing an act.[58] States must legislate to punish these acts, 'in particular where they are intended or calculated to provoke a state of terror in the general public or in a group of persons or particular persons'. While deriving from a 1994 General Assembly definition, itself similar to the 1937 League definition, the notion of a 'state of terror' is not an element of the offences, nor are the offences defined as 'nuclear terrorism' as such.

The 1999 Terrorist Financing Convention adds the notion of intimidation to the idea of compulsion found in these treaties, and comes closest to furnishing an essential definition of terrorism.[59] The Convention prohibits the financing of:

Any other act intended to cause death or serious bodily injury to a civilian, or to any other person not taking an active part in the hostilities in a situation of armed conflict, when the purpose of such act, by its nature or context, is to *intimidate* a population, or to *compel* a government or an international organization to do or to abstain from doing any act.[60]

The idea of compulsion was included even though a number of States preferred referring only to intimidation,[61] or eliminating any purposive element.[62]

---

[54] 2005 Protocol to the 1988 Rome Convention, Art 3*bis*; 2005 Protocol to the 1988 Rome Protocol, Art 2*bis*. Both 2005 Protocols were adopted under the auspices of the IMO on 14 Oct 2005.   [55] 1980 Rome Convention, Art 7(1)(g)(ii), as amended by the 2005 Amendment.

[56] With the intent to cause death or serious bodily injury, or to cause substantial damage to property or the environment: Art 2(1).

[57] Or using or damaging a nuclear facility in a manner which releases or risks the release of radioactive material.

[58] Art 1(b)(iii). Ancillary offences are established in Arts 2(2)(a)–(b), 3, and 4(a)–(c). The distinction between the 1980 and 2005 treaties is explained above in n 38.

[59] *Suresh v Canada (Minister of Citizenship and Immigration)* [2002] 1 SCR; 2002 SCC 1, paras 96–98.   [60] 1999 Terrorist Financing Convention, Art 2(1)(b) (emphasis added).

[61] UNGA (54th Sess) (6th Committee), Measures to Eliminate International Terrorism: Working Group Report, 26 Oct 1999, UN Doc A/C.6/54/L.2, 23 (Austria), 40 (Brazil), 51 (Kuwait); Ad Hoc Committee Report (1999), n 38, 12, 15 (France), 33 (Guatemala), 38 (Germany), 29, 31 (Austria).

[62] Working Group Report (1999), ibid, 61–62 (Chair).

Drafting proposals to refer expressly to acts intended to provoke terror, designed to terrorize, or of a terrorist nature, were also not accepted,[63] with intimidation the preferred term.

Similarly, the 1997 Terrorist Bombings Convention did not embody drafting proposals to limit its scope to bombings 'for a terrorist purpose',[64] nor to extend its scope to bombings likely to 'create a state of terror'[65] or have 'psychological effects'.[66] In addition, the 1997 Terrorist Bombings Convention differs from the 1999 Terrorist Financing Convention by also rejecting proposals to define terrorist bombings as those designed to 'seriously intimidate'[67] or to 'intimidate, coerce or retaliate' or compel.[68] Instead, the Convention is limited to physical acts of bombing,[69] regardless of any ulterior aim or purpose. At best, Article 5 requires States to ensure that criminal bombings are not considered justifiable 'in particular' where such acts 'are intended or calculated to provoke a state of terror in the general public or in a group of persons or particular persons'. This reference to the 1994 General Assembly definition is located in a qualifying provision which does not form part of the definition of offences, nor is there further definition of 'a state of terror'.

The common element in the Hostages, Rome, UN Personnel, and Terrorist Financing treaties is, therefore, the requirement that the prohibited physical acts be committed to intimidate or compel another to do or refrain from doing any act. The motive of the acts—in the sense of motive as the end, purpose, or object of an act[70]—is coercion of specified targets. In contrast, proof of a motive in another juridical sense—as an emotion prompting an act[71] (such as political or private motives)—is not required. For example, while hostage-taking is often motivated by a specific ideological or political belief, the definition does not require evidence of such reasons, and thus covers such acts committed for private reasons (such as financial gain). This approach avoids the difficulty of having to identify and prove the motives underlying violence in order to secure a conviction.

---

[63] ibid, 24 (Costa Rica and Mexico) and 39–40 (Syria); Ad Hoc Committee Report (1999), n 38, 58 (Rapporteur).

[64] UNGA (52nd Sess) (6th Committee), Measures to Eliminate International Terrorism: Working Group Report, 10 Oct 1997, UN Doc A/C.6/52/L.3, 20 (China); Ad Hoc Committee Report (1997), n 38, 51.

[65] Ad Hoc Committee Report (1997), ibid, 5–6, 13 (revised Bureau text); see also Working Group Report (1997), ibid, 37 (revised text by Friends of Chair).

[66] Working Group Report (1997), ibid, 51 (Rapporteur's informal summary of Working Group discussions).

[67] ibid, 20 (China) and 42 (Russia) respectively.

[68] ibid, 23 (France for seven industrialized countries and Russia).

[69] 1997 Terrorist Bombings Convention, Art 2(1). The definition excludes accidental bombings and lawful uses of explosives, such as demolitions of buildings, controlled explosions, and hostage rescues: Ad Hoc Committee Report (1997), n 38, 51–52 (Rapporteur).

[70] *Hyam v DPP* [1975] AC 55, 73.   [71] ibid.

Many of the anti-terrorism treaties are built on the principle of 'prosecute or extradite' (*aut dedere aut judicare*), a treaty-based principle emerging as a customary norm in relation to some terrorist offences.[72] The treaties do not give rise to individual criminal responsibility for terrorist-type activities in international law *stricto sensu* (before international criminal tribunals), but rely on domestic prosecutions, facilitated by transnational judicial co-operation.[73] Only the two most recent treaties expressly exclude the political offence exception to extradition,[74] while preserving a non-discrimination clause (and remaining subject to the customary prohibition of *refoulement* to torture). The political offence exception was historically a source of much international anxiety about terrorism,[75] yet only the most recent treaties have secured agreement on its removal in the face of long-standing concerns about delivering up political opponents to oppressive regimes. The treaties contain

[72] Higgins, n 1, 26; MC Bassiouni, 'An International Control Scheme for the Prosecution of International Terrorism: An Introduction' in A Evans and J Murphy (eds), *Legal Aspects of International Terrorism* (ASIL, Washington, DC, 1979) 485, 487; D Freestone, 'International Cooperation against Terrorism and the Development of International Law Principles of Jurisdiction' in Higgins and Flory (eds), n 1, 43, 44; cf Y Dinstein, 'Terrorism as an International Crime' (1989) 19 IYBHR 55, 70; C Shachor-Landau, 'Extraterritorial Penal Jurisdiction and Extradition' (1980) 29 ICLQ 274, 277–278.

[73] Guillaume, n 1, 6; N Boister, 'Transnational Criminal Law?' (2003) 14 EJIL 953, 955, 962; on the modalities of cooperation, see A Maged, 'International Legal Cooperation: An Essential Tool in the War Against Terrorism' in W Heere (ed), *Terrorism and the Military: International Legal Implications* (Asser Press, The Hague, 2003) 157.

[74] 1997 Terrorist Bombings Convention, Art 11; 1999 Terrorist Financing Convention, Art 14. In addition, some regional treaties exclude the exception: 1971 OAS Convention, Art 2 (regarding offences as common crimes); 1977 Council of Europe Convention, Art 1; 1987 SAARC Convention, Arts I, III(1); 1998 Arab League Convention, Art 2(b) (subject to Art 6(a)); 1999 OIC Convention, Art 2(b) (subject to Art 6(a)); 1999 CIS Treaty, Art 4.

[75] See G Gilbert, *Transnational Fugitive Offenders in International Law: Extradition and Other Mechanisms* (Martinus Nijhoff, Dordrecht, 1998); C Van den Wijngaert, *The Political Offence Exception to Extradition* (Kluwer, Boston, 1980); MC Bassiouni, *International Extradition and World Public Order* (AW Sijthoff, Leiden, 1974) 370–428; A Sofaer, 'The Political Offence Exception and Terrorism' (1986) 15 Den JILP 125; M Sapiro, 'Extradition in the Era of Terrorism' (1986) 61 NYU LR 654; B Banoff and C Pyle, 'To Surrender Political Offenders' (1984) 16 NYU JILP 169; L Fields, 'Bringing Terrorists to Justice' in R Lillich (ed), *International Aspects of Criminal Law* (Michie Co, Charlottesville, 1981); S Lubet and M Czaczkes, 'The Role of the American Judiciary in the Extradition of Political Terrorists' (1980) 71 JCLC 193; J Paust, 'Extradition and United States Prosecution of the Achille Lauro Hostage-Takers' (1987) 20 Van JTL 235; A Rubin, 'Extradition and "Terrorist" Offenses' (1987) 10 *Terrorism* 83; A Evans, 'The Realities of Extradition and Prosecution' in Y Alexander and S Finger (eds), *Terrorism: Interdisciplinary Perspectives* (John Jay Press, New York, 1977) 128; C Schlaefer, 'American Courts and Modern Terrorism' (1981) 13 NYU JILP 617; K Wellington, 'Extradition: A Fair and Effective Weapon in the War on Terrorism' (1990) 51 Ohio SLJ 1447; W Hannay, 'International Terrorism and the Political Offence Exception to Extradition' (1980) 18 Col JTL 381; B Larschan, 'Extradition, the Political Offence Exception and Terrorism' (1986) 4 Buffalo JIL 231; A Petersen, 'Extradition and the Political Offence Exception in the Suppression of Terrorism' (1992) 67 *Indiana Law Journal* 767; A Washington, 'Terrorism: United States Policy on Immigration and Extradition' (1996) 21 *Marshall Law Review* 291; O Lagodny, 'The Abolition and Replacement of the Political Offence Exception' (1989) 19 IYBHR 317.

'widely differing approaches to jurisdiction',[76] including resort to the territoriality, nationality, passive personality, and protective principles, and sometimes to a type of 'subsidiary' or 'quasi' universal jurisdiction.[77] The treaties
do not, however, establish priority of jurisdiction,[78] nor do they specify
whether prosecution or extradition takes priority.[79]

In the absence of empirical research, it is hard to assess the effectiveness of
these treaties in combating terrorism. Sectoral treaties are generally silent on
remedies for breach of treaty obligations by States,[80] although occasionally
States have resorted to counter-measures, sometimes through political
agreements, in response to breaches.[81] While many States have implemented
their obligations in national law, global statistics on prosecutions and extradi-
tions under these treaties are not available,[82] and only spectacular cases of
enforcement failure command international attention. The formal framework
of cooperation in criminal matters has also been frequently circumvented
by discretionary measures of deportation or summary expulsion.[83] Such
measures by-pass the legal protections for suspects under extradition law,
although some national courts have insisted that deportation cannot be used
as a substitute for extradition law.[84] Since late 2001, 'irregular rendition' has
been used by the US precisely to evade the 'traditional systems of criminal or

[76] S Peers, 'EU Responses to Terrorism' (2003) 52 ICLQ 227, 233; see also R Kolb, 'The
Exercise of Criminal Jurisdition over International Terrorists' in A Bianchi (ed), *Enforcing Inter-
national Law Norms against Terrorism* (Hart, Oxford, 2004) 227. The jurisdiction provisions are
set out in the 1970 Hague Convention, Arts 4–5; 1971 Montreal Convention, Arts 1, 3, 5; 1973
Protected Persons Convention, Art 3; 1979 Hostages Convention, Art 5; 1980 Vienna Conven-
tion, Art 8; 1988 Rome Convention, Art 6; 1988 Rome Protocol, Art 3; 1997 Terrorist Bombings
Convention, Art 6; 1999 Terrorist Financing Convention, Art 7; 2005 Nuclear Terrorism
Convention, Art 9.

[77] Guillaume, n 1, 6–7; Freestone, n 72, 58; Higgins, n 1, 24; N Schrijver, 'Responding to
International Terrorism: Moving the Frontiers of International Law for "Enduring Freedom"?'
(2001) 48 Netherlands ILR 271, 275; Freestone, n 1, 202.

[78] Peers, n 76, 233; Halberstam, n 12, 366.

[79] MC Bassiouni and E Wise, *Aut Dedere Aut Judicare* (Martinus Nijhoff, Dordrecht, 1995)
62.

[80] Cassese, n 19, 593; MC Bassiouni, *International Criminal Law* (Sijthoff & Noordhoff, The
Netherlands, 1980) 23; Falvey, n 19, 338–341.

[81] eg under the Summit Seven's Bonn Declaration against Afghanistan in the 1980s: Levitt,
n 11, 108–118.

[82] C Harding, 'The Concept of Terrorism and Responses to Global Terrorism: Coming to
Terms with the Empty Sky', Paper at Sept 11 Conference, University of Sussex, 21–22 Mar 2003,
3–6.

[83] See, eg, T Stein, 'Rendition of Terrorists: Extradition Versus Deportation' (1989) 19
IYBHR 281; MC Bassiouni, 'Unlawful Seizures and Irregular Rendition Devices as Alternatives
to Extradition' (1973) 7 Van JTL 25.

[84] See *Mohamed v South Africa* (2001) 3 SA 893 (the South African Constitutional Court held
that deporting a suspect in the 1998 bombing of the US embassy in Tanzania was unlawful and
extradition law applied); *R v Horseferry Road Magistrates Court, ex p Bennett* [1994] 1 AC 42
(Lord Griffiths) (obtaining informal custody through rendition is a 'serious abuse of process'
where extradition law applies); *R v Hartley* [1978] 2 NZLR 199; *S v Ebrahim*, 1991 (2) SA 553
(Sth African Ct App).

military justice' which the US believes do not apply to terrorists.[85] It mirrors the converse unlawful practice of abducting suspects from foreign territory or the high seas.[86]

Nevertheless, as Guillaume writes, 'over the past forty years, international criminal law has made significant progress in the combat against international terrorism . . . Most of the normative work has been accomplished'.[87] Effectiveness depends 'on the will of States' and 'it cannot be denied that certain difficulties may arise, either because certain States are unable to maintain their authority on their own territory, or because of wrongful conduct by the States themselves'.[88]

The sectoral treaties have also influenced the development of customary law. It is well accepted that treaty provisions are a 'recognized method' of custom formation, although this is 'not lightly . . . attained'[89] and treaties have no capacity to bind third States. Customary law is evidenced 'primarily in the actual practice and *opinio juris* of States', although treaties may have 'an important role' in recording, defining, or developing customary rules.[90] In developing custom, a treaty provision must 'be of fundamentally norm-creating character as could be regarded as forming the basis of a general rule of law'.[91] State practice must also be 'extensive and virtually uniform' and 'show a general recognition that a rule of law or legal obligation is involved'.[92] Nonetheless, 'a very widespread and representative participation in the convention might suffice of itself, provided it included that of States whose interests were specially affected'.[93] The degree of ratification is thus clearly relevant.

[85] US Secretary of State C Rice, quoted in S Goldenberg and L Harding, 'Detainee flights have saved European lives', *Guardian Weekly*, 9–15 Dec 2005, 1; see S Borelli, 'The Rendition of Terrorist Suspects to the United States: Human Rights and the Limits of International Cooperation' in Bianchi (ed), n 76, 331.

[86] See, eg, *Attorney-General of Israel v Eichmann* (1961) 36 ILR 5 (Distr Ct Jerusalem); *US v Alvarez-Machain* (1992) 31 ILM 902; B Thrush, 'US Sanctioned Kidnappings Abroad' (1994) 11 Ariz JICL 181; J Gurule, 'Terrorism, Territorial Sovereignty, and the Forcible Apprehension of International Criminals Abroad' (1994) 17 *Hastings International and Comparative Law Review* 457; J Quigley, 'Our Men in Guadalajara and the Abduction of Suspects Abroad' (1993) 68 *Notre Dame Law Review* 723; M Halberstam, 'International Kidnapping' (1992) 86 AJIL 736; J Bush, 'How Did We Get Here? Foreign Abduction after *Alvarez-Machain*' (1993) 45 *Stanford Law Review* 939; M Glennon, 'State Sponsored Abduction' (1992) 86 AJIL 746; M Matorin, 'Unchaining the Law: The Legality of Extraterritorial Abduction in Lieu of Extradition' (1992) 41 *Duke Law Journal* 907; J Gentin, 'Government-Sponsored Abduction of Foreign Criminals Abroad' (1991) 40 *Emory Law Journal* 1227; C Fisher, 'US Legislation to Prosecute Terrorists: Antiterrorism or Legalized Kidnapping?' (1985) 18 Van JTL 915; M Garcia-Mora, 'Criminal Jurisdiction of a State over Fugitives Brought from a Foreign Country by Force or Fraud' (1957) 32 *Indiana Law Journal* 42; C Whitlock, 'Police retrace CIA's expensive Italian job', *Sydney Morning Herald*, 27 June 2005.

[87] Guillaume, n 1, 13.   [88] ibid.

[89] *North Sea Continental Shelf* cases (1969) ICJ Reports 3, 41.

[90] *Continental Shelf* case *(Libya v Malta)* (1985) ICJ Reports 13, 29–30, para 27.

[91] *North Sea*, n 89, 42–43, para 72.   [92] ibid, 43, para 74.

[93] ibid, 42, para 73 and 43, para 74.

In creating new rules to confront the challenges of modern terrorism, the sectoral treaties filled gaps in the existing customary law and thus played a significant role in developing new and parallel rules of customary law. Three treaties have been ratified by more than 90 per cent of States: the 1963 Tokyo Convention, the 1970 Hague Convention, and the 1971 Montreal Convention. A further three treaties have been ratified by more than 80 per cent of States: the 1973 Protected Persons Convention, the 1979 Hostages Convention, and the 1988 Montreal Protocol. Parties to these treaties include numerous States specially affected by terrorism. State practice in general is consistent with the norms in these treaties, which States also regard as legally obligatory. It is thus probable that the core provisions of these treaties are now reflected in parallel customary rules.

The customary status of the remaining treaties is more doubtful, with five treaties having ratification levels below 65 per cent.[94] While the 1997 Terrorism Bombings Convention and the 1999 Terrorist Financing Convention have both been ratified by more than 75 per cent of States, it is probably too soon to judge whether State practice as a whole is consistent with the rules in those treaties. On the other hand, conformity with the 1999 Terrorist Financing Convention has been greatly accelerated by the incorporation of its substantive provisions into Security Council Resolution 1373 (2001). This resolution binds all States and thus renders the substantive norms of the Convention applicable even to non-party States, with implementation supervised by the UN Counter-Terrorism Committee. Restrictions on terrorist financing are also reflected in the practice of regional organizations.[95] In combination, these factors suggest that the key provisions of the 1999 Terrorist Financing Convention already reflect customary law due to the focused attention paid to such measures after 11 September 2001, and despite the relatively short period of time since the adoption of the Convention in 1999.

C. TREATIES OF REGIONAL ORGANIZATIONS

Unlike the international treaties, a number of treaties concluded by member States of regional or other organizations define specifically 'terrorist' offences.[96] These treaties have a limited sphere of operation, governing

[94] 1980 Vienna Convention; 1988 Rome Convention; 1988 Rome Protocol; 1991 Montreal Convention; 1994 UN Personnel Convention.

[95] See, eg, 1999 OIC Convention, Art 2(d); EU Common Position of Dec 2001, n 195; 2002 Inter-American Convention, Arts 4–6; 2004 SAARC Additional Protocol; 2004 African Union Protocol, Art 3; 2005 Council of Europe Convention on Laundering, Search, Seizure and Confiscation of the Proceeds from Crime and on the Financing of Terrorism.

[96] Including those of the SAARC, Arab League, OIC, OAU (now AU) and EU; see below; see also K Graham, 'The Security Council and Counter-terrorism: Global and Regional Approaches to an Elusive Public Good' (2005) 17 *Terrorism and Political Violence* 37, 49–52.

relations between members of geographically regional organizations (who have become parties to the treaty),[97] or between members of organizations defined by religious or cultural affiliation (such as the Organization of the Islamic Conference (OIC) and the Arab League). Whereas regional treaties on terrorism were once rare,[98] now nine such treaties have been adopted.

Aust observes that the concept of 'regional' treaties has no legal significance[99] and the same might be said of treaties adopted by organizations typified by religious or cultural affiliation. However, such treaties may furnish evidence of local or regional custom over time[100] (or of custom observed by States grouped according to other principles), which in turn may contribute to the evolution of international customary law. Lauterpacht writes that 'the regional experience is a stage in the evolution towards the more complete integration of international society'.[101] Regionalism in security matters has been seen as increasingly important in recent years,[102] with the Security Council specifically urging regional organizations to enhance the effectiveness of their counter-terrorism efforts.[103]

Other than the 1977 European Convention, little scholarly attention has been paid to most of these treaties, many of which have been adopted since 1998. Cumulatively, these organizations have international normative significance because many of them are long-established and involve a large number of States.[104] In addition, other intergovernmental organizations—such as the Commonwealth, the North Atlantic Treaty Organization, the Organization for Security Cooperation in Europe, and the Association of South East Asian Nations—have adopted specific measures, short of treaties, in response to terrorism.[105]

The definitions of terrorism in regional treaties contribute to the normative

---

[97] Not all organizations are 'regional arrangements' under the UN Charter, Art 52(1); see P Sands and P Klein, *Bowett's Law of International Institutions* (5th edn, Sweet and Maxwell, London, 2001) 152–154.

[98] Cassese, n 19, 592.

[99] A Aust, *Modern Treaty Law and Practice* (CUP, Cambridge, 2000) 15.

[100] The ILC lists treaties as a form of State practice: (1950-II) ILCYB 368–372. Constant and uniform usage, in the practice of a group of States, may establish regional custom: *Asylum* case *(Columbia v Peru)* (1950) ICJ Reports 266, 276–277; see also *Right of Passage* case *(Portugal v India)* (1960) ICJ Reports 6, 39–43.

[101] H Lauterpacht, *International Law and Human Rights* (Stevens, London, 1950) 462–463.

[102] See, eg, UNGA (60th Sess), 2005 World Summit Outcome, UN Doc A/60/L.1 (20 Sept 2005) para 170; UN High-Level Panel on Threats, Challenges and Change, *A more secure world: Our shared responsibility*, 2 Dec 2004, UN Doc A/59/565, paras 220, 270–273; UN Secretary-General's Report, *In larger freedom: towards development, security and human rights for all*, UNGA (59th Session), 21 Mar 2005, UN Doc A/59/2005, paras 213–215.

[103] UNSC Resolution 1631 (2005), para 6.

[104] See Table 3.2 below, although there is overlap in the memberships of the Arab League and the OIC, and the Council of Europe and the EU.

[105] These are not considered here. See, eg, S Tay and Tan Hsien Li, 'Southeast Asian Cooperation on Anti-Terrorism: The Dynamics and Limits of Regional Responses' in V Ramraj, M Hor and K Roach (eds), *Global Anti-Terrorism Law and Policy* (CUP, Cambridge, 2005) 399.

debates about definition in international law, supplying concrete examples of definitions which might be accepted, modified, or contested on the international plane and which influence State practice. Their customary significance partly depends on the extent to which they shape State behaviour, including that of non-State Parties to the treaties. Since many of the treaties are relatively recent, it is premature to gauge their effects on State practice, or to anticipate their likely effects over time.

At present, the sheer diversity of regional definitions is sufficient to militate against the view that there is any embryonic customary definition of terrorism. While some of the more recent treaties include generic definitions of terrorism, other recent treaties have deliberately refrained from generic definition, following the approach of the older regional treaties. Among those treaties which include generic definitions, it is further difficult to discern any underlying shared conception of terrorism. As the ICJ stated in the *Asylum* case, these treaties reflect 'so much uncertainty and contradiction, so much fluctuation and discrepancy . . . that it is not possible to discern in all this any constant and uniform usage, accepted as law'.[106] While the ICJ stated in the *Fisheries* case that 'too much importance need not be attached to a few uncertainties or contradictions',[107] the differences between the definitions of terrorism in regional treaties are not merely penumbral, but reflect fundamental disagreements about the permissibility and classification of political violence. Each of these treaties is considered below, according to their adopting organizations. The different elements of generic definitions are then compared and contrasted.

As Table 3.2 (page 145) shows, some of the regional treaties have been ratified by a large proportion of member States of the adopting regional organization, with universal or near-universal ratification of the Council of Europe, SAARC, and EU instruments. However, less than half of the Organization of American States (OAS) member States have ratified the OAS Convention after more than thirty years. About three-quarters of Arab League members have ratified that organization's terrorism convention, although all States are signatories and it was only adopted in 1998.

The remaining treaties are too recent (since 1999) to effectively gauge their real levels of participation. Least successful so far is the OIC Convention, with slightly more than 20 per cent of OIC members currently parties, and only a handful more signatories. About 70 per cent of the Organization of African Unity (OAU) members are parties to the OAU Convention, and most remaining members have signed it; half of the Commonwealth of Independent States (CIS) members are parties to the CIS Treaty; and all members of the Shanghai Cooperation Organization (SCO) are parties to its treaty. While

---

[106] *Asylum* case, n 100, 277.
[107] *Anglo-Norwegian Fisheries* case *(UK v Norway)* (1951) ICJ Reports 116, 131.

Table 3.2. Status of Regional Anti-Terrorism Treaties [108]

Convention	States Parties	Signed but Unratified	Organization Membership
Organization of American States			35
1971 Convention	17	4	
2002 Inter-American Convention	14	20	
Council of Europe			46
1977 Convention	44	1	
2003 Protocol (not in force)	19 ratifications	25	
2005 Terrorism Convention (not in force)	0 ratifications	20	
2005 Financing Convention (not in force)	0 ratifications	16	
South Asian Association of Regional Countries			7
1987 SAARC Convention	7	0	
2004 Additional Protocol (not in force)	2 ratifications	5	
1998 Arab League Convention	17	5	22
1999 OIC Convention	10	8	57
Organization of African Unity			53
1999 Convention	36	10	
2004 Protocol (not in force)	0 ratifications	1	
1999 CIS Treaty	6	0	12
2001 Shanghai Convention	6	0	6
2002 EU Framework Decision	25	0	25

about 40 per cent of OAS members are parties to the Inter-American Convention, nearly all are signatories and the treaty was only adopted in 2002.

1. *Organization of American States: 1971 and 2002 Conventions*

One of the least controversial regional instruments is the 1971 Organization of American States (OAS) Convention,[109] which was a response to the growth of terrorism—mainly kidnapping, ransom, and extortion—in Central and South America in the early 1970s, usually to raise funds for urban guerilla movements or to secure the release of prisoners.[110] Although there was initially support for generically defining terrorism in a treaty,[111] the Convention

---

[108] Status of treaties according to depositories as at 16 Nov 2005.
[109] 1971 OAS Convention to Prevent and Punish Acts of Terrorism Taking the Form of Crimes against Persons and Related Extortion that are of International Significance.
[110] McWhinney, n 19, 144.
[111] B van Ginkel, 'The United Nations: Towards a Comprehensive Convention on Combating Terrorism' in M van Leeuwen (ed), *Confronting Terrorism* (Kluwer, The Hague, 2003) 207, 213.

as adopted is limited in scope to protected persons. It is really a regional precursor to the 1973 Protected Persons Convention, though it uses broader language. Article 1 requires States to 'prevent and punish acts of terrorism, especially kidnapping, murder, and other assaults against the life or physical integrity of those persons to whom the State has the duty according to international law to give special protection, as well as extortion in connection with those crimes'. The offences are 'considered common crimes of international significance, regardless of motive'.[112]

The term 'acts of terrorism' in Article 1 is open-ended and lacks definition, although ambiguity might be cured in national implementation. Article 1 lists certain prohibited acts as *examples* of 'acts of terrorism' rather than as definitive components of it (the duty is to 'prevent and punish acts of terrorism, *especially* . . .' (emphasis added)). In contrast, the 1973 Protected Persons Convention makes no mention of the term 'terrorism', instead exhaustively spelling out the physical elements of offences. The OAS Convention therefore permits States to establish a wider crime of 'terrorism' in national law, although the crime is limited to acts against protected persons.

By 1995, there was again some support in the OAS for defining terrorism generically in a comprehensive regional convention. An internal draft convention prepared by the OAS Secretariat of Legal Affairs in 1995 defined terrorism, *inter alia*, as violence 'intended to generate widespread fear, intimidation, or alarm' in the population.[113] The events of 11 September 2001 generated renewed impetus for new legal instruments, and an OAS Declaration condemned terrorism generically as 'the targeting of innocent persons to promote ideological objectives'.[114]

However, the US and Canada soon succeeded in arguing for a 'pragmatic and operational' or 'complementary' approach to a new instrument.[115] The US explained that attempts at generic definition would result in deadlock and detract from the agreement already reached through sectoral treaties.[116] States were conscious of the impasse affecting the Draft UN Comprehensive Convention since 2000, although a counter-argument was that the national liberation debate did not affect the western hemisphere to the same extent.[117] It

---

[112] 1971 OAS Convention, Art 2.

[113] Doc OEA/Sec.Gral. DDI/Doc.12/01 (26 Sept 2001); see M Scalabrino, 'Fighting against International Terrorism: The Latin American Response' in Bianchi (ed), n 76, 183–185.

[114] OAS, Declaration of Solidarity from the House of the Americas, 18 Oct 2001, OAS Doc OEA/Ser.F/11.23/RC.23/DEC.1/01 rev.1, corr.1, para 3.

[115] E Lagos and T Rudy, 'Preventing, Punishing, and Eliminating Terrorism in the Western Hemisphere: A Post–9/11 Inter-American Treaty' (2003) 26 Fordham ILJ 1619, 1628.

[116] ibid, 1629.

[117] ibid, 1630–31. Domestic insurgency has been more common in Latin America: Scalabrino, n 113, 172.

was, however, easier to avoid the ideological debate altogether, by focusing on terrorist *acts* rather than the definition of terrorism.[118]

As a result, the 2002 Inter-American Convention against Terrorism, as adopted, does not require States to criminalize any generic terrorist offences,[119] nor does it define terrorism even for the limited purposes of cooperation or extradition. While it aims 'to prevent, punish, and eliminate terrorism' (Article 1), it serves chiefly to encourage States to become parties to, and implement, the existing sectoral treaties, including by criminalizing their offences.[120] A similar approach had been recommended by the American Bar Association as early as 1983.[121] There are also provisions against terrorist financing,[122] reflecting Security Council measures, and provisions for co-operation on border control, law enforcement, mutual legal assistance, and transfer of custody.[123] Article 11 excludes the political offence exception for offences in the sectoral anti-terrorism treaties, although Article 14 preserves a non-discrimination clause. States must also exclude suspected terrorists from refugee status,[124] even though sectoral offences may not always be of sufficient gravity to warrant exclusion.

2. *Council of Europe: 1977 Convention, 2003 Protocol, and 2005 Convention*

A more ambitious regional response to terrorism is the Council of Europe's 1977 Convention on the Suppression of Terrorism, which aimed to facilitate the extradition of persons suspected of terrorist offences.[125] The European Convention was a response to violence, after the 1968 student protests, by groups such as the Baader-Meinhof Gang in West Germany and the Red Brigade in Italy.[126]

Article 1 *requires* States to exclude listed offences from the political offence exception to extradition. The offences included those in three international anti-terrorism treaties;[127] and an 'offence involving the use of a bomb, grenade, rocket, automatic firearm or letter or parcel bomb if this use

---

[118] OAS, Legal Aspects of Terrorism, 21 Feb 1996, OAS Doc OAS/Ser.G/CP/CAJP–1069/96, 11.

[119] OAS General Assembly (2nd Plenary Sess), AG/RES 1840 (XXXII-O/02), 3 June 2002, OAS Doc OAE/Ser.P/AG/doc 4143/02; see Lagos and Rudy, n 115. For the broader Latin American response to terrorism, see Scalabrino, n 113, 163.

[120] 2002 Inter-American Convention, Art 3 (treaties listed in Art 2). States must 'endeavour' to become parties.

[121] ABA, Model American Convention on the Prevention and Punishment of Series Forms of Violence (ABA, Washington, DC, 1983) Arts 1–2.

[122] ibid, Arts 4–6.   [123] ibid, Arts 7–10 respectively.   [124] ibid, Arts 12–13.

[125] 1977 Council of Europe Convention on the Suppression of Terrorism and Explanatory Memorandum; see also 1979 Dublin Agreement and 2003 Protocol; M Baker, 'The Western European Legal Response to Terrorism' (1987) 13 Brookings JIL 1; V Lowe and J Young, 'Suppressing Terrorism under the European Convention' (1978) 25 Netherlands ILR 305.

[126] McWhinney, n 19, 145–146.

[127] 1970 Hague Convention, 1971 Montreal Convention, 1973 Protected Persons Convention.

endangers persons'.[128] Article 2(1) allows States also not to regard as a political offence 'a serious offence involving an act of violence . . . against the life,
physical integrity or liberty of a person', while Article 2(2) applies the same
option to 'a serious offence involving an act against property . . . if the act
created a collective danger for persons'.

The 1977 European Convention expanded offences beyond those in the
then existing international anti-terrorism treaties to include a variety of acts
commonly committed by terrorists. However, it does not use or define the
term terrorism,[129] despite referring to 'acts of terrorism' in its preamble.
There is no reference to any generic elements of terrorism in the substantive
offences, such as an intention to instil terror or intimidate a group, or political
motives or objectives. Nor does the Convention require domestic criminalization of the enumerated offences. It simply establishes a list of prohibited acts,
often committed by terrorists (but not exclusively), to facilitate extradition,
but subject to reservations and a non-discrimination clause.[130] Prosecution is
conditioned on a refusal to extradite and is thus subsidiary.

Following the adoption in 2002 of an EU Framework Decision on Combating Terrorism and an associated Decision establishing a common European
arrest warrant, the 1977 European Convention is likely to diminish in importance. It is not, however, obsolete, because as an instrument of the Council of
Europe, it encompasses a much larger number of States than the EU. Even after
EU enlargement in 2004, the Convention will still govern extradition between
European member States outside the EU, and between EU and non-EU States
in Europe. Indeed, the 1977 Convention was revitalized by a 2003 amending
Protocol, which updated the list of sectoral treaties in Article 1, strengthened
implementation measures, placed procedural constraints on reservations,
and precluded extradition to torture or to face the death penalty.[131]

The 2003 Protocol was adopted after a review in the Council of Europe of
how to strengthen the effectiveness of existing international terrorism conventions after 11 September 2001. The question of drafting a comprehensive
regional convention against terrorism was also raised,[132] but the relevant
expert bodies concluded that the issue was not within their mandate.[133]

---

[128] 1977 European Convention, Art 1(d).

[129] Murphy, n 32, 21.

[130] J Lodge and D Freestone, 'The European Community and Terrorism: Political and Legal
Aspects' in Y Alexander and K Myers (eds), *Terrorism in Europe* (Croom Helm, London, 1982)
81.

[131] 2003 Protocol amending the European Convention on the Suppression of Terrorism (ETS
No 190, Strasbourg, 15 May 2003).

[132] Parliamentary Assembly Recommendations 1550 (2002) and 1644 (3004) and Opinion No
242 (2003); 25th Conference of the European Ministers of Justice, Sofia, 9–10 Oct 2003.

[133] Multidisciplinary Group on International Action against Terrorism (GMT), superseded by
the Committee of Experts on Terrorism (CODEXTER) from Oct 2003; see Explanatory Report
on Council of Europe Convention on the Prevention of Terrorism, adopted by the Committee of
Ministers, 925th mtg of the Council of Europe, paras 5–12.

Instead, it was decided that incremental steps should be taken to fill gaps in the legal framework, rather than taking a comprehensive approach to definition in a new treaty. One such step was the adoption of a convention on the proceeds of crime and terrorist financing in 2005.[134]

In addition, the 2005 Council of Europe Convention on the Prevention of Terrorism was adopted in Warsaw in May 2005.[135] It requires State Parties to adopt three new criminal offences with effective, proportionate, and dissuasive penalties: 'public provocation to commit a terrorist offence', recruitment for terrorism, and training for terrorism.[136] The Convention also contains provisions on prevention; compensation for victims; and international cooperation.[137] It imposes a duty to investigate the offences and to extradite (preferred) or prosecute.[138] The offences are made extraditable and are excluded from the political offence exception, subject to the protection of a non-discrimination clause and a requirement to respect human rights in implementation.[139] The Convention establishes mandatory territoriality and nationality jurisdiction, and optional bases for extending jurisdiction.[140]

For the purposes of the Convention, terrorism is defined in Article 1 as any offence in ten listed sectoral treaties (although States not party to particular treaties can declare their non-applicability). While there is thus no attempt to generically or comprehensively define terrorism, the preamble recalls that:

... acts of terrorism have the purpose by their nature and context to seriously intimidate a population or unduly compel a government or an international organization to perform or abstain from performing any act or to seriously destabilize or destroy the fundamental political, constitutional, economic or social structures of a country or an international organization. ...

Implicitly invoking the EU's definition of terrorism is not, however, intended to require its purposive motives as an element of the Convention's offences.[141] A Council of Europe Parliamentary Assembly recommendation to use the EU definition in a Common Position of 27 Dec 2001 was not accepted by the expert drafting committee.[142] The Council of Europe now has divergent definitions of terrorist-type activity between its 1977 and 2005 Conventions and the position is complicated further by the preambular reference to the EU's different definition.

---

[134] 2005 Council of Europe Convention on Laundering, Search, Seizure and Confiscation of the Proceeds from Crime and on the Financing of Terrorism (adopted at Warsaw, 24 June 2005).
[135] Opened for signature 16 May 2005, ETS No 196, Art 5(2) (not yet in force).
[136] Arts 5–7 respectively. It is not necessary that a terrorist offence is committed: Art 8. Art 9 establishes ancillary offences of complicity, organizing or directing, and conspiracy. Legal entities are also liable under Art 10. The nature of the penalties is described in Art 11.
[137] Arts 3, 13, 17 respectively.   [138] Arts 15 and 18 respectively.
[139] Arts 19–21 (extradition), 12 (human rights).
[140] Art 14.   [141] Explanatory Report, n 133, para 46.
[142] ibid, para 48. European Council, Common Position, 27 Dec 2001 (2001/931/CFSP).

The most controversial aspect of the 2005 Convention is its criminalization of 'public provocation' of terrorism. 'Public provocation' is defined as 'the distribution, or otherwise making available, of a message to the public, with the intent to incite the commission of a terrorist offence, where such conduct, whether or not directly advocating terrorist offences, causes a danger that one or more such offences may be committed' (Article 5(1)). The provision stemmed from a working group and expert report which considered both '*apologie du terrorisme*' and 'incitement to terrorism'.[143] *Apologie du terrorisme* was understood as the public expression of praise, support, or justification of terrorism.[144] It is thus broader than ordinary incitement to commit a crime (including terrorism), which is already an offence in many European countries.

The drafters intended that the new offence of 'public provocation' should extend beyond direct incitement to cover *indirect* incitement and *apologie*. The purported rationale for criminalizing such statements is that they create 'an environment and psychological climate conducive to criminal activity',[145] though they may fall short of any specific connection to the commission of an actual offence.

Examples of conduct that might be covered include 'presenting a terrorist offence as necessary and justified', and 'the dissemination of messages praising the perpetrator of an attack, the denigration of victims, calls for funding of terrorist organisations or other similar behaviour'.[146] Such conduct must be accompanied by the specific intent to incite a terrorist offence. It must also cause a credible danger that an offence might be committed, and this may depend on 'the nature of the author and of the addressee of the message, as well as the context'.[147] These qualifications (specific intent and causing danger) substantially narrow the offence, such that merely justifying or praising terrorism, without more, is not criminalized.

Moreover, the drafters insisted that the crime must be viewed in the light of the quality and integrity of European judicial systems, the availability of effective remedies, and the guarantee of a fair trial.[148] In particular, agreement on criminalizing public provocation was only reached because of mutual confidence in the system of institutional and legal protection of human rights in Europe.[149] The drafters were conscious that criminalizing incitement or

---

[143] CODEXTER, 'Apologie du terrorisme' and 'incitement to terrorism': Analytical Report by O Ribbelink, Secretariat Memorandum by the Directorate General of Legal Affairs, CODEXTER 3rd mtg, Strasbourg, 6–8 July 2004, CODEXTER (2004) 04 rev, Strasbourg, 24 June 2004.

[144] ibid, 5.

[145] M Kremnitzer and K Ghanayim, 'Incitement, Not Sedition' in D Kretzmer and F Hazan (eds), *Freedom of Speech and Incitement against Democracy* (Kluwer, The Hague, 2000) 147, 197.

[146] Explanatory Report, n 133, paras 98, 95 respectively.

[147] ibid, paras 99–100.   [148] CODEXTER, n 143, 31.

[149] Explanatory Report, n 133, paras 27–30.

apologie might interfere in freedom of expression, but argued that it could nonetheless constitute a legitimate restriction.[150] It seems that the drafters intended media transmissions of the statements to be excluded.

Even so, a great deal of discretion is given to the courts in evaluating the context and circumstances of a message, and since the intention behind messages will often be obscure, there is a danger that courts may too readily impute intentions without specific evidence. This danger is acute where a person is accused of making inflammatory, offensive, or shocking statements at odds with the prevailing values of the majority, where judges may face considerable pressure to conform to social morality in the face of public fear of terrorist violence. Further, the Convention does not expressly exempt statements made reasonably and in good faith for an academic, artistic, scientific, research, religious, journalistic, or other public interest purpose (as is common in defences to anti-vilification offences banning racial incitement).[151]

Human rights concerns about the scope of such offences were raised regarding the British Prime Minister's proposed new offence of 'condoning or glorifying terrorism' in the UK or abroad, announced in August 2005,[152] partly to implement the 2005 Council of Europe Convention.[153] Following considerable criticism, including by an independent expert appointed to review the proposals,[154] the proposal was replaced in the Terrorism Act 2006 (UK) with a narrower offence of 'encouragement of terrorism'.[155] Even so, the UK provision may have a wider reach because it is linked to the generic UK definition of terrorism, rather than to the narrower definition based on sectoral treaties in the 2005 Council of Europe Convention.

In a related development, in September 2005 the UK sponsored UN Security Council Resolution 1624 which called on States to: 'Prohibit by law incitement to commit a terrorist act or acts', prevent incitement, and deny safe haven or entry to inciters.[156] The preamble also repudiates 'attempts at the justification or glorification (*apologie*) of terrorist acts that may incite

---

[150] CODEXTER, n 143, 31.

[151] See, eg, Racial Discrimination Act 1975 (Australia), s 18D; Anti-Discrimination Act 1977 (NSW, Australia), s 20C(2); Racial and Religious Tolerance Act 2001 (Victoria, Australia), s 11.

[152] Prime Minister Blair, Statement on Anti-Terror Measures, 5 August 2005, para 2.

[153] Previously, UK law only prohibited incitement to terrorism within the UK or abroad, but not the broader offence of condoning or glorifying terrorism: see Terrorism Act 2000 (UK) ch 11, ss 59–61; C Walker, *Blackstone's Guide to the Anti-Terrorism Legislation* (OUP, Oxford, 2002) 175–177.

[154] Lord Carlile of Berriew QC, Report by the Independent Reviewer on Proposals by Her Majesty's Government for Changes to the Laws against Terrorism, Oct 2005.

[155] Terrorism Act 2006 (UK), s 1. It is an offence to publish a statement (including a statement which glorifies terrorism) where members of the public are likely to understand it as a direct or indirect encouragement or inducement to commit, prepare, or instigate terrorist acts, and the person intends for members of the public to be encouraged.

[156] UNSC Resolution 1624 (2005), para 3.

further terrorist acts'. The resolution does not go as far as the Council of Europe, since it calls for the *criminalization* of incitement, but merely *repudiates* the justification or glorification (*apologie*) of terrorism. Nonetheless, it ambiguously refrains from defining 'incitement', so it is unclear whether this term extends to indirect incitement, private incitement, or even vague *apologie* for terrorism. This lack of definition is of concern given that the Security Council has also failed to define terrorism itself,[157] allowing governments to unilaterally and subjectively define the scope of criminal liability. In the absence of a binding universal human rights system as in Europe, encouraging all States to criminalize incitement may encourage some States to excessively restrict free expression without any remedial restraints.

3. SAARC: 1987 Convention and 2004 Protocol

The 1987 SAARC Convention stemmed from a Sri Lankan proposal in 1985.[158] Under the Convention, specified offences according to national law are 'regarded as terroristic' and not as political offences for the purposes of extradition.[159] Offences include those in three international anti-terrorism treaties;[160] offences in treaties to which SAARC members are parties; and, in Article 1(e): 'Murder, manslaughter, assault causing bodily harm, kidnapping, hostage-taking and offences relating to firearms, weapons, explosives and dangerous substances when used as a means to perpetrate indiscriminate violence involving death or serious bodily injury to persons or serious damage to property.' The Convention imposes no duty on States to criminalize the listed offences; its provisions on extradition only operate if member States have enacted the necessary offences. The designation of specified treaty crimes in Article 1 as 'terroristic' is not in itself problematic, given that the treaties themselves define the offences. By regarding terrorism as constituted by common crimes, the drafters sought to avoid conferring any special political status on offenders.[161]

The SAARC Convention presents *indiscriminate violence* as a defining characteristic of 'terrorist' crimes, appearing to exclude discriminate attacks on designated (rather than random) targets. The acts listed as 'terroristic' also encompass forms of violence not commonly considered terrorist. Acts designed 'to perpetrate indiscriminate violence involving death or serious

---

[157] See B Saul, 'Definition of "Terrorism" in the UN Security Council: 1985–2005' (2005) 4 Chinese JIL 141 and Ch 4 below.

[158] R Perera, 'Suppression of Terrorism: Regional Approaches to Meet the Challenges' (2004) 16 Sri Lanka JIL 19, 20–21.

[159] 1987 SAARC Regional Convention on Suppression of Terrorism, Art 1.

[160] 1970 Hague Convention, 1971 Montreal Convention and 1973 Protected Persons Convention.

[161] Perera, n 158, 22.

bodily injury to persons or serious damage to property' could conceivably cover 'ordinary' criminal acts such as serial killing or mass murder, neither of which are typically committed for political motives or objectives (although such acts may intend to cause great fear). Similarly, the use of the listed methods to seriously damage property could include wayward expressions of democratic political protest which lack a terrorist character.

Soon after 11 September 2001, SAARC took steps to draft a new instrument to implement Security Council Resolution 1373 (2001) and the 1999 Terrorist Financing Convention.[162] As a result, the 2004 SAARC Additional Protocol to the 1987 Convention was adopted in Islamabad in early 2004.[163] It requires States to create a new offence of directly or indirectly providing or collecting funds with the intention or knowledge that they will be used for terrorism.[164] For the purposes of the Protocol, terrorism is defined as offences in ten listed sectoral treaties or 'any' SAARC treaty (necessarily including those not relating to terrorism), but also more generally as: 'Any other act intended to cause death or serious bodily injury to a civilian, when the purpose of such act, by its nature or context, is to intimidate a population, or to compel a Government or an international organization to do or to abstain from doing any act'.[165] As with the 2005 Council of Europe Protocol, the consequence is that SAARC has created divergent definitions of terrorism for different purposes in its 1987 and 2004 instruments. The definition derives from that in the 1999 Terrorist Financing Convention and thus establishes consistency with the international treaty regime governing terrorist financing. An attempt to distinguish national liberation movements from terrorism during the drafting was not pursued following the 'growing rapprochement' between India and Pakistan by the end of 2002.[166] Other provisions in the Protocol deal with regulatory measures to prevent, suppress, and eradicate financing; the seizure and confiscation of funds or assets; and predicate offences to money laundering.[167]

---

[162] SAARC Standing Committee, 28th Sess, Kathmandu, 19–20 Aug 2002; SAARC Council of Ministers, 23rd Sess, Kathmandu, 21–22 Aug 2002; drafting sessions were held in Sri Lanka and Bangladesh.

[163] Adopted at the 12th SAARC Summit, Islamabad, 4–6 Jan 2004.

[164] Art 4(1). The Convention also provides for the ancillary or inchoate offences of attempt, complicity, organizing or directing, and conspiracy: Art 4(4)–(5). Legal entities are also liable: Art 6.

[165] Art 4(1). Art 5 encourages States to become parties to the existing sectoral treaties.

[166] Perera, n 158, 24.

[167] Arts 7–9. The remaining provisions relate to cooperation, mutual legal assistance, extradition (including the exclusion of the political offence exception, subject to non-discrimination), denial of refugee status to financers, and technical cooperation: Arts 10–17, 20.

4. *League of Arab States: 1998 Convention*

One of the broadest definitions of terrorism appears in the 1998 Arab Convention on the Suppression of Terrorism,[168] which defines 'terrorism' in Article 1(2) as:

Any act or threat of violence, whatever its motives or purposes, that occurs in the advancement of an individual or collective criminal agenda and seeking to sow panic among people, causing fear by harming them, or placing their lives, liberty or security in danger, or seeking to cause damage to the environment or to public or private installations or property or to occupying or seizing them, or seeking to jeopardise a national resource.

Article 1(3) defines 'terrorist offences' as: 'Any offence or attempted offence committed in furtherance of a terrorist objective in any of the Contracting States, or against their nationals, property or interests, that is punishable by their domestic law.' The article additionally lists offences in six international treaties which are regarded as 'terrorist offences',[169] as well as the provisions on piracy on the high seas in the 1982 UN Convention on the Law of the Sea. The concept of terrorism in this Convention includes not only creating grave fear through acts or threats of violence, but any act or threat of violence, in pursuit of a criminal agenda, which endangers human life, liberty, or security, or which damages public or private property. It is difficult to see how the latter conduct can genuinely be described as terrorist, since it encompasses most ordinary violent crime.

The definition of terrorism in Article 1(2) is evidently very broad. Amnesty International argues that this definition 'can be subject to wide interpretation and abuse, and in fact does not satisfy the requirements of legality'.[170] The definition is based closely on Article 86 of the Egyptian Penal Code, adopted in 1992, which the UN Human Rights Committee describes as encompassing diverse acts of varying gravity.[171] The term 'violence' is not defined and it is unclear whether it refers only to unlawful acts of violence rather than to all violent acts. 'Threats' of violence may count as terrorism, but it is not clear how credible a threat must be. The meanings of 'to sow panic among people' and 'causing fear by harming them' are subjective and potentially arbitrary. It is not obvious what level of danger

---

[168] 1998 Arab Convention on the Suppression of Terrorism; see generally L Welchman, 'Rocks, Hard Places and Human Rights: Anti-Terrorism Law and Policy in Arab States' in Ramraj et al (eds), n 105, 581, 588–591; national implementation of the Convention varies: see Welchman, above, 591–606.

[169] 1963 Tokyo Convention, 1970 Hague Convention, 1971 Montreal Convention and 1988 Montreal Protocol, 1973 Protected Persons Convention, 1979 Hostages Convention.

[170] Amnesty International, 'The Arab Convention for the Suppression of Terrorism: A Serious Threat to Human Rights' (2002), AI Index: IOR 51/001/2002, 18.

[171] UNHRC, Comment on Egypt's Second Periodic Report on Implementation of the ICCPR, 9 Sept 1993, UN Doc CCPR/C/79/Add.23, para 8.

is envisaged by the expression 'placing ... lives, liberty or security in danger'.

Moreover, the expression 'seeking to cause damage to the environment or to public or private installations or property' does not require the commission of actual damage, and may also criminalize acts permitted by IHL in non-international armed conflict.[172] It is uncertain how 'seeking to cause damage' relates to concepts in international criminal law such as attempt. Merely 'occupying or seizing' public or private installations or property will not necessarily be for terroristic reasons, particularly in the context of democratic political protest or civil disobedience actions. 'Seeking to jeopardise national resources' is unhelpfully broad, since neither 'jeopardise' nor 'national resources' is defined.

Article 2(b) excludes the offences in Article 1 from being regarded as political offences for the purposes of extradition. Article 2(c)–(h) lists additional offences not as political offences, 'even if committed for political motives'. These include attacks on protected persons;

Premeditated murder or theft accompanied by the use of force directed against individuals, the authorities or means of transport and communications; Acts of sabotage and destruction of public property ... even if owned by another Contracting State; [and] the manufacture, illicit trade in or possession of weapons, munitions or explosives, or other items that may be used to commit terrorist offences.

While the definition makes terrorism extraditable 'whatever its motives or purposes', a contradictory disclaimer appears in Article 2(a), which states that: 'All cases of struggle by whatever means, including armed struggle, against foreign occupation and aggression for liberation and self-determination, in accordance with ... international law, shall not be regarded as an offence.' The self-serving exclusion in Article 2(a) is the statement that the 'provision shall not apply to any act prejudicing the territorial integrity of any Arab State'. Thus terrorist acts in pursuit of self-determination against *non*-Arab States are justifiable and lawful—but they are prohibited against Arab States.

On the other hand, the Convention does not expressly prevent the return of terrorist suspects to a State where they would be at risk of torture in contrast to the 2003 Council of Europe Protocol. Civil society groups have criticized the Convention for attempting to 'contract around' the international prohibition on return to torture by implicitly permitting it in the region.[173] Plainly, regional treaty frameworks are circumscribed by peremptory norms of

---

[172] Amnesty International, n 170, 20.

[173] Human Rights Watch, 'Black Hole: The Fate of Islamists Rendered to Egypt' (2005) 17(5) HRW Report 1, 9; Arab Center for the Independence of the Judiciary and the Legal Profession, 'Commentary on the Arab Convention Against Terrorism', Cairo, 7 May 1998; see also International Federation for Human Rights, Ankara Declaration, Regional Seminar on the Post-September 11 Era, 18–21 Dec 2003.

international law, including non-refoulement to torture. Nonetheless, the absence of an express protection to this effect in the Convention is of concern given the substantial evidence of the return of suspects to torture in the region in the US-led 'war' on terror.[174] The Arab Convention has been frequently used to deliver suspects in the region.[175]

5. *Organization of the Islamic Conference: 1999 Convention*

Resembling the 1998 Arab Convention is the 1999 Organization of the Islamic Conference (OIC) Convention.[176] The treaties are similar largely due to the substantial overlap in the memberships of the Arab League and the OIC, although the OIC also includes non-Arab Muslim States, including prominent victims of terrorism such as Pakistan, Indonesia, and Turkey. Article 1(2) of the OIC Convention defines 'terrorism' as:

... any act of violence or threat thereof notwithstanding its motives or intentions perpetrated to carry out an individual or collective criminal plan with the aim of terrorizing people or threatening to harm them or imperiling their lives, honour, freedoms, security or rights or exposing the environment or any facility or public or private property to hazards or occupying or seizing them, or endangering a national resource, or international facilities, or threatening the stability, territorial integrity, political unity or sovereignty of independent States.

Article 1(3) defines a 'terrorist crime' as 'any crime executed, started or participated in to realise a terrorist objective in any State party, or against its nationals, assets or interests or foreign facilities and nationals residing in its territory punishable by its internal law'. Article 1(4) additionally lists offences in twelve international treaties as terrorist crimes.[177] Like the Arab League Convention, the OIC Convention also deems much ordinary criminal activity as terrorist, including any act of violence, pursuing a criminal plan, which threatens to harm people or imperil their lives, honour, freedoms, security, or rights. This encompasses conduct from mugging to burglary.

Article 2(a) excludes from consideration as terrorism: 'Peoples' struggle including armed struggle against foreign occupation, aggression, colonialism,

---

[174] See, eg, Human Rights Watch, ' "Empty Promises": Diplomatic Assurances No Safeguard against Torture' (2004) 16(4) HRW Report; J Fitzpatrick, 'Rendition and Transfer in the War against Terrorism: Guantanamo and Beyond' (2003) 25 *Loyola Los Angeles International and Comparative Law Review* 457; Canadian Commission of Inquiry into the Actions of Canadian Officials in Relation to Maher Arar: <www.ararcommission.ca> (last accessed 7 Feb 2006).

[175] A Maged, 'International Legal Cooperation: An Essential Tool in the War Against Terrorism' in Heere (ed), n 73, 157, 177.

[176] 1999 OIC Convention on Combating International Terrorism.

[177] 1963 Tokyo Convention, 1970 Hague Convention, 1971 Montreal Convention and 1988 Protocol, 1973 Protected Persons Convention, 1979 Hostages Convention, 1982 UNCLOS (piracy provisions), 1980 Vienna Convention, 1988 Rome Convention and 1988 Protocol, 1991 Montreal Convention, and 1997 Terrorist Bombings Convention.

hegemony, aimed at liberation and self-determination in accordance with . . . international law.' As in the 1998 Arab Convention, this exclusion exists despite the declaration in Article 1(2) that the 'motives or intentions' behind an act are irrelevant to its terrorist character.

Article 2(b) establishes that none of the offences 'shall be considered political crimes' in extradition law. Further offences to be treated as non-political are listed in Article 2(c) and are very similar to those found in Article 2(c)–(h) of the Arab League Convention. In addition, Article 2(d) states that: 'All forms of international crimes, including illegal trafficking in narcotics and human beings [and] money laundering aimed at financing terrorist objectives shall be considered terrorist crimes.'

The definition of terrorism is broader than the already wide definition in the 1998 Arab Convention. The 'aim' of violence or its threat must be 'terrorizing people or threatening to harm them or imperiling their lives, honour, freedom, security or rights', introducing numerous vague and subjective elements. The term 'violence' is not defined or limited by reference to criminal or unlawful acts, nor to the severity of the violence. It is not clear what amounts to exposing the environment or any facility or property to a 'hazard'. As in the 1998 Arab Convention, there are difficulties with the concept of 'occupying or seizing' property in the light of legitimate democratic protest, and 'endangering a national resource' is of potentially broad scope.

The greatest ambiguity lies in the abstract and political concept of 'threatening the stability, territorial integrity, political unity or sovereignty of independent states'. Since many of the elements of the definition in Article 1(2) are *not* cumulative, a mere threat of a criminal act against State 'stability', 'integrity', 'unity', or 'sovereignty' could be treated as a 'terrorist crime'. There is a serious danger of the abusive use of terrorist prosecutions against political opponents, ordinary criminals, and persons threatening public order or national security.

6. *Organization of African Unity: 1999 Convention and 2004 Protocol*

A narrower definition of terrorism is found in the 1999 OAU Convention, which requires States to criminalize enumerated offences.[178] Article 1(3)(a) defines a 'Terrorist act' as any domestic criminal act 'which may endanger the life, physical integrity or freedom of, or cause serious injury or death to, any person, any number or group of persons or causes or may cause damage to public or private property, natural resources, environmental or cultural heritage'. Such an act must be conjunctively 'calculated or intended to':

---

[178] 1999 OAU Convention on the Prevention and Combating of Terrorism, Art 2(a). See generally Roch Gnahoui David, 'Le terrorisme: cadre juridique au plan de l'Union Africaine' in SOS Attentats (ed), *Terrorisme, victimes et responsabilité pénale internationale* (Calmann-Lévy, Paris, 2003) 102.

(i) intimidate, put in fear, force, coerce or induce any government, body, institution, the general public or any segment thereof, to do or abstain from doing any act, or to adopt or abandon a particular standpoint, or to act according to certain principles; or
(ii) disrupt any public service, the delivery of any essential service to the public or to create a public emergency; or
(iii) create general insurrection in a State.

The OAU Convention is drafted more restrictively than the Arab League and OIC Conventions. It establishes a concept of terrorism which hinges on the intimidation or coercion of protected targets, or the disruption of public services, through violent criminal acts. Criminal acts must produce a fairly high minimum threshold of danger to the public before being considered as terrorist offences. It is similar in some respects to definitions of terrorist offences in the 2002 EU Framework Decision and the UN Draft Comprehensive Convention.

Nonetheless, it still defines terrorism very broadly. The protected targets are very wide and ill-defined. 'Inducing' a government to adopt or abandon a particular standpoint is a basic aim of democratic politics, sometimes occasioned by overzealous acts of protest which amount to criminal violence but fall short of the idea of terrorism and which ought not be treated as such. Regarding acts which create a 'public emergency' or a 'general insurrection' as terrorism conflates national security or emergency laws with terrorism laws, eroding any distinction between these categories.

Like the Arab League and OIC Conventions, the OAU Convention states in Article 3(1) that 'the struggle waged by peoples in accordance with the principles of international law for their liberation or self-determination, including armed struggle against colonialism, occupation, aggression and domination by foreign forces shall not be considered as terrorist acts'. Again this exclusion exists despite Article 3(2) stating that: 'Political, philosophical, ideological, racial, ethnic, religious or other motives shall not be a justifiable defence against a terrorist act.' The national liberation provision operates, therefore, as an exclusion from the definition of terrorist acts, rather than as an immunity or defence to terrorism, although the practical consequence— impunity—is the same.

The definition and exclusion provisions in the 1999 Convention also supply the operative definition for a 2004 African Union Protocol to the Convention.[179] The 2004 Protocol creates no new offences, but aims to enhance the implementation of the Convention and to coordinate and harmonize African efforts to prevent and combat terrorism.[180] States undertake to implement a range of measures on terrorist training and financing, mercenarism, weapons

---

[179] Adopted by the African Union Assembly, 3rd Ordinary Sess, Addis Ababa, 8 July 2004.
[180] 2004 Protocol, Art 2(2), and pursuant to the 2002 Protocol Relating to the Establishment of the Peace and Security Council of the African Union (adopted 1st Ordinary Sess of the African Union Assembly, Durban, 9 July 2002) Art 3(g).

of mass destruction (WMDs), compensation for victims of terrorism, preventing the entry of terrorists, and the exchange of information and cooperation.[181] It forbids the torture or degrading or inhumane treatment of terrorist suspects, but asks States to 'take all necessary measures to protect the fundamental human rights of their populations against all acts of terrorism'.[182] It tasks the African Union's Peace and Security Council with harmonizing and coordinating African counter-terrorism, and States undertake to submit regular reports to the Council.[183]

7. Commonwealth of Independent States: 1999 Treaty

With the disintegration of the Soviet Union in the late 1980s, complex conflicts, some involving terrorist methods, developed in parts of Russia and the newly independent republics. With this physical fragmentation came new obstacles to law enforcement, as new national boundaries frustrated the once hegemonic Soviet police State. In 1999, the CIS Treaty was adopted to deal with judicial cooperation, exchange of information, and cross-border anti-terrorism operations.[184] States must cooperate in preventing, uncovering, halting, and investigating terrorism (Article 2), but the treaty does not require States to criminalize terrorist offences.

For the purposes of cooperation and extradition, 'terrorism' is defined in Article 1 as the commission of a specified criminal act 'for the purpose of undermining public safety, influencing decision-making by the authorities or terrorizing the population'.[185] The specified acts include violence or threats of violence against natural or juridical persons, and certain acts against protected persons.

Specified acts against property in Article 1 include destroying or damaging, or threatening to destroy or damage, property and other material objects to endanger lives; or causing substantial harm to property or 'other consequences dangerous to society'. The final type of specified act includes 'Other acts classified as terrorist' under national law or in 'universally recognized' international anti-terrorism treaties.

The definition of terrorism in the CIS Treaty is a composite of quite different offences—undermining public safety; influencing official decision-making; or terrorizing the population. It contains novel elements such as prohibiting violence for private motives such as 'revenge', in addition to

---

[181] Art 3(1). The Convention also supplies a basis for extradition (Art 8) and contains a dispute settlement provision: Art 7.

[182] Art 3(1)(k) and (a) respectively.

[183] Arts 4–5 and 3(1)(h)–(i) respectively. Regional mechanisms play a complementary role: Art 6.

[184] 1999 CIS Treaty on Cooperation in Combating Terrorism.

[185] 'Technological terrorism' is separately and lengthily defined in the CIS Treaty, Art 1.

political motives. It covers a wide range of activity, without limiting terrorist offences to very serious conduct (such as *seriously* undermining public safety or *intimidating*, rather than merely influencing, decision-makers). There is also vagueness in the notion of causing 'other consequences dangerous to society'. The CIS Treaty permits States a wide latitude in unilaterally defining terrorist offences, since it declares that it also covers 'Other acts classified as terrorist under the national legislation of the Parties'.

The CIS Treaty requires States not to regard acts of terrorism 'as other than criminal' for extradition purposes (Article 4). Nonetheless, a State may decline extradition if it believes that fulfilling the request 'may impair its sovereignty, security, social order or other vital interests or is in contravention of its legislation or international obligations', or the act does not satisfy the double criminality rule (Article 9). In practice therefore, the political offence exception survives under another name, to the extent that it exists to protect the sovereignty, security, social order, or vital interests of the requested State.

8. Shanghai Cooperation Organization: 2001 Convention [186]

Five CIS member States are also members of the Shanghai Cooperation Organization (SCO), an intergovernmental organization established in 2001 by six States in Central Asia: Kazakhstan, China, Kyrgyzstan, the Russian Federation, Tajikistan, and Uzbekistan. The SCO aims to strengthen relations between member States and to promote political, security, and economic cooperation,[187] and its political significance lies in the powerful combination of Russia and China in a single organization.

The SCO Convention on Combating Terrorism, Separatism and Extremism was adopted on the same day that the SCO was founded, indicating the importance of security matters to the Organization. The preamble states that 'terrorism, separatism and extremism constitute a threat to international peace and security [and] the promotion of friendly relations among States' and that such acts should be prosecuted 'regardless [of] their motives, [and] cannot be justified under any circumstances'. The Convention immediately signals a blurring of terrorism with other phenomena, even though separatist movements, for example, need not use terrorist methods.

The Parties to the Convention undertake to cooperate and assist in preventing, identifying, and suppressing terrorism, separatism, and extremism and to consider such acts as extraditable offences, although extradition and

---

[186] Shanghai Convention on Combating Terrorism, Separatism and Extremism (adopted in Shanghai on 15 June 2001, entered into force 29 March 2003). All six members of the SCO are State Parties.
[187] As well as cooperation on science, culture, education, energy, transport, tourism, and environmental protection; and to create a 'democratic, just, reasonable new international political and economic order': see <www.sectsco.org>.

legal assistance remain in accordance with international treaties and national law.[188] Most importantly, the parties must take all necessary measures, including legislation, to ensure that terrorism, separatism, and extremism are 'in no circumstances ... subject to acquittal based upon exclusively political, philosophical, ideological, racial, ethnic, religious or any other similar considerations and that they should entail punishment proportionate to their gravity'.[189] The Convention thus implicity requires the criminalization of terrorism, separatism, and extremism.

The Convention defines 'terrorism' in Article 1(1)(1) as: (a) offences in annexed treaties or (b) certain other violent criminal acts against persons or property 'when the purpose of such act, by its nature or context, is to intimidate a population, violate public security or to compel public authorities or an international organization to do or to abstain from doing any act'. Acts against persons must be 'intended to cause death or serious bodily injury to a civilian, or any other person not taking an active part in the hostilities in a situation of armed conflict', while acts against property must be intended to 'cause major damage to any material facility'.[190] The Convention thus excludes attacks on combatants in armed conflicts from being treated as terrorist and this exclusion appears to extend to both international and non-international conflicts. This may be significant to the extent that the violence in Chechnya is characterized (by the parties) as an armed conflict.

The generic part of the Convention shares elements in common with the 1999 Terrorist Financing Convention and the 2002 EU Framework Decision (including intimidating a population or compelling a government or international organization, and the qualifying phrase 'by its nature or context'). However, the Convention goes significantly further by adding the vague alternative element of violating 'public security', which is nowhere defined. The definition of terrorism accordingly extends to cover violence against people or property which is not designed to terrorize, intimidate, or coerce, but simply to interfere with public order or security.

The scope of the Convention is further widened by the definition of 'separatism' in Article 1(1)(2) as criminal violence 'intended to violate [the] territorial integrity of a State including by annexation of any part of its territory or to disintegrate a State'. In addition, Article 1(1)(3) defines 'extremism' as criminal violence 'aimed at seizing or keeping power', changing the 'constitutional regime of a State', encroaching on public security, or organizing or participating in 'illegal armed formations' for such purposes.

---

[188] Art 2(1)–(3). The remainder of the Convention provides for detailed measures of cooperation and assistance, the exchange of information, requests for assistance, and technical assistance. It also foreshadows the establishment of a Regional Counter-Terrorist Structure, based in Bishek, to combat terrorism: Arts 5–11.

[189] Art 3.

[190] Organizing, planning, aiding, or abetting such acts is also covered by the definition.

These definitions seek to suppress both secession and more limited domestic rebellions, and there is no exclusion for violence against combatants in internal armed conflicts. This effectively negates the benefit of the exclusion in the terrorism definition, since what is not classified as terrorism can be treated as separatism or extremism. These definitions might, for example, cover violent unrest by Uighurs in China's Xinjiang province or other radical groups in the region,[191] some of which is motivated by resistance to government repression or marginalization.[192] Concerns have already been raised about the impact on freedom of expression and the media of Kyrgyzstan's law banning extremism.[193]

9. *European Union: 2002 Framework Decision*[194]

A more targeted regional approach to criminalizing terrorism was adopted by the EU Council in its hastily drafted 2002 Framework Decision on Combating Terrorism,[195] which defines 'terrorist offences' to enable a common European arrest warrant and the mutual recognition of legal decisions and verdicts among EU States.[196] It required the approximation of the (hitherto

---

[191] On unrest in the region, see M Singh (ed), *International Terrorism and Religious Extremism: Challenges to Central and South Asia* (Anamika Publishers, New Delhi, 2003).

[192] F Hill, 'Central Asia: Terrorism, Religious Extremism, and Regional Stability', The Brookings Institution, Testimony before the US Congress, House Committee on International Relations (Subcommittee on the Middle East and Central Asia), 23 July 2003.

[193] Law on Counteraction of Extremist Activities (adopted by the Kyrgyzstan Parliament on 30 June 2005, approved by the President on 17 Aug 2005); see Moscow Media Law and Policy Institute, quoted in ICJ Bulletin on Counter-Terrorism and Human Rights, No 8, Geneva, Nov 2005.

[194] While not formally a treaty in public international law, the EU Framework Decision is considered here because it serves the similar purpose of imposing binding legal obligations on member States. Framework Decisions are binding under the EU third pillar of Police and Judicial Cooperation in Criminal Matters: EU Treaty, Arts 29–32. Such decisions are made cooperatively by member States (and thus more closely resemble treaties) rather than within European Community law-making processes.

[195] 2002 EU Framework Decision on Combating Terrorism; see also EU Commission, Proposal for a Council Framework Decision on Combating Terrorism, Brussels, 19 Sept 2001, COM(2001) 521 Final, 2001/0217 (CNS); European Parliament, Sess Doc, Consultation Procedure Reports on Commission Proposals, 14 Nov 2001, FINAL A5–0397/2001, and 9 Jan 2002, FINAL A5–0003/2002; Human Rights Watch, Open Letter to EU President, 12 Oct 2001; Amnesty International, Comments on a Proposal by the Commission for a Council Framework Decision on Combating Terrorism, Brussels, 19 Oct 2001; Peers, n 76; B Saul, 'International Terrorism as a European Crime: The Policy Rationale for Criminalization' (2003) 11 *European Journal of Crime, Criminal Law and Criminal Justice* 323; E Symeonidou-Kastanidou, 'Defining Terrorism' (2004) 12 *European Journal of Crime, Criminal Law and Criminal Justice* 14.

[196] 2002 EU Framework Decision on the European Arrest Warrant and the Surrender Procedures. For the broader EU response to terrorism, see J Monar, 'Anti-Terrorism Law and Policy: The Case of the European Union' in Ramraj et al (eds), n 105, 425; F Gregory, 'The EU's Response to 9/11' (2005) 17 *Terrorism and Political Violence* 105; A Reinisch, 'The Action of the European Union to Combat International Terrorism' in Bianchi (ed), n 85, 119; M den Boer, 'The EU Counter-Terrorism Wave: Window of Opportunity or Profound Policy Transformation?' in M van Leeuwen (ed), *Confronting Terrorism* (Kluwer, The Hague, 2003) 185.

disparate)[197] domestic terrorism offences of EU States by 31 December 2002.[198] The definition of terrorism in the Framework Decision also identifies individuals and entities subject to asset freezing under EU legislation implementing Security Council measures.[199] The Framework Decision is not limited to international terrorism, extending to domestic and EU terrorism, and imposes wide extraterritorial jurisdiction on EU States.[200]

The definition of terrorism in the Framework Decision is modelled on an identical definition in an EU Council Common Position of December 2001, which served the limited purpose of implementing Security Council Resolution 1373 (2001) to freeze the funds and assets of listed terrorist suspects and associates.[201] The Framework Decision definition distinguishes terrorism from ordinary crime by focusing on the aims or motives of offenders.[202] In tortuous language, Article 1(1) defines 'terrorist offences' as:

... offences under national law, which, given their nature or context, may seriously damage a country or an international organization where committed with the aim of:
— seriously intimidating a population, or
— unduly compelling a Government or international organization to perform or abstain from performing any act, or
— seriously destabilising or destroying the fundamental political, constitutional, economic or social structures of a country or an international organization ...

Motive is ordinarily irrelevant to criminal responsibility in most legal systems. The EU understands motive as the specific purpose behind committing prohibited acts—intimidation, compulsion, or destabilization—rather than as a particular ideological, political, or religious cause motivating the offence. This approach to motive contrasts with a 1996 resolution of the EU Parliament, which referred to terrorism politically as acts or threats of violence 'intended to create a state of terror' with 'motives lying in separatism, extremist ideology, religious fanaticism or subjective irrational factors'.[203]

The wording of the definition is 'complex and uncertain'.[204] It draws

---

[197] A Vercher, *Terrorism in Europe* (Clarendon, Oxford, 1992) 297–303.
[198] 2002 EU Framework Decision, Art 11(1). Framework Decisions adopted under the EU 'third pillar' are not directly applicable and, like EC directives, require national implementation.
[199] EU Council, Common Position on the Application of Specific Measures to Combat Terrorism (2001/931/CFSP), 27 Dec 2001 [2001] OJ L344/93, Art 1(3), implemented by Reg 2580/2001 [2001] OJ L344/70 and Decision 2001/927 [2001] OJ L344/83; all implementing UNSC Resolution 1373 (2001). See A Reinisch, 'Some Problematic Aspects of Recent EU Financial Anti-Terrorism Measures' (2002) Austrian RIEL 7.
[200] Peers, n 76, 233.
[201] EU Council Common Position 2001/931/CFSP, n 199, Art 1(3). Another EU measure gives effect to UNSC Resolution 1333 (2000) to freeze the funds and assets of Osama bin Laden and associates: EU Council Common Position 2001/154/CFSP (1), 26 Feb 2001.
[202] EU Commission Proposal, n 195, 6–7.
[203] European Parliament, Resolution on Combating Terrorism in the EU [1997] OJ C55/27, preamble (C).
[204] Guillaume, n 1, 4.

heavily on Article 2(1)(b) of the 1999 Terrorist Financing Convention, although it is 'far wider'.[205] It modifies the comparable provision of that Convention by requiring that the *aim* (rather than 'purpose') of offences must be to *seriously* intimidate a population or *unduly* compel a government or international organization to perform or abstain from doing any act. This modification raises the threshold of terrorist aims and ensures that less serious intimidation or compulsion will not fall within the Framework Decision's offences. There is, however, no protection from compulsion for non-governmental organizations (NGOs), other non-international groups, or natural or juridical persons other than States or international organizations, just as such proposals were excluded from the 1999 Terrorist Financing Convention.[206]

Further, the Framework Decision requires that offences 'may seriously damage a country or an international organization' in addition to having a terrorist aim, a requirement which is not present in the 1999 Terrorist Financing Convention. However, *actual* damage is seemingly unnecessary ('may' damage); a likelihood or even a possibility of damage is sufficient. The Framework Decision adds a third possible aim of terrorist offences— seriously destabilizing the fundamental structures of a country or an international organization—which is not found in the 1999 Terrorist Financing Convention.[207] The idea of 'fundamental structures' is particularly imprecise. A further addition is the qualifying phrase 'given their nature or context', which provides flexibility in appreciating what conduct constitutes terrorism. While some argue that this qualifying phrase narrows the definition,[208] to the contrary, it may widen the scope of offences by eliminating the need to prove an intention to intimidate, compel, or destabilize.[209]

The prohibited acts in Article 1(1), linked to the generic part of definition, fall into five basic groups: offences against the person; offences against property; weapons offences; offences by other prohibited means; and threats to commit such offences. They are drawn from identical provisions in the EU Common Position of 2001.[210] In short, the Decision prohibits three types of acts against the person in Article 1(1): '(a) attacks upon a person's life which

---

[205] Peers, n 76, 232: 'particularly as regards: the personal scope of prohibited death and injury; the scope of prohibited damage to property and the means by which such damage is caused; individual acts related to biological and chemical weapons; release of dangerous substances or causing fires and floods; interfering with resources; and threatening to commit the great majority of these acts'.

[206] Working Group Report (1999), n 61, 40 (Brazil), 44 (India); Ad Hoc Committee Report (1999), n 38, 33 (Guatemala).

[207] Peers, n 76, 231.

[208] ibid, 232.

[209] The expression 'by its nature or context' in the 1999 Terrorist Financing Convention was intended to remove the need to prove a subjective mental state: Working Group Report (1999), n 49, 62 (Chair).

[210] EU Common Position 2001/931/CFSP, n 199, Art 1(3)(a)–(i).

may cause death; (b) attacks upon the physical integrity of a person; [and] (c) kidnapping or hostage taking'. Concerning property, Article 1(1)(d) establishes the terrorist offence of 'causing extensive destruction to a Government or public facility, a transport system, an infrastructure facility, including an information system, a fixed platform located on the continental shelf, a public place or private property likely to endanger human life or result in major economic loss.'

Article 1(1)(e) creates the further property offence of the 'seizure of aircraft, ships or other means of public or goods transport', reflecting offences in existing anti-terrorism treaties.[211] The idea of 'causing extensive destruction' was adapted from the 1997 Terrorist Bombings Convention and the targets protected are similar,[212] although the Framework Decision extends protection to fixed platforms (embodying the 1988 Rome Protocol) and *private* property, increasing the risk of violent demonstrations in democratic societies being regarded as terrorism.[213]

Indeed, the Framework Decision was initially intended to cover situations of 'urban violence',[214] and Italy hoped the definition of terrorism would cover anti-globalization protests such as those against the G8 in Genoa.[215] Such coverage would blur terrorism offences with other offences against public order and political violence, and ultimately the preamble to the Framework Decision stated that the Decision cannot be interpreted to restrict fundamental rights such as the right to strike and demonstrate, and freedoms of assembly, association, or expression.[216]

It is not at all clear, however, that violence such as the widespread suburban riots in Paris and other French cities of November 2005[217] would be excluded from the definition. Such violence involved extensive property damage and may have aimed to intimidate the population, coerce the French government, or destabilize fundamental political, constitutional, economic, or social structures in France, while also seriously damaging France. The difficulty here is that conduct which satisfies the legal definition of terrorism is not widely *perceived* as terrorism either in France or abroad; rather, it is an experience of urban (and racialized) violence by disaffected or disenfranchised segments of the population, also well-known in French history.

---

[211] 1963 Tokyo Convention, 1970 Hague Convention, 1971 Montreal Convention and 1988 Rome Convention.

[212] 2002 EU Framework Decision, Art 2.

[213] Peers, n 76, 237.

[214] EU Commission Proposal, n 195, 9.

[215] J Monar, 'The European Union's Response to September 11', Paper at Sept 11 Conference, University of Sussex, 21–22 Mar 2003.

[216] 2002 EU Framework Decision, recital 10.

[217] 'Emegency laws subdue French violence', *The Guardian*, 9 Nov 2005. Consider also the small scale 'riots' by indigenous people in the Australian suburb of Redfern in 2004: 'Sydney riots over Aborigine death', BBC News, 16 Feb 2004.

Regarding serious attacks on property as terrorism expands the scope of terrorism beyond direct attacks on people. Whereas the 1997 Terrorist Bombings Convention rejected proposals to regard attacks on private property as terrorism,[218] the Framework Decision includes private property. The concern in 1997 was that reference to private property would criminalize acts governed by national law.[219] The idea of 'extensive destruction' to property in the Framework Decision is similar to the grave breach of 'extensive destruction' in the 1949 Fourth Geneva Convention.[220]

Article 1(1)(f) creates a bundle of weapons and explosives offences, while Article 1(1)(g) prohibits the 'release of dangerous substances, or causing fires, floods or explosions the effect of which is to endanger human life'. A further offence in Article 1(1)(h) prohibits 'interfering with or disrupting the supply of water, power or any other fundamental natural resource the effect of which is to endanger human life'. Threatening to commit any of the forgoing acts is an offence in Article 1(1)(i). The remaining offences include 'offences linked to terrorist activities' (aggravated theft, extortion, or drawing up false documents with a view to committing a terrorist offence)[221] and 'inciting or aiding or abetting' or 'attempting' to commit an offence.[222]

A recital to the Framework Decision excludes the actions of armed forces during armed conflict from being regarded as terrorist offences, since such actions are governed by IHL.[223] The recital also excludes actions by *State* armed forces 'in the exercise of their official duties' and 'inasmuch as they are governed by other rules of international law'. This provision reflects the 1999 Terrorist Bombings Convention,[224] although it takes the form of a recital, rather than an operative provision, and its legal effect is thus uncertain.[225] An attempt to exclude persons analogous to freedom fighters in Europe in the Second World War is even more uncertain.[226]

(a) Terrorist group offences

The Framework Decision also establishes terrorist group offences, an innovation not found in other regional treaties. A 'terrorist group' is defined in Article 2(1) to mean 'a structured group of more than two persons, established over a period of time and acting in concert to commit terrorist

---

[218] Working Group Report (1997), n 64, 19 (Germany); Ad Hoc Committee Report (1997), n 38, 5–6, 13 (Revised Bureau text), 50 (Rapporteur).
[219] Ad Hoc Committee Report (1997), ibid, 52 (Rapporteur).
[220] 1949 Fourth Geneva Convention, Art 147 (where not justified by military necessity and carried out unlawfully and wantonly).
[221] 2002 EU Framework Decision, Art 3(a)–(c) respectively.
[222] ibid, Art 4(1) and (2) respectively.   [223] ibid, recital 11.
[224] 1997 Terrorist Bombings Convention, Art 19(1); Peers, n 76, 234.
[225] ibid, 234. In contrast, human rights protections are located in Art 1(2).
[226] See Ch 2 above.

offences'; a 'structured group' is also defined.[227] The definition is identical to that in the EU's earlier Common Position of 2001.[228] The general definition of terrorist groups cures the danger of statutory lists of proscribed groups inadvertently or tardily omitting certain groups, such as in the UK, where members of the Real IRA, responsible for the Omagh bombing, were acquitted of membership offences because only the IRA was proscribed.[229] It also ensures that the failure to proscribe a group does not imply its legitimacy or lawfulness.

Article 2(2) requires States to punish intentionally (a) 'directing a terrorist group' and (b) 'participating in the activities of a terrorist group'.[230] Participation is defined to include the supply of information or material resources, or by funding the group's activities in any way, 'with knowledge of the fact that such participation will contribute to the criminal activities of the terrorist group'. Clearly, mere membership is not sufficient to attract liability,[231] and these offences do not amount to collective punishment or guilt by association, since liability is for the crimes of direction or participation, not for the crimes of the group. Most such conduct would already be covered by ancillary and inchoate offences such as complicity or conspiracy, so that the offences are largely symbolic. They are based on Article 5 of the UN Convention against Transnational Organized Crime, and are narrower than group offences in UK legislation[232] and those prosecuted at Nuremberg,[233] but wider

---

[227] A 'structured group' is then defined as 'a group that is not randomly formed for the immediate commission of an offence and that does not need to have formally defined roles for its members, continuity of its membership or a developed structure'; see similarly 2000 UN Convention against Transnational Organized Crime, Art 2(c).

[228] EU Council Common Position 2001/931/CFSP, n 199, Art 1(3).

[229] M Taylor, 'Real IRA is not illegal: judge', *The Guardian*, 27 May 2004.

[230] See similarly EU Common Position 2001/931/CFSP, n 199, Art 1(3)(j)–(k).

[231] In national law, mere membership of a criminal group is not usually sufficient to amount to criminal complicity: see, eg, *Yugoslav Terrorism* case (1978) 74 ILR 509 (Germany).

[232] The Terrorism Act 2000 (UK) establishes various offences relating to a proscribed organization: belonging or professing to belong to it (s 11(1)), inviting support for it (s 12(1)), arranging, managing, or assisting in arranging or managing, a meeting of it (s 12(2)), addressing a meeting to encourage support for or further the activities of it (s 12(3)), and appearing in public displaying allegiance with or support for it (s 13(1)); directing an organization is also an offence, which does not require proscription (s 56); see Walker, n 153, 60–64. The UK law has a low threshold for 'supporting' terrorist organizations; one man was convicted of membership for wearing a ring inscribed with the initials of the Ulster Volunteer Force: *James Rankin v Procurator Fiscal, Ayr*, Scottish High Ct of Justiciary (Appeal Ct), Appeal No XJ343/03, 1 June 2004.

[233] 1945 Nuremberg Charter, Art 9 gave the International Military Tribunal at Nuremberg (IMT) power to declare organizations criminal in the trial of any individual member, while Art 10 allowed national authorities to prosecute individuals for membership of such organizations, whose criminality could not then be challenged (incorporated in Control Council Law No 10, Art II(1)(d)). The IMT declared criminal the Nazi Leadership Corps, Gestapo, SD, and SS. However, to avoid mass punishment, the IMT interpreted these provisions as requiring personal guilt, voluntary association, and criminal knowledge; and likened them to a criminal conspiracy (requiring an organized group with a common criminal purpose): *Nuremberg Judgment* 1946 (1947) 41 AJIL 172, 250–251; see also *Altstoetter (Justice* case*)* (1947) US Military Tribunal at Nuremberg, *Trial of War Criminals before the Nuremberg Military Tribunals*, vol III, 1030; see

than US anti-mafia legislation.[234] Membership offences are preferable to indefinite detention of terrorist suspects where there is insufficient evidence to prosecute for an ordinary offence.

However, the first offence of directing a terrorist group problematically criminalizes *all* directions, 'even if lawful and, indeed, even if desirable', such as a direction to surrender, observe a cease-fire or to disarm.[235] Further, that offence does not require that the person have knowledge of the criminal activities of the group. The second offence, participation, does not require a person to have *specific* knowledge of *particular* group crimes, nor does it demand that the person know of the group's *terrorist* crimes, as opposed to its ordinary ones. This may result in unfairness where, for instance, a person donates money for charitable purposes to a group which performs mixed charitable and terrorist functions, such as some Palestinian groups.[236] There is also no requirement that participation in a terrorist group must be *voluntary*, raising the prospect that persons coerced into participating may be held liable.[237]

D. ATTEMPTS AT DEFINITION IN TREATY LAW 1930–2006

On a number of occasions since the 1920s, the international community has attempted to arrive at a generic definition of terrorism for the purposes of prohibition and/or criminalization, suggesting that it attaches considerable importance to definition. As Brownlie notes: 'Even an unratified treaty may be regarded as evidence of generally accepted rules, at least in the short run.'[238] While these sources do not carry great weight as evidence of custom, they illustrate the recurring normative and political disputes surrounding definition and elucidate the basic features of terrorism.

K Kittichaisaree, *International Criminal Law* (OUP, Oxford, 2001) 248–249; Cassese (2003), n 5, 138. In numerous cases, the US Military Tribunal at Nuremberg found defendants guilty of membership of criminal organizations (mainly the SS): *Medical* case *(USA v Karl Brandt et al)* (1947); *Pohl* case *(USA v Oswald Pohl et al)* (1947); *Milch* case *(USA v Erhard Milch)* (1947); *Justice* case *(USA v Josef Altstoetter et al)* (1947); *Flick* case *(USA v Friedrich Flick et al)* (1947); *IG Farben (USA v Carl Krauch et al)* (1948); *RuSHA* case *(USA v Ulrich Greifelt et al)* (1947–48); *Einsatzgruppen* case *(USA v Otto Ohlendorf et al)* (1948); *Ministries* case *(USA v Ernst von Weizsaecker et al)* (1949). However, constructive knowledge of the activities of a criminal organization could be imputed to an individual by virtue of that person's position in the organization: *Justice* case, above, 1170, 1176; *Flick* case, above, 1122.

[234] Racketeer Influences and Corrupt Organizations (RICO), 18 USC §§1961–68; J Atkinson, 'Criminal Law: Racketeer Influences and Corrupt Organizations: Broadest of the Federal Criminal Statutes' (1978) 69 JCLC 1. RICO does not criminalize group participation *per se* but enhances penalties for the commission of two or more ordinary criminal offences.

[235] Walker, n 153, 170.

[236] Reuters, 'EU resists Israeli pressure to ban Hamas political wing', *Sydney Morning Herald*, 19 July 2003; W Laqueur, *The New Terrorism: Fanaticism and the Arms of Mass Destruction* (Phoenix, London, 2001) 137 (Hezbollah provides social services).

[237] Subject to the criminal law defence of duress: see Ch 2 above.

[238] Brownlie, n 14, 12.

1. 1920s and 1930s Unification of Criminal Laws

Attempts to exclude terrorist 'outrages'—such as the assassination of State officials—from the political offence exception to extradition had been steadily made in some national laws from the late nineteenth century, beginning with the Belgian *attentat* clause. Yet the idea of systematically defining terrorism as an international criminal offence only gathered momentum in the 1920s and 1930s. In 1926, Roumania asked the League of Nations to consider drafting a 'convention to render terrorism universally punishable' but the request was not acted on.[239]

Terrorism was more systematically considered in a series of International Conferences for the Unification of Criminal Law between 1930 and 1935.[240] The term 'terrorism' first appeared at the Third Conference in Brussels in 1930:

The intentional use of means capable of producing a common danger that represents an act of terrorism on the part of anyone making use of crimes against life, liberty or physical integrity of persons or directed against private or state property with the purpose of expressing or executing political or social ideas will be punished.[241]

The political or social motives behind specified violent acts, and the risk of producing a common danger, were the defining features of terrorism.[242] At the Fourth Conference in Paris in 1931, two rapporteurs proposed different definitions, although each shared the core element of imposing a political or social doctrine through criminal violence.[243] Ultimately a resolution was adopted which avoided reference to political or social objectives, and instead emphasized the effects of specified violent acts:

Whoever, for the purpose of terrorizing the population, uses against persons or property bombs, mines, incendiary or explosive devices or products, fire arms or other deadly or deleterious devices, or who provokes or attempts to provoke, spreads or attempts to spread an epidemy, a contagious disease or other disaster, or who interrupts or attempts to interrupt a public service or public utility will be punished . . .[244]

The Fourth Conference also recommended the adoption of a convention 'to assure the universal repression of terrorist attempts'.[245]

---

[239] LoN, Committee of Experts for the Codification of International Criminal Law, Replies of Governments 1927, LoN Doc C.196.M.70.1927.V, 221.

[240] Terrorism was discussed at the 3rd (Brussels 1930), 4th (Paris 1931), 5th (Madrid 1933) and 6th (Copenhagen 1935) International Conferences for the Unification of Criminal Law: G Bouthoul, 'Definitions of Terrorism' in Carlton and Schaerf (eds), n 1, 72; B Zlataric, 'History of International Terrorism and its Legal Control' in Bassiouni (ed), n 32, 474, 478–482; T Franck and B Lockwood, 'Preliminary Thoughts towards an International Convention on Terrorism' (1974) 68 AJIL 69, 75–76.

[241] Final Commission Proposal, quoted in Zlataric, n 240, 479.

[242] Zlataric, ibid, 479.

[243] Definitions quoted in Zlataric, ibid, 479–480.

[244] ibid, 480.   [245] ibid.

At the Fifth Conference in Madrid in 1934, terrorism and crimes creating a common danger were considered separately and the discussion focused on terrorism. Whereas Rapporteur Roux concentrated on the definition from the Fourth Conference, Rapporteur Lemkin avoided the notion of terrorism and instead developed the idea of *crimina juris gentium* (including provoking international catastrophe, destroying art works, and participating in massacres or collective atrocities against the civilian population).[246] While notions of political and social terrorism were discussed, ultimately only social rather than political terrorism formed part of the concept adopted by the Conference: 'He, who with the hope of undermining social order, employs any means whatsoever to terrorize the population, will be punished.'[247] The Fifth Conference accordingly reduced the notion of terrorism to the crime of anarchy,[248] avoiding earlier references to political motives or aims.

In 1935, the Sixth Conference at Copenhagen adopted model national legislation for the repression of terrorism.[249] Article 1 proposed the offence of 'intentional acts directed against the life, physical integrity, health or freedom' of specified protected persons, where the perpetrator has created 'a common [or public] danger, or state of terror that might incite a change or raise an obstacle to the functioning of public bodies or a disturbance in international relations'.[250] Article 2 listed acts which create a common danger or provoke a state of terror.[251]

The Copenhagen Draft was similar to early draft provisions developed by the League of Nations' expert Committee for the International Repression of Terrorism (CIRT) in 1935, suggesting that the Copenhagen Conference approved the approach taken by the CIRT. Importantly, the preamble of the Copenhagen Draft stated that

. . . it is necessary that certain acts should be punished as special offences, apart from any general criminal character which they may have under the laws of the State, whenever such acts create a public danger or a state of terror, of a nature to cause a change in or impediment to the operation of the public authorities or to disturb international relations, more particularly by endangering peace . . .[252]

This approach to treating terrorism as a discrete crime was markedly at odds with a 'preliminary draft convention' prepared by the International Criminal Police Commission in Vienna, which elaborated on a 1934 French

---

[246] ibid, 480.   [247] ibid.   [248] ibid, 481.
[249] LoN CIRT, 'Texts adopted by the 6th International Conference for the Unification of Criminal Law (Copenhagen, 31 Aug–3 Sept 1935)', Geneva, 7 Jan 1936, LoN Doc CRT.17 ('Copenhagen Draft').
[250] Quoted in Zlataric, n 240, 482.
[251] Including instigating a catastrophe or calamity, polluting drinking water, spreading contagious diseases, destroying public utilities, and using explosives in a public place.
[252] Copenhagen Draft, n 249, 1.

proposal to the League, and was submitted to the CIRT at its first session.[253] The prohibited acts in the Vienna Draft differed from the French Proposal only in elaboration: protected persons and property were specified in more detail; the list of prohibited weapons was expanded; and methods of incitement were listed. Significantly, the Vienna Draft stated that 'acts of terrorism' are enumerated offences punishable 'as ordinary crimes'. In contrast, the Copenhagen Draft stated that 'it is necessary that certain acts should be punished as special offences, apart from any general criminal character'.[254]

2. 1937 League of Nations Convention

The most significant early modern attempt to define terrorism as an international crime was undertaken by the League of Nations between 1934 and 1937.[255] In October 1934, King Alexander I of Yugoslavia was assassinated by Croatian separatists while on a State visit to France;[256] the French Foreign Minister, Louis Barthou, and two bystanders were also killed. The suspects fled to Italy, and France requested their extradition under a treaty of 1870, which excluded political crimes from extradition. The Court of Appeal of Turin refused to surrender the accused on the grounds that the offences were politically motivated and thus non-extraditable.[257] The Court found that 'the assassination of a sovereign is a political crime if it is prompted by political motives . . . and offends against a political interest of a foreign state', as are 'crimes committed or attempted in the course of the said regicide'.[258]

The League of Nations faced immediate political pressure to respond.

---

[253] LoN (CIRT), 'Preliminary Draft Convention drawn up by the Executive Bureau of the International Criminal Police Commission', Geneva, 11 Apr 1935, LoN Doc CRT.3 ('Vienna Draft'), 9.

[254] Copenhagen Draft, n 249, 1.

[255] H Donnedieu De Vabres, 'La repression internationale du terrorisme—les conventions de Genève (16 novembre 1937)' (1938) 19 *Revue de Droit International Législation Comparée* 37; A Sottile, 'Le terrorisme international' (1938–III) 65 *Recueil des Cours de l'Académie de Droit International* 116; J Starke, 'The Convention for the Prevention and Punishment of Terrorism' (1938) 19 BYBIL 214; H Mosler, 'Die Konferenz zur internationalen Bekämpfung des Terrorismus' (1938) 8 Zaö RV 99; V Pella, 'Les Conventions de Genève pour la prévention et la répression du terrorisme et pour la création de la Cour pénale internationale' (1938) 18 *Revue de droit pénal et de criminology* 402; P Kovacs, 'La Société des Nations et son action après l'attentat contre Alexandre, roi de Yougoslavie' (2004) 6 *Journal of History and International Law* 65; G Marston, 'Early Attempts to Suppress Terrorism: The Terrorism and International Criminal Court Conventions of 1937' (2002) 73 BYBIL 293; B Saul, 'The Legal Response of the League of Nations to Terrorism' (2006) 4 JICJ 78.

[256] F Walters, *A History of the League of Nations* (OUP, London, 1969) 599.

[257] *In re Pavelic and Kwaternik* (1933–34) Ann Dig and Reports of PIL Cases, Case No 158, 372; B Ferencz, *An International Criminal Court: vol I* (Oceana, London, 1980) 48; Walters, n 256, 602.

[258] Cited in *R v Governor of Pentonville Prison, ex p Cheng* [1973] AC 931.

The memory of the assassination of Chancellor Dolfuss of Austria three months earlier in July 1934 was still fresh,[259] as was an attempt on the life of Romanian Minister Duca.[260] The League had faced a similar international crisis in 1923, when General Tellini of Italy was assassinated while delimiting the frontier between Albania and Greece, resulting in Italy's bombardment and occupation of Corfu.[261] Seasoned diplomats had not forgotten the assassination of Archduke Franz Ferdinand in Sarajevo in 1914 and its catastrophic consequences for global peace.[262]

Following two months of intensive diplomacy, in a resolution of December 1934, the League Council noted that 'the rules of international law concerning the repression of terrorist activity are not at present sufficiently precise to guarantee efficiently international co-operation'.[263] It established an expert committee, CIRT, to draft a preliminary international convention 'to assure the repression of conspiracies or crimes committed with a political and terrorist purpose'. The terms 'terrorist activity' and 'political and terrorist purpose' were not defined. The CIRT comprised eleven States and met in three sessions between April 1935 and April 1937.[264]

The Committee was further guided by a League Assembly resolution of October 1936, which stated that the proposed convention must be founded 'upon the principle that it is the duty of every State to abstain from any intervention in the political life of a foreign State'. The resolution confined the scope of the convention further by stating that it should have 'as its principal objects': '(1) To prohibit any form of preparation or execution of terrorist outrages upon the life or liberty of persons taking part in the work of foreign public authorities and services'; (2) to prevent and detect such outrages; and (3) to punish terrorist outrages which 'have an international character'.[265]

The convention was drafted in a number of phases between 1935 and 1937.[266] An international diplomatic conference met in November 1937 to draft and adopt a convention based on the final draft submitted by CIRT. The Final Act of the diplomatic conference adopted two international

---

[259] Walters, n 256, 604.   [260] Zlataric, n 240, 481.

[261] Walters, n 256, 244–255.   [262] ibid, 246, 600.

[263] LoN, Committee for the International Repression of Terrorism (CIRT), Geneva, 10 Apr 1935, LoN Doc CRT 1.

[264] 1st Sess, Apr–May 1935; 2nd Sess, Jan 1936; 3rd Sess, Apr 1937. Members included Belgium, UK, Chile, France, Hungary, Italy, Poland, Roumania, USSR, Spain, and Switzerland.

[265] By virtue of the place of preparation or execution, or the nationality of perpetrators or victims: LoN, International Conference Proceedings on the Repression of Terrorism, Geneva, 1–16 Nov 1937, LoN Doc C.94.M.47.1938.V, Annex I, 183.

[266] LoN (CIRT), Reports to Council, Geneva: 1st Sess (8 May 1935, LoN Doc C.184.M.102.1935.V); 2nd Sess (10 Feb 1936, LoN Doc A.7.1936.V); 3rd Sess (26 Apr 1937, LoN Doc V. Legal 1937.V.1); see also LoN Assembly (17th Ordinary Sess), Records— Committee Meetings (1st Committee Constitutional and Legal Questions), Geneva, (1936) LoN OJ (Special Supp) 156.

conventions—the first defining international terrorist offences, and the second creating an international criminal court to punish the offences in the first treaty.[267]

The first treaty, the 1937 Convention for the Prevention and Punishment of Terrorism, required States to criminalize terrorist offences and encouraged States to exclude the offences from the political offence exception to extradition.[268] It attracted twenty-four signatories: twelve were European States, seven were Caribbean, Central or South American States, and five others included major States from other regions.[269] The Convention was only ratified by one (colonial) State—India, which had separate League membership to Britain[270]—and never entered into force. The Second World War diverted attention from the Convention and with the demise of the League of Nations, interest in the Convention never revived.

Despite never entering into force, the 1937 League Convention indicates the early views of States on terrorism. Article 1(1) reaffirms as a 'principle of international law' that it is 'the duty of every State to refrain from any act designed to encourage terrorist activities directed against another State and to prevent acts in which such activities take shape'. States were, however, careful to implicitly exclude armed forces from the scope of the Convention, including acts committed in civil wars.[271]

Article 1(2) cumulatively defines 'acts of terrorism' as 'criminal acts directed against a State and *intended or calculated to create a state of terror in the minds of* particular persons, or a group of persons or the general public' (emphasis added). Article 2 then enumerates the criminal acts which States must criminalize, where they are committed on that State's territory, directed against another contracting State, and 'if they constitute acts of terrorism

---

[267] LoN Final Act of Conference, Geneva, 16 Nov 1937, LoN Doc C.548.M385.1937.V; (1938) 19 LoN OJ 23; in Y Alexander et al (eds), *Control of Terrorism: International Documents* (Crane Russak, New York, 1979) 19; Ferencz, n 257, 380.

[268] 1937 League Convention, in International Conference Proceedings, n 266, Annex I, 5; and 1937 Convention for the Creation of an International Criminal Court, in International Conference Proceedings, above, 19. The latter treaty attracted fewer signatories and never came into force. A State party was entitled, instead of prosecuting, or extraditing a suspect to another State party, to send the suspect for trial before the international criminal court.

[269] European States: Albania, Belgium, Bulgaria, Czechoslovakia, France, Greece, Monaco, the Netherlands, Norway, Romania, Spain, Yugoslavia. American States: Argentina, Cuba, Dominican Republic, Ecuador, Haiti, Peru, Venezuela. Other regions: USSR, Turkey, (British) India and Egypt, along with a small State, Estonia. Monaco signed later: Starke, n 255, 214.

[270] Starke, ibid, 215.

[271] 3rd Sess Report, n 266, 2; 1st Committee Records, n 266, 30 (Roumania), 36 (Yugoslavia), 38 (Sweden); LoN (CIRT), Observations by Governments (Series I), 7 Sept 1936, LoN Doc A.24.1936.V (Norway); LoN (CIRT), Observations by Governments, 30 March 1937, LoN Doc C.194.M.139.1937.V), 1–2 (Czechoslovakia); Letters from H McKinnnon-Wood (UK Foreign Office, Geneva) to L Brass (UK Home Office, London) and J Fischer-Williams (Oxford), 30 Mar 1937, LoN Archives Geneva Doc 3A/20521/15085/XIX.

within the meaning of Article 1'. The acts include crimes against persons and property, weapons offences, and ancillary offences.[272]

Consequently, terrorism is defined by the intended aim (a state of terror), the ultimate target (a State), and the prohibited means used, but not by reference to political motives or coercive objectives.[273] Proposals to define terrorism as a means to a political end were not accepted.[274] 'Acts of terrorism' was defined circularly or tautologically by reference to 'a state of terror',[275] despite objections that the term was ambiguous and open to abuse.[276] The meaning of a 'state of terror' is not explained in the treaty or in the drafting record.

On a literal construction, it suggests acute or extreme fear, with the words 'a state of' indicating a more durable or continuing fear than the word 'terror' on its own. At the time, some States thought a 'state of terror' did not mean a subjective fear in the mind of one person, but a more objective state involving many individuals.[277] However, the text of the provision refers to 'a state of terror *in the minds of particular individuals*' (emphasis added), which envisages that a subjective state of terror in the minds of a small number of persons could amount to terrorism.[278]

It is also unclear from the record whether acts 'directed against a State' narrowly referred to attempts to overthrow the State,[279] or encompassed acts against broader State interests, including State 'honour', security, or public order.[280] Further, only acts directed against a State, and not against private persons or groups, were regarded as terrorism. A French proposal to criminalize attacks on 'private persons by reason of their political attitude' (such as political activists, academics, suffragettes, or trade unionists) was not

---

[272] Including wilfully: 'causing death or grievous bodily harm or loss of liberty' to protected persons and public officials (Art 2(1)); destroying or damaging public property of another State (Art 2(2)); endangering the lives of the public (Art 2(3)); attempting to commit offences (Art 2(4)); manufacturing, obtaining, possessing, or supplying arms, ammunition, explosives or harmful substances with a view to committing an offence in any country (Art 2(5)); and conspiracy, incitement, direct public incitement, wilful participation, and knowing assistance (Art 3).

[273] International Conference Proceedings, n 265, 72 (Yugoslavia), 63 (Spain).

[274] LoN CIRT, 'Legislation regarding political terrorist crimes: Study by T Givenovitch', Geneva, 3 May 1935, LoN Doc CRT.9, 4.

[275] International Conference Proceedings, n 265, 81 (Yugoslavia), 80 (Spain), 78 (France).

[276] 1st Committee Records, n 266, 32 (Belgium); Observations by Governments (1937), n 271, 2 (Czechoslovakia); 2nd Sess Report, n 266, Appendix III, 16 (Roumania).

[277] Observations by Governments (1937), n 271, 3 (Czechoslovakia); 1st Committee Records, n 266, 45 (Roumania); International Conference Proceedings, n 265, 77 (Netherlands), 75 (Poland).

[278] International Conference Proceedings, n 265, 75–76 (UK, USSR, Poland).

[279] As proposed in the 2nd Sess Draft, Art 2, in 2nd Sess Report, n 266; and by the UK: CIRT, 'Suggestion by the British expert for an article to be inserted in the draft convention', Geneva, 1 May 1935, LoN Archives Doc 3A/17592/15085/VII.

[280] International Conference Proceedings, n 265, 72 (Yugoslavia) and 2nd Sess Report, n 266, Appendix III, 15 (Roumania).

accepted. (Likewise, a Latvian proposal to regard attacks on private property as terrorism was not accepted.)[281]

As a result, the killings of Karl Liebknecht and Rosa Luxemburg in Weimar Germany in 1919[282] would not be considered terrorism, despite the German Social Democratic Party, exiled in Prague, bringing assassinations of its members in the 1920s and 1930s to the attention of the CIRT in 1937.[283] With chilling prescience, Leon Trotsky, exiled in Mexico, also warned the League of Soviet terrorism against its enemies—just a few years before he was assassinated by Soviet agents.

The utility of the Convention was always doubtful because its extradition provisions did not exclude terrorism from the political offence exception.[284] In a climate of mounting authoritarianism, many States were reluctant to confine their sovereign discretion in extradition matters, including the scope of political offences,[285] and were at pains to protect asylum from degradation.[286] The drafting of the Convention was primarily a means of averting the escalation of the international crisis precipitated by King Alexander's assassination,[287] rather than a progressive process of legal reform. A contemporary writer viewed its provisions as not of 'major importance', and suggested that practical cooperation was more important than 'stiffening' the law.[288] Despite definition, the term 'terrorism' remained open to abuse, with Hitler justifying the Nazi occupation of Bohemia and Moravia in March 1939 as designed to disarm 'terrorist bands threatening the lives of [German] minorities'.[289]

Nonetheless, the Convention is normatively significant in the debate about defining terrorism, since its drafting elucidated major substantive issues which remained relevant in the post-war period. Its definition served for many years as a benchmark definition of terrorism, surfacing early in the drafting of the 1954 ILC Draft Code of Offences,[290] and most influentially, shaping a much cited 1994 General Assembly Declaration.[291] In 1996, the League definition was approved by an English judge to limit the scope of the exclusion clauses in the 1951 Refugee Convention.[292] It is significant that

---

[281] 2nd Sess Report, n 266, Appendix III, 14.

[282] E Hobsbawm, *Age of Extremes* (Abacus, London, 1995) 68.

[283] Letter from the Sozialdemokratischen Partei Deutschlands (Prague) to CIRT (Geneva), 30 Oct 1937, LoN Archives Doc 3A/15105/15085/XIII.

[284] 1937 League Convention, Art 8.

[285] 1st Committee Records, n 266, 40 (UK); International Conference Proceedings, n 265, 53 (UK), 54 (Norway); 62 (Belgium); Observations by Governments (Series I), n 271, 3 (Belgium).

[286] 1st Committee Records, n 266, 48 (Finland), 37 (Norway); 39 (Netherlands), 41 (Sweden, France), 33, 43 (Belgium); Observations by Governments (Series I), n 271, 11 (Netherlands).

[287] Walters, n 256, 605.   [288] Starke, n 255, 215.

[289] Quoted in I Brownlie, *International Law and the Use of Force by States* (Clarendon, Oxford, 1963) 340.

[290] See '3 1954 ILC Draft Code of Offences' below.

[291] UNGA Resolution 49/60 (1994), annexed Declaration on Measures to Eliminate International Terrorism, para 3.

[292] *T v Home Secretary* [1996] AC 742 (Lord Mustill).

the main dispute surrounding the drafting was the scope of the extradition provisions, rather than difficulties with the definition of terrorism itself. It is certainly possible that a treaty may reflect custom even if it has not entered into force,[293] and the process of drafting treaties focuses world opinion and influences State behaviour and legal conviction.[294] Nonetheless, the practice of States (including specially affected States) on the definition of terrorism since 1937 has been far from consistent with the Convention's approach to definition.

3. 1954 ILC Draft Code of Offences

The next major attempt to codify terrorism was made by the International Law Commission (ILC) when drafting its 1954 Draft Code of Offences against the Peace and Security of Mankind (Part I).[295] Terrorism was explicitly linked to the concept of aggression. Article 2(6) defines an offence 'against the peace and security of mankind' of the 'undertaking or encouragement by the authorities of a State of terrorist activities in another State, or the toleration by the authorities of a State of organized activities calculated to carry out terrorist acts in another State'. Under Article 1, offences in the Code 'are crimes under international law, for which the responsible individuals shall be punished'. The offence only covers conduct by those acting for the State,[296] and not the activities of non-State actors, despite an early 1950 draft provision covering acts of private persons.[297] Further, it only covers State toleration of terrorist activities where those activities are sufficiently 'organized' to affect peace (such as acts of political parties directed against another State), thus excluding acts of single persons without any organized connection.[298] Further, arguments to include private terrorism with international effects were not accepted,[299] the requirement being that acts be directed against another State.[300]

As the UK noted at the time, the terms 'terrorist activities' and 'terrorist

---

[293] *Continental Shelf* case *(Libya v Malta)* (1985) ICJ Reports 13, 33, para 34.

[294] J-M Henckaerts and L Doswald-Beck (eds), *Customary International Humanitarian Law* (CUP, Cambridge, 2004) vol I: *Rules*, xliii; K Wolfke, *Custom in Present International Law* (2nd edn, Martinus Nijhoff, Dordrecht, 1993) 71.

[295] 1954 ILC Draft Code of Offences against the Peace and Security of Mankind (Part I), in ILC 6th Sess Report (3 Jun–28 Jul 1954), UN Doc A/2693, as requested by UNGA Resolution 177(II) (1947).

[296] (1950–II) ILCYB 59.

[297] 1950 Draft Code, crime no IV, in Report by Special Rapporteur Spiropoulos, 26 Apr 1950, UN Doc A/CN.4/25, (1950–II) ILCYB 253, 263; see also (1950–I) ILCYB 127–128 (Rapporteur Spiropoulos).

[298] (1950–I) ILCYB 126 (Rapporteur Spiropoulos), 166 (Cordova); (1950–II) ILCYB 58, 253 (Rapporteur Spiropoulos), the latter conduct being left to national law. A proposal to delete 'organized' was not accepted: (1950-I) ILCYB 127 (François).

[299] (1950–I) ILCYB 129, 166 (ILC Chairperson).

[300] ibid, 129 (Amado).

acts' are not defined,[301] and one ILC member stated that the first expression was as vague as another expression that had been rejected—'fifth column'.[302] In contrast, the Special Rapporteur argued that terrorism had a 'fairly precise meaning in international law', deriving from the 1937 League Convention,[303] which, while not in force, expressed the legal views of 40 States.[304] The Rapporteur decided, however, to make the provision more general in character than the 1937 definition.[305] At the same time, the drafting record also refers to concepts of terrorism developed elsewhere:[306] 'systematic terrorism' developed in 1919; the war crime of 'indiscriminate mass arrests for the purpose of terrorizing the population' from 1944; and terrorism in national law.[307]

Yet some ILC members found references to terrorism too vague unless linked to the 'excellent' 1937 definition.[308] As a result, a 1951 draft provision incorporated the League definition,[309] but this disappeared after objections that the 1937 expression 'a state of terror' was 'too literary' and antiquated, and would embarrass a judge,[310] with the modern term 'terrorist activities' preferred.[311] Others also questioned the meaning of the 1937 definition, or found the draft definition too confused.[312] As such, it was omitted from the 1954 provision, but contextualizes the meaning of terrorism.

Higgins argues that the inclusion of terrorism in the 1954 ILC Draft Code in relation to State aggression serves only as a 'term of convenience' or political expediency.[313] In her view, this is because international law on the use of force and the law of State responsibility already address terrorist acts, or support for such acts, by States of the kind envisaged by Draft Article 2(6). Consequently, the description of such acts as terrorist is considered legally redundant, particularly in the absence of any definition of 'terrorist activities' in Article 2(6).

Higgins' analysis is accurate to the extent that there is no normative void in international law in relation to responsibility for the acts of States envisaged by Article 2(6). The law of State responsibility and law on the use of force undoubtedly already apply to unlawful acts committed in these circumstances.[314] Draft Article 2(6) merely particularizes forms of aggression and the scope of State responsibility.

---

[301] (1954–II) ILCYB 117 (UK).   [302] (1954–I) ILCYB 130.
[303] ibid, 131.   [304] (1950–I) ILCYB 218 (Alfaro).
[305] ibid, 126.   [306] (1950–II) ILCYB 253, 264–266.
[307] See, respectively, Ch 5; UN War Crimes Commission, Legal Committee Report, 9 May 1944; Australian War Crimes Act 1945, s 3(ii): 'murder or massacres—systematic terrorism', and Chinese Law, 24 Oct 1946, art III(1): war crime of 'Planned slaughter, murder or other terrorist action'.
[308] (1950–I) ILCYB 127 (Hudson, François).
[309] 1951 Draft Code, Art I(5), in (1950–II) ILCYB 58.
[310] (1950–I) ILCYB 63 (Alfaro and Kerno respectively).
[311] ibid.   [312] ibid, 127–128 (Amado and Yepes respectively).
[313] Higgins, n 1, 26–27.   [314] See Ch 4 below.

On the other hand, the purpose of Article 2(6) was to establish *individual criminal responsibility* for the State commission, encouragement, or toleration of 'terrorist activities'. Individual criminal responsibility is a different type of international legal liability than that provided for by the law of State responsibility or the law on the use of force. Reference to terrorism may thus serve a useful legal function for the purpose criminal liability, quite apart from whether it remains a term of convenience for the other purpose of State responsibility. The article on terrorism was adopted by the ILC by 10 votes to 0, with 3 abstentions, suggesting that ILC members believed reference to terrorism served some useful purpose. Further, the view that the provision was similar to a draft provision on civil strife did not result in the amalgamation of the provisions as suggested,[315] indicating that the ILC felt justified in preserving a distinct provision on terrorism.

Due to insurmountable disagreement about the definition of aggression, in 1954 the General Assembly postponed further consideration of the 1954 ILC Draft Code until a Special Committee on defining aggression had reported.[316] Subsequent attempts to define aggression have eschewed any reference to terrorism and severed the early linkage between these concepts. A (non-exhaustive) General Assembly resolution defining 'aggression' in 1974 makes no reference to terrorism,[317] nor does the definition in the 1996 ILC Draft Code or in the 1998 Draft Rome Statute.[318]

4. *1991 and 1996 ILC Draft Code of Crimes*

The ILC resumed consideration of the Draft Code in 1982.[319] Following nine reports by a Special Rapporteur between 1983 and 1991, the ILC adopted a first reading of a Draft Code in 1991.[320] Article 24 of the 1991 ILC Draft Code, based on Article 2(6) of the 1954 Draft Code,[321] proposed an offence where a State agent or representative commits or orders the 'undertaking, organizing, assisting, financing, encouraging or tolerating acts against another State directed at persons or property and *of such a nature as to create a state of terror in the minds of* public figures, groups of persons or the general public'.[322] Compared with the 1954 draft, this provision partially incorporated the 1937 League definition; added the notions of 'organizing',

---

[315] (1950–I) ILCYB 127 (El Khoury).   [316] UNGA Resolution 897 (IX) (1954).
[317] UNGA Resolution 3314 (XXIX) (1974).
[318] ICC PrepCom Report, UN Diplomatic Conference of Plenipotentiaries on an ICC, Rome, 15 June–17 July 1998, UN Doc A/Conf.183/2/Add.1 (14 Apr 1998), Art 5. Aggression may be defined by future amendment to the 1998 Rome Statute.
[319] UNGA Resolution 36/106 (1981).
[320] (1991–II) ILCYB, para 175; see also ILC (47th Sess), 13th Report of Special Rapporteur (1995), UN Doc A/CN.4/466.
[321] (1990) ILCYB 336.
[322] Emphasis added. Draft Art 16(1) of 1990 is similar: (1990) ILCYB 336.

'assisting', and 'financing'; and expressly covered acts against property. Some ILC members objected that the definition was tautological and that it would be better to refer to 'a state of fear' rather than a 'state of terror'.[323] The difficulty of proving subjective fear was also raised.[324]

The proposed offence did not apply to private individuals and required a State connection.[325] Some ILC members thought, however, that groups of individuals could threaten peace and security,[326] and regretted that acts by liberation movements, and international corporations, were not covered.[327] Some governments also believed that terrorism should cover private as well as State conduct.[328] Other governments felt that the provision was too imprecise to impose criminal liability,[329] or that terrorism was too sensitive to be entrusted to an international tribunal.[330]

In 1995, a renumbered draft Article 24 retained similar wording to the 1991 draft, but added that acts must be committed 'in order to compel' the victim State 'to grant advantages or to act in a specific way'.[331] While this narrowed the scope of the offence, it had the disadvantage of excluding nihilist or other violence designed to terrorize but not also to compel.[332] Some thought it better to avoid altogether any reference to the subjective motives or objectives of the act.[333]

As alternatives to a 'state of terror', reference was made to 'a state of fear' or a 'state of dread'. New offences of 'ordering' or 'facilitating' terrorist acts emerged, while the offence of 'assisting' from 1991 disappeared. While some ILC members continued to insist that the meaning of terror was generally understood,[334] others maintained that the term was imprecise and the provision should be deleted.[335] Suggestions to refer to the sectoral anti-terrorism treaties, or to designate terrorism as a crime against humanity, were not accepted, nor was the view that the determination of terrorism should be left to the Security Council.[336]

The final ILC Draft Code (Part II) was adopted in 1996.[337] While earlier

---

[323] (1990) ILCYB 338 (Koroma), 339 (Pellet, Rao).   [324] ibid (Koroma).

[325] ibid, 338 (Mahiou, Calero Rodriguez); L Sunga, *The Emerging System of International Criminal Law* (Kluwer, The Hague, 1997) 200.

[326] ibid, 338 (Njenga), 339 (Benama).

[327] ibid, 338 (Pellet, Tomuschat, Njenga) and 338 (Pellet) respectively. cf 1999 Terrorist Financing Convention, Art 5, establishing corporate liability where a person 'responsible for the management or control' of a financial entity 'in that capacity' commits a financing offence.

[328] ILC (45th Sess), Comments and Observations from Governments (1993), UN Doc A/CN.4/448; Sunga, n 325, 202 (Belarus, Denmark, Finland, Iceland, Norway, Paraguay, Sweden, and the UK).

[329] Sunga, ibid, 202 (referring to Australia and the Netherlands).   [330] ibid.

[331] ILC, Report on 47th Sess (2 May–21 July 1995), UNGAOR Supp 10, UN Doc A/50/10, 58.

[332] (1995–I) ILCYB 38 (Al-Khasawneh).

[333] ibid, 18 (Vargas Carreño).   [334] ibid, 45 (Chairperson Rao).

[335] ibid, 41 (Rosenstock) and 6–7 (Pellet), 8 (Rosenstock), 15 (Mikulka) respectively.

[336] ibid, 21 (Jacovides), 26 (Kramer); 40 (Razafindralambo); 8 (Rosenstock) respectively.

[337] ILC, Report on 48th Sess (6 May–26 Jul 1996), UN Doc A/51/10, ch II(2) paras 46–48.

drafts between 1990 and 1995 had included distinct articles on 'international terrorism',[338] a discrete terrorist offence was subsumed by, and recast within, final Article 20 on 'war crimes' (discussed in Chapter 5).[339] The war crime of 'acts of terrorism' in Article 20 embodied the simple prohibition in Article 4(2)(d) of Protocol II.[340] There was no longer any broader offence of creating a state of terror outside armed conflict.

5. *1998 Draft Rome Statute*

While the 1996 ILC Draft Code was not adopted as a treaty, the General Assembly drew it to the attention of the Preparatory Committee on the Establishment of an International Criminal Court (PrepCom).[341] Ultimately, Article 5 of the 1998 Draft Rome Statute, presented to the 1998 Rome Diplomatic Conference,[342] included 'crimes of terrorism' comprising three distinct offences. The first offence was:

Undertaking, organizing, sponsoring, ordering, facilitating, financing, encouraging or tolerating acts of violence against another State directed at persons or property and *of such a nature as to create terror, fear or insecurity in the minds of* public figures, groups of persons, the general public or populations, for whatever considerations and purposes of a political, philosophical, ideological, racial, ethnic, religious or such other nature that may be invoked to justify them . . . (emphasis added)

This first offence resembles that in the 1991 ILC Draft Code and was not limited to armed conflict (as in the 1996 ILC Draft Code). It also shares elements of the 1937 League definition and a 1994 General Assembly working definition. The second offence comprised any offence in six sectoral treaties.[343] The third offence involved 'the use of firearms, weapons, explosives and dangerous substances when used as a means to perpetrate indiscriminate violence involving death or serious bodily injury to persons or groups or persons or populations or serious damage to property'.

Thirty-four States spoke in favour of including terrorism,[344] particularly

---

[338] See 1990 Draft, Art 16, in ILC, Report on 42nd Sess (1990), UN Doc A/45/10, ch II paras 20–158; 1991–1995 Drafts, Art 24, ILC 43rd—47th Sess, in 13th Report of Special Rapporteur, n 256, and ILC, Report on 47th Sess, n 267, ch II(B)(1)–(3) paras 41–125, 126–139.

[339] ILC, Report on 47th Sess, ibid, ch II, paras 27–143.

[340] ILC, Report on 48th Sess, n 338, ch II, commentary on draft Art 20, para 14.

[341] UNGA Resolution 51/160 (1996).

[342] 1998 Draft Rome Statute, Art 5, in *Official Records* of the UN Diplomatic Conference of Plenipotentiaries on an ICC, Rome, 15 June–17 July 1998, UN Doc A/CONF.183/13, vol III, 21; see also ICC PrepCom Report, UN Doc A/Conf.183/2/Add.1 (14 Apr 1998) 2.

[343] 1971 Montreal Convention; 1970 Hague Convention; 1973 Protected Persons Convention; 1979 Hostages Convention; 1988 Rome Convention and 1988 Rome Protocol.

[344] *Official Records*, n 342, vol II: Albania, 82; Algeria, 73, 148, 177, 283; Armenia, 78; Barbados, 248, 354; Benin, 286; Bolivia, 347; Burundi, 118; Cameroon, 181; Comoros, 287; Congo, 117; Costa Rica, 175; Cuba, 181; Dominica, 248, 354; Egypt, 281; Ethiopia, 288; India, 87, 177–178, 323; Jamaica, 328; Kuwait, 289; Kyrgyzstan, 77; Libya, 102; Macedonia, 86; New

those that had been its victims. Those in favour of including terrorism argued that it shocked the conscience of humanity; had grave consequences for human suffering and property damage; occurred increasingly frequently and on a larger scale; and threatened peace and security.[345] The option of referring terrorism to the ICC was also intended to avoid jurisdictional disputes between States, and supply the Security Council with a means of referring terrorist threats for resolution.[346]

Among States that supported the inclusion of terrorism, there was variation in the approach to definition and criminalization. Some States thought that terrorism should be included as a crime against humanity.[347] Russia thought the offence should be limited only to the most serious terrorist crimes; Turkey believed systematic and prolonged terrorism against a civilian population should be covered; and Albania argued that institutionalized State terrorism should be included.[348] Though in favour of including terrorism, Egypt sought to exclude national liberation movements, while a number of Islamic States impliedly urged the same result by invoking the 1999 Arab League Convention as a model approach to definition.[349]

One alternative definition of terrorism presented at the Diplomatic Conference defined 'an act of terrorism' as serious crimes within the sectoral treaties, but also as:

An act of terrorism, in all its forms and manifestations involving the use of indiscriminate violence, committed against innocent persons or property intended or calculated to provoke a state of terror, fear and insecurity in the minds of the general public or populations resulting in death or serious bodily injury, or injury to mental or physical health and serious damage to property irrespective of any considerations and purposes of a political, ideological, philosophical, racial, ethnic, religious or of such other nature that may be invoked to justify it, is a crime . . .[350]

Zealand, 178; Nigeria, 111; Pakistan, 173; Russia, 115, 177, 289; Saudi Arabia, 179, 293; Sri Lanka, 123, 176, 288, 339; Tajikistan, 92; Thailand, 332; Trinidad and Tobago, 248, 354; Tunisia, 174, 292; Turkey, 106, 124, 179, 276, 330; United Arab Emirates, 177; Yemen, 178. See also Kittichaisaree, n 233, 227; C Silverman, 'An Appeal to the United Nations: Terrorism must come within the Jurisdiction of an International Criminal Court' (1998) 4 *New England and Comparative Law Annual*: <www.nesl.edu/intljournal/VOL4/CS.HTM>.

[345] ICC PrepCom, Summary of Procs, 25 Mar–12 Apr 1996, UN Doc A/AC.249/1 (7 May 1996) para 66.

[346] ibid.

[347] Algeria, Comoros, India, Sri Lanka, Tunisia, Turkey. See *Official Records*, n 342, vol III, 242 (proposal of India, Sri Lanka, and Turkey).

[348] *Official Records*, n 342, vol II, 115, 177, 289 (Russia); 106, 124, 179, 276, 330 (Turkey); 82 (Albania).

[349] ibid, 281 (Egypt); 177 (United Arab Emirates); 178 (Yemen); 179, 293 (Saudi Arabia); 289 (Kuwait).

[350] *Official Records*, n 342, vol III, 222 (Coordinator draft), 242 (draft of India, Sri Lanka, and Turkey); 248, 354 (draft of Barbados, Dominica, India, Jamaica, Sri Lanka, Trinidad and Tobago, and Turkey).

This partly circular definition differs in substance from draft Article 5 mainly in its requirement of 'indiscriminate violence' and its omission of any reference to the 'undertaking, organizing, sponsoring, ordering, facilitating, financing, encouraging or tolerating acts of violence against another State'. Removing the nexus to another State means that non-international terrorism could be covered. On the other hand, removing reference to the various methods of preparing, supporting, or committing terrorism narrows the scope of the offence, although much of this conduct would be covered by applying the Rome Statute's provisions on the modes of criminal participation.[351]

Ultimately, terrorism was not included in the 1998 Rome Statute as adopted. A conference resolution 'regretted' that 'despite widespread international condemnation of terrorism, no generally acceptable definition ... could be agreed upon'.[352] Terrorism was not included for a variety of reasons: its legal novelty and lack of prior definition; disagreement about national liberation violence; and a fear that it would politicize the ICC.[353] More pragmatically, some States felt that terrorism was better suited to national prosecution, due to investigative complexities and the need for immunities.[354] The US felt that investigation, rather than prosecution, was the main problem in combating terrorism.[355] Others believed that terrorism was not always serious enough to be internationally prosecuted.[356] Of the 23 States which spoke against including terrorism,[357] many of them agreed that terrorism was a serious crime but preferred to defer its inclusion until it was defined more clearly in future. These included developed States as well as those who supported an exception for self-determination movements. Sri Lanka and Turkey abstained from voting on the Rome Statute partly because terrorism was excluded.[358] The omission of terrorism from the Rome Statute is normatively

---

[351] 1998 Rome Statute, Art 25(3) (including committing, ordering, soliciting, inducing an offence, as well as complicity and the inchoate offences of conspiracy and attempt).

[352] Resolution E, annexed to the Final Act of the UN Diplomatic Conference of Plenipotentiaries on an ICC, 17 July 1998, UN Doc A/Conf.183/10.

[353] ICC PrepCom, n 346, para 67; Kittichaisaree, n 233, 227–228; Cassese (2003), n 5, 125; see also N Boister, 'The Exclusion of Treaty Crimes from the Jurisdiction of the Proposed International Criminal Court: Law, Pragmatism, Politics' (1998) 3 JACL 27.

[354] M Arsanjani, 'The 1998 Rome Statute of the International Criminal Court' (1999) 93 AJIL 22, 29; Cassese (2003), n 5, 125; see also ICC PrepCom, n 346.

[355] D Scheffer, 'Developments at Rome Treaty Conference', Testimony of US Ambassador at Large for War Crimes Issues and Head of US Delegation to the Rome Conference, US Senate Foreign Relations Committee, Washington, DC, 23 Jul 1998.

[356] Cassese (2003), n 5, 125; Cassese (2001), n 5, 994.

[357] *Official Records*, n 342, vol II, Bahrain, 284; Bangladesh, 181; Belgium, 174; Brazil, 277; France, 177; Ghana, 278; Greece, 175, 281; Guatemala, 291; Iraq, 174; Japan, 290; Morocco, 173; the Netherlands, 181, 269; Norway, 172; Oman, 180; Republic of Korea, 175, 277; Senegal, 176; Spain, 181, 329; Sweden, 176; Syria (speaking also for the Arab League), 172, 271; UK, 272; Ukraine, 176; US, 123, 176, 280; Uruguay, 283.

[358] Kittichaisaree, n 233, 227.

significant, since the Statute represents the most recent and 'authoritative expression of the legal views of a great number of States' on international criminal law.[359] The conference affirmed, however, that the Statute provides for future expansion of jurisdiction, which might provide an opportunity for the future inclusion of terrorism.[360] Agreement on the definition of crimes was intended 'to reflect existing customary international law, and not to create new law';[361] but nor was such agreement intended to preclude the emergence of new crimes.

In addition, the Rome Conference responded to terrorism in a different sense. In Article 7(2)(a) of the Rome Statute, crimes against humanity require 'multiple commission of acts . . . pursuant to or in furtherance of a State or organizational policy to commit such attack'. The reference to organizations was 'intended to include such groups as terrorist organizations',[362] although express reference to terrorism as a crime against humanity was not adopted. Thus terrorist groups which commit acts constituting crimes against humanity are liable. This includes acts in armed conflict or peacetime, as long as the conduct is 'part of a widespread or systematic attack directed against any civilian population, with knowledge of the attack'.[363] Such attacks need not be both widespread *and* systematic; either is sufficient.[364] Prosecution of such acts is, of course, subject to the jurisdictional and other limitations of the ICC.[365]

---

[359] ibid, 38; *Furundzija*, ICTY–95–17/1–T (10 Dec 1998) para 227. The Statute was the culmination of a long process of codification begun by the ILC in its 1954 Draft Code of Offences against the Peace and Security of Mankind (ILC Report (6th Sess, 1954), UN Doc A/2693) and revitalized in the 1990s: see W Schabas, *An Introduction to the International Criminal Court* (CUP, Cambridge, 2001) ch 1.

[360] Resolution E, n 354; see also V Proulx, 'Rethinking the Jurisdiction of the International Criminal Court in the Post-September 11th Era: Should Acts of Terrorism Qualify as Crimes against Humanity?' (2004) 19 AUILR 1009; F McKay, 'US Unilateralism and International Crimes: The International Criminal Court and Terrorism' (2004) 36 Cornell ILJ 455; A Rubin, 'Legal Response to Terror: An International Criminal Court?' (2002) 43 Harvard ILJ 65; T Sailer, 'The International Criminal Court: An Argument to Extend its Jurisdiction to Terrorism and a Dismissal of US Objections' (1999) 13 *Temple International and Comparative Law Journal* 311; 'The United States and the World Need an International Criminal Court as an Ally in the War against Terrorism' (1997) 8 *Indiana International and Comparative Law Review* 159; G Abi-Saab, 'The Proper Role of International Law in Combating Terrorism' (2002) 1 Chinese JIL 305, 311–312; Cassese (2003), n 5, 131.

[361] P Kirsch, 'Foreword' in K Dörmann, *Elements of War Crimes under the Rome Statute of the International Criminal Court: Sources and Commentary* (CUP, Cambridge, 2003) xiii.

[362] Arsanjani, n 354, 31.   [363] 1998 Rome Statute, Art 7.

[364] Arsanjani, n 354, 31.

[365] See M Morris, 'Prosecuting Terrorism: The Quandaries of Criminal Jurisdiction and International Relations' in Heere (ed), n 73, 133 (particularly acts committed by non-State party nationals in their own States, or by non-party nationals in other non-party States); M Morris, 'Arresting Terrorism: Criminal Jurisdiction and International Relations' in Bianchi (ed), n 76, 63; M Morris, 'Terrorism and the Politics of Prosecution' (2005) 5 Chinese JIL 405; C Van den Wyngaert, 'Jurisdiction over Crimes of Terrorism' in Heere (ed), above, 147.

6. 2000—Draft Comprehensive Convention

Not long after definition was deferred in the context of the ICC, attempts to comprehensively define terrorism resurfaced in the Ad Hoc Committee established by the UN General Assembly in 1996.[366] Between 1997 and 2005, the Ad Hoc Committee successfully drafted the 1997 Terrorist Bombings Convention, the 1999 Terrorist Financing Convention, and the 2005 Nuclear Terrorism Convention. In 2000, India informally circulated in the Committee a revised draft comprehensive treaty originally submitted to the Sixth Committee in 1996.[367] Earlier in 1994, Algeria had argued for a comprehensive convention to consolidate sectoral treaty offences,[368] but the Indian draft went further by proposing a generic approach to definition. While Sudan endorsed the Indian proposal in 1997, only after the terrorist attacks on US embassies in Africa in 1998 did more than 37 States support the Indian approach.[369] By 2000, India's proposal had been supported by the Non-Aligned Movement, the Group of Eight and the EU.[370]

Substantial drafting progress on the comprehensive convention was made in the Ad Hoc Committee in 2001–02, spurred on by the 'shock of recognition' of September 11,[371] and by 2002 agreement was reached on most of the 27 articles.[372] By 2003, however, some States had reached their 'bottom-line' on disputed matters.[373] The Coordinator believed that resolving outstanding issues—the preamble, definitions in Article 1 and definition of offences in Article 2[374]—would depend on resolving Article 18 (application to armed forces and armed conflict).[375] The drafting mandate was renewed again in

---

[366] UNGA Resolution 54/110 (1999); Ad Hoc Committee Report (2000), n 38; see generally van Ginkel, n 111; S Subedi, 'The UN Response to International Terrorism in the Aftermath of the Terrorist Attacks in America and the Problem of the Definition of Terrorism in International Law' (2002) 4 *International Law Forum* 159; L Bondi, 'Legitimacy and Legality: Key Issues in the Fight against Terrorism', Fund for Peace, Washington, DC, 11 Sept 2002, 26–30; F Andreu-Guzmán (ed), *Terrorism and Human Rights* (ICJ, Geneva, 2002) 202–208; B Broomhall, 'State Actors in an International Definition of Terrorism from a Human Rights Perspective' (2004) 36 Case Western Reserve JIL 421, 430–440.

[367] Ad Hoc Committee Report (2000), n 38, 4; see UN Doc A/C.6/55/1 (28 Aug 2000) and the original 1996 draft in UN Doc A/C.6/51/6 (11 Nov 1996).

[368] Report of the UN Secretary-General, UN Doc A/49/257 (25 July 1994); see van Ginkel, n 111, 216.

[369] Van Ginkel, n 121, 217–218 (Algeria, Angola, Bahrain, Bangladesh, Brazil, Canada, China, Coast Rica, Croatia, Cuba, Domincan Republic, DR Congo, El Salvador, Ethiopia, Ghana, Guatemala, Honduras, Indonesia, Iran, Japan, Kuwait, Lebanon, Liechtenstein, Macedonia, Malawi, Malaysia, Mongolia, Nicaragua, Panama, Qatar, Slovakia, South Africa, Syria, Tanzania, Turkey, Uganda, Vietnam).

[370] Van Ginkel, ibid, 219.   [371] Abi-Saab, n 359, 311–312.

[372] See Ad Hoc Committee Report (2001), n 38; UNGA (57th Sess) (6th Committee), Measures to Eliminate International Terrorism: Working Group Report, 16 Oct 2002, A/C.6/57/L.9, Annex II, 7–8.

[373] Ad Hoc Committee Report (2003), n 38, 8.   [374] ibid, 6.

[375] UNGA, Ad Hoc Committee, 'Finalizing Treaty Requires Agreement on "Armed Forces", "Foreign Occupation", Anti-Terrorism Committee Told', PR L/2993, 1 Feb 2002.

2004, 2005, and 2006.[376] Negotiations were given further impetus by the recommendations to define terrorism by the UN High-Level Panel on Threats, Challenges and Change (2004), the UN Secretary-General's report *In larger freedom* (2005), the Madrid Summit (2005), and the UN World Summit (2005).[377]

The preamble to the Draft Comprehensive Convention condemns 'all acts, methods and practices of terrorism as criminal and unjustifiable, wherever and by whomever committed'.[378] Draft Article 2(1) proposes an offence if a person 'unlawfully and intentionally' causes: 'Death or serious bodily injury to any person'; 'Serious damage to public or private property'; or 'Damage to property, places, facilities, or systems . . . resulting or likely to result in major economic loss'.[379] The purpose of any such conduct, 'by its nature or context', must be 'to intimidate a population, or to compel a Government or an international organization to do or abstain from doing any act'.[380] Put another way, the prohibited acts must be motivated by purposes of intimidation or compulsion, but there is no requirement that acts be motivated by political aims or objectives. The treaty proposes to exclude the offences from the political offence exception to extradition.[381]

Unlike the 1997 Terrorist Bombings Convention, the Draft Convention proposes to protect private property as well as public property. It captures a wider range of acts against property than the EU Framework Decision, by referring to 'serious *damage*' rather than 'extensive *destruction*'. Like the Bombings Convention, the Draft Convention protects only States or international organizations from compulsion, and not NGOs, political parties, corporations, or other social groups.

While there was a basic consensus on the definition of offences,[382] disagreement arose when Malaysia, on behalf of the OIC, sought to exclude

---

[376] UNGA Resolutions 58/81 (2004) paras 14–19; 59/46 (2004) paras 17–20; 60/53 (2005).

[377] UN High-Level Panel, n 102; UN Secretary-General, n 102; Club of Madrid, 'The Madrid Agenda', International Summit on Democracy, Terrorism and Security, 11 Mar 2005 (supporting the definition proposed by the UN High-Level Panel). The World Summit was unable to reach agreement on a definition of terrorism and merely stressed the need to reach agreement on the Draft Comprehensive Convention during the 60th Session of UNGA, and acknowledged the possibility of convening a high-level UN conference: 2005 World Summit Outcome, n 102, paras 83–84.

[378] Ad Hoc Committee Report (2002), n 38, Annex I (Discussion paper by the Bureau).

[379] UNGA (56th Sess) (6th Committee), Measures to Eliminate International Terrorism: Working Group Report, 29 Oct 2001, UN Doc A/C.6/56/L.9, Annex I, 16 (informal Coordinator texts); Ad Hoc Committee Report (2002), n 38, 6–7.

[380] Ancillary offences are in Draft Comprehensive Convention, Art 2(2), (3) and (4)(a)–(c).

[381] Draft Comprehensive Convention, Art 14.

[382] Although NGOs have raised concerns about aspects of the definition in Arts 2 and 18: Amnesty International, 'Draft Comprehensive Convention on International Terrorism: A Threat to Human Rights Standards', Statement to UNGA 56th Sess (2002), AI Index: IOR 51/009/ 2001, 22 Oct 2001; Amnesty International and Human Rights Watch, 'Comprehensive Convention against International Terrorism', Joint Letter to Ambassadors, 28 Jan 2002.

'people's struggle including armed struggle against foreign occupation, aggression, colonialism, and hegemony, aimed at liberation and self-determination.'[383] The aim was to balance the exclusion of the activities of State armed forces by also excluding national liberation forces. The proposal was taken from Article 2 of the 1999 OIC Convention and is significant in voting terms because the OIC comprises 56 States, and was also supported by Arab States and the Non-Aligned Movement. Other States objected to the proposal, believing that 'a terrorist activity remained a terrorist activity whether or not it was carried out in the exercise of the right of self-determination'.[384] Further, the obvious point had been made that self-determination was already governed by existing law, including obligations to comply with IHL in Protocol I.[385]

No such exclusionary provision was included in the 1997 Terrorist Bombings Convention or the 2005 Nuclear Terrorism Convention, both of which were drafted by the same Ad Hoc Committee. When Pakistan lodged a reservation purporting to exclude the application of the 1997 Convention from self-determination struggles, numerous States formally objected.[386] The UK and the US stated that the reservation amounted to a unilateral limitation on the scope of the Convention, contrary to its object and purpose (suppressing terrorist bombings, irrespective of location or perpetrator).[387] It was further objected that the reservation was contrary to Article 5 of the Convention, which requires criminalization regardless of any justifications.

A remaining critical dispute is the application of the Convention to armed forces and armed conflicts. The 1997 Terrorist Bombings Convention, the 2005 Nuclear Terrorism Convention, and the 2005 Amendment to the 1980 Vienna Convention all exclude the 'activities of armed forces during an armed conflict' from those Conventions, as well as the activities of State military forces exercising their official duties 'inasmuch as they are governed by other rules of international law'.[388] This approach is also followed in the EU Framework Decision.[389] Part of the 1999 Financing Convention protects 'civilians' or 'any other person not taking an active part in the hostilities in a situation of armed conflict'. The sectoral treaties addressing maritime and

---

[383] Subedi, n 366, 163.   [384] ibid.   [385] ibid, 165.

[386] Austria, Australia, Canada, Denmark, Finland, France, Germany, India, Israel, Italy, Japan, the Netherlands, New Zealand, Norway, Spain, Sweden, the UK, and the US.

[387] 1969 Vienna Convention on the Law of Treaties, Art 19(c), does not permit reservations which are incompatible with the object and purpose of a treaty.

[388] 2005 Nuclear Terrorism Convention, Art 4; 1997 Terrorist Bombings Convention, Art 19(2); 1980 Vienna Convention, Art 2(4)(b); also stating that 'armed forces' and 'armed conflict' are understood according to, and governed by, IHL. Thus non-State armed forces may also be covered: Witten, n 13, 780. Some State bombings outside armed conflict, and not by armed forces in their official duties, might still be unlawful, such as France's bombing of the *Rainbow Warrior* in New Zealand in 1986: R Marauhn, 'Terrorism: Addendum' in R Bernhardt (ed), *Encyclopaedia of PIL: vol 4* (North Holland, Amsterdam, 2000) 849, 853.

[389] 2002 EU Framework Decision, recital 11.

aerial violence do not apply to ships or aircraft used for military, customs, or police purposes.[390]

Proposed Article 18 of the Draft Comprehensive Convention is based on the 1997 Terrorist Bombings Convention, but is subject to three basic disagreements that also delayed the adoption of the 2005 Nuclear Terrorism Convention between 1997 and 2005.[391] One disputed element is whether the Draft Convention should exclude the activities of the 'parties'—rather than the 'armed forces'—during an armed conflict, since reference only to 'armed forces' might exclude other participants in armed conflict under IHL, particularly as 'parties' are mentioned in the Hague Regulations and the Geneva Conventions.[392] Reference to the 'parties' is specifically aimed at exempting organizations such as the PLO, Hamas, Islamic Jihad, and Hezbollah.[393] This could preclude civilians taking part in hostilities from being regarded as 'terrorists'.[394]

The International Committee of the Red Cross (ICRC) suggested that the term 'armed forces' should be defined to cover both government forces and those of organized armed groups,[395] which would seem an appropriate approach. The 1997 Terrorist Bombings Convention refers to armed forces 'as understood' under IHL, but definition in the Draft Convention itself would provide further clarity, particularly concerning its application to non-State forces in non-international armed conflicts under Protocol II.[396] Clearly, reference to the 'parties' would be too broad,[397] since it would exclude all

---

[390] 1963 Tokyo Convention, Art 1(4); 1970 Hague Convention, Art 3(2); 1971 Montreal Convention, Art 4(1); 1988 Rome Convention, Art 2.

[391] Ad Hoc Committee Report (2003), n 38, 11–12; Ad Hoc Committee Report (1998), n 38, Annex III, 50. Some States wanted the Nuclear Terrorism Convention to apply to the activities of State armed forces and/or State-sponsored nuclear terrorism, particularly given that States are the primary possessors of nuclear material and that the legality of the use of nuclear weapons is contested and might benefit from codification. Lesser disagreements surrounded: whether radioactive dumping should be covered (Ad Hoc Committee Report (2003), above, 11–12); whether reference to the 'environment' should be retained (Ad Hoc Committee Report (1998), above, Annex III, 46, 47); the relationship to other instruments, particularly the nuclear non-proliferation regime (above, 45); and whether the offence of using or damaging a nuclear facility might criminalize peaceful protests (above, 47, 49).

[392] OIC proposal, in Ad Hoc Committee Report (2002), n 38, 17 and Ad Hoc Committee Report (2004), n 38, 11, para 6 respectively.

[393] S von Schorlemer, 'Human Rights: Substantive and Institutional Implications of the War on Terror' (2003) 14 EJIL 265, 272; C Walter, 'Defining Terrorism in National and International Law' in C Walter et al (eds), *Terrorism as a Challenge for National and International Law* (Springer, Heidelberg, 2003) 23, 39–40.

[394] UNGA 6th Committee, Report of the Working Group on Measures to Eliminate International Terrorism (8 Oct 2004) UN Doc A/C.6/59/L.10.

[395] ICRC Report, 'Terrorism and International Law: Challenges and Responses: The Complementary Nature of Human Rights Law, International Humanitarian Law and Refugee Law', Geneva, 2002, 5.

[396] Walter, n 393, 17–18.

[397] Ad Hoc Committee Report (2003), n 38, 9.

State activity in armed conflict—not just military activities—as well as numerous non-State armed groups.[398]

A second disagreement concerns the issue of whether situations of 'foreign occupation' should also be excluded from the Convention, in addition to 'armed conflict'.[399] This is part of the same OIC proposal to exclude the activities of the 'parties' and is intended to cover situations where there are no hostilities and IHL may not strictly apply. Politically, it is aimed at excluding non-State violence against Israel in the Palestinian Occupied Territories and against India in Kashmir.[400]

It has been argued that this OIC proposal would 'eviscerate' the convention, by reintroducing a national liberation exception.[401] Other States wanted even more explicit exemptions for self-determination movements.[402] Since many terrorist acts take place in armed conflict or under foreign occupation, this proposal would neuter much of the treaty's purpose. Such acts would remain punishable under national law, or under IHL to the extent that it applies, but would not be punishable as terrorism. In calling for 'moral clarity' in the drafting of the Convention, the UN Secretary-General has also implicitly criticized this approach.[403] Others have called for liberation fighters to be exempted only to the extent that they do not terrorize civilians.[404]

A third cause of disagreement is whether State military forces exercising their official duties[405] are excluded from the Convention if they are merely 'governed' by international law or required to be 'in conformity' with it. The OIC proposes that military forces would be liable for terrorism if they were not 'in conformity' with international law, including the law on genocide, torture, IHL, or State responsibility. These States felt that the convention should cover State and State-sponsored terrorism, notwithstanding the application of existing international law to State conduct.[406] The OIC proposal

---

[398] Ad Hoc Committee Report (2004), n 38, 11, para 7.

[399] OIC proposal, in Ad Hoc Committee Report (2002), n 38, Annex IV, 17.

[400] N Rostow, 'Before and After: The Changed UN Response to Terrorism since September 11th' (2002) 35 Cornell ILJ 475, 489, 488.

[401] Halberstam, n 12, 582.

[402] Working Group Report (1997), n 64, 19 (Syria), 31 (Egypt); Ad Hoc Committee Report (1997), n 38, 38 (Pakistan).

[403] UN Sec-Gen, 'Addressing Assembly on Terrorism, Calls for "Immediate, Far-Reaching Changes" in UN Response to Terror, UN PR, UN Doc SG/SM/7977 GA/9920, 1 Oct 2001.

[404] Ad Hoc Committee Report (2004), n 38, 7, para 16; 11, para 8.

[405] In the 1997 Terrorist Bombings Convention, 'military forces of a State' is defined in Art 1(4) as 'the armed forces of a State which are organized, trained and equipped under its internal law for the primary purpose of national defence or security and persons acting in support of those armed forces who are under their formal command, control and responsibility'. Proposals to refer explicitly to official duties such as law enforcement, evacuation operations, peace operations, UN operations, or humanitarian relief were not adopted: Working Group Report (1997), n 64, 58 (Australia, Germany), 59 (Republic of Korea, Costa Rica, NZ).

[406] Including IHL, human rights law, international criminal law, the law on the non-use of force and non-intervention, and the law of State responsibility.

lacks balance since the activities of non-State forces are not similarly classified as terrorism if they are not in conformity with international law.

In response, the ICRC warned of the danger of criminalizing acts that are not already unlawful in IHL.[407] The ICRC stated that as a result, 'third states would be under an obligation to prosecute or extradite persons who have not in fact committed an unlawful act under IHL'.[408] The preferred position of the ICRC was to exclude acts covered by IHL (committed in the course of an armed conflict) from the scope of the convention.[409] As discussed in Chapter 5, acts of terror committed in armed conflict are already prohibited and criminalized in IHL.

The ICRC position aims to maximize clarity and simplicity in the Draft Convention's relationship to IHL. On one hand, criminalizing political violence against civilians as terrorism would seldom conflict with the objectives of IHL, just as prohibitions on genocide, crimes against humanity, and torture apply concurrently with IHL and complement it. An alternative approach would be to exclude the application of the Convention only where it directly conflicts with IHL.[410] Yet since the Draft Convention also criminalizes violence against 'any' person and against property, its application to situations covered by IHL would interfere with the carefully constructed parameters of violence set by IHL, unravelling compliance with it.

The case for applying terrorist offences to the activities of State armed forces is strongest in situations where IHL does not apply, and the conduct in question does not rise to the level of crimes against humanity. Such application would confer legitimacy on the Convention for the many States, and others, who object to 'State terrorism'. Under the present draft, only acts of State armed forces outside their official duties, and not covered by IHL, may be regarded as terrorism.[411] Deliberate or 'official' State action designed to terrorize remains excluded.

Finally, the relationship between the Draft Comprehensive Convention and sectoral anti-terrorism treaties is undecided. Some States preferred no provision at all,[412] in which case the sectoral treaties would only apply to the extent that they are compatible with the Draft Convention, as a treaty later in time.[413] In contrast, Article 2 *bis* presently states that where the Convention and a sectoral treaty would apply to the same act, between parties to both, the sectoral treaty prevails,[414] thus being regarded as *lex specialis*. While this provision was widely supported, some States objected that since it was

---

[407] ICRC, n 395.   [408] ibid.
[409] ibid.   [410] Walter, n 393, 18–19.
[411] See discussion of an identical provision in the 1997 Terrorist Bombings Convention: Ad Hoc Committee Report (1997), n 38, 53 (Rapporteur).
[412] Working Group Report (2002), n 372, Annex II, 8.
[413] 1969 Vienna Convention on the Law of Treaties, Art 30.
[414] Ad Hoc Committee Report (2002), n 38, 7; an approach adopted by the 1972 US Draft Convention.

designed to 'fill gaps' in the existing law, the Draft Convention established 'a separate and autonomous regime' applicable 'in parallel with' the sectoral treaties.[415] This view correctly recognizes that terrorism is a special offence with additional and distinct elements to sectoral offences—that the Draft Convention itself is *lex specialis*. The provision may depend on resolving other disagreements.[416]

E. CONCLUSION

Despite the many international attempts to define terrorism generically, there is still no such crime as terrorism in international treaty law. Although some regional treaties have adopted general definitions, the variation in these definitions militates against the emergence of any shared international conception of terrorism. Some regional definitions are so broad as to be indistinguishable from other forms of political violence, or public order or national security offences. The divergent definitions also reflect the political preoccupations of particular regional groupings, especially concerning the validity of exclusions from any definition of terrorism. The next chapter examines whether customary law recognizes a generic definition of terrorism.

---

[415] Ad Hoc Committee Report (2003), n 38, 9; Ad Hoc Committee Report (2004), n 38, 12, para 14.

[416] Particularly Draft Comprehensive Convention, Art 18.

4

Terrorism in Customary International Law

A. INTRODUCTION

In the absence of a generic treaty crime of terrorism, analysis of customary law confirms that there is no distinct international crime, or unified legal concept, of terrorism. There is little in the literature on whether universal jurisdiction over terrorism exists, and the predominance of 'soft law' sources on terrorism requires a broad inquiry.[1] A number of conflicting definitions of terrorism have emerged in the practice of the UN General Assembly and the Security Council, and in national case law and legislation. While there is a definite movement towards generic definition over time, the divergent approaches to definition, and persistent disagreement over the scope of exceptions, have inhibited the emergence of a customary crime. At best, there is international consensus on condemning terrorism, or support for a *prohibition* on terrorism, but which is insufficiently precise to support individual criminal liability.

B. UN GENERAL ASSEMBLY PRACTICE

General Assembly resolutions normally have no binding legal effect under the Charter,[2] nor is it admitted that they can give rise to 'instant custom'.[3] A Philippine proposal to vest the Assembly with legislative powers was decisively rejected at San Francisco.[4] Resolutions or a series of resolutions may, however, be declaratory of customary norms,[5] or evidence of emergent custom or *opinio juris*, depending on their content and conditions of adoption.[6] When framed as general principles they may help progressively to

---

[1] R Kolb, 'Universal Criminal Jurisdiction in Matters of International Terrorism' (1997) 1 *Revue Hellenique Droit International* 43, 46–47.

[2] UNGA issues non-binding recommendations under Arts 10–11 of the Charter; see B Simma (ed), *The Charter of the United Nations: A Commentary* (OUP, New York, 2002) 237–241.

[3] See, eg, H Thirlway, *International Customary Law and Codification* (AW Sifthoff, Leiden, 1972), 72–77; cf B Cheng, 'United Nations Resolutions on Outer Space: "Instant" International Customary Law?' (1965) 5 Indian JIL 23.

[4] R Falk, 'On the Quasi-Legislative Competence of the General Assembly' (1966) 60 AJIL 782, 783.

[5] *Tadic (Interlocutory Appeal)* ICTY–94–1 (2 Oct 1995) para 112. On the diverse effects of resolutions, see M Öberg, 'The Legal Effects of Resolutions of the UN Security Council and General Assembly in the Jurisprudence of the ICJ' (2005) 16 EJIL 879.

[6] *Legality of the Threat or Use of Nuclear Weapons* (1996) 35 ILM 809, 826; *Military and Paramilitary Activities (Nicaragua v US)* (1986) ICJ Reports 14, para 188; *Texaco v Libya* (1978)

develop and consolidate customary norms.[7] They may also promote the adoption of treaties which elaborate upon the principles they espouse.[8] Resolutions may express 'common interests' and the 'general will',[9] and are an important concentration of opinion in an international community of many States.[10] Resolutions may be especially important where other sources of customary law are unclear.[11]

The normative significance of resolutions depends on a variety of factors: their subject matter, objectives and context; the generality and normativity of their language (including whether it is declaratory, obligatory, or recommendatory); the voting pattern (including bloc voting and the votes of specially affected States) and explanations of votes; and the position of the Security Council.[12] States do not necessarily vote out of a sense of legal obligation,[13] and the Assembly is foremost a political body expressing political opinions.[14] Even resolutions adopted by consensus need not signify universal acceptance of their provisions as law, since States may not object because they believe a resolution is non-binding,[15] or because agreement was secured due to the inclusion of vague language open to divergent interpretations.[16] Resolutions should not be considered in isolation but as merely 'one manifestation' of State practice. While they provide an accelerated and 'very concentrated focal point for state practice',[17] what must be examined is the

17 ILM 1, 28, para 83; R Higgins, *The Development of International Law through the Political Organs of the United Nations* (OUP, Oxford, 1963) 5; I Brownlie, *Principles of Public International Law* (5th edn, Clarendon, Oxford, 1998) 14; P Sands and P Klein, *Bowett's Law of International Institutions* (5th edn, Sweet and Maxwell, London, 2001) 29; C Parry, *The Sources and Evidence of International Law* (MUP, Manchester, 1965) 113; Falk, n 4; see generally J Castaneda, *Legal Effects of United Nations Resolutions* (Columbia University Press, New York, 1969).

[7] Brownlie, ibid, 14.

[8] *Tadic (Interlocutory)*, n 5, para 112.

[9] O Schachter, *International Law in Theory and Practice* (Martinus Nijhoff, Dordrecht, 1991) 85.

[10] L Hannikainen, 'Customary Law: Are Rumours of its Death Exaggerated?', Paper at ESIL Conference, Florence, 13–15 May 2004; Higgins, n 6, 2.

[11] K Skubiszewski, 'Normative Functions of Resolutions of the General Assembly of the United Nations' (Institute of International Law) (1985) Annuaire de l'Institute de Droit International 29, 327–328.

[12] See Falk, n 4, 786–789; Brownlie, n 6, 15; I Shearer, *Starke's International Law* (11th edn, Butterworths, London, 1994) 47; M Shaw, *International Law* (4th edn, CUP, Cambridge, 1997) 90; see E Sloan, 'The Binding Force of a "Recommendation" of the General Assembly of the United Nations' (1948) 25 BYBIL 1.

[13] Schachter, n 9, 88; K Wolfke, *Custom in Present International Law* (2nd edn, Martinus Nijhoff, Dordrecht, 1993) 84; M Villiger, *Customary International Law and Treaties* (Martinus Nijhoff, Dordrecht, 1985) 29.

[14] P Van Krieken, *Terrorism and the International Legal Order* (Asser, The Hague, 2002) 121.

[15] Wolfke, n 13, 63; Villiger, n 13, 9.

[16] M Peterson, 'Using the General Assembly' in J Boulden and T Weiss (eds), *Terrorism and the UN: Before and After September 11* (Indiana University Press, Bloomington, 2004) 173, 174.

[17] Higgins, n 6, 2.

'collective practice ... in all its complex manifestations',[18] particularly whether State behaviour outside the UN conforms to even a unanimous resolution.[19]

Resolutions framed as *declarations* may have direct legal effect as authoritative interpretations of the Charter.[20] A declaration is 'a formal and solemn instrument, suitable for rare occasions when principles of great and lasting importance are being enunciated'.[21] Declarations may be authoritative statements of the international community,[22] expressing a 'general consensus',[23] creating an expectation of adherence, and potentially becoming binding as embodying customary norms.[24] The legal authority of declarations does not, however, stem from their designation as declarations but from their usual function of restating well-settled customary norms.[25]

1. 1970 Declaration on Friendly Relations and 1965 Declaration

The first major General Assembly resolutions referring to terrorism were adopted in 1965 and 1970. In interpreting the Charter obligation to refrain from the use of force, the 1970 Declaration on Friendly Relations, adopted without objection,[26] states that:

Every State has the duty to refrain from organizing, instigating, assisting or participating in acts of civil strife or *terrorist acts* in another State or acquiescing in organized activities within its territory directed towards the commission of such acts, when the acts referred to ... involve a threat or use of force.[27]

There is no definition of 'terrorist acts' and the matter received little attention during the drafting. A related provision of the 1970 Declaration notes the duty of States 'to refrain from organizing or encouraging the organization of

---

[18] R Higgins, *Problems and Processes: International Law and How We Use It* (Clarendon, Oxford, 2003) 23–24.

[19] ibid, 26–27; R Jennings and A Watts (eds), *Oppenheim's International Law: vol I* (9th edn, Longman, London, 1992) 45; see also G Arangio-Ruiz, 'The Normative Role of the General Assembly of the United Nations and the Declaration of Principles of Friendly Relations' (1972–III) 137 *Recueil des cours* 419, 431; S Schwebel, 'The Effect of Resolutions of the UN General Assembly on Customary International Law' (1979) ASIL Proceedings 301; Falk, n 4, 786–789.

[20] Brownlie, n 6, 15; Schachter, n 9, 85; Shearer, n 12, 46–47.

[21] UN Office of Legal Affairs, Memorandum (1962) 34 UNESCOR Supp 8, 15, UN Doc E/CN.4/1/610.

[22] E Schwelb, *Human Rights and the International Community* (Quadrangle Books, Chicago, 1964) 70.

[23] Jennings and Watts (eds), n 19, 45.

[24] UNOLA, n 21; see also Arangio-Ruiz, n 19.

[25] Wolfke, n 13, 85.

[26] 1970 Declaration on Principles of International Law concerning Friendly Relations and Cooperation among States in accordance with the Charter of the UN, annexed to UNGA Resolution 2625 (XXV) (1970) (hereinafter '1970 Declaration').

[27] 1970 Declaration, Principle of Prohibition on Threat or Use of Force, para 9 (emphasis added).

irregular forces or armed bands, including mercenaries, for incursion into the territory of another State'.[28] Both provisions were intended to confront indirect uses of force after 1945.[29] The reference to 'irregular forces or armed bands' was non-exhaustive and intended to apply to 'all categories of irregular forces, irrespective of their composition'[30] and even if 'not expressly mentioned'.[31] As such, those terms arguably encompass terrorist groups.

In the *Nicaragua* case, the ICJ held that the above provisions referred to 'less grave forms of the use of force' below the level of an 'armed attack',[32] which may also violate the principle of non-intervention.[33] Accordingly, in elaborating on the Charter obligation of *non-intervention*, the 1970 Declaration states that 'no State shall organize, assist, foment, finance, incite or tolerate subversive, *terrorist* or armed activities directed towards the violent overthrow of the regime of another State, or interfere in civil strife in another State'.[34] There has equally been little judicial explication of 'terrorist' activities. The principle of non-intervention was designed to protect political independence, at the insistence of Eastern European and Latin American States.[35] Although some western States were sceptical of its legal status, it was eventually supported. The US noted that indirect intervention had become the most prevalent kind since 1945.[36]

The principle was drawn verbatim from the 1965 Declaration on the Inadmissibility of Intervention.[37] In 1966, a committee to draft the 1970 Declaration asserted that the 1965 Declaration 'reflects a universal legal conviction which qualifies it to be regarded as an authentic and definite principle of international law'.[38] This was contested by western States, which thought that the 1965 Declaration was too imprecise and reflected political rather than legal consensus.[39] There was much disagreement about the scope of non-intervention, and accommodation was reached on the basis of the Organization of American States (OAS) Charter and a generalizing of western hemisphere norms.[40]

---

[28] ibid, para 8.

[29] R Rosenstock, 'The Declaration of Principles of International Law Concerning Friendly Relations: A Survey' (1971) 65 AJIL 713, 720.

[30] UNGAOR (25th Sess) Supp 18 (1970), UN Doc A/8018, para 147 (France), para 171 (Canada); UNGAOR (25th Sess) (6th Committee), 1181th mtg, 25 Sept 1970, para 7 (NZ).

[31] UNGAOR Supp 18 (1970), n 30, para 86 (drafting Special Committee).

[32] *Nicaragua*, n 6, para 191.   [33] ibid, para 205.

[34] 1970 Declaration, Principle of Non-Intervention, para 2 (emphasis added).

[35] Rosenstock, n 29, 726, 728.   [36] ibid, 727.

[37] 1965 Declaration on the Inadmissibility of Intervention in the Domestic Affairs of States and the Protection of their Independence and Sovereignty, annexed to UNGA Resolution 2131(XX) (1965) (109 votes to 0, with 1 abstention).

[38] UNGAOR 21st Sess (1966) Annexes, UN Doc A/6230, para 341 (Special Committee); see also UNGAOR Supp 18 (1970), n 30, Special Committee Report, paras 58–59.

[39] (1965) UNYB 93 (Australia, Belgium, Canada, France, Italy, NZ, Spain, the UK); Rosenstock, n 29, 728.

[40] Rosenstock, ibid, 729.

There is little guidance in the drafting record on the meaning of 'terrorist' activities in either Declaration. In 1965, States referring to terrorism were heavily influenced by Cold War politics.[41] Charges were made that the Vietcong and North Vietnam were terrorists, and counter-charges that the Vietnamese were victims of terrorism.[42] The US spoke of the infiltration of agents who terrorize innocent people and impose the will of a foreign government and ideology, while Albania objected that the US financed terrorism against socialist States.[43] Some States referred to Latin America as a victim of terrorism, while others condemned it for exporting terrorism.[44] Colombia and Kenya emphasized State terrorism, whereas Brazil objected to liberation terrorism.[45] Terrorism and subversion were often referred to interchangeably as forms of intervention.

In the absence of definition, it is significant that both uses of 'terrorist' in the 1970 Declaration refer to 'acts' or 'activities', rather than to terrorist groups or bands. The term is used adjectivally to qualify the nature of acts violating the non-use of force or non-intervention, not as a noun to describe a separate legal category of persons. It relates to, and elaborates on, the *jus ad bellum* (resort to force) rather than the *jus in bello* (means of force), and is only helpful in that it strengthens prohibitions on indirect force and intervention. Proposals to include State support for 'terrorist' acts in the 1974 Definition of Aggression were not, however, accepted,[46] although the Commission on Human Rights has since designated terrorism as aggression.[47]

Ultimately the precise meaning of 'terrorist' in the 1970 Declaration may not be legally important, because it is the use of force or intervention by a State (rather than the particular terrorist *methods*) which violates

[41] See UNGAOR (20th Sess) Annexes (1965) 77–142: Special Committee Report, UN Doc A/ 5746; UNGAOR (20th Sess) (1st Committee) mtgs 1395–1406, 1420, 1422–23, 3–20 Dec 1965.
[42] 1st Committee, ibid, 1399th mtg, 7 Dec 1965, para 16 (Australia); 1406th mtg, 10 Dec 1965, para 5 (US) and 1398th mtg, 6 Dec 1965, para 45 (China) respectively.
[43] Ibid, 1396th mtg, 3 Dec 1965, para 8 (US); 1405th mtg, 9 Dec 1965, paras 66, 68 (Albania).
[44] Ibid, 1400th mtg, 7 Dec 1965, para 18 (Brazil); para 28 (Honduras) respectively.
[45] Ibid, 1395th mtg, 3 Dec 1965, para 28 (Colombia); 1402th mtg, 8 Dec 1965, para 21 (Kenya); 1400th mtg, 7 Dec 1965, para 13 (Brazil).
[46] Proposal by the US, the UK, Australia, Canada, Italy and Japan, quoted in B Ferencz, 'A Proposed Definition of Aggression: By Compromise and Consensus' (1973) 22 ICLQ 407, 420; UNGAOR (27th Sess) Supp 19 (1972), UN Doc A/8719, 15 (drafting committee).
[47] UNComHR Resolutions 1995/43, para 1; 1996/47, para 2; 1997/42, para 2; UNSub-ComHR Resolutions 1996/20, para 1; 1997/39, para 1. The prohibition in the 1974 Definition on States sending 'armed bands, groups, irregulars' to use armed force against another State (UNGA Resolution 3314 (XXIX) (1974) Annex, Art 3(g)) arguably encompasses terrorist groups, since reference to the specified groups was not intended to be exhaustive (*Nicaragua*, n 6, 14, para 168 (Schwebel J); G Fitzmaurice, 'The Definition of Aggression' (1952) 1 ICLQ 137, 143–144), but merely indicative of the kinds of groups which may use force (J Stone, 'Hopes and Loopholes in the 1974 Definition of Aggression' (1977) 71 AJIL 224, 237, referring to PLO terrorists). The category of 'armed bands' is a useful *clausula generalis* covering different uses of force: I Brownlie, 'International Law and the Activities of Armed Bands' (1958) 7 ICLQ 712, 713.

international law. The 1970 Declaration is declaratory of custom,[48] and an authoritative interpretation of the Charter.[49] It is restated or particularized in numerous resolutions on terrorism,[50] which reflect customary norms on State responsibility, the use of force, and non-intervention, rather than evidencing new obligations specifically governing terrorism.[51] The application of general customary rules to terrorism may indicate that that States did not consider there to be any specific rules of customary law governing terrorism.[52]

In particular, States owe long-established customary duties to diligently prevent and suppress the use of their territory for acts harmful to other States, including violence by private actors.[53] States are also responsible for injuring, or failing to diligently prevent or suppress private harm to, foreign nationals in their territory.[54] Both duties implicitly include harm caused by terrorist acts.[55] Thus in *Reparation for Injuries*, Israel was responsible for

[48] *Nicaragua*, ibid, para 188; O Schachter, 'United Nations Law' (1994) 88 AJIL 1, 3; Rosenstock, n 29, 714; see generally I Sinclair, 'The Significance of the Friendly Relations Declaration' in C Warbrick and V Lowe (eds), *The United Nations and the Principles of International Law* (Routledge, London, 1994) 1; G Arangio-Ruiz, *The United Nations Declaration on Friendly Relations and the System of the Sources of International Law* (Alphen aan den Rijn, Netherlands, 1979).

[49] Brownlie, n 6, 15; Shaw, n 12, 179; 1970 Declaration, para 3; 'Legal Questions' (1970) UNYB 787.

[50] UNGA Resolutions 3034 (XXVII) (1972); 32/147 (1977), preamble; 34/145 (1979), preamble, para 7; 38/130 (1983), para 4 (by consensus); 40/61 (1985), para 6; 42/159 (1987), paras 4, 5(a); 44/29 (1989), paras 3, 4(a); 46/51 (1991), paras 3, 4(a); 49/60 (1994), paras 4, 5(a); 51/210 (1996), para 5; 52/165 (1997), para 5; 53/108 (1999), para 5; 54/110 (2000), para 5; 55/158 (2001), para 5; 56/88 (2002), para 5; 57/27 (2003), para 5; 58/81 (2004), para 5; UNGA (60th Sess), 2005 World Summit Outcome, UN Doc A/60/L.1 (20 Sept 2005), para 86.

[51] cf R Schreiber, 'Ascertaining Opinio Juris of States Concerning Norms Involving the Prevention of International Terrorism: A Focus on the UN Process' (1998) 16 *Buffalo International Law Journal* 309, 325–326.

[52] *Nuclear Weapons (Advisory Opinion)*, n 6, para 72.

[53] See, eg, *Alabama Claims Arbitration* (1872) Moore 1 Int Arb 495; *Neer case (US v Mexico)* (1926) 4 RIAA 60, 61–62; *Caire Claim (France v Mexico)* (1929) 5 RIAA 516; *Texas Cattle Claims* (1944), in M Whiteman (1967) 8 Dig Intl L 749; *Corfu Channel* [1949] ICJ Reports 4; *Tehran Hostages Case* (1980) ICJ Reports 3, 31–32, paras 63, 67; *Nicaragua*, n 6; see also H Lauterpacht, 'Revolutionary Activities by Private Persons against Foreign States' (1928) 22 AJIL 105; Jennings and Watts, n 19, 391–406; H Kelsen, *Principles of International Law* (2nd edn, Holt, Rinehart and Winston, New York, 1966) 205–206; Brownlie, n 47, 729.

[54] See, eg, *British Property in the Spanish Zone of Morocco* (1924) 2 RIAA 640; *Tehran Hostages* ibid; *Janes Case (US v Mexico)* (1925) 4 RIAA 82, 87; *Youmans Case (US v Mexico)* (1926) 4 RIAA 110; *Solis* (1928) 4 RIAA 358, 361; *Texas Cattle Claims* ibid; *Home Missionary Society (US v Great Britain)* (1920) 6 RIAA 42; *Noyes Case (US v Panama)* (1933) 6 RIAA 308; see also R Lillich and J Paxman, 'State Responsibility for Injuries to Aliens Occasioned by Terrorist Activities' (1977) 26 AULR 217, 222–251, 262–270.

[55] Lillich and Paxman, ibid, 254–262, 276–307; L Condorelli, 'The Imputability to States of Acts of International Terrorism' (1989) 19 IYBHR 233, 240; S Malzahn, 'State Sponsorship and Support of International Terrorism: Customary Norms of State Responsibility (2002) 26 *Hastings International and Comparative Law Review* 83, 86; J McCredie, 'The Responsibility of States for Private Acts of International Terrorism' (1985) 1 *Temple International and Comparative Law Journal* 69; S Sucharitkul, 'Terrorism as an International Crime: Questions of Responsibility and Complicity' (1989) 19 IYBHR 247; L Kutner, 'Constructive Notice: A Proposal to End

failing to prevent the assassination of a UN mediator in Palestine, Count Bernadotte, by Jewish extremists in Israel.[56] A State is not, however, responsible for private acts that are not attributable to it, nor for harm caused by private acts where there is no failure of due diligence. It is the question of State control of private actors (or a breach of due diligence) that is decisive, not their status as armed bands, terrorists, or otherwise.[57]

Since 11 September 2001, the US has drawn no distinction between the acts of terrorists and the States that harbour, train, arm, fund, or supply them,[58] holding all 'equally guilty'.[59] Likewise, Israel allegedly killed twelve Palestinian police, staffing checkpoints in the West Bank, for failing to prevent the transit of 'terrorists' who killed six Israeli soldiers in 2002,[60] although it partly justified its action as a reprisal. It is too soon to judge the customary force of this view, but it exerts pressure to modify customary rules of State responsibility on attribution,[61] by holding States directly responsible for private acts even if a State does not 'effectively control' (or exercise 'overall control' over) the private actor.[62] Such a change may make the identification of 'terrorist' acts increasingly important, given the potential for triggering more frequent claims of self-defence against terrorism.

International Terrorism' (1974) 19 *New York Law Forum* 325; T Franck and D Niedermeyer, 'Accommodating Terrorism: An Offence against the Law of Nations' (1989) 19 IYBHR 75, 99–128; Y Dinstein, 'Terrorism as an International Crime' (1989) 19 IYBHR 55, 63; see also F Dubuisson, 'Vers un renforcement des obligations de diligence en matière de lutte contre le terrorisme?' in K Bannelier et al (eds), *Le droit international face au terrorisme* (Pédone, Paris, 2002) 141; P-M Dupuy, 'State Sponsors of Terrorism: Issues of International Responsibility' in A Bianchi (ed), *Enforcing International Law Norms against Terrorism* (Hart, Oxford, 2004) 3, 6–11 (considering the expansion of the range of subjects of international law to include non-State actors such as terrorists, and the broadening of the traditional criteria of attribution of conduct to States).

[56] *Reparation for Injuries Suffered in the Service of the United Nations (Advisory Opinion)* [1949] ICJ Reports 174.

[57] I Brownlie, *International Law and the Use of Force by States* (Clarendon, Oxford, 1963) 371–372.

[58] US President, 'President Shares Thanksgiving Meal with Troops', White House PR, Washington, DC, 21 Nov 2001; UNSC 56th Sess, 4370th mtg, Verbatim Record, 12 Sept 2001, UN Doc S/PV.4370, 7–8 (US); US President Bush, Address to UNGA, New York, 23 Sept 2003.

[59] US President Bush, Address to UNGA, New York, 10 Nov 2001.

[60] J Bennet, 'Israel Steps Up Counterstrikes; 22 Palestinians slain', *New York Times*, 21 Feb 2002.

[61] 2001 ILC Draft Articles on Responsibility of States for Internationally Wrongful Acts, Arts 4–11; *Nicaragua*, n 6, para 115; *Tadic (Appeal)* ICTY–94–1 (15 Jul 1999) paras 117–141, 158.

[62] D Jinks, 'State Responsibility for the Acts of Private Armed Groups' (2003) 4 Chinese JIL 83; R Wedgwood, 'The Fall of Saddam Hussein: Security Council Mandates and Preemptive Self-Defence' (2003) 97 AJIL 576, 583; G Travalio and J Altenburg, 'Terrorism, State Responsibility, and the Use of Military Force' (2003) 4 Chinese JIL 97, 102–110; A Cassese, 'Terrorism is Also Disrupting Some Crucial Legal Categories of International Law' (2001) 12 EJIL 993, 998–999.

2. The Munich Olympics and the 1972 US Draft Convention

While 'terrorism' had incidental significance in the 1970 and 1965 Declarations, the first concerted effort to address terrorism as a discrete subject in the General Assembly came in response to the killing of Israeli athletes at the Munich Olympics in early September 1972, and earlier attacks at an Israeli airport and on a Soviet diplomat in New York.[63] In late September, the US presented to the General Assembly a Draft Convention for the Prevention and Punishment of Certain Acts of International Terrorism,[64] although the proposed offences were designated as of 'international significance' rather than as 'terrorist' ones.[65]

Article 1 proposed three principal offences of unlawfully killing, causing serious bodily harm, or kidnapping, if such acts have an international dimension,[66] and are 'intended to damage the interests of or obtain a concession from a State or an international organization'.[67] Sectoral anti-terrorism treaties were to take precedence in the event of a conflict with the US Draft Convention.[68] The decision of whether to prosecute or to extradite was left to the discretion of the custodial State.

The US Draft Convention was limited to *international* rather than domestic acts of terrorism, excluding most acts by self-determination movements.[69] It was also designed to focus on individual terrorist acts, rather than State support for terrorist activity.[70] It excluded acts committed by, or against, 'a member of the Armed Forces of a State in the course of military hostilities',[71] and applicable IHL treaties would take precedence in case of a conflict.[72] The US Draft Convention further stated that it does not 'make an offence of any act which is permissible under' IHL, nor does it deprive any person of prisoner of war status if entitled to such status' in IHL.[73]

As a result, a prohibited act committed *against* a military member *in*

---

[63] A Sofaer, 'Terrorism and the Law' (1986) *Foreign Affairs* 901, 903; J Murphy, 'United Nations Proposals on the Control and Repression of Terrorism' in MC Bassiouni (ed), *International Terrorism and Political Crimes* (Charles C Thomas, Illinois, 1975) 496.

[64] UN Doc A/C.6/L.850 (1972), reprinted in (1972) 11 ILM 1382; see also J Moore, 'Toward Legal Restraints on International Terrorism' (1973) 67 ASIL Proceedings 88, 91–93; J Dugard, 'Towards the Definition of International Terrorism' (1973) 67 ASIL Proceedings 94, 98–100; G Wardlaw, *Political Terrorism: Theory, Tactics and Counter-measures* (CUP, Cambridge, 1982) 107–108.

[65] Murphy, n 63, 493, 505.

[66] Acts must be committed by a foreign national (Art 1(a)), and outside the target State, or inside the target State but against a foreign national (Art 1(b)). A State's territory includes all territory under its jurisdiction or administration: Art 2(c).

[67] 1972 US Draft Convention, Art 1(d).   [68] ibid, Art 14.

[69] J Murphy, 'Defining International Terrorism: A Way Out of the Quagmire' (1989) 19 IYBHR 13, 16; J Norton Moore, 'The Need for an International Convention' in Bassiouni (ed), n 63, 437, 443.

[70] Murphy, n 63, 496.   [71] 1972 US Draft Convention, Art 1(c).

[72] ibid, Art 13.   [73] ibid, Art 13(a)–(b).

peacetime may amount to terrorism. Secondly, a prohibited act committed *by* a military member in peacetime may amount to terrorism, so admitting the punishment of 'State terrorism' (subject to State immunities). Acts committed by non-state forces in the course of military hostilities are not privileged by exclusion from the Convention, so guerilla, national liberation, or self-determination forces may be punished as terrorists in some circumstances. Since the Convention was proposed in 1972, its exclusionary provisions in relation to IHL did not refer to the recognition extended to non-state forces in the 1977 Protocols.

Despite these limitations, the US Draft Convention envisaged broad liability, since the concept of intending to damage the 'interests' of a State is ambiguous and open-ended. There need only be an *intention* to damage; no *actual* damage is required. The idea of 'damage' is not limited by any minimum degree of severity. States have any number of 'interests' of varying importance and there was no attempt to circumscribe the types of interests deserving special protection. There is similarly no gradation of the concept of 'concessions' in terms of their political significance. There were, however, no property offences in the Convention,[74] which focused on threats to life, and few States except Israel expressed support for protecting property.[75]

There was little support for the US initiative in a General Assembly deadlocked by Cold War politics and the ideological divide between developed and developing States, particularly over self-determination. The US sought to convene a treaty conference, but was opposed by Arab and African States, and China, which believed that it was an attempt to criminalize self-determination movements.[76] The timing of the US proposal ensured its defeat, given the 'heated atmosphere engendered by the Munich killings and by the charges and countercharges passing between Israel and the Arab States'.[77]

3. *Resolution 3034 (XXVII) (1972)*

In place of the American proposal, UN Secretary-General Waldheim proposed an agenda item in the General Assembly on: 'Measures to prevent terrorism and other forms of violence which endanger or take innocent human lives or jeopardize fundamental freedoms'.[78] There was opposition to addressing terrorism without considering its causes, and the item was amended to include a 'study of the underlying causes of those forms of terrorism and acts of violence which lie in misery, frustration, grievance and

---

[74] T Franck and B Lockwood, 'Preliminary Thoughts towards an International Convention on Terrorism' (1974) 68 AJIL 69, 76.
[75] ibid.   [76] Murphy, n 69, 17; Murphy, n 63, 493, 499.
[77] ibid, 502.   [78] Quoted in Sofaer, n 63, 903.

despair and which cause some people to sacrifice human lives, including their own, to effect radical changes'. An Italian compromise to both study the causes and request the ILC to prepare a draft treaty to criminalize terrorism was rejected.[79] In response to the agenda item, in Resolution 3034 (XXVII) of December 1972, the Assembly expressed deep concern about 'increasing acts of violence which endanger or take innocent human lives or jeopardize fundamental freedoms',[80] but refrained from condemning terrorism,[81] despite a draft proposal to that effect.[82] While the resolution was adopted by 76 votes to 35, with 17 abstentions,[83] some States not supporting the resolution, such as the US, did so because its language and measures were not strong enough, not from a reluctance to condemn terrorism.[84] Similar resolutions from 1976 to 1983 attracted more support, and many States voted against or abstained for similar reasons.[85]

In contrast, some States did not support the resolutions because of disagreements on defining terrorism, the relevance of its causes, and distinguishing liberation movements.[86] Particularly contentious was the affirmation in 1972 of:

... the inalienable right to self-determination and independence of all peoples under colonial and racist regimes and other forms of alien domination and ... the legitimacy of their struggle, in particular the struggle of national liberation movements in accordance with the principles and purposes of the Charter and the relevant resolutions of the organs of the United Nations ...[87]

Ambiguous affirmations of this kind were common in resolutions until 1993, and were often thought to imply either that terrorism is justifiable in pursuit of self-determination, or that acts of self-determination cannot be considered

---

[79] Murphy, n 63, 500.

[80] UNGA Resolution 3034 (XXVII) (1972), para 1; see also UNGA Resolution 31/102 (1976), para 1.

[81] M Halberstam, 'The Evolution of the United Nations Position on Terrorism: From Exempting National Liberation Movements to Criminalizing Terrorism Wherever and by Whomever Committed' (2003) 41 Col JTL 573, 574.

[82] (1972) UNYB 644–655; Schreiber, n 51, 317–318.

[83] (1972) UNYB 649–650; see E Evans, 'American Policy Response to International Terrorism: Problems of Deterrence' in M Livingston (ed), *International Terrorism in the Contemporary World* (Greenwood Press, Connecticut, 1978) 375, 376.

[84] Schreiber, n 51, 319; S Rosen and R Frank, 'Measures Against International Terrorism' in D Carlton and C Schaerf (eds), *International Terrorism and World Security* (Croom Helm, London, 1975) 60, 68.

[85] Schreiber, n 51, 319–320; Halberstam, n 81, 574; see UNGA Resolutions 31/102 (1976) (by 100 votes to 9, with 27 abstentions); 32/147 (1977) (by 91 votes to 9, with 28 abstentions); 32/148 (1977) (by consensus); 36/109 (1981); 38/130 (1983).

[86] Schreiber, n 51, 320–321; (1977) UNYB 969 (Afghanistan, Cuba, Iran, Libya and the USSR).

[87] UNGA Resolution 3034 (XXVII) (1972) para 3; see also 31/102 (1976) para 3; 32/147 (1977) para 3; 34/145 (1979) preamble; 36/109 (1981) preamble; 38/130 (1983) preamble; 40/61 (1985) preamble; 42/159 (1987) preamble; 44/29 (1989) preamble; 46/51 (1991) preamble.

terroristic at all.[88] So too did the emphasis in Resolution 3034 (XXVII) (1972) on condemning only State terrorism: 'repressive and terrorist acts by colonial, racist and alien regimes in denying peoples their legitimate right to self-determination and independence and other human rights'.[89]

One writer described Resolution 3034 (XXVII) as 'a victory for those who supported the right to use all available measures to advance the ends of self-determination and wars of national liberation'.[90] That conclusion is difficult to sustain from the text of the resolution. Although the title of the resolution problematically assumes that there is a causal relationship between terrorism and underlying causes, nothing in the resolution asserts that terrorism is a *lawful* means of pursuing just causes, or even that those causes justify or excuse terrorism, rather than simply explain it.[91]

After 1991, resolutions on terrorism refrained from reaffirming self-determination.[92] Proposals for an international conference to distinguish national liberation from terrorism have never been accepted, despite some support for this approach.[93] Attempts to include liberation exceptions in sectoral treaties, such as the 1973 Protected Persons Convention and the 1979 Hostages Convention, were unsuccessful.[94] Since 1977, many States have accepted Protocol I[95]—which decriminalized violence by qualifying liberation movements, that complied with IHL—as resolving the 'freedom fighter' problem.[96]

The 1972 resolution established an Ad Hoc Committee of 35 States to make recommendations for eliminating terrorism.[97] The Committee reported

[88] J Dugard, 'Terrorism and International Law: Consensus at Last?' in E Yakpo and T Boumedra (eds), *Liber Amicorum Judge Mohammed Bedjaoui* (Kluwer, The Hague, 1999) 159, 164; Van Krieken, n 14, 223; Halberstam, n 81, 577; A Cassese, *Terrorism, Politics and Law: The Achille Lauro Affair* (Polity, London, 1989) 7–8; R Marauhn, 'Terrorism: Addendum' in R Bernhardt (ed), *Encyclopaedia of PIL: vol 4* (North Holland, Amsterdam, 2000) 849, 850; J Lambert, *Terrorism and Hostages in International Law* (Grotius, Cambridge, 1990) 31.

[89] UNGA Resolution 3034 (XXVII) (1972) para 4; see also UNGA Resolutions 31/102 (1976) para 4; 32/147 (1977) para 4; 34/145 (1979) para 4.

[90] Sofaer, n 63, 905.

[91] See Ch 2 above.

[92] Halberstam, n 81, 575, 577; A Cassese, *International Criminal Law* (OUP, Oxford, 2003) 124.

[93] B van Ginkel, 'The United Nations: Towards a Comprehensive Convention on Combating Terrorism' in M van Leeuwen (ed), *Confronting Terrorism* (Kluwer, The Hague, 2003) 207, 215–217 (particularly by Belarus, Bolivia, Brunei, Cuba, Cyprus, Ecuador, Guyana, Iraq, Libya, Qatar, Syria, Tunisia, Venezuela).

[94] Lambert, n 88, 48, 62–65; A Falvey, 'Legislative Responses to International Terrorism: International and National Efforts to Deter and Punish Terrorists' (1986) 9 BC ICLR 323, 336. However, some States lodged reservations excluding liberation movements: Sofaer, n 63, 918.

[95] There were 163 parties to Protocol I at April 2005: Swiss Federal Department of Foreign Affairs.

[96] Cassese, n 88, 123; see generally Ch 5, and E Chadwick, *Self-Determination, Terrorism and the International Humanitarian Law of Armed Conflict* (Martinus Nijhoff, The Hague, 1996).

[97] UNGA Resolution 3034 (XXVII) (1972) paras 9, 10; mandate renewed in UNGA Resolutions 31/102 (1976) paras 7–11 and 32/147 (1977) paras 7–11.

in 1973, 1977, and 1979,[98] examining the definition of terrorism, its causes, and preventive measures, although there was disagreement about whether definition was a precondition for studying the causes or taking preventive measures.[99] The debate about causes is examined in Chapter 2. The measures recommended in 1979 provided a template for future resolutions: condemning terrorism; eliminating its causes; respecting the 1970 Declaration; implementing sectoral treaties and developing new ones; encouraging cooperation, information exchange, prosecution, and extradition; and involving the UN, specialized and regional agencies.[100] A series of later resolutions has also addressed the human rights implications of terrorism and counter-terrorism,[101] in particular requiring anti-terrorism measures to comply with international law, including human rights, humanitarian, and refugee law.

The balance of this chapter focuses on the Assembly's initial condemnation of terrorism and its attempts to define it. There was little normative progress in the 1970s and early 1980s, due to ideological differences between non-aligned, communist and developed States.[102] However, as moderate Arab States and developing and communist States increasingly became victims of

[98] UNGAOR (28th Sess), Ad Hoc Committee Report (1973) Supp 28, UN Doc A/9028; UNGAOR (32nd Sess), Ad Hoc Committee Report (1977) Supp 37, UN Doc A/32/37; UNGAOR (34th Sess) Ad Hoc Committee Report (1979) Supp 39, UN Doc A/34/39; see also (1979) UNYB 1146.

[99] Ad Hoc Committee Report (1973) ibid, 4, para 9; 6, para 17; 11, para 35; 13–14, paras 42–43; 15, para 48; 17, para 53; Ad Hoc Committee Report (1977) ibid, 4, para 4; 18–19, para 12 (Hungary); 20, para 4 (France); 21, para 9 (Japan); Ad Hoc Committee Report (1979) ibid, 4, para 10; 11, paras 33, 35; 13, para 42; 18, paras 62–63; 19, para 67; 24, para 86; Lambert, n 88, 36–39.

[100] Ad Hoc Committee Report (1979), n 98, 32–33, para 118, adopted by UNGA Resolution 34/145 (1979) paras 2, 5–6; see also Resolutions 36/109 (1981); 38/130 (1983); 40/61 (1985); 42/22 (1987), annexed Declaration; 42/159 (1987); 44/29 (1989); 46/51 (1991); 48/122 (1993); 49/60 (1994), annexed Declaration; 49/185 (1994); 50/53 (1995); 50/186 (1995); 51/210 (1996), annexed Declaration; 52/133 (1997); 52/165 (1997); 53/108 (1999); 54/110 (2001); 54/164 (2000); 55/158 (2002); 56/88 (2002); 57/27 (2003); 58/81 (2004); 59/153 (2005). Before 1979, see Resolutions 3034 (XXVII) (1972); 31/102 (1976); 32/147 (1977); UN Sec-Gen, Reports on Measures to Eliminate International Terrorism (1981–2004).

[101] UNGA Resolutions 48/122 (1993); 49/185 (1994); 50/186 (1995); 52/133 (1997); 54/164 (1999); 56/160 (2002); 57/219 (2003); 58/174 (2004); 58/187 (2004); 59/191 (2005); 59/195 (2005); UNComHR Resolutions 1994/46; 1995/43; 1996/47; 1997/42; 1998/47; 1999/27; 2000/30; 2001/37; 2002/35; 2003/37; 2003/68; 2004/44; 2004/87; UNSubComHR Resolutions 1994/18; 1996/20; 1997/39; 1998/29; 1999/26; 2001/18; 2002/24; 2003/6; UN Com Status of Women Resolution 36/7 (1992). See also UN Sec-Gen, Reports on Human Rights and Terrorism, UN Docs A/50/685 (1995); A/54/439 (1999); A/56/190 (2001); A/58/266 (2004); A/58/533 (2004); A/59/404 (2004); UNSubComHR (Special Rapporteur K Koufa), Progress Report on Terrorism and Human Rights, UN Doc E/CN.4/Sub.2/2001/31, Preliminary Report, UN Doc E/CN.4/Sub.2/1999/27. The UN Commission on Human Rights created an independent expert in 2004 to consider human rights and counter-terrorism by States: UNComHR Resolution 2004/87, para 10.

[102] E McWhinney, *Aerial Piracy and International Terrorism* (Martinus Nijhoff, Dordrecht, 1987) 139; Rosen and Frank, n 84, 61; Lambert, n 88, 30.

terrorism,[103] the ideological polarization and permissive international attitudes towards terrorism began to diminish.

(a) General condemnation of terrorism

Numerous resolutions since 1979 have condemned international terrorism without defining it. In the Ad Hoc Committee, some States believed condemnation would 'exert considerable moral influence', while others believed it dangerous to condemn terrorism without first determining its scope.[104] The earliest is Resolution 34/145, which 'unequivocally' condemned 'all acts of international terrorism which endanger or take human lives or jeopardize fundamental freedoms',[105] and condemned State terrorism in the same way as the 1972 resolution.[106] The resolution was a breakthrough of sorts, prompted by détente after the Vietnam war and the emergence of non-western victims of terrorism, such as in the OPEC hostage-taking.[107]

The term 'unequivocally' implies that no justifications for terrorism are permissible. However, since some States understood terrorism to exclude acts furthering just causes *ab initio*, a resolution 'unequivocally' condemning terrorism could still be supported. The resolution attracted significant support (118 votes to 0, with 22 abstentions, including the US and the UK). Unequivocal condemnation of terrorism became a common refrain in later resolutions, with important accretions.

First, Resolutions 40/61 and 42/159 condemned 'as criminal, all acts, methods and practices of terrorism, wherever and by whomever committed'.[108] Terrorism, rather than only 'international' terrorism, was condemned; it was designated 'criminal' for the first time; and there was greater specification ('all acts, methods and practices'; 'wherever and by whomever committed'). While this language impliedly excludes justifications for terrorism, this was not the understanding of States that perceived terrorism to exclude just causes.[109] Second, from Resolution 44/29 onwards, terrorism was routinely condemned as both 'criminal and unjustifiable'.[110]

This cumulatively modified formula was adopted in the Assembly's 1994

---

[103] J Murphy, 'United Nations Proposals on the Control and Repression of Terrorism' in MC Bassiouni (ed), *International Terrorism and Political Crimes* (Charles C Thomas, Illinois, 1975) 493, 504.
[104] Ad Hoc Committee Report (1973), n 98, 18, paras 59–60.
[105] UNGA Resolution 34/145 (1979) para 3.
[106] ibid, para 4.   [107] Lambert, n 88, 42.
[108] UNGA Resolutions 40/61 (1985), para 1 (by consensus); 42/159 (1987), para 1 (153 votes to 2 (Israel and the US); 1 abstention).
[109] Sofaer, n 63, 905 (Angola, Bulgaria, Kuwait, Sri Lanka); Murphy, n 69, 19.
[110] UNGA Resolutions 44/29 (1989) para 1 (by consensus); 46/51 (1991) preamble (by consensus); 50/53 (1995) para 1 (by consensus); 51/210 (1996) para 1 (by consensus); 52/165 (1997) para 1 (by consensus); 54/110 (2000) para 1 (by 149 votes to 0; 2 abstentions); 55/158 (2001) para 1 (by 151 votes to 0; 2 abstentions).

Declaration on Measures to Eliminate International Terrorism.[111] Many later resolutions further strengthened this condemnation by referring to 'all acts, methods and practices of terrorism *in all its forms and manifestations*, wherever and by whomever committed'.[112] This additional language suggests that novel forms of terrorism, such as those facilitated by new technologies or by organized crime, are also condemned. UN subsidiary bodies have condemned terrorism in similar terms.[113]

The designation of terrorism as criminal in 1985 was a significant turning point. One writer argues that the description of terrorist acts as 'criminal' is evidence of implicit customary universal jurisdiction over terrorism.[114] While resolutions have not expressly posited terrorism as an international crime, Cassese writes that most international crimes originated as prohibitions on certain conduct, which did not specify the criminal consequences of such conduct,[115] or precisely define its elements. Reference to criminality generally, rather than to sectoral treaty offences, may indicate a belief by States in the existence of underlying customary norms.[116]

However, it is not clear from the resolutions whether terrorism itself is considered 'criminal', or whether that designation refers to the ordinary crimes or sectoral offences which typically comprise terrorist acts. It is also unclear whether criminality refers to the international or domestic legal order, although Van den Wyngaert accepts that the term 'criminal' refers to the international level rather than domestic law.[117] There is, however, room for some doubt, since the emphasis in resolutions has been on transnational judicial cooperation for national prosecutions, which may relate to domestic crimes rather than to any special international ones.

Further, the condemnation of terrorism as 'criminal' is hortatory,[118] and does not carry with it an international obligation to criminalize terrorism

---

[111] UNGA Resolutions 49/60 (1994) annexed Declaration, para 1; 51/210 (1996), annexed Declaration, para 1; 53/108 (1999) para 1 (by consensus); 56/88 (2002) para 1 (by consensus); 56/160 (2002) para 3; 57/27 (2003) para 1; 57/219 (2003) preamble; 58/81 (2004) para 1; 59/46 (2004) para 1; 1999 Terrorist Financing Convention, preamble.

[112] UNGA Resolutions 48/122 (1993) para 1 (by consensus) (emphasis added); 49/185 (1994) para 1; 50/186 (1995) para 2; 52/133 (1997) para 3; 54/164 (2000) para 2; 57/219 (2003) preamble; 58/81 (2004) para 1; 59/153 (2005) preamble; World Summit Outcome (2005), n 50, para 81.

[113] UNComHR Resolutions 1995/43, para 1; 1996/47, para 2; 1997/42, para 2; 1998/27, para 3; 1999/27, para 1; 2000/30, para 1; 2001/37, para 1; 2002/35, para 1; 2003/37, para 1; 2003/68, preamble; UNSubComHR Resolutions 1996/20, para 1; 1997/39, para 1; also 1994/18, para 1; 2001/18, preamble; 2002/24, preamble.

[114] Schreiber, n 51, 326.   [115] Cassese, n 88, 17.

[116] In *Tadic (Interlocutory)*, n 5, para 116, resolutions referred to 'international humanitarian law' rather than the treaty law of the Geneva Conventions and were held to be 'clearly articulating the view that there exists a corpus of general principles and norms on internal armed conflict embracing common Article 3 but having a much greater scope'.

[117] C Van den Wyngaert, 'The Political Offence Exception to Extradition: How to Plug the "Terrorist Loophole" Without Departing from Fundamental Human Rights' (1989) 19 IYBHR 297.

[118] Dinstein, n 55, 56–57.

domestically, or to prosecute or extradite offenders. Resolutions have not purported to impose duties of this kind (nor could they), nor to suggest that such duties exist in custom. At most, resolutions have encouraged States to apprehend and prosecute or extradite perpetrators,[119] cooperate and/or exchange information,[120] and conclude agreements on prosecution and extradition.[121] States have also been urged to establish jurisdiction to prosecute terrorism, but only for offences in sectoral treaties.[122] Another resolution has stressed accountability for 'aiding, supporting or harbouring the perpetrators, organizers and sponsors' of terrorism.[123] Despite asking States to exclude terrorism from the political offence exception to extradition, the Assembly has recognized the sovereign primacy of national law in extradition.[124]

(b) Specific condemnations of terrorism

From 2001, the Assembly began to condemn particular incidents as terrorism, an approach followed earlier by the Security Council. Resolution 56/1 condemned the 'heinous acts of terrorism, which . . . caused enormous loss of human life, destruction and damage' in the US on 11 September 2001.[125] Resolution 57/27 condemned terrorist acts in Bali and Moscow.[126] The common feature of these attacks was the indiscriminate killing of civilians for political reasons, outside the theatre of hostilities in any armed conflict. It is significant that the Moscow attack was characterized as terrorism, rather than as a treaty-offence of hostage-taking, or a crime against humanity, and that the Assembly involved itself in domestic terrorism.

A resolution of 2003 condemned the 'atrocious and deliberate attack' on the UN Office in Baghdad, which killed the UN High Commissioner for Human Rights, fifteen UN staff, and seven others.[127] It called for

---

[119] UNGA Resolutions 38/130 (1983) para 6; 40/61 (1985) para 8; 42/159 (1987) para 5(b); 44/29 (1989) para 4(b); 46/51 (1991) para 4(b); 46/51 (1991) para 4(b); 1994 Declaration, para 5(b); 1996 Declaration, para 5. UNComHR Resolutions have urged States to bring terrorists to justice: 1999/27, para 7; 2000/30, para 7; 2001/37, para 7; 2002/35, para 7; 2003/37, para 7.

[120] UNGA Resolutions 34/145 (1979) para 11; 40/61 (1985) para 7; 42/159 (1987) paras 5(c)–(d), 7; 42/22 (1987) annexed Declaration, para 23; 44/29 (1989) para 4(c)–(d); 46/51 (1991) para 4(c)–(d); 1994 Declaration, paras 5(c)–(d), 6; 52/165 (1997) para 4; 53/108 (1999) para 4; 54/110 (2000) para 4; 48/122 (1993) para 3; 49/185 (1994) para 3; 50/186 (1995) para 4; 52/133 (1997) para 5; 54/164 (2000) para 5; 50/53 (1995) paras 5–6; 52/165 (1997) para 4; 53/108 (1999) para 4; 54/110 (2000) para 4; 51/210 (1996) paras 3(a), 3(e), 4, reiterated in 52/165 (1997) para 3; 53/108 (1999) para 3; 54/110 (2000) para 3; 55/158 (2001) paras 3–4; 58/81 (2004) preamble, para 4; 1996 Declaration, para 8.

[121] UNGA Resolutions 34/145 (1979) para 11; 42/159 (1987) para 5(c); 44/29 (1989) para 4(c); 46/51 (1991) para 4(c); 1994 Declaration, paras 5(c), 6.

[122] UNGA Resolutions 55/158 (2001) para 7; 58/81 (2004) para 7.

[123] UNGA Resolution 56/1 (2001) para 4.

[124] UNGA Resolution 51/210 (1996) annexed Declaration, paras 6–7.

[125] UNGA Resolution 56/1 (2001) para 1; reaffirmed in 58/81 (2004) preamble (by consensus).

[126] UNGA Resolution 57/27 (2003), preamble (by consensus).

[127] UNGA Resolution 57/338 (2003) para 1; reaffirmed in 58/81 (2004) preamble.

cooperation to bring to justice the perpetrators, organizers, and sponsors of the attack, and to prevent and eradicate terrorism.[128] It is significant that the attack was categorized as terrorism, rather than as treaty offences against protected persons or UN personnel,[129] or as war crimes in IHL, and it is unclear which offences the Assembly had in mind in calling for cooperation.

(c) Definition in the Ad Hoc Committee on international terrorism

In its final report, the Ad Hoc Committee refrained from defining terrorism due to the persistent disagreement among States. Terrorism was described as a 'loaded term' and 'liable to diverse interpretations', as well as a 'highly emotional' and imprecise term 'encompassing many forms of violence linked to war and political oppression'.[130] Others thought that no definition could accommodate the divergent views, and that terrorism was 'extremely difficult to define'.[131] The methodology of definition was also controversial, such as whether it should be general, abstract, and comprehensive; enumerative, analytical, and pragmatic; or mixed (combining generic elements with listed acts).[132] Yet others thought the 'substance' or 'framework' of terrorism could be identified for taking preventive measures,[133] without requiring precise definition.

In proposing definitions, some States emphasized violence for political motives or objectives,[134] or for coercive (but not necessarily political) ends.[135] Venezuela proposed the twin aims of instilling terror *and* achieving a political objective, thus narrowing the definition. For some, acts motivated by 'material gain or personal satisfaction' were not terrorism,[136] whereas other proposals explicitly included private motives.[137] All proposals specified an international element, commonly by reference to territory or nationality.[138] Some of the proposals specified the perpetrators and/or the victims of terrorism,[139] or listed serious violent acts, in conjunction with generic elements.[140]

---

[128] UNGA Resolution 57/338 (2003) paras 4–5.

[129] 1973 Protected Persons Convention; 1994 Convention on UN and Associated Personnel.

[130] Ad Hoc Committee Report (1979), n 98, 25, para 88 and Ad Hoc Committee Report (1973), n 98, 5, para 13 respectively.

[131] Ad Hoc Committee Report (1979), n 98, 11, para 34 and 26, para 90 respectively.

[132] Respectively: Ad Hoc Committee Report (1973), n 98, 6, para 14 and Ad Hoc Committee Report (1979), n 98, 11, para 33; Ad Hoc Committee Report (1973), n 98, 6, para 15; Ad Hoc Committee Report (1973), n 98, 11, para 36.

[133] Ad Hoc Committee Report (1973), n 98, 12, para 36.

[134] ibid, 7, para 19; 15, para 48; Annex, 22 (Haiti); 23 (Venezuela).

[135] ibid, Annex, 21 (France); 22 (Greece); Ad Hoc Committee Report (1979), n 98, 13, para 43.

[136] Ad Hoc Committee Report (1973), n 98, 7, para 19.

[137] ibid, Annex, 21 (Non-Aligned States), 22 (Greece).

[138] ibid, Annex, 21 (France) 11, 36 (Greece); 22 (Haiti); 23 (Venezuela).

[139] ibid, Annex, 22 (Greece, Haiti); 23 (Venezuela).

[140] ibid, Annex, 23 (Venezuela); 26 (Greece); 28–33 (US).

Some States simply enumerated objective violent acts considered terrorist, without generic elements.[141]

Among the most divisive issues was the belief that 'State terrorism' was the most harmful, noxious, cruel, pernicious, or dangerous form of terrorism.[142] Conversely, violent struggles were seen as 'a negation of terrorism' and an attempt to secure human rights and a just legal order.[143] A very wide range of activity was considered State terrorism.[144] This included violations of existing legal norms on aggression, use of force, self-determination, apartheid, discrimination, foreign occupation, colonial domination, non-intervention, non-interference, subversion and infiltration, mercenaries, acts of terror against civilians, terror bombing, torture, massacres, mass imprisonments, and reprisals.

It also included more ambiguous, extra-legal acts, such as oppression, serfdom, hegemony, use of defoliants, economic destruction, preventive action, banditry by fascists or intelligence services, and the nuclear 'balance of terror'. Concrete examples of State terrorism suggested included Israeli occupation of Palestine, armed provocation by Israel against Arab States and Uganda, and acts of Zionists, national immigrant centres and fascist groups.[145] Rhodesia and South Africa were also accused of ruling by terror.[146]

While a number of proposed definitions included State terrorism,[147] other States sought to limit terrorism to non-State violence. The principal objection was that State violence was already regulated by existing norms (including the UN Charter, the 1970 Declaration, self-determination, and human rights law) and institutions (such as the Security Council), and it was therefore 'unnecessary and inappropriate to revert to those questions'.[148] It was also

---

[141] ibid, Annex, 23 (Nigeria); 33–34 (Uruguay);

[142] ibid, 8, para 24; 18, para 62; Ad Hoc Committee Report (1977), n 98, 14, para 11 (Algeria); Ad Hoc Committee Report (1979), n 98, 8, para 26.

[143] Ad Hoc Committee Report (1979), n 98, 9, para 28.

[144] ibid, 8, para 26; 9, para 28; 12, paras 39–40; Ad Hoc Committee Report (1973), n 98, Annex, 24 (Algeria).

[145] Ad Hoc Committee Report (1979), n 98, 7, para 23; Ad Hoc Committee Report (1977), n 98, 31, para 15 (USSR), para 20 (Tunisia).

[146] Ad Hoc Committee Report (1977), n 98, 31, para 20 (Tunisia).

[147] Ad Hoc Committee Report (1973), n 98, Annex, 21 (Non-Aligned States: Algeria, Congo, Democratic Yemen, Guinea, India, Mauritania, Nigeria, Syria, Tunisia, Tanzania, Yemen, Yugoslavia, Zaire, and Zambia); 22–23 (Iran); 23 (Venezuela); 24 (Algeria).

[148] ibid, 8, para 24; see also 12, para 38; 19, paras 64–66; Ad Hoc Committee Report (1977), n 98, 4, para 2; 34, para 29 (UK); Ad Hoc Committee Report (1979), n 98, 8 para 27; 26, para 90; 28, para 105; 29, paras 108–109 (Sweden). See also UNComHR (53rd Sess), Terrorism and Human Rights: Progress Report by Special Rapporteur K Koufa, 27 June 2001, UN Doc E/CN.4/Sub.2/2001/31, 14, 18; Franck and Lockwood, n 74, 74; Murphy, n 69, 34; K Skubiszewski, 'Definition of Terrorism' (1989) 19 IYBHR 39, 45; D Pokempner, 'Terrorism and Human Rights: The Legal Framework' in M Schmitt and G Beruto (eds), *Terrorism and International Law* (IIHL and George C Marshall European Center for Security Studies, San Remo, 2003) 19, 22; R Friedlander, 'Terrorism' in Bernhardt (ed), n 88, 845, 847, 849.

argued that the acts of armed forces in armed conflict were extensively covered by IHL and human rights law.[149]

Apart from resolutions reiterating the 1970 Declaration and the 1974 Definition of Aggression, few resolutions have explicitly referred to State terrorism. A 1984 resolution was devoted entirely to the 'Inadmissibility of the policy of State terrorism',[150] but the acts it describes are no more than a political relabelling of State responsibility for violations of existing legal norms mentioned in the resolution.[151] It is not evidence of separate customary norms on State terrorism, nor does it define it. It must also be interpreted in the light of its large number of abstentions.[152]

The other divisive issue was the attempt to exclude self-determination, liberation, or independence movements from the prohibition of terrorism.[153] The USSR also sought to exclude demonstrations by workers opposed to exploitation.[154] Exclusion provisions are found in a number of proposed definitions.[155] Other States thought this amounted to double standards 'based on ideological criterion [sic] and vestiges of the cold war' and argued for no exceptions.[156] The inability to agree on the exception partially accounts for the failure to reach agreement on definition.

(d) Subsequent Resolutions on definition

The deep division on definition prevented the Assembly from addressing the question for many years. In Resolution 42/159, the Assembly recognized that a 'generally agreed definition' would make the struggle against terrorism more effective.[157] Yet no concrete definition was forthcoming until 1994. In the meantime, some resolutions indicated some of the characteristics of terrorism. A preliminary step was Resolution 48/122, which did not define terrorism but described some of its attributes, as:

---

[149] Ad Hoc Committee Report (1973), n 98, 8, para 24; 12, para 37; see also Ad Hoc Committee Report (1977), n 98, 15, para 14 (Sweden); 23, para 16 (Italy); 34, para 29 (UK).

[150] UNGA Resolutions 39/159 (1984).

[151] ibid, preamble, including the non-use of force, territorial integrity and political independence, non-intervention, self-determination, and sovereignty over natural resources.

[152] UNGA Resolution 39/159 (1984) was adopted by 117 votes to 0, with 30 abstentions.

[153] Ad Hoc Committee Report (1973), n 98, 12, para 37; Ad Hoc Committee Report (1977), n 98, 27, para 37 (Haiti); 26–27, para 35 (Yugoslavia); 26, para 33 (Ukraine); 28, para 2 (Czechoslovakia); 30, para 13 (Venezuela); 30, para 15 (USSR); Ad Hoc Committee Report (1979), n 98, 24, para 82.

[154] Ad Hoc Committee Report (1979), n 98, 5–6, para 16; Ad Hoc Committee Report (1977), n 98, 30, para 15 (USSR).

[155] Ad Hoc Committee Report (1973), n 98, Annex, 22 (Greece), 23 and 27 (Nigeria), 21 (Iran).

[156] Ad Hoc Committee Report (1979), n 98, 7, para 23 and 24, para 83.

[157] UNGA Resolution 42/159 (1987) preamble; see also 44/29 (1989) preamble; 46/51 (1991) preamble.

. . . activities aimed at the destruction of human rights, fundamental freedoms and democracy, threatening the territorial integrity and security of States, destabilizing legitimately constituted Governments, undermining pluralistic civil society and having adverse consequences on the economic and social development of States . . .[158]

The resolution also characterized terrorism as the killing, massacre, and maiming of innocent persons 'in indiscriminate and random acts of violence and terror, which cannot be justified under any circumstances'.[159] A more comprehensive definition was provided in the 1994 Declaration on Measures to Eliminate International Terrorism:

Criminal acts intended or calculated to provoke a state of terror in the general public, a group of persons or particular persons for political purposes are in any circumstance unjustifiable, whatever the considerations of a political, philosophical, ideological, racial, ethnic, religious or any other nature that may be invoked to justify them . . .[160]

Although the provision was not expressly presented as a definition,[161] it implicitly serves that function, at least as a working premise for the Assembly. The 1994 Declaration has been affirmed in later resolutions,[162] and partly reflects the definition in the 1937 League Convention.

Cassese argues that the 1994 Declaration is evidence of 'broad agreement' on the 'general definition of terrorism',[163] influenced also by the 1999 Terrorist Financing Convention and IHL provisions on terror.[164] This partly underpins a wider argument that terrorism is a customary crime with distinct elements: (1) violent (national) criminal acts; (2) a special intent (*mens rea*) to spread terror (or fear or intimidation) by violence or threats of violence against the State, the public or a group; and (3) a political, religious, ideological, or other (non-private) motive.[165] For Cassese, there is general agreement on a definition, but the scope of exceptions remains contentious.[166] Kolb agrees that there is nascent universal jurisdiction over terrorism.[167] In

---

[158] UNGA Resolutions 48/122 (1993) para 1; 49/185 (1994) para 1; 50/186 (1995) para 2; 52/133 (1997) para 3; 54/164 (2000) para 2; 56/160 (2002) para 3; 57/219 (2003) preamble; 58/174 (2004) para 1; 58/187 (2004) preamble; 59/191 (2005) preamble; 59/195 (2005), para 1.
[159] UNGA Resolution 48/122 (1993) preamble; see also preambles to UNGA Resolutions 48/122 (1993); 49/185 (1994); 50/186 (1995); 52/133 (1997); 54/164 (2000); 56/160 (2002) preamble; 58/174 (2004) para 3; 59/195 (2005) para 4; UNComHR Resolutions 1995/34; 1996/47; 1997/42; 1998/47; 1999/27; 2000/30; 2001/37; 2002/35; 2003/37; UNSubComHR Resolutions 1994/18; 1996/20; 1997/39; 1999/26; 2001/18; 2002/24.
[160] UNGA Resolution 49/60 (1994) annexed Declaration, para 3 (emphasis added).
[161] Halberstam, n 81, 576.
[162] UNGA Resolutions 50/53 (1995) para 2; 51/210 (1996) para 2; 52/165 (1997) para 2; 53/108 (1999) para 2; 54/110 (2000) para 2; 55/158 (2001) para 2; 56/88 (2002) para 2; 57/27 (2003) para 2; 58/81 (2004) para 2; 59/46 (2004), para 3.
[163] A Cassese, *International Law* (OUP, Oxford, 2001) 246.   [164] Cassese, n 88, 121–122.
[165] Cassese, n 62, 994; Cassese, n 163, 246, 259; Cassese, n 88, 120–131.
[166] Cassese, n 88, 121.
[167] Kolb, n 1, 87–88; cf R Kolb, 'The Exercise of Criminal Jurisdition over International Terrorists' in Bianchi (ed), n 55, 227, 276–278.

theory, the assertion by States of excuses or justifications for violations of a customary rule need not challenge or undermine the existence of the rule itself.[168]

The normative weight of the 1994 definition must be evaluated in the light of a number of factors. On one hand, as a Declaration it is of greater importance than ordinary resolutions. It was adopted without a vote, suggesting a degree of consensus among States, and has been reiterated in numerous later resolutions.[169] The reference to 'criminal acts' invokes normative language, rather than mere exhortation or aspiration. On the other hand, there is little support for the view that the definition declares custom. The Declaration itself emphasizes the need to progressively develop and codify the law on terrorism,[170] far from purporting to reflect existing rules. Adoption by consensus does not guarantee unanimity among States, just that there are no formal objections.[171] States may also have supported it for non-legal reasons.

Indeed, in the Sixth Committee, a number of States proposed legal definitions, or gave concrete examples, of terrorism at variance with the 1994 Declaration.[172] More importantly, many States argued that there was still a need to define terrorism and/or to adopt a comprehensive treaty,[173] and to distinguish self-determination struggles.[174] Subsequently, the many States of the Non-Aligned Movement and the OIC have insisted on legal definition and the differentiation of liberation struggles—even while approving the 1994 Declaration.[175]

The statement in the 1994 Declaration that terrorist acts are 'unjustifiable' must be cautiously interpreted in this light. While other States dismissed the

---

[168] J-M Henckaerts and L Doswald-Beck (eds), *Customary International Humanitarian Law*, vol I (CUP, Cambridge, 2004) xxxviii.

[169] UNGA Resolutions 50/53 (1995) para 2; 51/210 (1996) para 2; 52/165 (1997) para 2; 53/108 (1999) para 2; 54/110 (2000) para 2; 55/158 (2001) para 2; 56/88 (2002) para 2; 57/27 (2003) para 2.

[170] 1994 Declaration, para 12.

[171] E Suy, 'The Meaning of Consensus in Multilateral Diplomacy' in R Akkerman, P Van Krieken, and C Pannenborg (eds), *Declarations on Principles: A Quest for Universal Peace* (Leyden, Groningen, 1977) 259, 272.

[172] UNGAOR (49th Sess) (6th Committee), 13th mtg, 19 Oct 1994, para 3 (Germany); 14th mtg, 20 Oct 1994, para 5 (Sudan); para 23 (Pakistan); paras 74, 78 (Turkey); 15th mtg, 21 Oct 1994, paras 44–45, 60 (Kuwait); para 59 (Iraq); para 25 (Libya); para 26 (US).

[173] ibid, 14th mtg, 20 Oct 1994, para 5 (Sudan), 13 (India), 27 (Algeria), 71 (Nepal); 15th mtg, 21 Oct 1994, para 4 (Sri Lanka), 9 (Iran), 18–19 (Libya),

[174] ibid, 14th mtg, 20 Oct 1994, para 6 (Sudan), 20 (Syria), 24 (Pakistan); 15th mtg, 21 Oct 1994, para 9 (Iran), 18–19 (Libya).

[175] NAM, XIV Ministerial Conference, Final Doc, Durban, 17–19 Aug 2004, paras 98–99, 101–102, 104; NAM, XIII Conference of Heads of State or Government, Final Doc, Kuala Lumpur, 25 Feb 2003, paras 105–106, 108, 115; NAM, XIII Ministerial Conference, Final Doc, Cartagena, 8–9 Apr 2000, paras 90–91; OIC Resolutions 6/31–LEG (2004), para 5; 7/31–LEG (2004), preamble, paras 1–2; 6/10–LEG (IS) (2003), para 5; 7/10–LEG (IS) (2003), paras 1–2; OIC, Islamic Summit Conference (10th Sess), Final Communiqué, Malaysia, 16–17 Oct 2003, para 50; OIC (Extraordinary Session of Foreign Ministers), Declaration on International Terrorism, Kuala Lumpur, 1–3 Apr 2002, paras 8, 11, 16 and Plan of Action, paras 2–3.

need for a definition and/or a convention,[176] the 1994 definition must be viewed as a compromise formula, which identifies a minimal political agreement on the scope of terrorism, but falls short of a legal definition, left to another day. There is further a 'lack of universal *opinio juris*' on the scope of terrorism *ratione personae*, as to whether a crime is limited to private actors or also encompasses State conduct.[177] State practice reveals that States remain 'profoundly divided' on definition, notwithstanding resolutions evidencing 'a clear sign of deep concern regarding the problem'.[178]

Cassese also relies too heavily on resolutions as evidence of custom. The resolutions must be interpreted cautiously, since parallel UN treaty negotiations since 2000 have been unable to reach agreement on a legal definition. Against that background, it is difficult to interpret resolutions as sufficient evidence of a customary crime, particularly since the 1994 definition is quite different to that in the Draft Comprehensive Convention.

Further, treaties negotiated after 1994—including the 1999 Terrorist Financing Convention and regional treaties—have adopted different definitions, suggesting that the definition of terrorist crimes remains contested. While Cassese states that the 1994 definition 'is not far from, and indeed to a large extent dovetails with' the definition in the 1999 Terrorist Financing Convention,[179] that is a misdescription. The 1994 Declaration defines terrorism as criminal acts intended to provoke terror in certain persons for political purposes. In contrast, the 1999 definition refers to serious violent acts for the purpose of intimidating a population, or compelling a government or international organization.[180] The first definition focuses on a mental state inflicted for a political purpose, whereas the second focuses on coercive or intimidatory objectives for whatever purpose—including non-political ones. The 1999 definition should also be read cautiously since it does not establish general terrorist offences, but triggers only financing offences. In any event, Cassese's proposed definition lacks reference to the element of compelling a government or international organization, at least where such compulsion does not *also* intimidate or terrorize.

Cassese further relies on the terrorism provisions in IHL to support the contention that there is a customary crime of terrorism. Yet, as Chapter 5 explains, terrorism has a distinctive meaning in armed conflict and States have not abstracted and generalized that definition to create a general crime of terrorism outside the context of armed conflicts. More specifically, terrorism

---

[176] UNGAOR (49th Sess) (6th Committee), 14th mtg, 20 Oct 1994, para 18 (Sweden for Nordic States), 38 (Romania), 41 (Israel), 56 (Venezuela); 15th mtg, 21 Oct 1994, para 40 (Hungary), 57 (Germany for EU).

[177] G Abi-Saab, 'The Proper Role of International Law in Combating Terrorism' in Bianchi (ed), n 55, xiii, xx.

[178] *Nuclear Weapons (Advisory Opinion)*, n 6, paras 67 and 71 respectively.

[179] Cassese, n 88, 124.

[180] 1999 Terrorist Financing Convention, Art 2(1)(b).

in armed conflict has not been interpreted to require a political, religious, ideological, or other motive, which Cassese claims is a core part of the customary definition of terrorism.

There have been few extradition requests or prosecutions pursuant to the 1994 definition, which has only marginally influenced national laws.[181] At best, the definition reflects nascent political agreement on a shared concept of terrorism, but not legal agreement evidencing a customary crime. Voting support for such resolutions may have been conditioned on the understanding that they did not generate criminal liability. It would be surprising if the protracted disputes on definition in the treaty context could be circumvented by a relatively recent series of non-binding resolutions, unsupported by State behaviour in conformity with the 1994 definition.

(e) Particular manifestations of terrorism

Occasionally, the Assembly has addressed particular types of terrorism. Indeed, many of the sectoral treaties were adopted under its auspices.[182] Other resolutions have called for the prevention of hostage-taking,[183] and addressed the detection of explosives and harmful substances.[184] States have also been encouraged to prevent terrorists from using electronic systems; abusing social, cultural and charitable groups (including for financing terrorism); and being involved with organized crime.[185]

In 2003–04, three resolutions were devoted to preventing terrorists from acquiring weapons of mass destruction (WMDs) and their means of delivery.[186] The emphasis on prevention indicates States' concerns at the consequences of even a single use of WMDs; the preambles call the problem a 'threat to humanity'.[187] This judgment is borne out by the literature on terrorism and WMDs,[188] which, while sometimes alarmist and unsubstantiated by

---

[181] See 'E. National Terrorism Legislation' below.

[182] An Ad Hoc Committee created by UNGA Resolution 31/103 (1976) drafted the 1979 Hostage Convention, annexed to UNGA Resolution 34/146 (1979). Another Ad Hoc Committee, created by UNGA Resolution 51/210 (1996), drafted the 1997 Terrorist Bombings Convention, the 1999 Terrorist Financing Convention, and the 2005 Nuclear Terrorism Convention: UNGA Resolutions 52/164 (1997), 54/109 (2000) and 59/290 (2005) respectively.

[183] UNGA Resolutions 44/29 (1989) paras 7–8; 46/51 (1991) paras 7–8.

[184] UNGA Resolutions 51/210 (1996) para 3(b), 52/165 (1997) para 3; 53/108 (1999) para 3; 54/110 (2000) para 3; 55/158 (2001) para 3.

[185] UNGA Resolutions 51/210 (1996) para 3(c)–(d) and (f), 52/165 (1997), para 3; 53/108 (1999) para 3; 54/110 (2000) para 3; 55/158 (2001) para 3.

[186] UNGA Resolutions 57/83 (2003) paras 1–3; 58/48 (2004) paras 1–3; 59/80 (2004), paras 1–2.

[187] UNGA Resolutions 57/83 (2003), preamble; 58/48 (2004), preamble.

[188] N Gurr and B Cole, *The New Face of Terrorism: Threats from Weapons of Mass Destruction* (IB Tauris, London, 2002); W Laqueur, *The New Terrorism: Fanaticism and the Arms of Mass Destruction* (Phoenix Press, London, 2001) 49–78; L Johnson, 'The Threat of Nuclear Terrorism and September 11th: Wake-up Call to Get the Treaties Right' (2002) 31 Den JILP 80; D Fidler, 'Bioterrorism, Public Health and International Law' (2002) 3 Chinese JIL 7; L Beres,

evidence of particular threats, holds that the risk of WMDs warrants a firm precautionary approach.

4. Summary of Assembly practice

Attempts in the Assembly to define terrorism in the 1970s were unsuccessful, largely due to Cold War politics and differences over decolonization. Over time, gradual progress was made towards definition, as terrorism was condemned as criminal and unjustifiable; the early emphasis on State terrorism dissipated; and the implicit exemption of self-determination movements was eliminated from resolutions.

In 1994, political agreement was reached on a working definition of terrorism—instilling fear for political purposes—but falling short of a legal definition. There is not yet sufficient evidence of a customary crime based on this definition, given the absence of wider State practice (such as national prosecutions or laws), and the ongoing disagreement on definition in the treaty negotiation context. It is, however, plausible that a customary prohibition on terrorism, as minimally defined in 1994, has emerged, but not yet criminal liability for breaches of that prohibition.

Customary norms are, however, reflected in early Assembly declarations, often reiterated, which affirm States' duties not to support terrorism against other States amounting to a use of force or an intervention. Yet State responsibility for terrorism is a subset of the long-established customary rule that States are responsible for unlawful harm caused to other States, although, in practice, the identification of 'terrorist' actors may be necessary for purposes of attribution and/or self-defence. While fulfilling these duties may require domestic criminalization or extradition of terrorists,[189] divergences in national definitions preclude the existence of a customary crime.

C. UN SECURITY COUNCIL PRACTICE

The question of terrorism was largely consigned to the General Assembly prior to 2001,[190] reflecting the structural dichotomy between the Assembly as the 'soft UN' and the Council as the 'hard UN'.[191] There has been

---

'On International Law and Nuclear Terrorism' (1994) 24 Geo JICL 1; R Friedlander, 'The Ultimate Nightmare: What if Terrorists Go Nuclear?' (1982) 12 Den JILP 1.

[189] Schreiber, n 51, 327–328.

[190] N Rostow, 'Before and After: The Changed UN Response to Terrorism since September 11th' (2002) 35 Cornell ILJ 475, 479; E Rosand, 'Security Council Resolution 1373, the Counter-Terrorism Committee, and the Fight Against Terrorism' (2003) 97 AJIL 333.

[191] M Koskenniemi, 'The Police in the Temple: Order, Justice and the UN: A Dialectical View' (1995) 6 EJIL 325, 336.

little scrutiny of the breadth of Council resolutions on terrorism before 11 September 2001.[192] Until then, resolutions did not impose measures against terrorism generally, nor did they define it. However, various resolutions after 1985 designated specific incidents, and types of violence by and against various actors, as terrorism. The first part of this section deductively and incrementally identifies the substantive content of 'terrorism' in Council practice, notwithstanding the lack of consistency in the designation of acts as terrorism.[193]

The second part examines radical shifts in the Council's approach after September 2001.[194] Since then, the Council has imposed binding, quasi-legislative measures against terrorism in general,[195] unconnected to specific incidents, and unlimited in time. The Council has also regarded 'any' act of terrorism as a threat to peace and security, regardless of its severity, or international effects. Yet, the Council failed to define terrorism until late 2004, despite using it as an operative legal concept with serious consequences for individuals and entities. For three years, States could unilaterally define terrorism and assert universal jurisdiction over it, despite wide divergences in national definitions. The Council's 2004 definition raises other problems, since it is non-binding (allowing States to preserve unilateral definitions) and potentially conflicts with multilateral treaty negotiations on defining terrorism.

1. Legal implications of Council resolutions

Council resolutions do not formally create international law, but are normative obligations on member States under the Charter.[196] The Council is 'a political organ having legal consequences',[197] determined by the terms of a resolution, surrounding discussions, the Charter provisions invoked, and all

---

[192] D Malone, 'The Security Council in the Post-Cold War Era: A Study in the Creative Interpretation of the UN Charter' (2003) 35 *International Law and Politics* 487, 501; C de Jonge Oudraat, 'The Role of the Security Council' in J Boulden and T Weiss (eds), *Terrorism and the UN: Before and After September 11* (University of Indiana Press, Bloomington, 2004) 151.

[193] R Higgins, 'The General International Law of Terrorism' in R Higgins and M Flory (eds), *Terrorism and International Law* (Routledge, London, 1997) 13, 19.

[194] See generally K Graham, 'The Security Council and Counter-terrorism: Global and Regional Approaches to an Elusive Public Good' (2005) 17 *Terrorism and Political Violence* 37; J Dhanapala, 'The United Nations Response to 9/11' (2005) 17 *Terrorism and Political Violence* 17.

[195] J Stromseth, 'The Security Council's Counter-Terrorism Role: Continuity and Innovation' (2003) 97 ASIL Proceedings 41; P Szasz, 'The Security Council Starts Legislating' (2002) 96 AJIL 901; Rosand, n 190; S Talmon, 'The Security Council as World Legislature' (2005) 99 AJIL 175, 177–178.

[196] M de Brichambaut, 'The Role of the United Nations Security Council in the International Legal System' in M Byers (ed), *The Role of International Law in International Politics* (OUP, Oxford, 2001) 268. On the diverse effects of resolutions, see Öberg, n 5.

[197] ibid.

the circumstances.[198] Resolutions may also assist in interpreting the Charter;[199] evidence general principles of law;[200] or reflect *opinio juris*, 'provided that their subject-matter is not restricted to particular circumstances'.[201] Unanimous Council resolutions may be of 'great relevance to the formation of *opinio juris*'.[202] Even non-binding resolutions may influence State behaviour[203] or evidence general principles of law.[204] The Council's repeated reference to terrorism over time may, therefore, be of normative significance to the development of that concept in customary law. However, given the Council's unrepresentativeness, evidence of more general acceptance (or acquiescence) is required.[205] Resolutions alone will seldom reflect the necessary *opinio juris* and generality of State practice.[206]

In applying legal rules to specific situations over time, resolutions may have precedential effects in equivalent situations,[207] notwithstanding the absence of any doctrine of precedent in international law. The application of a norm to a specific case is inevitably a 'law-creative act'.[208] Precedents are especially important in relation to security because 'the body of principles is still so fragmentary and abstract': 'Such precedents contribute the specificity which is essential to convert the "soft" law of the Charter into the "hard" law needed for effective implementation. Greater precision through case law may also contribute to more rational treatment of particular problems.'[209] In applying legal rules to specific situations over time, resolutions contribute to 'the stream of authoritative decisions which are looked to as a source of law'.[210] Caution is, however, warranted, given that the Council is foremost a political decision-maker rather than a judicial body applying legal principles and there is not always proper consideration of relevant legal issues.[211] While there are risks in developing international law through 'the ad hoc and piecemeal reactions of a political organ to particular crises', this may not be so 'different from the process by which law ingests the haphazard practice of States'.[212] Coordinated consideration of a problem by the Council may

---

[198] *Namibia (Advisory Opinion)* (1971) ICJ Reports 41.

[199] G Nolte, 'The Limits of the Security Council's Powers and its Functions in the International Legal System: Some Reflections' in Byers (ed), n 196, 315, 320, 324.

[200] P Hulsroj, 'The Legal Function of the Security Council' (2002) 1 Chinese JIL 59, 70.

[201] de Brichambaut, n 196, 273.

[202] *Tadic (Interlocutory)*, n 5, para 133.

[203] O Schachter, 'The Quasi-Judicial Role of the Security Council and the General Assembly' (1964) 58 AJIL 960, 963.

[204] Hulsroj, n 200, 70.

[205] Nolte, n 199, 325; V Gowlland-Debbas, 'The Functions of the United Nations Security Council in the International Legal System' in Byers (ed), n 196, 277, 300.

[206] Gowlland-Debbas, n 205, 300.

[207] Schachter, n 203, 963–964; M Reisman, 'The Constitutional Crisis in the United Nations' (1993) 87 AJIL 83, 85; Hulsroj, n 200, 69; R Higgins, 'The Place of International Law in the Settlement of Disputes by the Security Council' (1970) 64 AJIL 1, 6.

[208] Schachter, n 203, 964.   [209] ibid.   [210] Higgins, n 207, 6.

[211] ibid, 6–7.   [212] Gowlland-Debbas, n 205, 301.

sometimes promote more legal coherence than the unsystematized, unilateral reactions of individual States.

The Council's presidential statements, adopted by consensus, do not generally create binding obligations on States, although they may bind the Council, its members, and the UN Secretariat on organizational and procedural matters.[213] In principle, a Council 'decision' binding States under Articles 25 and 27 and Chapter VII of the Charter could be taken in the form of a Presidential Statement, although this has not yet occurred.[214] Nonetheless, the terms of statements should be closely examined and they may reinforce and implement binding resolutions.[215]

2. *Council resolutions before 1985*

Until the 1990s, the Council was reluctant to regard terrorist acts as threats to peace and security, although this was attributable more to Cold War politics than to an absence of terrorist threats. Some of the most flagrant terrorist acts, such as the attack on Israeli athletes at the Munich Olympics in 1972, or the Air France flight hijacked to Entebbe in 1976,[216] failed to produce any action by the Council. In cases involving State violence against civilian aircraft,[217] and non-State aircraft hijacking and hostage-taking,[218] the Council treated such acts within the legal frameworks on the use of force and on international civil aviation (including the 1944 Chicago Convention), without reference to 'terrorism', allowing it to avoid the political and ideological disputes surrounding that term.

The Council's response to the occupation of the US Embassy in Tehran by revolutionary students in November 1979 similarly avoided referring to 'terrorism'. Instead, a series of resolutions dealt with the incident within the legal frameworks of diplomatic and consular immunities and State responsibility.[219] The Council's involvement was overtaken by a negotiated settlement in January 1981, resulting in the release of the hostages, and overshadowing

---

[213] S Talmon, 'The Statements by the President of the Security Council' (2003) 2 Chinese JIL 419, 449.

[214] ibid, 450.

[215] ibid, 454–458.

[216] F Boyle, 'The Entebbe Hostage Crisis' (1982) 29 Netherlands ILR 32; F Boyle, 'The Entebbe Hostage Crisis' in H Han (ed), *Terrorism and Political Violence: Limits and Possibilities of Legal Control* (Oceana, New York, 1993) 267.

[217] eg UNSC Resolutions 262 (1968) (Israel attacked Beirut airport); 616 (1988) (US destroyed an Iran Air flight; an ICJ action was discontinued after a settlement: *Aerial Incident of 3 July 1988 (Iran v US) (Order of Discontinuance)* 22 Feb 1996); 1067 (1996) (Cuba shot down two civil aircraft).

[218] UNSC Resolutions 286 (1970) (appealing for the release of hostages held in hijackings and calling on States to prevent hijackings); 337 (1993) (condemning Israel for forcibly diverting and seizing an Iraqi Airways aircraft from Lebanese air space).

[219] UNSC Resolutions 457 (1979) and 461 (1979).

Iran's non-compliance with an adverse ICJ judgment of May 1980.[220] Reparations proceedings before the ICJ were discontinued in May 1981 and later dealt with through a bilateral claims process.[221]

3. Hostage-taking in the 1980s

The first Council resolution to use the term 'terrorism' was Resolution 579 of 1985, in response to a spate of terrorist acts in the preceding year.[222] On the day of the resolution, Palestinian suicide bombers killed twenty people at US and Israeli check-in desks at Rome and Vienna airports. Resolution 579 condemned 'all acts of hostage-taking and abduction' as 'manifestations of international terrorism'.[223] Hostage-taking and abduction (and impliedly, terrorism) were considered 'offences of grave concern to the international community', endangering human rights and friendly relations.[224]

In 1988, Resolution 618 condemned the abduction of a UN military observer in Lebanon and demanded his release.[225] The Council President reported in 1989 that the UN observer 'may have been murdered' and called for international action against hostage-taking and abductions as 'unlawful, criminal and cruel acts'.[226] Resolution 638 was adopted unanimously soon after, condemning hostage-taking and abduction in general and demanding the release of all victims.[227] States were urged to become parties to relevant treaties, and to prevent, prosecute, and punish 'all acts of hostage-takings and abductions as manifestations of terrorism'.[228]

The classification of *all* hostage-takings and abductions as terrorism discounts political motives, an intent to instil fear, or intimidatory or coercive aims, as the defining elements of terrorism. Instead, it is objectively defined by the prohibited *methods* of hostage-taking and abduction—even if done for private ends—and despite the political motives underlying the specific incidents the Council was responding to.

The preamble to Resolution 638 also stated that such acts were 'serious violations' of IHL, indicating that the Council regarded those acts as governed by an existing legal framework when committed in armed conflict. That

---

[220] *Tehran Hostages*, n 53.
[221] *Tehran Hostages* case *(Order of Discontinuance)*, 12 May 1981.
[222] Including the hijackings of a Kuwaiti aircraft in December 1984; a Jordanian aircraft, a Middle East Airlines flight, and a TWA flight in June 1985; an Egyptair flight in November 1985; the seizure of the Achille Lauro in October 1985; and the seizure of 25 Finnish UN soldiers by the South Lebanon Army in June 1985.
[223] UNSC Resolution 579 (1985) paras 1 and 5; see also UNSC Pres Stat (9 Oct 1985).
[224] UNSC Resolution 579 (1985) preamble; see also 638 (1989) preamble.
[225] UNSC Resolution 618 (1988) preamble and paras 1–2 respectively.
[226] UNSC Pres Stat (31 July 1989), para 3.
[227] UNSC Resolution 638 (1989) paras 1–3.
[228] ibid, paras 4–5.

is the approach of the 1979 Hostages Convention, which excludes hostage-taking constituting a grave breach of the Geneva Conventions and Protocols.[229] Thus hostage-taking in armed conflict, including by liberation movements,[230] is treated as a war crime rather than as the general treaty crime of hostage-taking.

There are numerous IHL provisions prohibiting hostage-taking in armed conflict.[231] Traditionally, hostage-taking aimed to intimidate a resisting enemy population, to ensure its obedience and secure control of occupied territory.[232] It was thus a deliberately political use of violence. In contrast, a wider definition is given to the hostage-taking offences in the 1998 Rome Statute, which requires that the 'perpetrator intended to compel a State, an international organization, a natural or legal person or a group of persons to act or refrain from acting as an explicit or implicit condition for the safety or the release of such person or persons'.[233] This definition is similar to that in the 1979 Hostages Convention, suggesting a harmonization of the meaning of hostage-taking in armed conflict and in peacetime. The modern view covers any hostage-taking to obtain a concession or advantage, including for private reasons, such as financial gain.[234] It thus loses some of the specificity of its earlier linkage to explicitly political violence. The modern view is consistent with the Council's approach to regarding *all* hostage-taking as forbidden. It is also supported by the customary prohibition on hostage-taking (whether military or civilian) and complemented by the human right to be free from arbitrary detention.[235]

In later Resolution 1502 (2003), on the protection of UN, humanitarian and associated personnel in conflict zones, the Council strongly condemned:

. . . forms of violence, including, *inter alia*, murder, rape and sexual assault, intimidation, armed robbery, abduction, hostage-taking, kidnapping, harassment and illegal arrest and detention to which those participating in humanitarian operations are increasingly exposed, as well as attacks on humanitarian convoys and acts of destruction and looting of their property . . .[236]

---

[229] 1979 Hostages Convention, Art 12.

[230] Lambert, n 88, 263–298.

[231] 1949 Geneva Conventions, common Art 3(1)(b); 1949 Fourth Geneva Convention, Art 34; 1977 Protocol II, Art 4(2)(c); 1993 ICTY Statute, Art 2(h); ICTR Statute, Art 4(c); 1998 Rome Statute, Art 8(2)(a)(viii) (international conflicts) and Art 8(2)(c)(iii) (non-international conflicts).

[232] *Hostages* case (1953) 15 Ann Dig 632, 644; J Pictet (ed), *The Geneva Conventions of 12 August 1949: Commentary* (ICRC, Geneva, 1958) 229 (on 1949 Fourth Geneva Convention, Art 34).

[233] 1998 Rome Statute: Elements of Crimes (2002): common element 3, Art 8(2)(a)(viii) and (c)(iii).

[234] *Blaškic* ICTY–95–14–T (3 Mar 2000) para 158; K Kittichaisaree, *International Criminal Law* (OUP, Oxford, 2001) 154–155.

[235] ICRC Study, n 168, 336.

[236] UNSC Resolution 1502 (2003) preamble.

What is significant here is the omission of any reference to 'terrorism' against UN personnel in armed conflict. This may suggest that by 2003, the Council had retreated from categorizing the hostage-taking of UN personnel, such as the abduction of a UN observer in Lebanon in 1988, as terrorism, instead invoking more established legal categories under humanitarian, human rights and refugee law.[237] On the other hand, a resolution in the same year condemned a 'terrorist attack' on UN headquarters in Baghdad,[238] indicating that violence against UN staff may still be regarded as terrorist.

4. *Assassinations in Lebanon: 1989 and 2005–06*

In 1989, the Council President condemned the assassination of Lebanese President Rene Muawad in Beirut as a 'cowardly, criminal and terrorist act' and 'an attack upon the unity of Lebanon, the democratic processes and . . . national reconciliation'.[239] It is significant that the Council regards assassination as terrorism. To the contrary, some argue that since assassination targets individuals, it is not capable of causing terror generally.[240] Such a conclusion is suspect, because assassination *is* likely to terrify (at least) other politicians and their supporters, who share the victim's political beliefs. While an isolated assassination does not necessarily put the public in fear, it may have that effect. If prohibiting terrorism aims to protect peaceful, deliberative politics,[241] then assassination will often qualify as terrorism, and is popularly regarded as such.

Sixteen years later in 2005, the former Lebanese Prime Minister, Rafiq Hariri, was assassinated in Beirut, with many others killed or injured. A Council Presidential Statement unequivocally condemned the 'terrorist bombing' and called on the Lebanese government 'to bring to justice the perpetrators, organizers and sponsors of this heinous terrorist act'.[242] The Council was concerned that the murder would jeopardize the holding of parliamentary elections in 'transparent, free and democratic conditions' and destabilize Lebanon and its democracy. The assassination arguably had the converse effect, hastening a complete Syrian withdrawal from Lebanon.[243]

A fact-finding mission to Lebanon involving the UN Secretary-General concluded soon after that 'the Lebanese investigation process suffers from

---

[237] UNSC Resolution 1502 (2003) para 3.

[238] UNSC Resolution 1511 (2003) para 18.

[239] UNSC Pres Stat (22 Nov 1989) S/20988.

[240] G Guillaume, 'Terrorism and International Law', Grotius Lecture, British Institute of International and Comparative Law, London, 13 Nov 2003, 5; Lambert, n 88, 18; A Rubin, 'International Terrorism and International Law' in Y Alexander and S Finger (eds), *Terrorism: Interdisciplinary Perspectives* (John Jay Press, New York, 1977) 121, 122.

[241] See Ch 1 above.

[242] UNSC Pres Stat 2005/4 (15 Feb 2005); reiterated in UNSC Resolution 1595 (2005) para 2.

[243] See UNSC Pres Stat 2005/17 (4 May 2005) (including military and intelligence personnel).

serious flaws and has neither the capacity nor the commitment to reach a satisfactory and credible conclusion'.[244] In response, Council Resolution 1595 of April 2005 established an independent international investigation Commission, based in Lebanon, 'to assist the Lebanese authorities in their investigation of all aspects of this terrorist act, including to help identify its perpetrators, sponsors, organizers and accomplices'.[245] The Commission was empowered to collect evidence, interview witnesses, move freely in Lebanon, and enjoy the necessary facilities and cooperation from the authorities.[246] It could also determine its own procedures of investigation, 'taking into account the Lebanese law and judicial procedures'.[247] The creation of the Commission is significant because it inserts an international investigative body into a domestic justice system, although Lebanon remained responsible for any prosecutions and was required only to take into account the investigation's findings.[248]

In Resolution 1636 of October 2005, the Council was concerned at the Commission's conclusion that Syrian and Lebanese officials were involved in the assassination,[249] commended Lebanon for arresting former security officials suspected of involvement, and extended the Commission's mandate.[250] It imposed travel bans on, and froze the funds, assets, and resources of, individuals designated by Lebanon or the Commission as involved in the assassination.[251] Such steps were intended to assist in the investigation and not to prejudice judicial determination of responsibility.[252]

Further, Syria was required to cooperate fully and to detain any officials or individuals whom the Commission suspected of involvement and to make them available for interview by the Commission.[253] The Council also insisted that Syria should not interfere in Lebanese affairs, and warned that any State involvement in the assassination would violate States' obligations 'to prevent and refrain from supporting terrorism' and to respect Lebanon's sovereignty and political independence.[254] The Council warned of 'further action' in the event of Syrian non-compliance.[255]

Despite these strong measures, assassinations continued in Lebanon in

---

[244] UNSC Resolution 1595 (2005) preamble.
[245] UNSC Resolution 1595 (2005) para 1.
[246] UNSC Resolution 1595 (2005) para 3.
[247] UNSC Resolution 1595 (2005) para 6.
[248] UNSC Resolution 1595 (2005) para 2.
[249] UNSC Resolution 1636 (2005), para 2: 'there is converging evidence pointing at the involvement of both Lebanese and Syrian officials in this terrorist act, and that it is difficult to envisage a scenario whereby such complex assassination could have been carried out without their knowledge'.
[250] UNSC Resolution 1636 (2005) para 9; see also L Noueihed, 'Four generals charged over Hariri assassination', *Sydney Morning Herald*, 3–4 Sept 2005, 20.
[251] UNSC Resolution 1636 (2005) para 3(a), subject to the approval of a Security Council Committee.   [252] ibid, para 3.   [253] ibid, paras 11 and 5.
[254] ibid, paras 12 and 4–5.   [255] ibid, para 12.

2005, consolidating a long history of the practice in that country. Council Presidential Statements condemned the separate assassinations of Lebanese journalist Samir Qassir ('a symbol of political independence and freedom') and former Communist Party leader George Hawi in June 2005.[256] A Statement in December 2005 condemned a 'terrorist bombing' in Beirut that killed 'Lebanese member of Parliament, editor and journalist Gebrane Tueni, a patriot who was an outspoken symbol of freedom' and of Lebanese sovereignty and independence.[257] These statements confirm that the Council regards 'political assassinations' as 'terrorist acts' which 'undermine security, stability, sovereignty, political independence and . . . civil accord'.[258] They also call on Lebanon to bring to justice those responsible for the attacks and for other States to respect Lebanon's sovereignty, territorial integrity, unity, and political independence.

Soon after, Council Resolution 1644 of December 2005 extended the Commission's mandate to June 2006 and demanded that Syria cooperate 'unconditionally' and respond 'unambiguously and immediately' with the Commission's investigation.[259] On Lebanon's request, the Council expanded the Commission's mandate to investigate terrorist attacks in Lebanon since October 2004,[260] when Minister Marwan Hamade was killed. In addition, the Council acknowledged Lebanon's request that those responsible for killing Prime Minister Hariri be tried by 'a tribunal of an international character' and requested the Secretary-General to identify the assistance needed.

The latter measure did not specify for which crimes those responsible might be tried. International tribunals typically prosecute international crimes rather than domestic crimes such as murder. Yet, there is no international crime of 'assassination' as such, although a pattern of organized political killings may amount to the crime against humanity of murder, where it is part of a systematic attack on the civilian population, and particularly where a foreign State such as Syria is involved. There is, however, room for doubt, and isolated or sporadic assassinations may not meet the threshold of crimes against humanity. Alternatively, it is open to the Council to confer jurisdiction over crimes of 'international terrorism' on an international tribunal, although that would arguably amount to retrospective punishment in the absence of any existing treaty or customary crime of terrorism as such.

In his report to the Security Council on 21 March 2006, the Secretary-General recommended establishing a mixed or hybrid tribunal with both Lebanese and 'significant' international participation. He noted that Lebanon would prefer to apply Lebanese substantive criminal law, although

---

[256] UNSC Pres Stat 2005/22 (7 Jun 2005) and 2005/26 (22 Jun 2005) respectively.
[257] UNSC Pres Stat 2005/61 (12 Dec 2005).
[258] UNSC Pres Stats 2005/22 (7 Jun 2005); 2005/61 (12 Dec 2005).
[259] UNSC Resolution 1644 (2005) para 2–4.
[260] ibid, para 6–7.

specific charges would depend on the results of the investigation. Thus, the assassinations and bombings in Lebanon may ultimately be prosecuted simply as murder or other common crimes, although there are also terrorism offences in Lebanese law. The Secretary-General further observed that security concerns would make it difficult to establish an effective tribunal within Lebanon itself, such that any tribunal may need to be located elsewhere. In response to his report, Security Council Resolution 1664 (2006) asked the Secretary-General to negotiate with Lebanon with the aim of 'establishing a tribunal of an international character based on the highest international standards of criminal justice' and in light of the Secretary-General's report.

5. *Plastic explosives 1989*

In Resolution 635 (1989), the Council raised 'the implications of acts of terrorism for international security'[261] in the context of detecting plastic explosives. While not naming the incident, the resolution was prompted by an attack on a civilian aircraft over the Sahara, which killed 400 people.[262] The resolution called on States 'to prevent all acts of terrorism' and urged the International Civil Aviation Organization (ICAO) to intensify its efforts to prevent terrorism against civil aviation,[263] particularly the drafting of a treaty on plastic explosives, adopted two years later.[264] The resolution implies that the unlawful use of plastic explosives may amount to terrorism, suggesting a definition based on prohibited means, rather than political motives, or intimidatory or coercive aims.

6. *Iraq 1991–2005*

After the 1991 Gulf War, the 'permanent ceasefire' resolution required Iraq 'to inform the Council that it will not commit or support any act of *international terrorism* or allow any organization directed towards the commission of such acts to operate within its territory and to condemn unequivocally and renounce all acts, methods and practices of *terrorism*'.[265] This obligation was later asserted to constitute a ceasefire condition in the dispute about disarming Iraq from 1991 to 2003.[266] The Council does not specify which Iraqi acts constitute terrorism, and the invasion of Kuwait was a classic case of interState aggression. However, the resolution also invoked the 1979 Hostages

---

[261] UNSC Resolution 635 (1989) preamble.

[262] L Sunga, *The Emerging System of International Criminal Law* (Kluwer, The Hague, 1997) 197–198.

[263] UNSC Resolution 635 (1989) paras 2 and 4 respectively.

[264] 1991 Plastic Explosives Convention.

[265] UNSC Resolution 687 (1991) para 32 (emphasis added).

[266] See B Saul, 'Legality of the Use of Force against Iraq in 2001' (2003) 8 *UCLA Journal of International Law and Foreign Affairs* 267.

Convention and condemned the taking of hostages,[267] some of whom were used as human shields.[268] It is still unclear why the Council designated such conduct as terrorism rather than as violations of IHL, or of obligations concerning hostage-taking or protected persons.

After 11 September 2001, the US and the UK sought to prove links between Iraq and the terrorist group Al-Qaeda, although little evidence of links emerged, even after the overthrow of Saddam Hussein in 2003.[269] This was so despite the aberrant finding of a US judge in 2003, in a civil case for damages, that there was a 'conclusive link' between Iraq and Al-Qaeda concerning the September 11 attacks.[270] There was, however, evidence of Iraq funding Palestinian suicide bombings.[271]

Normatively, the resolution is significant because of its binding character under Chapter VII and because it admits not only State-sponsored terrorism, but also direct State terrorism (by requiring Iraq not to 'commit' it). It is doubtful whether this description adds anything to the legal framework of States' obligations,[272] since the law on the use of force, non-intervention, and State responsibility for transboundary harm by non-State actors already governs international violence by, or supported by, States. Most such violence is inherently political in purpose, so it is not possible to distinguish between State *uses of force* and State *terrorism* as separate categories on the basis of political motivation alone. There is no evidence that the resolution was intended to create individual criminal liability for State terrorism by Iraq, unless it obliquely refers to liability under IHL for acts of terror or spreading terror. No crime of terrorism was included in the 2003 Statute of the Iraqi Special Tribunal for Crimes against Humanity.[273]

[267] UNSC Resolution 687 (1991) preamble; see J Paust, 'Suing Saddam: Private Remedies for War Crimes and Hostage-Taking' (1991) 31 Van JIL 351.

[268] Others argue that Iraq's destruction of oil wells in retreat from Kuwait amounted to 'eco-terrorism' (but it is difficult to see how that would terrify a population): L Edgerton, 'Eco-Terrorist Acts during the Persian Gulf War: Is International Law Sufficient to Hold Iraq Liable?' (1992) 22 Geo JICL 151; J Seacor, 'Environmental Terrorism: Lesson from the Oil Fires of Kuwait' (1994) 10 AUJILP 481.

[269] US Senate (108th Congress) (Select Committee on Intelligence), *Report on the US Intelligence Community's Prewar Intelligence Assessments on Iraq* (Washington, DC, 7 July 2004) 346 (conclusion 93), 347 (conclusion 96), 348 (conclusion 97); UK Parliament (Intelligence and Security Committee), *Report on Iraqi Weapons of Mass Destruction: Intelligence and Assessments* (HMSO, London, Sept 2003) 34–35; Report by Privy Counsellors' Committee, *Review of Intelligence on Weapons of Mass Destruction* (HMSO, London, 14 July 2004) para 484; L Freedman, 'War in Iraq: Selling the Threat' (2004) 46 *Survival* 7, 18–21.

[270] P Hurtado, 'Baghdad liable for September 11: judge', *Sydney Morning Herald*, 9 May 2003 (citing default judgment of January 2003, and damages of US$104m in May 2003, for Iraq's 'material support' to Al-Qaeda); see also J Pedigo, 'Rogue States, Weapons of Mass Destruction, and Terrorism: Was Security Council Approval Necessary for the Invasion of Iraq?' (2004) 32 Geo JICL 199.

[271] P McGeough, 'Saddam stokes war with suicide bomber cash', *Sydney Morning Herald*, 26 Mar 2002.   [272] Higgins, n 193, 20–21.

[273] Coalition Provisional Authority, Order No 49, Delegation of Authority regarding an Iraqi Special Tribunal, 10 Dec 2003, annexed Statute, Arts 11–14 (crimes within jurisdiction).

After the overthrow of the Iraqi government, the Council shifted its emphasis to non-State terrorism in Iraq. In Resolution 1511, on UN involvement in occupied Iraq, the Council condemned the 'terrorist bombings' of the Jordanian and Turkish embassies, UN headquarters in Baghdad, and a mosque in Najaf.[274] It also condemned the murder of a Spanish diplomat and the assassination of an Iraqi leader, and emphasized that those responsible must be brought to justice.[275] The preamble called these 'attacks on the people of Iraq, the United Nations, and the international community', and the assassination as an attack on Iraq's future.

The resolution emphasized the need for effective Iraqi police and security forces to combat terrorism, and called on States to prevent the transit, arming, and financing of terrorists in Iraq.[276] The resolution does not define terrorism, although the acts it condemns partly illustrate its conception of terrorism—including attacks on embassies and diplomats, UN premises, political leaders, and religious sites—despite most of these acts already being covered by IHL and sectoral treaties.

In Resolution 1546, the Council endorsed the formation of a sovereign interim Iraqi government from 30 June 2004. The resolution condemns 'all acts of terrorism in Iraq' and refers to States' obligations to prevent 'terrorist activities in and from Iraq or against its citizens'.[277] The resolution reaffirmed the authorization of the multinational force established in Resolution 1511, and gave the force 'the authority to take all necessary measures to contribute to the maintenance of security and stability in Iraq . . . including by preventing and deterring *terrorism*'.[278] This is the first Council resolution to give explicit authority to States to use force against 'terrorism', albeit limited to a connection with Iraq, and contingent on the (not entirely consensual) 'Iraqi request for the continued presence of the multinational force'.[279] The resolution does not define terrorism, implicitly conferring a discretion on the multinational force to determine for itself the meaning of terrorism. In November 2005, the Council extended the mandate of the multinational force until the end of 2006,[280] based on a request by Iraq which specifically noted the threat of 'forces of terrorism that incorporate foreign elements'.[281]

---

[274] UNSC Resolution 1511 (2003), para 18. The bombing of UN headquarters was also condemned as a 'terrorist attack' 'against the international community as a whole' in Pres Stat S/PRST/2003/13 (20 Aug 2003).
[275] UNSC Resolution 1511 (2003) para 18.
[276] ibid, paras 16, 19; see also UNSC Resolution 1546 (2004) para 17.
[277] UNSC Resolution 1546 (2004) para 17.
[278] ibid, para 10 (emphasis added).
[279] ibid, para 10; see C Le Mon, 'Legality of a Request by the Interim Iraqi Government for the Continued Presence of United States Military Forces', *ASIL Insights*, June 2004.
[280] UNSC Resolution 1637 (2005) para 1.
[281] Letter of 27 Oct 2005 from the Prime Minister of Iraq to the President of the Council, Annex I to UNSC Resolution 1637 (2005).

The Council itself affirmed that terrorism must not be allowed to disrupt Iraq's political and economic transition.[282]

Yet it is unclear which activities amount to 'terrorism' in Iraq. Following the US invasion, a variety of irregular forces continued to resist occupation. Not all of these forces can be characterized as terrorists, since some may qualify as combatants in an international armed conflict—either as irregular forces resisting occupation,[283] or as civilians *levée en masse*. This was implicitly recognized in an amnesty offer to Iraqi insurgents by the incoming Iraqi government,[284] an approach which the Council seems to have endorsed:

The Security Council calls on those who use violence in an attempt to subvert the political process to lay down their arms and participate in the political process. It encourages the Iraqi authorities to engage with all those who renounce violence and to create a political atmosphere conducive to national reconciliation and political competition through peaceful means.[285]

Further, some acts labelled as terrorism by the US are difficult to accept as such. For instance, given the privatization of military functions, a plot to bomb a civilian passenger airliner, contracted to transport US troops to Iraq,[286] may be a legitimate military action.

It seems unlikely either that the references to terrorism are intended to carefully reflect the limited IHL prohibitions on terror, and the Statute of the Iraqi Special Tribunal does not recognize acts of terror, or spreading terror, as war crimes. Rather, such references derive from earlier unsubstantiated links between Iraq and terrorism, and paradoxically address the appearance of non-State terrorism in Iraq where, pre-invasion, there was none.[287]

Further guidance on the Council's conception of terrorism in Iraq emerges from the Council's response to violence in Iraq in 2005. Presidential Statements condemned the separate assassinations of an Egyptian and two Algerian diplomats in July 2005, and the attempted assassinations of diplomats from Bahrain and Pakistan.[288] The statements called for those responsible to be brought to justice and emphasized that 'there can be no justification for such terrorist acts'. Council Resolution 1618 of August 2005 further condemned the 'shameless and horrific' terrorist attacks that killed over one hundred people, including children, electoral employees, and persons

---

[282] UNSC Resolution 1637 (2005) preamble.

[283] F Kaplan, 'This is not terrorism', *The Guardian*, 3 Apr 2003.

[284] R McCarthy, S Goldenberg, and N Watt, 'Amnesty for Iraqi insurgents', *The Guardian*, 5 July 2004.

[285] UNSC Pres Stat 2005/5 (16 Feb 2005); see also UNSC Resolution 1637 (2005) preamble.

[286] T Shanker, 'Planes moving troops are in terrorists' sights, says US', *Sydney Morning Herald*, 14 Jan 2003.

[287] J Record, 'Threat Confusion and its Penalties' (2004) 46 *Survival* 51, 62; R Norton-Taylor, 'Occupation has boosted al-Qaida, says thinktank', *The Guardian*, 26 May 2004.

[288] UNSC Pres Stat 2005/29 (8 July 2005); 2005/37 (27 July 2005).

involved in drafting a new Iraqi Constitution.[289] The resolution also condemned attacks on diplomats, including murder and kidnapping.[290]

7. *Libya 1992–2003*

In 1992, Resolution 731 condemned the destruction of a civil airliner over Lockerbie in Scotland. It deplored Libya's failure to cooperate in establishing responsibility for these 'terrorist acts', and urged Libya to help eliminate 'international terrorism'.[291] The resolution implicitly required Libya to surrender two nationals for trial,[292] a significant interference in the sovereign operation of national extradition law in circumstances where Libya did not extradite nationals.[293] While terrorism is not defined, it is clear that the Council considers violence against civil aviation (by explosives) to be terrorism, regardless of ulterior motives or aims.

Following non-compliance, Resolution 748 demanded Libyan compliance with requests from France, the UK and the US, and imposed aircraft, military, and diplomatic sanctions.[294] It also required Libya itself to 'cease all forms of terrorist action and all assistance to terrorist groups' and 'demonstrate its renunciation of terrorism', and all States to deny freedom of movement to Libyans involved in terrorism.[295] The resolution did not define terrorism, nor was there any list of terrorist groups.

Resolution 883 also demanded compliance and imposed further financial and aircraft sanctions.[296] Suspension of sanctions was conditioned on Libya surrendering those charged for trial in a UK or US court, satisfaction of French judicial authorities, and compliance with earlier resolutions.[297] The preamble noted the Council's determination to bring to justice 'those responsible for acts of international terrorism'.

In constantly referring to 'terrorism', these resolutions avoided invoking the 1971 Montreal Convention, which is evidently an important legal framework governing violence against civil aviation. The deliberate, repeated use of the term suggests that the Council attributed normative importance to it—perhaps because it more fittingly captured the shocking nature of the incident than the more technical law on air safety, or because it supplied a political trigger for Council involvement. Given the suspected responsibility of Libyan

[289] UNSC Resolution 1618 (2005) para 1–2.
[290] UNSC Resolution 1618 (2005) para 3.
[291] UNSC Resolution 731 (1992) paras 2–3.   [292] Reisman, n 207, 86.
[293] D Türk, 'Law and Policy: Security Council's Ability to Innovate' (2002) 97 ASIL Proceedings 51, 52; Gowlland-Debbas, n 205, 90.
[294] UNSC Resolution 748 (1992) para 1 and paras 4–7 respectively. The UK and the US also demanded that Libya disclose all knowledge and evidence of the crime, and pay compensation: US, Statement Regarding the Bombing of Pan Am 103, 27 Nov 1991, UN Doc S/23308.
[295] UNSC Resolution 748 (1992) para 2 and para 6(c) respectively.
[296] UNSC Resolution 883 (1993) paras 1–7, 9–10.   [297] ibid, para 16.

officials in the bombing, the Council implicitly accepted that States could perpetrate terrorism.[298]

The Council's demands conflicted with Libya's attempt to rely on its obligation to prosecute the suspects (as an alternative to extradition, since Libya does not extradite nationals) under the 1971 Montreal Convention. In 1992, the ICJ declined a Libyan request for provisional measures to prevent Libya being forced to transfer the suspects.[299] Since all States are required, under Articles 25 and 103 of the Charter, to carry out Council decisions over other treaty obligations, the ICJ found that the treaty rights claimed by Libya were no longer 'appropriate for protection' and 'would be likely to impair' rights enjoyed by the UK and the US in Resolution 748.[300]

In contrast, at the preliminary objections phase in 1998, the ICJ rejected the argument that Libya's treaty rights could not be exercised because they were superseded by Resolutions 748 and 883.[301] Those resolutions were adopted after Libya's application was filed in March 1992, and later resolutions could not affect ICJ jurisdiction once established. Resolution 731, adopted before the application, was non-binding and thus did not render the application inadmissible.

The incident was ultimately resolved in a settlement, formalized in Resolution 1192 (1998). Libya handed over two suspects for trial in a Scots law court sitting in the Netherlands.[302] In 2003, Libya accepted responsibility for the acts of Libyan officials, paid compensation, renounced terrorism, and committed to cooperation.[303] In Resolution 1506, the Council lifted sanctions

---

[298] Marauhn, n 88, 851; Higgins, n 193, 23.

[299] *Lockerbie (Libya v UK) (Provisional Measures)* (1992) ICJ Reports 3; W Czaplinski, 'The Lockerbie Case: Comments' (1993) 20 Pol YBIL 37; M McWhinney, 'The International Court as Emerging Constitutional Court and the Co-ordinate UN Institutions (especially the Security Council): Implications of the Aerial Incident at Lockerbie' (1993) 30 Can YBIL 261; V Gowlland-Debbas, 'The Relationship between the International Court of Justice and the Security Council in the Light of the Lockerbie Case' (1994) 88 AJIL 643; S Shubber, 'The Destruction of Aircraft in Flight over Scotland and Niger: The Question of Jurisdiction and Extradition under International Law' (1995) BYBIL 239.

[300] *Lockerbie (Libya v UK) (Provisional Measures)*, n 299, paras 39–41.

[301] *Lockerbie (Libya v UK) (Preliminary Objections)* (1998) ICJ Reports 9, paras 38, 44; see A Paulus, 'Jurisprudence of the International Court of Justice: Lockerbie Cases, Preliminary Objections' (1998) 9 EJIL 550; P Bekker, 'Questions of Interpretation and Application of the 1971 Montreal Convention arising from the Aerial Incident at Lockerbie' (1998) 92 AJIL 503.

[302] See 'Netherlands–UK: Agreement between the Government of the Kingdom of The Netherlands and the Government of the United Kingdom of Great Britain and Northern Ireland Concerning a Scottish Trial in The Netherlands' (1999) 38 ILM 926; 'UK High Court of the Justiciary (Proceedings in the Netherlands) (UN) Order 1998' (1999) 38 ILM 942; 'The Great Compromise: Where to Convene the Trial of the Suspects Implicated in the Pan Am Flight 103 Bombing over Lockerbie, Scotland' (1999) 23 *Suffolk Transnational Law Review* 131; M Kamminga, 'Comment: Trial of Lockerbie Suspects before a Scottish Court in the Netherlands' (1998) 45 Netherlands ILR 417.

[303] UNSC Resolution 1506 (2003) preamble. Compensation was also subsequently paid for the 1986 bombing of a West Berlin disco: AP, 'Libya paying out for bombing', *The Guardian*, 4 Sept 2004; see D Turndorf, 'The US Raid on Libya: A Forceful Response to Terrorism' (1988) 14

and removed the item from its agenda.[304] The ICJ cases were discontinued in 2003,[305] removing the possibility of an ICJ merits review of the legal effects of Council resolutions.[306] Doubt remains about the lawfulness of the Council's adopting binding measures in support of an unlawful UK/US threat to use force if Libya did not comply with their demands.[307] Questions also remain about whether Libya's actions really constituted a threat to the peace.[308]

8. Presidential Statements 1992–94

Presidential Statements have highlighted the Council's concern at terrorism as a threat to peace and security. In 1992 at the first Council meeting of Heads of State and Government, the Council President expressed 'deep concern over acts of international terrorism' and emphasized the need to deal with them effectively.[309] This generalized statement of concern about terrorism was facilitated by the possibilities of cooperation opened up by the end of the Cold War. In 1994, the President condemned 'terrorist attacks' in Buenos Aires and London, demanded 'an immediate end to' such attacks, and stressed the need for cooperation and 'to prevent, combat and eliminate all forms of terrorism, which affect the international community as a whole'.[310] While terrorism was not defined, the attacks involved killings of civilians by organized groups (such as the IRA) for political purposes. Condemnation of terrorism in Presidential Statements rather than in resolutions may be a matter of convenience as a much as a calibrated judgment about the seriousness of the threat and the appropriate form of response.

9. Sudan 1996–2001

In Resolution 1044, the Council condemned 'the terrorist assassination attempt' on the President of Egypt in Ethiopia in 1995, which violated

Brookings JIL 187; W Warriner, 'The Unilateral Use of Coercion under International Law: A Legal Analysis of the United States Raid on Libya on April 14, 1986' (1986) 37 *Naval Law Review* 49.

[304] UNSC Resolution 1506 (2003) paras 1–3.

[305] *Lockerbie (Libya v UK) (Order of Discontinuance)* 10 Sept 2003; *Lockerbie (Libya v US) (Libya v UK) (Order of Discontinuance)* 10 Sept 2003.

[306] B Martenczuk, 'The Security Council, the International Court and Judicial Review: What Lessons from Lockerbie?' (1999) 10 EJIL 517, 518; see also M Plachta, 'The Lockerbie Case: The Role of the Security Council in Enforcing the Principle Aut Dedere Aut Judicare' (2001) 12 EJIL 125; D Arzt, 'The Lockerbie "Extradition by Analogy" Agreement: "Exceptional Measure" or Template for Transnational Criminal Justice?' (2002) 18 AUILR 163.

[307] A Orakhelashvili, 'The Impact of Peremptory Norms on the Interpretation and Application of United Nations Security Council Resolutions' (2005) 16 EJIL 59, 71.

[308] Koskenniemi, n 191, 342.

[309] UNSC Pres Stat (31 Jan 1992) S/23500.

[310] UNSC Pres Stat (29 July 1994) S/PRST/1994/40.

Ethiopia's sovereignty and integrity and disturbed regional peace and secur-ity.[311] The resolution called on Sudan to comply with Organization of African Unity (OAU) requests to extradite three suspects to Ethiopia and to: 'Desist from ... assisting, supporting and facilitating terrorist activities and from giving shelter and sanctuaries to terrorist elements.'[312]

Facing non-cooperation, the Council adopted Resolution 1054 under Chapter VII, which demanded compliance with its earlier requests within two weeks, after which it would impose diplomatic sanctions and travel restrictions.[313] In Resolution 1070, the Council repeated its demands and imposed sanctions on Sudanese aircraft.[314] The Council's management of the incident was interrupted by US air strikes on a pharmaceutical factory in Khartoum,[315] wrongly thought to be producing chemical weapons for terror-ist use. Sudan had expelled Bin Laden in 1996. After requests by the OAU, Egypt, and Ethiopia, sanctions were finally lifted by Resolution 1372 (2001).

10. *Kosovo 1998–99*

Four resolutions on Kosovo have referred to terrorism, condemning 'terror-ism in pursuit of political goals by any group or individual, and all external support for such activities in Kosovo, including the supply of arms and train-ing for terrorist activities', as well as its financing.[316] Resolution 1160 charac-terized terrorism as a non-State activity by condemning 'all acts of terrorism by the Kosovo Liberation Army (KLA) or any other group or individual', while in contrast, Serbian police violence against civilians was condemned only as 'the use of excessive force'.[317]

Three resolutions asked Kosovar Albanian leaders alone 'to condemn all terrorist action' and stressed that their community should pursue its goals peacefully.[318] One resolution required all States to 'prevent arming and train-ing for terrorist activities' in Kosovo, but implicitly recognized underlying causes by stating that 'the way to defeat violence and terrorism in Kosovo is for the authorities in Belgrade to offer the Kosovar Albanian community a genuine political process'.[319]

---

[311] UNSC Resolution 1044 (1996) paras 1–2; reiterated in UNSC Resolution 1070 (1996) preamble.
[312] UNSC Resolution 1044 (1996) para 4(a)–(b).
[313] UNSC Resolution 1054 (1996) paras 1–4.
[314] UNSC Resolution 1070 (1996) para 3.
[315] R Wedgwood, 'Responding to Terrorism: The Strikes against Bin Laden' (1999) 24 Yale JIL 559; L Campbell, 'Defending against Terrorism: A Legal Analysis of the Decision to Strike Sudan and Afghanistan' (2000) 74 *Tulane Law Review* 1067.
[316] Preambles to UNSC Resolutions 1199 (1998) and 1203 (1998); and 1160 (1998) respectively.
[317] UNSC Resolution 1160 (1998) preamble.
[318] UNSC Resolutions 1160 (1998) para 2; 1199 (1998) para 6; 1203 (1998) para 10.
[319] UNSC Resolution 1160 (1998) para 8 and para 3 respectively.

Resolution 1244 suggested that State forces may also commit terrorism, by condemning 'all terrorist acts by any party'.[320] Nonetheless, the Council avoided invoking the IHL of non-international armed conflicts, characterizing the Kosovars as terrorists rather than as belligerent forces in a civil conflict. Even during the NATO bombing of 1999, the KLA was not recognized as an internal self-determination movement.[321] Yugoslavia even claimed that NATO illegally trained KLA terrorists.[322]

11. Kenya and Tanzania 1998

In Resolution 1189, the Council condemned 'terrorist bomb attacks' in Kenya and Tanzania, which killed hundreds, injured thousands, and caused massive property destruction.[323] It called on all States to assist investigations in Kenya, Tanzania, and the US, 'to apprehend the perpetrators of these cowardly criminal acts and to bring them swiftly to justice'.[324] More generally, States were called on to prevent terrorism and prosecute and punish the perpetrators.[325] The resolution does not define terrorism, but the preamble describes some of its characteristics as 'indiscriminate and outrageous' bomb attacks against civilians.

The resolution did not attribute responsibility for the attacks, nor did it authorize a military response.[326] It is the first resolution to describe terrorism as 'criminal'. Yet by mentioning national investigations, it is most likely referring to national crimes or sectoral offences, and not a generic international crime. Still, it is normatively significant that the attacks, which targeted US embassies, were described as terrorism, rather than breaches of the inviolability of diplomatic premises. Without complicity between the host States and terrorists, responsibility could not be attributed to those States, and private groups do not have obligations of diplomatic protection.

12. Afghanistan, the Taliban, and Al-Qaeda 1998–2005

Soon after, the Council adopted a series of resolutions demanding that the factions in the Afghan conflict, particularly the Taliban, refrain from harbouring, providing sanctuary for, and training terrorists, and cooperate in bringing indicted terrorists to justice,[327] including Bin Laden.[328] Resolution

---

[320] UNSC Resolution 1244 (1999) preamble.

[321] L Green, *The Contemporary Law of Armed Conflict* (2nd edn, MUP, Manchester, 2000) 63.

[322] C Gray, *International Law and the Use of Force* (OUP, Oxford, 2000) 35 (argument made in the *Genocide* case).

[323] UNSC Resolution 1189 (1998) para 1.   [324] ibid, para 3.   [325] ibid, para 5.

[326] A Roberts, 'Law and the Use of Force After Iraq' (2003) 45 *Survival* 31, 37.

[327] UNSC Resolutions 1193 (1998) para 15; 1214 (1998) para 13; 1267 (1999) para 1; 1333 (2000) para 1, preamble; UNSC Pres Stats (22 Oct 1999) S/PRST/1999/29; (7 Apr 2000) S/PRST/2000/12.   [328] UNSC Resolutions 1267 (1999) preamble; 1333 (1999) preamble.

1214 also condemned the Taliban's capture and murder of Iranian diplomats and a journalist as 'flagrant violations of international law' (but not as terrorism), and asked the Taliban to investigate and prosecute these crimes and the killings of three UN workers.[329]

Resolution 1267 demanded that the Taliban surrender Bin Laden for trial for the bombings, to a State (such as the US)[330] where he had been indicted, or would be surrendered or tried.[331] The Taliban had one month to comply, after which aircraft and financial sanctions would be imposed, monitored by a committee.[332] The preamble recalled treaty obligations 'to extradite or prosecute terrorists',[333] indicating that sectoral treaties and national law were the appropriate frameworks governing terrorism, particularly given US charges for conspiracy to kill US citizens abroad.

Following non-compliance, later resolutions imposed further military, diplomatic, aircraft, and travel sanctions on the Taliban.[334] The most far-reaching provisions require States to freeze the funds and assets of Bin Laden and associated individuals and entities, including Al-Qaeda, as listed by the 1267 Committee.[335] Resolution 1390 extended sanctions beyond Afghan territory after the fall of the Taliban, focusing on the global activities of Bin Laden, Al-Qaeda, and 'associates'.[336] At the end of 2005, more than 200 individuals and 100 entities were proscribed as associated with Al-Qaeda,[337] and over 140 individuals with the Taliban, including in areas of separatist or religious conflict such as Bosnia, Kosovo, Chechnya, Palestine, North Africa, Sudan, Kurdistan, and South-East Asia. Despite its sweeping reach, the sanctions regime is not based on a generalized proscription of 'terrorists', but on a connection to specific groups such as the Taliban or Al-Qaeda.

Concern has been expressed about the procedural unfairness of the

---

[329] UNSC Resolutions 1214 (1998) para 5; 1267 (1999) preamble; 1333 (1999) preamble; UNSC Pres Stats (22 Oct 1999) S/PRST/1999/29; (7 Apr 2000) S/PRST/2000/12.

[330] UNSC Resolution 1267 (1999) preamble; also UNSC Resolutions 1333 (2000) preamble; 1390 (2002) preamble; see 'Efforts to Obtain Custody of Osama Bin Laden' (2000) 94 AJIL 366.

[331] UNSC Resolution 1267 (1999) para 2, reiterated in UNSC Resolutions 1333 (2000) para 2; see also UNSC Pres Stats (22 Oct 1999) S/PRST/1999/29; (7 Apr 2000) S/PRST/2000/12.

[332] UNSC Resolution 1267 (1999) paras 3, 6 ('1267 Committee'), and subject to humanitarian exceptions: para 4.

[333] UNSC Resolutions 1267 (1999) preamble; 1333 (1999) preamble.

[334] UNSC Resolution 1333 (2000) paras 5–6 (military) paras 7–8(a) (diplomatic), paras 8(b), 11–12 (aircraft), para 14 (travel), subject to humanitarian exceptions: paras 11–12; 1452 (2002) para 1–4. Detailed provisions govern implementation and supervision: UNSC Resolutions 1333 (2000) paras 15–26; 1363 (2001) paras 1–8; 1388 (2002); 1390 (2002); 1452 (2002); 1455 (2003) paras 1–15; 1526 (2004).

[335] UNSC Resolution 1333 (2000) paras 8(c), 16(b).

[336] UNSC Resolutions 1390 (2002) para 1; 1617 (2005); Stromseth, n 195, 42–43; N Krisch, 'The Rise and Fall of Collective Security: Terrorism, US Hegemony, and the Plight of the Security Council' in C Walter et al (eds), *Terrorism as a Challenge for National and International Law* (Springer, Berlin, 2003) 23, 33.

[337] UNSC (1267 Committee), Consolidated List of Individuals and Entities Belonging to or Associated with the Taliban and Al-Qaida Organization (6 Dec 2004).

sanctions regime,[338] particularly the low standard of proof in listing 'associated' individuals and entities (initially based on 'information provided' to the Committee); the lack of definition of 'association'; and the lack of a hearing at the listing or delisting stage. A wide range of entities has been regarded as 'associated with' Al-Qaeda or the Taliban, including those constituted lawfully under domestic law, such as banking and financial institutions, businesses, and humanitarian relief and charitable organizations. Potentially, the degree of association with Al-Qaeda may not be sufficiently serious to warrant proscription. Some Islamic charitable organizations, for instance, primarily provide humanitarian relief and assistance, while only a small part of their operations is engaged in supporting terrorism. Further, no distinction is drawn between association with Al-Qaeda (a terrorist group) and the Taliban (a quasi-governmental authority). There is also the potential for unrelated terrorist organizations or even militant groups to be wrongly drawn into the orbit of 'associates' of Al-Qaeda.

Over time, some improvements to the standard of proof and to the procedure have been made,[339] including requiring better particulars from States and allowing for affected individuals or entities to petition their governments. However, the diplomatic protection model underlying the de-listing process remains ill-suited to protecting the interests of non-State actors— particularly where political opponents lack effective protection by their State, and third States have no interest in objecting to a listing.[340] The Council seems willing to suspend procedural fairness for the purposes of preventive security. One Taliban individual and eight Taliban entities, and five Al-Qaeda individuals and three entities, had been removed from the Consolidated List by the 1267 Committee by December 2005,[341] suggesting a significant error rate.

It may be preferable, on grounds of procedural fairness, to accord limited

[338] J Fitzpatrick, 'Speaking Law to Power: The War against Terrorism and Human Rights' (2003) 14 EJIL 241, 260–264; Krisch, n 336, 11–12; E Miller, 'The Use of Targeted Sanctions in the Fight against International Terrorism: What about Human Rights?' (2003) 97 ASIL Proceedings 46, 46, 49–50. There have also been challenges in Europe to the EU's implementation of these measures: see, eg, *Abdirisak Aden v Commission* Case T–306/01 (10 Dec 2002); *Ahmed Ali Yusuf and Al Barakaat International Foundation and Yassin Abdullah Kadi v Council of the European Union and Commission of the European Communities* ECJ (Crt of First Instance), Case T–306/01, and Case T–315/01 (21 Sept 2005).

[339] UNSC Resolutions 1526 (2004) paras 16–18; 1617 (2005) paras 4–6, 18; UNSC (1267 Committee) Guidelines of the Committee for the Conduct of its Work, 7 Nov 2002, amended 10 Apr 2003, para 5(b) (requiring of States 'a narrative description of the information that forms the basis or justification for taking action'). A higher standard of proof is required for listing in the EU by Common Position 2001/931/CFSP, Art 1(4) (listing is 'based on serious and credible evidence or clues, or condemnation for such deeds').

[340] The diplomatic protection model is restricted because a claim cannot be made by a petitioned government where the designating government objects.

[341] UNSC (1267 Committee), Consolidated List of Individuals and Entities Belonging to or Associated with the Taliban and Al-Qaida Organization (6 Dec 2004).

legal personality to individuals and entities that are threatened with listing, by providing them with the opportunity to be heard or to present evidence. As it stands, punitive measures may be imposed without any opportunity to respond to untested allegations. Procedural mechanisms for handling sensitive or secret intelligence information could be used.[342] At a minimum, if a prospective hearing is not provided, those affected should have an opportunity to appeal and to seek review of their listing.[343]

13. *Terrorist attacks of 11 September 2001*

(a) Resolution 1368

The sanctions regime was still in place when the US was attacked on 11 September 2001. In Resolution 1368 the next day, under Chapter VII, the Council condemned 'in the strongest terms the horrifying terrorist attacks' and regarded 'such acts, like any act of international terrorism, as a threat to international peace and security'.[344] The attacks involved hijacking of aircraft and their use, or intended use, as weapons against civilian buildings (the World Trade Center), government offices (the White House and Congress), and military headquarters (the Pentagon). All States were called on to 'bring to justice the perpetrators, organizers and sponsors' and hold accountable 'those responsible for aiding, supporting or harbouring' them, and to 'prevent and suppress terrorist acts'.[345]

The preamble recognized 'the inherent right of individual or collective self-defence in accordance with the Charter',[346] but it did not explicitly state that the US had a right of self-defence against the attacks.[347] Indeed the Council called the attacks a 'threat to the peace' rather than an 'armed attack'.[348] Most Council members did not immediately conceptualize September 11 as an armed attack, instead invoking a criminal law paradigm by speaking of *bringing the perpetrators to justice* or referring to *crimes* rather than acts of war.[349]

---

[342] See, eg, Miller, n 338, 49.   [343] ibid.

[344] UNSC Resolution 1368 (2001) para 1; reaffirmed in 1373 (2001) preamble.

[345] UNSC Resolution 1368 (2001) paras 3–4 respectively.

[346] Reaffirmed in UNSC Resolution 1373 (2001) preamble; see generally B Fassbender, 'The UN Security Council and International Terrorism' in Bianchi (ed), n 55, 83.

[347] F Mégret, ' "War"? Legal Semantics and the Move to Violence' (2002) 13 EJIL 361, 374. Self-defence against terrorism is not considered here: see generally M Byers, 'Terrorism, the Use of Force and International Law after September 11' (2002) 51 ICLQ 401; Franck, *Recourse to Force* (CUP, Cambridge, 2002) 53–68; Gray, n 322, 115–119; Cassese, n 62; R Wedgwood, 'Responding to Terrorism: The Strikes against Bin Laden' (1999) 24 Yale JIL 559; O Schachter, 'The Lawful Use of Force by a State against Terrorists in Another Country' (1989) 19 IYBHR 209.

[348] Cassese, n 62, 996; Mégret, n 347, 375.

[349] UNSC 56th Sess, 4370th mtg, Verbatim Record, 12 Sept 2001, UN Doc S/PV.4370, 3 (Mauritius), 4 (Tunisia), 5 (Ireland, China, Russia), 6 (Jamaica, Norway); see also Fassbender, n 346, 86.

It was only later that explicit claims of armed attack and self-defence were articulated,[350] which soon gained acceptance.[351]

The resolution reflects the ambivalence felt by States about whether to conceptualize the attacks within a law enforcement or use of force paradigm.[352] A day after the attacks, the Council was confronted with the difficult legal question of whether an 'armed attack' can be committed by non-State actors,[353] along with complex factual questions such as whether the scale and effects of the conduct amounted to an 'armed attack';[354] whether the attack was continuing;[355] and who was responsible for the attacks, including whether they were attributable to a State.[356] Indeed, nothing in the resolution attributed responsibility to any individuals or entities, which would have been necessary for the Council to endorse a right of self-defence.[357] This omission assumed particular importance in the light of later US claims that it 'will make no distinction between the terrorists who committed these acts and those who harbour them',[358] suggesting an attenuation of existing principles of State responsibility for the unlawful use of force.

In spite of expressing 'readiness to take all necessary steps to respond to the terrorist attacks . . . and to combat all forms of terrorism',[359] the Council did not authorize military action in Resolution 1368. Instead, the Council deferred to the unilateral, defensive response of a victim State,[360] losing the opportunity to manage collectively the forcible response, including its targets and duration.[361] Questions soon emerged about the immediacy of the US's defensive response, since there was much deliberation prior to actual military action being taken on 7 October 2001, indicating a tendency towards punitive reprisals rather than self-defence.[362] The proportionality of the response was

[350] NATO, Press Release 124 (12 Sept 2001); E Katselli and S Shah, 'September 11 and the UK Response' (2002) 52 ICLQ 245, 248; UN Doc S/2001/947 (7 Oct 2001) (UK); Conclusions and Plan of Action of the Extraordinary European Council Meeting, 21 Sept 2001, SN140/01.

[351] E Myjer and N White, 'The Twin Towers Attack: An Unlimited Right to Self-Defence?' (2002) 7 JCSL 1, 8–9; C Gray, 'The Use of Force and the International Legal Order' in M Evans (ed), *International Law* (OUP, Oxford, 2004) 589, 604.

[352] Abi-Saab, n 177, 307.

[353] Myjer and White, n 351, 7; T Franck, 'Terrorism and the Right of Self-Defense' (2001) 95 AJIL 839, 840.

[354] Myjer and White, ibid, 7.   [355] Franck, n 353, 839–840.

[356] Myjer and White, n 351, 7.

[357] Abi-Saab, n 177, 309; see also Myjer and White, n 351, 9–10.

[358] UNSC 56th Sess 4370th mtg, Verbatim Record, 12 Sept 2001, UN Doc S/PV.4370, 7–8 (US).

[359] UNSC Resolution 1368 (2001) para 5, see also 1373 (2001) preamble.

[360] M Byers, 'Terrorism, the Use of Force and International Law after September 11' (2002) 51 ICLQ 401, 413; Cassese, n 62, 999–1000; R Falk, *The Great Terror War* (Arris, Gloucestershire, 2003) 59.

[361] Abi-Saab, n 177, 309; J Brunnée, 'Terrorism and Legal Change: An International Law Lesson' in R Daniels et al (eds), *The Security of Freedom* (University of Toronto Press, Toronto, 2001) 341, 343.

[362] Myjer and White, n 351, 8.

also questioned, since the response to localized attacks in the US involved attacking an entire State (Afghanistan) and overthrowing its government.[363] The Council only became involved in authorizing military force *after* major powers achieved their objectives. Thus the Council authorized the International Security Assistance Force to assist the Afghan interim government to maintain security in a limited area around Kabul, after the US occupied the country.[364] The Council was reduced to 'mopping up' operations on behalf of powerful States.

Further, the US stated soon after 11 September 2001 that its self-defence may require 'further actions with respect to other organizations and other states', beyond Al-Qaeda and the Taliban.[365] The Council's abdication of control arguably encouraged US adventurism in Iraq in 2003. In that situation, the unilateral US response to September 11 exceeded the margins of self-defence and entered the realm of pre-emption, partly on the pretext that links existed between Iraq, WMDs, and Al-Qaeda.[366] Although renunciation of 'terrorism' was a cease-fire condition in Resolution 687 (1991), credible evidence of Iraqi links to terrorism was largely absent at the time of the invasion and was confirmed following the invasion.

The Council's failure to control forcible responses to terrorism may have inadvertently encouraged other States to use force against unrelated terrorist problems,[367] despite US double standards in insisting on its exceptional defensive claims.[368] Collective security has been marginalized in the military response to terrorism—subordinated to the interests of a powerful State— with the Council performing 'quiet background functions' of regulation and 'low politics'.[369] The UN is relegated to performing the 'peripheral' or 'cosmetic' roles of legitimating unilateral action, while forgoing active management of international threats.[370] The sidelining of the Council may also have longer-term consequences for the Council's legitimacy.[371]

---

[363] ibid.

[364] UNSC Resolution 1386. Similarly, the Council later authorized a multinational assistance force in Iraq after the US coalition occupied it, in part to combat terrorism: UNSC Resolutions 1511 (2003), 1546 (2004).

[365] US Ambassador J Negroponte, UN Doc S/2001/946 (7 Oct 2001).

[366] Statement by US Secretary of State C Powell, in 'Ministerial-Level Security Council Meeting Calls for Urgent Action to Prevent, Suppress All Support for Terrorism: Declaration in Resolution 1456 (2003) adopted unanimously', UNSC (4688th mtg) Press Release SC/7638, 20 Jan 2003; Roberts, n 326, 39.

[367] Falk, n 360, 55.

[368] H Koh, 'On American Exceptionalism' (2003) 55 *Stanford Law Review* 1479, 1487.

[369] Krisch, n 336, 2, 16–17, 20; see also J Charney, 'The Use of Force against Terrorism and International Law' (2001) 95 AJIL 835.

[370] Myjer and White, n 351, 1, 16.   [371] Fassbender, n 346, 100–102.

(b) Resolution 1373

In Resolution 1373, the Council required States, under Chapter VII, to suppress terrorism, implicitly approving earlier General Assembly recommendations.[372] In a bout of legislative and regulatory activism,[373] States are foremost *required* to prevent, suppress, freeze, and criminalize terrorist financing.[374] States must also: (a) refrain from supporting terrorists; (b) prevent terrorist acts; (c) deny safe haven to those who finance, plan, support, or commit terrorist acts, or harbour them; and (d) prevent the use of their territory for international terrorism.[375]

Further, States are *required* to: (e) bring to justice those who finance, plan, prepare, perpetrate or support terrorist acts, *and establish such terrorist acts as serious criminal offences in domestic laws with proportionate penalties*; (f) assist other States in criminal investigations or proceedings; and (g) prevent the movement of terrorists by controls on borders, documentation, and counterfeiting.[376] The resolution prefers criminal law and regulatory measures over military responses.[377]

Other provisions are framed as *requests* rather than obligations.[378] The Council declared that committing, financing, planning, and inciting terrorism are contrary to UN purposes and principles,[379] potentially leading to exclusion from refugee status under the 1951 Refugee Convention.[380] The Council was determined 'to take all necessary steps' to implement the resolution.[381] A Counter-Terrorism Committee (CTC) monitored implementation, including through mandatory State reporting,[382] which diverted a large proportion of

---

[372] Szasz, n 195, 903.

[373] Guillaume, n 240, 8; Krisch, n 336, 3, 5–6, 13; Rosand, n 190, 334; Szasz, n 195, 903; Myjer and White, n 351, 6.

[374] UNSC Resolution 1373 (2001), para 1; see generally I Bantekas, 'The International Law of Terrorist Financing' (2003) 97 AJIL 315; W Perkel, 'Money Laundering and Terrorism' (2004) 41 *American Criminal Law Review* 183; S Chenumolu, 'Revamping International Securities Laws to Break the Financial Infrastructure of Global Terrorism' (2003) 31 Geo JICL 385; J Norton and H Shams, 'Money Laundering Law and Terrorist Financing: Post-September 11 Responses' (2002) 36 *International Lawyer* 103; A Srivastava, 'The Steps Being Taken to Tighten Up Money Laundering Regulation Worldwide in the War against Terrorism' (2001) NLJ 1466; M Kantor, 'The War on Terrorism and the End of Banking Neutrality' (2001) 118 *Banking Law Journal* 891.

[375] UNSC Resolution 1373 (2001) para 2.

[376] ibid.   [377] Myjer and White, n 351, 6.

[378] UNSC Resolution 1373 (2001) paras 3–4: States are *called upon* to exchange information, cooperate, adopt, and implement treaties and resolutions, and deny refugee status and the political offence exception to terrorists. The Council was also concerned about links between terrorism and transnational organized crime, drugs and arms trafficking, money-laundering, and illegal movements of WMDs.

[379] UNSC Resolution 1373 (2001) para 5.

[380] 1951 Refugee Convention, Art 1F(c).

[381] UNSC Resolution 1373 (2001) para 8.

[382] Ibid, para 6, confirmed and structured in UNSC Pres Stat (15 Apr 2002) S/PRST/2002/10; (8 Oct 2002) S/PRST/2002/26; (17 Dec 2002) S/PRST/2002/38; (4 Apr 2003) S/PRST/2003/3; (30 Mar 2004) S/PRST/2004/8; 2004/26 (19 Jul 2004); 2004/37 (19 Oct 2004); 2005/3

UN documentation resources from other activities.[383] In requiring extensive legislative and administrative changes, the resolution imposed a heavy burden on States, with smaller States particularly 'overwhelmed'.[384] The CTC has not sanctioned States for non-compliance, instead pursuing a cooperative, non-threatening, technical, and regulatory approach.[385] Its primary role is to strengthen the infrastructure against terrorism and to provide technical assistance, rather than to identify particular terrorist acts.[386] There has been a high level of cooperation, compliance, and reporting by States.[387] There remain concerns that these counter-terrorism efforts have diverted resources from more pressing developmental needs and distorted assistance in favour of predominantly western interests.[388] There is also unease about the indefinite duration of the CTC.[389] As the CTC Chairman stated: 'Do not expect us to declare any member state compliant, because 1373 is open-ended, and the threats posed by various forms of terrorism will evolve'.[390] By positing itself as a regulatory body with perpetual competence, the CTC renders

(18 Jan 2005); UNSC Resolution 1535 (2004); see Rosand, n 190, 334–337; Rostow, n 190, 482; C Ward, 'Building Capacity to Combat International Terrorism: The Role of the United Nations Security Council' (2003) 8 JCSL 289, 298–304; UNSC, Pres Note, Annex: CTC Report on Implementation Problems, 26 Jan 2004, UN Doc S/2004/70, 15; UNODC (Terrorism Prevention Branch), Global Programme against Terrorism, Current Developments, Vienna, Aug 2003; ECOSOC (Commission on Crime Prevention and Criminal Justice), Sec-Gen Report on Strengthening international cooperation and technical assistance in preventing and combating terrorism, 13th Sess, Vienna, 11–20 May 2004, UN Doc E/CN.15/2004/8 (17 Mar 2004).

[383] Dhanapala, n 194, 19 (citing UN Sec-Gen's statement of 18 Jan 2002).

[384] Ward, n 382, 298–299; see also UNSC, Note by the President, Annex: Report by the Chair of the Counter-Terrorism Committee on the problems encountered in the implementation of Security Council Resolution 1373 (2001), 26 Jan 2004, UN Doc S/2004/70, 15.

[385] Rosand, n 190, 335–7. The CTC works through three subcommittees, assisted by experts. It operates by consensus, thus allowing all member States the power of veto. The CTC is not a sanctions committee nor a UN subsidiary organ with delegated decision-making powers under Art 29 of the Charter.

[386] Rosand, n 190, 337. Indeed, the Council cannot delegate its power to determine that a threat to, or breach of, the peace exists or ceases to exist: D Sarooshi, *The United Nations and the Development of Collective Security* (OUP, Oxford, 2003) 32–33. The UN Office on Drugs and Crime and the G8 have worked closely with the CTC to provide technical assistance: UNODC (Terrorism Prevention Branch), Global Programme against Terrorism, Current Developments, Vienna, Aug 2003; ECOSOC (Commission on Crime Prevention and Criminal Justice), Sec-Gen Report on Strengthening international cooperation and technical assistance in preventing and combating terrorism, 13th Sess, Vienna, 11–20 May 2004, UN Doc E/CN.15/2004/8 (17 Mar 2004); the 2003 G8 summit in Evian, France, also adopted a G8 action plan 'Building International Political Will and Capacity to Combat Terrorism'.

[387] Rosand, n 190, 337. In its first 18 months (to April 2003) the CTC had received first reports from 189 member States and five others; 131 States had submitted second reports; and third reports were received from 28 States: Ward, n 382, 298.

[388] Ward, ibid, 302, countering that 'there are development and economic related benefits which accrue from putting in place the legal and administrative infrastructure required by the resolution'.

[389] Rostow, n 190, 482.

[390] CTC Chair (Ambassador Greenstock), Symposium on Combating International Terrorism: The Contribution of the United Nations', Vienna, 3–4 June 2002.

compliance 'manifestly uncertain',[391] although it has structured compliance into different phases.[392]

As Judge Kooijmans observed in the *Israel Wall Advisory Opinion*, the 'completely new element' in these resolutions is classifying 'acts of international terrorism, without any further qualification, a threat to international peace and security . . . without ascribing these acts of terrorism to a particular State'.[393] The general proscription of terrorism eliminates the selectivity in the Council's previous ad hoc approach,[394] which disregarded 'the principle of equal treatment'.[395] The serious consequences of the Council's failure to define terrorism were discussed in Chapter 1, along with concerns about the validity of not identifying specific threats.

Concerns have also been raised that the Council and the CTC have not paid due regard to human rights obligations in supervising States' implementation of counter-terrorism measures. In later resolutions, the Council belatedly insisted that States 'ensure that any measure taken to combat terrorism comply with all their obligations under international law . . . in particular international human rights, refugee, and humanitarian law',[396] as well as the law of Charter.[397] Proper implementation of human rights law can mitigate the excesses of unilateral definitions of terrorism.[398] The CTC also interacts with the UN High Commissioner for Human Rights[399] and its communications with States refer to their human rights obligations.[400] However, concerns about the impact of the CTC's work on human rights protection remain, and the CTC rejected an offer from the UN High Commissioner for Human Rights to appoint a human rights expert to advise the CTC.[401] The CTC has made it very clear that monitoring human rights is not part of its mandate.[402]

[391] Rosand, n 190, 335.
[392] Rosand, ibid, 335–336; Stromseth, n 195, 43–44.
[393] *Israel Wall Advisory Opinion*, ICJ Case 131 (9 Jul 2004) para 35 (separate opinion of Kooijmans J).
[394] See generally A Bianchi, 'Ad-hocism and the Rule of Law' (2002) 13 EJIL 263, 271–272.
[395] J Habermas, *The Inclusion of the Other* (Polity Press, Cambridge, 2002) 180.
[396] UNSC Resolutions 1456 (2003), annexed Declaration, para 6; also 1535 (2004) preamble. See generally E Flynn, 'Counter-Terrorism and Human Rights: The View from the United Nations' [2005] Issue 1 EHRLR 29; A Schmid, 'Terrorism and Human Rights: A Perspective from the United Nations' (2005) 17 *Terrorism and Political Violence* 25; C Gearty, 'Terrorism and Human Rights' [2005] 1 EHRLR 1.
[397] UNSC Resolutions 1455 (2003), preamble; 1526 (2004), preamble.
[398] See the discussion on the specificity of offences in Ch 1 above.
[399] UNSC (4512th mtg), UN Doc S/PV.4512, 15 April 2002, 3; Greenstock, n 391.
[400] Ward, n 382, 298; 269–297.
[401] Rosand, n 190, 340; see also Stromseth, n 195, 44.
[402] Rostow, n 190, 484.

(i) Legislative action by the Council

The other legally significant feature of the Council's response is the quasi-legislative and/or regulatory nature of its response.[403] In requiring all States to adopt provisions drawn from the 1999 Terrorist Financing Convention, not then in force, Resolution 1373 'rendered certain purely treaty rules binding' on all UN members and 'thus assumed the role of a true international legislator'.[404] In addition, the resolution requires States to pursue broad legislative change in relation to terrorism generally.[405] The trend towards legislative action has been criticized as 'difficult to reconcile with the general role of the Security Council's enforcement powers under the UN Charter, which is more of an executive kind and follows a police model'.[406]

Yet, as long as the Council has lawfully identified a specific threat to security under Chapter VII of the Charter, it is difficult to sustain any legal objection to its use of legislative measures in response to that threat.[407] Resolutions clearly cannot be 'legislative in the sense of applying outside the framework of particular cases of restoration of international peace and security'.[408] But as the International Criminal Tribunal for the former Yugoslavia (ICTY) stated in *Tadic*, the Council 'has a broad discretion in deciding on the course of action and evaluating the appropriateness of the measures to be taken', whether that discretion derives from the wide reach of Articles 41 and 42 of the Charter, or 'general powers to maintain and restore international peace and security under Chapter VII at large'.[409] The Council's enforcement powers under Articles 41 and 42 of the Charter list illustrative but non-exhaustive measures.[410] Domestic legislation may be necessary for States to fulfil their Charter duty to implement binding resolutions,[411] and the Council is not limited to directing 'enforcement action only against the state responsible for a threat'.[412] In past practice, the Council has required 'adaptation of legislation and even constitutions'.[413]

States have uniformly and rapidly accepted the obligations in Resolution 1373, indicating agreement on Charter norms through State practice or

[403] Guillaume, n 240; see also Myjer and White, n 351, 6; Krisch, n 336, 5, 13.
[404] Guillaume, n 240; see also Krisch, n 336, 6; Rosand, n 190, 334; Szasz, n 195, 903.
[405] Rosand, n 190, 334.
[406] Krisch, n 336, 6.
[407] See, eg, Talmon, n 195, 183 (requiring a 'genuine link' between the threat and the measure); Orakhelashvili, n 307, 61; Szasz, n 195, 904.
[408] Gowlland-Debbas, n 205, 300.
[409] *Tadic (Interlocutory)*, n 5, para 31; see also Türk, n 293, 52.
[410] cf Türk, ibid, 52 (invoking the *eiusdem generis* doctrine—*inclusio unius est exclusion alterius*).
[411] V Gowlland-Debbas, 'Security Council Enforcement Action and Issues of State Responsibility' (1994) 43 ICLQ 55, 84–85.
[412] Kelsen, n 53, 788.
[413] Gowlland-Debbas, n 205, 293.

acquiescence.[414] This builds on acceptance of the Council's expanding use of legislative measures in the 1990s.[415] States have also accepted the quasi-administrative rule-making authority of the CTC, which issues guidelines interpreting resolutions and strengthens the Council's executive powers.[416] This is so even though the Council has allowed the CTC a great deal of discretion in managing its own activities.[417]

The Council should, however, exercise prudence in assuming the mantle of a global legislator. By requiring States to criminalize terrorism in domestic law, the Council is substituting itself for—or at least interfering in—conventional law-making processes.[418] Criminalization of harmful trans-national conduct normally takes place in multilateral treaty negotiations, a process marked by broader participation (than 15 unrepresentative Council members)[419] and greater precision (of elements of offences, jurisdictional principles and penalties—which resolutions are silent on). Further, Council negotiations on the drafting of legislative resolutions are not publicly recorded,[420] creating further uncertainty about the intended meaning of 'terrorism'. Ultimately, if Council measures become too intrusive, such as by requiring States to pass excessive legislation, then States may refuse to implement the Council's decisions, further damaging its authority and legitimacy and thus undermining its effectiveness.[421]

14. Terrorist acts 2002–05

From 2002, the Council adopted a series of formulaic resolutions condemning a particular terrorist bomb attack (Bali and Kenya in 2002, Bogota and Istanbul in 2003, Madrid in 2004, and London in 2005), hostage-taking (Moscow in 2002), or missile attack (Kenya).[422] The resolutions regard such acts 'like any act of international terrorism, as a threat to international peace and security'; urge States to bring the perpetrators, organizers, and sponsors to justice; and express 'determination to combat all forms of terrorism'.[423]

---

[414] Krisch, n 336, 7.   [415] Nolte, n 199, 325.

[416] Krisch, n 336, 7. See CTC, Guidelines of the Committee for the Conduct of its Work, Note by the Chair, 16 Oct 2001, UN Doc S/AC.40/2001/CRP.1; CTC, Guidance for the Submission of Reports pursuant to Paragraph 6 of UNSC Resolution 1373 (2001) of 28 Sept 2001, Note by Chair.

[417] Rosand, n 190, 335; Stromseth, n 195, 43.   [418] Rostow, n 190, 482.

[419] cf Talmon, n 195, 179 (Council decisions to use force are open to the same criticism, but this is not a basis for opposing Chapter VII actions).

[420] Talmon, ibid, 186.   [421] Gowlland-Debbas, n 205, 312.

[422] UNSC Resolutions 1438 (2002) para 1; 1450 (2002) para 1 (14 votes to 1); 1465 (2003) para 1; 1516 (2003) para 1; 1611 (2005) para 1; 1530 (2004) para 1; 1440 (2002) para 1 respectively.

[423] UNSC Resolutions 1438 (2002) paras 1, 3–4; 1440 (2002) paras 1, 4–5; 1450 (2002) paras 1, 3–4; 1465 (2003) paras 1, 3–4; 1516 (2003) paras 1, 3–4; 1530 (2004) paras 1, 3–4; 1611 (2005) paras 1, 3–4.

The Moscow Resolution 1440 (2002) also demanded the release of hostages. That resolution is significant because the Council involved itself in domestic terrorism, as did the resolution addressing the car bomb outside a Colombian social club.[424] Two presidential statements have also condemned internal terrorist attacks in Russia connected to the Chechen conflict. The first addressed a 'terrorist bomb attack' in Grozny in 2004, which killed the President of the Chechen Republic and others.[425]

The second responded to 'the heinous terrorist act' of hostage-taking at a school in Beslan in 2004, and 'other terrorist attacks' against 'innocent civilians' in Moscow and two Russian airliners.[426] Both statements urge all States to cooperate with Russia in bringing to justice those responsible for the attacks. While the statements did not attribute responsibility to Chechen rebels, investigations later did so. These attacks illustrate how serious acts of domestic terrorism can affect international interests or values, even in the absence of a strict connection to, or impact on, another State.

Only two of the resolutions attribute responsibility for terrorism. Whereas the Kenyan resolution is inconclusive, condemning only 'claims of responsibility' by Al-Qaeda in its preamble,[427] the Madrid resolution firmly attributes blame to 'the terrorist group ETA' in an operative paragraph.[428] Investigations soon showed that Al-Qaeda was responsible, and the hasty attribution to ETA, on the day of the bombing, was based on erroneous Spanish advice.[429] The Council abandoned its previously cautious approach in a rush to act, making an avoidable mistake.

The Council's error raises the wider problem of the evidentiary standard used in Council decision-making.[430] O'Connell writes that there is no 'well-established set of rules governing evidence in international law in general'[431] and the Council has never specified its own standard of proof for decisions about responsibility for breaches of, or threats to, peace and security. The ILC Articles on State responsibility are purposely silent on evidentiary issues,

---

[424] UNSC Resolution 1465 (2003); see M Sossai, 'The Internal Conflict in Colombia and the Fight against Terrorism' (2005) 3 JICJ 253, 257.

[425] UNSC Pres Stat (10 May 2004) S/PRST/2004/14.

[426] UNSC Pres Stat (1 Sept 2004) S/PRST/2004/31.

[427] Evidence suggests Al-Qaeda was indeed responsible: J Risen, 'US Suspects Qaeda Link to Bombing in Mombasa', *New York Times*, 30 Nov 2002.

[428] UNSC Resolution 1450 (2002) preamble and 1440 (2002) para 1 respectively.

[429] G Tremlett, 'Kofi Annan calls Aznar author of his own defeat', *The Guardian*, 18 Mar 2004.

[430] See generally M O'Connell, 'Evidence of Terror' (2002) 7 JCSL 19; S Scheideman, 'Standards of Proof in Forcible Responses to Terrorism' (2000) 50 *Syracuse Law Review* 249; After 11 September 2001, the US claimed it had 'clear and compelling information' about Al-Qaeda's responsibility: UNSC, Letter from the US Permanent Representative to the UNSC President, 7 Oct 2001, UN Doc S/2001/946.

[431] O'Connell, n 430, 21.

'which fall entirely outside the scope of the articles'.[432] Thus the standard of evidence is governed by the primary rules of State responsibility, and different standards may attach to different substantive obligations.

O'Connell suggests that a standard of 'clear and compelling' evidence of an armed attack is necessary before resort to force in self-defence,[433] because of the seriousness of the violent consequences flowing from judgments about responsibility for armed attacks. The standard of 'clear and compelling evidence' is drawn from the *Trail Smelter* case, which involved the lesser harm of transboundary environmental damage.[434] This standard is higher than the standard in civil cases in many common law jurisdictions (the balance of probabilities), but lower than the criminal standard (beyond reasonable doubt). Others speak of a standard of 'credible evidence'[435] or a 'prima facie' case.[436] The Council spoke of 'probable cause' for believing that Syria was involved in the assassination of the former Lebanese Prime Minister in 2005.[437] A fairly high standard is certainly implied by the *jus cogens* character of the prohibition on the use of force, and any exception to the prohibition requires a high threshold of justification.[438] Serious doubts were raised about the sufficiency of evidence on which the US relied to justify bombing Libya in 1986 and a factory in Sudan in 1998.[439]

An even higher standard of proof was demanded in the *Corfu Channel* case, in which the ICJ stated that the evidence must leave '*no room* for reasonable doubt'.[440] Although the ICJ drew on the criminal standard of proof, it allowed some flexibility in the nature of evidence admitted to prove this standard. The ICJ stated that the:

. . . exclusive territorial control exercised by a State within its frontiers has a bearing upon the methods of proof available to establish the knowledge of that State as to such events. By reason of this exclusive control, the other State, the victim of a breach of international law, is often unable to furnish direct proof of facts giving rise to responsibility. Such a State should be allowed a more liberal recourse to inferences of fact and circumstantial evidence . . .[441]

This view from 1949 is prescient in the context of international terrorism, where evidence of terrorist activity may be dispersed across multiple

---

[432] J Crawford, *The International Law Commission's Articles on State Responsibility: Introduction, Texts and Commentaries* (CUP, Cambridge, 2002) 124.

[433] O'Connell, n 431, 20; see also S Yee, 'The Potential Impact of the Possible US Responses to the 9–11 Atrocities on the Law regarding the Use of Force and Self-Defence' (2002) 1 Chinese JIL 287, 289.

[434] *Trail Smelter (US v Canada)* (1941) 3 RIAA 1905, 1963–1965.

[435] Charney, n 369, 836.   [436] Yee, n 434, 290.

[437] UNSC Resolution 1636 (2005) preamble.

[438] See generally J Lobel and M Ratner, 'Bypassing the Security Council: Ambiguous Authorizations to Use Force, Cease-fires and the Iraqi Inspection Regime' (1999) 93 AJIL 124.

[439] O'Connell, n 431, 20.

[440] *Corfu Channel* case (1949) ICJ Reports 4, 18.   [441] ibid.

jurisdictions, some of which (as with Libya in the Lockerbie dispute, or Afghanistan before 2001) refuse to cooperate transparently in international efforts to combat terrorism. It is arguable that in determining responsibility for terrorist acts as a precondition to international action, the Security Council is justified in relying on circumstantial evidence and inferences of fact, where harder evidence is difficult to come by. The catastrophic potential of terrorist acts further justifies the acceptance of such evidence.

At the same time, caution must be exercised when decisions are based on evidence which is incomplete due to the deliberate withholding of information by States, on the grounds that intelligence information is sensitive and sources need to be protected. As the US invasion of Iraq in 2003 illustrated, States which assert that the evidence justifies Council action, but which withhold details of that evidence, cannot always be trusted actually to possess reliable evidence. Political pressure on intelligence services in some States has compromised the impartiality and accuracy of such evidence that is presented publicly.

Lobel pragmatically observes that 'in the absence of an international judicial or other centralized fact-finding mechanism, the ad hoc manner in which nations evaluate factual claims is often decisive'.[442] This is also true of decisions made in the Council about questions of fact, since there is equally an absence of an established standard of proof or evidence in its practice. Yet, it is not sufficient for the Council to simply assert that it knows a threat to security when it sees it. The Council operates within legal boundaries, stipulated by the Charter and fundamental norms, and fulfilling its mandate requires it to make predictable, norm-based judgments about the existence of threats and responsibility for them. While there is inevitable political pressure on the Council to act decisively in response to terrorism, the Council's evidentiary sloppiness and undue haste in erroneously attributing responsibility for the Madrid bombings to ETA could be avoided if the Council were to adopt a rational and prospective evidentiary standard to guide its decision-making about terrorism.

In 2005, the Council made increased use of presidential statements to condemn terrorist attacks in Sharm el-Sheikh (Egypt), Bali (Indonesia), New Delhi (India), and Amman (Jordan).[443] Each statement followed the same formula of emphasizing the need to bring the perpetrators to justice and for all States to cooperate with the victim State; affirming the need to combat terrorism by all lawful means; expressing sympathy for the victims; and affirming that terrorism 'in all its forms and manifestations constitutes one of the most serious threats to international peace and security, and that any acts

---

[442] J Lobel, 'The Use of Force to Respond to Terrorist Attacks: The Bombing of Sudan and Afghanistan' (1999) 24 Yale JIL 537, 538.
[443] UNSC Pres Stats 2005/36 (27 July 2005), 2005/45 (4 Oct 2005), 2005/53 (31 Oct 2005), 2005/55 (10 Nov 2005) respectively.

of terrorism are criminal and unjustifiable, regardless of their motivation, wherever, whenever and by whomsoever committed'. There does not, however, appear to be any particular logic in the Council's choice of whether to condemn a terrorist attack in a resolution as opposed to a presidential statement.

15. *Terrorism in the Middle East 2002–05*

Despite the prevalence of terrorism in the Middle East for many years, few resolutions have condemned it, due to the political sensitivity of Palestinian self-determination. In 1995, the Council President condemned a 'terrorist attack' in Nordiya, Israel, in 1995, and 'terrorist attacks' in Jerusalem and Tel Aviv in 1996, and stated that these acts had 'the clear purpose of trying to undermine Middle East peace efforts'.[444] While terrorism was not defined, both attacks involved the targeting of civilians for political purposes. Unusually, the Council expressly mentioned the political motives behind the terrorist acts, which were intended to undermine the peace process.

Only since 2002, however, have *resolutions* mentioned terrorism. Resolution 1397, dealing with Israeli-Palestinian violence since the second intifadah from late 2000, demanded the 'immediate cessation of . . . all acts of terror',[445] reiterated in four later resolutions.[446] Resolution 1435 called on the Palestinian Authority (PA) to bring to justice persons responsible for terrorist acts, and condemned 'all terrorist attacks against any civilians, including the terrorist bombings in Israel' and 'in a Palestinian school in Hebron'.[447] Resolution 1402 expressed concern about 'suicide bombings' in Israel, which, given preambular references to terrorism, may be viewed as terrorism.

That resolution was also concerned about Israel's military attack on Arafat's headquarters, but did not qualify it as terrorism. Likewise, Resolution 1544 refers to housing demolitions and the killing of Palestinian refugees by Israel in Rafah, but does not classify these as terrorism. Nor does Resolution 1435, demanding that Israel cease destroying Palestinian infrastructure in Ramallah and that it withdraw from Palestinian cities. Resolutions addressing Israeli action have typically referred to the 'excessive use of force', as in Resolution 1322 (2000) dealing with Israel's response to the second Palestinian *intifadah* in 2000.[448]

---

[444] UNSC Pres Stats (30 May 1995) S/PRST/1995/3, (4 Mar 1996) S/PRST/1996/10.

[445] UNSC Resolution 1397 (2002) para 1.

[446] UNSC Resolutions 1402 (2002) para 2; 1435 (2002) para 1; 1515 (2003) preamble; 1544 (2004) preamble; see also UNSC Pres Stat 2005/12 (9 Mar 2005).

[447] UNSC Resolution 1435 (2002) para 4.

[448] Likewise, UNComHR Resolution S–5/1 (2000) condemned Israel's 'disproportionate and indiscriminate use of force' as human rights violations, crimes against humanity and war crimes and UNGA Resolution A/RES/ES–10/7 (2000) para 2 condemned Israel's 'excessive use of force'; see also K Graham, 'The Security Council and Counter-terrorism: Global and

Most references to terrorism do not ascribe responsibility for it, so it may be possible to interpret the condemnation of terrorism as applying equally to Israeli and Palestinian violence against civilians. This even-handed approach is reinforced by the Council's invocation of respect for IHL and the protection of civilians.[449] Sometimes the Council has attempted to depoliticize its terminology by using more neutral language: 'all Palestinians will stop all acts of violence against Israelis everywhere and . . . Israel will cease all its military activities against all Palestinians everywhere'.[450]

However, given the nature of some Palestinian violence, it is likely that the condemnation of terrorism is primarily directed against Palestinians. Resolution 1435 implies that non-State actors are the main perpetrators, when it calls on the PA to bring terrorists to justice. A statement by the 'Quartet' (the UN, the EU, the US, and Russia) involved in the Middle East 'Roadmap' peace process, and endorsed by the Security Council, refers to 'terrorism' by Palestinian groups and urges the Palestinian Authority to 'dismantle terrorist capabilities and infrastructure'.[451] In contrast, in nearby Lebanon, the Council has avoided mentioning terrorism and instead referred to the activities of 'armed militias'.[452] Similarly, in Afghanistan, reference has sometimes been made to 'illegal armed groups', 'extremist groups', and 'militia forces', or simply 'violence in any form intended to disrupt the democratic process'.[453]

16. Thematic resolutions 1999–2005

In addition to resolutions addressing specific terrorist acts or situations, since 1999 the Council has adopted one binding and three non-binding resolutions dealing with terrorism in more general terms.[454] Reflecting General Assembly resolutions, the Council unequivocally condemned 'all acts, methods and practices of terrorism as criminal and unjustifiable, regardless of their motivation, in all their forms and manifestations, wherever and by whomever

Regional Approaches to an Elusive Public Good' (2005) 17 *Terrorism and Political Violence* 37, 44. For examples of the differential labelling of Israeli and Palestinian violence by western States and the international media, see R Fisk, *The Great War for Civilization* (Fourth Estate, London, 2005) 464, 504–505, 551.

[449] UNSC Resolutions 1397 (2002) preamble; 1435 (2002) preamble; 1535 (2004) paras 1, 3; 1544 (2004) para 3.

[450] UNSC Pres Stat 2005/12 (9 Mar 2005).

[451] UNSC Pres Stat 2005/44 (23 Sept 2005), annexed Quartet Statement, New York, 20 Sept 2005.

[452] UNSC Resolution 1559 (2004) preamble, para 3.

[453] UNSC Resolutions 1589 (2005) preamble and 1623 (2005) preamble; UNSC Resolution 1589 (2005) para 12; and UNSC Pres Stat 2005/56 (23 Nov 2005) respectively.

[454] UNSC Resolutions 1269 (1999); 1377 (2001) annexed Ministerial Declaration; 1456 (2003) annexed Ministerial Declaration.

committed'.[455] All resolutions refer to the threat to peace and security posed by terrorism and its danger to life.[456] One resolution states that terrorism endangers human dignity and security, development, global stability, prosperity, and UN purposes and principles.[457]

These resolutions have urged States to prevent and suppress terrorism and its financing; bring perpetrators to justice; deny safe haven by apprehending, prosecuting or extraditing terrorists, and denying them refugee status; exchange information and cooperate; adopt and implement sectoral treaties and Council resolutions; and enhance the UN's role.[458] Two resolutions stressed the need to broaden 'understanding among civilizations' and address regional conflicts and global development.[459] One resolution warned of global links between terrorism, WMDs, and organized crime.[460]

While in 1999 the Council expressed 'its readiness to . . . take necessary steps . . . to counter terrorist threats',[461] the first three resolutions were non-binding, standard-setting instruments, influenced by Assembly resolutions, and lacking any compliance mechanisms.[462] The first resolution was largely ignored, since many States lacked the technical capacity or political will to take effective action.[463]

Resolution 1540 (2004), however, imposes obligations under Chapter VII to deal with the threat to peace and security posed by links between terrorism, non-State actors, and WMDs.[464] States must prohibit non-State actors from developing, acquiring, manufacturing, possessing, transporting, transferring, or using nuclear, chemical, or biological weapons and their means of delivery, 'in particular for terrorist purposes'.[465] The resolution establishes detailed control measures and a supervisory committee, and aims not to conflict with specialized WMD treaties and agencies.[466]

Unusually, in a footnote, the Council defines certain concepts for the purpose of the resolution, including 'means of delivery', 'non-State actor', and 'related materials'. Such definition is a helpful interpretive device in quasi-legislative resolutions, as long as the definition itself is not too vague,[467] but

---

[455] UNSC Resolutions 1269 (1999) para 1; 1377 (2001) annexed Declaration; 1456 (2003) annexed Declaration, preamble.

[456] UNSC Resolutions 1269 (1999) preamble, paras 1, 5; 1377 (2001), annexed Declaration; 1456 (2003), annexed Declaration, preamble; 1540 (2004) preamble.

[457] UNSC Resolutions 1269 (1999) para 3; 1377 (2001) annexed Declaration.

[458] UNSC Resolutions 1269 (1999); 1377 (2001); 1456 (2003).

[459] UNSC Resolutions 1377 (2001) annexed Declaration; 1456 (2003), annexed Declaration, para 10.

[460] UNSC Resolution 1456 (2003), annexed Declaration, preamble.

[461] UNSC Resolution 1269 (1999) para 6.

[462] Ward, n 382, 290.   [463] ibid.

[464] UNSC Resolution 1540 (2004) preamble.   [465] ibid, paras 1–2.

[466] ibid, paras 4–5 (referring to the 1968 Nuclear Non-Proliferation Treaty, 1993 Chemical Weapons Convention, and 1972 Biological and Toxin Weapons Convention; and the IAEA and Organization for the Prohibition of Chemical Weapons).

[467] Talmon, n 195, 190.

the device was not used here to define 'terrorism'. The regime targeting non-State actors is undermined, however, by double standards on the possession and monitoring of nuclear weapons by major nuclear States.[468]

17. *A working definition in 2004*

Three years after imposing measures against terrorism, the Council adopted a resolution generically defining it. While not expressly framed as a definition, Resolution 1566 of October 2004 recalls that the following acts are never justifiable:

> . . . criminal acts, including against civilians, committed with the intent to cause death or serious bodily injury, or taking of hostages, *with the purpose to provoke a state of terror* in the general public or in a group of persons or particular persons, *intimidate a population* or *compel a government or an international organization* to do or to abstain from doing any act, *which constitute offences within the scope of and as defined in the international conventions and protocols* relating to terrorism . . .[469]

States were urged to prevent such acts, and punish them 'by penalties consistent with their grave nature'. The resolution also created a working group to report on measures that could be imposed on individuals, groups, or entities involved in, or associated with, terrorist activities, *other than* those designated by the 1267 committee.[470] The resolution thus seeks to universalize (in a parallel regime) the proscription model developed by the 1267 Committee for the Taliban and Al-Qaeda. It was based on a Russian proposal to proscribe Chechen terrorists, which was opposed by Arab States objecting to the potential designation of Palestinian groups.[471]

The definition of terrorism provides explicit guidance to States (and the working group and CTC) on the meaning of terrorism, and may also exert pressure in the General Assembly to break the impasse on the Draft Comprehensive Convention. It presents a relatively narrow definition, limited to acts constituting sectoral offences (typically serious violence endangering life or property, and requiring an international element), which are *also* intended to create terror, intimidate a population, or coerce a government or organization. It thus combines elements of the definitions in the General Assembly's 1994 Declaration and the 1999 Terrorist Financing Convention.

The definition does not, however, require a political or other motive, thus encompassing private acts which terrorize, intimidate, or coerce.

---

[468] D Linzer, 'US backs out of nuclear inspections treaty', *Sydney Morning Herald*, 2 Aug 2004.

[469] UNSC Resolution 1566 (2004) para 3 (emphasis added).

[470] ibid, para 9: measures could include prosecution and extradition, asset freezing, and preventing movement and supply of weapons.

[471] M Farley, 'Chechens in frame as Russia asks UN to redefine terrorism', *Sydney Morning Herald*, 25–26 Sept 2004, 20.

Consequently, some of the distinctiveness of terrorism, explained in Chapter 1, is lost. Pragmatically, the definition may be too little, too late. In the three years to 2004, many States adopted laws implementing their obligations, and it is unlikely that they will further reform their laws to limit 'terrorism' in conformity with the resolution (which merely 'recalls' that certain acts are never justified and does not require law reform). As discussed earlier, there are also legitimacy costs in circumventing the treaty process.

18. Incitement, justification, and glorification of terrorism 2005

In September 2005 the Council adopted non-binding Resolution 1624 calling on States to: 'Prohibit by law incitement to commit a terrorist act or acts', prevent incitement, and deny safe haven or entry to inciters. The resolution also called for greater understanding between civilizations and for States to prevent the subversion of educational, cultural, and religious institutions by terrorists.[472] The CTC was tasked with reviewing implementation of the resolution.[473]

The preamble further repudiates 'attempts at the justification or glorification (*apologie*) of terrorist acts that may incite further terrorist acts'. It asserts that incitement 'poses a serious and growing danger to the enjoyment of human rights, threatens the social and economic development of all States, [and] undermines global stability and prosperity'. It further claims that inciting terrorism is contrary to UN purposes and principles, which may thus provide a basis for exclusion from refugee status under Article 1F(c) of the 1951 Refugee Convention.

The resolution does not go as far as the Council of Europe's 2005 Convention on the Prevention of Terrorism, since it calls for the *criminalization* of incitement but merely *repudiates* the justification or glorification of terrorism. Nonetheless, the resolution ambiguously refrains from defining 'incitement', so it is unclear whether this term is intended to encompass only direct and public incitement (as under the 1948 Genocide Convention), or whether it also extends to indirect incitement, private incitement, or even vague *apologie* for terrorism.

The lack of definition is of concern given that the Council in past resolutions has failed to define terrorism itself, resulting in a chain of ambiguous terms. Since incitement offences may interfere in freedom of expression,[474] the lack of definition may encourage some States to excessively restrict free

---

[472] UNSC Resolution 1624 (2005), para 3.

[473] ibid, para 6. The preamble also stresses that the media, civil and religious society, business, and educational institutions should foster an environment that is not conducive to incitement, and that States should prevent the exploitation of technology, communications, and resources for incitement.

[474] UNSC Resolution 1624 (2005) preamble.

expression. The lawfulness of any restriction on free expression will depend on how widely the crime of incitement is defined.[475] While the resolution was sponsored by the UK in the aftermath of the July 2005 terrorist bombings in London, a UK domestic proposal to criminalize condoning or glorifying terrorism[476] was amended to a lesser offence of 'encouragement' of terrorism, precisely because of freedom of speech concerns.[477]

19. Summary of Council practice

Prior to 1985, the Council refrained from using the term terrorism, while from 1985 to 2004, it qualified a variety of disparate activities as terrorism, many of them covered by sectoral treaties. In summary, conduct labelled as terrorist includes hostage-taking and hijacking; abduction of UN personnel; unlawful use of plastic explosives; assassination of heads of State or political leaders; destruction of, or attacks on, civilian aircraft; bombings of embassies and civilians; organized, non-State political violence in peacetime, including attacks on civilian, government, and military buildings; and attacks on religious sites in armed conflict. The acts of Al-Qaeda, including its destruction of property,[478] have also been described as terrorist, as has the use of WMDs by non-State actors.

It is too soon to judge whether the Council's measures have contributed to customary norms on terrorism. Before 2001, mention of terrorism was limited to specific situations, while generalized references were preambular and contributed marginally to custom formation, although resolutions often invoked customary norms reflected in the 1970 Declaration.[479] The frequent designation of terrorism as a threat to peace and security is significant,[480] but not evidence of delegated universal jurisdiction.[481] Reference to the obligation to prosecute or extradite terrorists is also deceptive, since many States prosecute terrorism as ordinary crime or sectoral offences.[482] It is

---

[475] B Saul, 'Speaking of Terror: Criminalizing Incitement to Violence' (2005) 28 *University of New South Wales Law Journal* 868 (generalized incitements which lack a proximate connection to imminent and probable serious harm are likely to be unjustifiable, unnecessary, and disproportionate restrictions on freedom of expression).

[476] UK Prime Minister Blair, 'Statement on Anti-Terror Measures', (5 Aug 2005) para 17. UK law already enables the prosecution of offences such as incitement to racial hatred or soliciting murder, of which the Muslim cleric Abu Hamza al-Masri was convicted in London in February 2006: 'Hamza jailed for seven years', *The Guardian*, 7 Feb 2006.

[477] See Ch 3, n 155; Lord Carlile of Berriew QC, *Report by the Independent Reviewer on Proposals by Her Majesty's Government for Changes to the Laws against Terrorism*, October 2005.

[478] Preambles to UNSC Resolutions 1390 (2002); 1455 (2003); 1526 (2004).

[479] Preambles to UNSC Resolutions 748 (1992); 1189 (1998); 1373 (2001).

[480] UNSC Resolutions 731 (1992); 748 (1992); 1044 (1996); 1054 (1996); 1070 (1996); 1189 (1998); 1193 (1998); 1267 (1999); 1368 (2001); 1373 (2001); 1390 (2002); 1455 (2003); 1511 (2003); 1526 (2004).

[481] Kolb, n 1, 77.   [482] See 'E. National Terrorism Legislation' below.

still premature to claim universal jurisdiction over terrorism, given the absence of an agreed definition, though its exercise might not give rise to protest.[483]

Mandatory anti-terrorism measures between 2001 and 2004 suffered from lack of definition, but in late 2004, the Council prospectively defined terrorism as serious (sectoral) criminal violence intended to provoke a state of terror, intimidate a population, or compel a government or organization. Following definition, in the long term, Council measures may gradually harmonize national criminal laws, which may in turn constitute evidence of State practice and *opinio juris*. Council practice is, however, but one element in the formation of customary norms on terrorism, notwithstanding that the Council has firmly taken hold of part of the international community's response to the subject. The next section examines judicial decisions and national laws for evidence of a customary definition of terrorism, outside UN practice.

D. JUDICIAL DECISIONS DEFINING TERRORISM

Judicial decisions are a subsidiary means for determining international legal rules under Article 38(1)(d) of the ICJ Statute.[484] No distinction is drawn between national and international decisions. On one hand, international decisions do not formally constitute State practice, since unlike national courts they are not State organs.[485] Even so, international decisions may constitute persuasive evidence of a customary rule and may have an (informal) precedential value,[486] although under Article 59 of the ICJ Statute the decisions of the ICJ have 'no binding force except between the parties and in respect of that particular case'. International decisions may also accelerate the ripening of practice into custom.[487] Decisions of international arbitral tribunals may carry less weight than those of courts, given the limited nature of such proceedings.

The decisions of domestic courts are generally less significant than those of international courts and tribunals. In the *Lotus* case, the inconsistency of national decisions was incidentally noted without any attempt to consider the customary significance of such decisions in general.[488] In contrast, dissenting Judge Finlay accorded 'great weight' to an English decision which applied international law.[489] National decisions have subsequently been considered by

---

[483] Kolb, n 1, 87–88.
[484] See also A D'Amato, *The Concept of Custom in International Law* (Cornell University Press, New York, 1971) 43.
[485] ICRC Study, n 168, xxxiv.		[486] ibid.
[487] Wolfke, n 13, 73.
[488] *Lotus* case (1927) PCIJ Series A, No 10, 28.		[489] ibid, 54.

international tribunals on numerous occasions. Recently, the ICJ took note of an Israeli Supreme Court decision which applied humanitarian law treaties to Israel's military activities in Rafah.[490]

The significance of national decisions as evidence of customary law may depend on the reputation of the court and whether particular decisions have been endorsed or acquiesced in by other States.[491] The value of domestic decisions may be limited by the restricted nature of the incorporation of international law into domestic law.[492] Inconsistent practices between different branches of government within a State may also neutralize the significance of the State's practice as a whole.[493]

Most international judicial decisions dealing with terrorist subject matter are silent on the legal status of terrorism, and instead treat the issue by recourse to other legal norms. Even if hijacking and hostage-taking are customary crimes of universal jurisdiction, these offences fall short of creating a generic terrorist crime. While numerous national judicial decisions address terrorist crimes in national law, few national decisions deal with the status of terrorism in international law. Some national decisions reject the view that terrorism is an international crime, although some judges have been willing to use international definitions of terrorism in non-criminal cases.

1. International decisions

In the *Tehran Hostages* case, ensuing from the 1979 revolutionary occupation of the US Embassy in Tehran, the ICJ found that Iran had violated obligations owed to the US under international treaties and general international law.[494] Despite the terroristic character of the incident, the judgment does not refer to terrorism and instead analyses the dispute within the framework of the law on diplomatic immunity and State responsibility. The ICJ's finding of illegality turned not on the characteristics of the offenders ('militants'),[495] but on the prohibited character of the acts and the protected nature of the targets. Similarly, the *Nicaragua* case 'is a striking example of how relevant subject-matter can be dealt with without the invocation of terrorism' or State terrorism.[496] The paramilitary activities of the contras were not described as terroristic in the judgment, but were dealt with within the framework of obligations on the non-use of force and non-intervention.[497]

The *Nicaragua* case does not, however, exclude terrorism from international law, since the ICJ approved the 1970 Declaration as evidence of customary norms on non-intervention and the non-use of force. The 1970 Declaration prohibits 'terrorist' acts and activities, and the Court did not

[490] *Israel Wall (Advisory Opinion)*, n 393, para 100.   [491] Wolfke, n 13, 74.
[492] ibid, 147.   [493] ICRC Study, n 168, xxxiv.
[494] *Tehran Hostages*, n 53, para 95.   [495] ibid, paras 57–58.
[496] Higgins, n 193, 20.   [497] *Nicaragua*, n 6.

qualify its approval of the 1970s Declaration's customary status by excluding those parts which refer to terrorism. It is also notable that *Nicaragua* was decided in 1986, before the normative shifts in State attitudes in the General Assembly from the mid-1990s, and the Security Council after 2001.

Both the *Tehran Hostages* and *Nicaragua* cases involved issues of State responsibility in a court with jurisdiction limited to disputes between States. Those cases were not dealing with the field of international law in which the precise definition of terrorism is most relevant—individual criminal responsibility. As such, it is not surprising that these decisions did not deal more explicitly with terrorism, since it is less important in resolving disputes between States on matters covered by existing norms.

The *Lockerbie* case in the ICJ also did not turn on any concept of terrorism, notwithstanding the terrorist character of the incident.[498] The case involved a dispute about whether the 1971 Montreal Convention or mandatory Security Council measures governed the response to the bombing. While the Council invoked terrorism in determining that the incident threatened peace and security, triggering enforcement measures, at neither the interim measures (1992) nor the preliminary objections (1998) phase did the ICJ inquire into whether the Council was justified in taking enforcement measures against 'terrorism'. The discontinuance of the case means the Council's discretion cannot now be challenged or reviewed at the merits phase.

The term 'terrorism' also featured in the *Israel Wall Advisory Opinion* of 2004. The ICJ majority did not invoke the term in any operative legal context, although it referred to Israeli arguments that Palestinian terrorism justified its security measures.[499] No mention was made of terrorism in three Separate Opinions.[500] In contrast, the Opinions of Judges Kooijmans and Owada, and the Dissenting Opinion of Judge Buergenthal, argued that the majority did not pay sufficient regard to the terrorist attacks on Israel in evaluating the lawfulness of the wall.[501] Yet such references were not legal usages so much as facts considered relevant in evaluating the legitimacy and proportionality of Israel's security response under IHL and human rights law.

More significantly, Judge Kooijmans elaborated a legal concept of terrorism for the first time in the ICJ, stating that attacks on a political opponent, by indiscriminately targeting civilians, are 'generally considered to be international crimes'.[502] Further: 'Deliberate and indiscriminate attacks against civilians with the intention to kill are the core element of terrorism which has

---

[498] *Lockerbie (Provisional Measures)*, n 299.

[499] *Israel Wall Advisory Opinion*, n 393, paras 46, 116, 127, 138 (majority decision); see also paras 23, 30 (Separate Opinion of Judge Owada) and para 3.2 (Separate Opinion of Judge Elaraby)

[500] ibid, (Separate Opinions of Judges Al-Khasawneh, Koroma, and Higgins).

[501] ibid, paras 4, 6, 11, 13 (Separate Opinion of Judge Kooijmans); para 31 (Separate Opinion of Judge Owada); paras 2–5 (Dissenting Opinion of Judge Buergenthal).

[502] ibid, paras 4–5 (Judge Kooijmans).

been unconditionally condemned by the international community regardless of the motives which have inspired them.'[503] In his view, every State has a right and a duty to protect its citizens against terrorist acts,[504] suggesting that identification of terrorists, through definition, is necessary for the exercise of security or defensive measures. In commenting on the Security Council's determination of 'terrorism' as a threat to peace and security, without definition,[505] Judge Kooijmans implicitly sought to limit the boundaries of mandatory Council measures.

2. National decisions

In the civil case of *Tel-Oren v Libya* (1984), a US federal appeals court found that terrorism was not an offence against the 'law of nations' under the Alien Tort Claims Act (US).[506] The case arose from an El Fatah attack on civilian vehicles in Israel in 1978, which killed 34 people and seriously injured 77 others.[507] Two judges found that there was insufficient international consensus on the definition of terrorism for it to constitute an offence against the law of nations.[508] As Judge Edwards stated: 'While this nation unequivocally condemns all terrorist acts, that sentiment is not universal. Indeed, the nations of the world are so divisively split on the legitimacy of such aggression as to make it impossible to pinpoint an area of harmony or consensus.'[509] The third judge believed that terrorism was a non-justiciable 'political question'.[510] The view of some writers that terrorism did constitute a law of nations violation[511] has not attracted much support. Meron argues that the court should have disentangled 'the cluster of norms involved in the terrorist attack . . . instead of focusing on the label of terrorism attached to the operation as a whole'.[512] Such was the case in a later US decision, *Yunis* (1991), in which the US Court of Appeals found (*obiter*) that the sectoral offence of aircraft hijacking was a crime of universal jurisdiction.[513]

---

[503] ibid, para 5; see similarly para 31 (Judge Owada).

[504] ibid, para 5 (Judge Kooijmans); see also 2 (Judge Buergenthal).

[505] ibid, para 35 (Judge Kooijmans).

[506] *Tel-Oren v Libyan Arab Republic* 726 F 2d 774 (DC Cir 1984) (separate concurring Opinions of Judges Edwards, Bork, and Robb), affirming *Tel-Oren* 517 F Supp 542 (DDC 1981). See also Alien Tort Claims Act, 28 USC, §1350 (1976).

[507] S Jetter, 'International Terrorism: Beyond the Scope of International Law: *Tel-Oren v Libyan Arab Republic*' (1986) 12 Brookings JIL 505, 505, 536.

[508] *Tel-Oren*, n 506, 795 (Judge Edwards), 806–807 (Judge Bork).

[509] ibid, 795 (Judge Edwards).

[510] ibid, 823 (Judge Robb).

[511] Jetter, n 507, 507, 545–552; see Note, 'Terrorism as a Tort in Violation of the Law of Nations' (1982) 6 Fordham ILJ 236.

[512] T Meron, 'When Do Acts of Terrorism Violate Human Rights?' (1989) 19 IYBHR 271, 273.

[513] *US v Yunis* 924 F 2d 1086 (DC Cir 1991) 1092; (1991) 30 ILM 403; see also *Burnett v Al Baraka Investment and Development Corporation* 274 F Supp 2d 86 (DDC 2003).

The US criminal case of *Yousef* (2003)[514] approved *Tel-Oren*. *Yousef* involved an appeal of convictions for conspiracy to bomb US airliners in Asia, and the 1993 bombing of the World Trade Center in New York.[515] On appeal, Yousef argued that customary law did not permit the US to exercise universal jurisdiction over the bombing of a Philippine Airlines flight,[516] outside the US and not harming US citizens. In the absence of an international definition of 'terrorism' and consensus on universal jurisdiction over it, Yousef argued that the US could not exercise jurisdiction under customary or domestic law.[517]

The US Court of Appeals swiftly rejected the view that US law was subordinate to customary law.[518] Even so, it found that US offences of the destruction of aircraft and aircraft piracy were based on the 1971 Montreal Convention.[519] Yousef's conviction was 'consistent with and required by' US treaty obligations, regardless of whether the bombing was termed 'terrorist' or amounted to 'terrorism'.[520] The Court also found that the protective, passive personality, and objective territorial principles permitted jurisdiction over a range of acts against aircraft and related activities.[521]

Although it was not decisive of the appeal, the Court agreed *obiter* that there was no universal jurisdiction over 'terrorism', finding that the District Court erred.[522] Universal jurisdiction could only be exercised over 'a limited set of crimes that cannot be expanded judicially'.[523] In contrast, the Court believed that terrorism 'is a term as loosely deployed as it is powerfully charged'.[524] The 'indefinite category' of terrorism was not condemned by all States, which had failed to achieve consensus on definition, particularly concerning State-sponsored terrorism and freedom fighters.[525] The Court noted that even US law contains several different definitions of terrorism.[526]

The Court of Appeal also criticized the District Court's reliance on the US Third Restatement as a source of customary law, which suggested that 'perhaps certain acts of terrorism' 'may' be subject to universal jurisdiction.[527] A Comment in an earlier Draft of the Restatement noted that terrorism was widely condemned, but there was no agreement on its definition.[528] The District Court erred further by drawing a judicial analogy between bombing an aircraft and other 'heinous' crimes subject to universal jurisdiction.[529]

The Court approved *Tel-Oren*, observing that: 'We regrettably are no closer

[514] *US v Yousef* 327 F 3d 56 (2d Cir 2003).
[515] *US v Yousef* 927 F Supp 673 (SDNY 1996)
[516] *Yousef*, n 514, 33.   [517] ibid, 34, 43.   [518] ibid, 34, 35–38.
[519] 18 USC §32 and 49 USC §46502 respectively.   [520] *Yousef*, n 514, 44.
[521] ibid, 34, 42–43; 64–65; see also *US v Bin Laden* 92 F Supp 2d 189, 193–197 (SDNY 2000) (US jurisdiction over the East Africa embassy bombings was based on the protective principle).
[522] *Yousef*, n 514, 34, 44.   [523] ibid, 53, 55–57.   [524] ibid, 57.
[525] ibid, 44.   [526] ibid, 59–60.   [527] ibid, 46.
[528] US Restatement of Foreign Relations §408 (10th Draft No L, 1981) comment (a).
[529] *Yousef*, n 514, 46.

now than eighteen years ago to an international consensus on the definition of terrorism or even its proscription.'[530] This conclusion is surprising because the Court relied heavily on sources that have become outdated since *Tel-Oren*. The Court failed to refer to the end of the Cold War and normative developments in the General Assembly in the 1990s (including political agreement on a working definition in 1994); the practice of the Security Council after 2001; or the adoption of new international and regional treaties in the 1990s. While there is not yet any firm international consensus, it was perhaps closer in 2003 than in 1984.

Finally, while the Court found that there was no definition of terrorism, it incidentally expressed its preferred approach. Noting that terrorism 'is defined variously by the perpetrators' motives, methods, targets, and victims', the Court criticized 'Motive-based definitions' for attempting to exempt self-determination struggles, which could potentially 'legitimate as non-terrorist certain groups nearly universally recognized as terrorist' (including in US case law, such as the IRA, Hezbollah, and Hamas).[531]

Outside the US, acts of terrorism have also rarely been prosecuted as crimes of international terrorism, rather than as sectoral or ordinary offences. In the *Ghaddafi* case (2001), the French Court of Cassation found that terrorism was not an international crime entailing the lifting of immunity for heads of State, and proceedings were quashed.[532] The charges included murder for complicity in a terrorist enterprise.[533] That case overturned an earlier appeals court decision that Libya's Head of State could be prosecuted for involvement in bombing a French aircraft over Niger in 1989.[534]

In the *Lockerbie* criminal trial under Scots law in the Netherlands, a suspect alleged to have destroyed an aircraft in flight was charged with, and convicted of, multiple murders. Despite early accusations of the 'commission of terrorism',[535] this was not charged at trial,[536] nor was it clear whether this expression

[530] ibid, 58–59.　　[531] ibid, 59–60.
[532] Bulletin des arrêts de la Cour de Cassation, Chambre criminelle, Mar 2001, No 64, 218–219; see S Zappala, 'Do Heads of State Enjoy Immunity from Jurisdiction for International Crimes? The *Ghaddafi* Case Before the French *Cour de Cassation*' (2001) 12 EJIL 595, 607–611.
[533] F Boitard (2001) 105 RGDIP 474.
[534] F Kirgis, 'French Court Proceedings against Muammar Qadhafi', *ASIL Insights*, Oct 2000.
[535] Higgins, n 193, 20.
[536] *Her Majesty's Advocate v Al Megrahi et al* (1999) (Scottish HC of Justiciary, Camp Zeist, The Netherlands) Case 1475/99, (2001) 40 ILM 581, para 1. The conviction was upheld in *Al Megrahi v Her Majesty's Advocate* (2002) (Scottish HC of Justiciary (App Ct)), Appeal No C104/01, 14 Mar 2002. The case has since been appealed to the ECHR; see also 'Verdict in the Trial of the Lockerbie Bombing Suspects' (2001) 95 AJIL 405; 'Lockerbie Criminal Trial Glossary' (1999) 11 *International Legal Perspectives* 41; A Aust, 'Lockerbie: The Other Case' (2000) 49 ICLQ 278; M Scharf, 'Terrorism on Trial: The Lockerbie Criminal Proceedings' (2000) 6 ILSA JICL 355; M Scharf, 'A Preview of the Lockerbie Case', *ASIL Insights*, May 2000; M Scharf, 'The Lockerbie Trial Verdict', *ASIL Insights*, Feb 2001; A Klip and M Mackarel, 'The Lockerbie Trial: A Scottish Court in the Netherlands' (1999) 70 *Revue international de droit penal* 777.

referred to domestic or international terrorism. At first instance, terrorism was descriptively referred to in the judgment four times,[537] and more often on appeal, but in neither case was the term used operatively to trigger legal consequences. The appeal judgment referred once to 'terrorist organizations', 13 times to a hypothetical 'terrorist' in expert testimony, once to an 'act of terrorism', and twice to 'terrorist activity'.[538]

After 11 September 2001, leading terrorist suspects in various jurisdictions have more commonly been charged with sectoral or ordinary offences than with terrorism. A US citizen captured in Afghanistan in 2001, John Walker Lindh, was charged with conspiracy to kill US citizens abroad.[539] The British 'shoe bomber', Richard Reid, was convicted in a US district court in 2003 of attempted murder and the attempted use of a WMD.[540] A German court convicted a Moroccan, Mounir el Motassadeq, of 3,066 counts of accessory to murder—but also for membership in a terrorist organization—for involvement in September 11.[541] The convictions were quashed in April 2003 because the US had refused to make available a key witness,[542] but a retrial will proceed following subsequent US cooperation.

More broadly, 52 suspects involved in suicide bombings in Casablanca in 2003, which killed 44 people, were charged in Morocco with 'forming a criminal band, acts against the security of the state, sabotage, homicide, and causing injuries'.[543] In Belgium, 23 Al-Qaeda suspects were charged with explosives, weapons and document fraud offences, and membership of a private militia, for planning to bomb US targets in Europe, and for the killing of an Afghan leader, Ahmed Shah Massood, in 2001.[544] When a German court convicted four Algerians of conspiracy to murder and to plant a bomb, and weapons offences concerning a planned attack on Strasbourg's Christmas market in 2000, charges of belonging to a terrorist organization were withdrawn to expedite trial.[545]

---

[537] *Al Megrahi* (1999), n 536, paras 42; 82: eg, there was 'no doubt' that certain organizations were involved in 'terrorist activities', but no evidence of their involvement 'in this particular act of terrorism'.

[538] *Al Megrahi* (2002), n 536, para 143; paras 204, 211, 258–262; para 261; and paras 362, 366 respectively.

[539] US Att-Gen Ashcroft, 'John Walker Lindh Press Conference', US Department of Justice, Washington, DC, 15 Jan 2002.

[540] P Belluck, 'Unrepentant shoe bomber sentenced to life', *New York Times*, 31 Jan 2003.

[541] D Butler, '9/11 accomplice guilty in germany', *New York Times*, 20 Feb 2003; 'First September 11 suspect on trial sentenced to 15 years', *Sydney Morning Herald*, 20 Feb 2003. In Feb 2004, Abdelghani Mzoudi was also acquitted of 3,000 counts of accessory to murder in relation to the same attacks for the same reason.

[542] D Rose, 'Germany to drop 9/11 plot charges', *Observer*, 18 July 2004.

[543] G Tremlett, '52 in court over suicide bombings', *The Guardian*, 22 July 2003.

[544] Press Association, 'Brussels terror trial begins amid high security', *The Guardian*, 22 May 2003.

[545] J Hooper and M Wainwright, 'British-based plotters are jailed for market bomb', *The Guardian*, 11 Mar 2003.

In Turkey, the PKK leader, Abdullah Ocalan, was prosecuted for acts intended to secede part of Turkish territory,[546] while Kurdish parliamentarians allegedly involved with the PKK were convicted of 'membership in an armed gang'.[547] In 2003, a suspect charged with bombing an Air India flight in 1985 pleaded guilty to 329 counts of manslaughter.[548] In Greece, 'November 17' members were convicted of murder in 2003.[549] In Indonesia, terrorism convictions for the Bali bombing were thrown into doubt after the Constitutional Court ruled in 2004 that the anti-terrorism law was retrospective.[550]

The '20th hijacker' on 11 September 2001, French citizen Zacarias Moussaoui, was, however, indicted in the US on charges which including conspiracy to commit acts of terrorism transcending national boundaries.[551] That offence falls short of evidence of universal jurisdiction over terrorism, since the offence of terrorism transcending national boundaries also requires harm to people or property within the US. Moussaoui ultimately pleaded guilty to the six conspiracy charges in April 2005, becoming the first person convicted in the US for the 11 September 2001 attacks. In relation to the same attacks, in September 2005, the Spanish High Court convicted 18 people, and acquitted six, of offences including conspiring on Spanish territory with the Al-Qaeda hijackers, terrorist homicide, and terrorist organization offences.[552]

One line of authority supports terrorism as an international crime. Spain has sought extradition of persons involved in 'dirty wars' in Chile, Argentina, Peru, and Guatemala,[553] under a law providing universal jurisdiction over

[546] *Ocalan v Turkey* ECHR, App No 46221/99 (12 Mar 2003).

[547] *Zana et al* (1994), State Security Court; retrial and conviction in Ankara State Security Court, Apr 2004; see International Commission of Jurists, 'Turkey: Guilty Verdict for Jailed Former Parliamentarians is a Setback for the Rule of Law', Press Release, 21 Apr 2004.

[548] C Krauss, 'Plea bargain in '85 blast on Indian jet', *New York Times*, 11 Feb 2003.

[549] 'Greek terror leaders convicted', *The Guardian*, 8 Dec 2003.

[550] M Moore, 'Bali bombers' convictions ruled illegal', *Sydney Morning Herald*, 24 July 2004; T Lindsey, S Butt, and R Clarke, 'Review is not a Release', *Australian*, 27 July 2004; R Clarke, 'Retrospectivity and the Constitutional Validity of the Bali Bombing and East Timor Trials' (2003) 5 *Australian Journal of Asian Law* 232; A Martyn, 'The Amrozi Bali Bombing Case: is Indonesia's Anti-terrorism Law Unconstitutional?', Research Note 14, Australian Parliamentary Library, 3 Oct 2003.

[551] 18 USC §2332b(a)(2) and (c); the other charges included conspiracy to: commit aircraft piracy, destroy aircraft, use weapons of mass destruction, murder US employees, and destroy property: see Indictment in *US v Moussaoui*, filed in the US District Court for the Eastern District of Virginia, 11 Dec 2001; see also US Att-Gen Ashcroft, 'DOJ To Seek Death Penalty Against Moussaoui', News Conference Transcript, US Department of Justice, Miami, 28 Mar 2002.

[552] *Barakat Yarkas et al* case, Spanish Sup Ct (Penal Section), Sentence No 36/2005, 26 Sept 2005.

[553] *Peruvian Genocide* case, Judgment No 712/2003, Spanish Sup Ct, 20 May 2003, (2003) 42 ILM 1200; *Menchú* case, Preliminary Inquiries 331/99, Edict (Judicial Decree), Spanish Fed Ct (Central Procs Ct No 1), Madrid, 27 Mar 2000; *Guatemala Genocide* case (Spanish Sup Ct) (2003) 42 ILM 686 and Spanish Constitutional Court appeal (26 Sept 2005) (overturning the lower court's limitation of jurisdiction by Spanish nationality); *Pinochet* case, Summary Proc

'terrorism'.[554] Terrorism is the commission of listed crimes (such as kidnapping, injuring, and killing) while 'acting in the service of, or collaborating with, armed bands, organizations or groups whose objective is to subvert constitutional order or to gravely alter public peace'.[555] The definition applies not only to order or peace in Spain, but also in other States. In the *Cavallo* case, Mexico authorized the extradition to Spain of a former Argentinian naval officer for his role in terrorism by the Argentine dictatorship in the 1970s and 1980s.[556]

Spain's assertion of universal jurisdiction over terrorism, as defined in Spanish law, is hard to reconcile with the absence of an international definition of terrorism. Rather, it reflects an assertion of extraterritorial, prescriptive jurisdiction over terrorism offences developed in a particular domestic context.[557] Although Mexico has recognized such jurisdiction in agreeing to extradite, that has more to do with similarities between Mexican and Spanish legal traditions than any solid foundation in international law.

The meaning of terrorism in national law has also been considered in situations where the statutory offence of 'terrorism' does not define it. In *Singh v State of Bihar*, in 2004 the Indian Supreme Court dismissed an appeal by multiple appellants against convictions under Indian anti-terrorism legislation.[558] The appellants argued that there was no evidence that they were terrorists, or had committed terrorist acts, under section 3 of the Terrorist and Disruptive Activities (Prevention) Act 1987 (India). The statute did not define terrorism and the Court found that precise definition was impossible. It observed that the problem of definition had 'haunted countries for decades', not least because of the difficulties posed by 'freedom fighters' and State-sponsored terrorism. The Court believed that 'Terminology consensus' would be necessary for agreement on a comprehensive international treaty, and

---

1/98-J, Audiencia Nacional (Central Investigatory Ct No 6), 20 Sept 1998; *Cavallo* case, Mexican Sup Ct, 10 June 2003; see J Méndez and S Tinajero-Esquivel, 'The Cavallo Case: A New Test for Universal Jurisdiction' (2000) 8 *Human Rights Brief; Scilingo* case, Spanish Audiencia Nacional, 14 Apr 2005 (upholding Spanish jurisdiction over crimes against humanity by Argentinians in Argentina, but rejecting charges of terrorism); see C Tomuschat, 'Issues of Universal Jurisdiction in the *Scilingo* Case' (2005) 3 JICJ 1074.

[554] 1985 Judicial Power Organic Law (Spain), art 23(4)(b); see earlier 1971 Code of Military Justice, art 17; R Wilson, 'Prosecuting Pinochet: International Crimes in Spanish Domestic Law' (1999) 21 *Human Rights Quarterly* 927, 961–963.

[555] Spanish Penal Code, arts 571–572; see also arts 573–580.

[556] Excerpts in (2003) 42 ILM 884; see M Becerra, 'The Cavallo Case: A Case of Universal Jurisdiction?', Paper at Oxford Public International Law Discussion Group, 4 Mar 2004.

[557] In *Pinochet*, counsel suggested that the offence of terrorism in Spanish law is reducible to conspiracy in English law, but the argument was not dealt with in the judgment: *Pinochet (No 3)* [2000] 1 AC 147, 153 (A Jones, C Greenwood, J Lewis, and C Lloyd-Jacob).

[558] *Madan Singh v State of Bihar* [2004] INSC 225 (2 Apr 2004). The appeal arose under s 19 of the Terrorist and Disruptive Activities (Prevention) Act ('TADA Act') 1987 (India) for offences under ss 302, 307, 149, 352 and 379 of the Indian Penal Code 1860, s 3 of the TADA Act, and s 27 of the Arms Act 1959 (India).

suggested that the 'lack of agreement' on definition had been 'a major obstacle to meaningful international countermeasures'.

The Court listed numerous definitions of terrorism without expressing its preference for any of them, including definitions from: the 1937 League of Nations Convention; General Assembly Resolution 51/210 (1996); Schmid's 1992 definition as the 'peacetime equivalent of a war crime'; an 'academic consensus definition' in Schmid's study of 1988;[559] and a range of definitions used by the US Federal Bureau of Investigation.[560] The Court did, however, suggest that Schmid's 1992 definition attempted to 'cut through the Gordian definitional knot' by regarding the core of war crimes—'deliberate attacks on civilians, hostage-taking and the killing of prisoners'—as a basis for an equivalent crime of terrorism in peacetime.

The Court then proceeded to offer a tentative descriptive definition of terrorism as the use of violence which causes physical or mental damage to victims but also a 'prolonged psychological effect' or potential effect on society as a whole. Beyond the physical harm of terrorist violence lies its 'main objective': 'to overawe the Government or disturb the harmony of the society or "terrorise" people and the society ... with a view to disturb the even tempo, peace and tranquility of the society and create a sense of fear and insecurity'.[561] In addition, the ordinary penal law was thought insufficient to address terrorism, since terrorism is 'in essence a deliberate and systematic use of coercive intimidation'. The Court also considered it to be a manifestation of 'increased lawlessness and cult of violence' and a 'revolt against a civilized and orderly society'. Terrorism is exploited by criminals aiming 'to achieve acceptability and respectability in the society' by being projected as

---

[559] 'Terrorism is an anxiety-inspiring, repeated violent action, employed by (semi-) clandestine individual, group or State actors, for idiosyncratic, criminal or political reasons, whereby—in contrast to assassination—the direct targets of violence are not the main targets. The immediate human victims of violence are generally chosen randomly (targets of opportunity) or selectively (representative or symbolic targets) from a target population, and serve as message generators. Threat—and violence—based communication processes between terrorist (organization), (imperilled) victims, and main targets are used to manipulate the main target, turning it into a target of terror, a target of demands, or a target of attention, depending on whether intimidation, coercion, or propaganda is primarily sought': see A Schmid and A Jongman, *Political Terrorism* (North Holland Publishing Co, Amsterdam, 1983).

[560] Including: 'Terrorism is the use or threatened use of force designed to bring about political change': B Jenkins. 'Terrorism constitutes the illegitimate use of force to achieve a political objective when innocent people are targeted': W Laqueur. 'Terrorism is the premeditated, deliberate, systematic murder, mayhem, and threatening of the innocent to create fear and intimidation in order to gain a political or tactical advantage, usually to influence an audience': J Poland. 'Terrorism is the unlawful use or threat of violence against persons or property to further political or social objectives. It is usually intended to intimidate or coerce a Government, individuals or groups, or to modify their behavior or politics': US Vice-President's Task Force, 1986. 'Terrorism is the unlawful use of force or violence against persons or property to intimidate or coerce a Government, the civilian population, or any segment thereof, in furtherance of political or social objectives': FBI.

[561] *Singh*, n 558.

heroes.[562] The Court equivocated on whether terrorism only includes attacks on non-combatants and excludes attacks on military targets.[563]

Courts have been more willing to use the term 'terrorism' in non-criminal cases. In the *Suresh* case (2002),[564] the Canadian Supreme Court accepted that there was an agreed international definition of terrorism for the limited purpose of interpreting and applying Canadian immigration law. The case involved an appeal against a denial of refugee status and a deportation order issued because Suresh was involved in 'terrorism'.[565] Terrorism was not defined in the legislation and the Court acknowledged the 'notoriously difficult' problem of definition, the absence of an authoritative international definition, and the factual difficulty of determining who falls within any definition.[566]

The Court observed that the absence of definition means 'the term is open to politicized manipulation, conjecture, and polemical interpretation'.[567] It gave the example of Mandela's ANC under apartheid, 'routinely labelled a terrorist organization' by South Africa and much of the international community.[568] Nonetheless, the Court found it unnecessary to 'exhaustively' define terrorism for the limited purpose of the immigration proceeding at hand.[569] Rather, it felt that 'the term provides a sufficient basis for adjudication and . . . is not inherently ambiguous "even if the full meaning . . . must be determined on an incremental basis" '.[570]

The Court approved the 'stipulative' definition in the 1999 Terrorist Financing Convention, which 'catches the essence of what the world understands by "terrorism" ', and is 'sufficiently certain to be workable, fair and constitutional', even if marginal cases provoke disagreement.[571] The Court rejected an argument that it should adopt a 'functional' definition—by listing specific acts—to 'minimize politicization'.[572] Conceding that the functional approach was strongly supported by jurists, States, and sectoral treaties, and that the stipulative approach was open to manipulation, the Court still

---

[562] Further: 'Crime became a highly politicised affair and greed compounded by corruption and violence enabled unscrupulousness and hypocrisy to reign supreme, supported by duplicity and deceitful behaviour in public life to amass and usurp public power to perpetuate personal aggrandizement, pretending to be for the common good': ibid.

[563] 'If terrorism is defined strictly in terms of attacks on non-military targets, a number of attacks on military installations and soldiers' residences could not be included in the statistics': ibid.

[564] *Suresh v Canada (Minister of Citizenship and Immigration)* [2002] 1 SCR; para 93.

[565] Immigration Act (Canada), s 19.

[566] *Suresh*, n 564, paras 93–95.   [567] ibid, para 94.

[568] ibid, para 95. Mandela himself admits that the ANC was prepared to use 'terrorism', and justified a perfidious attack on military targets in Pretoria which killed many civilians: N Mandela, *Long Walk to Freedom* (Little, Brown, London, 1994) 272, 506.

[569] *Suresh*, n 564, para 93.   [570] ibid, para 93; also para 96.

[571] ibid, paras 96–98.   [572] ibid, para 97.

believed that a functional list 'may change over time' and ultimately require a term like terrorism to distinguish some illicit acts from others.[573]

The Court's belief that there is core global agreement on the definition of terrorism, except in marginal cases, glosses over the very real and wide differences between States. As discussed above, apparent political agreement on a basic definition in the General Assembly masked deep divisions about any definition for the purpose of imposing criminal liability. In this case, the equally serious legal consequences of a security deportation caution against conceptual leaps of judicial reasoning which transpose definitions from one area to a different context. As explained earlier, agreement on the generic definition in the 1999 Terrorist Financing Convention was reached only because the definition triggered financing offences, and not any broader criminal liability or other serious legal disability.

In the UK House of Lords, a similar case arose involving exclusion from refugee status. In *T v Home Secretary*, Lord Mustill relied on the 1937 League Convention definition of terrorism to limit the meaning of 'serious non-political' crime in Article 1F(b) of the 1951 Refugee Convention. While cautious about using the contested term 'terrorism' in exclusion cases, he preferred it to more subjective tests such as remoteness, causation, atrocity, and proportionality, since it 'concentrates on the method of the offence, rather than its physical manifestation'.[574] Lord Mustill stated that 'terrorism is not simply a label for violent conduct of which the speaker deeply disapproves . . . [but] is capable of definition and objective application'.[575]

In his view, a terrorist targets civilians indiscriminately, rather than striking at 'the tyrants whom he opposes'.[576] In international law, Lord Mustill found 'a recognition that terrorism is an evil in its own right, distinct from endemic violence, and calling for special measures of containment'.[577] He was 'content to adopt' the 1937 League definition as 'serviceable' for exclusion purposes.[578] Lord Slynn agreed, adding that terrorism may also include acts 'likely to cause injury to persons who have no connection with the government'.[579] The views of Lords Mustill and Slynn were not the majority, and courts have generally been reluctant to deploy definitions of terrorism in exclusion cases.[580] The finding that terrorism is a discrete concept in international law is overly-optimistic, given ongoing disagreements about definition.

---

[573] ibid.
[574] *T v Home Secretary* [1996] AC 742, 772 (Lord Mustill).
[575] ibid, 773.   [576] ibid, 772.   [577] ibid, 773.
[578] ibid.   [579] ibid, 776 (Lord Slynn).
[580] See B Saul, 'Exclusion of Suspected Terrorists from Asylum: Trends in International and European Refugee Law', IIIS Discussion Paper 26, Dublin, July 2004.

E. NATIONAL TERRORISM LEGISLATION

National laws may be evidence of State practice and *opinio juris*; or embody general principles of law.[581] Definitions of terrorism are increasingly found in national law and may contribute to the formation of an international customary definition, and universal jurisdiction over terrorism.[582] Cassese writes that numerous national laws prohibit terrorism and 'substantially converge', contributing to a customary definition, although he only provides examples from four similar western democracies.[583] Yet close attention to national laws shows that wide divergences in national definitions make it difficult to ascertain any common, customary definition.

The picture is complicated by the use of different definitions for different purposes,[584] including in a single jurisdiction. While this creates uncertainty,[585] there may be legitimate reasons for using different definitions for different preventive or repressive purposes. Often national definitions do not establish offences or 'serve as a legal term of art upon which liberty depends',[586] but are used for jurisdictional, budgetary, or administrative purposes. These include special investigative or prosecutorial powers; different evidentiary rules (such as lower standards of proof, or reversing the onus of proof); reducing lawyer-client confidentiality; enhanced penalties; and forfeiture or freezing of assets.[587] Where terrorism offences are defined to require a political motive, it may be advantageous to remove the motive element in relation to powers to investigate terrorism,[588] since evidence of motive may take some time to establish and it may be necessary to act preventively in the meantime.

Further, definitions may trigger emergency laws and restrictions on, or derogation from, human rights or constitutional protections.[589] In UK

---

[581] *Hostages* case, VIII UNWCC Law Reports, 34, 49; *Lotus* case, n 488, 96 (Separate Opinion of Judge Altamira); Wolfke, n 13, 77, 148.

[582] P Macklem, 'Canada's Obligations at International Criminal Law' in Daniels et al (eds), n 362, 353.

[583] Cassese, n 88, 122; see also A Cassese, 'Terrorism as an International Crime' in Bianchi (ed), n 55, 213 (referring to the US, the UK, Canada, and Australia).

[584] In the US, different definitions of terrorism are used by the State Department, the Defence Department, the FBI, the CIA, and others. Some of these are discussed in *Flatow v Iran* 999 F Supp 1, 17 (DDC 1998).

[585] C Walter, 'Defining Terrorism in National and International Law' in Walter et al (eds), n 337, 23.

[586] C Walker, *Blackstone's Guide to the Anti-Terrorism Legislation* (OUP, Oxford, 2002) 21.

[587] MC Bassiouni, 'Effective National and International Action against Organized Crime and Terrorist Criminal Activities' (1990) 4 *Emory International Law Review* 9, 26–27, 41; D Freestone, 'Legal Responses to Terrorism: Towards European Cooperation?' in J Lodge (ed), *Terrorism: A Challenge to the State* (Martin Robertson, Oxford, 1981) 195, 199.

[588] N Keijzer, 'Terrorism as a Crime' in W Heere (ed), *Terrorism and the Military: International Legal Implications* (Asser Press, The Hague, 2003) 115, 121.

[589] Bassiouni, n 587, 27.

immigration law, definition of terrorism permitted non-citizens suspected of terrorism to be indefinitely detained if deportation was impossible, until the House of Lords declared the law was impermissibly discriminatory.[590] There have also been attempts to exclude terrorists from refugee status automatically, or to return recognized refugees to persecution after admission, even though terrorism is undefined and may not be serious enough to warrant exclusion or *refoulement* in international refugee law. Reference to terrorism may even trigger war—after the Beslan attacks, the Russian Duma considered a law allowing war to be declared in response to a terrorist act threatening national security.[591]

In federal States, the divergences in criminal law definitions may be acute. In the US, the Oklahoma City bomber was prosecuted in a state court for 160 counts of murder.[592] In contrast, the 'Washington snipers' were prosecuted under Virginian law for terrorism, a crime 'with the intent to intimidate the civilian population at large or influence the conduct or activities of the government of the United States, a state or locality through intimidation'.[593]

1. National criminal laws on terrorism

Historically, it was difficult to compare national criminal definitions of terrorism due to the methodological difficulty of accessing national laws.[594] Since late 2001, national approaches can be gleaned from mandatory State reports to the CTC,[595] which detail national compliance with Council Resolution 1373, including the obligation to criminalize terrorist acts domestically (including financing, planning, preparing, and perpetrating such acts), with proportionate penalties.[596] By 30 June 2004, the CTC had received 515 reports from States and international organizations.[597]

---

[590] Anti-Terrorism, Crime and Security Act 2001 (UK), ss 21–23, upheld in *A v Home Secretary* [2003] 1 All ER 816; but declared incompatible with the Human Rights Act 1998 (UK) in *A v Home Secretary* [2004] UKHL 56 (the *Belmarsh* case); see also UK Parliament (Joint Committee on Human Rights), Continuance in Force of ss 21–23 of the Anti-Terrorism, Crime and Security Act 2001, 5th Report of Sess 2002–03, HL Paper 59, HC 462.

[591] ICJ, 'Russia: Chief of Staff Announces Pre-emptive Strikes', ICJ E-Bulletin on Counter-Terrorism and Human Rights, No 2, Sept 2004.

[592] AP, 'Nichols faces trial in state court in the Oklahoma City bombing', *New York Times*, 14 May 2003 (despite an earlier federal conviction).

[593] J Blair, 'Sniper case will be first test of Virginia antiterrorism law', *New York Times*, 17 Dec 2002.

[594] While the UN Sec-Gen had been tasked by UNGA with collecting national laws, a compilation was not published until after 11 Sept 2001, and was incomplete and out-of-date: see National Laws and Regulations on the Prevention and Suppression of International Terrorism: Part I, UN Legislative Series, New York, 2002, UN Doc ST/LEG/SER.B/22.

[595] CTC (Chair), Guidance Note for the Submission of Reports: UNSC Resolution 1373 (2001) para 3(2).

[596] UNSC Resolution 1373 (2001) para 2(e).

[597] UNSC (CTC), CTC Work Program (1 July–30 Sept 2004), UN Doc S/2004/541 (6 Jul 2004), 4.

Analysis of State reports reveals three main patterns in national criminal responses to terrorism:[598] 87 States lack special terrorism offences and hence use ordinary offences; 46 States have *simple generic* terrorism offences; and 48 States have *composite generic* terrorism offences. Each category is examined below. (Fifteen States provided insufficient information on criminal laws,[599] while a further 18 States possess terrorism offences but their definition is unclear from their reports.)[600]

(a) Ordinary offences approach

Despite rapid legislative change in many jurisdictions since September 2001,[601] historical patterns in national legal approaches to terrorism remain fairly clear. Eighty-six States prosecute terrorism as ordinary crime, without any special terrorism offences.[602] Thus terrorism may be prosecuted as murder, assault, false imprisonment, and so on. The physical harm, or threat of harm, is the decisive factor in the legal response, rather than the presence of generic elements such as a political motive or intimidatory aim. Some States treat terrorism as ordinary crime to avoid legitimizing violent terrorists as extraordinary 'political' offenders.[603] Most States supplement this approach by incorporating many of the sectoral treaty offences, a process much accelerated after 2001.

Many States also possess broad laws on national security, public emergency, public order, unlawful association, armed bands, hostile expeditions, subversion, treason, sedition, or threats to constitutional order. Terrorist acts

---

[598] State Reports to CTC available at: <www.un.org/Docs/sc/committees/1373/submitted_reports. html>. For reasons of space, citations to each of the 515 State reports have been omitted.
[599] Bangladesh, Bosnia and Herzegovina, Burkina Faso, Cape Verde, Central African Republic, Chad, Comoros, Cook Islands, Equatorial Guinea, Ethiopia, Honduras, Liberia, Mali, Mauritania, and Togo.
[600] Bulgaria, Costa Rica, Cambodia, Dominican Republic, Gambia, Guinea Bissau, Guyana, Iraq, Liechtenstein, Malawi, Marshall Islands, Mauritius, Monaco, Norway, Oman, Tajikistan, Uganda, and the UAE.
[601] J Zelman, 'Recent Developments in International Law: Anti-Terrorism Legislation' (2001) 11 JTLP 183, 184.
[602] Afghanistan, Andorra, Angola, Antigua and Barbuda, Argentina, Bahamas, Bahrain, Barbados, Benin, Bhutan, Botswana, Brazil, Brunei Darussalam, Burundi, Cameroon, China, Costa Rica, Cote D'Ivoire, Cuba, Dominica, DPR Korea, DR Congo, Eritrea, Fiji, Gabon, Ghana, Grenada, Guatemala, Haiti, Indonesia, Jamaica, Japan, Kenya, Kiribati, Kuwait, Lao PDR, Lesotho, Libya, Madagascar, Malaysia, Malta, Micronesia, Moldova, Myanmar, Namibia, Nauru, NZ, Niger, Nigeria, Niue, Palau, Panama, Papua New Guinea, Paraguay, Philippines, Poland, Rep Congo, Rep Korea, Rwanda, St Kitts and Nevis, Saint Lucia, Sao Tome and Principe, Samoa, San Marino, Saudi Arabia, Senegal, Seychelles, Sierra Leone, Singapore, Solomon Islands, Somalia, South Africa, Sri Lanka, Suriname, Swaziland, Switzerland, Tanzania, Timor Leste, Trinidad and Tobago, Tuvalu, Ukraine, Uruguay, Vanuatu, Venezuela, Yemen, Zambia.
[603] Walker, n 586, 164 (UK); C Walker, 'Irish Republic Prisoners, Political Detainees, Prisoners of War or Common Criminals?' (1984) 19 *Irish Jurist* 189.

often fall within—and are subsumed by—the sovereign, prerogative scope of these wide protective laws, rendering a specific offence of terrorism pragmatically unnecessary. Jurisdiction to prescribe such offences is usually territorially limited, or extended by the objective territorial and protective principles, but universal jurisdiction is not usually exercised.

Some States which prosecute terrorism as ordinary crime possess offences which roughly approximate terrorism, without naming it as such. These include offences such as public intimidation (Argentina); creating panic (Kuwait); and intimidation (Japan, Sri Lanka, and Venezuela). Spreading terror is an element of the crime of collective endangerment in Brazil, and of public intimidation in Guatemala; while in Lesotho, putting the public in fear is an element of subversion.

Occasionally, States have terrorism offences on the books, but terrorism is prosecuted as ordinary crime. In South Africa, an apartheid-era definition has fallen into disuse, and prosecutors rely on ordinary offences[604]—though ironically, members of Afrikaans for Boer Forces were charged with terrorism in 2003, for anti-State violence, including a plot to kill President Mandela.[605] It is rare for ordinary crimes to be categorized as terrorism, without that description adding anything substantive. Thus, Sri Lanka has 'terrorism' offences which simply list objective criminal acts, without any generic or purposive elements. Similarly, 'terroristic' or subversive 'indiscriminate mass murder' in Japan merely describes aggravated common crime.

After September 2001, most States relying on ordinary offences intended to reform their legal approach to terrorism, and few States maintain that ordinary offences are now sufficient.[606] A small number of States consider reform unlikely due to parliamentary opposition to, or rejection of, government proposals.[607] While treating terrorism as common crime is the historically dominant approach, and remains so, this pattern is likely to change as further reforms take place.

(b) Generic definitions of terrorism

Historically, few States generically defined terrorist crimes, or combined generic elements with the enumeration of specific acts. Since 2001, however, States have increasingly adopted generic offences. The CTC has pressured States to criminalize terrorism, without supplying an international definition, or objecting to the unilateral, generic national definitions which go beyond the sectoral treaty offences.

Generic offences fall into two broad categories: simple generic offences, comprising a single generic element; and composite or compound generic

---

[604] CTC Report: South Africa, UN Doc S/2001/1281 (8 Jan 2002).
[605] AFP, 'Court postpones trial of white right-wingers', *Sydney Morning Herald*, 20 May 2003.
[606] eg Singapore.   [607] eg Paraguay, NZ, and Switzerland.

offences, constituted by cumulative or conjunctive generic elements. Almost all generic offences require an intent to commit an objective, serious, violent and/or criminal act, to life or property, although the specification of violent acts varies greatly. The focus of this analysis is on the generic elements of terrorist offences, in furtherance of which violence is committed, rather than on the myriad forms violence may take.

To aid analysis, the different language used in national definitions for similar concepts has been simplified into overarching descriptors. Thus the idea of 'putting civilians in fear', used below, is variously formulated in national law as creating panic or anxiety, terrorizing, frightening, or intimidating. Reference to 'civilians' is shorthand for various protected targets in national law: individuals, entities, populations, peoples, and so on. The limited purpose of this analysis is to appreciate general patterns, rather than to interrogate the precise meaning of different terms. State reports to the CTC often do not make it clear whether terrorism definitions relate to domestic or international terrorism offences. This analysis considers both types of definition together, on the basis that the generic *purposive elements* of terrorism (terror, intimidation, coercion, compulsion, and so on) can be analysed independently of whether the *targets* of terrorism are domestic or international.[608]

(i) Simple generic terrorism offences

At the narrow end of the spectrum of simple generic offences, nine States define terrorism as violence intended to terrorize or intimidate people.[609] These definitions resemble those in the 1937 League Convention and in IHL, which focus on the grave psychological impact of acts. Also at the narrow end are three States defining terrorism as coercing or intimidating a State or international organization,[610] regardless of whether it is politically or privately motivated. Eight States define terrorism as either putting civilians in fear, *or* coercing a government or organization, thus presenting the first two simple generic definitions as alternatives and broadening the definition.[611] That approach reflects the 1999 Terrorist Financing Convention.[612]

At the broader end of the spectrum, 10 States define terrorism as violent acts which damage, weaken, or oppose the State, constitutional, or public order.[613] These definitions more closely approximate broad national security

---

[608] A more refined analysis which distinguishes international from national definitions would be useful, but is beyond the scope of this research.

[609] Albania, Algeria, Colombia (aggravated if done to hinder elections), Cyprus, Ecuador, El Salvador, Lebanon, Syrian Arab Republic, and Tunisia.

[610] Hungary, Latvia, and Mongolia.

[611] Azerbaijan, Belarus, Bolivia, Chile, Lithuania, Mozambique, Thailand, and Tonga.

[612] 1999 Terrorist Financing Convention, Art 2(1)(b).

[613] Czech Republic, Armenia, Guatemala, Malaysia (emergency powers only), Nicaragua, Slovakia, South Africa, Spain, Turkey, Vietnam, and Zimbabwe.

or public order offences, labelled as terrorism. Zimbabwe has a crime of 'insurgency, banditry, sabotage or terrorism'—without distinguishing the terms—involving insurrection or resistance, or coercion against the State. South Africa's 1982 definition covers acts with intent to (a) overthrow or endanger State authority, (b) achieve 'any constitutional, political, industrial, social or economic aim or change' in the State, or (c) coerce the State in some way.[614] Turkey defines terrorism as organized violence to change the State's constitutional, political, legal, social, secular or economic order, impair territorial or national integrity, endanger the State's existence or authority, eliminate basic rights or freedoms, or damage safety, public order, or the State's health.[615] Israel defines a 'terrorist organization' simply as any group violence or threat of violence 'calculated to cause death or injury to a person', irrespective of motive.[616]

The broadest end of the spectrum includes definitions presenting, as alternatives, multiple simple generic definitions. Six States define terrorism as violence putting civilians in fear, *or* harming interests such as public order, safety, security, democracy, or the State,[617] the environment, public facilities, or resources.[618] A further seven States define terrorism as violence putting civilians in fear, *or* coercing a government or international organization, *or* harming public safety, order, security, independence, integrity, or the State's foundations.[619] One State defines terrorism as violence putting civilians in fear, *or* for political ends;[620] while another defines it as violence motivated by politics or religion, *or* to provoke war or conflict.[621]

(ii) Composite generic terrorism offences

Composite generic offences require proof of multiple generic elements. The elements are similar to those in simple generic definitions, but composite offences are narrower because multiple, conjunctive elements must be present. Thirteen States define terrorism as violence putting civilians in fear, *in order to* disrupt public order, safety, peace, the State, or constitution; or conversely define terrorism as disrupting order to put civilians in fear.[622] One

---

[614] Internal Security Act 1984 (South Africa), s 54.
[615] Law No 3713 on Suppression of Terrorism (Turkey), s 1.
[616] Prevention of Terrorism Ordinance, No 33 of 5708–1948 (Israel), s 1.
[617] Egypt, Italy, Myanmar, Nepal, and India (Prevention of Terrorism Act 2002 since repealed.
[618] Sudan.
[619] Kazakhstan, Kyrgyzstan, Russia, Turkmenistan, Finland, Portugal, Iceland, and Moldova (emergency powers only).
[620] Maldives.   [621] Estonia.
[622] Denmark, Djibouti, Macedonia, France, Guinea, Jordan, Morocco, Peru, Qatar, Romania, Senegal, Serbia and Montenegro, and Slovenia. The Peruvian Constitutional Court, however, declared too broad a definition of terrorism referring to spreading anxiety, alarm, or fear in the population to change the power structure (by installing a totalitarian government): Decision of 3 Jan 2003, cited in CTC Report: Peru, UN Doc S/2003/896 (17 Sept 2003), 2.

State defines terrorism as putting civilians in fear to coerce a government or international organization,[623] while another defines it in the same way but adds the alternative of jeopardizing the constitutional, political, or economic values of a State or an organization.[624] A further State refers to putting civilians in fear to either coerce a government, disturb the peace, or undermine State authority.[625]

Five States define terrorism as violence for a political or other motive, aiming to (a) coerce a government or international organization, or (b) intimidate a population or civilians.[626] This category resembles the 1994 General Assembly definition, but broadens it by adding the alternative of coercing a government or international organization. Twenty-five EU States define terrorism as acts which seriously damage a State and (a) intimidate a population; (b) coerce a government or international organization; or (c) destroy fundamental structures.[627] Unlike the previous category, there is no requirement of a political or other motive. Another State similarly defines terrorism as violence affecting public security or State interests, by putting civilians in fear, or coercing a State or organization.[628] Finally, one State defines terrorism as coercing a State or international organization for the purpose of disturbing international relations, causing war, or destabilizing the State.[629]

(iii) Summary of analysis

The dominant approach in national laws—almost half of all States—is to prosecute terrorism as ordinary crime. The remaining half of States defines terrorism generically—half simple generic (one quarter of States), and half composite generic (also one quarter). Some generic definitions were the result of reforms after September 2001, increasing the historically small number of States which defined terrorism generically.

Nonetheless, the divergence in generic definitions militates against abstracting—by teleological reduction[630]—a minimum core definition of terrorism in State practice. Even the basic element of an intent to create terror is not found in all definitions. Further, the influence of international definitions (as in the 1999 Terrorist Financing Convention, the 1994 Declaration, Council resolutions, and the 1937 League Convention) on national criminal laws has been fairly limited.

---

[623] Iran.   [624] Croatia.   [625] Mexico.

[626] Australia, Belize, Canada, Pakistan, the UK (investigative powers only), and NZ (emergency powers only). A draft crime of terrorism in South Africa contains similar elements, but adds that violence must pursue a cause *and* threaten the unity or territorial integrity of the State: Draft Anti-Terrorism Bill, Nov 2003.

[627] 2002 EU Framework Decision, Art 1. There is, however, variation in national implementing legislation. The UK continues to prosecute terrorism as ordinary crime: CTC Report: UK, UN Doc S/2002/787 (19 July 2002) 6.

[628] Georgia.   [629] Uzbekistan.   [630] Kolb, n 1, 57.

Where definitions do not include terrorizing or intimidating people as an element, they lose their distinctiveness and differentiation from other political violence. For instance, violence for political ends, or to coerce a government, is conceptually different from violence to intimidate the public or put it in fear.[631] Unless terrorism is pinned to the idea of terrorizing people—whether or not in addition to political motives, or coercive aims—then such a crime is better described as subversion, coercion, or otherwise.

(c) Jurisdiction over terrorism

The duty to criminalize terrorism in Resolution 1373 is silent on the scope of prescriptive jurisdiction, illustrating the danger of circumventing treaty-making process—which would stipulate bases of jurisdiction—in establishing an international crime. While States clearly must criminalize terrorist acts committed or prepared in their territory, it is not clear what wider bases of jurisdiction the Council envisages.

In requiring States to 'bring to justice' and 'deny safe haven' to terrorists, Resolution 1373 may simply be referring to a duty to extradite in relation to existing sectoral offences or other serious crimes. On the other hand, by referring specifically to 'terrorism' rather than to treaty offences, it may implicitly require the exercise of universal jurisdiction over 'terrorism' *per se*, despite not defining its scope. Indeed the CTC encouraged States to extend jurisdiction over domestic terrorism to cover international terrorism.[632] One CTC expert describes this 'unilateral' process as evidence of emergent universal jurisdiction over terrorism: 'that the State concerned considers these criminal acts to be of such gravity that they either threaten the peace, security and well-being of the world, that they constitute such atrocities that they deeply shock the conscience of humanity'.[633] Yet the process is more complex than a recognition by States that terrorism is universally punishable, in view of the Council's pressure to widen jurisdiction, and thus hasten the development of universal jurisdiction. It is difficult to accept universal jurisdiction over terrorism when States define it in radically different ways. Universal jurisdiction presupposes criminalization of common conduct, not widely divergent acts artificially compacted under the nominal umbrella of 'terrorism'. It is still too early to tell, however, whether the Council's 2004 definition of terrorism will gradually harmonize national definitions over time.

---

[631] R Scruton, *A Dictionary of Political Thought* (2nd edn, Macmillan, London, 1996) 546; J-M Sorel, 'Some Questions about the Definition of Terrorism and the Fight against its Financing' (2003) 14 AJIL 365, 371; Lambert, n 88, 18.
[632] Greenstock, n 390.
[633] W Gehr, 'Recurrent Issues: CTC Briefing for Member States', 4 Apr 2002.

F. CONCLUSION

Arguments that terrorism is a customary international crime are premature. Attempts in the General Assembly to define terrorism in the 1970s were unsuccessful, although the end of Cold War,[634] and the near completion of decolonization, allowed progress to be made. Whereas the communist bloc long regarded anti-terrorism efforts as an ideological excuse for anti-Sovietism,[635] by 1987 Gorbachev proposed that a UN tribunal be established to investigate terrorism,[636] and in 1994 Russia remarked that the end of the Cold War had opened up prospects for cooperation.[637] While political consensus was reached on a working definition of terrorism in 1994, disagreement over a national liberation exception hindered agreement on a binding prohibition.

In the Security Council, reference to specific acts or incidents of terrorism was common after 1985, and generalized references with legal consequences appeared after 2001. Yet terrorism has remained legally undefined in Council practice, despite a non-binding definition of late 2004. Most judicial decisions are silent on the international legal status of terrorism, and instead resolve disputes about terrorist-type conduct by recourse to existing legal norms, although some decisions invoke international definitions of terrorism for non-criminal law purposes. National definitions of terrorism, while gradually drifting towards generic definition, are still too divergent to support the existence of a customary international definition or crime of terrorism.

---

[634] M Flory, 'International Law: An Instrument to Combat Terrorism' in Higgins and Flory (eds), n 193, 30, 35; H Gasser, 'Acts of Terror, "Terrorism" and International Humanitarian Law' (2002) 84 IRRC 547, 549.

[635] I Blishchenko and N Zhdanov, *Terrorism and International Law* (Progress, Moscow, 1984) 44.

[636] J Quigley, 'Perestroika and International Law' (1988) 82 AJIL 788, 794.

[637] UNGAOR (49th Sess) (6th Committee), 13th mtg, 19 Oct 1994, para 11.

5

Terrorism in International Humanitarian Law

A. INTRODUCTION

It is commonly asserted that terrorism 'is not a discrete topic of international law with its own substantive legal norms', and is even 'a term without legal significance'.[1] Yet this orthodox position, expressed by two scholar-judges of the ICJ, has consistently overlooked the 'absolute and unconditional ban on terrorism' in armed conflict.[2] There is a long history of efforts to establish discrete concepts of terrorism in IHL, with specific and constitutive reference to the terms 'terrorism' and 'terror'. The omission of these efforts from the orthodox analysis is perhaps due to the specialized branch of law from which these efforts derive—IHL. Yet even in the specialist legal literature, little attention has been paid to these efforts.[3] This chapter examines the emergence of the prohibition on terrorism in armed conflict, grounded in the First and Second World Wars and the inter-war period, as well as in the modern law of Geneva, as developed through modern tribunals and national laws. It also articulates the distinctive features of, and purposes behind, these prohibitions.

B. EARLY DEVELOPMENTS 1919–38

At the end of the First World War, the Paris Peace Conference established a Commission on the Responsibility of the Authors of the War and on Enforcement of Penalties, to investigate violations of the laws and customs of

---

[1] R Higgins, 'The General International Law of Terrorism' in R Higgins and M Flory (eds), *Terrorism and International Law* (Routledge, London, 1997) 13–14 and 28; see also G Guillaume, 'Terrorism and International Law', Grotius Lecture, BIICL, London, 13 Nov 2003, 5.

[2] H Gasser, 'Prohibition of Terrorist Acts in International Humanitarian Law' (1986) No 253 IRRC 200.

[3] Key sources include: ibid; H Gasser, 'Acts of Terror, "Terrorism" and International Humanitarian Law' (2002) 84 IRRC 547; H Gasser, 'International Humanitarian Law, the Prohibition of Terrorist Acts, and the Fight against Terrorism' in IPA (ed), *Responding to Terrorism* (IPA, New York, 2002) 49; F Kalshoven, ' "Guerilla and "Terrorism" in Internal Armed Conflict' (1984) 33 AULR 67, 73–80; S Oeter, 'Means and Methods of Combat' in D Fleck (ed), *The Handbook of Humanitarian Law in Armed Conflicts* (OUP, Oxford, 2004) 105, 169–180; H Levie, *Terrorism in War: The Law of War Crimes* (Oceana, New York, 1993); J-M Henckaerts and L Doswald-Beck (eds), *Customary International Humanitarian Law* (CUP, Cambridge, 2004) vol I: *Rules*, 8–11; vol II: *Practice*, 67–78.

war by Germany and its allies.[4] In its 1919 report, the Commission identified 32 categories of war crimes, the first being 'Murders and massacres; systematic terrorism' of civilians.[5] Given its pre-eminent position in the list, it is evident that the Commission considered 'systematic terrorism' among the most serious of war crimes committed during the war,[6] although such a crime was not prosecuted at the ineffective Leipzig trials.[7]

The Commission also gave as an example of this crime the 'Massacres of Armenians by the Turks', in particular the 'More than 200,000 victims assassinated, burned alive, or drowned in the lake of Van, the Euphrates or the Black Sea'.[8] Attempts to establish a tribunal to prosecute this conduct as violations of 'the law of nations, as they result from the usages established among civilised peoples, from the laws of humanity, and the dictates of the public conscience' (reflecting the Martens clause in the preamble to the 1907 Hague Convention) were thwarted by US resistance.[9]

The concept of terrorism in armed conflict next arose at the 1922 Washington Conference on the Limitation of Armaments, which created a Commission of Jurists to consider legal responses to new methods of warfare since the 1907 Hague Conference, and specifically to prepare rules on aerial warfare.[10] The 1899 Hague Declaration and the succeeding 1907 Hague Declaration dealt largely with the use of balloons in warfare[11]—such as launching of projectiles or explosives—although the 1907 Declaration also referred to 'other new methods of a similar nature', which could include aircraft.[12] While binding, the 1907 Declaration was undermined by a lack of participation by major air powers, its temporariness, contrary State practice,

[4] UN War Crimes Commission, *History of the United Nations War Crimes Commission and the Development of the Laws of War* (HMSO, London, 1948) ch III; Commission on the Responsibility of the Authors of the War and on Enforcement of Penalties, Report to the Preliminary Peace Conference, 29 Mar 1919, in (1920) 14 AJIL 95, 113.

[5] UN War Crimes Commission, ibid, 34–35.

[6] In its report, the Commission asserted that the belligerents had executed a 'system of terrorism carefully planned and carried out to the end' and had 'deliberately sought to strike terror into every heart for the purpose of repressing all resistance': Commission on Responsibility, n 4, 113.

[7] *Galic* ICTY–98–29–T (5 Dec 2003) para 116; see also UN War Crimes Commission, n 4, 48–51; C Mullins, *The Leipzig Trials* (HF & G Witherby, London, 1921) 224.

[8] Commission on Responsibility, n 4, Annex II. The Armenian massacres had earlier been condemned by a Declaration of the Triple Entente as 'crimes against humanity and civilisation' on 24 May 1915.

[9] See MC Bassiouni, 'World War I: "The War to End All Wars" and the Birth of a Handicapped International Criminal Justice System' (2002) 30 Den JILP 244, 262–265. The US argued that the 1919 Commission exceeded its mandate to consider only war crimes; the Martens clause was too vague to establish liability; and there were no established procedures for a tribunal to apply.

[10] The Commission comprised representatives of the US, France, UK, Italy, Japan and the Netherlands.

[11] 1899 Hague Declaration 1; 1907 Hague Declaration (XIV).

[12] A Roberts and R Guelff, *Documents on the Laws of War* (3rd edn, OUP, Oxford, 2002) 139.

and the practical obsolescence of balloons.[13] Existing prohibitions on *wanton* destruction in war also did not cover deliberate or *purposive* terror bombing.[14] The 1907 Hague Regulations did, however, prohibit attacks on undefended locations 'by whatever means',[15] which was intended to cover aerial bombardment.

The Commission of Jurists produced the 1923 Hague Draft Rules of Aerial Warfare, Article 22 of which prohibited, *inter alia*: 'Aerial bombardment for the purpose of terrorizing the civilian population.'[16] The prohibition was also implied in the doctrine of the military objective,[17] and related to the prohibition in Article 24(3) on bombing military objectives if this would also result in the indiscriminate bombing of civilians.[18] The prohibition of terror bombing was also linked to prohibitions on using poisonous gases (in the Washington Convention) and chemicals (in the Hague Declaration), given the potential for terrorizing civilians using such weapons.[19]

The emergence of 'total war' and large-scale civilian suffering in the First World War, brought about by new technology (including aircraft),[20] was at the forefront of the Commission's decision to ban indiscriminate bombing of civilians: 'The conscience of mankind revolts against this form of making war in places outside the actual theater of military operations, and the feeling is universal that limitations must be imposed.'[21] Italy was among the first countries to order aerial bombardment of civilians, bombing Arab villages in the Turko-Italian war of 1911–12.[22] Britain used air power in policing its empire from the early 1920s, attacking tribal villages in Somaliland, Mesopotamia, the north-west frontier in India, Baluchistan, Palestine, South Arabia, and Southern Sudan.[23] Air 'frightfulness' was intended to undermine the morale of any resistance to British rule.[24] Such attacks were often justified as reprisals (preceded by warnings), rather than based on any legal right to

---

[13] ibid.

[14] W Royse, *Aerial Bombardment and the International Regulation of Warfare* (Harold Vinal, New York, 1928) 214.

[15] 1907 Hague Regulations Respecting the Laws and Customs of War on Land, Art 25.

[16] 1923 Hague Draft Rules Concerning the Control of Wireless Telegraphy in Time of War and Air Warfare (1923) 17 AJIL Supp 245; see also W Hall, *A Treatise on International Law* (8th edn, Clarendon, Oxford, 1924) 632.

[17] J Spaight, *Air Power and War Rights* (Longmans, Green & Co, London, 1924) 213.

[18] 1923 Hague Draft Rules, n 16, Art 24(3).

[19] Royse, n 14, 217–219.

[20] E Hobsbawm, *Age of Extremes* (Abacus, London, 1994) 28.

[21] Commission of Jurists to Consider and Report upon the Revision of the Rules of Warfare, General Report, Part II: Rules of Aerial Warfare (1938) 32 AJIL Supp 12, 22.

[22] Royse, n 14, 211.

[23] B Simpson, *Human Rights and the End of Empire: Britain and the Genesis of the European Convention* (OUP, Oxford, 2001) 71–74; see also D Omissi, *Air Power and Colonial Control: The Royal Airforce 1919–1939* (MUP, Manchester, 1990); C Bowyer, *RAF Operations 1918–1938* (W Kimber & Co, London, 1988); C Townshend, *Britain's Civil Wars: Counter-insurgency in the Twentieth Century* (Faber & Faber, London, 1986) 93–99.

[24] See sources quoted in Simpson, ibid, 72–73.

attack civilians or their property. They also invoked a theory of collective (tribal) responsibility for the acts of individuals.[25]

In the First World War, despite official denials, a number of belligerents used aerial bombing for its moral, political, or psychological effect, rather than for its military effect.[26] Germany 'employed aerial bombardment for psychological purposes, as openly stated by both Hindenburg and Ludendorf',[27] bombing European and Russian cities to terrorize and demoralize the enemy population and hasten victory.[28] German raids on England alone killed 1,413 persons and wounded 3,408, the majority being civilians.[29]

The Allies followed a similar policy, bombing 305 German cities from the air and causing mainly civilian casualties.[30] British raids in Germany 'spread terror and panic through widespread areas far outside the actual objective of the attack',[31] and bombing to demoralize enemy civilians was advocated by some British officers.[32] In 1917, Britain refused a Spanish initiative to develop restraints on aerial warfare.[33]

Given the rudimentary technology of aerial bombardment in the First World War, bombing in populated areas was inherently indiscriminate.[34] Officially, France claimed that it only bombed civilians in retaliation; Britain and Italy argued that they bombed only military objectives (and thus civilian casualties were incidental); and Germany presented both justifications, primarily bombing military targets but increasingly bombing in retaliation.[35] As one jurist put it: 'The right of general devastation for political or psychological ends . . . was not officially claimed by any of the belligerents in the late war.'[36] Only the exceptional doctrine of reprisal provided a legal basis on which to deliberately bomb civilian centres, or terrorize civilians.[37]

Thus, although aerial bombardment to terrorize civilians was practised by both sides during the First World War, *opinio juris* did not exist establishing a legal right to bomb for this purpose. As early as 1918, one writer argued that bombing 'for the purpose of terrorizing the population and not for a military object, is contrary to the universally recognised principles of the law of war'.[38] This view was shared by a leading authority in 1924, who argued further that intentionally bombing civilian objectives was an individual criminal breach of international law, and should also be banned as means of

---

[25] Simpson, ibid, 74.   [26] Spaight, n 17, 5, 16,   [27] Royse, n 14, 214.
[28] ibid, 175–183; Spaight, n 17, 9–10; Hall, n 16, 631.
[29] Royse, n 14, 181.   [30] ibid, 183–184.   [31] Spaight, n 17, 11; 10–12.
[32] F Taylor, *Dresden: Tuesday 13 Feb 1945* (Bloomsbury, London, 2004) 84–85.
[33] D Watt, 'Restraints on War in the Air before 1945' in M Howard (ed), *Restraints on War* (OUP, Oxford, 1979) 57, 63.
[34] Royse, n 14, 185–187; Spaight, n 17, 17.
[35] Royse, n 14, 189–190; Spaight, n 17, 198–201.   [36] Royse, n 14, 192.
[37] Spaight, n 17, 42–44; H Lauterpacht (ed), *Oppenheim's International Law: vol II* (8th edn, Longmans, Green and Co, London, 1955) 525.
[38] F Smith, *International Law* (5th edn, JM Dent and Sons, London, 1918) 214.

reprisal.[39] By late in the war, 'The demand for some international agreement banning aerial bombardment of cities outside the war zone made itself heard with growing voice' in German parliaments.[40]

The Commission on Responsibilities was conscious that 'the aircraft is a potent engine of war' for States, which cannot risk fettering their 'liberty of action' in legitimately and effectively attacking an enemy.[41] The Commission had great difficulty agreeing on legitimate objects of attack,[42] which partly accounts for the refusal of States to adopt the 1923 Hague Draft Rules as a treaty. In contrast, the Commission had 'no difficulty' agreeing 'that there are certain purposes for which aerial bombardment is inadmissible',[43] including terrorizing civilians.

The Commission's report was not endorsed by States, some of which actively opposed its acceptance, and the 1923 Hague Draft Rules were never adopted as a treaty.[44] Some States did not want to fetter their freedom of action to bomb civilians if necessary. In 1926, the US Air Service Tactical School stated that 'bombardment is an efficient weapon to . . . weaken the morale of the enemy people by attacks on centers of population', though only in reprisal.[45] France expressed similar sentiments.[46] Bombing to demoralize civilians continued after the war, with British air action over Somaliland in 1919, and bombing civilians was a policing method in the colonies.[47] The Italian, Giulio Douhet, explicitly advocated deliberately targeting civilians.[48]

Nevertheless, the 1923 Hague Draft Rules have come to be regarded as 'an authoritative attempt to clarify and formulate rules of law governing the use of aircraft in war'.[49] They carried the authority of the eminent jurists who drafted them;[50] many of the rules reflected existing customary rules and principles;[51] and others were transposed from existing maritime and land warfare rules.[52] The rules affected subsequent State practice[53] and soon gained acceptance by those States which declared that they would comply with them.[54] Courts have also taken notice—in *Shimoda*, a case about the use of atomic weapons against Japan, the Tokyo District Court treated the 1923 Hague Draft Rules as equivalent to a binding treaty.[55]

---

[39] Spaight, n 17, 19, 30, 44–46; see also Royse, n 14, 193.   [40] Spaight, ibid, 10–11.
[41] Commission of Jurists, n 21, 22; see also Royse, n 14, 193.
[42] Commission of Jurists, ibid.   [43] ibid, 23.
[44] Roberts and Guelff, n 12, 140 (the Netherlands, France and Britain).
[45] Quoted in Royse, n 14, 215.
[46] Royse, ibid, 214–215.   [47] Watt, n 33, 69.
[48] G Douhet, *The Command of the Air* (1921), cited in Taylor, n 32, 85–87.
[49] Lauterpacht, n 37, 519.
[50] J Spaight, *Air Power and War Rights* (3rd edn, Longmans, Green & Co, London, 1947) 42.
[51] Roberts and Guelff, n 12, 139.
[52] Spaight, n 17, 36; see also Lauterpacht, n 37, 520.
[53] Spaight, n 50, 42.   [54] Roberts and Guelff, n 10, 140.
[55] *Shimoda v Japan* (1964) Japanese Ann IL 212; R Falk, 'On the Quasi-Legislative Competence of the General Assembly' (1966) 60 AJIL 782, 783.

After 1923, inter-war efforts to create binding treaty norms on aerial bombardment came to nothing. Although one jurist proposed individual criminal liability for breaches,[56] this was never established. In 1936, Britain expressed interest in a treaty on air warfare, but the Second World War intervened.[57] Yet support for the 1923 Hague Draft Rules was expressed until the outbreak of war. In July 1932, a resolution of the General Commission of the Disarmament Conference stated that 'air attack against the civilian population shall be absolutely prohibited',[58] and similar statements were issued by the US and Japan.[59]

During the Spanish Civil War (1936–39), Picasso's *Guernica* (1937) famously depicted the terror of an aerial attack by Germany's Condor Legion, assisting Franco's Nationalists, on a neutral Basque village in Spain.[60] A League of Nations Council resolution of May 1937 condemned 'methods contrary to international law and the bombing of open towns' in Spain.[61] The Council did not, however, formally discuss the lawfulness of bombardments such as Guernica and efforts towards 'humanizing the war' through the Council were sometimes rebuffed.[62] Though condemned, aerial bombing was not declared a violation of international law by the League Council.[63]

In contrast, in June 1937, the 27 governments comprising the International Committee for Non-Intervention in Spain urged belligerents to 'abstain from the destruction of all open towns and villages . . . whether by bombardment from the air . . . or by any other means'.[64] In September of that year, US Secretary of State Hull stated that the general bombing of large civilian populations is contrary to international law and humanity.[65] Similarly, in 1938, the British Prime Minister condemned as unlawful any deliberate attack on civilian populations, in the aftermath of attacks by German and Italian air forces on civilians in Spain, and by Japanese air forces in China.[66] In March 1938, British Prime Minister Chamberlain protested the bombing of Barcelona, stating in Parliament:

---

[56] Spaight, n 17, 48.   [57] Watt, n 33, 72.

[58] LoN Doc 1932.IX.63, (1932) Docs 179, 268.

[59] Lauterpacht, n 37, 523.

[60] Taylor, n 32, 88–91. Two-thirds of the town was destroyed and one-third of its population killed or wounded (about 1,600 people).

[61] LoN Council, Resolution on the Spanish Appeal against Foreign Intervention, 29 May 1937, LoN [1937] OJ 333–334; see also statements in support by Britain, France and Sweden, above, 317–320.

[62] N Padelford, *Interrnational Law and Diplomacy in the Spanish Civil War* (Macmillan, New York, 1939) 129.

[63] ibid, 141.

[64] Appeal published in the *The Times* (London), 19 June 1937, quoted in Padelford, n 62, 95.

[65] Statement of 27 Sept 1937, cited in I Detter, *The Law of War* (2nd edn, CUP, Cambridge, 2000) 285.

[66] Lauterpacht, n 37, 523.

The one definite rule of international law, however, is that the direct and deliberate bombing of non-combatants is in all circumstances illegal . . . the bombardment of Barcelona, carried on apparently at random and without special aim at military objectives, was in fact of this nature.[67]

Further, in September 1938, the League of Nations Assembly adopted a unanimous resolution in response to the Spanish and the Sino-Japanese wars, stating:

. . . on numerous occasions public opinion has expressed through the most authoritative channels its horror of the bombing of civilian populations . . . [and] this practice, for which there is no military necessity and which, as experience shows, only causes needless suffering, is condemned under recognised principles of international law . . .[68]

The Assembly called on States to conclude an agreement on the issue and declared a series of principles to guide the adoption of any regulations:

1. The intentional bombing of civilian populations is illegal;
2. Objectives aimed at from the air must be legitimate military objectives and must be identifiable;
3. Any attack on legitimate military objectives must be carried out in such a way that civilian populations in the neighbourhood are not bombed through negligence.[69]

To this effect, the 1938 Amsterdam Draft Convention for the Protection of Civilian Populations against New Engines of War had repeated verbatim the relevant language of Article 22 of the 1923 Hague Draft Rules.[70] Overall, in the *Tadic* case the International Criminal Tribunal for the former Yugoslavia (ICTY) concluded that a prohibition of the intentional bombing of civilians was recognized during the Spanish war.[71] The prohibition was not, however, universally recognized; in a work on the Spanish war published in 1939, one jurist wrote simply that there were 'no universal or conventional rules of international law regarding aerial bombing even in time of international warfare'.[72] The only limits on such bombing were said to arise from the rules of State responsibility concerning damage to neutral foreign property.[73]

---

[67] 333 House of Commons Debates, col 1177 (23 Mar 1938); see also 337 House of Commons Debates, cols 937–938 (21 June 1938): 'it is against international law to bomb civilians as such and to make deliberate attacks upon civilian populations. That is undoubtedly a violation of international law. In the second place, targets which are aimed at from the air must be legitimate military objectives and must be capable of identification. In the third place, reasonable care must be taken in attacking those military objectives so that by carelessness a civilian population in the neighbourhood is not bombed.'

[68] LoN, [1938] OJ Spec Supp 183, 135–136.   [69] ibid.

[70] 1938 Amsterdam Draft Convention for the Protection of Civilian Populations against New Engines of War, Art 4, in D Schindler and J Toman, *The Laws of Armed Conflicts* (Martinus Nihjoff, Dordrecht, 1988) 223–229.

[71] *Tadic (Interlocutory Appeal)* ICTY–94–1 (2 Oct 1995) para 100.

[72] Padelford, n 62, 38.   [73] ibid, 39.

In addition to the Spanish conflict, in the late 1930s deliberate or indiscriminate aerial bombing of civilians was committed in a number of other conflicts. In Ethiopia (1935–36), Italy dropped tear gas and mustard gas from aircraft onto vast areas of territory, 'drenching not only soldiers but also women, children, cattle, rivers, lakes and pastures with this "deadly rain", systematically killing all living creatures'.[74] While the UN War Crimes Commission reluctantly agreed to consider 10 war crimes cases during this period,[75] Ethiopia faced political pressure from Britain to abandon prosecutions. Ethiopia pressed ahead against two leading suspects—Marshal Pietro Badoglio (commander of Italian forces in East Africa) and Marshal Rodolfo Graziani (Viceroy of Ethiopia)—but was unable to obtain custody. The Ethiopian War Crimes Commission and the Ethiopian government considered these suspects most responsible for the Italian policy of 'systematic terrorism' in Ethiopia, including by using poison gas and aiming to destroy the Amhara and Abyssinian peoples.[76] Following Japan's invasion of China (1937–39), in the *Tokyo Judgment* the International Military Tribunal for the Far East also found that, in July 1939, Japan adopted a policy of indiscriminate bombing to terrorize the Chinese.[77]

In the absence of a treaty on air warfare,[78] the 1923 Draft Rules were important evidence of a customary prohibition on terrorizing civilians. Given the paucity of case law, however, the caution expressed in 1928 is still valid: 'It remains for the future to determine the full meaning of terrorization as produced by aerial bombardment and to define more strictly the limitations to be placed upon such practices.'[79] The tactics of belligerents in that war sorely tested the normative pull of the 1923 Draft Rules.

C. THE SECOND WORLD WAR AND AFTERMATH 1939–48

1. State practice during the War

During the Second World War, the German air force inflicted large casualties on the civilian populations of major cities across Europe, the UK, and the Soviet Union.[80] Japanese bombing in Burma was designed to 'spread panic and alarm' among the civilian population.[81] British and US air forces attacked major German cities, often using incendiary devices and

---

[74] UN War Crimes Commission, n 4, 189.   [75] ibid, 483.

[76] See R Pankhurst, 'Italian Fascist War Crimes in Ethiopia: A History of Their Discussion, from the League of Nations to the United Nations (1936–1949)' (1999) 6 *Northeast African Studies* 83, 127–129.

[77] B Röling and C Rüter (eds), *The Tokyo Judgment:* vol I (University Press Amsterdam, Amsterdam, 1977) 394.

[78] Roberts and Guelff, n 12, 139.   [79] Royse, n 14, 220–221.

[80] R Overy, *Russia's War* (Allen Lane, London, 1998) 89.   [81] Spaight, n 50, 281.

delayed fuses to increase demoralization,[82] killing 300,000 civilians and injuring 780,000.[83] In Japan, the US firebombed Tokyo, killing 100,000 in March 1945, and used rudimentary (and thus indiscriminate) atomic weapons on Hiroshima and Nagasaki, killing 100,000 and injuring a further 100,000.[84]

There is substantial historical evidence that the Allies deliberately adopted a policy of 'terror bombing' against Germany and Japan, without individually assessing the military necessity of attacking particular targets, the proportionality of the means used, or the minimization of civilian casualties. During the war, the British government shifted its policy from 'precision' to 'area' bombing, raining inaccurate incendiary bombs on highly populated urban areas to undermine the morale of industrial and munitions workers.[85] In the view of Arthur Harris of British Bomber Command, 'air frightfulness'—which 'terrified German leaders' (not to mention the German people)—was necessary to win the war: 'In spite of all that happened at Hamburg, bombing proved a comparatively humane method . . . it saved the flower of the youth of this country and of our allies from being mown down by the military in the field.'[86] For Harris, causing terror to demoralize the enemy was the aim—not merely an unintended side-effect—of bombing policy.[87] Although he thought causing civilian casualties is 'specially wicked', 'all wars have caused casualties among civilians' and the blockade of Germany killed many more Germans (800,000) than aerial bombing (305,000).[88] Bombing was also considered the only effective weapon available.[89]

Similarly, US military documents suggest that the selection of Japanese targets for atomic attack was driven by the 'great importance' of 'obtaining the greatest psychological effect against Japan' and 'making the initial use sufficiently spectacular for the importance of the weapon to be internationally recognized'.[90] Any use of atomic weapons against a military objective was to be 'located in a much larger area subject to blast damage

---

[82] M Connelly, *Reaching for the Stars* (IB Tauris, London, 2001) 90, 99–120.

[83] M Walzer, *Just and Unjust Wars* (3rd edn, Basic Books, New York, 2000) 255. Other estimates are higher, with 593,000 German civilians killed: Detter, n 67, 285.

[84] J Glover, *Humanity* (Jonathan Cape, London, 1999) 102.

[85] A Harris, *Bomber Offensive* (Collins, London, 1947) 76–77, 82, 89; Glover, n 84, 69–88. cf the UK Air Council's official denial: 'widespread devastation is not an end in itself but the inevitable accompaniment of an all-out attack on the enemy's means and capacity to wage war': quoted in Connelly, n 82, 116.

[86] Harris, ibid, 176.   [87] Connelly, n 82, 115.

[88] Harris, n 85, 176–177; see also H Probert, *Bomber Harris* (Greenhill, London, 2001) 339–340; Glover, n 84, 77, 88.

[89] Harris, n 85, 112.

[90] Target Committee, Minutes of 2nd mtg, Los Alamos, 10–11 May 1945; US National Archives, Record Group 77, Records of the Office of the Chief of Engineers, Manhattan Engineer District, TS Manhattan Project File 42–46, folder 5D Selection of Targets, 2 Notes on Target Committee Meetings, point 7A.

in order to avoid undue risks of the weapon being lost'.[91] As Lauterpacht writes, the 'main object' of atomic weapons is 'to wreak havoc, terror and devastation among vast centres of population as a means of winning the war'.[92]

At first sight, the extensive use of 'terror bombing' by both sides suggests that the belligerents did not recognize any customary law prohibitions on aerial bombing to terrorize civilians. Indeed, 'the practice of indiscriminate bombardment challenged the application of the most fundamental principles developed in respect of air warfare'.[93] Harris believed that there was 'no international law at all' on air warfare, and reasoned analogously that it was common practice in war to besiege or bombard defended cities.[94]

Yet 'both Axis and Allies powers proclaimed their adherence to the 1923 Hague Draft Rules and made accusations of their violation'.[95] There is some state practice supporting a prohibition on terror bombing. On 1 September 1939, US President Roosevelt requested that Britain, France, Italy, Germany, and Poland declare that their 'armed forces shall in no event and under no circumstances undertake bombardment from the air of civilian populations or unfortified cities, upon the understanding that the same rules of warfare shall be scrupulously observed by all their opponents'.[96] An Anglo-French declaration of 2 September 1939 accepted these conditions, while Germany similarly stated that it would confine its attacks to military targets.[97] Germany characterized its air raids on London as reprisals for British raids on German cities,[98] implying that such raids were ordinarily unlawful but for the prior illegality of Britain. Britain also claimed to be acting out of reprisal, or revenge.[99]

In domestic debates, senior British officials expressed reservations about the lawfulness (and morality) of terror bombing.[100] In the House of Lords in 1944, Bishop Bell of Chichester stated that the 'progressive devastation of cities is threatening the roots of civilization'.[101] The perceived illegality of terror bombing was also implied by the German response to Allied raids. Goering alleged that Hitler demanded the lynching of Allied 'terror fliers', while Himmler and Kaltenbrunner ordered police and security forces not to interfere.[102] Even the High Command of the German Army ordered the

---

[91] ibid, point 8A.   [92] Lauterpacht, n 37, 349.
[93] Roberts and Guelff, n 12, 141.   [94] Harris, n 85, 177.
[95] ibid, 140.   [96] Quoted in Spaight, n 50, 259.
[97] Spaight, ibid, 259–260; Lauterpacht, n 37, 527–528.
[98] Spaight, ibid, 48.
[99] Walzer, n 83, 256–257.   [100] ibid, 257.
[101] Quoted in Glover, n 84, 87.
[102] *Nuremberg Judgment*, International Military Tribunal, 1 Oct 1946 (1947) 41 AJIL 172, 313, and Spaight, n 50, 61 respectively.

military not to prevent civilian lynchings of 'terror flyers'.[103] There was a persistent post-war German view that defeat was due to Allied 'terror fliers'.[104] Captured US 'terror fliers' were also lynched by civilians in Japan and by Japanese military personnel in the Pacific.[105]

According to Spaight, area bombing was not unlawful if it was the only means of destroying the enemy's armament and munitions centres (often indistinguishable from worker housing), passed the test of military effectiveness, and there was no 'direct intent' to injure innocent civilians (other than incidental casualties).[106] Area bombing also ended the horrors of the concentration camps sooner, possibly saved two million Allied combat casualties, and was publicly popular.[107] The same author condemned atomic bombing as unlawful because it did not aim at military objectives, but disproportionately attacked whole cities without exhausting other means.[108]

At a minimum, the terror bombing campaigns of the Second World War sorely tested the existence of any customary restraints on terrorizing civilians from the air, reducing 'to the vanishing point the protection of the civilian population from aerial bombardment'.[109] No defendant was charged at Nuremberg with indiscriminate bombing of civilians,[110] probably because the victors feared being accused of double standards. The US Military Tribunal at Nuremberg incidentally observed in the *Einsatzgruppen* case that the Allied bombing of German cities was merely a response to German raids; that cities were bombed for tactical military purposes with only collateral civilian casualities; and that atomic bombs aimed to overcome military resistance and not to kill non-combatants.[111] For Lauterpacht, aerial bombing of cities obliterated the distinction between combatants and non-combatants in conflict.[112]

Writers have noted that: 'To the extent that such practices continue, the significance of certain principles embodied in the 1923 Hague Draft Rules will be called into greater question.'[113] Soon after the Second World War, Britain continued to use air power in colonial policing in Malaya (1952), Kenya (1952–56), and Southern Arabia (in the 1950s),[114] although targeting

---

[103] Levie, n 3, 313. There were a number of post-war US military trials for such lynchings, including *Erich Heyer* (*Essen Lynching* case), UNWCC Law Reports, vol I (HMSO, London, 1947) 88; *Wilhem von Leeb* (*German High Command* case), UNWCC Law Reports, vol XII, 1; see also the cases of *Albrecht*, *Borkum Island* case, *Goetz, Schmidt, Kohn, Back*, the *Justice* case, the *Ministries* case: all summarized in Levie, above, 314–318; *Bury* and *Hafner*, UNWCC Law Reports, vol III (HMSO, London, 1947) 62.

[104] Spaight, n 50, 48.

[105] See, eg, *Nisuke Masuda* (*Jaluit Atoll* case), UNWCC Law Reports, vol I (HMSO, London, 1947), 71; *Noburu Seki* case, in Levie, n 3, 318.

[106] Spaight, n 50, 271–272 (munitions workers were also not regarded as 'innocent').

[107] ibid.   [108] ibid, 274.   [109] Lauterpacht, n 37, 529.

[110] ibid, 529–530; UNWCC Law Reports, vol XV, (HMSO, London, 1949) 110.

[111] *Einsatzgruppen* case *(Ohlendorf and others)* (1953) 15 Ann Dig 656.

[112] Lauterpacht, n 37, 207, 350, 527.   [113] Roberts and Guelff, n 12, 141.

[114] Simpson, n 23, 74.

gradually became more discriminating and less directed against civilians. There are certainly egregious examples since the Second World War of States failing to comply with the prohibition on terror bombing. US 'carpet bomb- ing' in the Viet Nam War (and in Cambodia) in the 1960s and 1970s is one notorious example;[115] so too is the strafing and bombing of southern Sudanese villages by the northern Arab government in the 1980s and 1990s.

Yet these are relatively isolated examples in overall State practice since the Second World War—and examples which have been recognized as unlawful when they occurred. Most States have accepted a prohibition on deliberate air bombardment 'for the purpose of instilling terror',[116] including in civil wars; as early as 1964, the Prime Minister of the Democratic Republic of the Congo declared: 'For humanitarian reasons, and with a view to reassuring . . . the civilian population which might fear that it is in danger . . . the Congo- lese Air Force will limit its action to military objectives'.[117] Despite the absence of a specific international agreement on air warfare, the increasingly detailed treaty regulation of armed conflict since the Second World War supplies general principles applicable to air action—including principles of distinction, military necessity, proportionality, humanity, and limits on means and methods of war.[118] Indiscriminate area bombardment of popu- lated civilian areas is ruled out in both international and non-international armed conflicts under treaty and customary law, and is forbidden by numer- ous military manuals.[119]

2. *Legal efforts to confront terrorism during the War*

Despite the frequent practice of terror bombing during the war, post-war international criminal trials did not attempt to prosecute individuals for such conduct. Nonetheless, the concept of terrorism occasionally appeared in Allied efforts to respond to war atrocities. On 25 October 1941, US President Roosevelt stated in London: 'The Nazis might have learned from the last war the impossibility of breaking men's spirit by terrorism. Instead, they develop their lebensraum and new order by depths of frightfulness which even they have never approached before . . . Frightfulness can never bring peace to Europe.'[120] In 1942, nine European States issued a declaration on the

---

[115] Detter, n 65, 285.   [116] Lauterpacht, n 37, 526.

[117] Quoted in *Tadic (Interlocutory)*, n 71, para 105.

[118] See generally J Guisández Gómez, 'The Law of Air Warfare' (1998) 323 IRRC 347. 1977 Protocol I, Art 51 forbids indiscriminate attacks or bombardment 'by any method or means' and incidental casualties are prohibited unless outweighed by concrete and direct military advantage.

[119] See Protocol I, Art 51(5)(a); Protocol II, Art 13(2); Amended Protocol II to the Convention on Certain Conventional Weapons, Art 3(9); ICRC Study, n 3, vol I, 43–45.

[120] Punishment for War Crimes: The Inter-Allied Declaration, St James's Palace, London, 13 Jan 1942 and Relative Documents (HMSO, Inter-Allied Information Committee), 15; in UN War Crimes Commission, n 4, 88.

punishment of German war crimes, alleging that Germany had 'instituted in the occupied territories a regime of terror characterized ... by imprisonments, mass expulsions, the execution of hostages and massacres'.[121] The Moscow Declaration by Stalin, Churchill and Roosevelt on 1 November 1943 noted that under Hitler, Germany and occupied Europe 'suffered from the worst form of government by terror'.[122] These usages of 'terror' and 'terrorism' were, however, descriptive, rhetorical, and political, rather than legal.

In 1942–43, the quasi-governmental London International Assembly (LIA) examined legal responsibility for war crimes during the war, including the establishment of an international criminal tribunal.[123] The LIA based its work on the list of war crimes drawn up by the 1919 Commission on Responsibilities. In its final draft of October 1943, the LIA proposed jurisdiction over the crime of 'systematic terrorism',[124] which had appeared in the 1919 list, where committed by heads of State, or in several countries, or against the nationals of several countries.[125] Apart from keeping the issue of responsibility for war crimes alive during the war, the LIA did not have much wider influence on the course of post-war prosecutions.

The 1919 list of war crimes, however, continued to prove durable, being adopted as a working instrument of the UN War Crimes Commission in December 1943—including the foremost crime of 'Murder and massacres—systematic terrorism'—although the list did not exhaustively enumerate all violations of the laws and customs of war.[126] In May 1944, the Legal Committee recommended adopting the further crime of 'Indiscriminate mass arrests for the purpose of terrorising the population, whether described as taking of hostages or not'.[127]

The official history states that this crime was duly added to the 1919 list, although the appendix which reproduces the amended list of 2 December 1943 only includes the additional crime of 'Indiscriminate mass arrests'.[128] The qualifying phrase ('for the purpose of terrorising the population ...') was omitted—apparently widening the offence by eliminating the purposive requirement—though the qualifying element was intended in the drafting.

---

[121] 1942 Declaration of the Inter-Allied Commission on the Punishment of War Crimes (Belgium, Czechoslovakia, France, Greece, Luxembourg, Norway, the Netherlands, Poland, and Yugoslavia), in UN War Crimes Commission, n 120, 90. The same States referred to the 'invader's acts of oppression in terrorism' in a note of July 1942 to the British Government: Punishment for War Crimes: Collective Notes to Great Britain, the USSR and the USA and Relative Correspondence, in UN War Crimes Commission, above, 93.

[122] Quoted in UN War Crimes Commission, n 121, 107.

[123] The LIA was an unofficial body under the auspices of the League of Nations Union, although its members were designated by Allied governments, to which they reported: UN War Crimes Commission, n 121, 99. In 1942, the proceedings of the 1937 League of Nations Terrorism Conference were drawn to the attention of the LIA: above, 102.

[124] ibid, 100.   [125] ibid, 103.   [126] ibid, 171, 477–478.   [127] ibid, 172.

[128] ibid, 172 and 478 respectively.

After its investigation of war atrocities, on 16 May 1945 the UN War Crimes Commission recommended the seeking out of 'the leading criminals responsible for the organisation of criminal enterprises including *systematic terrorism*, planned looting and the general policy of atrocities against the peoples of the occupied States, in order to punish all the organisers of such crimes.'[129] In its approach to atrocities, the UN War Crimes Commission squarely regarded 'systematic terrorism' as an international legal concept, although the Commission's mandate was primarily investigative, rather than judicial or prosecutorial.

3. *1945 Nuremberg Charter*

The foremost judicial attempt to address atrocities involved the drafting of the Nuremberg Charter. In a preparatory report of June 1945, US Justice Jackson had descriptively referred to terrorism in accusing the Nazi leadership, the SS, and Gestapo of establishing themselves in Germany 'by terrorism and crime'.[130] On 20 July 1945, at the International Conference on Military Trials in London, the UK proposed that a post-war international military tribunal should, *inter alia*, try 'Systematic atrocities against or systematic terrorism or ill-treatment or murder of civilians'.[131] The proposal derived from the 1919 notion of 'systematic terrorism'.[132]

No explanation of 'terrorism' accompanied the British proposal; there is no recorded discussion of its meaning; and it was not referred to in earlier or later drafts. In contrast, the crimes of atrocities, ill-treatment, and murder in the UK proposal were subsumed by the category of 'crimes against humanity' in the Charter.[133] Although the USSR drew the 1937 League of Nations Convention on terrorism (signed by the USSR eight years earlier) to the attention of the International Conference,[134] the Conference did not see fit to include its terrorism offences in the Nuremberg Charter.

The idea of terrorism did, however, cross-cut other categories of crime discussed at the International Conference. Nazi terrorism was viewed by the US and the UK as *evidence* of the common criminal plan or conspiracy

[129] ibid, 43 (emphasis added).
[130] R Jackson, Report to the US President on Atrocities and War Crimes, 7 June 1945.
[131] UK Proposed Revision of Definition of 'Crimes', 20 July 1945, draft Art 6(2), in Report of R Jackson, International Conference on Military Trials, London, 1945; International Organization and Conference Series; II European and British Commonwealth 1; Dept State Pub 3080 (GPO, Washington, DC, 1949) 312.
[132] *Galic*, n 7, para 117.
[133] Agreement for the Prosecution and Punishment of the Major War Criminals of the European Axis, London, 8 Aug 1945, annexed Charter of an International Military Tribunal at Nuremberg, Art 6(c). In *Galic*, n 7, the ICTY suggests that the terrorism proposal was subsumed by the later notion of 'atrocities' and the subsequent category of war crimes.
[134] Minutes of International Conference on Military Trials: London, 2 July 1945 (Nikitchenko).

of preparing, launching, and waging an aggressive war, including by eliminating domestic dissent.[135] While 'terrorism' was rejected as a distinct crime, it underlay some of the thinking about the content, and proof, of aggression and crimes against humanity.

4. Nuremberg International Military Tribunal

Although terrorism was not established as a discrete crime in the Nuremberg Charter, numerous references to terrorism appear in the Nuremberg Indictment and Judgment. The 22 volumes of transcripts of the proceedings are littered with the term and its variants. These many references are typically used to describe Nazi activities, rather than as legal terms of art (or liability), although the 1919 crime of 'systematic terrorism' was cited in a discussion of the historical development of war crimes.[136]

In the Indictment, in alleging the particulars of a common plan or conspiracy to wage aggressive war, the Nazi use of 'terrorism' was asserted to be a first step in acquiring totalitarian control of Germany.[137] The establishment and extension of a 'system of terror' allegedly consolidated Nazi control over Germany.[138] Crimes of murder and ill-treatment of civilians were allegedly committed 'for the purpose of systematically terrorizing the inhabitants' of occupied territories, including a 'premeditated campaign of terrorism' in Denmark and a 'program of terror'.[139] The prosecution clearly believed that 'terrorism' was relevant for evidentiary purposes in proving criminal charges, notwithstanding that terrorism was not an offence. The concept of terrorism in the Indictment refers to indiscriminate attacks on civilians, intended to put them in grave fear, and thereby to subdue resistance to Nazi rule.

In the Nuremberg Judgment, frequent reference was made to Nazi terrorism.[140] In relation to war crimes and crimes against humanity

---

[135] US Revised Draft Agreement and Memorandum, 30 June 1945 (terrorism was a manifestation of the master plan to attack international peace); US Memorandum, San Francisco, 30 Apr 1945: II(a) and (c); Memorandum to US President Roosevelt from the Secretaries of State and War and the Att-Gen, 22 Jan 1945, III; UK Illustrative Draft of Indictment, 17 July 1945; R Jackson, Reports to the US President, 6 June 1945 and 7 Oct 1946, point (6); Minutes of Conference Sessions, 29 June 1945 (Jackson) and 23 July 1945 (Maxwell Fyfe and Jackson); Planning Memorandum to Delegations at London Conference, June 1945, IV: Outlines of Proof: 6(a)(2).
[136] Trial of German Major War Criminals, Nuremberg, 7–19 Jan 1946, 36th day, 17 Jan 1946, Part 8, 370.
[137] Nuremberg Indictment, count 1: IV. Particulars of the Nature and Development of the Common Plan or Conspiracy: (D) The Acquiring of Totalitarian Control of Germany: Political: 1. First steps in acquisition of control of State machinery; see also *Nuremberg Judgment*, n 103, 222.
[138] Nuremberg Indictment, count 1, ibid: 3. Consolidation of control: (b).
[139] ibid, count 3: (A) Murder and Ill-Treatment of Civilian Populations of or in Occupied Territory and on the High Seas.
[140] Lauterpacht, n 37, 576, also mentions German 'terror' in the Second World War.

(particularly murder and ill-treatment of civilians), the Judgment describes the Nazi dictatorship in Germany and occupied Europe as founded on a 'reign of terror'; the 'systematic rule of . . . terror'; 'methods of terror'; the 'organized use of terror' (through killing hostages, destroying towns, and massacring civilians); and 'terrorizing' civilians'.[141] The Judgment also describes a pre-war 'policy of terror' in Germany 'carried out on a vast scale . . . [which] was organized and systematic'.[142]

In discussing Nazi organizations, the Nuremberg Judgment found that the SS was created to 'terrorise political opponents', while the SA 'played an important role in establishing a Nazi reign of terror in Germany'.[143] The use of concentration camps is described as: 'One of the most notorious means of terrorising the people in occupied territories.'[144] The Judgment quotes Nazi documents specifically ordering the military to spread 'terror' or 'terrorism' to eradicate civilian resistance.[145] The Judgment also attributes responsibility for 'terror' or 'terrorism' against civilian populations to a number of defendants, indicating that terrorist methods included the indiscriminate shooting of civilians and hostages, deportation of labour, use of concentration camps, mass killings of Jews, and stripping occupied territories of food and materials.[146]

Linguistically, most of the uses of terms such as terror, terrorism, and terrorist in the Judgment are descriptive or evaluative, in the same way that the Judgment applies terms such as 'horror' or 'cruelty' to Nazi activities.[147] They were not, however, used as legal terms to trigger criminal liability. Some of the physical acts causing terror in civilians were themselves crimes under the Charter, while conversely evidence of terrorism helped to prove the commission of Charter crimes.

The only tenuously *legal* notion of terrorism emerging from the Nuremberg Judgment is in reference to Nazi (national) law. For example, a Gestapo order of 12 June 1942 authorized the use of 'third degree' interrogation methods on 'Communists, Marxists, Jehovah's witnesses, saboteurs, *terrorists*, members of resistance movements, parachute agents, anti-social elements, Polish or Russian loafers or tramps'.[148] The Security Police and the SD executed without trial persons charged as terrorists and saboteurs.[149] In July 1944 Hitler also ordered that resistance to German occupation should be combated as 'acts of terror and of sabotage'.[150] 'Terror' and terrorism in these senses referred to political opponents of, or militant resistance to, German

[141] *Nuremberg Judgment*, n 103, 289, 229, 182, 231, 231 respectively.
[142] ibid, 249.   [143] ibid, 177 and 267 respectively.
[144] ibid, 231.   [145] ibid, 232, 283 (defendant Keitel).
[146] ibid, 289–290 (Frank in Poland); 293 (Frick in Bohemia and Moravia); 319 (Seyss-Inquart in the Netherlands); 288 (Rosenberg in the Eastern Occupied Territories).
[147] ibid, 224, 249.   [148] ibid, 230 (emphasis added).   [149] ibid, 260.
[150] Terrorist and Sabotage Decree, 30 July 1944: see *High Command* case; Levie, n 3, 318–319.

occupation; thus one Nazi commander described the Jewish uprising in the Warsaw ghetto as the work of 'Polish terrorists'.[151] Members of the French resistance were also shot by the Germans as 'terrorists'.[152]

5. National post-war trials

In the *Hostages* case, the US Military Tribunal at Nuremberg used the term 'terrorism' in similar ways to the International Tribunal. In the Indictment, German defendants allegedly 'terrorized, tortured and murdered' non-combatants in Greece, Yugoslavia and Albania in retaliation for attacks on German forces.[153] These 'acts of collective punishment' were described as 'part of a deliberate scheme of terror and intimidation ... in flagrant violation of the laws and customs of war'.[154] Executing hostages was the primary means of implementing a 'scheme of terror and intimidation' or 'pacification-through-terror scheme'.[155] The defendants were charged with war crimes and crimes against humanity under Article II of Control Council Law No 10, by 'the murder, torture, and systematic terrorization ... of the civilian populations',[156] and prosecutors frequently referred to terrorism in argument.

In its Judgment, the US Military Tribunal chiefly used 'terrorism' in descriptive rather than legal senses. It warned that shooting innocent civilians in reprisal 'can progressively degenerate into a reign of terror', and noted three times that 'terrorism and intimidation' were used to subjugate opposition. The Judgment concedes that the defendants protested against the 'plan of terrorism and intimidation', but notes that they were continually advised by subordinate units of 'the policy of terrorism and intimidation' carried out in the field. There is no discussion, however, of any distinct crime of terrorism in the Judgment, despite the charge being laid.

Terrorism was only referred to as a legal concept in the US Military Tribunal at Nuremberg in the cases of *Becker* and *Weber*. The defendants were convicted of the French crime of illegal arrests and the Tribunal incidentally observed that indiscriminate mass arrests may constitute 'systematic terrorism' where they are committed repeatedly and as part of a deliberate pattern.[157] The Tribunal expressly invoked the linkage between indiscriminate mass arrests and systematic terrorism in the UN War Crimes Commission's

---

[151] Stroop Report, 'The Warsaw Ghetto is No More', Nazi Conspiracy and Aggression, vol 3 Doc 1061–PS.

[152] *Holstein*, UNWCC Law Reports, vol VIII, 22, 26.

[153] *List and others* (*Hostages* case), US Military Tribunal at Nuremberg, 19 Feb 1948 (1953) 15 Ann Dig 632, indictment, count 1(2).

[154] ibid, count 1(3); see also count 1(4).

[155] ibid, counts 1(4) and 2(8), 3(12)(c) respectively.

[156] ibid, count 4(14).

[157] *Becker* and *Weber*, UNWCC Law Reports, vol VII (HMSO, London, 1948) 67, 68–69.

1944 list of war crimes.[158] Criminal liability in these cases did not, however, turn on the concept of 'systematic terrorism'.[159]

As in many post-war US trials,[160] the term terrorism was also used descriptively in the trial of the Nazi leader Adolf Eichmann in Israel, following his abduction from Argentina. The court found that Eichmann had used threats of terror to force the emigration of Jews from Vienna, Prague, and Berlin, including threats to send them to concentration camps.[161] The policy of forced emigration constituted a crime against humanity and 'terror' served a descriptive or evidentiary, but non-legal, purpose.

In contrast, the concept of 'systematic terrorism'—stemming from the 1919 Commission, the proposals of the London International Assembly in 1943 and the UN War Crimes Commission in 1945, and the draft British proposal of 1945—produced a small number of post-war prosecutions in other tribunals. First, the former Governor of Crete, General Bruno Brauer, was charged with 'systematic terrorism' before a Greek military court in Athens, for the deaths of 3,000 persons in Crete under German occupation.[162] The defendant was sentenced to death in December 1946 and shot in May 1947, although other charges contributing to this sentence included murders and massacres, deportations, pillage, wanton destruction, torture, and ill-treatment of civilians.[163]

Second, a court martial in the Netherlands East Indies, established to prosecute Japanese war crimes in the region, had jurisdiction based on the war crimes specified by the 1919 Commission and the 1944 Commission, including over '[s]ystematische terreur', which was listed as a crime separate from 'murder and massacres' (unlike in the 1919 list).[164] In the *Motomura* case of 1947, 13 of 15 defendants were convicted of 'systematic terrorism practiced against civilians', achieved through (a) indiscriminate mass arrests for the purpose of terrorizing the population; and (b) the torture and

---

[158] See text to nn 127–128.

[159] Similarly, in *Buhler* the US Military Tribunal described various German orders in Poland as 'systematic terrorism': *Buhler*, UNWCC Law Reports, vol XIV (HMSO, London, 1949) 23, 28.

[160] *Krauch (IG Farben)*, UNWCC Law Reports, vol X, 1, 5 (accused terrorized slave labourers); *Krupp*, UNWCC Law Reports, vol X, 69, 74 (civilians 'terrorised' into working for Krupp industries); *Zuehlke*, UNWCC Law Reports, vol XIV, 139, 140 (Jewish prisoners terrorized by warder); *Greisner*, UNWCC Law Reports, vol XIII, 73 (Polish population persecuted by being kept in constant fear).

[161] *Att-Gen of the Government of Israel v Eichmann* (1961) 36 ILR 5 (Dist Ct Jerusalem), para 185; see also para 62 (Austrian Jews lived in an 'atmosphere of terror' following Hitler's entry into Vienna) and para 64 (Jews were robbed of capital by 'terrorist measures').

[162] Cited in UN War Crimes Commission, n 4, 525.

[163] ibid.

[164] Decree No 44 (1946), in *Staatsblad van Nederlandsch-Indië*, 1946, Art 1(2); see also UNWCC Law Reports, vol XI, annex, 93. The decree also added the offence identified by the UNWCC of 'Indiscriminate mass arrests for the purpose of terrorising the population': see text to nn 127–128.

ill-treatment of civilian internees.[165] Mass arrests terrorized the population because 'nobody, even the most innocent, was any longer certain of his liberty, and a person once arrested, even if absolutely innocent, could no longer be sure of health and life'.[166] Torture was also a particular form of terrorism because it was systematically applied and involved 'psychological and physical compulsion paralysing the resistance of the persons under interrogation ... who were entirely innocent'.[167]

A third prosecution took place before the Supreme National Tribunal of Poland in June and July 1948. In the *Joseph Buhler* case, the Deputy-Governor of German-occupied Poland was charged with being part of a government that ordered 'systematic terrorism' against the population.[168] On conviction, Buhler was sentenced to death. Until 2003, these cases were the only recorded prosecutions for the crime of terrorism in armed conflict.[169]

Other attempts to prosecute for terrorism were less successful. In August 1944, the French authorities sent a statement of charges to the UN War Crimes Commission alleging that a Gestapo leader in Lyon, Klaus Barbie, had committed 'murder and massacres, systematic terrorism, and execution of hostages'.[170] Barbie eluded capture by fleeing to South America and was convicted *in absentia* of war crimes by the Lyon military tribunal in 1952 and 1954.[171] Following his expulsion to France, he was convicted of crimes against humanity in 1985, but not of war crimes.[172] The crime of terrorism was not charged in any of these proceedings.

---

[165] *Trial of Shigeki Motomura and 15 Others*, UNWCC Law Reports, vol XIII, (HMSO, London, 1949) 138, 140, 143–144. Seven defendants were sentenced to death and the remainder imprisoned for between one and 20 years. The indictment alleged the following conduct: 'systematic terrorism taking the form of repeated, regular and lengthy torture and/or ill-treatment, the seizing of men and women on the grounds of wild rumours, repeatedly striking them with the hand and with sticks during their interrogation, kicking them with the shod foot, hanging them up by the arm or leg, burning them with glowing cigarettes and bicycle bells, wrenching their knee joints apart, stripping women and exposing them in this condition to the public view, withholding food from arrestees ... the aforesaid acts having led or at least contributed to the death, severe physical and mental suffering of many'.
[166] ibid, 143.   [167] ibid, 144.
[168] In Levie, n 3, 124–125.   [169] *Galic*, n 7, para 66.
[170] UN Archives: UNWCC Charge Files 192/FR/G/40 and 184/Fr/G/42.
[171] See Judgment of 6 Oct 1983, Cass crim, 1984 DS Jur 113, GP Nos 352–54 (18–20 Dec 1983), 1983 JCP II G, No 20 107, JDI 770 (1983).
[172] *Klaus Barbie* (20 Dec 1985), 78 ILR 136; upheld on Appeal, Court of Cassation: (3 June 1988), ILR 332 and 336. Gaz Pal 1988, II, 745; see generally L Wexler, 'The Interpretation of the Nuremberg Principles by the French Court of Cassation: From Touvier to Barbie and Back Again' (1995) 32 Col JTL 289; J-O Viout, 'The Klaus Barbie Trial and Crimes against Humanity' (1999) 3 *Hofstra Law and Policy Symposium* 155; N Doman and R Nicholas, 'Aftermath of Nuremberg: The Trial of Klaus Barbie' (1989) 60 *Colorado Law Review* 449; G Binder, 'Representing Nazism: Advocacy and Identity at the Trial of Klaus Barbie' (1989) 98 *Yale Law Journal* 1321.

D. 1949 GENEVA CONVENTIONS AND 1977 PROTOCOLS

The repeated references to terrorism in the context of war crimes suggest that freedom from terror was historically considered an international value worthy of protection. Another operative legal reference to terrorism in the immediate post-war period is found in the 1946 Constitution of the International Refugee Organization (IRO), which excluded from the IRO's mandate persons who had 'participated in any terrorist organization' since the end of the Second World War[173]—such as Zionist IRGUN members in Palestine[174]—but the exclusion did not apply to wartime 'terrorism'. While the British authorities in the mandate territory of Palestine were attacked by Jewish 'terrorist' groups in the 1940s (such as Irgun Tsvai Leumi and the Stern Gang or 'Lehi'),[175] Britain responded using broad emergency powers and the criminal law,[176] without usually creating special legal categories or liabilities for 'terrorism' or 'terrorists'. One exception is in the definition of an 'unlawful association' in regulation 84 of the *Defence (Emergency) Regulations* 1945, which included any body of persons which advocates, incites, or encourages 'acts of terrorism' against servants of the UK or Palestine government, or against the UK High Commissioner. The substance of those regulations continued to be used by the new Israeli State after independence

---

[173] 1946 Constitution of the International Refugee Organization (18 UNTS 3, adopted by UNGA Resolution 77 of 15 Dec 1946, entered into force 20 Aug 1948), Annex I, Part II, Art 6(a).

[174] IRO, *Manual for Eligibility Officers* (IP, Geneva, 1950) 39(1), para 42, Case No Geneva 4495.

[175] eg Lehi (Lohamei Herut Israel or 'Fighters for the Freedom of Israel') assassinated Lord Moyne in Cairo in 1944 and the UN mediator Count Bernadotte in 1948 (some suspects received amnesties in 1949 and two enjoyed a State funeral in 1975); Lehi and Irgun killed more than 100 Arab villagers at Deir Yassin in 1948; Irgun bombed the British military and civilian headquarters at the King David Hotel in Jerusalem in 1946, killing 91 people (mainly civilians); see RIIA, *Great Britain and Palestine 1915–1945* (RIIA, London, 1946) 138–139; *Hansard*, House of Commons, 6 Dec 1944, cols 557–561; J Bowyer Bell, *Terror Out of Zion: Irgun Zvai Leumi, Lehi and the Palestine Underground 1929–1949* (Avon, New York, 1977). Many Arab killings of Jewish civilians in Palestine could similarly be considered terrorist: see, eg, N Shepherd, *Ploughing Sand: British Rule in Palestine 1917–1948* (John Murray, London, 1999) 179–243; T Kapitan, 'Terrorism in the Arab-Israeli Conflict' in I Primoratz (ed), *Terrorism: The Philosophical Issues* (Palgrave Macmillan, Hampshire, 2004) 175. Equally, in extrajudicially executing two British soldiers, Sergeants Paice and Martin, in July 1947, an Irgun 'Court' found the soldiers guilty of 'Belonging to a British Terrorist Criminal Organization known as the British Military Occupation Forces': see R Fisk, *The Great War for Civilization* (Fourth Estate, London, 2005) 458.

[176] See, eg, *Palestine (Defence) Order in Council* 1931 under the Emergency Powers Act 1920 (UK); Government of Palestine, *Ordinances, Regulations, Rules, Orders and Notices* 1936, ii, 259; *Palestine Martial Law (Defence) Orders in Council* 1936 and 1937; Defence (Emergency) Regulations 1945 under the Emergency Powers (Defence) Act 1945, 8 & 9 Geo. VI c 31; see Simpson, n 23, 84–85, 88–89; N Bethell, *The Palestine Triangle: The Struggle between the British, the Jews, and the Arabs 1935–1948* (Deutsch, London, 1979).

in 1948 to combat Israel's perceived 'permanent emergency'. It was, however, in post-war IHL treaties that the tentative legal concept of terrorism in armed conflict was cemented in international law.

1. Measures of terrorism: 1949 Fourth Geneva Convention

Article 33(1) of the Fourth Geneva Convention 1949 prohibits 'collective penalties and likewise all measures of intimidation or of terrorism' against protected persons in international armed conflict. The protection applies to persons 'in the hands of a Party to the conflict',[177] but not to civilians in territory not occupied by the adverse Party. It protects civilians in occupied territory or detained by an adverse party, removing 'all doubt as to the illegality of practices . . . applied widely in occupied territories during World War II'.[178]

The meaning of 'terrorism' in Article 33(1) is not defined and there is little recorded debate from the Diplomatic Conference.[179] The ICRC Commentary observes that in past conflicts, belligerents inflicted collective penalties and measures of intimidation and terrorism to prevent hostile acts by protected persons, although: 'Far from achieving the desired effect . . . such practices, by reason of their excessive severity and cruelty, kept alive and strengthened the spirit of resistance.'[180] Such acts 'strike at guilty and innocent alike' and 'are opposed to all principles based on humanity and justice'.[181] The specific prohibition in Article 33 is a particularization of, or complement to, the 'general prohibition' in Article 27 on violence and inhumane treatment against civilians.[182] It is also part of a general movement in IHL towards limiting reprisals against civilians. Given its historical origins, the notion of 'terrorism' in the provision has 'a narrower meaning than in present-day language'.[183]

2. Developments in the 1950s and 1960s

Further development of the concept of terrorism in armed conflict took place in 1954, when the ICRC Board of Governors asked the ICRC to propose a

---

[177] 1949 Fourth Geneva Convention, Art 4.

[178] Kalshoven, n 3, 74; see also Gasser (2002), n 3, 558.

[179] Kalshoven, n 3, 73–74; *Final Record of the Diplomatic Conference of Geneva of 1949* (Swiss Federal Political Dept, Berne) vol 1, 118; vol 2A, 648–651; vol 2B, 406; see also ICRC Report, 'Terrorism and International Law: Challenges and Responses: The Complementary Nature of Human Rights Law, International Humanitarian Law and Refugee Law', Geneva, 2002, 4; E-C Gillard, 'The Complementary Nature of Human Rights Law, International Humanitarian Law and Refugee Law', M Schmitt and G Beruto (eds), *Terrorism and International Law* (IIHL and George C Marshall European Center for Security Studies, San Remo, 2003) 50, 52.

[180] J Pictet (ed), *The Geneva Conventions of 12 Aug 1949: Commentary* (ICRC, Geneva, 1958) vol IV.

[181] ibid. 1949 Fourth Geneva Convention, Art 27, states in part that protected persons 'shall be protected especially against all acts of violence or threats thereof'.

[182] H-P Gasser, 'Protection of the Civilian Population', in Fleck (ed), n 3, 209, 219.

[183] Gasser (2002), n 3, 558; Gillard, n 179, 52.

text to protect civilian populations from atomic, chemical, and bacterio-logical warfare. In 1956, the ICRC produced Draft Rules for the Limitation of the Dangers incurred by the Civilian Population in Time of War, which restated and defined the limits on the use of armed force 'by the requirements of humanity and the safety of the population', complementing existing IHL.[184]

Article 6 of the ICRC Draft Rules prohibited: 'Attacks directed against the civilian population, as such, whether with the object of terrorizing it or for any other reason.' Although the meaning of 'terrorizing' was not defined, Article 6 further stated that 'In consequence' of the prohibition, 'it is also forbidden to attack dwellings, installations or means of transport, which are for the exclusive use of, and occupied by, the civilian population'. It appears, therefore, that such attacks were non-exhaustively listed as examples of acts which aim to terrorize civilians.

The Draft Rules were an attempt to extend the scope of protection under the Geneva Conventions, since it was proposed that they would apply in any armed conflict, including non-international ones.[185] In 1957, the ICRC Draft Rules were submitted to the XIXth International Conference of the Red Cross in New Delhi, but there was little support from States to develop the text further.[186] The Draft Rules were, however, influential in shaping the content of provisions in the 1977 Protocols.

In 1969, the Institute of International Law adopted a similar resolution stating that: 'Existing international law prohibits, irrespective of the type of weapon used, any action whatsoever designed to terrorise the civilian population.'[187] There was no definition of what it meant to 'terrorize' the population, but the resolution is significant because it intended to state exist-ing law and attracted wide support (60 votes to 1, with 2 abstentions). Less successful was a proposal abandoned at a 1972 Conference of Government Experts in Geneva, which sought to prohibit 'acts of terrorism, consisting of acts of violence directed intentionally and indiscriminately against civilians taking no active part in the hostilities'.[188]

---

[184] 1956 ICRC Draft Rules for the Limitation of the Dangers incurred by the Civilian Population in Time of War, preamble, Art 5.

[185] ibid, Art 2(a)–(b).

[186] Conference Resolution XIII encouraged the ICRC to submit the text and amendments to States.

[187] Institute of International Law, 'The Distinction between Military Objectives and Non-Military Objectives in General and Particularly the Problems Associated with Weapons of Mass Destruction', Edinburgh, 9 Sept 1969, rule 6.

[188] Conference of Government Experts, Report: vol I, Geneva, 1972, 75, draft Art 5(b) (Reactional Committee); see also J Toman, 'Terrorism and the Regulation of Armed Conflicts' in M Bassiouni (ed), *International Terrorism and Political Crimes* (Charles C Thomas, Illinois, 1975) 133, 149.

3. *Spreading terror among civilians: 1977 Protocols I and II*

Ultimately, a limited concept of terrorism in armed conflict was included in Article 51(2) of 1977 Protocol I, and Article 13(2) of 1977 Protocol II. These identical provisions prohibit 'acts or threats of violence the primary purpose of which is to spread terror among the civilian population'. The innovative prohibition[189] in Protocol I applies 'to all cases of partial or total occupation of the territory of a High Contracting Party, even if the said occupation meets with no armed resistance'.[190] It thus extends the protection available under the Fourth Geneva Convention, since it applies to civilians in international conflict (including self-determination conflicts) who are not 'in the hands' of the adverse Party.[191] The protection in Protocol II applies to civilians in *non*-international armed conflicts.[192] In both cases, there may be difficulties in determining when low-intensity, non-State violence (such as terrorism) crosses the threshold of armed conflict and triggers the application of IHL.[193]

Both provisions are part of wider treaty prohibitions on attacking the civilian population or individual civilians,[194] and terrorizing is just one type of 'particularly reprehensible' attack on civilians.[195] In the first international decision applying Article 51(2) of Protocol I,[196] in the *Galic* case the ICTY stated that 'the prohibition against terror is a specific prohibition within the general prohibition of attack on civilians', the latter of which constitutes 'a peremptory norm of customary international law'.[197] It includes bombardment (aerial or other) of civilians where 'deliberately intended to intimidate the adversary and the enemy civilian population'.[198]

The ICRC Commentary on Article 51(2) acknowledges that violent acts in war 'almost always give rise to some degree of terror among the population and sometimes also among the armed forces', and that 'attacks on armed forces are purposely conducted brutally in order to intimidate the enemy soldiers and persuade them to surrender'.[199] While violence 'is inherent in war', some violence is 'licit' and some 'illicit',[200] depending on the legal status

---

[189] Gasser (1986), n 3.

[190] 1977 Protocol I, Art 1(3); 1949 Geneva Conventions, common Art 2.

[191] *Galic*, n 7, para 120; Gasser (2002), n 3, 559, 563.

[192] Reaffirmed in the Declaration of General Rules in Non-International Armed Conflicts, 14th Roundtable on Humanitarian Law, San Remo, 1989, rule 3 (1989) 10 IRRC 278, 404.

[193] UNSubComHR (53rd Sess), Terrorism and Human Rights: Progress Report by Special Rapporteur K Koufa, 27 June 2001, UN Doc E/CN.4/Sub.2/2001/31, 19–22.

[194] 1977 Protocol I, Art 51(2) and 1977 Protocol II, Art 13(2): 'The civilian population as such, as well as individual civilians, shall not be the object of attack. Acts or threats of violence the primary purpose of which is to spread terror among the civilian population are prohibited.'

[195] Y Sandoz et al (eds), *Commentary on the 1977 Protocols* (ICRC, Geneva, 1987) para 4785; Oeter, n 3, 169.

[196] *Galic*, n 7, para 66.   [197] ibid, para 98.   [198] Oeter, n 3, 169; 219.

[199] Sandoz et al (eds), n 195, para 1940 (1977 Protocol I, Art 51(2)); see also para 4786 (1977 Protocol II, Art 13(2)); Gasser (2004), n 182, 219–220.

[200] Gasser (2002), n 3, 554.

of the person committing it and compliance with restrictions on means and methods of warfare.[201] Terrorism in armed conflict thus has a 'different legal connotation' to acts of terrorism in peacetime,[202] because of the special rules regulating violence in armed conflict.

The prohibition on terror is not intended to address forms of accepted violence (and the inevitable terror they cause) in war, but rather refers to 'acts of violence the primary purpose of which is to spread terror among the civilian population without offering substantial military advantage'.[203] Proposals to limit the provision only to acts which *actually* spread terror were not accepted during the drafting.[204] The prohibition also extends to threats of terror, recalling 'proclamations made in the past threatening the annihilation' of civilians.[205]

Article 13(2) of Protocol II, which applies to non-international armed conflicts, is worded identically to Article 51(2) of Protocol I. The ICRC Commentary observes that attacks aimed at terrorizing 'are particularly reprehensible', occur frequently and 'inflict particularly cruel suffering upon the civilian population'.[206] The provision is intended to broaden the prohibition on terrorizing civilians by aerial bombardment in the 1923 Hague Draft Rules, by prohibiting 'Acts or threats of violence' in order 'to cover all possible circumstances'.[207] It particularizes the more general protection of civilians in Article 13(1) of Protocol II.[208] Whereas an earlier draft had referred to an 'intention' to spread terror,[209] that more subjective notion was replaced by the term 'purpose' in the final provision.[210]

The decisive element in the identical prohibitions in Protocol I and II is the *primary purpose* to spread terror.[211] While belligerents frequently claim responsibility for particular acts of violence and publicly proclaim their purposes,[212] this element may give rise to difficulties. In some cases, evidence of the subjective purpose behind violent acts may be hard to discover, especially where motives are undeclared, or where practice departs from declared

---

[201] ibid; even lawful combatants may become criminally liable for terrorism if they violate IHL.

[202] Gasser (1986), n 3.

[203] Ibid; Gasser (2004), n 182, 219–220; see also Y Dinstein, 'Terrorism as an International Crime' (1989) 19 IYBHR 55, 62; Kalshoven, n 3, 76, 78.

[204] *Galic*, n 7, para 100.   [205] Ibid; Gasser (2002), n 3, 556.

[206] Sandoz et al (eds), n 195, para 4785 (1977 Protocol II, Art 13(2)).

[207] ibid.

[208] 1977 Protocol II, Art 13(1): 'The civilian population and individual civilians shall enjoy general protection against the dangers arising from military occupation'; see also Kalshoven, n 3, 75.

[209] Diplomatic Conference on the Reaffirmation and Development of International Humanitarian Law Applicable in Armed Conflicts, *Official Records* (ICRC, Geneva, 1974–77) vol 1, 16.

[210] Kalshoven, n 3, 76.

[211] Gasser (2004), n 182, 220; Gasser (2002), n 3, 556; Kalshoven, n 3, 76.

[212] Kalshoven, ibid, 79.

motives.[213] Where mixed purposes underlie violence,[214] it may be difficult to weigh those purposes to uncover which is *primary*. Further, it is not clear whether the provisions prohibit violence against *military* objectives where the primary purpose is to spread terror among civilians.[215] The randomness of indiscriminate attacks may also conceal underlying purposes.[216]

Nevertheless, the 'primary purpose' standard is more appropriate than an 'exclusive purpose' standard. For example, Lauterpacht argued that Allied strategic bombing in the Second World War was not so objectionable because it was not done 'for the exclusive purpose of spreading terror and shattering the morale of the population at large'.[217] Demanding that causing terror must be the *exclusive* purpose of bombing sets the standard too high, given that attacks often have multiple aims.

4. *Acts of terrorism: 1977 Protocol II*

Protocol II regulates a further limited concept of terrorism in Article 4(2)(d), which prohibits 'acts of terrorism' in *non-international* armed conflicts 'at any time and in any place whatsoever', as well as threats to commit such acts.[218] The provision is modelled on Article 33 of the Fourth Geneva Convention,[219] but applies to non-international conflicts. Article 4 is a fundamental guarantee in Protocol I, permitting no derogation. Thus, as the ICRC Commentary notes, 'Even unlawful acts on the part of the adverse party cannot justify such measures' and denunciation of the Protocol is ineffective until the end of the armed conflict.[220] The provision is a further specific restriction on resort to reprisals against civilians.

An earlier ICRC draft had prohibited 'acts of terrorism in the form of acts of violence committed against those persons'. The simpler language of the final provision extends its scope to cover 'not only acts directed against people, but also acts directed against installations which would cause victims as a side-effect'.[221] Acts or threats of violence aimed *solely* at terrorizing *civilians* 'constitute a special type of terrorism' specifically prohibited in Article 13 of Protocol II.[222] Contrary to Green's assertion, the prohibition in Article 4 of Protocol II is not used in a non-technical sense equivalent to its

---

[213] eg the IRA and PLO have denied deliberately targeting civilians, claiming that civilians are incidental casualties of attacks on military objectives: AFP, 'IRA says sorry for 30 years of killing', *Sydney Morning Herald*, 17 July 2002; AFP, 'Arafat condemns terrorist actions targeting civilians', *Sydney Morning Herald*, 14 Apr 2002.

[214] MC Bassiouni, 'A Policy Oriented Inquiry into the Different Forms and Manifestations of "International Terrorism" ' in MC Bassiouni (ed), *Legal Responses to International Terrorism* (Martinus Nijhoff, Dordrecht, 1988) xv, xxx.

[215] Kalshoven, n 3, 76–79.   [216] ibid, 77, 79.   [217] Lauterpacht, n 37, 528.

[218] 1977 Protocol II, Art 4(2)(h).

[219] Sandoz et al (eds), n 195, para 4538 (1977 Protocol II, Art 4(2)(d)); Kalshoven, n 3, 73.

[220] ibid, para 4784 (1977 Protocol II, Art 13(2)).

[221] ibid, para 4538 (1977 Protocol II, Art 4(2)(d)).   [222] ibid.

meaning in Article 13 of Protocol II.[223] The Commentary makes plain that it was intended to be wider provision.

There is a further significant distinction between these provisions. Article 13(2) of Protocol II and Article 51(2) of Protocol I prohibit acts or threats 'the primary purpose of which is to spread terror', but there is no requirement that the act or threat actually *result* in terror. In contrast, Article 4(2)(d) of Protocol II prohibits actual 'acts of terror', so that acts which intend to terrorize but fail to do so are not prohibited. Consequently, Article 4(2)(d) is a wider provision in that it does not limit the prohibition on terror to people, but narrower in requiring the commission of actual terror.

The change in wording in the final Article 4(2)(d) of Protocol II was not, however, intended to remove the requirement in the original draft that an act of terrorism must be a violent one.[224] At the Diplomatic Conference, the US had observed that 'terrorism was an excessively vague word of which no satisfactory definition existed' and insisted that it referred only to physical violence,[225] although threats to commit physical violence were also ultimately prohibited.

In this sense, there is an intimate connection between Article 4(2)(d) of Protocol II and Article 4(2)(a), the latter prohibiting types of violence to life. Kalshoven argues that Article 4(2)(d) is not really 'a separate category entirely independent of article 4(2)(a)' and that no special legal consequences flow from a finding of terrorism, rather than of violence to life.[226] The only difference is one of 'gravity', so that the vagueness of 'terrorism' is not of great concern.[227]

This interpretation, however, renders Article 4(2)(d) nugatory and contradicts its plain textual meaning. Putting a person in extreme fear is distinct from any underlying physical violence, as a separate *intention* and in *moral* distinctiveness. Even a difference in *gravity* entails different legal consequences—at the very least, in the form of enhanced penalties; at most, in the greater stigma of conviction for a recognizably distinct (and possibly more serious) offence. Kalshoven's admission that 'if one so wishes, one may regard an act of terrorism as an aggravated form' of violence to life[228] is not an entirely satisfactory analysis.

5. *General considerations*

Referring to the various terrorism provisions in IHL, Cassese writes that:

. . . if all these treaties speak of 'terrorism' or 'acts of terrorists' without specifying what is covered by this notion, it means that the draftsmen had a fairly clear idea of

---

[223] L Green, *The Contemporary Law of Armed Conflict* (2nd edn, MUP, Manchester, 2000) 324.
[224] *Official Records*, n 209, vol 8, 412, paras 4–7; Kalshoven, n 3, 74.
[225] *Official Records*, n 209, 426, para 30 (USA); Kalshoven, n 3, 74.
[226] Kalshoven, ibid, 75, 80.   [227] ibid.   [228] ibid.

what they were prohibiting . . . they either deliberately or unwittingly were referring to a general notion underlying treaty provisions and laid down in customary rules.[229]

Any 'general notion' is, however, implicit, and must be understood according to the principles of treaty interpretation. There are few judicial decisions interpreting these provisions. The terms 'terror', 'terrorizing', and 'terrorism' must be given their ordinary textual meaning, in their context and in the light of their object and purpose.[230] The ordinary meaning of 'terror' refers to 'intense fear, fright or dread'; 'terrorism' refers to a 'policy intended to strike with terror those against whom it is adopted; [or] the employment of methods of intimidation'.[231]

Significantly, however, there is no wider notion of terrorizing for an ulterior political purpose, objective, or motive,[232] such as coercing a government or political institutions to do or refrain from doing something. There is similarly no requirement that terror be motivated by any political aims; it is sufficient that terror against civilians is committed or threatened. The meaning of terrorism in IHL is thus more limited than many definitions of terrorism outside the context of armed conflict.[233]

The case-by-case identification of particular acts which spread terror assists in the pragmatic interpretation of the prohibitions. The ICRC gives the example of the aerial carpet bombing of cities in the Second World War[234] and some national military manuals expressly forbid bombardment for the purpose of terrorizing civilians.[235] A Swiss military manual regards the 'threat of nuclear attack against urban centres' as a prohibited means of spreading terror among civilians.[236]

Further, in the *Galic* case the ICTY found that a campaign of deliberately sniping and shelling besieged civilians in Sarajevo violated the prohibition on spreading terror in Article 51(2) of Protocol I.[237] Writers support the view that Serbian violence in Croatia (1991), Bosnia (1992), and Kosovo (1998–99), including 'ethnic cleansing' and mass expulsions, amounted to terrorism as understood in IHL.[238] The US State Department asserted, in 1994, that Bosnian Serb militias were using rape to terrorize populations, while a UN

---

[229] A Cassese, *International Criminal Law* (OUP, Oxford, 2003) 121.
[230] 1969 Vienna Convention on the Law of Treaties, Art 31(1).
[231] Oxford English Dictionary (online edition), definitions of 'terror' and 'terrorism'.
[232] Kalshoven, n 3, 76 (referring to 1977 Protocol II, Art 13(2)).
[233] See Chs 3 and 4 above.   [234] ICRC Report, n 179, 3.
[235] Belgium, *Law of War Manual* (1983), 31; Ecuador, *Naval Manual* (1989) s 6.2.5; Netherlands, *Military Manual* (1993) V–4, XI–6; US, *Naval Handbook* (1995) s 11.3.
[236] Switzerland, *Basic Military Manual* (1987) art 27(2).
[237] See discussion below.
[238] Oeter, n 3, 170; Green, n 223, 324; see also UNGA Resolutions 49/196 (1994) para 7; 53/164 (1998) preamble; UNComHR Resolutions 1992/S–2/1, para 7; 1993/7, para 12; 1994/72, para 7; 1995/89, para 5; OSCE, *Kosovo/Kosova, as seen as told: An analysis of the human rights findings of the OSCE Kosovo Verification Mission, October 1998 to June 1999* (OSCE, Warsaw, 1999); Helsinki Watch, *War Crimes in Bosnia-Herzegovina*, vol II (New York, 1993) 11.

Special Rapporteur has characterized 'the use of sexual violence . . . as an effective way to terrorise and demoralise members of the opposition' during war.[239]

Moreover, Oeter writes of terror that 'this particularly barbarian variant of "total" warfare is unfortunately used regularly by military actors in practice',[240] such as by the Soviet Union in Afghanistan in the 1980s, and by Iraqi 'Scud' missiles fired at Saudi Arabia and Kuwait in the 1991 Gulf War.[241] Gasser suggests additional examples from the Algerian war of independence; Soviet repression of independence movements; conflicts in Indochina and Northern Ireland; civil wars in Sri Lanka, Africa, and Colombia; and wars in the Middle East and Palestine.[242] The UN Sub-Commission on Human Rights has identified the use of 'death squads' in El Salvador as a means of terrorizing the population,[243] while Human Rights Watch criticized the spreading of terror among civilians by both sides in a conflict in Yemen.[244] The ICRC lists a variety of types of violence against civilians during conflicts which may cause terror and has specifically urged parties to respect the prohibition on terror in conflicts in the Middle East (1973), Yugoslavia (1991), Nagorno-Karabakh (1993), Angola (1994), and the Near East (2000).[245] The videotaping and beheading ('exhibition killing') of aid workers in Iraq in 2003–04,[246] and the bombing of UN headquarters, may also qualify, both designed to terrorize those groups of people.

The meaning of the terrorism provisions cannot be divorced from related IHL provisions, including the unequivocal, peremptory prohibition of reprisals against the civilian population and civilian objects,[247] and prohibitions on the use of incendiary weapons against civilians, or military objectives located within concentrations of civilians.[248] The terrorism provisions are further linked to stronger principles of distinction and discrimination,[249]

---

[239] US State Department, *Bosnia-Herzegovina Human Rights Practice 1993*, 31 Jan 1994, 2; UN Special Rapporteur on Systematic Rape, Sexual Slavery and Slavery-like Practices during Wartime, Update to final report to UNSubComHR, UN Doc E/CN.4/Sub.2/2000/21 (6 June 2000), para 20; see also Human Rights Watch, *Global Report on Women's Human Rights* (New York, 1995) 1.

[240] Oeter, n 3, 170.

[241] ibid; Israel also claimed that SCUD missiles aimed to terrorize civilians and breached international law: Israel, Letter to UN Sec-Gen, UN Doc S/22160 (29 Jan 1991) 2.

[242] Gasser (2002), n 3, 547–548.

[243] UNSubComHR Res 1989/9, preamble.

[244] Human Rights Watch, Letter to Yemeni Government, New York, 19 May 1994.

[245] ICRC Study, n 3, vol I, 11; vol II, 76–77.

[246] See, eg, O Mahdi and R Carroll, 'Where daily killings come free on DVD', *Guardian Weekly*, 26 Aug–1 Sept 2005, 3; although many kidnappings in Iraq were committed by criminal groups for purely financial not political motives: H Esmaeili, 'Hostage to murky forces', *The Australian*, 16 May 2005.

[247] 1977 Protocol I, Arts 51(6) and 52(1); Oeter, n 3, 170; Gasser (2002), n 3, 556.

[248] 1980 Protocol III on Prohibitions or Restrictions on the Use of Incendiary Weapons, Art 2.

[249] eg 1977 Protocol I, Arts 51(4) and 52; Oeter, n 3, 172–180; Gasser (2002), n 3, 255.

detailed rules on persons out of combat and enemy civilians,[250] and on cultural property and installations containing dangerous forces.[251]

Clearly, certain acts prohibited as terroristic against civilians may be permissible acts of violence when committed against combatants during hostilities.[252] However, as Gasser notes, 'the right of parties . . . to choose methods or means of warfare is not unlimited'[253] and certain weapons or methods of warfare—which might terrorize combatants—are prohibited.[254] In particular, it is prohibited to use weapons or methods 'of a nature to cause superfluous injury or unnecessary suffering',[255] while some acts regarded as terroristic may amount to the war crime of perfidy.[256]

A controversial application of terror tactics against military forces is the US doctrine of 'Shock and Awe' used in the Iraq war in 2003.[257] Its architects in the Pentagon hope that shock and awe tactics will intimidate adversaries, overwhelm their perception and paralyse their will to fight.[258] It draws expressly on precedents such as shell shock in the First World War, the atomic bombing of Hiroshima and Nagasaki, massive aerial bombardment and blitzkrieg in the Second World War, assassination and reprisals.[259] Its authors argue: 'While there are surely humanitarian considerations that cannot or should not be ignored, the ability to Shock and Awe ultimately rests in the ability to frighten, scare, intimidate, and disarm'.[260]

To the extent that such tactics respect the laws of war and human rights standards applicable in armed conflicts, there is nothing innately unlawful about terrorizing enemy combatants. However, the aggressive emphasis on psychological dominance and overwhelming force may result in an inexorable drift towards using excessive means or attacking protected targets. Further, although physical force is directed against military targets, it may also be designed to incidentally intimidate or overwhelm civilians and their support for the military effort.[261]

---

[250] Gasser (2002), n 3, 557–560; W Mallison and S Mallison, 'The Control of State Terror through the Application of the International Humanitarian Law of Armed Conflict' in M Livingston (ed), *International Terrorism in the Contemporary World* (Greenwood Press, Westport, 1978) 325.

[251] eg 1954 Convention for the Protection of Cultural Property in the Event of Armed Conflict, Art 4; 1977 Protocol I, Arts 53 and 56; Gasser (2002), n 3, 557.

[252] Gasser (2002), n 3, 557.

[253] 1977 Protocol I, Art 35(1).

[254] Such as enemy civilians planting a bomb in an officers' mess with the specific intent of spreading terror among combatants: Cassese, n 229, 127.

[255] 1977 Protocol I, Art 35.

[256] 1977 Protocol I, Art 37 (feigning civilian status in an attack).

[257] 'Iraq faces massive US missile barrage', CBS News, 24 Jan 2003.

[258] H Ullman and J Wade, *Shock and Awe: Achieving Rapid Dominance* (Defense Group Inc, US National Defense University, 1996) ch 2: 'Shock and Awe'.

[259] ibid.   [260] ibid, 34.

[261] K Graham, 'The Security Council and Counter-terrorism: Global and Regional Approaches to an Elusive Public Good' (2005) 17 *Terrorism and Political Violence* 37, 40.

E. INTERNATIONAL CRIMINAL TRIBUNALS SINCE 1993

1. Terrorism in tribunal statutes

Individual criminal liability for breaches of IHL prohibitions on terrorism have been expressly established in the statutes of some recent international criminal tribunals. Article 4(d) of the 1994 ICTR Statute embodies Article 13(2) of Protocol II, by conferring jurisdiction over 'Acts of terrorism' committed in Rwandan territory, or by Rwandan citizens in neighbouring States, between 1 January and 31 December 1994.[262] Similarly, Article 3(d) of the Statute of the Special Court for Sierra Leone enables the prosecution of 'Acts of terrorism',[263] which is listed among violations of common Article 3 of the four Geneva Conventions and of Protocol II.

In contrast, 'terrorism' appears in neither the 1993 ICTY Statute, nor the 1998 Rome Statute of the ICC. Its omission from the Rome Statute is normatively significant, since the Statute represents the most recent and 'authoritative expression of the legal views of a great number of States' on international criminal law.[264] The Rome Conference rejected a broader proposed crime of terrorism *outside* the context of armed conflict,[265] yet it also excluded a proposed *war crime* of terrorism.

The proposed war crime of terrorism was found in the 1996 ILC Draft Code of Crimes against the Peace and Security of Mankind,[266] drawn to the attention of the ICC Preparatory Committee by the UN General Assembly.[267] Draft Article 20(f) described as a 'war crime' both the 'taking of hostages' and 'acts of terrorism', where committed in violation of IHL applicable in non-international armed conflict and 'in a systematic manner or on a large scale'.[268] The phrase 'acts of terrorism' was not defined, although the provision resembles that in Article 4(2)(d) of Protocol II.

Although the draft provision was not adopted, Article 10 of the Rome Statute declares that the Statute cannot limit or prejudice 'in any way existing or developing rules of international law for purposes other than this Statute'.

---

[262] 1994 ICTR Statute, Art 4(2)(d).

[263] Agreement between the UN and Sierra Leone pursuant to UNSC Resolution 1315 (2000), annexed Statute.

[264] *Furundzija* ICTY–95–17/1–T (10 Dec 1998) para 227; K Kittichaisaree, *International Criminal Law* (OUP, Oxford, 2002) 38. The Statute was the culmination of a long process of codification begun by the ILC in its 1954 Draft Code of Offences against the Peace and Security of Mankind (ILC Report (6th Sess, 1954), UN Doc A/2693) and revitalized in the 1990s: see W Schabas, *An Introduction to the International Criminal Court* (CUP, Cambridge, 2001) ch 1.

[265] See Ch 3 above.

[266] 1996 ILC Draft Code of Crimes against the Peace and Security of Mankind (Part II), in ILC Report (48th Sess, 6 May–26 July 1996) UN Doc A/51/10, ch II(2), paras 46–48.

[267] UNGA Resolution 51/160 (1996).

[268] ILC Report (47th Sess, 2 May–21 July 1995), UN Doc A/50/10.

As the ICTY stated in the *Furundzija* case, the Statute is not a perfect expression of customary law but depending on the issue, 'may be taken to restate, reflect or clarify customary rules or crystallize them, whereas in some areas it creates new law or modifies existing law'.[269] Thus although violations of the terrorism prohibitions in the Geneva Conventions and Protocols cannot be tried in the ICC, prosecutions in customary law (or other tribunals) are not precluded. Still less does the exclusion of terrorism from the Statute prejudice the future development of such a customary crime.

2. The Galic *case in the ICTY*

This position is supported by ICTY practice. While the ICTY Statute does not mention terrorism, Article 3 allows prosecution of violations of 'the laws and customs of war', and jurisdiction is not limited to the offences listed—in contrast to the exhaustive enumeration of crimes in the Rome and ICTR Statutes. Thus in the *Galic* case, the ICTY prosecutor alleged multiple violations of the laws and customs of war by 'unlawfully inflicting terror upon civilians', under Article 51 of Protocol I and Article 13 of Protocol II.[270] The prosecutor argued the 'principal objective of the campaign of sniping and shelling of civilians [in Sarajevo] was to terrorize the civilian population'.[271] The intent to spread terror was evident from the widespread targeting of civilian activities, the manner of the attacks, and their timing and duration.[272]

Three judges of the Trial Chamber first considered the case in a decision on an acquittal motion of October 2002.[273] The defence admitted that the civilian population had experienced terror, but contended that it was a consequence of urban warfare rather than specifically intended by the accused.[274] Yet the ICTY rejected the defence argument that the prosecution had failed to offer sufficient evidence of specific intent to terrorize, and allowed that charge to proceed to trial.[275]

In its merits judgment of December 2003, the ICTY found that a 'crime of terror against the civilian population', or more simply 'the crime of terror', was committed at Sarajevo.[276] The legal basis of the crime was Article 51 of Protocol I, which applied to the Bosnian conflict by an international

---

[269] *Furundzija*, n 264, para 227.
[270] *Galic*, Indictments, ICTY–98–29–T (26 Mar 1999 and 24 Apr 1998, unsealed 2 Nov 2001). Identical charges were laid in the Amended Indictments in *Mladic* IT–95–5/18–I (11 Oct 2002) (counts 9 and 14) and *Karadzic* IT–95–5/18 (31 May 2000) (count 10) (both cases involving the sniping and shelling of civilians).
[271] *Galic*, Prosecutor's Pre-Trial Brief, 23 Oct 2001, Case No IT–98–29–I, paras 22–25.
[272] ibid.
[273] *Galic (Acquittal Motion Decision)* ICTY–98–29–T, 3 Oct 2002, para 32.
[274] ibid.   [275] ibid.
[276] *Galic*, n 7, paras 65, 597; see D Kravetz, 'The Protection of Civilians in War: The ICTY's *Galic* Case' (2004) 17 Leiden JIL 521.

agreement of 22 May 1992. It was consequently unnecessary to decide if Protocol I applied due to its 'inherent conditions of application' (in Article 1), or if Protocol II also applied.[277] The ICTY repeatedly emphasized that its judgment was based on the *treaty* crime of terror, and did not consider whether parallel customary rules existed, or constituted peremptory norms.[278] Further, the ICTY did not decide whether it had jurisdiction over terrorism resulting from threats of violence, or violence not causing death or injury.[279] In these respects, it avoided answering some of the most difficult questions in this area.

There was, however, significant discussion of the elements of the crime, which were found to comprise: (1) acts of violence against the civilian population or civilians not taking direct part in hostilities, causing death or serious injury to body or health; (2) wilfully making civilians the object of the violence; and (3) committing the offence 'with the primary purpose of spreading terror among the civilian population'.[280] On the facts, the *actus reus* consisted of violence against civilians, in particular 'a campaign of sniping and shelling' of civilians in Sarajevo.[281]

The distinctive feature of the crime of terror is its *mens rea* element: 'the primary purpose of spreading terror'.[282] The ICTY regards terror as a crime of 'specific intent', which excludes '*dolus eventualis* or recklessness from the intentional state specific to terror'.[283] The perpetrator must have been aware of the possibility or likelihood that terror would result from acts of violence, and that such terror was the result specifically intended.[284] This position accords with the view of the drafting committee at the 1974–77 Diplomatic Conference, which excluded unintended or incidental terror arising from lawful acts of warfare with another primary objective.[285]

Contrary to the prosecution's argument, the ICTY found that the *actual* infliction or spreading of terror is not a necessary element.[286] During the drafting of Article 51, some believed it preferable to prohibit particular methods which in fact spread terror, since proving intent to spread terror would be too difficult.[287] That view did not gain acceptance. The ICTY also acknowledged that *threats* (rather than acts) of violence 'could also involve grave consequences for the victim', but did not address the matter because it was not at issue in the *Galic* case.[288]

---

[277] *Galic*, n 7, para 95.
[278] ibid, paras 69, 97, 113; and para 98 respectively.
[279] ibid, para 130.   [280] ibid, para 133.   [281] ibid, para 597.
[282] ibid.   [283] ibid.   [284] ibid.
[285] *Official Records*, n 209, vol XV, 274; see also vol XIV, 65 (France) and vol XIV, 64 (Iran).
[286] *Galic*, n 7, paras 65, 76, 134.   [287] *Official Records*, n 209, vol XV, 241.
[288] *Galic*, n 7, para 110.

3. *The meaning of 'terror' in* Galic

In interpreting the term 'terror', the ICTY accepted the prosecution's definition of 'extreme fear'.[289] The prosecution drew this interpretation from a dictionary definition and the testimony of an expert witness (a psychiatrist), and nothing in the *travaux préparatoires* of Protocol I contradicted it.[290] The defence unsuccessfully argued for more restrictive interpretation, submitting that 'extreme fear' understated the notion, which had to be 'of the highest intensity', 'long term', 'direct', and 'capable of causing long-term consequences'.[291] That view sets the bar too high, since terror will often be transient given the ebb and flow of hostilities.

Despite defining 'terror' as 'extreme fear', the decision does not satisfactorily explain how the courts will determine what kinds of acts are likely to cause extreme fear. Since proof of actual terror is not required, empirical evidence of terror adduced through the testimony of affected civilians (about their state of mind) may not be available. Even if it is available, the more difficult question remains as to how 'terror' is to be accurately measured. While both parties in the *Galic* case relied extensively on the expert evidence of psychiatrists to assist in measuring 'terror', the ICTY's judgment neither evaluates this evidence nor assesses its significance.

Since the ICTY implicitly accepted the prosecution's definition,[292] it is important to examine its basis. The prosecution's expert, a British psychiatrist, prepared a report on the relationship between events such as the shelling and sniping at Sarajevo and 'the production of terror'.[293] The report defined terrorism as 'extreme fear' and then investigated how psychiatry identifies and measures 'fear'. The report considered 'realistic' terror rather than neurotic or phobic fear, and how terror affects people with 'normally robust personality structures'.[294] It found that deliberate disasters generated more fear than accidental ones; and that non-combatants were not as prepared for violence as combatants and thus experienced fear differently. It also noted that a range of factors affects the ability of civilians to *cope* with fear.

The report indicates that factors likely to induce terror in civilians include: violence which is intense and dangerous, repeated and continuing, and uncontrollable and unpredictable; attempts to disrupt sleep (including by loud noise) or essential services (such as food and water, transport, medicine, electricity, or communications); propaganda; interfering with grieving (such as by sniping at funerals); targeting cultural icons (such as mosques or Red Cross hospitals); and disrupting the daily lives of civilians (including

---

[289] ibid, para 137. [290] ibid, paras 75 and 137 respectively.
[291] ibid, para 83. [292] ibid, para 137.
[293] S Turner, Report for the ICTY Case No IT–98–29–T, Prosecution Exhibit P3716, 6 May 2002 (tendered 24 June 2002).
[294] ibid, paras 13, 16.

shopping, schooling, or going to cafes). Such acts create a sense of help-lessness and vulnerability. Fear may be expressed in different ways: panic, apathy, depression, detachment, disassociation, numbness, or hopelessness. It may also be manifested as acute stress disorder or post-traumatic stress disorder, or through increased drug use, suicide, and greater hostility among children.

The defence called a Serbian psychiatrist, who attacked the methodology used by the prosecution's expert on a variety of grounds.[295] The defence argued that that there was no common experience of fear in Sarajevo, but that individuals felt it differently and differences in the structure, age, gender, education, and mental condition of the population had to be taken into account. The defence argued that the fear felt was neither extreme (since there was no widespread panic, 'shell shock' or 'bent man' syndrome), nor experienced by the majority. It was asserted that fear in a civil war is normal in a siege situation, where civilians live among military objectives. It was also argued that civilian activities continued in Sarajevo, including schools, hospitals, and restaurants, with no major increases in suicide or malnutrition.

The defence's arguments on the meaning and measuring of 'terror' made little impression on the ICTY, despite heavily contesting the findings of the prosecution's expert. While the latter expert was a more qualified and highly regarded psychiatrist, it is troubling that the ICTY glossed over the critical issues of what causes 'terror' and how it should be measured. 'Terror' is not a concept known to psychiatry or psychology and simply interpreting 'terror' as a heightened form of 'fear' may not be analytically sound in the absence of further rigorous scientific investigation.

The crime of terror may be committed if terror is intended but does not actually result, and possibly even where terror is merely threatened. Judges must make speculative, predictive, and subjective judgments about what kinds of acts are likely to produce terror in a target population, in the absence of empirical testimony as to how that population actually felt. Since juries are absent in international criminal trials and most national military trials, the likelihood of terror is not being evaluated by what an ordinary or reasonable person in the community believes would cause terror. For this reason, judges are more reliant on expert testimony about terror (in addition to their own intuitive or 'common sense' views about what causes terror). This makes

---

[295] Dr B Kuljic, Expert Opinion of 14 Jan 2002 and ICTY testimony in transcript of 4–6 Mar 2003. It was claimed that the prosecution's report was flawed because it: failed to conduct interviews, surveys, or questionnaires of the affected population, or to consider their medical records; lacked random sampling or control questions; did not use tests for measuring PTSD or acute stress disorder, or consider comparative data; relied too heavily and selectively on secondary literature; and was tainted by dependence on selective extracts of witness testimony provided by the prosecution.

it all the more important for the courts to properly resolve conflicting expert evidence (and the many lingering questions) about the causes and symptoms of 'terror'.

F. INDIVIDUAL CRIMINAL RESPONSIBILITY FOR 'TERRORISM'

The IHL terrorism provisions are textually framed as *prohibitions*, rather than as *crimes*. The prohibition in Article 33(1) of the Fourth Geneva Convention is not expressly included among the 'grave breaches' in Article 147 of that Convention. Nor are the prohibitions in Protocol I identified as grave breaches under Article 85 of that Protocol,[296] while Protocol II contains no provisions establishing grave breaches.

Nonetheless, the *Galic* case confirms that serious violations of the prohibition on terrorism may attract individual criminal responsibility. Following the conditions established in the *Tadic* case,[297] the ICTY found that spreading terror is both 'serious' (breaching a basic rule protecting important values and involving grave consequences for the victim) and entails individual criminal responsibility.[298] Although the indictment did not charge spreading terror as a grave breach, the ICTY found that persons seriously violating the prohibition were criminally liable if it caused serious injury or death: 'In such cases the acts of violence qualified, in themselves, as grave breaches of Protocol I. Therefore the violation seen in all its elements (attack plus intent to terrorize) could not have been qualified as less criminal than a grave breach.'[299] The ICTY believes that terrorism is a compound offence comprising other crimes or grave breaches under Article 85 of Protocol I, in particular wilfully 'making the civilian population or individual civilians the object of attack' and 'causing death or serious injury to body or health'.[300] The universal acceptance of Article 85 at the Diplomatic Conference, combined with the 'unanimous and unqualified condemnation' of spreading terror, is 'clear proof' that relevant violations of Article 51(2) have been criminalized.[301] Leading writers support the implicit grave breach theory,[302] including in non-international armed conflict under Protocol II.[303]

The argument that serious acts of terrorism *implicitly* amount to grave breaches is not entirely persuasive and misrepresents the legal character of the prohibition on terror. While the underlying physical acts may be grave breaches (such as unlawful killings), the distinctive feature of the prohibition

---

[296] Gillard, n 179, 52.

[297] *Tadic (Interlocutory)*, n 71, para 94; see C Greenwood, 'International Humanitarian Law and the Tadic Case' (1996) 7 EJIL 265, 279–281.

[298] *Galic* n 7, paras 106–108, 130; and 127, 130 respectively.

[299] ibid, para 127.   [300] ibid, para 128.   [301] ibid.

[302] Gasser (2002), n 3, 556, 560, 565; Oeter, n 3, 169.   [303] Gasser, ibid, 562.

on terror is the special intent to commit physical violence *for the purpose of* spreading terror. IHL treaties do not treat terror, *as such*, as a grave breach and the ICTY conflates the distinct prohibition of terror with the physical acts partially comprising it. Ireland, for example, treats any 'minor breach' of Article 51(2) of Protocol I as still being an offence.[304]

G. CUSTOMARY CRIMES OF TERRORISM IN ARMED CONFLICT

A better legal argument is to avoid artificially characterizing terrorism as an implied grave breach, and instead to regard the prohibition as a crime in customary law. As the US Military Tribunal stated in the *Hostages* case: 'It is not essential that a crime be specifically defined and charged in accordance with a particular ordinance, statute or treaty if it is made a crime by international convention, recognized customs and usages of war, or the general principles of criminal justice common to civilized nations generally.'[305] The penal aspect of IHL is 'still rudimentary' and 'When treaties fail to clearly define the criminality of prohibited acts . . . customary law and internal penal law . . . supply the missing links'.[306] The system of grave breaches in more recent IHL treaties does not exclude the existence of other war crimes in customary law, just as the absence of grave breaches in earlier treaties did not preclude criminal liability.[307] The notion of grave breaches may be more relevant to treaty-based obligations concerning jurisdiction, prosecution and extradition than to criminality *per se*.[308]

In the *Galic* case, the ICTY majority refrained from examining whether the treaty prohibitions also constituted customary rules, as argued by the prosecution. In dissent, Judge Nieto-Navia found that the limited criminalization of terrorism in State practice was insufficient to establish individual criminal liability in customary law, and as a result, the offence of terrorizing civilians was not within the ICTY's jurisdiction.[309] The ICRC study of customary IHL accepts the existence of a customary prohibition on 'acts or threats of violence the primary purpose of which is to spread terror among the civilian population',[310] but does not examine whether it also constitutes a customary crime.

---

[304] Geneva Conventions Act (1962, as amended) (Ireland), s 4.

[305] *Hostages* case, n153, 634–635; see also *Nuremberg Judgment*, n 102, 221; Green, n 223, 303.

[306] T Meron, 'International Criminalization of Internal Atrocities' (1995) 89 AJIL 554, 563.

[307] ibid, 564; see also Greenwood, n 297, 279.   [308] Meron, n 306, 566.

[309] *Galic* (dissent of Judge Nieto-Navia), n 7, paras 108–113 (the 1992 agreement was not considered sufficient).

[310] ICRC Study, n 3, vol I: *Rules*, 8–11; vol II: *Practice*, 67–78; see also International Institute of Humanitarian Law (IIHL), 1990 Rules of Humanitarian Law Governing the Conduct of Hostilities in Non-International Armed Conflicts (1990) No 278 IRRC 388, Rule A2; Institute for Human Rights (Åbo Akademi), 1990 Declaration of Minimum Humanitarian Standards (1991) No 282 IRRC 332, Art 6.

Determining the existence of customary humanitarian law requires consideration of States' official pronouncements, military manuals and judicial decisions,[311] particularly where observation of States' actual practice is rendered difficult by lack of independent access to the theatre of hostilities.[312] The practice of international organizations such as the ICRC is also important.[313] The legal significance of the practice of non-State actors is unclear,[314] although in the *Tadic* case the behaviour of 'insurgents' was a relevant consideration.[315]

As the majority in *Galic* admitted, there are few examples of national or international criminal prosecutions for violations of treaty or customary prohibitions on terrorizing civilians. Ordinarily, more than a few isolated cases are necessary to establish a customary crime, and widespread evidence of prosecutions in State practice and the attendant *opinio juris* is required.[316] Where the case law and statutes are silent, recourse to military manuals, national legislation and judicial practice, and general principles of justice assumes greater importance.[317] The observation in the *Galic* case that 'evidence of terrorization of civilians has been factored into convictions on other charges' in international tribunals[318] only marginally supports an argument that terrorism is a customary war crime.

Nevertheless, there is some evidence that the treaty prohibitions on terrorism are emerging as customary crimes. First, the origins of liability for terrorism in IHL extend as far back as the 1919 list of war crimes adopted by the Commission on Responsibilities. Second, these provisions influenced a number of attempts to establish criminal liability during the Second World War, and provided the basis for a number of national post-war prosecutions.[319]

Third, there was widespread support for the terrorism provisions during the drafting of the 1949 Geneva Conventions and the 1977 Protocols, which have been widely ratified.[320] During the drafting of Article 51(2) of Protocol I,

---

[311] *Tadic (Interlocutory)*, n 71, para 99; see also ICRC Study, n 3, vol 1, xxxi–xlv.
[312] *Tadic (Interlocutory)*, n 71, para 99.
[313] ibid, para 109; ICRC Study, n 3, vol 1, xxxv.   [314] ibid, vol 1, xxxvi.
[315] *Tadic (Interlocutory)*, n 71, para 108.   [316] Cassese, n 229, 51.   [317] ibid.
[318] *Galic*, n 7, para 66. eg the 'atmosphere of terror' in detention camps was evidence of war crimes such as torture, cruel or inhuman treatment (*Delalic* ICTY–96–21–T (16 Nov 1998), paras 976, 1056, 1086–1091, 1119; *Blaškic* ICTY–95–14–T (3 Mar 2000), paras 695, 700, 732–733) and the crime against humanity of persecution (*Nikolic (Rule 61 Decision)* ICTY–94–2 (20 Oct 1995), paras 67, 109, 111, 119, 177, 206). The terrorizing of civilians by intensive shelling was evidence of crimes of 'unlawful attack' on civilians, and persecution and inhumane acts (*Blaškic*, above, paras 630, 505, 511 and *Krstic* ICTY–98–33–T (2 Aug 2001) paras 533, 122 respectively). Terrorizing civilians, through threats, insults, looting and burning houses, beatings, rapes, and murders, was also evidence of persecution and inhumane acts (*Krstic* above, paras 150, 607). In *Martic*, the use of cluster bombs was not designed to hit military targets, but to terrorize civilians in Zagreb (*Martic (Rule 61 Decision)* ICTY–95–11 (8 Mar 1996) paras 23–31), while the shelling of civilian targets in Sarajevo allegedly had a similar purpose in *Dukić*, Initial Indictment (29 Feb 1996) para 7, count 2.   [319] See 'B (5) National Post-War Trials' above.
[320] There are 188 Parties to each of the four 1949 Geneva Conventions; 155 Parties to 1977 Protocol I; and 148 Parties to 1977 Protocol II: Roberts and Guelff, n 12, 362, 498.

the ICRC stated that it 'merely reaffirmed existing international law', and Article 51 as a whole was adopted by 77 votes to 1, with 16 abstentions.[321] Byelorussia stated that 'spreading terror among the civilian population is well known to be one of the infamous methods widely resorted to by aggressors seeking to attain their criminal ends'.[322] Mexico rejected reservations to Article 51 as inconsistent with the object and purpose of Protocol I, while the UK regarded Article 51(2) as a reaffirmation of customary law.[323]

Fourth, some of the treaty prohibitions on terrorism are reflected in the Statutes of the ad hoc criminal tribunals for Rwanda and Sierra Leone, and the practice of the ICTY. The statutes of international criminal tribunals may be evidence of a customary crime, despite a paucity of prosecutions.[324] Up to the end of 2005, all 13 indictments in the Special Court for Sierra Leone contained charges of 'acts of terrorism' or 'terrorizing the civilian population', as war crimes arising under common Article 3 of the 1949 Geneva Conventions and Protocol II.[325]

In the indictment of Charles Taylor, it is asserted that as leader of the National Patriotic Front of Liberia and Liberian President, Taylor supported, encouraged, organized, and led a campaign to terrorize the civilian population of Sierra Leone, and did terrorize them.[326] The acts comprised in the campaign included many of the other charges: unlawful killings, sexual and physical violence, use of child soldiers, abductions and forced labour, looting, and burning.[327] The indictments against many other defendants are similarly structured, with other war crimes or crimes against humanity supplying the *actus reus* of the overarching war crime of terrorism.

Fifth, national legislation and case law lends support to a customary crime of terror. At least 23 national military manuals prohibit acts or threats of violence designed to terrorize the civilian population in international conflicts, while 18 States make breaches of the prohibition an offence.[328] As early as 1945, Australia had criminalized 'murder or massacres—systematic

---

[321] *Galic*, n 7, para 99; *Official Records*, n 209, vol XIV, 36 and vol VI, 163 respectively.
[322] *Official Records*, ibid, vol VI, 177; see also 201 (Ukraine); *Galic*, n 7, para 103.
[323] *Official Records*, vol VI, 193 (Mexico); 164 (UK).
[324] Cassese, n 229, 51.
[325] *Taylor* SCSL–2003–01 (3 Mar 2003); *Sankoh* SCSL–2003–02; *Koroma* SCSL–2003–03; *Bockarie* SCSL–2003–04; *Sesay* SCSL–2004–15–PT; *Brima* SCSL–2004–16–PT; *Kallon* SCSL–2004–15–PT; *Norman* SCSL–2004–14–PT; *Gbao* SCSL–2004–15–PT; *Kamara* SCSL–2004–16–PT; *Fofana* SCSL–2004–14–PT; *Kondewa* SCSL–2004–14–PT; *Kanu* SCSL–2004–16–PT. The indictments against Sankoh and Bockarie were withdrawn in December 2003 following their deaths.
[326] *Taylor*, ibid, count 1: Acts of Terrorism.   [327] ibid, counts 3–13.
[328] ICRC Study, n 3, vol I: *Rules*, 8–9; vol II: *Practice*, 69–72 (offences in Argentina, Australia, Bangladesh, Bosnia and Herzegovina, China, Colombia, Côte d'Ivoire, Croatia, Czech Republic, Ethiopia, Ireland, Lithuania, the Netherlands, Norway, Slovakia, Slovenia, Spain, and Yugoslavia). At least 17 military manuals prohibit terror in non-international conflict, while 12 States make it an offence: ibid, vol I, 9–10.

terrorism',[329] while a 1946 Chinese Law defined war crimes to include 'Planned slaughter, murder or other terrorist action'.[330] By 1995, the Colombian Constitutional Court had accepted the customary status of Article 13 of Protocol II, including its prohibition of terror.[331] In 1997, in the *Radulovic* case the Split County Court in Croatia convicted Serbian fighters for 'a plan of terrorising and mistreating the civilians', 'with the goal to terrorise', under Article 33 of the Fourth Geneva Convention, Article 51 of Protocol I, and Article 13 of Protocol II.[332] The acts included indiscriminately firing at civilian areas and threats to demolish, and demolishing, a dam with the intention of drowning 30,000 people.

Plainly not all violations of IHL attract individual criminal liability,[333] such as certain administrative or regulatory matters.[334] As a matter of policy, factors relevant in determining whether an international prohibition also gives rise to criminal liability include: 'The extent to which the prohibition is addressed to individuals, whether the prohibition is unequivocal in character, the gravity of the act, and the interest of the international community.'[335] Applying these criteria, the terrorism prohibitions in IHL treaties, which are not specifically listed as grave breaches, are: (a) addressed to individual conduct; (b) unequivocal, since terrorism is not even permitted in reprisal; (c) responding to extremely grave violence against civilians; and (d) safeguarding a vital international interest—the protection of civilians from violence in armed conflict.[336] Moreover, the imposition of international criminal responsibility 'is also fully warranted from the point of view of substantive justice and equity'.[337]

H. US MILITARY COMMISSIONS AND TERRORISM

In April 2003, the US Department of Defence issued an Instruction specifying the criminal jurisdiction of US military commissions in the US 'war on

---

[329] War Crimes Act 1945 (Australia), s 3, crimes as defined in a 1945 Board of Inquiry Instrument: see (1950–II) ILCYB 253, 265; (1950–II) ILCYB 253, 265; UNWCC Law Reports, vol V, annex, 95.

[330] Chinese Law, 24 Oct 1946, art III(1): see (1950–II) ILCYB 253, 266.

[331] Ruling No C–225/95, excerpted in M Sassòli and A Bouvier (eds), *How Does Law Protect in War?* (ICRC, Geneva, 1999) 1366, para 30; see also Colombian Penal Code, art 144.

[332] *Radulovic et al*, Split County Court, Rep Croatia, K–15/95, 26 May 1997. Terrorizing civilians was a crime under the 1960 and 1976 Yugoslavian Criminal Codes and was prohibited by 1988 Yugoslavian military regulations: *Galic*, n 7, paras 121–123.

[333] *Tadic (Interlocutory)*, n 71, para 94; Cassese, n 242, 50–51.

[334] Meron, n 306, 570.

[335] ibid, 562.

[336] The UN Secretary-General has identified the interests protected in *Galic* as among the fundamental standards of humanity: UNComHR (60th Sess), Report of the Secretary-General: Fundamental Standards of Humanity, 25 Feb 2004, UN Doc E/CN.4/2004/90, para 17.

[337] *Tadic (Interlocutory)*, n 71, para 135.

terror'.[338] The listed crimes ostensibly 'derive from' and 'constitute violations of' the law of armed conflict, or are offences 'consistent with that body of law'.[339] The Instruction purports to be 'declarative of existing law' and so allows trials for conduct prior to the date of the Instruction, but not for offences which did not previously exist.[340] The crimes are divided into three overarching categories of 'war crimes' (eighteen offences), 'other crimes triable by military commissions' (eight offences), and 'other forms of liability and related offences' (seven inchoate or ancillary offences).

The crime of 'terrorism' is listed in the Instruction as a substantive offence within the second category of 'other offences triable'.[341] Although no definition of terrorism is provided, the Instruction outlines its 'elements' as: (1) intentionally or recklessly killing or inflicting bodily harm, or destroying property; (2) such conduct was *intended to intimidate or coerce a civilian population, or to influence the policy of a government by intimidation and coercion*'; and (3) the conduct occurred 'in the context of and was associated with armed conflict'.[342]

The elements are not cumulative, since: 'Each element need not be specifically charged.' However, the offence would not be coherent as a distinct offence of 'terrorism' if the elements are *not* cumulative. Unless the second element always comprises part of the offence, the offence becomes indistinguishable from other war crimes such as unlawful killing or inflicting bodily harm on civilians.

The offence in the Instruction departs from the more limited crime of terror in IHL.[343] Mere 'intimidation' or 'coercion' of civilians by violence falls well short of the standard of 'extreme fear' established in the *Galic* case, and inferred from the ordinary meaning of 'terrorism'. Moreover, the prohibition of terror in IHL aims solely to protect civilians in armed conflict, not to a wider insulation of government policy from influence by coercion or intimidation—notwithstanding the Instruction's exclusion of attacks on lawful military objectives, by State military forces exercising official duties.[344]

As a result, the US Military Instruction exceeds its self-imposed limitations. Its offence of terrorism does *not* derive from the law of armed conflict, or declare existing law,[345] and thus permits punishment for an offence which

[338] US Department of Defence, Military Commission Instruction No 2: Crimes and Elements for Trials by Military Commission', 30 Apr 2003.
[339] ibid, 1.   [340] ibid.
[341] ibid, 13. The other offences in this category include: hijacking or hazarding a vessel or aircraft; murder by an unprivileged belligerent; destruction of property by an unprivileged belligerent; aiding the enemy; spying; perjury or false testimony; and obstruction of justice related to military commissions.
[342] ibid, 12–13 (emphasis added). Element (1) includes causing death or bodily harm, even indirectly.
[343] F Kirgis, 'US Charges and Proceedings against Two Guantanamo Detainees for Conspiracy to Commit Crimes Associated with Armed Conflict', *ASIL Insight*, Mar 2004.
[344] US Military Instruction, n 338, 13.   [345] ibid, 1.

did not exist at the time the conduct took place.[346] The first two Guantanamo Bay detainees charged in February 2004 were accused of terrorism under the Instruction,[347] giving rise to grave concerns about retrospective punishment and an unfair trial.

The definition of terrorism in the Instruction draws inspiration from the 1999 Terrorist Financing Convention, which, *inter alia*, prohibits the financing of acts 'intended to cause death or serious bodily injury . . . when the purpose . . . is to intimidate a population, or to compel a government'.[348] However, that Convention only requires States to criminalize the *financing* of such acts, and not the acts themselves. Further, the Convention does not apply to persons actively participating in hostilities in an armed conflict. In addition, outside armed conflict, there is no generic treaty or customary crime of terrorism.[349] Consequently, the Instruction is not grounded in any general international crime of terrorism outside IHL, although it conflates different meanings of terrorism within and outside armed conflict.

I. NO SEPARATE CATEGORY OF TERRORIST

The prohibitions on terror in armed conflict do not give rise to any special legal status for suspected violators. The legal *status* of 'terrorists' in IHL has been exhaustively discussed in connection with the 'war on terror'[350] and is not considered here. It is sufficient to note that—unlike for spies and mercenaries—there is no distinct legal category of 'terrorist' in IHL, just as those who commit the war crimes of pillage or rape are not separately categorized as 'pillagers' or 'rapists'.[351]

Rather, combatants and non-combatants (including unlawful participants in hostilities) are equally bound by the prohibitions on terror. They may be

---

[346] ibid.

[347] N Lewis, 'US charges two at Guantánamo with conspiracy', *New York Times*, 25 Feb 2004.

[348] 1999 Terrorist Financing Convention, Art 2(1)(b).   [349] See Chs 3 and 4 above.

[350] M Sassòli, 'The Status of Persons Held in Guantanamo under International Humanitarian Law' (2004) 2 JICJ 96; S Palmer, 'Arbitrary Detention in Guantanamo Bay: Legal Limbo in the Land of the Free' [2003] 62 *Cambridge Law Journal* 6; K Dörmann, 'The Legal Situation of "Unlawful/Unprivileged Combatants" ' (2003) 85 IRRC 45; J Klabbers, 'Rebel with a Cause? Terrorists and Humanitarian Law' (2003) 14 EJIL 299; D Vagts, 'Which Courts Should Try Persons Accused of Terrorism?' (2003) 14 EJIL 313; G Aldrich, 'The Taliban, Al Qaeda, and the Determination of Illegal Combatants' (2002) 96 AJIL 892; see national cases such as: *Hamdi v Rumsfeld* (US Sup Ct, 28 June 2004); *Rasul v Bush* (US Sup Ct, 28 June 2004); *Coalition of Clergy, Lawyers and Professors v Bush* (US Sup Ct, 19 May 2003); *Abassi v Foreign Secretary* [2002] EWCA Civ 1598.

[351] The Council of Europe has not ruled out developing new categories of combatants concerning terrorist groups: Venice Commission (57th Plenary Sess), Opinion on the Possible Need for Further Development of the Geneva Conventions, 17 Dec 2003, Opinion No 245/2003, CDL-AD (2003) 18, 23.

criminally liable for terrorist acts amounting to war crimes, while non-combatants are also liable for terrorist violations of national law. Persons who unlawfully participate in hostilities by committing terrorist acts become legitimate objects of attack *during the course of* armed engagements, although once *hors de combat*, they regain protected status.[352] It is necessary, however, to distinguish terrorist acts during hostilities from other terrorist acts committed in wartime, but unrelated to the conflict, or outside the theatre of hostilities.[353]

J. CONCLUSION: PROVING TERROR, AVOIDING DUPLICATION

Fear is endemic in war, and instilling fear in enemy combatants through lawful methods is normal, even expected.[354] At the same time, the violence of any conflict—even one strictly fought between combatants—inevitably produces psychological insecurity in civilians. But the international community has agreed that deliberately terrorizing civilians warrants condemnation, as it rises above the ordinary level of fear tolerated in war as an incident of military necessity.

After a series of early efforts before 1949, there are now well-established—if infrequently invoked—prohibitions of 'terrorism' and 'terror' in IHL, which derive meaning from their ordinary textual interpretation, drafting history and historical usage, and relevant case law. Developments in customary law have also given rise to individual criminal responsibility for breaches of some of these prohibitions.

In an essay on fear, Montaigne wrote: 'I have hardly any idea of the mechanisms by which fear operates in us'.[355] Despite the subjectivity of an emotional state such as 'terror', justiciable methods of proving the existence, or likelihood, of a state of grave fear are available. Just as national tort laws cope with concepts of nervous shock, emotional distress, mental suffering, post-traumatic stress, psychosis, and other psychological conditions, diagnosing 'terror' (and identifying acts that produce it) is not beyond medical science.

As in the *Galic* case, expert witnesses may assist in determinations; while in

---

[352] Gasser (2002), n 3, 566. See generally G Rona, 'Interesting Times for International Humanitarian Law: Challenges from the "War on Terror" ' (2005) 17 *Terrorism and Political Violence* 157.

[353] Dinstein, n 203, 64; Koufa (2001), n 193, 21–22. Consider the conflicts in Sri Lanka, Chechnya, and Kashmir, which involve territorial armed conflicts and terrorist acts outside the theatre of hostilities.

[354] G Bouthoul, 'Definitions of Terrorism' in D Carlton and C Schaerf, *International Terrorism and World Security* (Croom Helm, London, 1975) 50–51; C Greenwood, 'Terrorism and Humanitarian Law: The Debate over Additional Protocol I' (1989) 19 IYBHR 187, 188–189; ICRC Report, n 179, 3.

[355] M de Montaigne, 'On Fear' in M de Montaigne, *The Complete Essays* (trans M Screech, Penguin, London, 1991) 81.

the *Nikolic* case, the mental trauma suffered was evidence of terror in detention.[356] In a civil analogy, in 2002 a US court held a Bosnian Serb responsible for intentionally inflicting emotional distress.[357] Since different people have different thresholds of terror,[358] courts should consider the degree of fear that a reasonable person, of ordinary firmness of mind, might be expected to resist; as well as any cultural (or other relevant) differences affecting the ability of particular populations or sub-populations to cope with fear.

A doctrinal question remains as to whether prohibiting terror is superfluous in the light of more direct prohibitions on violence against civilians.[359] An intent to spread terror will almost always only exist in connection with other unlawful acts or threats, such as sniping and shelling in the *Galic* case, or aerial bombing in both world wars. Proof of intentional physical attacks does not require showing a further underlying purpose, which may be difficult to prove. The variety of motives includes: reaching combatants hiding among civilians; depopulating or capturing territory; undermining civilian support for the military; terrorizing civilians into submission; reprisal or punishment; discrimination or persecution; extermination or genocide; even sadism or base cruelty.

Yet it is the business of IHL and criminal law to draw precise distinctions between different types of attacks on civilians. Simple protections against physical attacks do not capture the idea that the some attacks are deliberately designed to achieve more than their immediate objective of physical harm. A range of other crimes and prohibitions address ulterior purposes behind physical attacks on civilians, including discrimination, persecution, extermination, genocide, reprisal, and collective punishment. These too are already covered by simple prohibitions on attacking civilians, but still exist to protect other values infringed by such attacks.

In the same way, there is something profoundly disturbing or shocking to moral sensibility about acts or threats of violence which deliberately seek to put civilians in grave fear for their lives or safety. Spreading terror among non-combatants is a particular kind of cruelty and viciousness which deserves explicit and specific condemnation. This is an inherently moral position which may not be shared by all. But it does seem borne out by the experience of civilian suffering in war.

[356] *Nikolic*, n 318, para 69; also paras 109, 177.
[357] Decision of Dist Ct of Northern District of Georgia, 29 Apr 2002, in 'National Implementation of International Humanitarian Law: Biannual Update: Jan–Jun 2002' (2002) No 847 IRRC 701, 713.
[358] P Wilkinson, *Terrorism and the Liberal State* (Macmillan, London, 1977) 47.
[359] eg 1949 Fourth Geneva Convention, Art 27; 1977 Protocol I, Art 51(2); 1977 Protocol II, Art 13(2).

CONCLUSION
The Promise of Restraint

Undoubtedly, terrorism commands disproportionate attention relative to the harm it causes[1] and other kinds of violence—particularly by States, and even by common criminals—cause greater harm.[2] Since the 1960s, global casualties of international terrorism have averaged a few thousand deaths per decade, in contrast to the many tens of millions killed in wars, internal conflicts, and by repressive States.[3] Clearly, 'the quantum of harm' caused by terrorism 'is not what shapes perceptions of [the] threat'[4] and terrorism may well indulge western anxieties in the absence of real emergencies.[5] The spectacular nature of terrorist acts, the vulnerability of civilian targets, the frequent victimization of the United States and Israel, and mass media publicity have shaped a powerful discourse of public panic and transnational anxiety surrounding terrorism. In some western media, there is little questioning of the official labelling of 'terrorists', analysis of the causes of terrorism, attention to State violence precipitating terrorism, or responsiveness to non-State explanations for violence.[6] Exaggeration of the terrorist threat is significant because those who fear terrorism the most also tend to support more aggressively militant responses to it.[7]

While it is simplistic to claim that the attacks of 11 September 2001 were a 'predictable and inevitable . . . act of retaliation against constant and systematic manifestations of state terrorism' by the US,[8] in some cases, root causes underlie and explain—but do not necessarily justify or excuse—resort to

[1] MC Bassiouni, 'A Policy-Oriented Inquiry into the Different Forms and Manifestations of "International Terrorism" ' in MC Bassiouni (ed), *Legal Responses to International Terrorism* (Martinus Nijhoff, Dordrecht, 1988) xv, xvii, xxvi; J Lambert, *Terrorism and Hostages in International Law* (Grotius, Cambridge, 1990) 24.

[2] N Chomsky, 'Terror and Just Response' in J Sterba (ed), *Terrorism and International Justice* (OUP, Oxford, 2003) 69, 70–71; P Wilkinson, *Terrorism and the Liberal State* (Macmillan, London, 1977) 197; J Pilger, 'The attack on Iraq is another chapter of terrorism from the West', *Sydney Morning Herald*, 23 Mar 2004.

[3] L Pojman, 'The Moral Response to Terrorism and Cosmopolitanism' in Sterba (ed), n 2, 135. US Department of Justice (FBI), *Terrorism in the US 1999* (DOJ, Washington, DC, 2000) 15 (there were an estimated 14,000 international terrorist attacks between 1968 and 1999, resulting in 10,000 deaths).

[4] MC Bassiouni, 'Terrorism: The Persistent Dilemma of Legitimacy' (2004) 36 Case Western Reserve JIL 299, 302.

[5] C Gearty, *The Future of Terrorism* (Phoenix, London, 1997) 14.

[6] G Philo, 'What you get in 20 seconds', *The Guardian*, 14 July 2004; 'Mid-East coverage baffles Britons', BBC News, 22 June 2004.

[7] L Weinberg, A Pedahzur, and D Canetti-Nisim, 'The Social and Religious Characteristics of Suicide Bombers and Their Victims' (2003) 15 *Terrorism and Political Violence* 139, 147–148.

[8] H Pinter, Speech on receipt of an Honorary Doctorate at Turin, 27 Nov 2002.

terrorism. Legal controls perform only cosmetic functions, or merely treat symptoms, unless structural grievances are also addressed.[9] In particular, inclusive political processes discourage violence[10]—even if it is not possible to bargain meaningfully with some people.[11] The preoccupation with terrorism also overshadows less spectacular international harms, including those which may generate terrorist impulses. As Koskenniemi writes:

It is hard to justify the attention given and the resources allocated to the 'fight against terrorism' in the aftermath of the attacks . . . in September 2001 in which nearly 3,000 people lost their lives, while simultaneously six million children under five years old die annually of malnutrition by causes that could be prevented . . . What becomes a 'crisis' in the world and will involve the political energy and resources of the international system is determined in a thoroughly Western-dominated process . . .[12]

The response to terrorism has, furthermore, distorted the allocation of the limited funds available for humanitarian assistance. In 2002, half of all global humanitarian aid went to Afghanistan[13]—the frontline in the 'war on terror'—and aid distribution was similarly distorted following the invasion of Iraq in 2003. Terrorism has thus come to dominate both security discourse and the field of humanitarian action.

The refashioning of terrorism as an international security threat has profoundly shaped the choice of legal responses, while conversely the choice of legal responses has influenced the characterization of terrorism as a security threat. Much has been written of the view that after 11 September 2001, it is no longer enough to serve terrorists with legal papers,[14] or that a 'third way' between crime and war is required.[15] The reliance on legal 'black holes' or 'loopholes' has been eloquently described elsewhere,[16] as a variety of

---

[9] C Harding, 'The Concept of Terrorism and Responses to Global Terrorism: Coming to Terms with the Empty Sky', Paper at Sept 11 Conference, University of Sussex, 21–22 Mar 2003, 1; see also G Abi-Saab, 'The Proper Role of International Law in Combating Terrorism' (2002) 1 Chinese JIL 305, 312; A Cassese, 'Terrorism is Also Disrupting Some Crucial Legal Categories of International Law' (2001) 12 EJIL 993, 1000–1001.

[10] J Stevenson, 'Irreversible Peace in Northern Ireland?' (2000) 42 *Survival* 5, 20.

[11] Wilkinson, n 2, 180.

[12] M Koskenniemi, 'What is International Law For?' in M Evans (ed), *International Law* (OUP, Oxford, 2003) 89, 95–96.

[13] A Horin, 'The forgotten victims of war on terrorism', *Sydney Morning Herald*, 10 June 2004.

[14] US President Bush, State of the Union Address, 20 Jan 2004.

[15] R Dworkin, 'Terror and the Attack on Civil Liberties', *NY Rev Books*, 6 Nov 2003. Others have bluntly argued for 'fourth generation' warfare against terrorists where 'the distinction between war and peace will be blurred to the vanishing point', along with the civilian-military distinction: S Lind et al, 'The Changing Face of War' (Oct 1989) *Marine Corps Gazette* 22–26; see generally R Grote, 'Between Crime Prevention and the Laws of War: Are the Traditional Categories of International Law Adequate for Assessing the Use of Force against International Terrorism?' in C Walter et al (eds), *Terrorism as a Challenge for National and International Law* (Springer, Heidelberg, 2004) 951.

[16] J Steyn, 'Guantanamo Bay: The Legal Black Hole' (2004) 53 ICLQ 1 and D Hovell, 'Of Black Holes and Loopholes: Human Rights and the "War against Terrorism" ' (2005) 14 *Human Rights Defender* 7 respectively; see also P Sands, *Lawless World* (Penguin, London, 2005) chs 7–9.

exceptional responses to terrorism proliferated: extrajudicial execution or assassination of suspects (often by foreign governments, outside conflict zones, and based on untested, secret evidence); torture and ill-treatment; extraordinary or irregular rendition; and regimes of preventive, executive, or incommunicado detention. Extra-legal approaches to countering terrorism are marked by their denial or restriction of procedural protections, access to remedies, and judicial supervision. Even where formal human rights protections apply, fear of terrorism has fostered a climate in which States may resort too readily to states of exception and derogation, while courts face pressure to allow 'margins of appreciation' or degrees of deference that are arguably too wide.

Set against the vain hope of pounding terrorists into oblivion through war, the criminal law offers the promise of restraint: individual rather than collective responsibility; a presumption of innocence; no detention without charge; proof of guilt beyond reasonable doubt; due process; the right to prepare and present an adequate defence; independent adjudication; and rational and proportionate punishment.[17] Criminal law responses to terrorism are not a panacea; for one thing, new anti-terrorism laws may have a 'marginal deterrent value',[18] although terrorist acts often occur because of law enforcement or intelligence failures rather than gaps in the law.[19] While the threat of terrorism may justify some modifications to regular criminal process, there is also a risk that rational principles of criminal law may be strained by reactive and emotive responses wrought by political pressures on governments.[20] Indeed, many States have modified regular criminal procedure or established expansive offences in terrorist cases, increasing the risk of wrongful convictions.[21] Whether defining terrorism is a good idea must depend on the uses to which it will be put, particular if it is designed to trigger radical measures outside the criminal law.

Despite these limitations, defining and criminalizing terrorism in international law would provide States with a functional, alternative response to terrorism. Expanding the armoury of regular legal responses may discourage the premature resort to extra-legal and military options. In the absence of any 'law of terrorism' in public international law,[22] it is not sufficient to leave definition of terrorism to individual governments, as the Security Council

---

[17] See, eg, K Roach, 'The Criminal Law and Terrorism' in V Ramraj, M Hor, and K Roach (eds), *Global Anti-Terrorism Law and Policy* (CUP, Cambridge, 2005) 129, 150–151.

[18] ibid, 150.   [19] ibid, 136.   [20] ibid, 132.

[21] ibid, 140. eg some States have made it easier to admit certain types of less reliable evidence; protected security sensitive evidence from disclosure to defendants or the court; modified the standard or burden of proof; removed the right to silence; overridden lawyer-client confidentiality; limited judicial supervision; and established broad preparatory or group-based terrorist offences.

[22] I Brownlie, *Principles of Public International Law* (6th edn, OUP, Oxford, 2003) 713.

has done.[23] Definition would not merely produce gains at the 'crude political level',[24] but could normatively express and articulate the wrongfulness of terrorism through the creation of a new international crime,[25] and restrain excessive national counter-terrorism responses. The term 'terrorism' holds powerful sway over public consciousness and, since the 1920s, has been often grappled with by jurists at the international level, suggesting that it captures and describes a phenomenon of some social and political importance.

DEFINING TERRORISM IN INTERNATIONAL LAW

In the light of the intense and persistent disagreement about defining terrorism over many years, it is crucial to first appreciate precisely what is so objectionable about terrorism. As shown in Chapter 1, the views and practice of States, evidenced through UN organs, indicate that the international community regards terrorism as a grave affront to fundamental human rights and freedoms, State authority and the political process, and international security. Terrorism is also perceived as distinguishable from private violence due to its political or public motivations, while a definition could structure and restrain the unilateral implementation of Security Council measures. These considerations, along with other incidental or subsidiary arguments, provide a coherent—but not unproblematic—basis on which to internationally define and criminalize terrorism.

Unless a pacifist position is accepted, any international definition of terrorism must ensure that legitimate forms of violent resistance to political oppression are not internationally criminalized. Chapter 2 argued that controversy about defining terrorism could be defused or depoliticized if similarly-situated self-determination movements were equally treated by the law, through the extension of Protocol I and recognition of combatant immunity. This does not mean that such movements could commit terrorist acts with impunity. Rather, IHL would apply to conduct committed in armed conflict, including liability for war crimes and for breaches of the specialized prohibitions on 'terrorism' in armed conflict (including where civilians are deliberately attacked). Far from legitimizing terrorists, the application of

---

[23] cf C Lim, 'The Question of a Generic Definition of Terrorism under General International Law' in Ramraj et al (eds), n 17, 37, 62–63 (arguing that national definition can progressively develop custom and produce greater precision in definition and wider participation by States).

[24] R Higgins, 'The General International Law of Terrorism' in R Higgins and M Flory (eds), *Terrorism and International Law* (Routledge, London, 1997) 13, 26.

[25] See also UN High-Level Panel on Threats, Challenges and Change, *A more secure world: Our shared responsibility*, 2 Dec 2004, UN Doc A/59/565, para 159: 'Lack of agreement on a clear and well-known definition undermines the normative and moral stance against terrorism and has stained the United Nations image'.

humanitarian law provides an incentive for them to comply with the law (since compliance is rewarded with treatment as prisoners of war). A similar approach could be adopted in internal conflicts involving political rebellions.

As for 'State terrorism', such conduct by governments is largely covered by other rules of international law, including human rights law, criminal law, humanitarian law (including specific offences of terrorism in the 1949 Geneva Convention and 1977 Protocols), and the law of State responsibility. In contrast, non-State actors have historically been subject to far less regulation, thus stimulating efforts to address some of their activities by defining them as terrorism. Even so, there is still a case for making State officials accountable for government violence which amounts to terrorism, since the above-mentioned laws applying to States do not always impose individual *criminal* liability for unlawful State violence (and instead only give rise to other remedies such as a duty to make reparation). This is so particularly where State violence is committed outside armed conflict (so war crimes law does not apply), and beneath the threshold of crimes against humanity (requiring conduct to be large scale or systematic). Only imposing liability for terrorism on non-State actors suffers from a lack of moral symmetry, undermining the legitimacy of any definition of terrorism. Thus extrajudicial assassinations of political opponents by State officials might gainfully be qualified as terrorism (such as the US assassination of enemies in Yemen, outside the theatre of hostilities), as might suicide bombings by non-State actors in peacetime.

At the same time, it makes sense to exclude the activities of State armed forces and non-State forces recognized under humanitarian law (as long as Protocol I is extended to liberation forces as argued earlier). Otherwise, criminalizing terrorism might interfere in the carefully constructed parameters of permissible violence in armed conflict, potentially unravelling compliance with the law of war and endangering civilians. (The alternative is to impose concurrent liability, just as crimes against humanity and genocide apply alongside war crimes law in armed conflicts).

Outside the context of armed conflicts, Chapter 3 found that, between 1963 and 2005, the international community strenuously avoided generic definition of terrorism in international treaties, instead preferring an objective, sectoral approach to regulating terrorist type acts. By the 1990s, that approach began to change as generic elements of definition found a place in the 1999 Terrorist Financing Convention, and the Draft UN Comprehensive Convention, but also in a number of treaties adopted by regional organizations. The diversity of regional definitions, however, militates against the emergence of a customary international crime. The many unsuccessful international attempts to define terrorism since the 1920s indicate that the international community has often regarded generic definition as normatively important. While some of these efforts took similar approaches to definition, others were more divergent, and most attempts were thwarted by political and ideological obstacles thrown up by decolonization and the Cold War.

As Chapter 4 shows, there is also insufficient evidence of State practice and *opinio juris* supporting a customary international definition or crime of terrorism. The General Assembly has condemned terrorism in increasingly strident tones since the late 1970s, and reached political agreement on a working definition by 1994. Yet many States conditioned support for these positions on an understanding that legal definition of terrorism, and agreement on exceptions to terrorism, were still necessary. For its part, from 1985 onwards, the Security Council incrementally identified particular acts or incidents as terrorist threats to peace and security, without providing advance definition of terrorism. Council measures from late 2001 responded to terrorism in a more generalized way, still without defining the scope of the problem. The serious legal consequences of Resolution 1373—including individual criminal liability for an ambiguous range of terrorist conduct—highlights the need for definition. A non-binding working definition of late 2004 is insufficient, and there are legitimacy costs in evading the usual treaty-making processes for transnational crimes.

Further, international and national judicial decisions seldom invoke terrorism as an operative international legal concept, usually treating terrorist-type conduct by recourse to more entrenched legal norms. Some national decisions, however, have deployed international definitions of terrorism for non-criminal purposes, such as in immigration proceedings or exclusion from refugee status. In national criminal legislation, almost half of States now define terrorism generically (either in simple or composite definitions), although half of States still treat terrorism as ordinary crime. The variation in national definitions precludes the identification of any international customary definition, although generic definition is increasingly common.

Finally, Chapter 5 explored the evolution and progressive codification of distinctive prohibitions on terrorism in armed conflict under IHL. Early prohibitions on aerial bombardment to terrorize civilians were generalized and universalized in the 1949 Geneva Convention and 1977 Protocols and have been affirmed in subsequent State practice and applied most recently as a basis for individual criminal liability in ad hoc international criminal tribunals. While there are difficulties in quantifying 'terror' in war and in differentiating it from the ether of fear which surrounds and permeates conflict, the international community has consciously condemned the deliberate terrorization of civilians as a tactic. The meaning of terrorism in IHL is distinct from the meaning of terrorism outside armed conflicts.

Utimately, attempts to abandon any legal use of the term 'terrorism', as pointless 'moralised name-calling',[26] are unrealistic in view of its popular resonance and powerful, enduring appeal. It is preferable to acknowledge that the term, once defined, can help to distinguish between different types of illegitimate violence[27] and to express international condemnation of acts of political violence which transgress the outermost ethical boundaries of legitimate violent resistance. Intellectually, definition would also supply clarity in studying terrorism, since the methodological difficulties of researching 'terrorism' stem partly from the conceptual confusion about its content.[28] Indeed, it is not possible coherently or systematically to describe, analyse, understand or ultimately counter the threat posed by terrorism unless there is basic agreement on what constitutes it.[29]

In the absence of definition, a lingering 'conceptual chaos or zone of passing turbulence in public or political language'[30] privileges those in the hegemonic position to define and interpret 'terrorism'—and to erratically brand it upon their enemies.

[26] G Wardlaw, *Political Terrorism: Theory, Tactics and Counter-Measures* (CUP, Cambridge, 1982) 8.

[27] ibid.

[28] A Silke, 'The Devil You Know: Continuing Problems with Research on Terrorism' (2001) 13 *Terrorism and Political Violence* 1, 2.

[29] See, eg, Wardlaw, n 26, 3.

[30] J Derrida, quoted in G Borradori, *Philosophy in a Time of Terror: Dialogues with Jürgen Habermas and Jacques Derrida* (University of Chicago Press, Chicago, 2003) 105.

Bibliography

'Documents Concerning the Aerial Incidents at Lockerbie and in Niger' (1992) 31 *International Legal Materials* 717.

'The Great Compromise: Where to Convene the Trial of the Suspects Implicated in the Pan Am Flight 103 Bombing over Lockerbie, Scotland' (1999) 23 *Suffolk Transnational Law Review* 131.

'Lockerbie Criminal Trial Glossary' (1999) 11 *International Legal Perspectives* 41.

'National Implementation of International Humanitarian Law: Biannual Update on National Legislation and Case Law: Jan–Jun 2002' (2002) 847 IRRC 701.

'The Passive Personality Principle and its Use in Combating International Terrorism' (1990) 13 Fordham ILJ 298.

'Terrorism as a Tort in Violation of the Law of Nations' (1982) 6 Fordham ILJ 236.

'The United States and the World Need an International Criminal Court as an Ally in the War against Terrorism' (1997) 8 *Indiana International and Comparative Law Review* 159.

Abbott, K, 'Economic Sanctions and International Terrorism' (1987) 20 Van JTL 289.

Abi-Saab, G, 'Wars of National Liberation in the Geneva Conventions and Protocols' (1979–IV) 165 *Recueil des Cours* 353.

—— 'Whither the International Community' (1998) 9 EJIL 248.

—— 'The Proper Role of International Law in Combating Terrorism' (2002) 1 Chinese JIL 305.

—— 'The Proper Role of International Law in Combating Terrorism' in Bianchi, A (ed), *Enforcing International Law Norms Against Terrorism* (Hart, Oxford, 2004) xiii.

Abresch, W, 'A Human Rights Law of Internal Armed Conflict: The European Court of Human Rights in Chechnya' (2005) 16 EJIL 741.

Abu-Lughod, I, 'Unconventional Violence and International Politics' (1973) 67 ASIL Proceedings 100.

Advisory Council of Jurists, Asia Pacific Forum of National Human Rights Institutions, Reference on the Rule of Law in Countering Terrorism, Background Paper, Aug 2003.

Akande, D, 'The International Court of Justice and the Security Council: Is There Room for Judicial Control of Decisions of the Political Organs of the United Nations?' (1997) 46 ICLQ 309.

Aldrich, G, 'The Taliban, Al Qaeda, and the Determination of Illegal Combatants' (2002) 96 AJIL 892.

Alexander, Y, 'Minorities and Terrorism: Some Legal and Strategic Perspectives' (1991) 21 IYHR 151.

—— 'Democracy and Terrorism: Threats and Responses' (1996) 26 IYBHR 253.

—— Browne M, and Nanes A (eds), *Control of Terrorism: International Documents* (Crane Russak, New York, 1979).

—— and Nanes, A (eds), *Legislative Responses To Terrorism* (Martinus Nijhoff, Dordrecht, 1986).

Allain, J, 'The Legacy of Lockerbie: Judicial Review of Security Council Actions or the First Manifestation of "Terrorism" as a Threat to International Peace?' (2004) 44 Indian JIL 74.

Allen, B, 'Talking "Terrorism": Ideologies and Paradigms in a Postmodern World' (1996) 22 Syra JILC 7.

Allison, M, 'The Hamas Deportation: Israel's Response to Terrorism during the Middle East Peace Process' (1994) 10 AUJILP 397.

Allott, P, 'The Concept of International Law' (1999) 10 EJIL 31.

Alvarez, J, 'Judging the Security Council' (1996) 90 AJIL 1.

Amarasinha, S and Isenbecker, M, 'Terrorism and the Right to Asylum under the 1951 Convention and the 1967 Protocol Relating to The Status of Refugees: A Contradiction in Terms or Do Opposites Attract?' (1996) 65 Nordic JIL 223.

Amnesty International, 'The Quest for International Justice: Defining the Crimes and Defences for the International Criminal Court', AI Index: IOR 40/006/1997, 1 Feb 1997.

—— Comments on a Proposal by the Commission for a Council Framework Decision on Combating Terrorism, Brussels, 19 Oct 2001.

—— 'Draft Comprehensive Convention on International Terrorism: A Threat to Human Rights Standards', Statement to UNGA 56th Sess (2002), AI Index: IOR 51/009/2001, 22 Oct 2001.

—— 'The Arab Convention for the Suppression of Terrorism: A Serious Threat to Human Rights' (2002), AI Index: IOR 51/001/2002, 9 Jan 2002.

—— 'Rights at Risk: Concerns Regarding Security Legislation and Law Enforcement Measures', AI Index: ACT 30/002/2002, 18 Jan 2002.

—— and Human Rights Watch, 'Comprehensive Convention against International Terrorism', Joint Letter to Ambassadors, 28 Jan 2002.

Anderson, B, *Imagined Communities: Reflections on the Origin and Spread of Nationalism* (Verso, London, 1983).

Anderson, S and Sloan, S, *Historical Dictionary of Terrorism* (Scarecrow Press, London, 1995).

Andreu-Guzmán, F (ed), *Terrorism and Human Rights* (ICJ, Geneva, 2002).

An-Na'im, A, 'Islamic Ambivalence to Political Violence: Islamic Law and International Terrorism' (1988) 31 Ger YBIL 307.

Ansah, T, 'War: Rhetoric and Norm Creation in Response to Terror' (2003) 43 Virginia JIL 797.

Arab Center for the Independence of the Judiciary and the Legal Profession, 'Commentary on the Arab Convention Against Terrorism', Cairo, 7 May 1998.

Arangio-Ruiz, G, 'The Normative Role of the General Assembly of the United Nations and the Declaration of Principles of Friendly Relations' (1972–III) 137 *Recueil des Cours* 419.

—— *The United Nations Declaration on Friendly Relations and the System of the Sources of International Law* (Alphen aan den Rijn, Netherlands, 1979).

Archibugi, D and Marion Young, I, 'Envisioning a Global Rule of Law' in Sterba, J, (ed), *Terrorism and International Justice* (OUP, Oxford, 2003) 158.

Arendt, H, *On Revolution* (Penguin, London, 1990).

Arsanjani, M, 'The 1998 Rome Statute of the International Criminal Court' (1999) 93 AJIL 22.

Arzt, D, 'The Lockerbie "Extradition by Analogy" Agreement: "Exceptional Measure" or Template for Transnational Criminal Justice?' (2002) 18 AUILR 163.

Ashworth, A, *Principles of Criminal Law* (3rd edn, OUP, Oxford, 1999).

Atkinson, J, 'Criminal Law: Racketeer Influences and Corrupt Organizations: Broadest of the Federal Criminal Statutes' (1978) 69 JCLC 1.

Aust, A, *Modern Treaty Law and Practice* (CUP, Cambridge, 2000).

—— 'Lockerbie: The Other Case' (2000) 49 ICLQ 278.

—— 'Counter-terrorism: A New Approach—The International Convention for the Suppression of the Financing of Terrorism' (2001) *Max Planck Yearbook of United Nations Law* 287.

—— Implementation Kits for the International Counter-Terrorism Conventions (Commonwealth Secretariat, London, 2002).

Austin, J, *Philosophical Papers* (Clarendon, Oxford, 1961).

Australian Law Reform Commission, *Principled Regulation: Civil and Administrative Penalties in Australia* (Report 95, Sydney, 2002).

Babievsky, K, 'Chemical Biological Terrorism' (1997) 6 *Low Intensity Conflict and Law Enforcement* 163.

Bailey, S, 'The UN Security Council and Terrorism' (1993) 11 *International Relations* 533.

Baker, M, 'The Western European Legal Response to Terrorism' (1987) 13 Brooklyn JIL 1.

Bali, A, 'Stretching the Limits of International Law: The Challenge of Terrorism' (2002) 8 ILSA JICL 403.

Bannelier, K, Christakis, T, Corten, O, and Delcourt, B (eds), *Le droit international face au terrorisme: Après le 11 septembre 2001* (Bruylant, Brussels, 2002).

Banoff, B and Pyle, C, 'To Surrender Political Offenders' (1984) 16 NYU JILP 169

Bantekas, I, 'The International Law of Terrorist Financing' (2003) 97 AJIL 315.

Bassiouni, MC, 'Unlawful Seizures and Irregular Rendition Devices as Alternatives to Extradition' (1973) 7 Van JTL 25.

—— *International Extradition and World Public Order* (AW Sijthoff, Leiden, 1974).

—— 'Methodological Options for International Legal Control of Terrorism' in Bassiouni, MC (ed), *International Terrorism and Political Crimes* (Charles C Thomas, Illinois, 1975) 485.

—— 'An International Control Scheme for the Prosecution of International Terrorism: An Introduction' in Evans, A and Murphy, J (eds), *Legal Aspects of International Terrorism* (ASIL, Washington, DC, 1979) 485.

—— 'Criminological Policy' in Evans, A and Murphy, J (eds), *Legal Aspects of International Terrorism* (ASIL, Washington, DC, 1979) 523.

—— *International Criminal Law: A Draft International Criminal Code* (Sijthoff and Noordhoff, Groningen, 1980).

—— 'International Control of Terrorism: Some Policy Proposals' (1981) *International Review of Criminal Policy* 44.

—— 'Terrorism, Law Enforcement and the Mass Media' (1981) 72 JCLC 1.

—— 'The Penal Characteristics of Conventional International Criminal Law' (1983) 15 Case Western Reserve JIL 27.

—— 'A Policy-Oriented Inquiry into the Different Forms and Manifestations of

"International Terrorism" ' in Bassiouni, MC (ed), *Legal Responses to International Terrorism: US Procedural Aspects* (Martinus Nijhoff, Dordrecht, 1988) xv.

—— 'Effective National and International Action against Organized Crime and Terrorist Criminal Activities' (1990) 4 Emory ILR 9.

—— *Crimes Against Humanity in International Criminal Law* (Martinus Nijhoff, Dordrecht, 1992).

—— 'International Terrorism' in Bassiouni, MC (ed), *International Criminal Law* (Translation Publishers, New York, 1999) 766.

—— *International Terrorism: Multilateral Conventions (1937–2001)* (Transnational Publishers, New York, 2001).

—— *International Terrorism: A Compilation of UN Documents (1972–2001)* (Transnational Publishers, New York, 2002).

—— 'World War I: "The War to End all Wars" and the Birth of a Handicapped International Criminal Justice System' (2002) 30 Den JILP 244.

—— 'Legal Control of International Terrorism: A Policy-Oriented Assessment' (2002) 43 Harvard ILJ 83.

—— 'Terrorism: The Persistent Dilemma of Legitimacy' (2004) 36 Case Western Reserve JIL 299.

—— and Wise, E, *Aut Dedere Aut Judicare: The Duty to Extradite or Prosecute in International Law* (Martinus Nijhoff, Dordrecht, 1995).

Baudrillard, J, 'Hypotheses on Terrorism' in Baudrillard, J, *The Spirit of Terrorism and Other Essays* (trans Turner, C, Verson, London, 2003) 49.

Baxter, R, 'A Skeptical Look at the Concept of Terrorism' (1974) 7 *Akron Law Review* 380.

—— 'The Geneva Conventions of 1949 and Wars of National Liberation', in Bassiouni, MC (ed), *International Terrorism and Political Crimes* (Charles C Thomas, Illinois, 1975) 120

Bayles, M, 'Reconceptualizing Necessity and Duress' in Corrado, M (ed), *Justification and Excuse in the Criminal Law* (Garland, New York, 1994) 492.

Becerra, M, 'The *Cavallo* Case: A Case of Universal Jurisdiction?', Paper at Oxford Public International Law Discussion Group, 4 Mar 2004.

Bedjaoui, M, *The New World Order and the Security Council: Testing the Legality of its Acts* (trans Noble, B, Martinus Nijhoff, Dordrecht, 1994).

Bekker, P, 'Questions of Interpretation and Application of the 1971 Montreal Convention arising from the Aerial Incident at Lockerbie' (1998) 92 AJIL 503.

Bell, B, *Terror Out of Zion: Irgun Zvai Leumi, Lehi and the Palestine Underground 1929–1949* (Avon, New York, 1977).

Berdal, M, 'The Security Council, Peacekeeping and Internal Conflict after the Cold War' (1997) 7 Duke JCIL 71.

Beres L, 'On International Law and Nuclear Terrorism' (1994) 24 Geo JICL 1.

—— 'The Legal Meaning of Terrorism for the Military Commander' (1995) 11 Connecticut JIL 1.

—— 'The Meaning of Terrorism: Jurisprudential and Definitional Clarifications' (1995) 28 Van JTL 239.

—— 'Israel's Freeing of Terrorism is Contrary to International Law' (1995) 73 *University of Detroit Mercy Law Review* 1.

—— 'Israel, the "Peace Process," and Nuclear Terrorism: A Jurisprudential

Perspective' (1996) 18 *Loyola Los Angeles International and Comparative Law Journal* 767.

Berlin, I, *The First and the Last* (Granta Books, London, 1999).

Berman, P, *Terror and Liberalism* (Norton, London, 2003).

Bethell, N, *The Palestine Triangle: The Struggle between the British, the Jews, and the Arabs 1935–1948* (Deutsch, London, 1979).

Bhatia, M, 'Fighting Words: Naming Terrorists, Bandits, Rebels and Other Violent Actors' (2005) 26 *Third World Quarterly* 5.

Bialos, J and Juster, K, 'The Libyan Sanctions: A Rational Response to State-Sponsored Terrorism?' (1986) 15 Virginia JIL 799.

Bianchi, A, 'Ad-hocism and the Rule of Law' (2002) 13 EJIL 263.

Bierzanek, R, 'Reprisals in Armed Conflicts' (1988) 14 Syra JILC 829.

Black, R, 'The Lockerbie Criminal Trial: The Scottish Rules of Evidence' (1999) 11 *International Legal Perspectives* 31.

Blakesley, C, *Terrorism, Drugs, International Law, and the Protection of Human Liberty* (Transnational Publishers, New York, 1992).

Blewitt, G, 'The Necessity for Enforcement of International Humanitarian Law' (1995) 89 *ASIL Proceedings* 298.

Blishchenko, I and Zhdanov, N, *Terrorism and International Law* (Progress Publishers, Moscow, 1984).

Bogdan, A, 'Cumulative Charges, Convictions and Sentencing in the Ad Hoc International Tribunals for the Former Yugoslavia and Rwanda' (2002) Melbourne JIL 1.

Boire, M, 'Terrorism Reconsidered as Punishment: Toward an Evaluation of Acceptability of Terrorism as a Method of Social Change or Maintenance' (1984) 20 Stanford JIL 45.

Boister, N, 'The Exclusion of Treaty Crimes from the Jurisdiction of the Proposed International Criminal Court: Law, Pragmatism, Politics' (1998) 3 *Journal of Armed Conflict Law* 27.

—— 'Transnational Criminal Law?' (2003) 14 EJIL 953.

Bondi, L, 'Legitimacy and Legality: Key Issues in the Fight against Terrorism', Fund for Peace, Washington, DC, 11 Sept 2002.

Bonnington, A, 'Scots Criminal Procedure and the Lockerbie Trial' (1999) 11 *International Legal Perspectives* 11.

Borelli, S, 'Terrorism and Human Rights: Treatment of Terrorist Suspects and Limits on International Cooperation' (2003) 16 Leiden JIL 803.

—— 'The Rendition of Terrorist Suspects to the United States: Human Rights and the Limits of International Cooperation' in Bianchi, A (ed), *Enforcing International Law Norms Against Terrorism* (Hart, Oxford, 2004) 331.

—— 'Casting Light on the Legal Black Hole: International Law and Detentions Abroad in the "War on Terror" ' (2005) 87 IRRC 39.

Bortz, S, 'Avoiding a Collision of Competence: The Relationship between the Security Council and the International Court of Justice in Light of *Libya v United States*' (1993) 2 *Florida State University Journal of International Law and Politics* 353.

Boulden, J and Weiss, T (eds), *Terrorism and the UN: Before and After September 11* (University of Indiana Press, Bloomington, 2004).

Bourgon, S, 'The Impact of Terrorism on the Principle of "Non-Refoulement" of

Refugees: The *Suresh* Case Before The Supreme Court of Canada' (2003) 1 JICJ 169.

Bouthoul, G, 'Definitions of Terrorism' in Carlton, D and Schaerf, C (eds), *International Terrorism and World Security* (Croom Helm, London, 1975) 50.

Bowett, D, 'The Impact of Security Council Decisions on Dispute Settlement Procedures' (1994) 5 EJIL 89.

Bowyer, C, *RAF Operations 1918–1938* (William Kimber & Co, London, 1988).

Boyle, F, 'The Entebbe Hostage Crisis' (1982) 29 Netherlands ILR 32.

Brady, D and Murphy, J, 'The Soviet Union and International Terrorism' (1982) 16 *International Lawyer* 139.

Brennan, D, 'International Terrorism and Domestic Law' (2002) 42 Indian JIL 173.

Brennan, M, 'Avoiding Anarchy: Bin Laden, Terrorism, the US Response, and the Role of Customary International Law' (1999) 59 *Louisiana Law Review* 1195.

Brierly, J, *The Outlook for International Law* (Clarendon, Oxford, 1944).

Bristol, M, 'The Laws of War and Belligerent Reprisals against Enemy Civilian Populations' (1979) 21 *Air Force Law Review* 397.

Broomhall, B, 'State Actors in an International Definition of Terrorism from a Human Rights Perspective' (2004) 36 Case Western Reserve JIL 421.

Brown, D, 'Holding Armed Rebel Groups and Terrorist Organisations Accountable for Crimes Against Humanity and War Crimes, and for "Terrorist Offences" under International Anti-Terrorist Conventions', Åbo Akademi Institute for Human Rights, 2002.

Brownlie, I, 'International Law and the Activities of Armed Bands' (1958) 7 ICLQ 712.

—— *International Law and the Use of Force by States* (Clarendon, Oxford, 1963).

—— 'The Decisions of the Political Organs of the United Nations and the Rule of Law' in MacDonald, R (ed), *Essays in Honour of Wang Tieya* (Martinus Nijhoff, Dordrecht, 1993) 91.

—— *Principles of Public International Law* (5th edn, Clarendon, Oxford, 1998).

Brudner, A, 'A Theory of Necessity' (1987) 7 OJLS 339.

Brunnée, J, 'Terrorism and Legal Change: An International Law Lesson' in Daniels, R, Macklem, P, and Roach, K (eds), *The Security of Freedom: Essays on Canada's Anti-Terrorism Bill* (University of Toronto Press, Toronto, 2001) 341.

Buergenthal, T, 'To Respect and to Ensure: State Obligations and Permissible Derogations' in Henkin, L (ed), *The International Bill of Rights: The Covenant on Civil and Political Rights* (Columbia University Press, New York, 1981) 72.

Bush, J, 'How Did We Get Here? Foreign Abduction after *Alvarez-Machain*' (1993) 45 *Stanford Law Review* 939.

Bushnell, P, *State Organized Terror: The Case of Violent Internal Repression* (Westview, Colorado, 1991).

Busuttil, J, 'The Bonn Declaration on International Terrorism: A Non-binding International Agreement on Aircraft Hijacking' (1982) 31 ICLQ 474.

Butler, P, 'Terrorism and Utilitarianism: Lessons From, and For, Criminal Law' (2002) 93 JCLC 1.

Byers, M, 'Terrorism, the Use of Force and International Law after September 11' (2002) 51 ICLQ 401.

Calnan, A and Taslitz, A, 'Defusing Bomb-Blast Terrorism: A Legal Survey of

Technological and Regulatory Alternatives' (1999) 67 *Tennessee Law Review* 177.

Campbell, L, 'Defending against Terrorism: A Legal Analysis of the Decision to Strike Sudan and Afghanistan' (2000) 74 *Tulane Law Review* 1067.

Carberry, J, 'Terrorism: A Global Phenomenon Mandating a Unified International Response' (1999) 6 *Indiana Journal of Global Legal Studies* 685.

Carcano, A, 'Sentencing and the Gravity of the Offence in International Criminal Law' (2002) 51 ICLQ 583.

Carcione, M, 'Terrorism and Cultural Property: A "Conflict" of a Non-International Character' (2002) 10 *Tilburg Foreign Law Review* 82.

Card, C, 'Rape as a Terrorist Institution' in Frey, R and Morris, C (eds), *Violence, Terrorism, and Justice* (CUP, Cambridge, 1991) 296.

—— 'Making War on Terrorism in Response to 9/11' in Sterba, J (ed), *Terrorism and International Justice* (OUP, Oxford, 2003) 171.

Lord Carlile of Berriew QC, *Report by the Independent Reviewer on Proposals by Her Majesty's Government for Changes to the Laws against Terrorism*, October 2005.

Carr, C, *The Lessons of Terror* (Little, Brown, London, 2002).

Carty, A, 'The Terrors of Freedom: The Sovereignty of States and the Freedom to Fear' in Strawson, J (ed), *Law after Ground Zero* (GlassHouse, London, 2002) 44.

Casey, D, 'Breaking the Chain of Violence in Israel and Palestine: Suicide Bombings and Targeted Killings under International Humanitarian Law' (2005) 32 Syra JILC 311.

Cassese, A, 'The Status of Rebels under the 1977 Geneva Protocol on Non-International Armed Conflicts' (1981) 30 ICLQ 416.

—— 'Terrorism and Human Rights' (1982) AULR 945.

—— 'The Geneva Protocols of 1977 on the Humanitarian Law of Armed Conflict and Customary International Law' (1984) 3 *UCLA Pacific Basin Law Journal* 55.

—— *Terrorism, Politics and Law: The Achille Lauro Affair* (Polity, Cambridge, 1989).

—— 'The International Community's "Legal" Response to Terrorism' (1989) 38 ICLQ 589.

—— *International Law in a Divided World* (Clarendon, Oxford, 1994).

—— *Self-Determination of Peoples: A Legal Reappraisal* (CUP, Cambridge, 1996).

—— *International Law* (OUP, Oxford, 2001).

—— 'Terrorism is Also Disrupting Some Crucial Legal Categories of International Law' (2001) 12 EJIL 993.

—— *International Criminal Law* (OUP, Oxford, 2003).

Castaneda, J, *Legal Effects of United Nations Resolutions* (Columbia University Press, New York, 1969).

Cayci, S, 'Countering Terrorism and International Law: The Turkish Experience' in Schmitt, M and Beruto, G (eds), *Terrorism and International Law: Challenges and Responses* (IIHL and George C Marshall European Center for Security Studies, San Remo, 2003) 137.

Chadwick, E, *Self-Determination, Terrorism and the International Humanitarian Law of Armed Conflict* (Martinus Nijhoff, The Hague, 1996).

Chamberlain, K, 'Collective Suspension of Air Services with States which Harbour Hijackers' (1982) 32 ICLQ 616.

Chan, S, *Out of Evil: International Politics and the New Doctrine of War* (IB Tauris, London, 2004).

Chan, W and Simester, A, 'Duress, Necessity: How Many Defences?' (2005) 16 KCLJ 121.

Chapman, F, 'Exclusivity and the Warsaw Convention: In Re Air Disaster at Lockerbie, Scotland' (1992) 23 *University of Miami Inter-American Law Review* 493.

Charlesworth, H, 'International Law: A Discipline of Crisis' (2002) 65 MLR 377.

Charney, J, 'The Use of Force against Terrorism and International Law' (2001) 95 AJIL 835.

Cheng, B, 'United Nations Resolutions on Outer Space: "Instant" International Customary Law?' (1965) 5 Indian JIL 23.

Chenumolu, S, 'Revamping International Securities Laws to Break the Financial Infrastructure of Global Terrorism' (2003) 31 Geo JICL 385.

Chesney, R, 'National Insecurity: Nuclear Material Availability and the Threat of Nuclear Terrorism' (1997) 20 *Loyola Los Angeles International and Comparative Law Journal* 29.

Chesterman, S, 'No Justice Without Peace? International Criminal Law and the Decision to Prosecute' in Chesterman, S (ed), *Civilians in War* (Lynne Rienner, Colorado, 2001) 145.

—— *Just War or Just Peace? Humanitarian Intervention and International Law* (OUP, Oxford, 2002).

Chinkin, C, 'Terrorism and Human Rights', Paper at ESIL Conference, Florence, 13–15 May 2004.

Chomsky, N, *The Culture of Terrorism* (South End Press, Boston, 1988).

—— 'Terror and Just Response' in Sterba, J (ed), *Terrorism and International Justice* (OUP, Oxford, 2003) 69.

Chung, C-P, 'China's "War on Terror": September 11 and Uighur Separatism' (Aug 2002) *Foreign Affairs* 8.

Cicero, 'No Fellowship with Tyrants' in Laqueur, W, *The Terrorism Reader* (Wildwood House, London, 1979) 16.

Clapham, A, *Human Rights in the Private Sphere* (Clarendon, Oxford, 1996).

Clarke, R, 'Retrospectivity and the Constitutional Validity of the Bali Bombing and East Timor Trials' (2003) 5 *Australian Journal of Asian Law* 232.

Coady, C, 'Defining Terrorism' in Primoratz, I (ed), *Terrorism: The Philosophical Issues* (Palgrave Macmillan, Hampshire, 2004) 3.

—— 'Terrorism, Morality and Supreme Emergency' in Primoratz, I (ed), *Terrorism: The Philosophical Issues* (Palgrave Macmillan, Hampshire, 2004) 80.

Coady, T and O'Keefe, M (eds), *Terrorism and Justice: A Moral Argument in a Threatened World* (MUP, Melbourne, 2002).

Cocuzza, C, 'State Involvement in Terrorist Activities and Economic Sanctions: The Libyan Case' (1988) 7 Italian YBIL 190.

Cohan, J, 'Formulation of a State's Response to Terrorism and State-Sponsored Terrorism' (2002) 14 Pace ILR 77.

Commission of Jurists to Consider and Report upon the Revision of the Rules of Warfare, General Report, Part II: Rules of Aerial Warfare (1938) 32 AJIL Supp 12.

Commission on the Responsibility of the Authors of the War and on Enforcement of Penalties, Report Presented to the Preliminary Peace Conference, Versailles, Mar 1919, Conference of Paris 1919, Carnegie Endowment for International

Peace, Division of International Law, Pamphlet 32, reprinted in (1920) 14 AJIL Supp 95.

Commonwealth Secretariat, Model Legislative Provisions on Measures to Combat Terrorism.

Condorelli, L, 'The Imputability to States of Acts of International Terrorism' (1989) 19 IYBHR 233.

Connelly, M, *Reaching for the Stars: A New History of Bomber Command in World War II* (IB Tauris, London, 2001).

Conquest, R, *The Great Terror: Stalin's Purge of the Thirties* (Pelican, Middlesex, 1971).

Constantinople, G, 'Towards a New Definition of Piracy: The Achille Lauro Incident' (1986) 26 Virginia JIL 723.

Corell, H, 'The International Instruments against Terrorism: The Record So Far and Strengthening the Existing Regime', Paper at Symposium on Combating International Terrorism: The Contribution of the UN, Vienna, 3–4 June 2002.

Council of Europe (European Commission for Democracy through Law), Opinion on the Possible Need for Further Development of the Geneva Conventions, Venice Commission, 57th Plenary Session, 17 Dec 2003, Opinion No 245/2003, CDL–AD (2003).

Coupland, R, 'Humanity: What Is It and How Does It Influence International Law?' (2001) 83 IRRC 969.

Crawford, J, 'The Right of Self-Determination in International Law: Its Development and Future' in Alston, P (ed), *Peoples' Rights* (OUP, Oxford, 2001) 7.

—— *The International Law Commission's Articles on State Responsibility: Introduction, Texts and Commentaries* (CUP, Cambridge, 2002).

—— and Olleson, S, 'The Nature and Forms of International Responsibility' in Evans, M (ed), *International Law* (OUP, Oxford, 2003) 445.

Crelinsten, R, Laberge-Altmejd, D, and Szabo, D (eds), *Terrorism and Criminal Justice: An International Perspective* (Lexington Books, Lexington, 1978).

Crisp, R and Warner, M, *Terrorism, Protest and Power* (Elgar, Aldershot, 1990).

Cronin, A, 'Rethinking Sovereignty: American Strategy in the Age of Terrorism' (2002) 44 *Survival* 119.

CTC Chair (Ambassador Greenstock), Presentation to Symposium: 'Combating International Terrorism: The Contribution of the United Nations', Vienna, 3–4 June 2002.

Cummings, R, 'The PLO Case: Terrorism, Statutory Obligations under Domestic and Public International Law' (1989) 13 *Hastings International and Comparative Law Review* 25.

Czaplinski, W, 'The Lockerbie Case: Comments' (1993) 20 Polish YBIL 37.

Czempiel, E-O, *Weltpolitik im Umbruch: Die Pax Americana, der Terrorismus und die Zukunft der internationalen Beziehungen* (Verlag Beck, Munich, 2003).

D'Amato, A, *The Concept of Custom in International Law* (Cornell University Press, New York, 1971).

—— and Rubin, A, 'What Does *Tel-Oren* Tell Lawyers?' (1985) 79 AJIL 92.

Dahl, A, 'The Legal Status of the Opposition Fighter in Internal Armed Conflict' (2004) 3–4 *Revue de Droit Militaire et Droit de la Guerre* 137.

Damaj, O, 'The Problem of Responding to Terrorism' in Schmitt, M and Beruto, G (eds), *Terrorism and International Law: Challenges and Responses* (IIHL and George C Marshall European Center for Security Studies, San Remo, 2003) 147.

Damrosch, L, 'Sanctions against Perpetrators of Terrorism' (1999) 22 Houston JIL 63.

Daniels, R, Macklem, P, and Roach, K (eds), *The Security of Freedom: Essays on Canada's Anti-Terrorism Bill* (University of Toronto Press, Toronto, 2001).

Darcy, S, 'The Evolution of the Law of Belligerent Reprisals' (2003) 175 *Military Law Review* 184.

Daudet, Y, 'International Action against State Terrorism' in Higgins, R and Flory, M (eds), *Terrorism and International Law* (Routledge, London, 1997) 201.

Davis, K, 'Cutting Off the Flow of Funds to Terrorists: Whose Funds? Which Funds? Who Decides?' in Daniels, R, Macklem, P, and Roach, K (eds), *The Security of Freedom: Essays on Canada's Anti-Terrorism Bill* (University of Toronto Press, Toronto, 2001) 299.

de Brichambaut, M, 'The Role of the United Nations Security Council in the International Legal System' in Byers, M (ed), *The Role of International Law in International Politics* (OUP, Oxford, 2001) 268.

de Jonge Oudraat, C, 'The Role of the Security Council' in Boulden, J and Weiss, T (eds), *Terrorism and the UN: Before and After September 11* (Indiana University Press, Bloomington, 2004) 151.

de Montaigne, M, *The Complete Essays* (trans Screech, M, Penguin, London, 1991).

de Wet, E, *The Chapter VII Powers of the United Nations Security Council* (Hart, Oxford, 2004).

Dean, A, 'Maritime Terrorism and Legal Responses' (1991) 19 Den JILP 529.

Dellapenna, J, 'Legal Remedies for Terrorist Acts' (1996) 22 Syra JILC 13.

Dempsey, P, 'Aviation Security: The Role of Law in the War Against Terrorism' (2003) 41 Col JTL 649.

den Boer, M, 'The EU Counter-Terrorism Wave: Window of Opportunity or Profound Policy Transformation?' in van Leeuwen, M (ed), *Confronting Terrorism* (Kluwer, The Hague, 2003) 185.

Denning, D, 'Cyberwarriors: Activists and Terrorists Turn to Cyberspace' (2001) 23 Harvard ILR 70.

Depippo, H, 'Criminal Remedies for Terrorist Acts' (1996) 22 Syra JILC 19.

der Bagdasarian, S, 'The Need for International Cooperation to Suppress Terrorism: The United States and Germany as an Example' (1999) 19 *NY Law School Journal of International and Comparative Law* 265.

Derby, D, 'Coming to Terms with Terrorism: Relativity of Wrongfulness and the Need for a New Framework' (1987) 3 *Touro Law Review* 151.

Dershowitz, A, *Why Terrorism Works: Understanding the Threat, Responding to the Challenge* (Yale University Press, New Haven, 2002).

Detter, I, *The Law of War* (2nd edn, CUP, Cambridge, 2000).

Dhanapala J, 'The United Nations Response to 9/11' (2005) 17 *Terrorism and Political Violence* 17.

Diaz, L and Dubner, B, 'On the Problem of Unilateral Action to Prevent Acts of Sea Piracy and Terrorism' (2004) 32 Syra JILC 1.

Dickson, B, 'Northern Ireland's Emergency Legislation' [1992] PL 592.

Dimitrijevic, V, 'L'eternel Retour: Terrorism: More of the Same' (2001) 10 *East European Constitutional Review* 84.

Dinstein, Y, 'International Cooperation in the Prevention and Suppression of Terrorism' (1986) 80 *ASIL Proceedings* 395.

—— 'Terrorism as an International Crime' (1989) 19 IYBHR 55.

Diplomatic Conference on the Reaffirmation and Development of International Humanitarian Law Applicable in Armed Conflicts, *Official Records* (ICRC, Geneva, 1974–1977).

Donnedieu de Vabres, H, 'La repression internationale du terrorisme—les conventions de Genève (16 novembre 1937)' (1938) 62 *Revue de droit international et de législation comparée* 45.

Dörmann, K, 'The Legal Situation of "Unlawful/Unprivileged Combatants" ' (2003) 85 IRRC 45.

—— *Elements of War Crimes under the Rome Statute of the International Criminal Court: Sources and Commentary* (CUP, Cambridge, 2003).

Douzinas, C, 'Postmodern Just Wars: Kosovo, Afghanistan and the New World Order' in Strawson, J (ed), *Law after Ground Zero* (GlassHouse Press, London, 2002) 29.

Draper, G, 'Wars of National Liberation and War Criminality' in Howard, M (ed), *Restraints on War: Studies in the Limitation of Armed Conflict* (OUP, Oxford, 1979) 135.

Drumbl, M, 'Judging the 11 September Terrorist Attack' (2002) 24 *Human Rights Quarterly* 323.

—— 'Terrorist Crime, Taliban Guilt, Western Victims, and International Law' (2002) 31 Den JILP 69.

Dubin, D, *International Terrorism: Two League of Nations Conventions, 1934–1937* (Kraus, New York, 1991).

Dubuisson, F, 'Vers un renforcement des obligations de diligence en matière de lutte contre le terrorisme?' in Bannelier, K, Christakis, T, Corten, O, and Delcourt, B (eds), *Le droit international face au terrorisme* (Bruylant, Brussels, 2002) 141.

Duez, D, 'De la définition à la labellisation: le terrorisme comme construction sociale' in Bannelier, K, Christakis, T, Corten, O, and Delcourt, B (eds), *Le droit international face au terrorisme* (Bruylant, Brussels, 2002) 105.

Duff, D, 'Charitable Status and Terrorist Financing: Rethinking the Proposed *Charities Registration (Security Information) Act*' in Daniels, R, Macklem, P, and Roach K (eds), *The Security of Freedom: Essays on Canada's Anti-Terrorism Bill* (University of Toronto Press, Toronto, 2001) 321.

Duffy, H, Responding to September 11: The Framework of International Law, *Interrights*, Oct 2001.

Dugard, J, 'International Terrorism: Problems of Definition' (1974) 50 *International Affairs* 67.

—— 'Towards the Definition of International Terrorism' (1973) 67 *ASIL Proceedings* 94.

—— 'Terrorism and International Law: Consensus at Last?' in Yakpo, E and Boumedra, T (eds), *Liber Amicorum Judge Mohammed Bedjaoui* (Kluwer, The Hague, 1999) 159.

Dupuy, P-M, 'State Sponsors of Terrorism: Issues of International Responsibility' in Bianchi, A (ed), *Enforcing International Law Norms against Terrorism* (Hart, Oxford, 2004) 3.

Dworkin, R, 'Terror and the Attack on Civil Liberties', *NY Rev Books*, 6 Nov 2003.

Dyzenhaus, D, 'The State of Emergency in Legal Theory' in Ramraj, V, Hor, M, and Roach, K (eds), *Global Anti-Terrorism Law and Policy* (CUP, Cambridge, 2005) 65.

EC, Guidelines on the Recognition of New States in Eastern Europe and in the Soviet Union, 16 Dec 1991 (1991) BYBIL 559.

ECOSOC (Commission on Crime Prevention and Criminal Justice), Sec-Gen Report on Strengthening International Cooperation and Technical Assistance in Preventing and Combating Terrorism, 13th Sess, Vienna, 11–20 May 2004, UN Doc E/CN.15/2004/8 (17 Mar 2004).

Eden, P and O'Donnell, T (eds), *11 September 2001: A Turning Point in International and Domestic Law?* (Transnational Publishers, New York, 2004).

Edgerton, L, 'Eco-Terrorist Acts during the Persian Gulf War: Is International Law Sufficient to Hold Iraq Liable?' (1992) 22 Geo JICL 151.

Ehrenreich Brooks, R, 'Law in the Heart of Darkness: Atrocity and Duress' (2003) 43 Virginia JIL 861.

Einisman, A, 'Ineffectiveness at its Best: Fighting Terrorism with Economic Sanctions' (2000) 9 *Minnesota Journal of Global Trade* 299.

Elagab, O (ed), *International Law Documents Relating to Terrorism* (Cavendish, London, 1997).

Enker, A, 'Duress, Self-Defence and Necessity in Israeli Law' (1996) 30 *Israel Law Review* 188.

EU Commission, Proposal for a Council Framework Decision on Combating Terrorism, Brussels, 19 Sept 2001, COM(2001) 521 Final, 2001/0217 (CNS).

EU Council, Common Position on Combating Terrorism (2001/930/CFSP), 27 Dec 2001, [2001] OJ L344/90.

Eubank, W and Weinberg, L, 'Terrorism and Democracy: Perpetrators and Victims' (2001) 13 *Terrorism and Political Violence* 155.

European Parliament, Sess Doc, Consultation Procedure Reports on Commission Proposals, 14 Nov 2001, FINAL A5–0397/2001, and 9 Jan 2002, FINAL A5–0003/2002.

Evans, A, 'Terrorism and Political Crimes in International Law' (1973) 67 AJIL 87.

—— 'The Realities of Extradition and Prosecution' in Alexander, Y and Finger, S (eds), *Terrorism: Interdisciplinary Perspectives* (John Jay Press, New York, 1977) 128.

—— 'Perspectives on International Terrorism' (1980) 17 *Willamette Law Review* 151.

Evans, E, 'American Policy Response to International Terrorism: Problems of Deterrence', in Livingston, M (ed), *International Terrorism in the Contemporary World* (Greenwood Press, Connecticut, 1978) 375.

Evans, G, 'The Global Response to Terrorism', Wallace Wurth Lecture, University of NSW, Sydney, 27 Sept 2005.

Evans, S, 'The Lockerbie Incident Cases: Libyan-Sponsored Terrorism, Judicial Review and the Political Question Doctrine' (1994) 18 *Maryland Journal of International Law and Trade* 21.

Falk, R, 'On the Quasi-Legislative Competence of the General Assembly' (1966) 60 AJIL 782.

—— *The Great Terror War* (Arris Books, Gloucestershire, 2003).

Falvey, A, 'Legislative Responses to International Terrorism: International and National Efforts to Deter and Punish Terrorists' (1986) 9 BC ICLR 323.

Fanon, F, *The Wretched of the Earth* (trans Farrington, C, Grove Press, New York, 1963).

Fassbender, B, 'The UN Security Council and International Terrorism' in Bianchi, A (ed), *Enforcing International Law Norms against Terrorism* (Hart, Oxford, 2004) 83.

Feinstein, B, 'The Interception of Civilian Vessels at Sea in the Fight against Terrorism: Legal Aspects: An Israeli View' (1991) 2 Finnish YBIL 197.

Fenwick, H, 'War and Terrorism: Legal Considerations' (2001) 8 *International Maritime Law* 87.

Ferencz, B, 'A Proposed Definition of Aggression: By Compromise and Consensus' (1973) 22 ICLQ 407.

—— *An International Criminal Court—A Step Toward World Peace—A Documentary History and Analysis, vol I* (Oceana, London, 1980).

Fidler, D, 'The Return of the Standard of Civilisation' (2001) 2 Chinese JIL 137.

—— 'Bioterrorism, Public Health and International Law' (2002) 3 Chinese JIL 7.

Fields, L, 'Bringing Terrorists to Justice' in Lillich, R (ed), *International Aspects of Criminal Law* (Michie Co, Charlottesville, 1981).

Fijnaut, S and Paoli, L (eds), *Organised Crime in Europe* (Springer, Berlin, 2004).

Final Record of the Diplomatic Conference of Geneva of 1949 (3 vols, Swiss Federal Political Department, Berne).

Finkelstein, M, 'Legal Perspectives in the Fight against Terror: An Israeli Perspective' (2003) 1 *Israeli Defence Forces Law Review* 341.

Finnis, J, 'Natural Law: The Classical Theory', in Coleman, J and Shapiro, S (eds), *Oxford Handbook of Jurisprudence and Legal Philosophy* (OUP, Oxford, 2002) 1.

Fiorita, D, 'Aviation Security: Have all the Questions been Answered?' (1995) 20-II *Annals of Air and Space Law* 69.

Fisher, C, 'US Legislation to Prosecute Terrorists: Antiterrorism or Legalized Kidnapping?' (1985) 18 Van JTL 915.

Fisk, R, *The Great War for Civilization: The Conquest of the Middle East* (Fourth Estate, London, 2005).

Fitzmaurice, G, 'The Definition of Aggression' (1952) 1 ICLQ 137.

Fitzpatrick, J, 'Speaking Law to Power: The War against Terrorism and Human Rights' (2003) 14 EJIL 241.

Fitzpatrick, P, 'Enduring Right' in Strawson, J (ed), *Law after Ground Zero* (GlassHouse Press, London, 2002) 37.

Fletcher, G, *Rethinking Criminal Law* (Little, Brown, Boston, 1978).

Flory, M, 'International Law: An Instrument to Combat Terrorism' in Higgins, R and Flory, M (eds), *Terrorism and International Law* (Routledge, London, 1997) 30.

Flynn, E, 'Counter-Terrorism and Human Rights: The View from the United Nations' [2005] 1 EHRLR 29.

Forster, M, 'Exclusionism and Terror: May Terrorists be Excluded from the Protection of the Human Rights Treaties?', Paper at All Souls-Freshfields Seminar, University of Oxford, 25 Mar 2004.

Forte, D, 'Terror and Terrorism: There is a Difference' (1986) Ohio NULR 39.

Fox, G, 'The Right to Political Participation in International Law' (1992) 17 Yale JIL 539.

—— and Roth, B (eds), *Democratic Governance in International Law* (CUP, Cambridge, 2000).

—— and Nolte, G, 'Intolerant Democracies' in Fox, G and Roth, B (eds), *Democratic Governance and International Law* (CUP, Cambridge, 2000) 389.

Francioni, F, 'Maritime Terrorism and International Law: The Rome Convention of 1988' (1988) 31 German YBIL 263.

Franck, T, 'International Legal Action Concerning Terrorism' (1978) 1 *Terrorism* 187.

—— *The Power of Legitimacy Among Nations* (OUP, Oxford, 1990).

—— 'The Emerging Right of Democratic Governance' (1992) 86 AJIL 46.

—— 'The "Powers of Appreciation": Who is the Ultimate Guardian of UN Legality?' (1992) 86 AJIL 519.

—— *Recourse to Force: State Action against Threats and Armed Attacks* (CUP, Cambridge, 2002).

—— and Rodley, N, 'Legitimacy and Legal Rights of Revolutionary Movements' (1970) 45 NYU LR 679.

—— and Lockwood, B, 'Preliminary Thoughts towards an International Convention on Terrorism' (1974) 68 AJIL 69.

—— and Senecal, S, 'Porfiry's Proposition: Legitimacy and Terrorism' (1987) 20 Van JTL 195.

—— and Niedermeyer, D, 'Accommodating Terrorism: An Offence against the Law of Nations' (1989) 19 IYBHR 75.

Frank, J, 'A Return to Lockerbie and the Montreal Convention in the Wake of the September 11th Terrorist Attacks: Ramifications of Past Security Council and International Court of Justice Action' (2002) 30 Den JILP 532.

Freedman, L, *Terrorism and International Order* (Routledge, London, 1986).

—— 'War in Iraq: Selling the Threat' (2004) 46 *Survival* 7.

Freestone, D, 'Legal Responses to Terrorism: Towards European Cooperation?' in Lodge, J (ed), *Terrorism: A Challenge to the State* (Martin Robertson, Oxford, 1981) 195.

—— 'International Cooperation against Terrorism and the Development of International Law Principles of Jurisdiction' in Higgins, R and Flory, M (eds), *Terrorism and International Law* (Routledge, London, 1997) 43.

French, S, 'Murderers, Not Warriors: The Moral Distinction Between Terrorists and Legitimate Fighters in Asymmetric Conflicts' in Sterba, J (ed), *Terrorism and International Justice* (OUP, Oxford, 2003) 31.

Friedlander, R, 'Terrorism and International Law: What Is Being Done?' (1977) 8 *Rutgers-Cambridge Law Journal* 383.

—— (ed), *Terrorism: Documents of International and Local Control* (6 vols, Oceana, New York, 1979).

—— 'Terrorism and National Liberation Movements: Can Rights Derive from Wrongs?' (1981) 13 Case Western Reserve JIL 281.

—— 'The Ultimate Nightmare: What If Terrorists Go Nuclear?' (1982) 12 Den JILP 1.

—— *Terror Violence: Aspects of Social Control* (Oceana, London, 1983).

—— 'The Orwellian Challenge: State Terrorism and International Law' (1984) 32 *Chitty's Law Journal* 4.

—— 'Punishing Terrorists: A Modest Proposal' (1986) 13 Ohio NULR 149.

—— 'Terrorism' in Bernhardt, R (ed), *Encyclopaedia of Public International Law: vol 4* (North Holland, Amsterdam, 2000) 845.

Fritz, N and Flaherty, M, 'Unjust Order: Malaysia's Internal Security Act' (2003) Fordham ILJ 1345.

Fry, J, 'Terrorism as a Crime against Humanity and Genocide: The Backdoor to Universal Jurisdiction' (2003) 7 UCLA JILFA 169.

Gaeta, P, 'The Armed Conflict in Chechnya before the Russian Constitutional Court' (1996) 7 EJIL 563.

Gaja, G, 'Measures against Terrorist Acts under International Law' in Ronzitti, N (ed), *Maritime Terrorism and International Law* (Martinus Nijhoff, Dordrecht, 1990) 15.

Gal-Or N, *International Cooperation to Suppress Terrorism* (St Martin's Press, New York, 1985).

Garapon, A, 'Three Challenges for International Criminal Justice' (2004) 2 JICJ 716.

Garcia-Mora, M, 'Criminal Jurisdiction of a State over Fugitives Brought from a Foreign Country by Force or Fraud: A Comparative Study' (1957) 32 *Indiana Law Journal* 427.

Gardner, J, 'The Gist of Excuses' (1997) 1 *Buffalo Criminal Law Journal* 575.

—— 'In Defence of Defences' in Asp, P, Herlitz, C, and Holmqvist, L (eds), *Flores Juris et Legum: Festskrift till Nils Jareborg* (Iustus Forlag, Uppsala, 2002).

Garrett, S, 'Terror Bombing of German Cities in World War II' in Primoratz, I (ed), *Terrorism: The Philosophical Issues* (Palgrave Macmillan, Hampshire, 2004) 141.

Gartenstein-Ross, D, 'A Critique of the Terrorism Exception to the Foreign Sovereign Immunities Act' (2002) 34 NYU JILP 887.

Gasser, H-P, 'Prohibition of Terrorist Acts in International Humanitarian Law' (1986) 253 IRRC 200.

—— 'International Humanitarian Law, the Prohibition of Terrorist Acts, and the Fight against Terrorism' in International Peace Academy (ed), *Responding to Terrorism: What Role for the United Nations?* (IPA, New York, 2002) 49.

—— 'Acts of Terror, "Terrorism" and International Humanitarian Law' (2002) 84 IRRC 547.

—— 'Protection of the Civilian Population' in Fleck, D (ed), *The Handbook of Humanitarian Law in Armed Conflicts* (OUP, Oxford, 2004) 209.

Gearty, C, *Terrorism* (Dartmouth, Aldershot, 1996).

—— *The Future of Terrorism* (Phoenix, London, 1997).

—— 'Terrorism and Morality' [2003] 4 EHRLR 377.

—— 'Terrorism and Morality' in Mileham, P (ed), *War and Morality* (Whitehall Paper 61, Royal United Services Institute, 2004), 19.

—— 'Terrorism and Human Rights', Paper at ESIL Conference, Florence, 13–15 May 2004.

—— 'Terrorism and Human Rights' [2005] 1 EHRLR 1.

—— and Kimbell, J, *Terrorism and the Rule of Law* (KCL Civil Liberties Research Unit, London, 1995).

Gehr, W, 'Recurrent Issues: CTC Briefing for Member States', 4 Apr 2002.

Gentin, J, 'Government-Sponsored Abduction of Foreign Criminals Abroad' (1991) 40 *Emory Law Journal* 1227.

Ghatate, N, 'Combating International Terrorism: A Perspective' (2002) 42 Indian JIL 194.

Gilbert, G, *Transnational Fugitive Offenders in International Law: Extradition and Other Mechanisms* (Martinus Nijhoff, Dordrecht, 1998).
—— 'Current Issues in the Application of the Exclusion Clauses' in Feller, E, Türk, V, and Nicholson, F (eds), *Refugee Protection in International Law* (CUP, Cambridge, 2003) 425.
Gilbert, T, 'The "Law" and "Transnational Terrorism" ' (1995) 26 Neth YBIL 33.
Gillard, E-C, 'The Complementary Nature of Human Rights Law, International Humanitarian Law and Refugee Law' in Schmitt, M and Beruto, G (eds), *Terrorism and International Law: Challenges and Responses* (IIHL and George C Marshall European Center for Security Studies, San Remo, 2003) 50.
Gilmore, K, ' "The War against Terrorism": A Human Rights Perspective', Speech by Amnesty International to the European Social Forum, Florence, 2002.
Glennon, M, 'State Sponsored Abduction: A Comment on *US v Alvarez-Machain*' (1992) 86 AJIL 746.
Glick, L, 'World Trade After September 11, 2001: The US Response' (2002) 35 Cornell ILJ 627.
Glover, J, *Humanity: A Moral History of the Twentieth Century* (Jonathan Cape, London, 1999).
Glover, J, *Responsibility* (Routledge and Kegan Paul, London, 1970).
Goldstone, R, 'International Law and Justice and America's War on Terrorism' (2002) 69 *Social Research* 1045.
Gooding, G, 'Fighting Terrorism in the 1980's: The Interception of the Achille Lauro Hijackers' (1987) 12 Yale JIL 158.
Goodwin-Gill, G, 'Crime in International Law: Obligations Erga Omnes and the Duty to Prosecute' in Goodwin-Gill, G and Talmon, S (eds), *The Reality of International Law: Essays in Honour of Ian Brownlie* (Clarendon, Oxford, 1999) 199.
—— 'Human Rights and the Challenges of Global Terrorism', Paper at All Souls-Freshfields Seminar, University of Oxford, 25 Mar 2004.
Goppel, A, 'Defining "Terrorism" in the Context of International Law', Working Paper 2005/1, Centre for Applied Philosophy and Public Ethics, University of Melbourne and Australian National University.
Gordon, A, 'Terrorism as an Academic Subject after 9/11' (2005) 28 *Studies in Conflict and Terrorism* 45.
Gordon, R, 'United Nations Intervention in Internal Conflicts: Iraq, Somalia and Beyond' (1994) 15 Michigan JIL 519.
Gowlland-Debbas, V, 'Security Council Enforcement Action and Issues of State Responsibility' (1994) 43 ICLQ 55.
—— 'The Relationship between the International Court of Justice and the Security Council in the Light of the Lockerbie Case' (1994) 88 AJIL 643.
—— 'The Functions of the United Nations Security Council in the International Legal System' in Byers, M (ed), *The Role of International Law in International Politics* (OUP, Oxford, 2001) 277.
Graefrath, B, 'Leave to the Court What Belongs to the Court: The Libyan Case' (1993) 4 EJIL 184.
Graham, K, 'The Security Council and Counter-terrorism: Global and Regional Approaches to an Elusive Public Good' (2005) 17 *Terrorism and Political Violence* 37.

Gray, C, *International Law and the Use of Force* (OUP, Oxford, 2000).
—— 'The Use of Force and the International Legal Order' in Evans, M (ed), *International Law* (OUP, Oxford, 2004) 589.
Green, L, 'The Nature and Control of International Terrorism' (1974) 4 IYHR 134.
—— 'Terrorism and Armed Conflict: The Plea and the Verdict' (1989) 19 IYBHR 131.
—— *The Contemporary Law of Armed Conflict* (2nd edn, MUP, Manchester, 2000).
Greenwood, C, 'Terrorism and Humanitarian Law: The Debate over Additional Protocol I' (1989) 19 IYBHR 187.
—— 'The Twilight of the Law of Belligerent Reprisals' (1989) 20 Netherlands YBIL 35.
—— 'International Humanitarian Law and the *Tadic* Case' (1996) 7 EJIL 265.
—— 'Scope of Application of Humanitarian Law' in Fleck, D (ed), *The Handbook of Humanitarian Law in Armed Conflicts* (OUP, Oxford, 2004) 39.
Gregory, F, 'The European Union's Response to 9/11' (2005) 17 *Terrorism and Political Violence* 105.
Greppi, E, 'The Evolution of Individual Criminal Responsibility under International Law' (1999) 81 IRRC 531.
Gressang, D, 'Terrorism and Sovereignty: Considering the Potential for Success' (2000) 9 *Low Intensity Conflict and Law Enforcement* 67.
Grote, R, 'Between Crime Prevention and the Laws of War: Are the Traditional Categories of International Law Adequate for Assessing the Use of Force against International Terrorism?' in Walter, C, Vöneky, S, Röben, V, and Schorkopf, F (eds), *Terrorism as a Challenge for National and International Law: Security versus Liberty* (Springer, Heidelberg, 2004) 951.
Guillaume, G, 'Terrorisme et droit international' (1989–III) 215 *Recueil des Cours* 287.
—— 'Terrorism and International Law', Grotius Lecture, British Institute of International and Comparative Law, London, 13 Nov 2003 (subsequently published in (2004) 53 ICLQ 537).
Guisández Gómez, J, 'The Law of Air Warfare' (1998) 323 IRRC 347.
Gupta, R, 'A Comparative Perspective on the Causes of Terrorism' (1998) 35 *International Studies* 23.
Gurr, N and Cole, B, *The New Face of Terrorism: Threats from Weapons of Mass Destruction* (IB Tauris, London, 2002).
Gurule, J, 'Terrorism, Territorial Sovereignty, and the Forcible Apprehension of International Criminals Abroad' (1994) 17 *Hastings International and Comparative Law Review* 457.
Gutierrez, G, 'The Ambiguity of "Megaterrorism" ' (2003) Cornell ILJ 367.
Habermas, J, *The Inclusion of the Other* (Polity, Cambridge, 2002).
Hailbronner, K, 'Rechtsfragen Der Internationalen Terrorismusbekampfung' (1990) 47 Swiss YBIL 11.
Halberstam, M, 'Terrorist Acts against and on Board Ships' (1989) 19 IYBHR 331.
—— 'International Kidnapping: In Defence of the Supreme Court Decision in *Alvarez-Machain*' (1992) 86 AJIL 736.
—— 'The Evolution of the United Nations Position on Terrorism: From Exempting National Liberation Movements to Criminalizing Terrorism Wherever and by Whomever Committed' (2003) 41 Col JTL 573.

Hall, W, *A Treatise on International Law* (8th edn, Clarendon, Oxford, 1924).

Hampson, F, 'Belligerent Reprisals and the 1977 Protocols to the Geneva Conventions of 1949' (1988) 37 ICLQ 818.

Han, H (ed), *Terrorism and Political Violence: Limits and Possibilities of Legal Control* (Oceana, New York, 1993).

Hannay, W, 'International Terrorism and the Political Offence Exception to Extradition' (1980) 18 Col JTL 381.

Hannikainen, L, 'Customary Law: Are Rumours of Its Death Exaggerated?', Paper at ESIL Conference, Florence, 13–15 May 2004.

Harding, C, 'The Concept of Terrorism and Responses to Global Terrorism: Coming to Terms with the Empty Sky', Paper at Sept 11 Conference, University of Sussex, 21–22 Mar 2003.

Harmon, C, *Terrorism Today* (Frank Cass, London, 2000).

Harper, K, 'Does the United Nations Security Council have the Competence to Act as a Court and Legislature?' (1995) 27 NYU JILP 103.

Harris, A, *Bomber Offensive* (Collins, London, 1947).

Hart, H, 'Legal Responsibility and Excuses' in Hart, H, *Punishment and Responsibility: Essays in the Philosophy of Law* (OUP, Oxford, 1984) 28.

—— 'Immorality and Treason' in Dworkin, R (ed), *The Philosophy of Law* (OUP, Oxford, 1986) 83.

—— 'Legal Responsibility and Excuses' in Corrado, M (ed), *Justification and Excuse in the Criminal Law: A Collection of Essays* (Garland, New York, 1994) 31.

—— *The Concept of Law* (2nd edn, OUP, Oxford, 1997).

Hathaway, J, *The Law of Refugee Status* (Butterworths, Ontario, 1991).

Hayward, K and Morrison, W, 'Locating "Ground Zero": Caught between the Narratives of Crime and War' in Strawson, J (ed), *Law after Ground Zero* (GlassHouse, London, 2002) 139.

Heikkilä, M, *Holding Non-State Actors Directly Responsible for Acts of International Terror Violence* (Institute for Human Rights, Åbo Akedmi University, 2002).

Heintze, H-J, 'On the Relationship between Human Rights Law Protection and International Humanitarian Law' (2004) 86 IRRC 789.

Helsinki Watch, *War Crimes in Bosnia-Herzegovina: vol II* (New York, 1993).

Henckaerts, J-M and Doswald-Beck, L (eds), *Customary International Humanitarian Law: Volume I: Rules and Volume II: Practice* (CUP, Cambridge, 2004).

Henham, R, 'The Philosophical Foundations of International Sentencing' (2003) 1 JICJ 64.

Herdegen, M, 'The "Constitutionalization" of the UN Security System' (1994) 27 Van JTL 135.

Heymann, P, 'International Cooperation in Dealing With Terrorism: A Review of Law and Recent Practice' (1990) 6 AUJILP 1.

Higgins, R, *The Development of International Law through the Political Organs of the United Nations* (OUP, Oxford, 1963).

—— 'The Place of International Law in the Settlement of Disputes by the Security Council' (1970) 64 AJIL 1.

—— 'The General International Law of Terrorism' in Higgins, R and Flory, M (eds), *Terrorism and International Law* (Routledge, London, 1997) 13.

—— *Problems and Processes: International Law and How We Use It* (Clarendon, Oxford, 2003).

Highet, K, 'The Irresistible Force and the Immovable Object: Reflections on the Recent PLO Controversies' (1989) 29 Virginia JIL 859.

Hirschmann, K, *Terrorismus* (Europäische Verlagsanstalt, Hamburg, 2003).

Hobsbawm, E, *Age of Extremes: The Short History of Twentieth Century 1914–1991* (Abacus, London, 1994).

Hocking, J, 'Counter Terrorism and the Criminalisation of Politics' (2003) 49 *Australian Journal of Politics and History* 355.

Hogan, G and Walker, C, *Political Violence and the Law in Ireland* (MUP, Manchester, 1989).

Holbrooke, R, 'Just and Unjust Wars: A Diplomat's Perspective' (2002) 69 *Social Research* 915.

Holmes, S, 'Why International Justice Limps' (2002) 69 *Social Research* 1055.

Honderich, T, *Three Essays on Political Violence* (Basil Blackwell, Oxford, 1976).

—— *Punishment: The Supposed Justifications* (Polity, Cambridge, 1989).

—— *After the Terror* (Edinburgh University Press, Edinburgh, 2003).

—— 'Is There a Right to Terrorism?', Lecture at the University of Leipzig, 19 Oct 2003.

Honoré, T, 'The Right to Rebel' (1988) 8 OJLS 34.

Horder, J, 'Occupying the Moral High Ground? The Law Commission on Duress' (1994) *Criminal Law Review* 334.

—— 'Self-Defence, Necessity and Duress: Understanding the Relationship' (1998) XI Can JLJ 143.

Hortatos, C, *International Law and Crimes of Terrorism against the Peace and Security of Mankind* (Sakkoulas Publishers, Athens, 1993).

Hostettler, P, 'Human Rights and the "War" against International Terrorism' in Schmitt, M and Beruto, G (eds), *Terrorism and International Law: Challenges and Responses* (IIHL and George C Marshall European Center for Security Studies, San Remo, 2003) 30.

Hovell, D, 'Of Black Holes and Loopholes: Human Rights and the "War against Terrorism" ' (2005) 14 *Human Rights Defender* 7.

Hudson, B, 'Punishing the Poor: A Critique of the Dominance of Legal Reasoning in Penal Policy and Practice' in Duff, A, Marshall, S, Dobash, RE, and Dobash, RP (eds), *Penal Theory and Practice: Tradition and Innovation in Criminal Justice* (MUP, Manchester, 1994) 302.

Hulsroj, P, 'The Legal Function of the Security Council' (2002) 1 Chinese JIL 59.

Human Rights Watch, *Global Report on Women's Human Rights* (New York, 1995).

—— ' "Empty Promises": Diplomatic Assurances No Safeguard against Torture' (2004) 16(4) HRW Report.

—— 'Black Hole: The Fate of Islamists Rendered to Egypt' (2005) 17(5) HRW Report.

Hunt, C, 'The Potential Contribution of the Chemical Weapons Convention to Combating Terrorism' (1999) 20 Michigan JIL 523.

Hutchinson M, *Revolutionary Terrorism: The FLN in Algeria 1954–1962* (Hoover Institution Press, Stanford, 1974).

ICC PrepCom Report, UN Diplomatic Conference of Plenipotentiaries on an ICC, Rome, 15 June–17 July 1998, UN Doc A/Conf.183/2/Add.1 (14 Apr 1998).

ICRC Report, 'Terrorism and International Law: Challenges and Responses: The Complementary Nature of Human Rights Law, International Humanitarian Law and Refugee Law', Geneva, 2002.

Ignatieff, M, 'Human Rights, the Laws of War, and Terrorism' (2002) 69 *Social Research* 1137.

—— *The Lesser Evil: Political Ethics in an Age of Terror* (Edinburgh University Press, Edinburgh, 2005).

Independent International Commission on Kosovo, *Kosovo Report: Conflict, International Response, Lessons Learned* (2000).

International Bar Association, *International Terrorism: Legal Challenges and Responses* (Transnational, New York, 2003).

—— (Human Rights Institute), *International Terrorism: Legal Challenges and Responses* (IBA, London, 2003).

International Commission of Jurists, Declaration on Upholding Human Rights and the Rule of Law in Combating Terrorism, Berlin, Aug 2004.

Intoccia, G, 'International Legal and Policy Implications of an American Counter-Terrorist Strategy' (1985) 14 Den JILP 121.

Ipsen, K, 'Combatants and Non-combatants' in Fleck, D (ed), *The Handbook of Humanitarian Law in Armed Conflicts* (OUP, Oxford, 2004) 65.

IRO, *Manual for Eligibility Officers* (Imprimeries Populaires, Geneva, 1950).

Jackson, D, 'Prevention of Terrorism and the Convention' in Jackson, D, *The United Kingdom Confronts the European Convention on Human Rights* (University Press of Florida, Florida, 1997).

Jackson, H, 'The Power to Prescribe Terrorist Organisations under the Commonwealth Criminal Code: Is It Open to Abuse?' (2005) 16 *Public Law Review* 134.

Jackson, R, *Writing the War on Terrorism: Language Politics and Counter Terrorism* (MUP, Manchester, 2005).

James, M, 'Keeping the Peace: British, Israeli, and Responses to Terrorism' (1997) 15 Dickinson JIL 405.

Jamieson, A (ed), *Terrorism and Drug Trafficking in the 1990s* (Dartmouth, Aldershot, 1994).

Jenkins, B, 'The Limits of Terror: Constraints on the Escalation of Violence' (1995) 17 Harvard ILR 44.

Jennings, R and Watts, A (eds), *Oppenheim's International Law: vol I* (9th edn, Longman, London, 1992).

Jessup, P, 'Diversity and Uniformity in the Law of Nations' (1964) 58 AJIL 341.

Jetter, S, 'International Terrorism: Beyond the Scope of International Law: *Tel-Oren v Libyan Arab Republic*' (1986) 12 Brookings JIL 505.

Jinks, D, '*People's Mojahedin Organization of Iran v United States Department of State*: DC Circuit Review of Designation of Terrorist Organizations' (2000) 94 AJIL 396.

—— 'International Human Rights Law and the War on Terrorism' (2002) 31 Den JILP 58.

—— 'State Responsibility for the Acts of Private Armed Groups' (2003) 4 Chinese JIL 83.

Johnson, L, 'The Threat of Nuclear Terrorism and September 11th: Wake-up Call to Get the Treaties Right' (2002) 31 Den JILP 80.

Johnson, V, 'The Declaration of the Rights of Man and of Citizens of 1789, the Reign of Terror, and the Revolutionary Tribunal of Paris' (1990) 13 BC ICLR 1.

Jones, C, *Global Justice: Defending Cosmopolitanism* (OUP, Oxford, 2001).

Joyner, C, 'The 1988 IMO Convention on the Safety of Maritime Navigation: Towards a Legal Remedy for Terrorism at Sea' (1988) 31 German YBIL 230.

—— 'Suppression of Terrorism on the High Seas: The 1988 IMO Convention on the Safety of Maritime Navigation' (1989) 19 IYBHR 343.

Kälin, W and Künzli, J, 'Article 1F(b): Freedom Fighters, Terrorists, and the Notion of Serious Non-Political Crimes' (2000) 12 IJRL (Special Supp) 46.

Kalshoven, F, *Belligerent Reprisals* (Sijthoff, Leiden, 1971).

—— ' "Guerilla" and "Terrorism" in Internal Armed Conflict' (1984) 33 AULR 67.

—— 'Belligerent Reprisals Revisited' (1990) 21 Netherlands YBIL 43.

Kamminga, M, 'Comment: Trial of Lockerbie Suspects before a Scottish Court in the Netherlands' (1998) 45 Netherlands ILR 417.

Kantor, M, 'Headnote: The War on Terrorism and the End of Banking Neutrality' (2001) 118 *Banking Law Journal* 891.

Kapitan, T, 'The Terrorism of "Terrorism" ' in Sterba, J (ed), *Terrorism and International Justice* (OUP, Oxford, 2003) 47.

—— 'Terrorism in the Arab-Israeli Conflict' in Primoratz, I (ed), *Terrorism: The Philosophical Issues* (Palgrave Macmillan, Hampshire, 2004) 175.

Kassam, Z, 'Can a Muslim be a Terrorist?' in Sterba, J (ed), *Terrorism and International Justice* (OUP, Oxford, 2003) 114.

Katselli, E and Shah, S, 'September 11 and the UK Response' (2002) 52 ICLQ 245.

Kautsky, K and Kerridge, W, *Terrorism and Communism: A Contribution to the Natural History of Revolution* (Allen and Unwin, London, 1920).

Keijzer, N, 'Terrorism as a Crime' in Heere, W (ed), *Terrorism and the Military: International Legal Implications* (Asser Press, The Hague, 2003) 115.

Kellman B, 'Catastrophic Terrorism: Thinking Fearfully, Acting Legally' (1999) 20 Michigan JIL 537.

—— 'Biological Terrorism: Legal Measures for Preventing Catastrophe' (2001) 24 *Harvard Journal of Law and Public Policy* 417.

Kelly, M, 'Cheating Justice by Cheating Death: The Doctrinal Collision for Prosecuting Foreign Terrorists—Passage of Aut Dedere Aut Judicare into Customary Law and Refusal to Extradite Based on the Death Penalty' (2003) 20 Ariz JICL 491.

Kelsen, H, *The Law of the United Nations* (Praeger, New York, 1950).

—— *Principles of International Law* (2nd edn, Holt, Rinehart and Winston, New York, 1966).

Kennedy, D, 'The Disciplines of International Law and Policy' (2000) 12 Leiden JIL 9.

Kennedy, R, '*Libya v United States*: The International Court of Justice and the Power of Judicial Review' (1993) 33 Van JIL 899.

Khan, A, 'A Legal Theory of International Terrorism' (1987) 19 *Connecticut Law Review* 945.

—— 'A Legal Theory of Revolutions' (1987) 5 BUILJ 1.

Kindt, J, *Eco-Terrorism: Strategic Environmental Terrorism and Potential International Legal Liability* (MH Nordquist, Florida, 1992).

King, C, 'Revolutionary War, Guerilla Warfare, and International Law' (1972) 4 Case Western Reserve JIL 91.

Kirgis, F, 'French Court Proceedings against Muammar Qadhafi', *ASIL Insights*, Oct 2000.

—— 'US Charges and Proceedings against Two Guantanamo Detainees for Conspiracy to Commit Crimes Associated with Armed Conflict', *ASIL Insights*, Mar 2004.

Kirschbaum, S (ed), *Terrorisme et sécurité internationale* (Bruylant, Brussels, 2004).

Kittichaisaree, K, *International Criminal Law* (OUP, Oxford, 2001).

Klabbers J, 'Rebel with a Cause? Terrorists and Humanitarian Law' (2003) 14 EJIL 299.

Klip, A and Mackarel, M, 'The Lockerbie Trial: A Scottish Court in the Netherlands' (1999) 70 *Revue international de droit penal* 777.

Knoops, G, *Defences in Contemporary International Criminal Law* (Transnational Publishers, New York, 2001).

Koch, H-J (ed), *Terrorismus: Rechtsfragen der äußeren und inneren Sicherheit* (Nomos Verlagsgesellschaft, Baden-Baden, 2002).

Koechler, H (ed), *Terrorism and National Liberation* (Peter Lang, Frankfurt-am-Main, 1988).

Koh, H, 'On American Exceptionalism' (2003) 55 *Stanford Law Review* 1479.

Kolb, R, 'Universal Criminal Jurisdiction in Matters of International Terrorism' (1997) 1 *Revue Hellenique Droit International* 43.

—— 'The Exercise of Criminal Jurisdition over International Terrorists' in Bianchi, A (ed), *Enforcing International Law Norms against Terrorism* (Hart, Oxford, 2004) 227.

Konstantinov, E, 'International Terrorism and International Law' (1988) 31 German YBIL 289.

Kooijmans, P, 'The Security Council and Non-State Entities as Parties to Conflicts' in Wellens, K (ed), *International Law: Theory and Practice—Essays in Honour of Eric Suy* (Martinus Nijhoff, The Hague, 1998) 333.

Koskenniemi, M, 'The Police in the Temple: Order, Justice and the UN: A Dialectical View' (1995) 6 EJIL 325.

—— 'What is International Law For?' in Evans, M (ed), *International Law* (OUP, Oxford, 2003) 89.

—— 'Hersch Lauterpacht and the Development of International Criminal Law' (2004) 2 JICJ 810.

Kovacs, P, 'La Société des Nations et son action après l'attentat contre Alexandre, roi de Yougoslavie' (2004) 6 *Journal of History and International Law* 65.

Kravetz, D, 'The Protection of Civilians in War: The ICTY's *Galic* Case' (2004) 17 Leiden JIL 521.

Kremnitzer, M and Ghanayim, K, 'Incitement, Not Sedition' in Kretzmer, D and Hazan, F (eds), *Freedom of Speech and Incitement against Democracy* (Kluwer, The Hague, 2000) 147.

Krisch, N, 'The Rise and Fall of Collective Security: Terrorism, US Hegemony, and the Plight of the Security Council' in Walter, C, Vöneky, S, Röben, V, and Schorkopf, F (eds), *Terrorism as a Challenge for National and International Law: Security versus Liberty* (Springer, Heidelberg, 2004) 879.

—— 'Hegemony and the Law on the Use of Force', Paper at ESIL Conference, Florence, 13–15 May 2004.

Kutner, L, 'Constructive Notice: A Proposal to End International Terrorism' (1974) 19 *New York Law Forum* 325.

—— 'A Philosophical Perspective on Rebellion' in Bassiouni, MC (ed), *International Terrorism and Political Crimes* (Charles C Thomas, Illinois, 1975) 51.

Kwakwa, E, 'Belligerent Reprisals in the Law of Armed Conflict' (1991) 27 Stanford JIL 49.

—— 'Article 1F(c): Acts Contrary to the Purposes and Principles of the United Nations' (2000) 12 IJRL (Special Supp) 79.

—— 'The International Community, International Law, and the United States: Three in One, Two against One, or One and the Same?' in Byers, M and Nolte, G (eds), *United States Hegemony and the Foundations of International Law* (CUP, Cambridge, 2003) 25.

Laborde, J-P, 'Les Nations Unies et la lutte contre le terrorisme: Aspects juridiques et pénaux' in SOS Attentats (ed), *Terrorisme, victimes et responsabilité pénale internationale* (Calmann-Lévy, Paris, 2003) 91.

Lackey, D, 'The Evolution of the Modern Terrorist State: Area Bombing and Nuclear Deterrence' in Primoratz, I (ed), *Terrorism: The Philosophical Issues* (Palgrave Macmillan, Hampshire, 2004) 128.

Lacoste, I, *Die Europäische Terrorismus Convention* (Schulthess Polygraphischer Verlag, Zürich, 1982).

Lagodny, O, 'The Abolition and Replacement of the Political Offence Exception' (1989) 19 IYBHR 317.

Lagos, E and Rudy, T, 'Preventing, Punishing, and Eliminating Terrorism in the Western Hemisphere: A Post-9/11 Inter-American Treaty' (2003) 26 Fordham ILJ 1619.

Lambert, J, *Terrorism and Hostages in International Law: A Commentary on the Hostages Convention 1979* (Grotius, Cambridge, 1990).

Laqueur, W, *Terrorism* (Weidenfeld and Nicolson, London, 1978).

—— 'Postmodern Terrorism' (1996) 75 *Foreign Affairs* 24.

—— 'Terror's New Face: The Radicalization and Escalation of Modern Terrorism' (1998) 20 Harvard ILR 48.

—— *The New Terrorism: Fanaticism and the Arms of Mass Destruction* (Phoenix, London, 2001).

Larschan, B, 'Extradition, the Political Offence Exception and Terrorism' (1986) 4 Buffalo JIL 231.

—— 'Legal Aspects to Control of Transnational Terrorism: An Overview' (1986) 13 Ohio NULR 117.

Larsson, J, *Understanding Religious Violence: Thinking Outside the Box on Terrorism* (Ashgate, Aldershot, 2003).

Lauterpacht, H, 'Revolutionary Activities by Private Persons against Foreign States' (1928) 22 AJIL 105.

—— *International Law and Human Rights* (Stevens, London, 1950).

—— (ed), *Oppenheim's International Law: vols I and II* (8th edn, Longmans, Green and Co, London, 1955).

Lavalle, R, 'The International Convention for the Suppression of the Financing of

Terrorism' (2000) 60 *Zeitschrift fur auslandisches offentliches Recht and Volkerrecht* 491.

Lawrence, T, *Seven Pillars of Wisdom: The Complete 1922 Oxford Text* (J and N Wilson, London, 2004).

Le Mon, C, 'Legality of a Request by the Interim Iraqi Government for the Continued Presence of United States Military Forces', *ASIL Insights*, June 2004.

Leach, E, *Custom, Law, and Terrorist Violence* (University Press, Edinburgh, 1977).

Legg, M, '*Rasul v Bush*: The War on Terrorism and the Right of Detainees to Access American Courts' (2005) 16 *Public Law Review* 89.

Lerner, N, 'Sanctions and Counter-Measures Short of the Use of Force against Terrorism' (1989) 19 IYBHR 259.

Levie, H, *Terrorism in War: The Law of War Crimes* (Oceana, New York, 1993).

—— 'Terrorism in War: The Law of War Crimes' (1994) 28 *George Washington Journal of International Law and Economics* 207.

Levine, M, 'Cuban Hijackers and the United States: The Need for a Modified Aut Dedere Aut Judicare Rule' (1994) 32 Col JTL 133.

Levitt, G, 'Combating Terrorism under International Law' (1986) 18 *University of Toledo Law Review* 133.

—— 'Is "Terrorism" Worth Defining?' (1986) 13 Ohio NULR 97.

—— 'International Counterterrorism Cooperation: The Summit Seven and Air Terrorism' (1987) 20 Van JTL 259.

—— 'Collective Sanctions and Unilateral Action' in Alexander, Y and Sochor, E (eds), *Aerial Piracy and Aviation Security* (Martinus Nijhoff, Dordrecht, 1990) 95.

Lietzau, W, 'Combating Terrorism: Law Enforcement or War?' in Schmitt, M and Beruto, G (eds), *Terrorism and International Law* (IIHL and George C Marshall European Center for Security Studies, San Remo, 2003) 75.

Lillich, R and Paxman, J, 'State Responsibility for Injuries to Aliens Occasioned by Terrorist Activities' (1977) 26 AULR 217.

Lim, C, 'The Question of a Generic Definition of Terrorism under General International Law' in Ramraj, V, Hor, M, and Roach, K (eds), *Global Anti-Terrorism Law and Policy* (CUP, Cambridge, 2005) 37.

—— and Elias, O, 'Sanctions without Law: The Lockerbie Case (Preliminary Objections)' (1999) 4 Austrian RIEL 204.

Liput, A, 'An Analysis of the Achille Lauro Affair: Towards an Effective and Legal Method of Bringing International Terrorists to Justice' (1986) 9 Fordham ILJ 328.

Livingstone, N, 'Terrorism: Conspiracy, Myth and Reality' (1998) 22 *Fletcher Forum of World Affairs* 1.

Lodge, J and Freestone, D, 'The European Community and Terrorism: Political and Legal Aspects' in Alexander, Y and Myers, K (eds), *Terrorism in Europe* (Croom Helm, London, 1982).

Long, P, 'In the Name of God: Religious Terrorism in the Millennium an Analysis of Holy Terror, Government Resources, and the Cooperative Efforts of a Nation to Restrain Its Global Impact' (2000) 24 *Suffolk Transnational Law Review* 51.

Lowe, V, 'Precluding Wrongfulness or Responsibility: A Plea for Excuses' (1999) 10 EJIL 405.

—— 'The Iraq Crisis: What Now?' (2003) 52 ICLQ 859.

—— and Young, J, 'Suppressing Terrorism under the European Convention' (1978) 25 Netherlands ILR 305.

Lubet, S and Czaczkes, M, 'The Role of the American Judiciary in the Extradition of Political Terrorists' (1980) 71 JCLC 193.

Lumumba-Kasongo, T, 'Laurent-Desire Kabila's Assassination: An Attempt to End Three Decades of a Nationalist's Political Struggle for Independence' (2001) 6 AJIAD 19.

MacFarlane, N, 'Charter Values and the Response to Terrorism' in Boulden, J and Weiss, T (eds), *Terrorism and the UN: Before and After September 11* (Indiana University Press, Bloomington, 2004) 27.

Mack, A, 'The Utility of Terrorism' (1981) 14 *Australian and New Zealand Journal of Criminology* 197.

Macklem, P, 'Canada's Obligations at International Criminal Law' in Daniels, R, Macklem, P, and Roach, K (eds), *The Security of Freedom* (University of Toronto Press, Toronto, 2001) 353.

Maged, A, 'International Legal Cooperation: An Essential Tool in the War against Terrorism' in Heere, W (ed), *Terrorism and the Military: International Legal Implications* (Asser Press, The Hague, 2003) 157.

Mahendra, B, 'Last Week's Ruling in the Afghan Hijackers Case' (2003) 7082 *New Law Journal* 809.

Mallison, W and Mallison, S, 'The Control of State Terror through the Application of the International Humanitarian Law of Armed Conflict' in Livingston, M (ed), *International Terrorism in the Contemporary World* (Greenwood Press, Westport, 1978) 325.

Malone, D, 'The Security Council in the Post-Cold War Era: A Study in the Creative Interpretation of the UN Charter' (2003) 35 *International Law and Politics* 487.

Maluwa, T, 'Treaty Interpretation and the Exercise of Prudential Discretion by the International Court of Justice: Some Reflections on the PLO Mission Case' (1990) 37 Netherlands ILR 330.

Malzahn, S, 'State Sponsorship and Support of International Terrorism: Customary Norms of State Responsibility' (2002) 26 *Hastings International and Comparative Law Review* 83.

Mandela, N, *Long Walk to Freedom* (Little, Brown, London, 1994).

Mani, V, 'International Terrorism: Is a Definition Possible? (1978) 18 Indian JIL 206.

—— 'Aviation Security, International Terrorism and the Law' (1992) 32 Indian JIL 1.

Marauhn, R, 'Terrorism: Addendum' in Bernhardt, R (ed), *Encyclopaedia of Public International Law: vol 4* (North Holland, Amsterdam, 2000) 849.

Marcuse, H, 'Ethics and Revolution' in Kent, E (ed), *Revolution and the Rule of Law* (Englewood Cliffs, NJ, 1971) 46.

Marks, S, 'The "Emerging Norm": Conceptualizing "Democratic Governance"' (1997) 91 *ASIL Proceedings* 372.

—— *The Riddle of All Constitutions: International Law, Democracy, and the Critique of Ideology* (OUP, Oxford, 2000).

Marshall, D, 'Narco-Terrorism: The New Discovery of an Old Connection' (2002) 35 Cornell ILJ 599.

Marston, G, 'Early Attempts to Suppress Terrorism: The Terrorism and International Criminal Court Conventions of 1937' (2002) 73 BYBIL 293.

Martenczuk, B, 'The Security Council, the International Court and Judicial Review: What Lessons from Lockerbie?' (1999) 10 EJIL 517.

Martin, J and Romano, A, *Multinational Crime: Terrorism, Espionage, Drug and Arms Trafficking* (Sage, California, 1992).

Martyn, A, 'The Amrozi Bali Bombing Case: Is Indonesia's Anti-terrorism Law Unconstitutional?', Research Note 14, Australian Parliamentary Library, 3 Oct 2003.

Marx, K and Engels, F, *Collected Works: vol 8* (Progress Publishers, Moscow, 1977).

Matorin, M, 'Unchaining the Law: The Legality of Extraterritorial Abduction in Lieu of Extradition' (1992) 41 *Duke Law Journal* 907.

McCarthy, J, 'The United States Should Prosecute Those Who Conspired to Assassinate Former President Bush in Kuwait' (1993)16 Fordham ILJ 1330.

McCormack, T and Robertson, S, 'Jurisdictional Aspects of the Rome Statute for the New International Criminal Court' (1999) 23 *Melbourne University Law Review* 635.

McCorquodale, R, 'The Individual and the International Legal System' in Evans, M (ed), *International Law* (OUP, Oxford, 2003) 299.

McCredie, J, 'The Responsibility of States for Private Acts of International Terrorism' (1985) 1 *Temple International and Comparative Law Journal* 69.

McCulloch, J and Pickering, S, 'Suppressing the Financing of Terrorism: Proliferating State Crime, Eroding Censure and Extending Neo-colonialism' (2005) 45 *British Journal of Criminology* 470.

McDonald, A, 'Terrorism, Counter-Terrorism and the Jus in Bello' in Schmitt, M and Beruto, G (eds), *Terrorism and International Law: Challenges and Responses* (IIHL and George C Marshall European Center for Security Studies, San Remo, 2003) 57.

McDonald, J, 'The United Nations Convention against the Taking of Hostages: The Inside Story' (1983) 6 *Terrorism* 54.

McDougal, M and Lasswell, H, 'The Identification and Appraisal of Diverse Systems of Public Order' (1959) 53 AJIL 1.

McForan, D, 'Terrorism: A Weapon of Soviet Subversion' (1989) 6 *International Journal of World Peace* 45.

McGinley, G, 'The Achille Lauro Affair: Implications for International Law (1985) 52 *Tennessee Law Review* 691.

McGinley, G, 'The ICJ's Decision in the Lockerbie Cases' (1992) 22 Geo JICL 577.

McGoldrick, D, *From '9–11' to the Iraq War 2003* (Hart, Oxford, 2004).

McKay, F, 'US Unilateralism and International Crimes: The International Criminal Court and Terrorism' (2004) 36 Cornell ILJ 455.

McWhinney, E, 'Aerial Piracy and International Terrorism: The Illegal Diversion of Aircraft and International Law, 1987' (1989) 27 Can YBIL 506.

—— *Aerial Piracy and International Terrorism: The Illegal Diversion of Aircraft and International Law* (Martinus Nijhoff, Dordrecht, 1987).

McWhinney, M, 'The International Court as Emerging Constitutional Court and the Co-ordinate UN Institutions (Especially the Security Council): Implications of the Aerial Incident at Lockerbie' (1993) 30 Can YBIL 261.

Mégret, F, ' "War"? Legal Semantics and the Move to Violence' (2002) 13 EJIL 361.
—— 'The Politics of International Criminal Justice' (2002) 13 EJIL 1261.
—— 'Justice in Times of Violence' (2003) 14 EJIL 327.
Mellor, J, 'Missing the Boat: The Legal and Practical Problems of the Prevention of Maritime Terrorism' (2002) 18 AUILR 341.
Méndez, J and Tinajero-Esquivel, S, 'The *Cavallo* Case: A New Test for Universal Jurisdiction' (2000) 8 *Human Rights Brief* 5.
Menefee, S, 'The New "Jamaica Discipline": Problems with Piracy, Maritime Terrorism and the 1982 Convention on the Law of the Sea' (1990) 6 Connecticut JIL 127.
Menon, R, 'The New Great Game in Central Asia' (2003) 45 *Survival* 187.
Meron, T, 'When Do Acts of Terrorism Violate Human Rights?' (1989) 19 IYBHR 271.
—— 'International Criminalization of Internal Atrocities' (1995) 89 AJIL 554, 563.
—— 'Is International Law Moving Towards Criminalization?' (1998) 9 EJIL 18.
—— 'The Humanization of Humanitarian Law' (2000) 94 AJIL 239.
Mertus, J, ' "Terrorism" as Ideology: Implications for Intervention' (1999) 93 *ASIL Proceedings* 78.
Mickolus, E, *The Literature of Terrorism: A Selectively Annotated Bibliography* (Westport Press, Connecticut, 1980).
Miller, A, 'Terrorism and Hostage Taking: Lessons from the Iranian Crisis' (1982) 13 *Rutgers-Camden Law Journal* 513.
Miller, E, 'The Use of Targeted Sanctions in the Fight against International Terrorism: What about Human Rights?' (2003) 97 *ASIL Proceedings* 46.
Mitchell, A, 'Does One Illegality Merit Another: The Law of Belligerent Reprisals in International Law' (2001) 170 *Military Law Review* 155.
Monar, J, 'The European Union's Response to September 11: Potential and Limits of a "New" Actor in the Fight against International Terrorism', Paper at Sept 11 Conference, University of Sussex, 21–22 Mar 2003.
—— 'Anti-Terrorism Law and Policy: The Case of the European Union' in Ramraj, V, Hor, M, and Roach, K (eds), *Global Anti-Terrorism Law and Policy* (CUP, Cambridge, 2005) 425.
Moore, J, 'Toward Legal Restraints on International Terrorism' (1973) 67 *ASIL Proceedings* 88.
Morris, M, 'Prosecuting Terrorism: The Quandaries of Criminal Jurisdiction and International Relations' in Heere, W (ed), *Terrorism and the Military: International Legal Implications* (Asser Press, The Hague, 2003) 133.
—— 'Arresting Terrorism: Criminal Jurisdiction and International Relations' in Bianchi, A (ed), *Enforcing International Law Norms Against Terrorism* (Hart, Oxford, 2004) 63.
—— 'Terrorism and the Politics of Prosecution' (2005) 5 Chinese JIL 405.
Morris, V and Scharf, M, *The International Criminal Tribunal for Rwanda: vol I* (Transnational Publishers, New York, 1998).
Mosler, H, 'Die Konferenz zur internationalen Bekämpfung des Terrorismus' (1938) 8 Zaö RV 99.
Muellerson, R, *Ordering Anarchy: International Law in International Society* (Martinus Nijhoff, The Hague, 2000).

Mullins, C, *The Leipzig Trials* (HF and G Witherby, London, 1921).

Mundis, D, 'Prosecuting International Terrorists' in Schmitt, M and Beruto, G (eds), *Terrorism and International Law: Challenges and Responses* (IIHL and George C Marshall European Center for Security Studies, San Remo, 2003) 85.

Murphy, J, 'United Nations Proposals on the Control and Repression of Terrorism' in Bassiouni, MC (ed), *International Terrorism and Political Crimes* (Charles C Thomas, Illinois, 1975) 493.

—— *Punishing International Terrorists: The Legal Framework for Policy Initiatives* (Rowman and Allanheld, New Jersey, 1985).

—— 'International Cooperation in the Prevention and Suppression of Terrorism' (1986) 80 *ASIL Proceedings* 386.

—— 'The Future of Multilateralism and Efforts to Combat International Terrorism' (1987) 25 Col JTL 35.

—— *State Support of International Terrorism: Legal, Political and Economic Dimensions* (Westview Press, Colorado, 1989).

—— 'Defining International Terrorism: A Way Out of the Quagmire' (1989) 19 IYBHR 13.

—— 'The Palestine Liberation Organization Mission Controversy' (1990) 82 *ASIL Proceedings* 534.

Murphy, S, 'International Law, the United States, and the Non-military "War" against Terrorism' (2003) 14 AJIL 347.

Mushkat, R, ' "Technical" Impediments on the Way to a Universal Definition of International Terrorism' (1980) 20 Indian JIL 448.

Myjer, E and White, N, 'The Twin Towers Attack: An Unlimited Right to Self-Defence?' (2002) 7 *Journal of Conflict and Security Law* 1.

Naert, F, 'The Impact of the Fight against International Terrorism on the Ius ad Bellum after "11 September" ' (2004) 3–4 *Revue de Droit Militaire et Droit de la Guerre* 55.

Nafziger, J, 'The Grave New World of Terrorism: A Lawyer's View' (2002) 31 Den JILP 1.

Nahlik, S, 'Belligerent Reprisals as Seen in the Light of the Diplomatic Conference on Humanitarian Law, Geneva, 1974–1977' (1978) 42 *Law and Contemporary Problems* 36.

Nanda, V, 'Combating International Terrorism' (2002) 31 Den JILP vi.

Naqvi, Y, 'Amnesty for War Crimes: Defining the Limits of International Recognition' (2003) 85 IRRC 583.

National Laws and Regulations on the Prevention and Suppression of International Terrorism: Part I, UN Legislative Series, New York, 2002, UN Doc ST/LEG/SER.B/22.

Nehru, J, *Jawaharlal Nehru: An Autobiography* (OUP, Oxford, 1989).

Netanyahu, B (ed), *Terrorism: How the West Can Win* (Weidenfeld and Nicolson, London, 1986).

Neuman, G, 'Comment: Counter-Terrorist Operations and the Rule of Law' (2004) 15 EJIL 1019.

Newman, D, 'A Human Security Council? Applying a "Human Security" Agenda to Security Council Reform' (2000) 31 *Ottawa Law Review* 213.

Nolte, G, 'The Limits of the Security Council's Powers and its Functions in the

International Legal System: Some Reflections' in Byers, M (ed), *The Role of International Law in International Politics* (OUP, Oxford, 2001) 315.

Norton, J and Shams, H, 'Money Laundering Law and Terrorist Financing: Post-September 11 Responses' (2002) 36 *International Lawyer* 103.

Norton Moore, J, 'The Need for an International Convention' in Bassiouni, MC (ed), *Legal Responses to International Terrorism: US Procedural Aspects* (Martinus Nijhoff, Dordrecht, 1988) 437.

Novogrod, J, 'Internal Strife, Self-Determination, and World Order' in Bassiouni, MC (ed), *International Terrorism and Political Crimes* (Charles C Thomas, Illinois, 1975) 98.

Nussbaum, M, 'Compassion and Terror' in Sterba, J (ed), *Terrorism and International Justice* (OUP, Oxford, 2003) 229.

O'Boyle, G, 'Theories of Justification and Political Violence: Examples from Four Groups' (2002) 14 *Terrorism and Political Violence* 23.

O'Brien, W, 'The Jus in Bello in Revolutionary War and Counterinsurgency' (1978) 18 Virginia JIL 193.

O'Connell, M, 'Evidence of Terror' (2002) 7 *Journal of Conflict and Security Law* 19.

O'Sullivan, N, *Terrorism, Ideology and Revolution* (Wheatsheaf, Brighton, 1986).

Öberg, M, 'The Legal Effects of Resolutions of the UN Security Council and General Assembly in the Jurisprudence of the ICJ' (2005) 16 EJIL 879.

Oeter, S, 'Terrorism and "Wars of National Liberation" from a Law of War Perspective' (1989) 49 *Zeitschrift fur auslandisches offentliches Recht und Volkerrecht* 445.

—— 'Means and Methods of Combat' in Fleck, D (ed), *The Handbook of Humanitarian Law in Armed Conflicts* (OUP, Oxford, 2004) 105.

Okowa, P, 'Defences in the Jurisprudence of International Tribunals' in Goodwin-Gill, G and Talmon, S (eds), *The Reality of International Law: Essays in Honour of Ian Brownlie* (Clarendon, Oxford, 1999) 389.

Omissi, D, *Air Power and Colonial Control: The Royal Airforce 1919–1939* (MUP, Manchester, 1990).

Orakhelashvili, A, 'The Impact of Peremptory Norms on the Interpretation and Application of United Nations Security Council Resolutions' (2005) 16 EJIL 59.

Orford, A, 'The Destiny of International Law' (2004) 17 Leiden JIL 441.

OSCE, *Kosovo/Kosova, As Seen As Told: An Analysis of the Human Rights Findings of the OSCE Kosovo Verification Mission, Oct 1998 to Jun 1999* (OSCE, Warsaw, 1999).

Overy, R, *Russia's War* (Allen Lane, London, 1998).

Ovey, C and White, R, *Jacobs and White: European Convention on the Human Rights* (3rd edn, OUP, Oxford, 2002).

Padelford, N, *International Law and Diplomacy in the Spanish Civil War* (Macmillan, New York, 1939).

Palmer, B, 'Codification of Terrorism as an International Crime' in Bassiouni, MC (ed), *International Terrorism and Political Crimes* (Charles C Thomas, Illinois, 1975) 507.

Palmer, S, 'Arbitrary Detention in Guantanamo Bay: Legal Limbo in the Land of the Free' [2003] 62 *Cambridge Law Journal* 6.

Panjabi, R, 'Terror at the Emperor's Birthday Party: An Analysis of the Hostage-taking Incident at the Japanese Embassy in Lima, Peru' (1997) 16 Dickinson JIL 1.

Parry, C, *The Sources and Evidence of International Law* (MUP, Manchester, 1965).

Partan, D, 'Terrorism: An International Law Offence' (1987) 19 *Connecticut Law Review* 751.

Patton, W, 'Preventing Terrorist Fundraising in the United States' (1996) 30 *George Washington Journal of International Law and Economics* 127.

Paulus, A, 'Jurisprudence of the International Court of Justice: Lockerbie Cases, Preliminary Objections' (1998) 9 EJIL 550.

—— 'The Influence of the United States on the Concept of the "International Community"' in Byers, M and Nolte, G (eds), *United States Hegemony and the Foundations of International Law* (CUP, Cambridge, 2003) 57.

Paust, J, 'A Survey of Possible Legal Responses to International Terrorism: Prevention, Punishment, and Cooperative Action' (1975) 5 Geo JICL 431.

—— 'The Human Right to Participate in Armed Revolution and Related Forms of Social Violence: Testing the Limits of Permissibility' (1983) 32 *Emory Law Journal* 545.

—— 'Aggression against Authority: The Crime of Oppression, Politicide and Other Crimes against Human Rights' (1986) 18 Case Western Reserve JIL 283.

—— 'An Introduction to and Commentary on Terrorism and the Law' (1987) 19 *Connecticut Law Review* 697.

—— 'The Link between Human Rights and Terrorism and Its Implications for the Law of State Responsibility' (1987) 11 *Hastings International and Comparative Law Review* 41.

—— 'Extradition and United States Prosecution of the Achille Lauro Hostage-Takers: Navigating the Hazards' (1987) 20 Van JTL 235.

—— 'Suing Saddam: Private Remedies for War Crimes and Hostage-Taking' (1991) 31 Vanderbilt JIL 351.

—— 'Legal Responses to International Terrorism' (1999) 22 Houston JIL 17.

—— 'Antiterrorism Military Commissions: Courting Illegality' (2001) 23 Michigan JIL 1.

—— 'Legal Responses to Terrorism: Security, Prosecution, and Rights' (2003) 97 *ASIL Proceedings* 13.

Pedigo, J, 'Rogue States, Weapons of Mass Destruction, and Terrorism: Was Security Council Approval Necessary for the Invasion of Iraq?' (2004) 32 Geo JICL 199.

Peers, S, 'EU Responses to Terrorism' (2003) 52 ICLQ 227.

Pella, V, 'Les Conventions de Genève pour la prévention et la répression du terrorisme et pour la création de la Cour pénale internationale' (1938) 18 *Revue de droit pénal et de criminology* 402.

Perera, R, 'Suppression of Terrorism: Regional Approaches to Meet the Challenges' (2004) 16 Sri Lanka JIL 19.

Perkel, W, 'Money Laundering and Terrorism' (2004) 41 *American Criminal Law Review* 183.

Petersen, A, 'Extradition and the Political Offence Exception in the Suppression of Terrorism' (1992) 67 *Indiana Law Journal* 767.

Petman, J, 'The Problem of Evil in International Law' in Petman, J and Klabbers, J (eds), *Nordic Cosmopolitanism: Essays in International Law for Martti Koskenniemi* (Martinus Nijhoff, Leiden, 2003) 111.

Pettit, P, 'Consequentialism and Respect for Persons' (1989) 100 *Ethics* 116.

Pfanner, T, 'Asymmetrical Warfare from the Perspective of Humanitarian Law and Humanitarian Action' (2005) 87 IRRC 149.

Pictet, J (ed), *The Geneva Conventions of 12 August 1949: Commentary* (ICRC, Geneva, 1958).

Pilgrim, C, 'Terrorism in National and International Law' (1990) 8 Dickinson JIL 147.

Plachta, M, 'The Lockerbie Case: The Role of the Security Council in Enforcing the Principle Aut Dedere Aut Judicare' (2001) 12 EJIL 125.

Plant, G, 'The Convention for the Suppression of Unlawful Acts against the Safety of Maritime Navigation' (1990) 39 ICLQ 27.

Pojman, L, 'The Moral Response to Terrorism and Cosmopolitanism' in Sterba, J (ed), *Terrorism and International Justice* (OUP, Oxford, 2003) 135.

Pokempner, D, 'Terrorism and Human Rights: The Legal Framework' in Schmitt, M and Beruto, G (eds), *Terrorism and International Law: Challenges and Responses* (IIHL and George C Marshall European Center for Security Studies, San Remo, 2003) 19.

Policy Working Group on the UN and Terrorism, Report, UN Doc A/57/273, S/2002/875.

Posner, E, 'Terrorism and the Laws of War' (2005) 5 Chinese JIL 423.

Poulantzas, N, 'International Terrorism: What Went Wrong?' (1988) *Revue Hellenique de droit international* 239.

Power, S, *A Problem from Hell: America and the Age of Genocide* (Flamingo, London, 2003).

Preparatory Committee on the Establishment of an International Criminal Court, Report, UN Diplomatic Conference of Plenipotentiaries on the Establishment of an International Criminal Court, Rome, 15 June–17 July 1998, UN Doc A/Conf.183/2/Add.1 (14 April 1998).

Pretzell, A, Krushner, D, and Hruschka, C, 'Terrorism and the 1951 UN Refugee Convention: The National and International Context' (2002) 16 *Tolleys Journal of Immigration, Asylum and Nationality Law* 148.

Primoratz, I, 'What Is Terrorism?' (1990) 7 *Journal of Applied Philosophy* 129.

—— 'What is Terrorism?' in Primoratz, I (ed), *Terrorism: The Philosophical Issues* (Palgrave Macmillan, Hampshire, 2004) 15.

Privy Counsellors Committee, Report, *Review of Intelligence on Weapons of Mass Destruction* (HMSO, London, 14 July 2004).

Probert, H, *Bomber Harris: His Life and Times* (Greenhill, London, 2001).

Proulx, V, 'Rethinking the Jurisdiction of the International Criminal Court in the Post-September 11th Era: Should Acts of Terrorism Qualify as Crimes against Humanity?' (2004) 19 AUILR 1009.

Pyle, C, 'International Cooperation in the Prevention and Suppression of Terrorism' (1986) 80 *ASIL Proceedings* 390.

Quénivet, N, 'The World after September 11: Has It Really Changed?' (2005) 16 EJIL 561.

Quigley, J, 'Perestroika and International Law' (1988) 82 AJIL 788.

—— 'Our Men in Guadalajara and the Abduction of Suspects Abroad: A Comment on *US v Alvarez-Machain*' (1993) 68 *Notre Dame Law Review* 723.

Raimo, T, 'Winning at the Expense of Law: The Ramifications of Expanding

Counter-Terrorism Law Enforcement Jurisdiction Overseas' (1999) 14 AUILR 1473.

Rama-Rao, T, 'State Terror as a Response to Terrorism and Vice Versa: National and International Dimensions' (1987) 27 Indian JIL 183.

Ramraj, V, Hor, M, and Roach, K (eds), *Global Anti-Terrorism Law and Policy* (CUP, Cambridge, 2005).

Ranstorp, M, 'Terrorism in the Name of Religion' (1996) 50 *Journal of International Affairs* 41.

Ratner, S and Abrams, J, *Accountability for Human Rights Atrocities in International Law: Beyond the Nuremberg Legacy* (2nd edn, OUP, Oxford, 2001).

Ravindran, P, 'Control of Terrorism in Air Space: Efforts by the International Community' (1997) 37 Indian JIL 27.

Rawls, J, *A Theory of Justice* (Clarendon, Oxford, 1972).

Ray, A, 'The Shame of It: Gender-Based Terrorism in the Former Yugoslavia and the Failure of International Human Rights Law to Comprehend the Injuries' (1997) 46 AULR 793.

Raz, J, *The Morality of Freedom* (Clarendon, Oxford, 1986).

Record, J, 'Threat Confusion and Its Penalties' (2004) 46 *Survival* 51.

Reed, A, 'Duress and Provocation as Excuses to Murder: Salutary Lessons from Recent Anglo-American Jurisprudence' (1997) 6 JTLP 51.

Reinisch, A, 'Some Problematic Aspects of Recent EU Financial Anti-Terrorism Measures' (2002) Austrian RIEL 7.

—— 'The Action of the European Union to Combat International Terrorism' in Bianchi, A (ed), *Enforcing International Law Norms Against Terrorism* (Hart, Oxford, 2004) 119.

—— 'Developing Human Rights and Humantarian Law Accountability of the Security Council for the Imposition of Economic Sanctions' (2001) 95 AJIL 851.

Reisman, M, 'Private Armies in a Global War System: Prologue to Decision' (1973) 14 Van JIL 1.

—— 'Sovereignty and Human Rights in Contemporary International Law' (1990) 84 AJIL 866.

—— 'The Constitutional Crisis in the United Nations' (1993) 87 AJIL 83.

—— 'International Legal Responses to Terrorism' (1999) 22 Houston JIL 3.

—— 'In Defense of World Public Order' (2001) 95 AJIL 833.

—— 'Aftershocks: Reflections on the Implications of September 11' (2003) 6 Yale HRDLJ 81.

Richardson, L, 'Global Rebels: Terrorist Organizations as Transnational Actors' (1998) 20 *Harvard International Review* 52.

Rieff, D, 'Fables of Redemption in an Age of Barbarism' (2002) 69 *Social Research* 1159.

Rifaat, A, 'Aggression and Terrorism: Two Legal Concepts' (1995) 51 *Revue Egyptienne de Droit International* 27.

Roach, K, 'The Criminal Law and Terrorism' in Ramraj, V, Hor, M, and Roach, K (eds), *Global Anti-Terrorism Law and Policy* (CUP, Cambridge, 2005) 129.

Roberts, A, 'Can We Define Terrorism?' (2002) 14 *Oxford Today* 18.

—— 'Counter-Terrorism, Armed Force and the Laws of War' (2002) 44 *Survival* 7.

—— 'Law and the Use of Force After Iraq' (2003) 45 *Survival* 31.

—— 'Righting Wrongs or Wronging Rights? The United States and Human Rights Post-September 11' (2004) 15 EJIL 721.

—— and Guelff, R, *Documents on the Laws of War* (3rd edn, OUP, Oxford, 2002).

Roberts, K, 'Second-Guessing the Security Council: The International Court of Justice and its Powers of Judicial Review' (1995) 7 Pace ILR 281.

Roberts, P and McMillan, N, 'For Criminology in International Criminal Justice' (2003) 1 JICJ 315.

Robinson, J, 'United States Practice Penalizing International Terrorists Needlessly Undercuts its Opposition to the Passive Personality Principle' (1998) 16 BUILJ 487.

Rodin, D, *War and Self-Defense* (Clarendon, Oxford, 2002).

Röling, B, 'The Legal Status of Rebels and Rebellion' (1976) 13 *Journal of Peace Research* 149.

—— and Rüter, C (eds), *The Tokyo Judgment: International Military Tribunal for the Far East: vol I* (University Press Amsterdam, Amsterdam, 1977).

Romano, J, 'Combating Terrorism and Weapons of Mass Destruction: Reviving the Doctrine of a State of Necessity' (1999) 87 *Georgetown Law Journal* 1023.

Romero, J, 'Prevention of Maritime Terrorism: The Container Security Initiative' (2003) 4 Chinese JIL 597.

Rona, G, 'Interesting Times for International Humanitarian Law: Challenges from the "War on Terror" ' (2005) 17 *Terrorism and Political Violence* 157.

Ronzitti, N, 'The Law of the Sea and the Use of Force against Terrorist Activities' in Ronzitti, N (ed), *Maritime Terrorism and International Law* (Martinus Nijhoff, Dordrecht, 1990) 1.

—— 'Maritime Terrorism and International Law' (1993) 30 Can YBIL 440.

Rorty, R, 'Is this the end of democracy?', *The Age*, 27 Apr 2004.

Rosand, E, 'Security Council Resolution 1373, the Counter-Terrorism Committee, and the Fight Against Terrorism' (2003) 97 AJIL 333.

Rosen, S and Frank, R, 'Measures Against International Terrorism' in Carlton, D and Schaerf, C (eds), *International Terrorism and World Security* (Croom Helm, London, 1975) 60.

Rosenne, S, 'The International Convention against the Taking of Hostages 1979' (1980) 10 IYBHR 109.

Rosenstock, R, 'The Declaration of Principles of International Law Concerning Friendly Relations: A Survey' (1971) 65 AJIL 713.

—— 'International Convention against the Taking of Hostages: Another International Community Step against Terrorism' (1980) 9 Den JILP 169.

Rosie, G, *The Dictionary of International Terrorism* (Mainstream Publishing, Edinburgh, 1986).

Rostow, N, 'Before and After: The Changed UN Response to Terrorism since September 11th' (2002) 35 Cornell ILJ 475.

Roth, B, 'Evaluating Democratic Progress: A Normative Theoretical Perspective' (1995) 9 *Ethics and International Affairs* 55.

—— *Governmental Illegitimacy in International Law* (Clarendon, Oxford, 1999).

Rothberg, B, 'Averting Armageddon: Preventing Nuclear Terrorism in the United States' (1997) 8 Duke JCIL 79.

Royal Institute of International Affairs, *Great Britain and Palestine 1915–1945* (RIIA, London, 1946).

Royse, W, *Aerial Bombardment and the International Regulation of Warfare* (Harold Vinal Ltd, New York, 1928).

Rubin, A, 'International Terrorism and International Law' in Alexander, Y and Finger, S (eds), *Terrorism: Interdisciplinary Perspectives* (John Jay Press, New York, 1977) 121.

—— 'Terrorism, "Grave Breaches" and the 1977 Geneva Protocols' (1980) 74 *ASIL Proceedings* 192.

—— 'Terrorism and the Laws of War' (1983) 12 Den JILP 219.

—— 'Current Legal Approaches to International Terrorism' (1984) 7 *Terrorism* 147.

—— 'Extradition and "Terrorist" Offenses' (1987) 10 *Terrorism* 83.

—— 'Legal Response to Terror: An International Criminal Court?' (2002) 43 Harvard ILJ 65.

Rubin, B, 'PLO Violence and Legitimate Combatancy: A Response to Professor Green' (1989) 19 IYBHR 167.

Sacerdoti, G, 'States' Agreements with Terrorists in Order to Save Hostages: Non-Binding, Void or Justified by Necessity?' in Ronzitti, N (ed), *Maritime Terrorism and International Law* (Martinus Nijhoff, Dordrecht, 1990) 25.

Sailer, T, 'The International Criminal Court: An Argument to Extend its Jurisdiction to Terrorism and a Dismissal of US Objections' (1999) 13 *Temple International and Comparative Law Journal* 311.

Sandoz, Y, Swinarski, C, and Zimmermann, B (eds), *Commentary on the Additional Protocols of 8 June 1977 to the Geneva Conventions of 12 August 1949* (Martinus Nijhoff and ICRC, The Hague and Geneva, 1987).

Sands, P, *Lawless World: America and the Making and Breaking of Global Rules* (Penguin, London, 2005).

—— and Klein, P, *Bowett's Law of International Institutions* (5th edn, Sweet and Maxwell, London, 2001).

Sassòli, M, 'The Status of Persons Held in Guantanamo under International Humanitarian Law' (2004) 2 JICJ 96.

—— and Bouvier, A (eds), *How Does Law Protect in War?* (ICRC, Geneva, 1999).

Saul, B, 'The International Crime of Genocide in Australian Law' (2000) 22 *Sydney Law Review* 527.

—— 'In the Shadow of Human Rights: Human Duties, Obligations and Responsibilities' (2001) 32 Col HRLR 565.

—— 'Was the Conflict in East Timor "Genocide" and Why Does It Matter?' (2001) 2 Melbourne JIL 477.

—— 'International Terrorism as a European Crime: The Policy Rationale for Criminalization' (2003) 11 *European Journal of Crime, Criminal Law and Criminal Justice* 323.

—— 'Legality of the Use of Force against Iraq in 2001' (2003) 8 *UCLA Journal of International Law and Foreign Affairs* 267.

—— 'Torturing Terrorists after September 11: Dershowitz' Torture Warrant' (2004) 27 *International Journal of Law and Psychiatry* 645.

—— 'Exclusion of Suspected Terrorists from Asylum: Trends in International and European Refugee Law', Institute for International Integration Studies, Discussion Paper 26, Dublin, July 2004.

—— 'Attempts to Define "Terrorism" in International Law' (2005) 52 Netherlands ILR 57.

—— 'Crimes and Prohibitions of "Terror" and "Terrorism" in Armed Conflict: 1919–2005' (2005) 4 *Journal of International Law, Peace and Armed Conflict* 264.

—— 'The Dangers of the United Nations' "New Security Agenda"' (2006) 1 *Asian Journal of Comparative Law* 147.

—— 'Definition of "Terrorism" in the UN Security Council: 1985–2004' (2005) 4 Chinese JIL 141.

—— 'Speaking of Terror: Criminalizing Incitement to Violence' (2005) 28 *University of New South Wales Law Journal* 868.

—— 'Reasons for Defining and Criminalizing Terrorism in International Law' (2006) 6 Mexican YBIL 419.

—— 'The Legal Response of the League of Nations to Terrorism' (2006) 4 JICJ 78.

Saxena, J, 'Relationship between International Terrorism, State Terror and Human Rights in the World Order' (1987) 27 Indian JIL 194.

Schabas, W, *An Introduction to the International Criminal Court* (CUP, Cambridge, 2002).

—— *Genocide in International Law* (CUP, Cambridge, 2002).

Schachter, O, 'The Quasi-Judicial Role of the Security Council and the General Assembly' (1964) 58 AJIL 960.

—— *International Law in Theory and Practice* (Martinus Nijhoff, Dordrecht, 1991).

—— 'United Nations Law' (1994) 88 AJIL 1.

Scharf, M, 'Clear and Present Danger: Enforcing the International Ban on Biological and Chemical Weapons through Sanctions, Use of Force, and Criminalization' (1999) 20 Michigan JIL 477.

—— 'A Preview of the Lockerbie Case', *ASIL Insights*, May 2000.

—— 'Terrorism on Trial: The Lockerbie Criminal Proceedings' (2000) 6 ILSA JICL 355.

—— 'Defining Terrorism as the Peace Time Equivalent of War Crimes: A Case of Too Much Convergence between International Humanitarian Law and International Criminal Law?' (2001) 7 ILSA JICL 391.

—— 'The Broader Meaning of the Lockerbie Trial and the Future of International Counter-Terrorism' (2001) 29 Syra JILC 50.

—— 'The Lockerbie Trial Verdict', *ASIL Insights*, Feb 2001.

—— 'Defining Terrorism as the Peacetime Equivalent of War Crimes: Problems and Prospects' (2004) 36 Case Western Reserve JIL 359.

Scheffer, D, 'Developments at Rome Treaty Conference', Testimony of US Ambassador at Large for War Crimes Issues and Head of US Delegation to the Rome Conference, US Senate Foreign Relations Committee, Washington, DC, 23 July 1998.

Scheideman, S, 'Standards of Proof in Forcible Responses to Terrorism' (2000) 50 *Syracuse Law Review* 249.

Scheuer, J, 'Moral Dimensions of Terrorism' (1990) 14 *Fletcher Forum of World Affairs* 145.

Schindler, D and Toman, J, *The Laws of Armed Conflicts* (Martinus Nihjoff, Dordrecht, 1988).

Schlaefer, C, 'American Courts and Modern Terrorism' (1981) 13 NYU JILP 617.

Schmid, A, 'Frameworks for Conceptualizing Terrorism' (2004) 16 *Terrorism and Political Violence* 197.

—— 'Terrorism: The Definitional Problem' (2004) 36 Case Western Reserve JIL 375.

—— 'Terrorism and Human Rights: A Perspective from the United Nations' (2005) 17 *Terrorism and Political Violence* 25.

—— and Jongman, A, *Political Terrorism: A Research Guide to Concepts, Theories, Data Bases and Literature* (North Holland Publishing Co, Amsterdam, 1983).

Schmitt, C, *The Concept of the Political* (trans Schwab, G, University of Chicago Press, Chicago, 1996).

Schmitt, M and Beruto, G (eds), *Terrorism and International Law: Challenges and Responses* (IIHL and George C Marshall European Center for Security Studies, San Remo, 2003).

Schofield, T, 'The Environment as an Ideological Weapon: A Proposal to Criminalize Environmental Terrorism' (1999) 26 BC EALR 619.

Schreiber, R, 'Ascertaining Opinio Juris of States Concerning Norms Involving the Prevention of International Terrorism: A Focus on the UN Process' (1998) 16 Buffalo ILJ 309.

Schrijver, N, 'Responding to International Terrorism: Moving the Frontiers of International Law for "Enduring Freedom"?' (2001) 48 Netherlands ILR 271.

—— 'September 11 and Challenges to International Law' in Boulden, J and Weiss, T (eds), *Terrorism and the UN: Before and After September 11* (Indiana University Press, Bloomington, 2004) 55.

Schumer, C, 'Terrorism Must Not Be Allowed to Hide Its Face' (1996) 22 Syra JIL and C 1.

Schwartz, R, 'Chaos, Oppression, and Rebellion: The Use of Self-Help to Secure Individual Rights under International Law' (1994) 12 BUILJ 255.

Schwarz, D, 'International Terrorism and Islamic Law' (1991) 29 Col JTL 629.

Schwarzenberger, G, *Terrorists, Hijackers, Guerrilleros and Mercenaries* (Current Legal Problems, London, 1971).

Schwebel, S, 'The Effect of Resolutions of the UN General Assembly on Customary International Law' (1979) *ASIL Proceedings* 301.

Schwelb, E, *Human Rights and the International Community* (Quadrangle Books, Chicago, 1964).

Scott, A, 'Criminal Jurisdiction of a State over a Defendant based upon Presence Secured by Force or Fraud' (1953) 37 *Minnesota Law Review* 91.

Scruton, R, *A Dictionary of Political Thought* (2nd edn, Macmillan, London, 1996).

Seacor, J, 'Environmental Terrorism: Lesson from the Oil Fires of Kuwait' (1994) 10 AUJILP 481.

Selth, A, *Against Every Human Law: The Terrorist Threat to Diplomacy* (ANU Press, Sydney, 1988).

Seton-Watson, H, *Nations and States: An Enquiry into the Origins of Nations and the Politics of Nationalism* (Westview Press, Colorado, 1977).

Shachor-Landau, C, 'Extraterritorial Penal Jurisdiction and Extradition' (1980) 29 ICLQ 274.

Shaikh, A, 'A Theoretical Approach to Transnational Terrorism' (1992) 80 *Georgetown Law Journal* 2131.

Shapiro, M, 'Extradition in an Era of Terrorism: The Need to Abolish the Political Offense Exception' (1986) 61 NYULR 654.

Shaw, M, *International Law* (4th edn, CUP, Cambridge, 1997).

Shearer, I, *Starke's International Law* (11th edn, Butterworths, London, 1994).

Shelton, D, 'Private Violence, Public Wrongs, and the Responsibility of States' (1990) 13 Fordham ILJ 1.

—— *Remedies in International Human Rights Law* (OUP, Oxford, 2000).

—— 'Shifting the Balance in United States Law between Liberty and Security: How Far is Too Far?', Paper at Sept 11 Conference, University of Sussex, 21–22 Mar 2003.

Shen, J, 'Terrorism and International Responses: Toward More Effective Suppression, Prevention and Elimination of Terrorism and Other Forms of Violence' (1999) 93 *ASIL Proceedings* 80.

Shepherd, N, *Ploughing Sand: British Rule in Palestine 1917–1948* (John Murray, London, 1999).

Shestack, J, 'Of Private and State Terror: Some Preliminary Observations' (1982) 13 *Rutgers Law Journal* 453.

Shook, K, 'State Sponsors of Terrorism Are Persons Too: The Flatow Mistake' (2000) 61 Ohio SLJ 1301.

Shubber, S, 'Sabotage and Attacks against Ships, Cargoes and Persons on Board: The Rome Convention 1988' (1992) 43 Austrian JPIL 139.

—— 'The Destruction of Aircraft in Flight over Scotland and Niger: The Question of Jurisdiction and Extradition under International Law' (1995) BYBIL 239.

Silke, A, 'The Devil You Know: Continuing Problems with Research on Terrorism' (2001) 13 *Terrorism and Political Violence* 1.

Silverman, C, 'An Appeal to the United Nations: Terrorism Must Come within the Jurisdiction of an International Criminal Court' (1998) 4 *New England and Comparative Law Ann*: <www.nesl.edu/intljournal/VOL4/CS.HTM>.

Simon, S and Benjamin, D, 'The Terror' (2002) 43 *Survival* 5.

Simpson, B, *Human Rights and the End of Empire: Britain and the Genesis of the European Convention* (OUP, Oxford, 2001).

Sinclair, I, 'The Significance of the Friendly Relations Declaration' in Warbrick, C and Lowe, V (eds), *The United Nations and the Principles of International Law: Essays in Memory of Michael Akehurst* (Routledge, London, 1994) 1.

Singh, M (ed), *International Terrorism and Religious Extremism: Challenges to Central and South Asia* (Anamika Publishers, New Delhi, 2003).

Skubiszewski, K, 'Normative Functions of Resolutions of the General Assembly of the United Nations' (Institute of International Law) (1985) *Annuaire de l'Institute de Droit International* 29.

—— 'Definition of Terrorism' (1989) 19 IYBHR 39.

Sliwowski, G, 'Legal Aspects of Terrorism' in Carlton, D and Schaerf, C (eds), *International Terrorism and World Security* (Croom Helm, London, 1975) 69.

Sloan, E, 'The Binding Force of a "Recommendation" of the General Assembly of the United Nations' (1948) 25 BYBIL 1.

Smith, F, *International Law* (5th edn, JM Dent and Sons, London, 1918).

Smith, J, *Smith and Hogan: Criminal Law* (10th edn, Butterworths, London, 2002).

Sofaer, A, 'Terrorism and the Law' (1986) *Foreign Affairs* 901.

—— 'The Political Offence Exception and Terrorism' (1986) 15 Den JILP 125.

Sorel, G, *Reflections on Violence* (trans Hulme, T, Peter Smith, New York, 1941).

Sorel, J-M, 'Existe-t-il une définition universelle du terrorisme?' in Bannelier, K, Corten, O, Christakis, T, and Delcourt, B (eds), *Le droit international face au terrorisme* (Pédone, Paris, 2002) 35.

—— 'Some Questions About the Definition of Terrorism and the Fight against its Financing' (2003) 14 AJIL 365.

Sornarajah, M-C, ' "Terrorism" Not Useful for Analyzing Random Violence' (1999) 93 *ASIL Proceedings* 79.

SOS Attentats, *Terrorisme, victimes et responsabilité pénale internationale* (Calmann-Lévy, Paris, 2003).

Sossai, M, 'UNSC Resolution 1373 (2001) and International Law-making: A Transformation in Nature of the Legal Obligations for the Fight against Terrorism?', Agorae Paper, ESIL Conference, Florence, 14 May 2004.

—— 'The Internal Conflict in Colombia and the Fight against Terrorism' (2005) 3 JICJ 253.

Sottile, A, 'Le terrorisme international' (1938-III) 65 *Recueil des Cours de l'Académie de Droit International* 116.

Soyinka, W, 'The Changing Mask of Fear', BBC Reith Lectures 2004: Climate of Fear, Lecture 1, <www.bbc.co.uk/radio4/reith2004> (9 Nov 2005).

Spaight, J, *Air Power and War Rights* (Longmans, Green and Co, London, 1924).

—— *Air Power and War Rights* (3rd edn, Longmans, Green and Co, London, 1947).

Sperduti, G, 'Responsibility of States for Activities of Private Law Persons' in Bernhardt, R (ed), *Encyclopaedia of Public International Law* (1987) 373.

Srivastava, A, 'The Steps Being Taken to Tighten up Money Laundering Regulation Worldwide in the War against Terrorism' (2001) NLJ 1466.

Starke, J, 'The Convention for the Prevention and Punishment of Terrorism' (1938) 19 BYBIL 214.

Stechel, I, 'Terrorist Kidnapping of Diplomatic Personnel' (1972) 5 Cornell ILJ 189.

Stein, T, 'Contempt, Crisis, and the Court: The World Court and the Hostage Rescue Attempt' (1982) 76 AJIL 499.

—— 'Rendition of Terrorists: Extradition Versus Deportation' (1989) 19 IYBHR 281.

—— 'International Measures against Terrorism and Sanctions by and against Third States' (1992) 30 *Archiv des Volkerrechts* 38.

Steinberg, M, 'The SEC and The Securities Industry Respond to September 11' (2002) 36 *International Lawyer* 131.

Steiner, H, 'International Protection of Human Rights' in Evans, M (ed), *International Law* (OUP, Oxford 2003) 757.

Steinhoff, U, 'How Can Terrorism Be Justified?' in Primoratz, I (ed), *Terrorism: The Philosophical Issues* (Palgrave Macmillan, Hampshire, 2004) 97.

Sterba, J, 'Terrorism and International Justice' in Sterba, J (ed), *Terrorism and International Justice* (OUP, Oxford, 2003) 206.

Stevenson, J, 'Pragmatic Counter-terrorism' (2002) 43 *Survival* 35.

Stock, M, 'Detainees in the Hands of America: New Rules for a New Kind of War' in Schmitt, M and Beruto, G (eds), *Terrorism and International Law: Challenges and Responses* (IIHL and George C Marshall European Center for Security Studies, San Remo, 2003) 119.

Stohl, M (ed), *The Politics of Terrorism* (Marcel Dekker, New York, 1979).

Stone, J, 'Hopes and Loopholes in the 1974 Definition of Aggression' (1977) 71 AJIL 224.

Strickler, N, 'Anti-History and Terrorism: A Philosophical Dimension' in Bassiouni, MC (ed), *International Terrorism and Political Crimes* (Charles C Thomas, Illinois, 1975) 47.

Stromseth, J, 'The Security Council's Counter-Terrorism Role: Continuity and Innovation' (2003) 97 *ASIL Proceedings* 41.

Subedi, S, 'The UN Response to International Terrorism in the Aftermath of the Terrorist Attacks in America and the Problem of the Definition of Terrorism in International Law' (2002) 4 ILF 159.

—— 'The Concept in Hinduism of "Just War" ' (2003) 8 JCSL 339.

Sucharitkul, S, 'Terrorism as an International Crime: Questions of Responsibility and Complicity' (1989) 19 IYBHR 247.

—— 'Jurisdiction, Terrorism and The Rule of International Law' (2002) 32 *Golden Gate University Law Review* 311.

Sunga, L, *The Emerging System of International Criminal Law: Developments in Codification and Implementation* (Kluwer, The Hague, 1997).

Surchin, A, 'Terror and the Law: The Unilateral Use of Force and the June 1993 Bombing of Baghdad' (1994) 5 Duke JCIL 457.

Suy, E, 'The Meaning of Consensus in Multilateral Diplomacy' in Akkerman, R, Van Krieken, P, and Pannenborg, C (eds), *Declarations on Principles: A Quest for Universal Peace* (Leyden, Groningen, 1977) 259.

Sweeney, J, 'State-Sponsored Terrorism: Libya's Abuse of Diplomatic Privileges and Immunities' (1986) 5 Dickinson JIL 133.

Symeonidou-Kastanidou, E, 'Defining Terrorism' (2004) 12 *European Journal of Crime, Criminal Law and Criminal Justice* 14.

Szasz, P, 'The Security Council Starts Legislating' (2002) 96 AJIL 901.

Tallgren, I, 'The Sense and Sensibility of International Criminal Law' (2002) 13 EJIL 561.

Talmon, S, 'The Statements by the President of the Security Council' (2003) 2 Chinese JIL 419.

—— 'The Security Council as World Legislature' (2005) 99 AJIL 35.

Taurek, J, 'Should the Numbers Count?' (1977) 6 *Philosophy and Public Affairs* 293.

Tay, S and Tan Hsien Li, 'Southeast Asian Cooperation on Anti-Terrorism: The Dynamics and Limits of Regional Responses' in Ramraj, V, Hor, M, and Roach, K (eds), *Global Anti-Terrorism Law and Policy* (CUP, Cambridge, 2005) 399.

Taylor, F, *Dresden: Tuesday 13 February 1945* (Bloomsbury, London, 2004).

Telhami, S, 'Conflicting Views of Terrorism' (2002) 35 Cornell ILJ 581.

Thirlway, H, *International Customary Law and Codification* (AW Sifthoff, Leiden, 1972).

Thompson, K, 'The Destabilization of Republican Regimes: The Effects of Terrorism on Democratic Societies' (1996) 5 *Low Intensity Conflict and Law Enforcement* 253.

Thrush, B, 'US Sanctioned Kidnappings Abroad: Can the US Restore International Confidence in its Extradition Treaties?' (1994) 11 Ariz JICL 181.

Tiefenbrun, S, 'A Semiotic Approach to a Legal Definition of Terrorism' (2003) 9 ILSA JICL 357.

Tierney, J, 'Terror at Home: The American Revolution and Irregular Warfare' (1977) 12 Stan JIL 1.

Timmeney, B, 'International Extraterritorial Jurisdiction—The Lockerbie Tragedy: Will Western Clout or International Convention Win the Extradition War?' (1993) 11 Dickinson JIL 477.

Todorov, T, 'The Limitations of Justice' (2004) 2 JICJ 711.

Toman, J, 'Terrorism and the Regulation of Armed Conflicts' in Bassiouni, MC (ed), *International Terrorism and Political Crimes* (Charles C Thomas, Illinois, 1975) 133.

Tomuschat, C, 'The Lockerbie Case before the International Court of Justice' (1992) No 48 *Review of the International Commission of Jurists* 38.

—— 'Issues of Universal Jurisdiction in the *Scilingo* Case' (2005) 3 JICJ 1074.

Torruella, J, 'On the Slippery Slopes of Afghanistan: Military Commissions and the Exercise of Presidential Power' (2002) 71 *Revista Juridica Universidad De Puerto Rico* 667.

Touret, D, 'Terrorism and Freedom in International Law' (1980) 2 Houston JIL 363.

Townshend, C, *Britain's Civil Wars: Counter-insurgency in the Twentieth Century* (Faber & Faber, London, 1986).

Transactional Records Access Clearinghouse (TRAC), 'Criminal Terrorism Enforcement since the 9/11/01 Attacks', Special Report, 8 Dec 2003.

Travalio, G and Altenburg, J, 'Terrorism, State Responsibility, and the Use of Military Force' (2003) 4 Chinese JIL 97.

Trotsky, L, *Terrorism and Communism: A Reply to Karl Kautsky* (New Park, London, 1975).

Tsairis, A, 'Lessons of Lockerbie' (1996) 22 Syra JILC 31.

Turndorf, D, 'The US Raid on Libya: A Forceful Response to Terrorism' (1988) 14 Brookings JIL 187.

Tyagi, Y, 'Political Terrorism: National and International Dimensions' (1987) 27 Indian JIL 160.

UK Parliament (Intelligence and Security Committee), *Report on Iraqi Weapons of Mass Destruction: Intelligence and Assessments* (HMSO, London, Sept 2003).

UK Parliament (Joint Committee on Human Rights), Continuance in Force of ss 21 to 23 of the Anti-Terrorism, Crime and Security Act 2001, 5th Report of Sess 2002–03, HL Paper 59, HC 462.

UN High-Level Panel on Threats, Challenges and Change, *A More Secure World: Our Shared Responsibility*, 2 Dec 2004, UN Doc A/59/565.

UN Secretary-General's Report, *In Larger Freedom: Towards Development, Security and Human Rights for All*, UNGA (59th Sess), 21 Mar 2005, UN Doc A/59/2005.

UN Special Rapporteur on Systematic Rape, Sexual Slavery and Slavery-like Practices during Wartime, Update to Final Report to UNSubComHR, UN Doc E/CN.4/Sub.2/2000/21 (6 June 2000).

UN War Crimes Commission, *History of the United Nations War Crimes Commission and the Development of the Laws of War* (HMSO, London, 1948).

UNDP, *Human Development Report 1994* (OUP, New York, 1994).

UNHCR, Handbook on Procedures and Criteria for Determining Refugee Status under the 1951 Convention and the 1967 Protocol relating to the Status of Refugees (Re-edited, Geneva, Jan 1992).

—— Guidelines on International Protection: Application of the Exclusion Clauses:

Article 1F of the 1951 Convention relating to the Status of Refugees, 4 Sept 2003, HCR/GIP/03/05.

UNHR Committee (16th Sess), General Comment No 8: ICCPR, Article 9, 30 June 1982.

—— Comment on Egypt's Second Periodic Report on Implementation of the ICCPR, 9 Sept 1993, UN Doc CCPR/C/79/Add.23.

—— General Comment No 31: Nature of the General Legal Obligation Imposed on States Parties to the Covenant, 26 May 2004, UN Doc CCPR/C/21/Rev.1/Add.13.

—— Concluding Observations: Belgium, 12 Aug 2004, UN Doc CCPR/CO/81/BEL.

Uniacke, S, 'Killing under Duress' (1989) 6 *Journal of Applied Philosophy* 53.

UNODC, Legislative Guide to the Universal Anti-Terrorism Conventions and Protocols (UN, New York, 2003).

UNSubComHR, Terrorism and Human Rights: Preliminary Report by Special Rapporteur K Koufa (1999), UN Doc E/CN.4/Sub.2/1999/27.

—— (53rd Sess), Terrorism and Human Rights: Progress Report by Special Rapporteur K Koufa, 27 June 2001, UN Doc E/CN.4/Sub.2/2001/31.

US Congress, Authorization for Use of Military Force, Pub L 107–40, 115 Stat 224 (18 Sept 2001).

US Dept of Justice (FBI), *Terrorism in the US 1999* (DOJ, Washington, DC, 2000).

US Senate (108th Congress) (Select Committee on Intelligence), *Report on the US Intelligence Community's Prewar Intelligence Assessments on Iraq* (Washington, DC, 7 July 2004).

Utley, T, *Terrorism and Tolerance: Flaws in the Liberal Tradition* (Centre for Policy Studies, London, 1985).

Vagts, D, 'Which Courts Should Try Persons Accused of Terrorism?' (2003) 14 EJIL 313.

Valsamis, M, 'Defining Organised Crime in the European Union: The Limits of European Law in an Area of "Freedom, Security and Justice" ' (2001) 26 ELR 565.

Van den Wijngaert, C, *The Political Offence Exception to Extradition* (Kluwer, Boston, 1980).

—— 'The Political Offence Exception to Extradition: How to Plug the "Terrorist' Loophole" Without Departing from Fundamental Human Rights' (1989) 19 IYBHR 297.

—— 'Jurisdiction over Crimes of Terrorism' in Heere, W (ed), *Terrorism and the Military: International Legal Implications* (Asser Press, The Hague, 2003) 147.

Van-Der-Vyver, J, 'State Sponsored Terror and Violence' (1988) 4 *South African Journal of Human Rights* 55.

Van Ginkel, B, 'The United Nations: Towards a Comprehensive Convention on Combating Terrorism' in van Leeuwen, M (ed), *Confronting Terrorism* (Kluwer, The Hague, 2003) 207.

Van Krieken, P (ed), *Terrorism and the International Legal Order* (Asser Press, The Hague, 2002).

Van Sliedregt, E, *The Criminal Responsibility of Individuals for Violations of International Humanitarian Law* (CUP, Cambridge, 2003).

Vercher, A, *Terrorism in Europe: An International Comparative Legal Analysis* (Clarendon, Oxford, 1992).

Verwey, W, 'The International Hostages Convention and National Liberation Movements' (1981) 75 AJIL 69.

Villiger, M, *Customary International Law and Treaties* (Martinus Nijhoff, Dordrecht, 1985).

Vogel, F, 'The Trial of Terrorists under Classical Islamic Law' (2002) 43 Harvard ILJ 53.

Volkan, V and Harris, M, 'The Psychodynamics of Ethnic Terrorism' (1995) 3 *International Journal of Group Rights* 145.

von Schorlemer, S, 'Human Rights: Substantive and Institutional Implications of the War on Terror' (2003) 14 EJIL 265.

Walker, C, 'Irish Republican Prisoners, Political Detainees, Prisoners of War or Common Criminals?' (1984) 19 *Irish Jurist* 189.

—— *The Prevention of Terrorism in British Law* (2nd edn, MUP, Manchester, 1992).

—— *Blackstone's Guide to the Anti-Terrorism Legislation* (OUP, Oxford, 2002).

—— 'Defining Terrorism in National and International Law' in Walter, C, Vöneky, S, Röben, V, and Schorkopf, F (eds), *Terrorism as a Challenge for National and International Law: Security versus Liberty* (Springer, Heidelberg, 2004) 23.

Walters, F, *A History of the League of Nations* (OUP, London, 1969).

Walzer, M, *Just and Unjust Wars* (3rd edn, Basic Books, New York, 2000).

Warbrick, C, 'The Principles of the European Convention on Human Rights and the Response of States to Terrorism', Study for the Council of Europe, Jan 2002.

—— 'The European Response to Terrorism in an Age of Human Rights' (2004) 15 EJIL 989.

Ward, C, 'Building Capacity to Combat International Terrorism: The Role of the United Nations Security Council' (2003) 8 JCSL 289.

Wardlaw, G, *Political Terrorism: Theory, Tactics and Counter-Measures* (CUP, Cambridge, 1982).

Wark, W, 'Managing the Consequences of Nuclear, Chemical, and Biological Terrorism' (1997) 6 *Low Intensity Conflict and Law Enforcement* 179.

Warriner, W, 'The Unilateral Use of Coercion under International Law: A Legal Analysis of the United States Raid on Libya on April 14, 1986' (1986) 37 *Naval Law Review* 49.

Washington, A, 'Terrorism: United States Policy on Immigration and Extradition' (1996) 21 *Marshall Law Review* 291.

Watson, G, 'Constitutionalism, Judicial Review, and the World Court' (1993) Harvard ILJ 1.

Watt, D, 'Restraints on War in the Air before 1945' in Howard, M (ed), *Restraints on War : Studies in the Limitation of Armed Conflict* (OUP, Oxford, 1979) 57.

Wattellier, J, 'Comparative Legal Responses to Terrorism: Lessons from Europe' (2004) 27 *Hastings International and Comparative Law Review* 397.

Waxman, D, 'Terrorism: The War of the Future' (1999) 23 *Fletcher Forum of World Affairs* 201.

Wedgwood, R, 'Responding to Terrorism: The Strikes against Bin Laden' (1999) 24 Yale JIL 559.

—— 'The Fall of Saddam Hussein: Security Council Mandates and Preemptive Self-Defence' (2003) 97 AJIL 576.

Wegner, A, 'Extraterritorial Jurisdiction under International Law: The *Yunis* Decision as a Model for the Prosecution of Terrorists in US Courts' (1991) 22 *Law and Policy in International Business* 409.

Weinberg, L, Pedahzur, A, and Canetti-Nisim, D, 'The Social and Religious Characteristics of Suicide Bombers and Their Victims' (2003) 15 *Terrorism and Political Violence* 139.

——, Pedahzur, A, and Hirsch-Hoefler, S, 'The Challenges of Conceptualizing Terrorism' (2004) 16 *Terrorism and Political Violence* 777.

Welchman, L, 'Rocks, Hard Places and Human Rights: Anti-Terrorism Law and Policy in Arab States' in Ramraj, V, Hor, M and Roach, K (eds), *Global Anti-Terrorism Law and Policy* (CUP, Cambridge, 2005) 581.

Weller, M, 'The Lockerbie Case: A Premature End to the "New World Order"?' (1992) 4 *African Journal of International and Comparative Law* 302.

Wellington, K, 'Extradition: A Fair and Effective Weapon in the War on Terrorism' (1990) 51 Ohio SLJ 1447.

Werner, W, 'Self-Determination and Civil War' (2001) 6 JCSL 171.

Whiteman, M, *Damages in International Law* (USGPO, Washington, DC, 1937).

Whittaker, D (ed), *The Terrorism Reader* (Routledge, London, 2001).

Wilder, S, 'International Terrorism and Hostage-taking: An Overview' (1981) 11 *Manitoba Law Journal* 367.

Wilkinson, P, *Terrorism and the Liberal State* (Macmillan, London, 1977).

—— *The Challenge of Terrorism to International Society and the Rule of Law* (Unitarian Publications, London, 1989).

—— *Terrorist Targets and Tactics* (Research Institute for the Study of Conflict and Terrorism, London, 2000).

—— *Terrorism Versus Democracy: The Liberal State Response* (Frank Cass, London, 2001).

Williams, B, *Morality* (CUP, Cambridge, 1972).

Williams, Glanville, 'The Theory of Excuses' [1982] Crim LR 732.

Williams, George and Golder, B, 'What is "Terrorism"? Problems of Legal Definition' (2004) 27 *University of New South Wales Law Journal* 270.

Williams, S, 'International Law and Terrorism: Age-old Problems, Different Targets' (1988) 26 Can YBIL 87.

Wilson, R, 'Prosecuting Pinochet: International Crimes in Spanish Domestic Law' (1999) 21 Human Rights Quarterly 927.

Wise, E, 'Terrorism and the Problems of an International Criminal Law' (1987) 19 *Connecticut Law Review* 799.

Wisgerhof, A, 'International Non-State Terrorism and the Transstate Paradigm' (1999) 8 *Low Intensity Conflict and Law Enforcement* 58.

Witten, S, 'The International Convention for the Suppression of Terrorist Bombings' (1998) 92 AJIL 774.

Wolfke, K, *Custom in Present International Law* (2nd edn, Martinus Nijhoff, Dordrecht, 1993).

Wortley, B, 'Political Crime in English Law and in International Law' (1971) BYBIL 234.

Yamamoto, J, 'Current Treaty Systems to Combat International Terrorism: Features and Domestic Implementation' (1989) *Japanese Annual of International Law* 34.

Young, R, 'Political Terrorism as a Weapon of the Politically Powerless' in Primoratz, I (ed), *Terrorism: The Philosophical Issues* (Palgrave Macmillan, Hampshire, 2004) 55.

Zaid, M, 'Combating International Terrorism into the 21st Century' (1996) 2 ILSA JICL 661.

Zamir, I, 'The Rule of Law and the Control of Terrorism' (1988) 8 *Tel Aviv University Studies in Law* 81.

Zappala, S, 'Do Heads of State Enjoy Immunity from Jurisdiction for International Crimes? The *Ghaddafi* Case Before the French *Cour de Cassation*' (2001) 12 EJIL 595.

Zard, M, 'Exclusion, Terrorism and the Refugee Convention' (2002) 13 FMR 32.

Zawati, H, 'Is Jihad a Just War? War, Peace and Human Rights under Islamic and Public International Law' (2002) 96 AJIL 1000.

Zegveld, L, *The Accountability of Armed Opposition Groups in International Law* (CUP, Cambridge, 2002).

Zelman, J, 'Recent Developments in International Law: Anti-Terrorism Legislation—Part One: An Overview' (2001) 11 JTLP 183.

Zlataric, B, 'History of International Terrorism and its Legal Control', in Bassiouni, MC (ed), *International Terrorism and Political Crimes* (Charles C Thomas, Illinois, 1975) 474.

Zolo, D, 'Peace through Criminal Law?' (2004) 2 JICJ 727.

Index

Lightning Source UK Ltd.
Milton Keynes UK
UKOW06f1304231015

261236UK00004B/79/P